"This book offers a rich illustration of the claim made by its editor that associations must now be viewed as an essential part of the 'toolkit' of those working on early Christianity. Taken together, this fascinating collection of essays by leading experts offers a window into the most innovative scholarship on Christ-groups today. These substantive studies bring new questions to the fore and expand our horizons on topics ranging from the world of work and trade, to the importance of sensory elements, to the significance of identifying wide-ranging factors which contribute to group durability and stability. Readers will discover sometimes-unexpected but illuminating ancient data from literary and material culture, leading them to think afresh about the shape of early Christianity."

—**Margaret Y. MacDonald**, *Professor, Department for the Study of Religion, Saint Mary's University, Halifax*

"Here is a state-of-the-art discussion of Greco-Roman associations and their importance for our understanding of early Christianity. Scholars have made great advances in recent years in the study of Greco-Roman associations. In this outstanding book, many of these advances are presented and drawn upon to help us think in new and stimulating ways about early Christ groups. By bringing our knowledge of associations and early Christ groups into conversation, we can better understand both the similarities and the differences between Christ-believers and other groups in their wider context. These cutting-edge essays open up new questions and new perspectives that will set the research agenda for decades to come."

—**Paul Trebilco**, *Professor of New Testament Studies, University of Otago, New Zealand*

"In recent decades, our understanding of the earliest Christ-groups, and early Christianity more generally, has been greatly illuminated by studies that examine these groups alongside other ancient associations. Engaging with this body of work, and both developing and challenging it, this rich and diverse collection of essays covers topics ranging from terminology and appropriate models through to meals, dress, fees, benefaction and mutual aid, and includes many studies of specific New Testament and early Christian texts. This volume will greatly help to enrich, challenge, and extend the scholarly conversation in this vibrant and vital area of research."

—**David G. Horrell**, *Professor of New Testament Studies, University of Exeter, United Kigndom*

Greco-Roman Associations, Deities, and Early Christianity

Bruce W. Longenecker

Editor

BAYLOR UNIVERSITY PRESS

Cover and book design by Kasey McBeath
Cover art: Unsplash/Jeremy Bezanger

The Library of Congress has cataloged this book under ISBN 978-1-4813-1516-6
Library of Congress Control Number: 2022940710

For John Barclay

Contents

II   Focal Points

Abbreviations for Epigraphic and Papyrological Collections

AE	*L'année épigraphique* (periodical).
AGRW	Philip Harland's website *Associations in the Greco-Roman World*, https://philipharland.com/greco-roman-associations/ (numbers that follow this abbreviation relate to the identification number of an item—inscription, papyrus, or ostracon—using WordPress' assigned post number).
ASSB	Runesson, Anders, Donald D. Binder, and Birger Olsson. *The Ancient Synagogue from Its Origins to 200 C.E.: A Source Book*. AGJU 72. Leiden: Brill, 2008.
BE	*Bullétin épigraphique*.
BGU	*Aegyptische Urkunden aus den Königlichen* (later *Staatlichen*) *Museen zu Berlin, Griechische Urkunden*. 15 vols. Berlin: Weidmann, 1895–1937.
CAPInv	*Inventory of Ancient Associations*. University of Copenhagen. https://ancientassociations.ku.dk/CAPI/.
CCCA	Vermaseren, M. J. *Corpus Cultus Cybelae Attidisque (CCCA)*. EPRO 50. 7 vols. Leiden: Brill, 1977–1989.
CCID	Hörig, M., and Elmar Schwertheim. *Corpus Cultus Iovis Dolicheni (CCID)*. EPRO 106. Leiden: Brill, 1987.
CGRN	Carbon, J.-M., S. Peels, and V. Pirenne-Delforge, eds. *A Collection of Greek Ritual Norms (CGRN)*. Liège: Collège de France and the University of Liège, 2016–. http://cgrn.ulg.ac.be/.

CIG	Boeckh, August, ed. *Corpus inscriptionum graecarum*. 4 vols. Berlin: Georg Reimer, 1828–1877.
CIJ	Frey, J. B., ed. *Corpus inscriptionum iudaicarum: recueil des inscriptions juives qui vont du IIIe siècle avant J.-C.* 2 vols. Rome: Pontificio istituto di archeologia cristiana, 1936–1952. Vol. 1, *Europe*, ed. J. B. Frey (1936); vol. 2, *Asia-Africa*, ed. J. B. Frey (1952).
CIL	*Corpus inscriptionum latinarum: Consilio et auctoritate Academiae litterarum regiae borussicae editum.* 17 vols. Berlin: Georg Reimer, 1863–1974.
CILA	Fernández, J. González. *Corpus de inscripciones latinas de Andalucía.* 4 vols. Seville: Dirección General de Bienes Culturales, 1991–2002.
CIMRM	Vermaseren, M. J., ed. *Corpus Inscriptionum et Monumentorum Religionis Mithriacae.* 2 vols. The Hague: Martin Nijhoff, 1956–1960.
CIRB	Struve, V. V., ed. *Corpus inscriptionum Regni Bosporani (CIRB). Korpus bosporskikh nadpisei.* Moscow: Nauka, 1965.
CJZC	Lüderitz, G., and J. M. Reynolds. *Corpus jüdischen zeugnisse aus der Cyrenaika.* Beihefte zum Tübinger Atlas des Vorderen Orients. Reihe B. Geisteswissenschaften 53. Wiesbaden: Dr. Ludwig Reichert, 1983.
CMRDM	Lane, E. *Corpus monumentorum religionis dei Menis (CMRDM).* EPRO 19. 4 vols. Leiden: Brill, 1971–1978. Vol. 1, *Monuments and Inscriptions*, by E. Lane (1971); vol. 2, *Coins and Gems*, by E. Lane (1975); vol. 3, *Interpretations and Testimonia*, by E. Lane (1976); vol. 4, *Supplementary Men-Inscriptions from Pisidia*, by E. Lane (1978).
CPJ	Tcherikover, Victor A., Alexander Fuks, M. Stern, Noah Hacham, and Tal Ilan, eds., in collaboration with M. M. Piotrkowski and Z. Szántó. *Corpus Papyrorum Judaicarum.* 4 vols. Cambridge, Mass.: Harvard University Press, 1957–2020. Vol. 1, ed. Victor A. Tcherikover, Alexander Fuks (1957); vol. 2, ed. Victor A. Tcherikover, Alexander Fuks (1960); vol. 3, ed. Victor A. Tcherikover, Alexander Fuks, M. Stern (1964); vol. 4, ed. Noah Hacham, Tal Ilan (2020).
GRA I–III	Kloppenborg, John S., Philip A. Harland, and Richard S. Ascough, eds. *Greco-Roman Associations: Texts, Translations, and Commentary.* 3 vols. Berlin: De Gruyter, 2011–2020. Vol. 1, *Attica, Central Greece, Macedonia, Thrace,*

ed. John S. Kloppenborg and Richard S. Ascough, BZNW 181 (2011); vol. 2, *North Coast of the Black Sea, Asia Minor*, ed. Philip A. Harland, BZNW 204 (2014); vol. 3, *Ptolemaic and Early Roman Egypt*, ed. John S. Kloppenborg, BZNW 246 (2020).

IAlexandriaK   Kayser, François. *Recueil des inscriptions grecques et latines (non funéraires) d'Alexandrie impériale.* Bibliothèque d'étude 108. Cairo: Institut français d'archéologie orientale du Caire, 1994.

IAnkyraM   Mitchell, Stephen, and David French. *From Augustus to the End of the Third Century AD.* Vol. 1 of *The Greek and Latin Inscriptions of Ankara (Ancyra).* Vestigia 62. Munich: C. H. Beck, 2012.

IApamBith   Corsten, Thomas. *Die Inschriften von Apameia (Bithynien) und Pylai.* Inschriften griechischer Städte aus Kleinasien 32. Bonn: Rudolf Habelt, 1987.

IAph   Reynolds, Joyce, Charlotte Roueché, and Gabriel Bodard. *Inscriptions of Aphrodisias.* King's College London, 2007. http://insaph.kcl.ac.uk/insaph/iaph2007/.

IBerenike   Reynolds, Joyce. "Inscriptions." Pages 233–54 in *Buildings, Coins, Inscriptions, Architectural Decoration.* Vol. 1 of *Excavations at Sidi Khrebish Benghazi (Berenice).* Edited by J. A. Lloyd. Supplements to Libya Antiqua 5. Libya: Department of Antiquities, Ministry of Teaching and Education, People's Socialist Libyan Arab Jamahiriya, 1977.

IBeroia   Gounaropoulou, L., and M. B. Hatzopoulos. *Inscriptiones Macedoniae Inferioris I: Inscriptiones Beroiae* (in Greek). Athens: Hypourgeio Politismou, 1998.

ICiliciaBM   Bean, George E., and Terence Bruce Mitford. I: *Journeys in Rough Cilicia 1962 and 1963.* Denkschriften der Osterreichischen Akademie der Wissenschaften in Wien, philosophisch-historische Klasse 85. Vienna: Hermann Böhlaus, 1965; II: *Journeys in Rough Cilicia 1964–1968.* Denkschriften der Österreichischen Akademie der Wissenschaften in Wien, philosophisch-historische Klasse 102.3. Vienna: Hermann Böhlaus, 1970.

ICosED   Mario, Segre, ed. *Iscrizioni di Cos.* 2 vols. Monografi e della Scuola archeologica di Atene e delle missioni italiane in Oriente 6. Rome: "L'Erma" di Bretschneider, 1993.

IDacia	Russu, Ioan I., Grigore Florescu, and Constantin C. Petolescu. *Inscriptiones Daciae Romanae.* 3 vols. Inscriptiones Daciae et Scythiae Minoris Antiquae. Bucharest: Editura Academiei Republicii Socialiste România, 1975–1988.
IDelos	Roussel, Pierre, and Marcel Launey. *Inscriptions de Délos: décrets postérieurs à 166 av. J.-C. (nos. 1497–1524). Dédicaces postérieures à 166 av. J.-C. (nos. 1525–2219).* Académie des Inscriptions et Belles-Lettres. Paris: Librairie Ancienne Honoré Champion, 1937.
IDionysosJ	Jaccottet, Anne-Françoise. *Choisir Dionysos: les associations dionysiaques, ou, La face cachée du dionysisme.* 2 vols. Akanthus crescens 6. Zürich: Akanthus, 2003.
IDR	Rossu, Ioan I., G. Florescu, C. C. Petolescu, D. M. Pippidi, I. Piso, and C. L. Băluță, eds. *Inscriptiones Daciae Romanae. Inscripțiile Daciei Romane.* 9 vols. Bucharest: Editura Academiei Republicii Socialiste România, 1975–2001.
IEph	Engelmann, H., H. Wankel, and R. Merkelbach. *Die Inschriften von Ephesos.* Inschriften griechischer Städte aus Kleinasien 11–17. 8 vols. Bonn: Rudolf Habelt, 1979–1984.
IG II²	Kirchner, Johannes, ed. *Inscriptiones Atticae Euclidis anno anteriores.* 4 vols. Berlin: De Gruyter, 1913–1940.
IG IV	Fränkle, M., ed. *Inscriptiones graecae Aeginae, Pityonesi, Cecryphaliae, Argolidis.* Berlin: Georg Reimer, 1902.
IG VII	Dittenberger, Wilhelm, ed. *Inscriptiones Megaridis et Boeotiae.* Berlin: Georg Reimer, 1892.
IG IX,1²	Klaffenbach, Gunther, ed. *Inscriptiones graeciae septentrionalis.* 2nd ed. 3 fascs. Berlin: De Gruyter, 1932–1968. Fasc. 1, *Inscriptiones Aetoliae* (1932); fasc. 2, *Inscriptiones Acarnaniae* (1957); fasc. 3, *Inscriptiones Locridis occidentalis* (1968).
IG IX,2	Kern, Otto, ed. *Inscriptiones graecae, IX,2. Inscriptiones Thessaliae.* Berlin: De Gruyter, 1908.
IG X,2.1	Edson, Charles, ed. *Inscriptiones Thessalonicae et viciniae.* Vol. 2, fasc. 1, in *Inscriptiones graecae Epiri, Macedoniae, Thraciae, Scythiae.* Berlin: De Gruyter, 1972.
IG XI,4	Roussel, Pierre. *Inscriptiones Deli liberae. Decreta, foedera, catalogi, dedicationes, varia.* Berlin: Georg Reimer, 1914.
IG XII,1–9	Hiller von Gaertringen, F., W. R. Paton, J. Delamarre, and E. Ziebarth, eds. *Inscriptiones insularum maris Aegaei praeter*

	Delum. 9 parts (part 6 never published). Berlin: Georg Reimer, 1895–1915.
IG XII,Suppl	Hiller von Gaertringen, F., ed. *Supplementum.* Berlin: De Gruyter, 1939.
IG XIV	Kaibel, Georg, ed. *Inscriptiones Siciliae et Italiae, additis Graecis Galliae, Hispaniae, Britanniae, Germaniae inscriptionibus.* Berlin: Georg Reimer, 1890.
IGBulg	Mikhailov, Georgi, ed. *Inscriptiones graecae in Bulgaria repertae.* 5 vols. Sofia: Academia Litterarum Bulgarica, 1956–1997. Vol. 1, *Inscriptiones orae Ponti Euxini*, ed. Georgi Mikhailov (1956); vol. 2, *Inscriptiones inter Danubium et Haemum repertae,* ed. Georgi Mikhailov (1958); vol. 3, pt. 1, *Inscriptiones inter Haemum et Rhodopem reperta: a territorio Philippopolis*, ed. Georgi Mikhailov (1961); vol. 3, pt. 2, *Inscriptiones inter Haemum et Rhodopem reperta: a territorio Philippopolitano usque ad oram Ponticam*, ed. Georgi Mikhailov (1964); vol. 4, *Inscriptiones in territorio Serdicensi et in vallibus Styrmonis Nestique repertae,* ed. Georgi Mikhailov (1966); vol. 5, *Inscriptiones novae, addenda et corrigenda*, ed. Georgi Mikhailov (1997).
IGLAM	Le Bas, Philippe, and William Henry Waddington. *Inscriptions grecques et latines recueillies en Asie Mineure.* Vol. 3 of *Voyage archéologique en Grèce et en Asie Mineure.* Paris: Firmin Didot Frères, 1870.
IGLSkythia	See *IHistria, IKallatis, ITomis.*
IGR/IGRR	Cagnat, R. L., J. F. Toutain, V. Henry, and G. L. Lafaye, eds. *Inscriptiones graecae ad res romanas pertinentes.* 4 vols. Paris: E. Leroux, 1911–1927.
IGUR	Moretti, L. *Inscriptiones graecae urbis romae.* 4 vols. Studi Pubblicati dall'Istituto Italiano per la Storia Antica 17, 22, 28, 47. Rome: Istituto Italiano per la Storia Antica, 1968.
IHadrianoi	Schwertheim, Elmar. *Die Inschriften von Hadrianoi und Hadrianeia.* Inschriften griechischer Städte aus Kleinasien 33. Bonn: Rudolf Habelt, 1987.
IHierapJ	Judeich, Walther. "Inschriften." Pages 67–181 in *Altertümer von Hierapolis.* Edited by Carl Humann, Conrad Cichorius, Walther Judeich, and Franz Winter. Jahrbuch des kaiserlich deutschen archäologischen Instituts, Ergänzungsheft 4. Berlin: Georg Reimer, 1898.

IHistria   Pippidi, D. M. *Inscriptiones Histriae et Viciniae*. Vol. 1 in
                Inscriptiones Scythiae Minoris graecae et latinae. Inscriptiones
                Daciae et Scythiae Minoris Antiquae. Bucharest: Academiei
                Scientiarum Socialum et Politicarum Dacoromana, 1983.

IJO   Noy, David, Alexander Panayotov, Hanswulf Bloedhorn, and
                Walter Ameling, eds. *Inscriptiones Judaicae Orientis*. 3 vols.
                Tübingen: Mohr Siebeck, 2004. Vol. 1, *Eastern Europe*, ed.
                David Noy, Alexander Panayotov, and Hanswulf Bloedhorn,
                TSAJ 101 (2004); vol. 2, *Kleinasien*, ed. Walter Ameling,
                TSAJ 99 (2004); vol. 3, *Syria and Cyprus*, ed. David Noy and
                Hanswulf Bloedhorn, TSAJ 102 (2004).

IKallatis   Avram, Alexander. *Callatis et territorium*. Vol. 3 in
                Inscriptiones Scythiae Minoris graecae et latinae. Inscriptiones
                Daciae et Scythiae Minoris Antiquae. Bucharest: Editura
                Enciclopedica, 2000.

IKibyra   Corsten, Thomas. *Die Inschriften von Kibyra*. Inschriften
                griechischer Städte aus Kleinasien 60. Bonn: Rudolf Habelt,
                2002.

IKlaudiupolis Becker-Bertau, Friedrich. *Die Inschriften von Klaudiu Polis*.
                Inschriften griechischer Städte aus Kleinasien 31. Bonn:
                Rudolf Habelt, 1986.

ILaodLyk   Corsten, Thomas. *Die Inschriften von Laodikeia am Lykos*.
                Inschriften griechischer Städte aus Kleinasien 49. Bonn:
                Rudolf Habelt, 1997.

ILCV   Diehl, Ernst. *Inscriptiones latinae christianae veteres*. 4 vols.
                Berlin: Weidmann, 1924–1931.

ILindos   Blinkenberg, C., ed. *Inscriptions*. Vol. 2 of *Lindos: fouilles et
                recherches, 1902–1913*. 2 vols. Berlin: De Gruyter, 1931–1941.

ILS   Dessau, Hermann. *Inscriptiones latinae selectae*. 3 vols.
                Berlin: Weidmann, 1892–1916. Repr., Dublin: Weidmann,
                1974; repr., Chicago: Ares, 1979.

ILTG   Wuilleumier, Pierre. *Inscriptions latines des Trois Gaules*.
                Paris: Centre National de la Recherche Scientifique, 1963.

IMakedD   Demitsas, M. G. Ἡ Μακεδονία ἐν λίθοις φθεγγομένοις
                καὶ μνημείοις σωζομένοις. Athens: Perre, 1896. Reprinted
                as *Sylloge inscriptionum graecarum et latinarum Macedoniae*.
                Chicago: Ares, 1980.

IMiletos   McCabe, Donald F., ed. *Miletos Inscriptions: Texts and List*.
                Princeton Project on the Inscriptions of Anatolia. Princeton:
                Institute for Advanced Study, 1984. Packard Humanities
                Institute CD no. 6, 1991.

IMT	Barth, Matthias, and Josef Stauber. *Inschriften Mysia und Troas.* Munich: Leopold Wenger-Institut, 1993.
IPalmyra	Yon, Jean-Baptiste. *Palmyre.* Vol. 17, fasc. 1 of *Inscriptions grecques et latines de la Syrie.* Bibliothèque archéologique et historique 195. Beirut: Institut français du Proche-Orient, 2012.
IPergamon	Fränkel, Max, ed. *Die Inschriften von Pergamon.* 2 vols. Berlin: W. Spemann, 1890–1895. Vol. 1, *Bis zum Ende der Königszeit,* ed. Max Fränkel (1890); vol. 2, *Römische Zeit,* ed. Max Fränkel (1895).
IPerinthos	Sayar, Mustafa Hamdi, ed. *Perinthos-Herakleia (Marmara Ereğlisi) und Umgebung. Geschichte, Testimonien, griechische und lateinische Inschriften.* Österreichische Akademie der Wissenschaften. Philosophisch-Historische Klasse. Denkschriften, 269 = Veröffentlichungen der kleinasiatischen Kommission 9. Vienna: Österreichischen Akademie der Wissenschaften, 1998.
IPessinous	Strubbe, J. H. M. *The Inscriptions of Pessinous.* Inschriften griechischer Städte aus Kleinasien 66. Bonn: Rudolf Habelt, 2005.
IPhilae	Bernand, André, and Étienne Bernand. *Les inscriptions grecques de Philae.* 2 vols. Paris: Éditions du Centre national de la recherche scientifique, 1969. Vol. 1, *Époque ptolemaïque* (nos. 1–127), by André Bernand (1969); vol. 2, *Haut et bas empire* (nos. 128–246), by Étienne Bernand (1969).
IPhilippiP II	Pilhofer, Peter. *Katalog der Inschriften von Philippi.* Vol. 2 of *Philippi.* WUNT 119. Tübingen: Mohr Siebeck, 2000 (2nd ed., 2009).
IPisidiaHM	Horsley, G. H. R., and Stephen Mitchell. *The Inscriptions of Central Pisidia.* Inschriften griechischer Städte aus Kleinasien 57. Bonn: Rudolf Habelt, 2000.
IPrusaOlymp	Corsten, Thomas, ed. *Die Inschriften von Prusa ad Olympum.* Inschriften griechischer Städte aus Kleinasien 39–40. 2 vols. Bonn: Rudolf Habelt, 1991–1993.
ISamos	McCabe, Donald F. *Samos Inscriptions. Texts and List.* The Princeton Project on the Inscriptions of Anatolia. Princeton: The Institute for Advanced Study, 1986.
IStratonikeia	Şahin, Mehmet Çetin. *Die Inschriften von Stratonikeia.* Inschriften griechischer Städte aus Kleinasien 21. 3 vols. Bonn: Rudolf Habelt, 1981–1990.

I. Thess	Decourt, Jean-Claude. *Inscriptions de Thessalie*. Vol. 1. *Les cités de la vallée de l'Énipeus*. Études épigraphiques, 3. Paris: École française d'Athènes, 1995.
ITomis	Stoian, Iorgu. *Tomis et territorium*. Vol. 2 in *Inscriptiones Scythiae Minoris graecae et latinae*. Inscriptiones Daciae et Scythiae Minoris Antiquae. Bucharest: Academiei Scientiarum Socialum et Politicarum Dacoromana, 1987.
JIGRE	Horbury, William, and David Noy. *Jewish Inscriptions of Graeco-Roman Egypt*. Cambridge: Cambridge University Press, 1992.
LSAM	Sokolowski, Franciszek. *Lois sacrées de l'Asie Mineure*. École française d'Athènes. Travaux et mémoires 9. Paris: Éditions de Boccard, 1955.
LSCG	Sokolowski, Franciszek. *Lois sacrées des cités grecques*. École française d'Athènes. Travaux et mémoires 18. Paris: Éditions de Boccard, 1969.
LSCGSup	Sokolowski, Franciszek. *Lois sacrées des cités grecques. Supplément*. École française d'Athènes. Travaux et mémoires 11. Paris: Éditions de Boccard, 1962.
LSJ	Liddell, Henry George, Robert Scott, and Henry Stuart Jones. *A Greek-English Lexicon*. 9th ed. with revised supplement. Oxford: Clarendon, 1996.
MAMA	Calder, W. M., E. Herzfeld, S. Guyer, and C. W. M. Cox, eds. *Monumenta Asiae Minoris antiqua*. 10 vols. American Society for Archaeological Research in Asia Minor. Publications 1–10. London: Manchester University Press, 1928–1993.
NewDocs I–V	Horsley, G. H. R., ed. *New Documents Illustrating Early Christianity*. 5 vols. Edited by S. R. Llewelyn. North Ryde: Ancient History Documentary Research Centre, Macquarie University, 1981–1989. Vol. 1, *A Review of the Greek Inscriptions and Papyri Published in 1976*, ed. G. H. R. Horsley (1981); vol. 2, *A Review of the Greek Inscriptions and Papyri Published in 1977*, ed. G. H. R. Horsley (1982); vol. 3, *A Review of the Greek Inscriptions and Papyri Published in 1978*, ed. G. H. R. Horsley (1983); vol. 4, *A Review of the Greek Inscriptions and Papyri Published in 1979*, ed. G. H. R. Horsley (1987); vol. 5, *Linguistic Essays*, ed. G. H. R. Horsley (1989).

OBodl | *Greek Ostraca in the Bodleian Library at Oxford and Various Other Collections.* 3 vols. Vol. 1, ed. J. G. Tait (1930); vol. 2, ed. J. G. Tait and C. Préaux (1955); vol. 3, ed. J. Bingen and M. Wittek (1964). London: Egypt Exploration Society, 1930–1964.

OCair GPW | Gallazzi, Claudio, Rosario Pintaudi, and Klaas A. Worp, eds. *Ostraka greci del Museo Egizio del Cairo.* Florence: Gonnelli, 1986.

OEdfou | Bruyère, B., J. Manteuffel, K. Michalowski, J. Sainte Fare Garnot, J. de Linage, C. Desroches, and M. Zejmo-Zejmis, eds. Papyri published in *Fouilles Franco-Polonaises* (series). 3 vols. Cairo: Institut Français d'Archéologie Orientale du Caire and the University of Warsaw, 1937–1939.

OGIS | Dittenberger, Wilhelm, ed. *Orientis graeci inscriptiones selectae. Supplementum Sylloge inscriptionum graecarum.* 2 vols. Leipzig: S. Hirzel, 1903–1905. Repr., Hildesheim: G. Olms, 1970.

OKrok | Cuvigny, Hélène, A. Büllow-Jacobsen, J. L. Fournet, and B. Redon. *Ostraca de Krokodilô.* 2 vols. Cairo: Institut français d'archéologie orientale, 2005–2019.

OLeid | Bagnall, Roger S., P. J. Sijpesteijn, and Klaus A. Worp. *Greek Ostraka: A Catalogue of the Greek Ostraka in the National Museum of Antiquities at Leiden, with a Chapter on the Greek Ostraka in the Papyrological Institute of the University of Leiden.* Zutphen: Terra, 1980.

OVleem | Vleeming, S. P. *Ostraka Varia: Tax Receipts and Legal Documents on Demotic, Greek and Greek-Demotic Ostraka, Chiefly of the Early Ptolemaic Period, from Various Collections.* Leiden: Brill, 1994.

OWilck | Wilcken, Ulrich. *Griechische Ostraka aus Aegypten und Nubien. Ein Beitrag zur antiken Wirtschaftsgeschichte.* 2 vols. Leipzig: Giesecke & Devrient, 1899. Vol. 1 (1899); vol. 2 (nos. 1–1624) (1899). Repr., Amsterdam: A. M. Hakkert, 1970, with addenda compiled by P. J. Sijpesteijn.

PAthen | Petropoulos, G. A., ed. *Papyri Societatis Archaeologicae Atheniensis.* Athens: Academia Scientarium Atheniensis, 1939.

PBagnall | Ast, Rodney, Hélène Cuvigny, Todd M. Hickey, and Julia Lougovaya, eds. *Papyrological Texts in Honor of Roger S. Bagnall.* American Studies in Papyrology 53. Durham, N.C.: American Society of Papyrologists, 2013.

PCair Service des Antiquités de l'Égypte, Catalogue Général des Antiquités égyptiennes du Musée du Caire. *Die Demotischen Denkmäler*. 3 vols. 1904–1932. Vol. 1, *Die Demotischen Inschriften*, ed. Wilhelm Spiegelberg (Leipzig, 1904); vol. 2, *Die Demotischen Papyrus* (nos. 30601–31270, 50001–50022), ed. Wilhelm Spiegelberg, part 1, *Text* (Strasbourg, 1908), part 2, *Plates* (Strasbourg, 1906); vol. 3, *Demotische Inschriften und Papyri* (nos. 50023–50165), ed. Wilhelm Spiegelberg (Berlin, 1932).

PCairZen Edgar, Campbell Cowan, ed. *Zenon Papyri: catalogue général des antiquités égyptiennes du Musée du Caire*. 5 vols. Cairo: Institut français d'archéologie orientale, 1925–1940.

PCount Clarysse, Willy, and Dorothy J. Thompson, eds. *Counting the People in Hellenistic Egypt*. 2 vols. Cambridge: Cambridge University Press, 2006. Vol. 1, *Population Registers (P.Count)*, ed. Willy Clarysse and Dorothy J. Thompson (2006); vol. 2, *Historical Studies*, ed. Willy Clarysse and Dorothy J. Thompson (2006).

PEnteuxeis Guéraud, Octave, ed. *ΕΝΤΕΥΞΕΙΣ: requêtes et plaintes addressées au roi d'Egypte au IIIe siècle avant J.-C.* Publications de la Société Royale Égyptienne de Papyrologie. Textes et documents 1. Cairo: Institut français d'archéologie orientale, 1931.

PGiss Eger, O., E. Kornemann, P. M. Meyer, and M. Kotyl, eds. *Griechische Papyri zu Giessen*. 2 vols. Berlin: Teubner, 1910–1912. Vol. 1, ed. O. Eger, E. Kornemann, and P. M. Meyer (1910); vol. 2, ed. M. Kotyl (1912).

PHamb Meyer, P. M., et al., eds. Griechische Papyrusurkunden der Hamburger Staats- und Universitätsbibliothek. Leipzig: Teubner, 1911–1984.

PHI Packard Humanities Institute numbers for Greek inscriptions. The Greek texts are available online at https://epigraphy.packhum.org/.

PHibeh Grenfell, Bernard P., Arthur S. Hunt, E. G. Turner, and M.-T. Lenger, eds. *The Hibeh Papyri*. 2 vols. Graeco-Roman Memoirs 7, 32. London: Egypt Exploration Society, 1906–1955. Vol. 1 (nos. 1–171), ed. B. P. Grenfell and Arthur S. Hunt (1906); vol. 2 (nos. 172–284), ed. E. G. Turner and M.-T. Lenger (1955).

PKöln	Kramer, B., and R. Hübner, et al., eds. *Kölner Papyri*. 45 vols. Cologne-Opladen: Westdeutscher, 1976–.
PLilleDem	Sottas, H., and François de Cenival., eds. *Papyrus démotiques de Lille*. Paris: Paul Geuthner, 1927–1984.
PMich	Edgar, Campbell Cowan, et al., eds. *Michigan Papyri*. 21 vols. Ann Arbor: University of Michigan Press; Amsterdam: J. C. Gieben, 1931–1996.
POxy	*The Oxyrhynchus Papyri*. 84 vols. Graeco-Roman Memoirs. London: Egypt Exploration Society, 1898–.
PPetaus	Hagedorn, Ursula, Dieter Hagedorn, Louise C. Youtie, and Herbert C. Youtie. *Das Archiv des Petaus (P.Petaus)*. Papyrologica Coloniensia 4. Cologne: Westdeutscher Verlag, 1969.
PPetr	Mahaffy, John P., ed. *The Flinders Petrie Papyri*. 3 vols. Dublin: Academy Press, 1891–1905.
PPrague	Pintaudi, Rosario, Růžena Dostálová, and Ladislav Vidman, eds. *Papyri Graecae Wessely Pragenses*. 3 vols. Firenze, 1988–2011.
PRyl	Johnson, J. M., V. Martin, Arthur S. Hunt, Colin H. Roberts, and E. G. Turner. *Catalogue of the Greek Papyri in the John Rylands Library, Manchester*. 4 vols. Manchester: Manchester University Press, 1911–1952.
PSI	*Papiri greci e latini. Pubblicazioni della Società italiana per la ricerca dei papiri greci e latini in Egitto*. 17 vols. Florence: F. Le Monnier, 1912–.
PStrass	Preisigke, Friedrich, ed. *Griechische Papyrus der Kaiserlichen Universitäts- und Landesbibliothek zu Strassburg*. 10 vols. Leipzig: J. C. Hinrichs, 1912–1989.
PTebt	Grenfell, Bernard P., Arthur S. Hunt, Edgar J. Goodspeed, J. G. Smyly, and Campbell Cowan Edgar. *The Tebtunis Papyri*. University of California Publications, Graeco-Roman Archaeology. 5 vols. London: Henry Frowde, 1902.
PTexas	Ptolemaic cartonnage papyri held by the Harry Ransom Humanities Research Center of the University of Texas, Austin.
PTorAmen	Pestman, P. W., ed. *L'Archivio di Amenothes figlio di Horos (P. Tor. Amenothes). Testi demotici e greci relativi ad una famiglia di imbalsamatori del secondo sec. a. C.* Milan: Istituto Editoriale Cisalpino, La Goliardica, 1981.

SB	Preisigke, Friedrich, F. Bilabel, E. Kiessling, and H.-A. Rupprecht, eds. *Sammelbuch griechischer Urkunden aus Ägypten.* 28 vols. Strasbourg: K. J. Trubner, 1915–.
SE	Alpers, Michael, and Helmut Halfmann, with the assistance of John Mansfield and Christoph Schafer, eds. *Supplementum Ephesium.* Hamburg: Deutschen Forschungsgemeinschaft, 1995.
SEG	Hondius, J. J. E., A. G. Woodhead, A. E. Raubitschek, H. W. Pleket, R. S. Stroud, J. H. M. Strubbe, Angelos Chaniotis, et al., eds. *Supplementum epigraphicum graecum.* 65 vols. Leiden: Brill, 1923–.
SIG³	Dittenberger, Wilhelm. *Sylloge inscriptionum graecarum.* 3rd ed. 4 vols. Leizpig: S. Hirzel, 1915–1924.
TAM	Österreichische Akademie der Wissenschaften. *Tituli Asiae Minoris.* 5 vols. Vienna: Hoelder, Pichler, Tempsky, 1901–1989. Vol. 1, *Tituli Lyciae lingua Lycia conscripti*, by Ernst Kalinka (1901); vol. 2, pts. 1–3, *Tituli Lyciae linguis Graeca et Latina conscripti*, by Ernst Kalinka (1920–1944); vol. 3, *Tituli Pisidiae linguis Graeca et Latina conscripti*, ed. Rudolf Heberdey (1941); vol. 4, *Tituli Bithyniae linguis Graeca et Latina conscripti*, ed. Friedrich Karl Dörner and Maria-Barbara von Stritzky (1978); vol. 5, pts. 1–2, *Tituli Lydiae linguis graeca et latina conscripti*, by Peter Herrmann (1981, 1989).
TDNT	Kittel, Gerhard, and Gerhard Friedrich, eds. *Theological Dictionary of the New Testament.* Translated by Geoffrey W. Bromiley. 10 vols. Grand Rapids: Eerdmans, 1964–1976.
UPZ	Wilcken, Ulrich, ed. *Urkunden der Ptolemäerzeit (ältere Funde).* 2 vols. Berlin: De Gruyter, 1927–1957.
ZPE	*Zeitschrift für Papyrologie und Epigraphik* (periodical).

Abbreviations of Ancient Sources

Abbreviations of most ancient works correspond to those given in the *SBL Handbook of Style*. Abbreviations not listed there appear below.

Ab urbe cond.	Livy, *Ab Urbe Condita*
Adv. nat.	Arnobius, *Adversus Nationes*
Apol.	Aristides, *Apology*
Diatr.	Musonius Rufus, *Diatribai*
Diff. puls.	Galen, *De Differentiis Pulsuum*
Dig.	*Digest of Justinian*
Ep.	Cyprian, *Epistles*
Epi.	Martial, *Epigrams*
Hist.	Polybius, *Historiae*
Hist.	Herodian, *History of the Empire from the Death of Marcus*
Hist. eccl.	Socrates, *Historia ecclesiastica*
Hist. eccl.	Sozomen, *Historia ecclesiastica*
Hist. rom.	Dio Cassius, *Historia Romana*
Instr.	Commodian, *Instructiones*
Med.	Marcus Aurelius, *Meditationes*
P.W.	Thucydides, *History of the Peloponnesian War*
Quaest.	Ambrosiaster, *Quaestiones Veteris et Novi Testamenti*
Vit. Mart.	Sulpicius Severus, *Life of St. Martin*
Vit. Porph.	Mark the Deacon, *Vita sancti Porphyrii*

1

Greco-Roman Associations and the Origins of Christianity

Taking Stock of Where We Are

Bruce W. Longenecker

Especially in the twenty-first century, the origins of Christianity have increasingly been studied in relation to the small groups that dotted the urban centers of the Roman world—groups generically referred to as "associations" in modern scholarly parlance. The contributions contained within this book seek to enlarge our conversations regarding the extent to which the study of Greco-Roman associations can shed light on features of Christian origins in the pre-Constantinian world.

Greco-Roman associations have already been shown to be relevant to any number of questions we might ask concerning the rise of Christ devotion in the Roman world, from micro-level questions about the interpretation of particular texts to macro-level questions about the spread of Christ devotion in the pre-Constantinian world and beyond. The big-picture question might be asked in this way: How did devotion to Jesus Christ grow from a small movement in the cultural outskirts of Roman Judea around 30 CE to become the lynchpin of a religiopolitical initiative that helped the emperor Constantine unify an empire in the early fourth century? What explains the expansion of Christ devotion, from a handful of people at the time of his crucifixion in Jerusalem to approximately six million people (estimates often suggest) spread throughout the Mediterranean basin three hundred years later?

Various answers have been proposed for macro-level questions of this kind. Often those explanations have involved appeals to some form of "Christian distinctiveness," illustrating how devotion to Jesus Christ was different from other phenomena of the pre-Constantinian Roman world, with that difference (or those differences) enabling it to endure, advance, and flourish, even through sporadic periods of persecution. In the words of Larry Hurtado, for instance, "Participation in the Christian faith must have offered things that attracted converts and compensated for the considerable social costs incurred in becoming an adherent" (2016, 35). The problem is that even when scholars see themselves to be historians primarily, their results often appear to be based on "ideological or theological assumptions concerning the supposed uniqueness and incomparability of early Christianity" (Harland 2009, 2).

The study of Greco-Roman associations offers the chance to pursue different angles of vision on long-standing issues about the rise of Christianity in the Roman world. The inner workings of these ancient groups are occasionally glimpsed in the material artifacts (especially associational inscriptions) that have survived the millennia, allowing us to see how associations of the Greco-Roman world organized themselves to maximize their chances of survival and enhancement. Paying attention to these data, new questions emerge regarding the origins of Christianity. For instance, instead of asking about the distinctives of Christ groups, historians can pursue other types of questions: How did groups in the Greco-Roman world maintain themselves? What practices and values fostered corporate stability? How can our understanding of those matters shed light on corporate maintenance among Christ groups in the pre-Constantinian world?

This is essentially to ask about sameness—that is, how Christ groups might have been similar, in fact, to other groups in the Roman world. In this regard, exploring the sinews of ancient associational life offers insight on the question of group construction and stability in general. Examining how associations structured themselves to maximize their stability and durability opens the possibility of inferring how pre-Constantinian Christ groups may have often structured themselves in order to maximize *their* stability and enhance *their* durability. Along the way, it might even be possible to catch a glimpse of distinctiveness here or there; as John Kloppenborg rightly notes, the "comparison of diverse associative practices can allow us to see both what was common" among Greco-Roman groups "and what was interestingly distinctive" about any particular group (2020b; cf. 2019, xi).[1] We might even begin to notice certain forms of distinctiveness coalescing among Christ groups amid a smorgasbord of attractions offered by the variety of associations of the Greco-Roman world.

In many ways, the conversation about these things seems to be in the relatively early stages. It wasn't too long ago, for instance, that probing the relevance of Greco-Roman associations for the study of pre-Constantinian Christianity looked to many like nothing more than a somewhat peripheral academic curiosity. But with a steady stream of publications emerging since the late 1990s or so, it is no longer possible to treat Greco-Roman associations simply as interesting curiosities on the periphery of historical analysis of early Christianity. Similarities, differences, comingled identities, financial viability, status identities of and within groups, relationships between similarly affiliated groups both within and between cities—these issues and more are currently in play in the study of associations and the early centuries of Christ devotion (having strong footholds within the essays that follow). No matter how scholarly conversations will develop from here, it is now clear that associations will need to be a part of the toolkit of those working at the coalface of the history of early Christianity.

HOW WE GOT HERE

If the study of Greco-Roman associations is now well positioned to enhance the study of the origins of Christianity, how did we get to this point?

Although serious study of Greco-Roman associations dates back to the nineteenth century, interest in the relevance of associational groups for the interpretation of Christian origins has waxed and waned since then. But that interest seems to have received a steroidal injection in the final years of the twentieth century, with the topic exercising increasing explanatory muscle in the early decades of the twenty-first century.

In the nineteenth and twentieth centuries, a few scholars thought that "funerary associations" of the poor may provide an interesting model through which to glimpse the inner life of Christ groups. But in general the scholarly pursuit was intent on recovering the attitude of Roman ruling authorities toward Greco-Roman associations in general—an interest driven by the common assumption that, as groups of poor people, associations must have

---

[1]   Kloppenborg places his interests in line with those of Jonathan Z. Smith; see especially Smith 1990. See Horrell 2020 for a nuance study of the possible attractions of early Christ groups. On studying New Testament texts alongside *comparanda*, see Barclay and White 2020.

been seen to threaten the structures of social stability of the urban world.[2] With some notable exceptions (e.g., Hatch 1881, 26–28), the tendency was to see Greco-Roman associations primarily as mechanisms of funerary insurance for the poor, without much of a "religious" dimension to them. And if they weren't primarily "religious," there wasn't much point thinking about them in relation to the early growth of a religious movement that came to be known as Christianity. Of course, some associations were characterized by devotion to particular deities, and this had drawn the attention particularly of some in the so-called "history of religions school" of the late nineteenth and early twentieth centuries. But interest in Greco-Roman associations as *comparanda* for Christ groups never gathered significant momentum. Discoveries of ancient documents relevant to the study of early Christianity captured scholarly attention—such as the Didache (discovered in 1873, published in 1883), the papyri at Oxyrhynchus (with excavations beginning in 1896), the Nag Hammadi library (discovered in 1945), and the Dead Sea Scrolls (discovered in 1947). Arguably this latter discovery (i.e., scrolls from a wilderness group still in existence in the first century and with strong similarities to the early Christ movement) played a significant role in shifting scholarly attention to the Judean (or Jewish) context of Christian origins—a context that seemed to share little overlap with Greco-Roman associations spread throughout the Mediterranean basin.

In the 1970s and 1980s, however, things began to shift. Classicists started to reevaluate the social functions of Greco-Roman associations. Instead of primarily being funerary groups populated by the poor or cultic groups in the worship of a deity, associations came to be seen as mechanisms for enhancing relationality among people who sought to enrich their interpersonal orbit—whether in a cultic group specifically formed to honor a particular deity or in some other form of corporate allegiance or identity. Associations were recognized as being enclaves of convivial camaraderie and social support, often funded by participants and others who commanded significant resources.[3] With a sizeable proportion of associational members being from middling economic groups (even if there were plenty of poorer members within them as well), association participants would often have had some social prominence within the civic context. Some were patronized by prominent authorities in the civic arena. Accordingly,

[2] Only some associations that presented themselves as having a notably "religious" character were, in this view, well placed to assuage the concerns of the elite, since some deities were linked to civic interests.

[3] See, for instance, MacMullen 1974, 68–87.

most associations came to be seen as firmly embedded within the social structures of the urban context in which their members often thrived.[4] Moreover, a "religious" component was recognized to have played a significant role in Greco-Roman associations of virtually every kind. Perhaps associations had more relevance for the study of the origins of Christianity than had previously been thought.

Although several studies in the 1970s and 1980s began to probe this area,[5] it was Wayne Meeks' influential book *The First Urban Christians* that largely set the tone on this matter in the aftermath of its appearance in 1983. Toward the beginning of a chapter entitled "The Formation of the Ekklēsia," Meeks sought to place early Christ groups within the context of other recognizable groups of their day to ascertain how groups in the Roman world came together and stayed intact. To avoid anachronistic reconstructions of Christ groups, Meeks studied the social structures of four historical *comparanda*, each selected because of its potential similarity with Christ groups in one way or another. Asking about the stability of groups in the Greco-Roman world, Meeks' four *comparanda*, which he called "models," were: households, "voluntary" associations, synagogues, and the philosophic or rhetorical schools.[6] Because all four models offer notable analogies to early Christ groups, Meeks thought that people in the Roman world might have interpreted Christ groups in relation to any of them. But Meeks ultimately concluded that none of these models was the template for the formation and continuance of early Christ groups; each *comparandum* left certain aspects of early Christ groups unexplained.[7] Without an institutional template to draw on for explanatory power, Meeks' chapter shifted its focus in the second half, where he introduced subsequent chapters of his book in relation to the issue of what might have made Christ groups distinctive within their historical context. Meeks' goal now was to try to identify what it was that gave early Christ groups their sense of identity in contradistinction

[4] MacMullen 1974, 76–77. He noted (76): "It followed that their internal organization should ape the high-sounding terminology of larger, municipal bodies . . . [so that] the larger craft associations constituted in every detail miniature cities."

[5] See especially Wilken 1971; Barton and Horsley 1981.

[6] Ascough used the same four institutions in his 1998 overview of the formation of Pauline assemblies.

[7] Meeks 1983, 74–84. If Meeks prioritized one *comparandum* over the others for its explanatory power in relation to the stability of Christ groups, it was the household, which offered structures that the other three *comparanda* often utilized, much like early Christ groups. But even recognizing that slight edge, Meeks imagined that none of these institutions offered a model for the formation of early Christ groups without remainder.

to other types of groups. In the end of the chapter, Meeks surmised that Christ groups may have been a relatively singular phenomenon on the cultural landscape of Roman world.[8]

Meeks' work has been highly influential and repays close attention even today. His view has often served as the default in the study of what Christ groups might have looked like on the ground. Consequently, there was little urgency within the study of Christian origins to inquire further into whether we could learn anything about early Christ groups by interpreting them in relation to Greco-Roman associations. But a few scholars didn't get that memo.

Consequently, toward the end of the twentieth century, some scholars began to give different answers to the agenda items that Meeks had registered. If certain parts of the historical picture are reconstructed differently to Meeks' handling of them, new possibilities emerge. A survey of the books most dedicated to the topic reveals the trend.

One of the first major studies in this regard was Thomas Schmeller's *Hierarchie und Egalität* (1995). Comparing Christ groups and associations in relation to hierarchical and egalitarian dynamics, Schmeller found both dynamics to be operative within Greco-Roman associations—a hierarchical dynamic with regard to patronage and group offices, and an egalitarian dynamic at work with regard to participants in general. According to Schmeller, much the same is evident within early Christ groups established by Paul. By noting the frequency of an egalitarian ethos within Greco-Roman associations, Schmeller facilitated a closer analogical fit between associations and early Christ groups.

The next year, a volume of essays was collected under the title *Voluntary Associations in the Graeco-Roman World*, edited by John S. Kloppenborg and Stephen G. Wilson (1996). Discussions within the book included not only Greco-Roman associations but also Judean groups and occasionally Christ groups as well. Five years later saw the publication of Anders Runesson's *The Origins of the Synagogue* (2001). Runesson argued that the origins of the synagogue in the diaspora cannot be explained without recourse to the influence of Greco-Roman associations. Within the span of five years, these two books had illustrated that discussion of Greco-Roman associations could be profitably applied to discussion of social structures within Judean

---

[8] Meeks (1983, 84) states the focus of his pursuit as being a determination of "the factors that contributed to their [Christ followers'] sense of belonging to a distinct group and the ways in which they distinguished that group from its social environment." He wondered whether, in fact, Christ groups "may after all have been unique."

(or "Jewish") synagogues of the diaspora.[9] This gave added impetus to the study of associations and early Christ groups, which themselves were closely associated with diaspora synagogues.

In the meantime, two doctoral projects had been written under the supervision of John Kloppenborg, each appearing in published form in 2003: Philip Harland's *Associations, Synagogues, and Congregations: Claiming a Place in Ancient Mediterranean Society* and Richard Ascough's *Paul's Macedonian Associations: The Social Context of Philippians and 1 Thessalonians*. Harland emphasized that associations often provided the means by which people found pockets of relational security within the civic context of the Greco-Roman world; by extension, early Christ groups should not be seen as staunchly sectarian but as groups fostering integration within their civic environments—precisely what the author of the Johannine apocalypse thought was contemptuous, because of the cultic dimension that permeated associational life. For his part, Ascough highlighted structural differences in the Christ groups of Philippi and Thessalonica, proposing that the Philippian Christ group approximated a religious association while the Thessalonian Christ group was more analogous to an association of professional workers.

Corinthian Christ groups were an important component of Stephen Chester's doctoral research, also published in 2003 as *Conversion at Corinth: Perspectives on Conversion in Paul's Theology and the Corinthian Church*. Although Chester saw differences between associations on the one hand and Paul's understanding of the Christ groups on the other, he argued that Corinthian Christ followers probably saw their participation in Christ groups to be much like membership with any other association—as an important component of their identity but not one that required them to relinquish other features of their civic life. This is reflected most clearly in their understanding of patronage, their observance of the Lord's Supper, the court litigations between believers, and their understanding of the Jerusalem collection as a feature of a trans-local relationality among associations. Ten years later, Éric Rebillard's *Christians and Their Many Identities in Late Antiquity* (2013) presented a different data set of evidence that nonetheless coincided with Chester's argument. According to Rebillard, third- through fifth-century data from North Africa offer glimpses of Christians negotiating their place in society by adopting various forms of identity in different social and civic

---

[9]   More recently, further studies have emerged that focus particularly on Judean groups in relation to ancient associations, including Gillihan 2012 and Eckhardt 2019. See also Harland's repeated interest in this area in several monographs (2003, 2009), as well as Last and Harland 2020.

contexts. Engaging with non-Christians and operating within society in ways that were strategically beneficial for them, Christians often participated as loyal members of associations beyond Christ groups, placing them in guilds and groups that venerated the traditional Greco-Roman deities.

Eva Ebel's study of Corinthian Christ groups appeared a year after Chester's—*Die Attraktivität früher christlicher Gemeinden: Die Gemeinde von Korinth im Spiegel griechisch-römischer Vereine* (2004). Noting that Christ groups would have been perceived as associations by their contemporaries, Ebel argued that Christ groups had certain attractions over other associational groups—with slaves, women, and the poor in particular appreciating the more socially diverse and economically supportive context of Christ groups (i.e., a weekly meal and the lack of obligatory membership fees) over against typical associations.[10]

In 2009, Philip Harland's second monograph on the subject appeared, entitled *Dynamics of Identity in the World of the Early Christians: Associations, Judeans, and Cultural Minorities*. Harland probed further aspects of associational identity. For instance, he drew attention to the use of fictive kinship language (i.e., "brother," "mother," and "father") in associations as a means of enhancing social cohesion;[11] he suggested that associations played a role of fostering Judean and gentile interaction and engagement, which may have benefited recruitment to Christ groups; and he noted that the non-exclusive character of associational membership may also have characterized some members of Christ groups. The following year, Valeriy A. Alikin argued that all sorts of practices that characterized communal practices in meetings of Christ followers from the first through third centuries have "counterpart[s] in customs practiced at banquets held by Graeco-Roman clubs and associations" (2010, 288).

Having written an article in 1998 contending that the Christ groups founded by Paul probably had written bylaws of constitution like other associations (referencing the phrase "do not go beyond what is written" in 1 Cor 4:6), James C. Hanges next turned his attention to Paul's stories of founding communities. In *Paul, Founder of Churches: A Study in Light of the Evidence for the Role of "Founder-Figures" in the Hellenistic-Roman Period* (2012), Hanges outlined the narrative contours of stories regarding associational founders and argued that Paul's own self-presentation as the founder

[10] This is all very much in line with the arguments of Pilhofer 2002. A similar interest in categorizing similarities and differences between Christ groups and associations among Germanic scholars animates the 2006 volume edited by Gutsfeld and Koch.

[11] See also Hemelrijk 2008.

of Christ groups falls well within those contours (e.g., his selection by a deity, his range of assigned responsibilities, the opposition from others, etc.).

Richard Last's doctoral research (supervised by John Kloppenborg) appeared in 2016 as *The Pauline Church and the Corinthian Ekklēsia: Greco-Roman Associations in Comparative Context*. According to Last, the Corinthian Christ group probably consisted of nine to twelve members who did not have a fixed place in which to meet (e.g., households) but gathered in rented spaces, collected membership fees from all, and had office-holding leaders (cf. 1 Thess 5:12-13; Phil 1:1; Did. 15.1–2) whom they elected on a regular and rotating basis, while also engaging in honorific practices of their leaders. Last's portrait shows little trace of the more traditional depictions of Christ groups generally tending toward egalitarian relationships and shunning honorifics while welcoming "freely" the poor and needy.

A similar assessment appears in Jin Hwan Lee's 2018 book *The Lord's Supper in Corinth in the Context of Greco-Roman Private Associations*. Lee focused especially on the particularities of associational meals to shed light on the observance of the Lord's Supper by Corinthian Christ followers and the cause of discord within that observance.[12] Another doctoral project supervised by John Kloppenborg, Lee's monograph postulated (on the basis of common associational practices) that the Corinthian Christ group funded the Lord's Supper through the payment of membership fees (rather than by householder resources or "potluck" arrangements) and met in rented accommodation (rather than in houses). According to Lee, things went wrong among the Corinthians when newly elected officials were humiliated by the previously elected officials (who were also more financially secure), who refuted the election results and, consequently, refused to relinquish their positions of honor where they enjoyed superior forms of experiencing the supper.

The year 2018 also saw the publication of *Juden, Christen und Vereine im Römischen Reich* by Benedikt Eckhardt and Clemens Leonhard (with a chapter contribution from Philip Harland). The authors offer case studies that consider the extent to which Greco-Roman associations provide a helpful analytical tool for studying groups of Judeans and Christ followers in the Roman world. Their findings are often cautionary, with the main authors generally demonstrating that the associational context can overpromise results for understanding Judean groups (i.e., synagogues, the Qumran community, the Therapeutae of Alexandria) and early Christ groups (i.e., the Christ groups founded by Paul in Corinth, Philippi, and Thessalonika).

---

[12] For earlier work on this subject, see Smith 2003 and Taussig 2009.

But in certain respects, associational data prove to be helpful for the task—especially when analyzing shared meal situations and economic scenarios. According to Eckhardt and Leonhard, the value of the associational backdrop very much depends on the kinds of questions one asks of the data.

The spring of 2020 saw yet another contribution from Richard Last and Philip A. Harland, in their coauthored monograph *Group Survival in the Ancient Mediterranean: Rethinking Material Conditions in the Landscape of Jews and Christians*. Delving into the nuts and bolts of associational socioeconomic realities and survival strategies, Last and Harland situated gatherings of Judeans and assemblies of Jesus followers firmly within the framework of relational networks evidenced in local groups of the Mediterranean basin.[13]

Six months earlier, John Kloppenborg's long-awaited book on the subject was published: *Christ's Associations: Connecting and Belonging in the Ancient City*. For the previous quarter of a century or so, Kloppenborg had produced a steady stream of studies on Greco-Roman associations and on their relevance to the study of early Christ groups. His influence in the field is evident not only in those contributions but also in his fostering of a new generation of scholars who have made their own explorations of associations and Christ groups. These developments came together in a stimulating fashion in this single book. Covering a wide range of issues, Kloppenborg presented associational data as "heuristic" material, insisting that associational data is "good to think with" when it comes to understanding early Christ groups; he did not contend for organic genealogy of any kind or even institutional influence, but noted simply that comparing Christ groups with associational mechanisms often adjusts our lens on those groups, offering focal depth and further clarity in our analysis. In many ways, Kloppenborg's book will do for the second quarter of the twenty-first century what Meeks' *First Urban Christians* did for the last quarter of the twentieth century. Even Meeks himself seems to have changed his tune in the intervening years. In a 2009 discussion of his earlier monograph, Meeks noted that he now found it completely acceptable to refer to early Christ groups as "associations of artificial immigrants"[14] (reiterating a view he first postulated in Meeks 2001). Perhaps, then, Meeks would now agree

---

[13] In the summer of that same year, the *Journal of Early Christian History* produced an issue half of which was dedicated to the topic of "Modelling Christian Cult Groups among Graeco-Roman Cults," with a focus on Christ groups and associations.

[14] Meeks 2009, 141. This followed on from Adams' suggestion that "the relevance of the associations to the study of Paul's churches can no longer be in doubt" (2009, 71).

with the claim Kloppenborg made in his presidential address to *Studiorum Novi Testamenti Societas* in 2019: "The study of ancient cultic associations coupled with network theory provides us with heuristic models to let us think more concretely about how the Christ cult spread in the period prior to Constantine."[15]

RESOURCING THE CONVERSATION

The overview of the preceding paragraphs is not intended to survey all that has been going on in relation to early Christ groups and Greco-Roman associations.[16] Highlighting books that have a sustained (or relatively sustained) focus on the topic, I have also omitted a number of books that have broader or other primary agendas, despite the fact that they do interact in some fashion along the way with Greco-Roman associations and early Christ groups.[17] I also have not surveyed the articles that have populated the field. But even this incomplete survey illustrates how the issue of associations in relation to Christ groups has gathered momentum over the past two decades, providing a strong vantage point from which to assess the contours of the origins of what was to become Christianity. Of course, there will be many degrees to which any particular historian will be onboard with this approach, but from the most vehement critic to the most vocal advocate, no scholar can turn a blind eye to this area of study. As Benedikt Eckhardt noted in 2016, interpreting texts and phenomena of early Christianity in relation to Greco-Roman associations "has now become a standard tool in religious studies and New Testament scholarship . . . open[ing] up new possibilities for understanding the social realities behind the Pauline epistles and other Christian texts, and it has stimulated new research into associations as well."[18]

Assisting in the advance of this area of study is the unprecedented availability of resources that this generation of scholarship currently enjoys. This includes edited collections of data pertaining to Greco-Roman associations, in particular:

- Richard S. Ascough, Philip A. Harland, and John S. Kloppenborg. 2012. *Associations in the Greco-Roman World: A Sourcebook*. Waco, Tex.: Baylor University Press.

---

[15] Kloppenborg 2020a, 350.
[16] For a fruitful survey, see especially Ascough 2015.
[17] These include (without being an exhaustive list) Downs 2008; Rebillard 2009; Corley 2010; Longenecker 2010.
[18] Eckhardt 2016, 646, 661, despite some cautions regarding the exercise.

- John S. Kloppenborg and Richard S. Ascough, eds. 2011. *Attica, Central Greece, Macedonia, Thrace.* BZNW 181. Vol. 1 of *Greco-Roman Associations: Texts, Translations, and Commentary.* Edited by John S. Kloppenborg, Philip A. Harland, and Richard S. Ascough. Berlin: De Gruyter.
- Philip A. Harland, ed. 2014. *North Coast of the Black Sea, Asia Minor.* BZNW 204. Vol. 2 of Kloppenborg, Harland, and Ascough, *Greco-Roman Associations.*
- John S. Kloppenborg, ed. 2020. *Ptolemaic and Early Roman Egypt.* BZNW 246. Vol. 3 of Kloppenborg, Harland, and Ascough, *Greco-Roman Associations.*
- two or three forthcoming volumes in Kloppenborg, Harland, and Ascough, *Greco-Roman Associations* (originally planned as a five-volume series, but that might grow to six)

Moreover, three invaluable databases are now available for online searches:

- Philip Harland's website *Associations in the Greco-Roman World* (https://philipharland.com/greco-roman-associations/)
- the Copenhagen Inventory of Ancient Associations project (https://ancientassociations.ku.dk/assoc/index.php)
- the Ghent Database of Roman Guilds and Occupation-Based Communities (GDRG), directed by Koenraad Verboven (https://gdrg.ugent.be/)

With no paucity of resource availability and with a selection of stimulating conversation pieces already establishing momentum, scholarly discussion of ancient associations is primed to move to the next stage, with an ever-increasing contingent of conversation partners.

Perhaps in the process the conversational focus will broaden. It is probably not an exaggeration to say that studies of early Christ groups in light of Greco-Roman associations gravitate, quite understandably, toward epistolary literature of the first century; while some work has been done with regard to gospel texts (especially canonical gospels) and other literature, it is the epistolary texts (especially the Pauline texts) that are especially amenable to the study of the corporate life of Christ groups in relation to Greco-Roman associations. Perhaps expanding the focus to other literary genres and to later time periods within the pre-Constantinian world is what lies ahead in this fertile field of academic conversation.

The essays in this book contribute to the burgeoning conversations in this emerging field of study. The essays have been written by a group of impressive scholars, who collectively represent interdisciplinary, intergenerational, and international contexts. Some scholars represented in this volume have already made significant contributions to the conversation for many years, even decisively shaping much of the contemporary context of discourse on the subject. Others have occasionally dipped a toe into associational waters, and still others are joining the conversation for the first time. Each contributor, however, is offering a fresh argument in one form or another, tightly bound to topics along the collective spine of this volume.[19] The authors obviously do not speak with a unanimous voice; they represent a symposium of voices, with each voice productively expanding our current conversations.

All contributors have been given a relatively short word limit, and have worked diligently to meet that target, sometimes needing to cut longer arguments to the prescribed length in the process. These essays are, then, focused exercises that explore features pertinent to the study of associations in relation to pre-Constantinian instances of Christ devotion (thus the title "Early Christianity" as opposed to "Early Christ Groups"). The essays have been grouped according to "angles of vision" and "focal points"—the former exploring a particular topic or trajectory through a selection of the data, the latter focusing more specifically on a particular text, set of texts, or group of inscriptions. These are not watertight compartments, but in general the essays tend to fall in one direction or the other.

I would like to thank the contributors for their fresh investigations for this volume. Each contributor joined the project with eagerness, and their contributions are productive. I look forward to seeing how their stimulating arguments impact further conversations in this fascinating field of study.[20]

[19] I have ensured that particular topics were discussed within the covers of this book. Other scholars were given *carte blanche* as to their topics, contributing to this volume in ways of their own choosing. Some whom I approached were, of course, unable to participate or were unable to remain in the project due to the Covid complications of 2020–2021. Several were hampered in their research by Covid restrictions and the lack of normal access to library facilities.

[20] I am grateful to the College of Arts and Sciences at Baylor University for providing a period of research leave, during which the editing of this book was one of the responsibilities undertaken. I am also indebted to the work of two impressive graduate students, Eric Brewer and Jeff Hubbard, who have helped enormously with the editing of this volume at various stages. Their future is bright, not simply as editors but as budding scholars and teachers. It has been a great pleasure to work closely with them on this project. I also thank John Kloppenborg for casting a helpful eye on this introduction. Any infelicities that remain are, of course, of my own making.

WORKS CITED

Adams, Edward. 2009. "First-Century Models for Paul's Churches: Selected Scholarly Developments since Meeks." Pages 60–78 in *After the First Urban Christians: The Social-Scientific Study of Pauline Christianity Twenty-Five Years Later*. Edited by Todd D. Still and David G. Horrell. London: T&T Clark.

Alikin, Valeriy A. 2010. *The Earliest History of the Christian Gathering: Origin, Development and Content of the Christian Gathering in the First to Third Centuries*. VCSup 102. Leiden: Brill.

Ascough, Richard S. 1998. *What Are They Saying about the Formation of Pauline Churches?* New York: Paulist Press.

———. 2003. *Paul's Macedonian Associations: The Social Context of Philippians and 1 Thessalonians*. WUNT 2/161. Tübingen: Mohr Siebeck.

———. 2015. "What Are They *Now* Saying about Christ Groups and Associations?" *CurBR* 13:207–44.

Ascough, Richard S., Philip A. Harland, and John S. Kloppenborg. 2012. *Associations in the Greco-Roman World: A Sourcebook*. Waco, Tex.: Baylor University Press.

Barclay, John M. G., and B. G. White, eds. 2020. *The New Testament in Comparison: Validity, Method, and Purpose in Comparing Traditions*. LNTS 600. London: T&T Clark.

Barton, S. C., and G. H. R. Horsley. 1981. "A Hellenistic Cult Group and the New Testament Churches." *JAC* 24:7–41.

Chester, Stephen J. 2003. *Conversion at Corinth: Perspectives on Conversion in Paul's Theology and the Corinthian Church*. London: T&T Clark.

Corley, Kathleen E. 2010. *Maranatha: Women's Funerary Rituals and Christian Origins*. Minneapolis: Fortress.

Downs, David J. 2008. *The Offering of the Gentiles: Paul's Collection for Jerusalem in Its Chronological, Cultural, and Cultic Contexts*. WUNT 2/248. Tübingen: Mohr Siebeck.

Ebel, Eva. 2004. *Die Attraktivität früher christlicher Gemeinden: Die Gemeinde von Korinth im Spiegel griechisch-römischer Vereine*. WUNT 2/178. Tübingen: Mohr Siebeck.

Eckhardt, Benedikt. 2016. "The Eighteen Associations of Corinth." *GRBS* 56:646–62.

———, ed. 2019. *Private Associations and Jewish Communities in the Hellenistic and Roman Cities*. JSJSup 191. Leiden: Brill.

Eckhardt, Benedikt, and Clemens Leonhard (with contributions by Philip A. Harland). 2018. *Juden, Christen und Vereine im Römischen Reich*. Berlin: De Gruyter.

Gillihan, Yonder Moynihan. 2012. *Civic Ideology, Organization, and Law in the Rule Scrolls: A Comparative Study of the Covenanters' Sect and Contemporary Voluntary Associations in Political Context*. STDJ 97. Leiden: Brill.

Gutsfeld, Andreas, and Dietrich-Alex Koch, eds. 2006. *Vereine, Synagogen und Gemeinden im kaiserzeitlichen Kleinasien.* Studien und Texte zu Antike und Christentum 25. Tübingen: Mohr Siebeck.

Hanges, James C. 1998. "1 Corinthians 4:6 and the Possibility of Written Bylaws in the Corinthian Church." *JBL* 117:275–98.

———. 2012. *Paul, Founder of Churches: A Study in Light of the Evidence for the Role of "Founder-Figures" in the Hellenistic-Roman Period.* Tübingen: Mohr Siebeck.

Harland, Philip A. 2003. *Associations, Synagogues, and Congregations: Claiming a Place in Ancient Mediterranean Society.* Minneapolis: Fortress.

———. 2009. *Dynamics of Identity in the World of the Early Christians: Associations, Judeans, and Cultural Minorities.* New York: Continuum; London: T&T Clark.

Hatch, Edwin. 1881. *The Organization of the Early Christian Churches: Eight Lectures Delivered before the University of Oxford, in the Year 1880.* London: Rivingtons.

Hemelrijk, Emily A. 2008. "Patronesses and 'Mothers' of Roman *Collegia.*" *ClAnt* 27:115–62.

Horrell, David G. 2020. "Why Were People Attracted to Paul's Good News?" Pages 260–77 in *The New Cambridge Companion to St. Paul.* Edited by Bruce W. Longenecker. Cambridge: Cambridge University Press.

Hurtado, Larry W. 2016. *Destroyer of the Gods: Early Christian Distinctiveness in the Roman World.* Waco, Tex.: Baylor University Press.

Kloppenborg, John S. 2019. *Christ's Associations: Connecting and Belonging in the Ancient City.* New Haven: Yale University Press.

———. 2020a. "Recruitment to Elective Cults: Network Structure and Ecology." *NTS* 66:323–50.

———. 2020b. Review of *Private Associations and Jewish Communities.* Edited by Benedikt Eckhardt. *RBL* 7.

Kloppenborg, John S., and Richard S. Ascough, eds. 2011. *Attica, Central Greece, Macedonia, Thrace.* BZNW 181. Vol. 1 of *Greco-Roman Associations: Texts, Translations, and Commentary.* Edited by John S. Kloppenborg, Philip A. Harland, and Richard S. Ascough. Berlin: De Gruyter.

Kloppenborg, John S., and Stephen G. Wilson, eds. 1996. *Voluntary Associations in the Graeco-Roman World.* London: Routledge.

Last, Richard. 2016. *The Pauline Church and the Corinthian Ekklēsia: Greco-Roman Associations in Comparative Context.* SNTSMS 164. Cambridge: Cambridge University Press.

Last, Richard, and Philip A. Harland. 2020. *Group Survival in the Ancient Mediterranean: Rethinking Material Conditions in the Landscape of Jews and Christians.* London: T&T Clark.

Lee, Jin Hwan. 2018. *The Lord's Supper in Corinth in the Context of Greco-Roman Private Associations*. Lanham, Md.: Lexington Books / Fortress Academic.

Longenecker, Bruce W. 2010. *Remember the Poor: Paul, Poverty, and the Greco-Roman World*. Grand Rapids: Eerdmans.

MacMullen, Ramsay. 1974. *Roman Social Relations, 50 B.C. to A.D. 284*. New Haven: Yale University Press.

Meeks, Wayne A. 1983. *The First Urban Christians: The Social World of the Apostle Paul*. New Haven: Yale University Press. 2nd ed., 2003.

———. 2001. "Corinthian Christians as Artificial Aliens." Pages 129–38 in *Paul beyond the Judaism/Hellenism Divide*. Edited by Troels Engberg-Pedersen. Louisville: Westminster John Knox.

———. 2009. "Taking Stock and Moving On." Pages 134–46 in Still and Horrell, *After the First Urban Christians*.

Pilhofer, Peter. 2002. "Die ökonomische Attraktivität christlicher Gemeinden der Frühzeit." Pages 194–216 in *Die frühen Christen und ihre Welt: Greifswalder Aufsätze 1996–2001*. WUNT 145. Tübingen: Mohr Siebeck.

Rebillard, Éric. 2009. *The Care of the Dead in Late Antiquity*. Translated by Elizabeth Trapnell Rawlings and Jeanine Routier-Pucci. Ithaca: Cornell University Press (the English translation of *Religion et sépulture: l'église, les vivants et les morts dans l'antiquité tardive*, Civilisations et sociétés 115 [Paris: Éditions de l'École des Hautes Études en Sciences Sociales, 2003]).

———. 2013. *Christians and Their Many Identities in Late Antiquity, North Africa, 200–450 CE*. Ithaca: Cornell University Press.

Runesson, Anders. 2001. *The Origins of the Synagogue: A Socio-historical Study*. ConBNT 37. Stockholm: Almqvist & Wiksell.

Schmeller, Thomas. 1995. *Hierarchie und Egalität: Eine sozialgeschichtliche Untersuchung paulinischer Gemeinden und griechisch-römischer Vereine*. Stuttgart: Katholisches Bibelwerk.

Smith, Dennis E. 2003. *From Symposium to Eucharist: The Banquet in the Early Christian World*. Minneapolis: Fortress.

Smith, Jonathan Z. 1990. *Drudgery Divine: On the Comparison of Early Christianities and the Religions of Late Antiquity*. Chicago: University of Chicago Press.

Taussig, Hal. 2009. *In the Beginning Was the Meal: Social Experimentation and Early Christian Identity*. Minneapolis: Fortress.

Wilken, Robert Louis. 1971. "Collegia, Philosophical Schools and Theology." Pages 268–91 in *The Catacombs and the Colosseum: The Roman Empire as the Setting of Primitive Christianity*. Edited by Stephen Benko and John J. O'Rourke. Valley Forge, Pa.: Judson Press.

I

Angles of Vision

2

House Church
or Association?

Some Reflections on Models and Usefulness

Peter Oakes

Discussion of models for early Christian groups has focused on whether associations, or other ancient groups such as synagogues or households, provide the closest model for the Christian groups (e.g., Ascough 2015; Gruen 2016; Ascough 2017). This is not a discussion that I have been part of. Brief points I have made that could be relevant to associations have functioned differently. "Nine Types of Church in Nine Types of Space in the Insula of the Menander" included discussion of what would be the implications for Christian groups of meeting in the dining facilities of a bar or in a large banqueting hall in an elite house, each of which could fit with association practices. I suggested that the possible moral reputation of the bar (subject to academic disagreements on that topic) could affect the composition of the group, and that patronage implications of dining in the elite house would affect how the group functioned (Oakes 2016, 40–42, 45–48; also as Oakes 2020, 46–48, 51–54). Although I have not been engaged in discussing whether various types of ancient groups were appropriate or inappropriate models for early Christian ones, I have engaged with models in a different sense. Using a type of spatial approach, I have modeled early Christian groups, deriving the models from archaeology of structures and other material culture. Similarly, many other scholars have, generally less explicitly, engaged in modeling of this type. Jerome Murphy-O'Connor, Carolyn Osiek, David Balch, and others have used ancient material culture as the basis for what are, effectively, constructed models of early Christian groups: models that are spatially based and, in most of their research, domestically focused. These scholars have put such models to work in various pieces of New Testament interpretation (Murphy-O'Connor 1983; Osiek and Balch 1997).

At the 2019 San Diego SBL Annual Meeting, a conversation with John Kloppenborg, after he had kindly chaired my paper, "A House-Church Account of Economics and Empire" (Oakes 2020, 3–30), set me off reflecting on the different directions we had taken in our application of ancient evidence to the study of early Christianity. I initially thought that this would involve weighing up the value of a domestic focus, comparing that with the value of an association focus, along with weighing the value of using general material evidence, as against concentrating more effort on the particular material evidence of inscriptions. However, I soon realized that there are quite different kinds of model in use in the two enterprises: in my case constructing model groups from ancient spaces; in Kloppenborg's case comparing Christian groups with actual known other groups, viewed as one particularly significant and informative model for the Christian groups (although I will try to reframe that, below, in terms of there being association models into which Christian groups could be argued to fit).

As Kloppenborg very reasonably argues in *Christ's Associations*, the key test of employment of comparative evidence is how useful it is for understanding the target academic domain (Kloppenborg 2019, 4–10). For him, this appears primarily to be understanding the early Jesus movement. For me, it is primarily interpreting New Testament texts. However, each of us is interested in both areas and there is, in any case, a very extensive overlap between them. Understanding the history of the followers of Jesus is regularly important for contextualizing New Testament texts. Proper New Testament interpretation is an important element in constructing history. In both areas, there are many possibilities for what kinds of effect are considered useful. This essay will focus primarily on a few possible effects of a fairly broad kind, involving general shifts in perception of the nature of early Christian groups and associated New Testament texts.

THINGS OR WORDS?

I considered writing this essay under the title "Things or Words? Which Archaeological Evidence Is More Useful for New Testament Interpretation?" There is a nice counterintuitive effect of even bothering to ask the question. The New Testament is a mass of words. Surely archaeologically preserved words are likely to be much more useful for New Testament interpretation than are structures and objects? Surely scholars such as Osiek, Balch, myself, and indeed the editor of the current volume (Longenecker 2020) would have been better spending our time as the Toronto projects associated with Kloppenborg largely were, amassing and interpreting epigraphic evidence from the New Testament period, rather than standing in ancient houses, staring at walls and at objects in museums on sites or nearby, trying to reflect on what various New Testament texts would have meant in such settings?

The answer, of course, is that each approach provides different benefits. Association inscriptions provide great amounts of evidence about how many kinds of predominantly non-elite groups organized themselves, conducted their meetings, and brought various kinds of benefits to their members. It is clearly a reasonable view that, even though first-century Christian groups did not produce any such inscriptions that are extant, there is a high probability that many practices of various Christian groups fitted within the repertoire of practices seen in the association inscriptions. Equally, it is clearly reasonable to suppose that lives of first-century Christians fell within the range of social situations indicated by predominantly nonverbal archaeological evidence from sites dating to that period (albeit usually interpreted with the help of literary or nonliterary textual evidence). It is reasonable both for Richard Ascough to assess 1 Thessalonians in relation to evidence of trade associations (Ascough 2003) and for Robert Jewett to assess what effects the nature of apartment blocks in Rome would have on Christian groups if they met in such a setting (Jewett 2007, 64–65).

There is, at least, useful piecemeal benefit to be gained from use of both nonverbal and verbal archaeological evidence. Individual New Testament passages can be considered in relation to archaeological evidence from a closely related cultural and social sphere and, in each case, we can evaluate whether the comparison is reasonable and is likely to be fruitful in terms of understanding the meaning of the text. To attempt to move beyond such piecemeal cases towards approaches that shed light on New Testament texts more broadly leads beyond the use of individual pieces of comparative evidence into the realm of considering overall models for the makeup and functioning of early Christian groups and asking how they could relate to the production of New Testament texts in that context.

CONTRASTING TYPES OF MODEL

Under some definitions of *association*, early Christian groups simply are associations. Ascough cites Kloppenborg's definition of them as groups of people "normally organized around a common ethnic identity, deity or cult, trade or profession, or neighborhood, and are to be distinguished from civic organizations" (Ascough 2015, 27, citing Kloppenborg 2009). Early Christian groups were groups organized around a deity or cult. They fit the definition. It is clear, though, that *association* becomes useful for analyzing Christian groups only when *association*, as a category, is given substance by collection of evidence: mainly epigraphic, but also from literary texts, papyri, and the remains of association meeting places and related finds. However, that evidence is full of differences as well as similarities. Analysts need to find patterns of sufficiently common features to make something recognizable as an "association." What is useful is an association model: a simplified representation of the evidence, making key commonalities visible and providing a framework within which variations can be set out (on models see Elliott 1993, 40–48). For Kloppenborg and others, various early Christian groups fit in various ways, in relation to various issues, into several variations of the association model (Kloppenborg 2019, 5–10, 23–54). As Kloppenborg insists, this is not the only model within which some Christian groups will fit: some may, for instance, look like philosophical schools for some issues (Kloppenborg 2019, 9). However, the association model works as a tool for analysis of early Christian groups when it gives an organized framework for deploying various instances of epigraphic evidence of association life to understand instances of such life in Christian groups, seen as belonging, with the group in the inscription, in a common model, in which the shared features are sufficiently substantial to enable progress on the interpretative issue in question.

The house church model is a very different type of model. There are no actual ancient non-Christian groups, of which we have textual or pictorial evidence, that are providing a model of organization within which the early Christian groups are seen as fitting. The house church model is constructed by juxtaposing various New Testament texts with ancient material and literary culture. In such an approach to the most prominent New Testament instance, that of the κατ᾽ οἶκον ἐκκλησία ("house assembly") of Rom 16:5, that phrase is juxtaposed with archaeological and textual evidence relevant to κατ᾽ οἶκον. What group results from the idea of assembling in a "house"? The result is a construct. I would see it as essentially a mathematical construct. It is the group that "fits" (in various physical, social, and cultural senses) into this ancient space.

This Christian group is not patterned on an actual known ancient group. That is not because meeting in houses was a uniquely Christian practice. All sorts of groups of ancient people undoubtedly met in houses. However, the house church model is not constructed by looking for instances of actual such meetings and trying to form a model from them. The house church model is constructed by asking questions about the size and nature of house spaces in which meetings could take place, what would be involved in meeting in such spaces, what it would mean for the household, what it would mean for people beyond the household to enter the space, who would be likely to enter the space, and so on. Construction of the house church model is performing a different task from construction of the association model and its application to early Christian groups. The house church model is a tool for deploying primarily the material culture within which Christians met. The association model is a tool for deploying primarily evidence drawn from known ancient groups.

As was the case for the issues of usefulness of general material culture compared with epigraphy, raised above, it might seem obvious that comparison with known ancient groups will always be more useful than use of constructs based on material culture. However, as in nonverbal vs verbal cases, both types of model quite notably have substantial uses, including cases in which the construct from material culture may be the more fruitful.

It is worth commenting that there are further valuable types of model that we could have brought into our discussion. One is what I would see as primarily a model of process, rather than of groups, namely, the dining model of early Christian activity. In this, New Testament texts are interpreted in light of ancient evidence of practices in banquets and symposia. Dennis Smith, Matthias Klinghardt, and others have given considerable impetus to this. The strongest richness of that model lies in its use of literary texts that depict various activities and ideas associated with dining, such as singing and mutual respect, that are seen in New Testament texts: texts that also explicitly depict dining together as a central group activity (Smith 2003; Klinghardt 1996; Smith and Taussig 2012). Another significant type of model is one of transformation of space. A prime example is a cultic one, in which Christian meetings, in the process of occurring, conceptually transform domestic (or related) spaces into spaces that can be compared with different settings, such as temples, in which devotion is offered to one or more divine figures. This type of model is exemplified in Jorunn Økland's *Women in Their Place*, in which she argues that, when early Christian meetings were happening, the transformation of domestic space into ritual space produced key changes to the conceptualization of women's participation in the meetings (Økland 2004).

A MODEL "HOUSE CHURCH"

If we are considering the sense of the κατ᾽ οἶκον ἐκκλησία of Prisca and Aquila in Rom 16:5, a couple of points need to be made. For translating ἐκκλησία in the New Testament, *assembly* usually has advantages over *church*, a term that sounds anachronistic and, to most people, suggests a building. However, *house church* would be more widely understood than *house assembly*. *House church* fits usage in modern Christian groups who do not have church buildings but meet in domestic spaces of various types (in the UK, *assembly* usually means a formal meeting of a school or regional parliament). My own use of it in my research stemmed from seeking to do more realistic work on ancient "house churches" than had been done in the well-established tradition of previous work on the topic. I argued for looking at non-elite houses rather than villas, and for looking at craftworker dwellings in particular. Then I sought to find archaeological instances of such dwellings and to consider what would be the implications of Christian groups meeting in such a setting, rather than in the villas that were prioritized in most earlier scholarship (Oakes 2009).

In fact, as Robert Jewett has argued, "tenement churches," rather than churches in houses, would be more typical in the city of Rome of Paul's day (Jewett 2007, 70). Following the tradition of Prisca and Aquila as craftworkers (Acts 18:3) and the broader scholarly view of many early Christian groups centering on people like craftworkers, my research looked at structures and loose finds in Pompeii that indicated spaces that craftworkers inhabited. Craftworkers' workshops usually included at least some living accommodation, ranging from small mezzanines or side rooms to quite substantial numbers of other rooms. The οἶκοι in which Prisca and Aquila's ἐκκλησία met in Ephesus and Rome (1 Cor 16:19; Rom 16:5) were probably variously in houses or apartments that combined living and craftwork space.

My "model craftworker house church" is a mathematical construct of social types of people that could be expected to be part of a group that met in a dwelling-cum-workshop at the upper end of the range of such dwellings, and that filled the largest meeting space there[1] (the model construct could also be

---

[1]   Pompeian model craftworker house church (based on Oakes 2009, table 3.6), which included forty people, comprising:

1. craftworker, wife, children, a few (male) craftworking slaves, (female) domestic slave, dependent relative;
2. several other householders (smaller houses), some spouses, children, slaves, other dependents;

used to explore what partial filling of the space would imply, especially as it varied the proportion of host household to outsiders in the group). Other scholars effectively model house churches in other ways. The key commonality is that these scholars develop New Testament work from looking at ancient houses or apartments and asking, Who would meet here? What would it involve? How would New Testament texts sound in such a context?

There were undoubtedly many other types of place in which early Christian groups met. Eddie Adams does an excellent job of gathering and analyzing the range of spaces for which there is evidence in texts by or about early Christians (Adams 2013). As mentioned above, I have also discussed a number of possible types of space and some of their consequences for group practices, formation, and ideology (Oakes 2016). However, fixing on a specific model, derived from a type of space that is clearly and repeatedly attested for first-century Christian meetings, gives us a basis for thinking through issues in group function and New Testament interpretation that raise questions and ideas in a way that a more generalized model would not. The interpretative issues raised by the model craftworker house church would also, in many cases, apply to many other models. In any case, the model craftworker house church will be the model mainly used on the "house church" side of our remaining discussion.

AVOIDING EXCEPTIONALISM

An area in which the association model has a clear advantage in usefulness over the house church model is in combating undue exceptionalism. Christian preachers and scholars have repeatedly sought to promote Christianity by claiming that various features of early Christian group life as implied by New Testament texts—features that are currently seen as positive—were unique to such groups in their day. The association model wins hands down over the house church model here because the association model deals with actual, attested groups, whereas the house church model is purely a construct. The association model compiles evidence from many actual associations: the house church model starts from archaeological evidence of housing, asking what makeup of group could we reasonably expect if this was its best meeting place.

---

3. a few members of families with non-Christian family heads;
4. a couple of slaves with non-Christian owners;
5. a couple of free or freed dependents of non-Christians; and
6. a couple of homeless people.

Before my first encounters with Kloppenborg, Alicia Batten, and others linked to the Toronto projects, I had quite a list of features, based on prior scholarship, that I thought were present in early Christian groups but not associations. One by one they were knocked out, notable casualties being moral instruction (Batten 2007) and wide social, gender, and status diversity (Kloppenborg 2019, 32). There are still ways in which the nature and proportion of these features probably differed, on average, between Christian groups and the non-Christian groups attested in association inscriptions, but there are very few absolutely unprecedented features of Christian groups except those directly involving or stemming from devotion specifically to Christ.

COMPLICATING GROUP BOUNDARIES

Another tendency among church leaders and Christian New Testament scholars, perhaps influenced by experience of highly structured present-day churches, has been to see early Christian groups as having very clear boundaries. Use of the association model is unlikely to challenge this, because the comparator groups are attested epigraphically and that epigraphic attestation is often in foundational documents. The public presentation inherent in most epigraphy, the act of committing anything to stone, and the nature of foundational ideas make it inevitable that this evidence will tend to convey ideas of clearly delineated membership. As well as foundational documents, there are many examples of membership lists, including some that were repeatedly updated (Kloppenborg 2019, 42–43). Again, these favor the idea of membership as a clear category.

In contrast, the nature of the house church model immediately raises extensive questions that complicate the issue of what belonging to a Christian group would mean. The starting point of the model is a host householder and his or her house or apartment. People gather in the space, offer devotion to Christ, eat, learn, and maybe hear prophecies. Who hears? Who eats? Who gathers? The New Testament enforces these questions by stories about household conversion (Acts 16:15, 33), as well as by passages directly addressed to people from childhood to old age (Eph 6:1-3; 1 John 2:12-14). The questions about the nature of membership are sharpest for the host household who are all, to some extent, present, whose identities are wrapped up in the identity of the householder, and all of whom may well have been baptized. What is it to talk about membership or belief among the range of people in such a group, present primarily by force of circumstances?

For people who came in from other households, there would presumably be more variability in how many from any particular household came to the meeting, especially since New Testament texts attest to some households including a mix of Christians and non-Christians (1 Cor 7:12; 1 Pet 3:1). For people who came to the meeting from beyond the host household we can expect that that more frequently involved deliberate choice than it did for people who lived where the group met. However, even so, the likely ambiguity of the concept of membership within the host household would probably be a paradigm for wider ambiguity about membership among other households or individuals who were, to some degree, linked to the house church.

The nature of first-century social networks, other than formally constituted ones such as epigraphically attested associations, typically made their limits and their patterns of level of commitment messy. Extended families, friendships, neighborhood relationships (other than as associations, explored in Last 2016), business relationships, extended networks of patronage: these and most other social networks would have had unclear boundaries and degrees of involvement. It is not just that we happen to lack membership lists for first-century Christian groups. My impression from New Testament texts is that the nature of participation in and allegiance to such groups would typically place them into the category not of formally constituted groups, with clearly measurable boundaries, but of informally constituted groups, the boundaries of which were not clear or consistent. Where modern churches look back at first-century Christian groups as paradigmatic, consideration of the house church model suggests that it is probably unwise to retroject into those early groups concepts of clear group boundaries and rules for membership.

IMAGINING LIFESTYLES AND DISAGGREGATING GROUPS

For interpretation of many New Testament texts, it is important to engage our imagination in an informed way, to think how the text would interact with aspects of first-century lifestyle, rather than with that of our time and place. Many problematic readings of New Testament texts have stemmed from failure to do that.

Both models can help here. A good example from the association model is about ways of collecting and distributing money. This is a major issue in various New Testament texts, especially Paul's letters. Association evidence offers a repertoire of ways in which these processes were set up in ancient groups of a variety of sizes and social makeups, and for a variety of purposes

(Kloppenborg 2019, 248–59). A particularly striking question that the associa-tion model raises for New Testament study is, What is happening about burial? Among the most common benefits that associations provided for members was proper burial. One of the common member duties was attendance at such rituals (Kloppenborg 2019, 267). In what ways, if any, do New Testament texts address this culturally prominent issue? Does New Testament teaching about death and afterlife somehow feed into this in a practical way?

Money provides a neat example of the different types of help that the association and house church models offer. Association inscriptions, and other evidence such as papyrus letters, give information of group subscrip-tions and expenditures. The archaeological evidence behind the house church model tells us exactly how much was in the purse of the male figure who died on the couch in the main reception room of a cabinet-maker's house in Pompeii (delineated as I.10.7). We also know the long list of all the specific belongings in the house, as well as other aspects of the structure, decoration, and craftworking operation (Oakes 2009, 15–32, drawing on Ling 1997; Ling and Ling 2004; Allison 2007). Such phenomenally detailed evidence that can, in principle, be replicated for many other craftworker dwellings, provides a very "thick description" (Geertz 1973) of aspects of life in types of setting that the New Testament suggests as likely to be fairly common among groups of its hearers. The craftworker house church model is constructed by combining this type of evidence with analysis of the socioeconomic structure of Pompeian society to provide a pattern for the type of group likely to meet in this house if that was the best space available to them. The model then provides an organized way of applying this to New Testament interpretation.

A key value of the house church model, in terms of lifestyle issues, is its demand that the group should be thought of in a socially differentiated way.[2] If a Christian group met in the home of a craftworker at the upper end of the socioeconomic range of such people, how many adult men would we expect in the group? How many women? How many children? How many enslaved persons? How many households would we expect to be involved? How many in the group would be able to read (at various levels) or would have various other skills or knowledge? Even though we cannot put specific numbers on our answers to these questions for any given group, evidence about first-century spaces, social structures, and culture do give important

---

[2] Ascough (2003) argues for a socially more uniform male trade-related Christian group in Thessalonica. Maybe that is the case (although I would argue probably not), but, even if so, there are other more clearly diverse groups, as Kloppenborg discusses (2019, 80–91).

contours to the kind of answers we would expect—answers that challenge assumptions that have been used by many New Testament interpreters. The questions also lead onto further qualitative ones. If the host householder rented the largest house in the group, what did that imply about other households? What were the power relationships, both within and between households? What would it mean for people from other households to enter the house? What would it mean to take part in various types of activity? Who in the group had use of money in their household? What would it mean for various group members to give money or time to group activities? These questions, and the answers that the house church model suggests for them, feed into many New Testament interpretative issues, most obviously those of social ethics but also of other practical issues in Christian life and, indeed, into issues about ideas such as "faith/trust/loyalty" (Oakes 2018; Oakes and Boakye 2021, 15–37), an issue also fruitfully raised by work on associations (Crook 2004, 244).

A further important aspect of the disaggregation of a Christian group into socially diverse component parts is that it encourages us to address the question of how the text would have sounded to each type of person. Taking the model house church as a basic audience for every New Testament text means addressing how that text related to issues facing women, issues facing enslaved persons, issues facing house church hosts, and so on. The literary theory concept of the "implied reader" cannot be a device that leads us into reading the texts only in relation to free adult males. Irrespective of how the rhetoric of a New Testament text is ostensibly constructed, in most cases it was probably expected to be heard by the kind of diverse group encapsulated in the model house church. Considering how it would have been heard by diverse people is a key task in the interpretative agenda.

UNSETTLING MODERN READINGS

A conversation that I would appreciate having some time with Kloppenborg is on his, and other association researchers', experiences of paradigm shifts in reading of the New Testament, brought about through their work on associations. I expect there will have been many. The effects of the UK university research impact agenda mean that some of this kind of data has been gathered for the house church model.

My and others' experience of using the house church model in New Testament interpretation in a range of student and public settings has seen significant changes in perception of the text. An important aspect of this, that

I expect the effects of the association model share, is to somewhat demystify the text. Encountering the text in relation to realia of first-century life takes it away from existing in something like a sacred contextual vacuum. In church reading and preaching, and in wider popular imagination, the text can feel as though it exists in a sphere separate from the concrete realities of life: as though it was written with only eternity in view, not the concrete daily lives of its expected hearers. By extension, the same can be true of the idea of the nature of early Christian groups—which, among other things, takes us back to our earlier discussion of exceptionalism.

CONCLUSIONS

This essay has generally stayed at a fairly broad level. It could, instead, have tried to count up the number of useful exegetical insights in particular passages that the many authors have suggested, using some kind of either association model or house church model (whether or not those authors have called it a model). However, this would result (given time!) in a blizzard of evidence that would be hard to weigh. In any case, it would also undoubtedly come to the same overall conclusion, that each approach has considerable, sometimes different, usefulness, both for understanding early Christian groups and for New Testament interpretation.

WORKS CITED

Adams, Edward. 2013. *The Earliest Christian Meeting Places: Almost Exclusively Houses?* Early Christianity in Context. LNTS 450. London: Bloomsbury T&T Clark.

Allison, Penelope M. 2007. *The Finds: A Contextual Study.* Vol. 3 of *The Insula of the Menander at Pompeii.* Oxford: Clarendon.

Ascough, Richard S. 2003. *Paul's Macedonian Associations: The Social Context of Philippians and 1 Thessalonians.* WUNT 2/161. Tübingen: Mohr Siebeck.

———. 2015. "Paul, Synagogues, and Associations: Reframing the Question of Models for Pauline Groups." *Journal of the Jesus Movement in Its Jewish Setting* 2:27–52.

———. 2017. "Methodological Reflections on Synagogues and Christ Groups as 'Associations': A Response to Erich Gruen." *Journal of the Jesus Movement in Its Jewish Setting* 4:118–26.

Batten, Alicia. 2007. "The Moral World of Greco-Roman Associations." *SR* 36:135–51.

Crook, Zeba A. 2004. *Reconceptualising Conversion: Patronage, Loyalty, and Conversion in the Religions of the Ancient Mediterranean.* BZNW 130. Berlin: De Gruyter.

Elliott, John H. 1993. *What Is Social Scientific Criticism?* Minneapolis: Fortress.

Geertz, Clifford. 1973. "Thick Description: Toward an Interpretive Theory of Culture." Pages 3–30 in *The Interpretation of Cultures: Selected Essays*. New York: Basic Books.

Gruen, Erich S. 2016. "Synagogues and Voluntary Associations as Institutional Models: A Response to Richard Ascough and Ralph Korner." *Journal of the Jesus Movement in Its Jewish Setting* 3:125–31.

Jewett, Robert. 2007. *Romans: A Commentary*. Edited by Eldon Jay Epp. Hermeneia. Minneapolis: Fortress.

Klinghardt, Matthias. 1996. *Gemeinschaftsmahl und Mahlgemeinschaft: Soziologie und Liturgie frühchristlicher Mahlfeiern*. Texte und Arbeiten zum neutestamentlichen Zeitalter 13. Tübingen: Francke.

Kloppenborg, John S. 2009. "Associations, Voluntary." Page 1062 in *Anim–Atheism*. Vol. 2 of *Encyclopedia of the Bible and Its Reception*. Edited by Dale C. Allison and Hans-Joseph Klauck. Berlin: De Gruyter.

———. 2019. *Christ's Associations: Connecting and Belonging in the Ancient City*. New Haven: Yale University Press.

Last, Richard. 2016. "The Neighborhood (*vicus*) of the Corinthian *ekklēsia*: Beyond Family-Based Descriptions of the First Urban Christ-Believers." *JSNT* 38:399–425.

Ling, Roger. 1997. *The Structures*. Vol. 1 of *The Insula of the Menander at Pompeii*. Oxford: Clarendon.

Ling, Roger, and Lesley Ling. 2004. *The Decorations*. Vol. 2 of *The Insula of the Menander at Pompeii*. Oxford: Clarendon.

Longenecker, Bruce W. 2020. *In Stone and Story: Early Christianity in the Roman World*. Grand Rapids: Baker Academic.

Murphy-O'Connor, Jerome. 1983. *St. Paul's Corinth: Texts and Archaeology*. GNS 6. Wilmington, Del.: Michael Glazier.

Oakes, Peter. 2009. *Reading Romans in Pompeii: Paul's Letter at Ground Level*. Minneapolis: Fortress.

———. 2016. "Nine Types of Church in Nine Types of Space in the Insula of the Menander." Pages 23–58 in *Early Christianity in Pompeian Light: People, Texts, Situations*. Edited by Bruce W. Longenecker. Minneapolis: Fortress.

———. 2018. "*Pistis* as Relational Way of Life in Galatians." *JSNT* 40:255–75.

———. 2020. *Empire, Economics, and the New Testament*. Grand Rapids: Eerdmans.

Oakes, Peter, and Andrew K. Boakye. 2021. *Rethinking Galatians: Paul's Vision of Oneness in the Living Christ*. London: Bloomsbury T&T Clark.

Økland, Jorunn. 2004. *Women in Their Place: Paul and the Corinthian Discourse of Gender and Sanctuary Space*. JSNTSup 269. London: T&T Clark.

Osiek, Carolyn, and David L. Balch. 1997. *Families in the New Testament World: Households and House Churches*. Louisville: Westminster John Knox.

Smith, Dennis E. 2003. *From Symposium to Eucharist: The Banquet in the Early Christian World*. Minneapolis: Fortress.

Smith, Dennis E., and Hal Taussig, eds. 2012. *Meals in the Early Christian World: Social Formation, Experimentation, and Conflict at the Table*. New York: Palgrave Macmillan.

3

Suspicion, Integration, and Roman Attitudes toward Associations

Eric J. Brewer

After years of scholarship emphasizing the subversive potential of Greco-Roman associations and the hostility of Roman authorities toward them, the tendency more recently has been instead to argue for the thorough integration of associations into society. In some ways this represents an important correction to a rather anachronistic understanding of Roman imperial authority. Ramsey MacMullen's claim that Roman "imperial power methodically controlled and discouraged" "people's attempts to organize themselves" (1966, 175), though not entirely without warrant, better describes a modern totalitarian state or (as suggested by Murray 1969) the McCarthyism of the 1950s than it does ancient Roman authorities. Without "people's attempts to organize themselves," particularly for the purposes of producing and distributing resources, the Roman Empire could not have functioned. At the same time, exclusive focus on the ways in which associations contributed and belonged to the social order can give an equally false impression of universal harmony and goodwill. A wealth of evidence points toward the thorough integration of associations into Greco-Roman society, but other, equally strong evidence attests to suspicions of their potential as sources of social unrest.

The same is true for early Christ assemblies. Evidence points both to suspicion of such assemblies (Pliny, *Ep. Tra.* 10.96) and to their integration into society (1 Cor 10:25-27; 1 Pet 2:17; cf. Harland 2000, 115–16). Accounting for such evidence is obviously important for understanding the early development of Christianity in the Greco-Roman world. It impinges on questions of why, how, and to what degree Christians were persecuted in this time period, as well as what factors may have encouraged or discouraged membership in the early Christian movement. A clearer understanding of Roman attitudes toward a variety of associations may provide additional insights into these questions about Christ assemblies.

In this essay, I will seek to reconcile the seemingly conflicting evidence regarding suspicion of associations and their integration into Roman society. Although one could perhaps consider a variety of kinds of suspicions, my focus will be on the concern that they might instigate social unrest. Most of this essay will consist of an analysis of evidence indicating that associations were suspected of instigating social unrest or at least possessing the potential to do so. This analysis will argue for the existence of such suspicions while also introducing a few important caveats. I will then supplement this with a brief section on the integration of associations into Roman society before concluding with my suggestions for how this seemingly disparate data may yield a coherent picture.[1]

SUSPICION OF ASSOCIATIONS

Most surveys of Roman suspicion of associations begin quite rightly with the infamous Bacchanalia crisis of 187–186 BCE (Ascough 2003, 42–46; Rulmu 2010, 399–403). Although we possess roughly contemporary evidence of the Senate's response to this crisis (*CIL* 1.2.581), our most thorough early narrative of the episode comes from Livy, writing roughly 150 years later. In Livy's telling (*Ab urbe cond.* 39.8–19), associations in Rome devoted to the worship Dionysus (known as Bacchus to the Romans) were suspected of conspiring to commit crimes, including ritual murders in the context of their nocturnal banquets. There were also fears that these associations were planning a revolt against the Senate (39.14), which responded by cracking down on the

---

[1]   Specialists may find that such a search for coherence across time periods and geographic regions fails to account adequately for differences in, for example, the administration of Rome and its colonies. In this essay I seek to offer more of a general framework for the question of suspicions of Greco-Roman associations and would commend numerous works from my list of works cited to those interested in the nuances of particular regions or time periods. See especially Arnaoutoglou 2002; 2005; Czajkowski 2019; Liu 2008.

Bacchic associations (39.16–17). Those wishing to continue to worship Bacchus had to receive permission from the Senate; could only gather in groups of five or fewer; and could not have a common fund, master of ceremonies, or priest (39.18). The veracity of Livy's account has been questioned (Gruen 1996, 34–78), but it became very influential in later Roman portrayals of associations as potentially subversive (see discussion of Pliny, *Ep. Tra.* 10.96 below).

Perhaps the best evidence of persistent suspicion that associations could disrupt society comes in the form of numerous occasions on which Roman authorities dissolved associations. Various historians describe the dissolving of associations by a number of Caesars, including Julius (Suetonius, *Jul.* 42; Josephus, *Ant.* 14.213–16), Augustus (Suetonius, *Aug.* 32.1), and Claudius (Dio Cassius, *Hist. rom.* 60.6.6–7).[2] It should be noted, however, that none of these appear to have been comprehensive bans on all associations. In his account of Julius' ban, for example, Suetonius writes that he excepted "those of ancient foundation" (*Jul.* 42 [Rolfe 1914]). Similarly, Augustus granted an exception for all associations that "were of long standing and formed for legitimate purposes" (*Aug.* 32.1 [Rolfe 1914]). Furthermore, Arnaoutoglou has demonstrated that despite these particular dissolutions, associations in Asia Minor and Egypt continued to be publicly active during the first and second centuries of the common era, apparently without receiving any special permission to do so, thus making it likely that these bans did not apply throughout the empire but perhaps only to Rome and its immediate environs (Arnaoutoglou 2002; 2005). Bans in other regions, such as that mentioned by Philo in *Flacc.* 1.4, appear to have been local, temporary, and responding to specific incidents of unrest (Arnaoutoglou 2005, 202–8; de Ligt 2000).

A similar pattern emerges in Tacitus' account of a riot that occurred in Pompeii in 59 CE during its prestigious games, resulting in the consuls dissolving "all associations formed in defiance of the laws" (*Ann.* 14.17 [Jackson 1937]). There is some debate as to the exact cause of this riot, so it is not at all clear that any association was directly responsible (Castrén 1975, 112; Sheppard 2019, 155–71, esp. 167). In spite of this, scholars have put forward a number of possible associational culprits, beginning with the suggestion of Della Corte (1924) that the *Iuvenes Venerii Pompeiani*, an association devoted to the physical and military education of relatively high-status young men, instigated the unrest. Moeller (1970) implicates the *Campani*, whom he identifies as supporters of the *Iuvenes Venerii Pompeiani*. Similarly, Franklin suggests that something like the fan clubs of gladiators were to

---

[2] For a more comprehensive survey, see Cotter 1996.

blame (1987, 106–7). Regardless of which if any association was responsible, the response of the consuls establishes a link between associations and social unrest. Evidently viewing associations as possessing sufficient potential to instigate unrest, they chose to dissolve at least some of them. At the same time, it again seems likely that they did not dissolve all associations. While the Latin text of *Ann.* 14.17, especially as it is punctuated in the Loeb edition (*collegiaque, quae contra leges instituerant, dissoluta*), could mean that all associations were unlawful and therefore were dissolved (e.g., "associations, which had been established contrary to the laws, were dissolved"), it is also open to the interpretation, found in Jackson's translation quoted above, that only those associations which had been established in contravention of the laws were dissolved. This latter interpretation certainly coheres better with the evidence provided in the previous paragraph indicating that bans did not apply to certain associations.

Similar suspicions of the socially disruptive potential of associations persisted into the second century, as three remarkable exchanges in Pliny's correspondence with Trajan amply demonstrate. The first pair of letters (Pliny, *Ep. Tra.* 10.33–34) begins with Pliny informing Trajan of a fire that broke out in Nikomedia and grew to enormous size in part because the residents of the town did nothing to fight it. Pliny has since taken measures to provide the town with firefighting equipment, but he concludes by asking Trajan for permission to form a guild of builders (*collegium fabrorum*), who would be responsible for fighting fires. Trajan, however, denies this permission (*Ep. Tra.* 10.34), reminding Pliny that such societies have disturbed his province in the past and warning that even associations which are legitimately formed inevitably devolve into political factions (*hetaeria*). As in the examples cited above, here again one finds Roman authorities suspecting associations of possessing the potential to incite civil unrest.

The same dynamic, though with a different outcome, appears in the second pair of letters, *Ep. Tra.* 10.92–93. There, Pliny submits to Trajan the request of the Amisenians, a city that had been granted a degree of autonomy through a formal treaty, to be allowed to form clubs (10.92). This time, Trajan grants this permission on the basis of their treaty while still expressing concern that the clubs use their funds for supporting the poor and not for "disturbances and illicit assembly" (*turbas et illicitos coetus, Ep. Tra.* 10.93 [Ascough, Harland, and Kloppenborg 2012, L40]). Trajan also indicates that he would not allow such clubs in cities subject to Roman law.

The final pair of letters is one of the most famous sources attesting to Christianity in the early second century (*Ep. Tra.* 10.96–97). The key text for our purposes comes near the end of Pliny's letter, where he shares what the examination of former Christians has taught him about Christ assemblies. According to their testimony:

> On a fixed day they used to meet before dawn and recite a hymn among themselves to Christ, as though he were a god. So far from binding themselves by oath to commit any crime, they swore to keep from theft, robbery, adultery, breach of faith, and not to deny any trust money deposited with them when called upon to deliver it. After this ceremony, they used to depart and meet again to take food, but of an ordinary and entirely harmless type. They also had ceased from this practice after the edict I issued, by which, in keeping with your orders, I banned all associations (*hetaeria*). (*Ep. Tra.* 10.96 [Ascough, Harland, and Kloppenborg 2012, L40])

Numerous scholars have called attention to the way in which this description of the meetings of Christ assemblies clearly evokes Livy's account of the Bacchanalia conspiracy, mentioned above (e.g., Grant 1948; Freudenberger 1967, 165–70). Pliny clearly indicates that the Christ assemblies were not of the same sort as those infamous Bacchic associations, but the fact that he does this likely indicates that he thinks they could have been misunderstood as such. The mention of *hetaeria* also supports this. Earlier, in *Ep. Tra.* 10.34, *hetaeria* referred to the kind of association that produces social unrest. Evidently, fear that Christ assemblies could be regarded as *hetaeria* led at least some Christians to cease from meeting together following Pliny's ban.[3]

Admittedly, resemblance to associations was not the only and perhaps not even the primary factor that made Christ assemblies and their members objects of suspicion. In Pliny's letter, charges of superstition (*superstitio*), stubbornness (*pertinacia*), and obstinacy (*obstinatio*) and hints of possible religious and economic impacts (*prope iam desolata templa coepisse celebrari*) loom larger. References to associations are also notably absent from Trajan's reply (*Ep. Tra.* 10.97). Nevertheless, Pliny's letter provides important evidence that Christ assemblies, like associations, were subject to suspicion that they might cause social unrest.

---

[3] For an argument that Pliny viewed Christ assemblies as associations, see Wilken 2003, 31–47. As for exactly who ceased from meeting, the "they" in the final sentence of the quotation is ambiguous. It could refer to all Christians or only to the former Christians whom Pliny had questioned. Either all Christians had ceased to meet together or only the former Christians had left their fellowship. The latter seems more likely but is not necessary for my argument in this essay.

Still later in the second century, *IEph* 215 may attest to a connection, real or perceived, between an association and an incident of social unrest.[4] This inscription, discovered near Magnesia but likely originating from Ephesus,[5] consists of an edict issued by the proconsul in response to "disorder and tumults" (ταραχὴν καὶ θορύβους) apparently instigated by the bakers of Ephesus. The proconsul notes that the bakers deserve to be arrested and tried but, being more concerned for the welfare of the city than the punishment of the bakers, he has chosen instead to warn them with an edict. He then forbids the bakers from "holding meetings as a faction or leading insolent activities" (συνέρχεσθαι τοὺς ἀρτοκ[ό]πους κατ᾽ ἑταιρίαν μήτε προεστηκότας θρασύνεσθαι) and commands them instead to obey regulations and supply the city with bread. The proconsul goes on to threaten any who disobey this order with arrest and punishment.

The central question, at least for our purposes, is whether the bakers constituted an association. The plural form of the name of an occupation, in this case ἀρτοκόποι, could refer to a formally organized guild or merely to the people who shared this occupation. *IEph* 215 lacks explicit terminology for an association, such as συνεργασία or σύνοδος, making it difficult to determine from the inscription itself whether the bakers were an association or merely sharers in a common trade (Arnaoutoglou 2002, 39–42; Zimmerman 2002, 84–85). On the other hand, strong evidence exists for bakers' guilds throughout the Roman Empire (*CIL* 14.4234; *GRA* III 204, 264), including in neighboring Thyatira (*CIG* 3495; Ascough, Harland, and Kloppenborg 2012, no. 138). Based on this, it seems likely that the ἀρτοκόποι of *IEph* 215 were in fact an occupational guild. In that case, this inscription would indicate that the Roman authorities (1) considered the bakers' guild responsible for some past incident of social unrest and (2) felt it necessary to take action to prevent the guild from causing further unrest. At the same time, however, the actual action taken appears to have amounted to little more than the issuing of this edict! As Buckler notes, according to the inscription itself, "(1) the offenders were not punished, but merely warned what punishment to expect in case of any further disobedience; (2) no penalty was threatened in the event of another strike; (3) while the bakers' union was forbidden to hold seditious meetings, there was no ban upon its ordinary business and no threat of its dissolution" (1923, 33). This is, therefore, a case of strong suspicion against an association accompanied by

---

[4]   For text, translation, and discussion, see Buckler 1923, 30–33; Merkelbach 1978; Börker and Merkelbach 1979, 27–28; Trebilco 1994, 338–40; Perry 2015.

[5]   The discovery near Magnesia of an inscription from Ephesus is explained by the presence of a railway running between these sites in the nineteenth century (Buckler 1923, 30, n. 1).

relative inaction. The reason for this seeming incongruity likely relates to the integration of the bakers into the city, so I will examine this case further in the final section of this essay.

All of the evidence to this point, from the Bacchanalia crisis to the Ephesian bakers, attests to the ways in which *Roman authorities* suspected associations of possessing the potential to incite social unrest. Based on this alone, one could hardly extrapolate to suppose that everyone in the Roman world regarded associations with suspicion. At the same time, some evidence attests to similar attitudes among other groups. For example, in his *Tarsica altera*, an oration delivered at Tarsus in the late first or early second century CE, Dio Chrysostom notes that the citizens of Tarsus sometimes regard the linen workers (λινουργούς)[6] as "responsible for the tumult and disorder in Tarsus" (τοῦ θορύβου καὶ τῆς ἀταξίας αἴτιον) and "instigators of insurrection and confusion" (στάσεως ἄρχειν καὶ ταραχῆς, *2 Tars.* 21 [Cohoon and Crosby 1940]).[7] It is by no means clear that the linen workers did in fact instigate any unrest, but the citizens of Tarsus evidently suspected that they did.[8] Here, not the Roman authorities but rather the citizens of the city suspected an association of potentially inciting civil disorder.

Suspicion of associations as socially disruptive also appears in at least two ways in Philo's *In Flaccum*. First, Philo blames an incident of civil unrest on associations (*Flacc.* 135–45). According to Philo, Alexandria was home to a large number of associations (θίασοι), also known as "synods" (σύνοδοι) or "couches" (κλῖναι; *Flacc.* 136).[9] Philo portrays these negatively as societies "whose fellowship is founded on no sound principle but on strong liquor and drunkenness and sottish carousing and their offspring, wantonness" (136 [Colson 1941]). Isidorus, whom Philo previously introduced as one of the lead conspirators in a plot against the Jews (20–21), occupied a prominent place in a large number of these associations and worked through them

---

[6] As with ἀρτοκόποι in *IEph* 215, λινουργοί could refer to a guild or to sharers in a common trade. Based on the prominence of linen work in Tarsus and the clear attestation for guilds of linen workers throughout Asia Minor (Ascough, Harland, and Kloppenborg 2012, nos. 172, 181, 207, 210; *TAM* 5.82), λινουργοί most likely refers to a formal guild of linen workers in this case.

[7] See discussion in Sommer 2008; Trebilco 1994, 340.

[8] If Dio were speaking to another group regarding the citizens of Tarsus, then one could legitimately question the degree to which his portrayal matched the views of the citizens of Tarsus or perhaps reflected more of his own interests in developing his argument. In this case, however, Dio is addressing the citizens of Tarsus themselves and thus likely would have articulated their views in a way that they themselves would readily accept.

[9] The last of these terms (κλῖναι) likely derives from the banquets that these associations shared.

whenever "he wished to get some worthless project carried out" (137 [Colson 1941]). In this particular case, Isidorus gathered the members of these various associations in the gymnasium and paid them to invent accusations against Flaccus, governor of Egypt (138–39). The plot was soon discovered, however (140–43), causing Isidorus to flee (142–45). Philo's portrayal of this incident indicates that he suspected associations of potential involvement in seditious activities.[10]

The second way in which *In Flaccum* attests to suspicions toward associations is in Philo's defense of Jewish synagogues. In this case, the suspicions are not Philo's but rather those of his broader Roman audience directed toward Jewish synagogues.[11] Throughout *Flacc.*, Philo is at pains to stress the loyalty of Alexandrian Jews to the Roman Empire (van der Horst 2003, 17–18). One way that he does this is by explaining that, though they do not contain images of the emperor, Jewish meetinghouses (προσευχαί) enable Jews to express their piety through the practice of dedicating these buildings to the emperor (*Flacc.* 41, 48). The absence of images might raise suspicions that the Jewish meetings that gathered in these buildings were subversive, but Philo dispels such suspicions by calling attention to these dedications.

Comparison with Philo's similar defense of Jewish synagogues in *Legatio ad Gaium* casts additional light on *In Flaccum*. There, Philo claims that Augustus "ordered that the Jews alone should be permitted by [the governors of Asia] to assemble in synagogues (εἰς τὰ συναγώγια συνέρχεσθαι). These gatherings (ταῦτα συνόδους), he said, were not based on drunkenness and carousing to promote conspiracy and so to do grave injury to the cause of peace, but were schools of temperance and justice" (311–12 [Colson 1941]). Both συναγωγή and σύνοδος are well-documented terms for Greco-Roman associations (Kloppenborg 2019, 19). Philo thus characterizes non-Jewish associations as based on "drunkenness and carousing" (μέθης καὶ παροινίας) and tending to incite disorder by promoting conspiracies. In contrast to this,

[10]   One's assessment of Philo's audience will play a major role in determining the significance of Philo's portrayal of associations in this incident. If *In Flaccum* is directed at Roman authorities as a cautionary tale against mistreating Jews, then Philo may be trying to conform his portrayal of associations to the views of those Roman authorities. This would confirm the evidence surveyed above indicating that Roman authorities sometimes regarded associations with suspicion, but it would not illuminate Philo's own views. If, on the other hand, *In Flaccum* is written for Philo's fellow Jews exhorting them to "keep the faith" in the face of persecution, then the portrayal of associations is much more likely to reflect his own views and perhaps those of other Jews. I follow van der Horst in viewing Philo's audience as including both Jews and a broader Roman audience (2003, 12).

[11]   See the previous note on the audience of *In Flaccum*. On synagogues as associations, see Czajkowski 2019.

Jewish synagogues promote temperance and justice and are therefore no threat to good public order. According to Philo, any suspicions that might fall on Jewish synagogues due to their superficial resemblance to non-Jewish associations are unfounded (Czajkowski 2019).[12]

The depiction of non-Jewish associations in *Legat.* 311–12 corresponds remarkably well with that of *Flacc.* 135–45. There, non-Jewish associations founded on drunkenness and carousing (μέθη καὶ παροινίαι) incite actual disorder through the promotion of a conspiracy. *Flacc.* 135–45 may not explicitly contrast Jewish synagogues with non-Jewish associations as in *Legat.* 311–12, but the reader need only recall earlier portrayals of Jewish synagogues as peaceable and submissive to Roman rule (*Flacc.* 48, 94) to appreciate that the non-Jewish associations of *Flacc.* 135–45 are behaving in a very different manner. Philo would not need to defend Jewish synagogues if they were not suspected of possibly being subversive, so his rhetoric in *In Flaccum* and *Legatio ad Gaium* attest to the presence of such suspicions in Roman society.

The evidence surveyed up to this point allows for three broad observations regarding suspicion of associations. First, most of our sources speak to the views of Romans authorities, indicating that they sometimes regarded associations as potentially subversive. At the same time, other evidence, such as Dio Chrysostom's *Tarsica altera* and Philo's defenses of Jewish synagogues, demonstrate that such views were by no means restricted to Roman officials. Second, a wide variety of associations, not just one type, appear to have been objects of suspicion. Religious associations, occupational guilds, and ethnic associations all appeared in the above survey. At the same time, this by no means indicates that equal suspicion was directed at all associations, which leads to my third and final observation. Old, established associations tended to be more trusted than new ones. Well-established associations were explicitly exempted from bans, and regulation of associations seems more often to have consisted in the refusal to allow new associations than in the dissolving of existing ones.

SOCIAL INTEGRATION OF ASSOCIATIONS

Even with the numerous caveats included in the preceding analysis, this depiction of associations as potentially subversive paints a fairly distorted picture of the place of associations in Roman society. In countless ways,

---

[12] Czajkowski (2019) provides an excellent analysis addressing whether the Romans viewed Jewish synagogues in Alexandria as associations as well as Philo's rhetoric surrounding Jewish and non-Jewish associations.

associations were thoroughly integrated into Roman society.[13] Inscriptional evidence indicates, for example, that legal documents were filed in city archives either by associations (*IDelos* 1522; Ascough, Harland, and Kloppenborg 2012, no. 220) or for their benefit (Ascough, Harland, and Kloppenborg 2012, nos. 149, 151, 152, 154, 158; *SEG* 65.651).[14] At least three associations appear even to have submitted a copy of their bylaws, preserved on papyrus, to the archive at Tebtynis (Ascough, Harland, and Kloppenborg 2012, nos. 300–302). These bylaws include provisions for the assessment of fines and punishments for failure to attend meetings, pay associational dues, or mourn at the passing of associational leaders. These associations relied on civil institutions like archives (for preserving such documents) and courts (for enforcing their provisions) and would have had a vested interest in preserving such institutions. Disruptions to social order would have posed a significant risk to such associations. They may have possessed the potential to instigate social unrest, but their dependence on civil institutions would have motivated them in exactly the opposite direction.

The countless honorific inscriptions commissioned by associations likewise attest to the integration of associations into society. To begin with, the mere presence of such inscriptions in public places demonstrate the desire of these associations to be recognized. Far from seeking to conceal their existence, membership, or activities, many associations effectively broadcast such information through public inscriptions (e.g., Ascough, Harland, and Kloppenborg 2012, nos. 47, 310; *CIL* 11.1355).[15] Perhaps even more significantly, these honorific inscriptions often name prominent benefactors (e.g., Ascough, Harland, and Kloppenborg 2012, nos. 5, 74; *GRA* III 244). A roster of boatmen of Ostia (*CIL* 14.250), for example, names four senatorial patrons and another five of equestrian rank (Kloppenborg 2019, 57–61). Such elite benefaction advertised the status of associations and cemented vertical social

---

[13] The most extensive work to date on this subject, especially as it relates to early Christianity, is Harland 2003. This is also one of the central themes of Kloppenborg 2019. See also Ascough 2022 and the section on "imperial allegiances" in Whitlark 2022.

[14] See the discussion of these inscriptions in Harland 2009, 123–42. Harland similarly interprets the mention of archives as evidence for the integration of these associations "within local society" (2009, 141).

[15] On the other hand, this may also reflect an associational response to suspicion by members of the public. It is noteworthy that we possess so many inscriptions from Bacchic associations, whose reputations likely required considerable rehabilitation thanks to the well-remembered Bacchanalia crisis (see previous section). Public inscriptions, especially those honoring Roman emperors or officials (Ascough, Harland, and Kloppenborg 2012, nos. 64, 116, 168, 173, 191, 264), would have countered rumors that Bacchic associations sought to subvert the social order by instead trumpeting their support of the authorities.

bonds between associations and their well-placed patrons (Kloppenborg 2019, 92). Even if relatively few associations could claim patronage from the equestrian and senatorial classes, the same dynamic applied to associations sponsored by local elites. Benefiting both financially and reputationally from connections with social elites, most associations would have been disinclined to risk losing such sponsorship by inciting social unrest.

ASSOCIATIONS: OBJECTS OF SUSPICION OR APPRECIATION?

Based on this evidence, suspicions of associations as socially subversive ought to be regarded as an important exception to the general rule of integration into society. In this period, associations were recognized as potentially useful for maintaining a functioning society (van Nijf 1997; Gutsfeld 1998; Venticinque 2016), but memories of the role of associations in various episodes of social unrest insured that they were never entirely free from suspicion. Suetonius' account of the actions of Augustus towards associations (as noted above) illustrates this particularly well. He describes how certain associations had been formed as façades for brigandage. In response, Augustus "disbanded all guilds (*collegia*), except such as were of long standing and formed for legitimate purposes" (*Aug.* 32.1 [Rolfe 1914]). Suetonius thus preserves the memory of associations as a potential threat to the Roman order while also indicating that Roman authorities recognized that associations "formed for legitimate purposes" were worth preserving.

Likewise, a more attentive reading of the correspondence between Pliny and Trajan analyzed above points to this same dynamic. Older scholars tended to focus on Trajan's opposition to the formation of a guild to fight fires while more recent scholars have instead called attention to the multiple associations which did in fact exist, apparently unhindered, in Asia Minor during this period (MacMullen 1966, 175; Arnaoutoglou 2002, 35–36). Neither has drawn sufficient attention to the letter from Pliny that prompted Trajan's response (*Ep. Tra.* 10.33). In it, Pliny makes a strong case for the formation of an association. Its size (*dumtaxat hominum CL*) and the composition (*ne quis nisi faber recipiatur*) of its membership will be limited. Its privileges will be limited to those necessary for their task of fighting fires (*neve iure concesso in aliud utatur*). All this will make the association easy to monitor (*nec erit difficile custodire tam paucos*). Such assurances are clearly addressed at concerns that associations could foment social unrest. At the same time, the fact that Pliny makes as strong a case as possible, even taking personal responsibility for the proper formation of the assembly (*Ego attendam*), indicates that he considered the benefits of such an association to outweigh the risks.

A similar weighing of risks and benefits likely explains the relative lack of punishment for the bakers mentioned in *IEph* 215. It will be remembered that the proconsul did not punish the bakers and only prohibited them from "holding meetings as a faction or leading insolent activities." They were not banned entirely from meeting. This could be evidence that the bakers did not meet regularly and thus were not a guild (Arnaoutoglou 2002, 40–41), but it could also reflect the proconsul's pragmatism. An absolute ban on meetings could have interfered with the bakers' ability to supply the city with bread, possibly resulting in famine. The bakers were too integrated into the life of the city to make drastic action against them practical.

This understanding of associations as generally trusted but not entirely free from suspicion coheres well with our current picture of Roman attitudes toward early Christianity. As new groups, Christ assemblies would have faced greater suspicion than older, established associations. Roman authorities likely regarded Christ assemblies with suspicion (when they noticed them at all), and at least some members of the general public would have held similar views. Such suspicions were not, however, strong enough to prevent Christ assemblies from gaining new members. At the same time, they may occasionally have contributed to both official and unofficial action against Christians (e.g., 1 Thess 2:14; 1 Peter; Pliny, *Ep. Tra.* 10.33). Such action was, however, sporadic and localized, just as bans of associations were local, temporary, and limited. Allowance ought to be made for the exclusive monotheism of Christianity, which may have limited its integration into Roman cities and increased the suspicion with which it was regarded, but even this would have only tipped the balance between trust and suspicion rather than eliminating one pole entirely.

WORKS CITED

Arnaoutoglou, Ilias N. 2002. "Roman Law and Collegia in Asia Minor." *RIDA* 49:27–44.

———. 2005. "*Collegia* in the Province of Egypt in the First Century AD." *Ancient Society* 35:197–216.

Ascough, Richard S. 2003. *Paul's Macedonian Associations: The Social Context of Philippians and 1 Thessalonians.* WUNT 2/161. Tübingen: Mohr Siebeck.

———. 2022. "Working with the Gods: Occupational Associations and Early Christ Groups." Pages 49–64 in *Greco-Roman Associations, Deities, and*

Early Christianity. Edited by Bruce W. Longenecker. Waco, Tex.: Baylor University Press.

Ascough, Richard S., Philip A. Harland, and John S. Kloppenborg. 2012. *Associations in the Greco-Roman World: A Sourcebook*. Waco, Tex.: Baylor University Press.

Börker, Christoph, and Reinhold Merkelbach, eds. 1979. *Die Inschriften von Ephesos*. Vol. 2. Bonn: Rudolf Habelt.

Buckler, W. H. 1923. "Labour Disputes in the Province of Asia." Pages 27–50 in *Anatolian Studies Presented to Sir William Mitchell Ramsay*. Edited by W. H. Buckler and W. M. Calder. Manchester: Manchester University Press.

Castrén, Paavo. 1975. *Ordo Populusque Pompeianus: Polity and Society in Roman Pompeii*. Acta Instituti Romani Finlandiae 8. Rome: Bardi.

Della Corte, Matteo. 1924. *Iuventus*. Arpino: Fraioli.

Cotter, Wendy. 1996. "The Collegia and Roman Law: State Restrictions on Voluntary Associations, 64 BCE–200 CE." Pages 74–89 in *Voluntary Associations in the Graeco-Roman World*. Edited by John S. Kloppenborg and Stephen G. Wilson. London: Routledge.

Czajkowski, Kimberley. 2019. "Jewish Associations in Alexandria?" Pages 76–96 in *Private Associations and Jewish Communities in the Hellenistic and Roman Cities*. Edited by Benedikt Eckhardt. JSJSup 191. Leiden: Brill.

Dio Chrysostom. 1940. *Discourses 31–36*. Translated by J. W. Cohoon and H. Lamar Crosby. LCL 358. Cambridge, Mass.: Harvard University Press.

Franklin, James L. 1987. "Pantomimists at Pompeii: Actius Anicetus and His Troupe." *AJP* 108:95–107.

Freudenberger, Rudolf. 1967. *Das Verhalten der römischen Behörden gegen die Christen im 2. Jahrhundert*. Munich: Beck.

Grant, Robert M. 1948. "Pliny and the Christians." *HTR* 41:273–74.

Gruen, Erich S. 1996. *Studies in Greek Culture and Roman Policy*. Leiden: Brill.

Gutsfeld, Andreas. 1998. "Das Vereinigungswesen und die Städte in der römischen Kaiserzeit." Pages 13–33 in *Gesellschaften im Vergleich: Forschungen aus Sozial- und Geschichtswissenschaften*. Edited by Hartmut Kaelbe and Jürgen Schriewer. Frankfurt am Main: Peter Lang.

Harland, Philip. A. 2000. "Honouring the Emperor or Assailing the Beast: Participation in Civic Life among Associations (Jewish, Christian and Other) in Asia Minor and the Apocalypse of John." *JSNT* 22:99–121.

———. 2003. *Associations, Synagogues, and Congregations: Claiming a Place in Ancient Mediterranean Society*. Minneapolis: Fortress.

———. 2009. *Dynamics of Identity in the World of the Early Christians: Associations, Judeans, and Cultural Minorities*. New York: Continuum; London: T&T Clark.

van der Horst, Pieter W. 2003. *Philo's Flaccus: The First Pogrom*. PACS 2. Leiden: Brill.

Kloppenborg, John S. 2019. *Christ's Associations: Connecting and Belonging in the Ancient City*. New Haven: Yale University Press.

de Ligt, Luuk. 2000. "Governmental Attitudes towards Markets and Collegia." Pages 237–52 in *Mercati permanenti e mercati periodici nel mondo romano: atti degli Incontri capresi di storia dell'economia antica (Capri 13–15 ottobre 1997)*. Edited by Elio Lo Cascio. Pragmateiai 2. Bari: Edipuglia.

Liu, Jinyu. 2008. "Pompeii and Collegia: A New Appraisal of the Evidence." *Ancient History Bulletin* 22:53–69.

MacMullen, Ramsay. 1966. *Enemies of the Roman Order: Treason, Unrest, and Alienation in the Empire*. Cambridge, Mass.: Harvard University Press.

Merkelbach, R. 1978. "Ephesische Parerga (18): Der Bäckerstreik." *ZPE* 30:164–65.

Moeller, Walter O. 1970. "The Riot of A. D. 59 at Pompeii." *Historia* 19:84–95.

Murray, Oswyn. 1969. Review of *Enemies of the Roman Order*, by Ramsay Macmullen. *JRS* 59:261–65.

van Nijf, Onno M. 1997. *The Civic World of Professional Associations in the Roman East*. Dutch Monographs on Ancient History and Archaeology 17. Amsterdam: J. C. Gieben.

Perry, Jonathan S. 2015. "'L'état intervint peu à peu': State Intervention in the Ephesian 'Bakers' Strike.'" Pages 183–205 in *Private Associations and the Public Sphere: Proceedings of a Symposium Held at the Royal Danish Academy of Sciences and Letters, 9–11 September 2010*. Edited by Vincent Gabrielsen and Christian A. Thomsen. Copenhagen: Royal Danish Academy of Sciences and Letters.

Philo. 1941. *Every Good Man Is Free. On the Contemplative Life. On the Eternity of the World. Against Flaccus. Apology for the Jews. On Providence*. Translated by F. H. Colson. LCL 363. Cambridge, Mass.: Harvard University Press.

———. 1962. *On the Embassy to Gaius. General Indexes*. Translated by F. H. Colson. Index by J. W. Earp. LCL 379. Cambridge, Mass.: Harvard University Press.

Rulmu, Callia. 2010. "Between Ambition and Quietism: The Socio-political Background of 1 Thessalonians 4,9–12." *Bib* 91:393–417.

Sheppard, Joe. 2019. "Mass Spectacles in Roman Pompeii as a System of Communication." PhD diss., Columbia University.

Sommer, Stephan. 2008. "Vereinigungen in Tarsos." Pages 131–48 in *A Roman Miscellany: Essays in Honour of Anthony R. Birley on His Seventieth Birthday*. Edited by Hans Michael Schellenberg, Vera Elisabeth Hirschmann, and Andreas Krieckhaus. Gdańsk: Foundation for the Development of Gdańsk University.

Suetonius. 1914. *Julius. Augustus. Tiberius. Gaius. Caligula*. Translated by J. C. Rolfe. Introduction by K. R. Bradley. Vol. 1 of *Lives of the Caesars*. LCL 31. Cambridge, Mass.: Harvard University Press.

Tacitus, Cornelius. 1937. *Annals: Books 13–16*. Translated by John Jackson. LCL 322. Cambridge, Mass.: Harvard University Press.

Trebilco, Paul. 1994. "Asia." Pages 291–362 in *The Book of Acts in Its Graeco-Roman Setting*. Edited by David W. J. Gill and Conrad Gempf. Vol. 2 of *The Book of Acts in Its First Century Setting*. Edited by Bruce W. Winter. Grand Rapids: Eerdmans.

Venticinque, Philip F. 2016. *Honor among Thieves: Craftsmen, Merchants, and Associations in Roman and Late Roman Egypt*. New Texts from Ancient Cultures. Ann Arbor: University of Michigan Press.

Whitlark, Jason A. 2022. "Reading Hebrews in a Roman *Vicus* with Voluntary Associations." Pages 359–75 in Longenecker, *Greco-Roman Associations, Deities, and Early Christianity*.

Wilken, Robert Louis. 2003. *The Christians as the Romans Saw Them*. 2nd ed. New Haven: Yale University Press.

Zimmerman, Carola. 2002. *Handwerkervereine im griechischen Osten des Imperium Romanum*. Mainz: Verlag des Römisch-Germanischen Zentralmuseums.

4

Working with the Gods

Occupational Associations and Early Christ Groups

Richard S. Ascough

There is evidence in early Christian texts suggesting that at least some Christ adherents were laborers. For example, Acts tells stories of women and men in various occupations, such as Tabitha the garment maker (9:39), Simon the tanner (9:43 and 10:6), Lydia the purple dealer (16:14), and Priscilla and Aquila the tentmakers (18:3). In his earliest letter, Paul recalls he and his retinue working "night and day" when with the Thessalonians (1 Thess 2:9),[1] although they are clearly "visiting" workers as they do not reside permanently in that city. In complaining about hardships to the Corinthians, Paul writes that he and his companions "grow weary from the work of our own hands" (1 Cor 4:12; see also 2 Cor 11:27) and later asks whether it is only he and Barnabas that must work for a living to support themselves (1 Cor 9:6).[2] While it is not clear whether he worked while in Corinth itself, Paul indicates that both before and after his time there manual labor was a primary means of supporting himself and, at least in Thessalonike, also a context in which he could proclaim his message about Christ.

---

[1]   This is a claim repeated in the second letter addressed to that city, with the added note that it was to save the Thessalonians from supporting him (2 Thess 3:8).
[2]   According to Acts, in a speech to the Ephesian elders in Miletus Paul claims, "I worked with my own hands to support myself and my companions" (20:34).

Given Paul's predilection for working with his hands, and the presentation in Acts that he (as well as Peter; Acts 9:43) contacted other laborers in cities he visited, this essay examines the broader context of mobile labor practices in Roman antiquity. Using network theory and evidence from occupational associations, we will give particular attention to how people such as Paul navigated finding temporary work in a new location. Paul's use of workshops as at least one venue for recruitment has implications for understanding the social status of resulting Christ adherents and the issue of cult practices in the workplace.

MOBILITY AND NETWORKS

In the first few centuries of the Roman imperial period, there was robust travel around and across the Mediterranean Sea. "The roads and sea ways were now thronged with traders . . . , armies, bureaucrats, couriers of the government post, and just plain tourists" (Casson 1994, 127), facilitated by the construction of new and better roads and less piracy due to Roman concern for security. Alongside the movement of goods was the movement of laborers—skilled or otherwise—looking for work outside of their home regions, either due to lack of economic opportunity there or (potentially) better opportunities elsewhere (de Ligt and Tacoma 2016, 9–10). Most of the inscriptional evidence, limited as it is, points to short-range mobility between towns or across regions. "Most migrants were male, and those with specific skills are easier to see than agricultural labourers" due to the nature of the documentation (e.g., craftsmen named on epitaphs; Woolf 2016, 454).[3] The long distances covered by Paul in his travels seem to be much rarer, even while he fits into the broader picture of mobile specialized laborers. Woolf speculates that only one out of every thousand people would make a long-distance journey necessitating sea travel every year (2016, 460), again pointing to the irregularity of Paul's mobility.

Although there were low-skill jobs to be had along the way, such as water carrier, vendor, or clothes stamping in a fullery, most occupations "required a certain proficiency, dexterity, and expertise, and therefore presupposed a

---

[3] Finding direct evidence for mobile traders is difficult as they did not leave a clear record. McDonald and Clackson use "linguistic minutiae" of inscribed names on ceramics to demonstrate how Greek traders and their wares spread across the Mediterranean prior to the Roman imperial period (2020, 97). Here we draw on later inscriptions, such as those highlighted in Broekaert 2011, to find similarly slight but potentially informative indications of itinerant traders.

period of training or schooling and preparation" (Landskron 2020, 179).[4] Zuiderhoek notes that "given the absence of institutionalized forms of professional schooling accessible to a fairly broad section of the non-elite population, skilled labour was scarce and expertise was mostly gained in private settings such as households or workshops" (2017, 23). In order to "work with their hands" in a trade, Paul and his companions would have acquired a set of skills and experiences that would be worth the wages they garnered in a shop. Although we do not have direct evidence from Paul's letters for what these skills might be, Acts 18:3 links Paul to "tentmaking" or "awning making" (σκηνοποιός), which has been understood to indicate that he is trained in leatherworking (see Still 2006, 781). That is, while his specialization could be making tents or awnings, Paul would have the requisite skills to work in a variety of shops producing leather goods even if he were not the master craftsman in that shop. For example, an establishment that focused on the production of shoes may have an expert cobbler oversee the operation and cut the leather to size (a highly skilled task) but would need people who were trained in the cutting and sewing of leather according to the wooden models used in the design process (Landskron 2020, 182; see also the analogy from the seventeenth and eighteenth centuries in Hawkins 2016, 94–95).

People like Paul would be in high demand not only for their skills but due also to the shortage of such persons around the empire. Although there was no empire-wide free labor market, "Roman artisans and entrepreneurs often made use of informal social network-type institutions and organizations" (Zuiderhoek 2017, 24). Thus, when Paul arrived in a city such as Thessalonike he would find employment not simply because of the abundance of work but also the lack of skilled workers. This might, we suspect, also have given him latitude in terms of the topics he could discuss with his fellow workers and the deities he could invoke. Discussing "religion and politics" in the workplace was not likely to get Paul "fired" given his particular specialized skillset.

This fits with John Kloppenborg's recent deployment of social network theory in studying ancient associations, including Christ groups (2019, 308–27; 2020). Weak ties, which exist among people of infrequent interactions or based on a single shared characteristic, are key to the diffusion of new ideas and beliefs across networks; "an acquaintance . . . is more likely to move in different circles than one's friends, and so have access to information that is not part of one's ego cluster" (Kloppenborg 2020, 328; Holleran 2017, 96). Paul was connected to at least one of his groups—the

---

[4]   On apprenticeships, see the overview in Liu 2017, 219–23.

Thessalonians—through his occupation (Ascough 2000) and consequentially through weak links generated by occupational guilds, which would provide what Kloppenborg identifies as the necessary "nudges" to propagate a new cult among them as part of a "complex contagion."[5] Alone, Paul would not be effective enough, but co-workers such as Silvanus and Timothy would also be nudging the Thessalonians and building their weak links into strong ties, so much so that Timothy could return to them as friend and emissary after the Pauline group departed (Kloppenborg 2020, 332).

Given the limited data on Roman collegia, Broekaert draws on comparisons with data from other preindustrial guilds, particularly medieval guilds, to argue that "the numerous professional organizations in the Roman empire, bringing together merchants and shippers and creating the possibility of valuable networking, also played a considerable part in enhancing the efficiency of Roman trade" (2011, 225). He draws on social network theories that identify two key factors in ensuring mutual trust and bonding within a network. The first is a shared set of interests, values, social rules, and convictions that make it a "closed" network insofar as members can control one another's behavior and ensure loyalty through formal or informal regulations. Bylaws of associations provide the formal scribing of such things, but the social pressures of group membership would extend the written rules. The other factor ensuring mutual trust and bonding within a network concerns multiplex relationships through which members are tied to one another through connections outside the social network, such as shared cultural norms, ethnic identities, religious practices, and the like. "The more ties, the closer the connection between the members and the more likely they are to help and protect each other" (Broekaert 2011, 227).

Ongoing labor shortages occurred due to the lack of skilled workers or temporary boosts in demand. For example, "The demand for goods in Rome fluctuated, as, consequently, did the demand for labour, both skilled and unskilled; short-term workers may then have been required to enable the

---

[5]   As with so many tradespeople, leatherworkers could form an association; see, e.g., Ascough, Harland, and Kloppenborg 2012, no. 131 (Thyatira, late first century CE); *IEph* 596 (Ephesos, second century CE); *TAM* 5.79 (Saittai, Lydia, 152/153 CE); *IGR* 4.790 (Apameia Kelainai, Phrygia, ca. 160 CE); *IEph* 2080 (Ephesos 200–210 CE); Ascough, Harland and Kloppenborg 2012, no. 259, and *IG* XII,2 109 (both Mytilene, Lesbos, undated); *CIL* 6.9053 (Rome, 70–200 CE). Among the many storefront mosaic advertisements of the forum of the corporations in Ostia (regio II,VII,4), on the east side, the guild of leather merchants identifies itself as *corpus pellion[um] Ost[iensium] et Por[tensium]* (*CIL* 14.4549, 2). Presumably inside the shop one could purchase leather goods of all sorts, either manufactured on-site or, more likely, imported from elsewhere (given the proximity of the forum to the docks and warehouses of Ostia).

completion of a particular order or to meet a period of high demand" (Holleran 2017, 100). The scarcity and difficulty of obtaining skilled laborers was linked in part to "the lack of reliable information on the trustworthiness of outside individuals" (Zuiderhoek 2017, 30), which is why network connections would be helpful, if not critical, to matching workers with opportunities. In her preliminary foray into understanding free workers in Rome, Holleran (2017) notes that, alongside those who found work independently, there must have been a labor market with mechanisms for employers and workers to find one another, including oral and written advertising, designated places where potential laborers could congregate, or connections made through patrons. Social networks would be critical for finding employment, and the more networks a person was connected to, the more likely they would find out about opportunities. Such networks could include family links, neighborhoods, religious practices, ethnicity, place of origin, and, of course, trade, although these categories could overlap (2017, 96). Migrants new to the city would rely on those who arrived before them, not only for settling into a new space and way of living (hence the clustering of ethnic groups in neighborhoods). The same could be said for travelers taking up temporary residence in the city.

One of the key networks for finding employment is found among people who share a common ethnic identity or religious practice. The writer of Acts imagines this in part when he has emissaries such as Paul and his companion arrive at a city and immediately seek out a synagogue. The writer's depiction is theologically motivated, to be sure, in linking the message of Jesus to the God of the Hebrew Bible, but it also reflects the practicality that was common in the ancient (and modern) world of finding ways to capitalize on extant social networks. People of like ethnicity, and in this case overlapping religious practice, are more likely to open their homes or at least share important information about settling into the city. For example, Paul connects in Corinth with Priscilla and Aquila because of their shared trade but also because of their shared *ethnos* (Judean; 18:3).[6] In this case, the lines between ethnicity and shared religious practice are blurred, for to be Judean is also to adhere to the Judean god—that is, unlike many (not all) ethnic groups, this one had an established deity to whom all members of the *ethnoi* were explicitly or implicitly bound.

---

[6] That women could take an active part in the leather goods industry is seen in a few inscriptions. The relief on the gravestone of Septimia Stratonice in Ostia depicts a woman holding either a shoe or its model in her extended right hand, while the inscription to the right of the relief records that her friend funded the memorial for her (*CIL* 14.4698-2, second century CE; text and interpretation in Landskron 2020, 180).

Paul seems to have understood his own adherence to Christ as a natural extension of this ethno-religious commitment, since for him Christ was the fulfillment of the promises of God (Rom 9–11).

Another key network for finding employment would be social venues such as the baths[7] or associations organized around common cult or occupation. Anyone new to a city and looking for work might find an entry into a cultic or occupational association through which they could acquire information and connections about employment opportunities (Holleran 2017, 99–100). Given the complicated and expensive process of finding reliable, skilled laborers, particularly in large urban areas, "the information networks of a *collegium* may have gone some way towards simplifying the process, enabling an employer to find reputable workers quickly and efficiently, and lowering the transaction costs associated with recruiting good skilled labour for short-term roles" (Holleran 2017, 100; see further Hawkins 2016, 73–79). One can find evidence of some merchant traders with links stretching from Spain to Rome, and surmise, as does Broekaert, that "when several *collegiate* were trading along the same routes, a merchant may ask a colleague, who was planning a business trip to the place where the agent was residing, to check on his reliability and local social credit" (Broekaert 2011, 231–32; 2012, 222, 247).[8] A reputation for trustworthiness and reliability would likely ensure an easier passage for goods and persons. In the same way, members of similar trades, particularly those whose network included shared collegial status, could pass on information about market conditions and employment opportunities as they traveled along trade routes. One can imagine Paul finding out about places to ply his trade in his next city of destination by sharing gossip with leatherworkers he passed along the way.

When an itinerant worker arrived in town, he not only brought with him his skill but also his reputation,[9] both of which would be important

---

[7] Apuleius observes that the artisans who met in the baths formed loose social networks; see *Metam.* 9.24; Hawkins 2016, 126.

[8] As Humphries notes, a trade network indicates "not simply the exchange of goods at market centres but the whole matrix of social relations associated with that trade" (1998, 204).

[9] I use the masculine pronoun here since most of the evidence we have points to males being the primary component of the *mobile* labor force. Although there is good evidence for women traveling, the evidence that they did so as artisans or traders is "rare" (Foubert 2016, 300). In this light, it is interesting to note that at least one mobile woman artisan appears in the biblical record. Pricilla joins Paul for part of his travels (Acts 18:18), along with her spouse Aquila, both of whom shared Paul's occupation. This couple makes an appearance in Corinth (1 Cor 16:19; Acts 18:1), Ephesos (Acts 18:19, 26), and Rome (Rom 16:3), suggesting that they too are mobile in their work, even if it is forced upon them by political circumstances (Acts 18:2). On women in the workforce in the Roman imperial period, see Treggiari 1976; 1979; Holman 2015; Larsson Lovén 2016; Landskron 2020.

for gaining work, especially in a trade in which associations were particularly key (which seems to be the majority). Locating potential workplaces would not prove difficult. "Given the spatial clustering of trades in an ancient city, it was relatively easy for a newcomer to a city to locate his trade, and once connected, a ready-made network was available" (Kloppenborg 2020, 334, n. 31).[10] For example, a single street might include a few different shops that all produce products made of leather such as shoes, shields, and awnings, so that they could collaborate and share access to the stock of base materials. In the case of Paul, whereas the writer of Acts has him engage with the diasporic Judean communities as his entryway into each urban center he visits, his own letters declare that he understands God commissioned him to speak to non-Judeans (Rom 11:13). Thus, when Paul and his companions enter a new city, rather than seek out a shared ethnic or religious network, the next natural network would be occupationally based, which would include, albeit not in a limiting way, the occupational association(s) linked to their profession. I have argued this to be the case at Thessalonike (Ascough 2000) but it might have likewise been so in other places. Kloppenborg summarizes a likely scenario: "The connections among the leatherworker guilds in Thessaloniki created by patronage and by physical proximity of workshops probably facilitated recruitment to the Christ cult. Thus, the Christ cult spread along the street through network connections" (2020, 337). Reading 1 Thess 1:8-10 in this light, Paul's elation that his reputation has preceded him from Thessalonike to Athens might be as much about his ability to find an entry point into the workshops of the city as it is about the change of religious affiliation of the group at Thessalonike.

Broekaert's examination of a few merchant associations in Gaul demonstrates that occupational associations were open to members who did not reside locally or were not from the town, but in order to protect the association's reputation they would need to ensure that such persons were themselves reputable and reliable, and would control their behavior, along with that of other members, through regulations (2011, 228–29, looking at inscriptions from Trier, Vienne, and Lyon). This was not just a social concern, but also linked to the commercial interests of the members of the association, for the bad behavior of any member, particularly in business dealings, might negatively impact all members of the association in their interactions with customers, suppliers, and business partners (Hawkins 2016, 115–22).

---

[10] On the phenomenon of clusters of crafts and trades in Roman cities, see Goodman 2016 and a partial list in Ruffing 2016, 121.

This would explain, in part, why many honorary inscriptions set up by occupational associations across the empire lead with a description of the social benefactions of the honorand and his personal characteristics (e.g., "generous," "pious," "zealous for honour," "fair," "humane," and even "their own savior and benefactor in everything" [*SEG* 34.1094]). This is a signal that the association has noted a person's credentials not only for inclusion in membership but now even more so for public honoring. It is their guarantee that this person is fair in their dealings, and in the case of some, generous to the group or even the city. Even those members not honored with statues—the majority—might also be similarly marked through the wearing of insignia that identified them as belonging to a trustworthy association, as was the case for the *utriclarii* in Gaul, from whom two personalized bronze tesserae have survived, each bearing the engraved name of the owner and his association (*CIL* 12.*136, *283; see Broekaert 2011, 229). As Konrad Verboven observes,

> Collegia were socially important not just because they were part of the structure of ancient cities, but because they institutionalized social mobility. They allowed successful businessmen to transform economic capital into social and symbolic capital—influence, honour and prestige. Thus the guilds laid out paths of social mobility that were firmly embedded in the civic community. (2017, 198)

Given this status, it would be important that any workshop, whether controlled by an association or not, employ reputable and skilled workers.

MEMBERSHIP STATUS

Almost a century ago, Krauss surveyed the epigraphic record for laborers in the Roman imperial period and referred to the majority being "in the unassuming guise of ordinary workingmen" and "the lowly that catered to the manifold wants of urban life" (1928, 161, 163). In framing the discussion this way, Krauss betrays not only his own implicit cultural biases against the working people of the Roman world but also his acceptance of the elite writings from that time in which men such as Cicero write of "craftsmen and shopkeepers and all that scum of the city" (*Flac.* 18).[11] Yet to his credit, Krauss was turning away from the elite writings themselves by focusing on the corpus of

---

[11] See further Verboven and Laes 2017, 1–2. In New Testament studies, Hock (1980) set the tone by arguing that although Paul himself worked with his hands, he accepted the elitist view disparaging artisans and thus used his status rhetorically to demonstrate his humility. Still (2006) rightly challenges this consensus view.

inscriptions that present an alternative, and more authentic, picture of people who work hard not only to make ends meet but to have enough disposable income for a few luxuries such as membership dues in an association and commemoration with a grave monument (from whence comes much of the epigraphic evidence). Continued investigation of these data has provided a much different perception of the self-understanding of laborers in the Roman world. For example, from her recent study of monuments and written sources concerning professions at Ostia, Landskron concludes that

> it can be said that the individuals depicted wished to be represented in their professional environment in a worthy and positive manner. In this regard, not only did pride in the practiced profession play a large role, but also the appropriate representation in the social setting. (2020, 197)

This is a far cry from a cringeworthy self-identity one might expect if the elite disparaging of tradespeople infused the professions themselves.[12]

Overall, it seems that "craftsmen and traders thus were not at all marginal people . . . they were well integrated into the urban community and, through their associations, maintained close ties with the urban elite" (Flohr and Wilson 2016, 12), or what Tran calls the "plebian elite" (2017, 268). These close ties are predicated on the customer base of many craftspersons and traders, with a correlation between a strong occupational identity and direct engagement with their customer base, and, in the case of an elite clientele, more chance of epigraphic commemoration (Flohr and Wilson 2016, 15). "These elites invested in trade and manufacturing because they wanted to get something out of it—socially or economically"—and yet left everyday operations in the hands of the craftspersons and traders (Flohr and Wilson 2016, 15). When correlated with association membership, this could lead to economic success, as Tran (2017) demonstrates for Arles, and Arnaoutoglou (2016) for Hierapolis.

The implications for Christ groups are important. For associations, it is "precisely because membership was costly" that "it not only barred a large number of the lower classes from entry but there was also no guarantee that all of the current members would be capable of maintaining membership" (Liu 2017, 210). One must also ask the same of early Christ groups, which too often have been presumed to have been the purview of the lowly and marginalized. While it is the case that the gospels portray Jesus as reaching out to some of the most marginalized

---

[12] This is not to suggest that some professions, such as tanning, prostitution, and mortuary work, were not disreputable, as Bond (2016) has so convincingly demonstrated.

people in his society—people with physical or mental infirmities that have been cast out—these people are not presented as forming the groups that would later receive letters from Paul and others. These groups are more reasonably comprised of people from the lower-middling order, those who could afford group membership. In addition, "while the monetary costs of membership in a Christ group were not very high . . . the 'signaling costs' imposed by behavioural demands were . . . more substantial" (Kloppenborg 2020, 342). For Paul and his ilk, these were strict ethical requirements, while for others it also extended to circumcision and even more restrictive food regulations and such of Torah (the so-called "Judiazers" against whom Paul takes much umbrage). Yet these ethical and social demands should not overshadow that membership in a Christ group still cost *something*. But beyond the financial cost, did such membership have a social cost, one that would impact both reputation and ability to travel in previous networks? To address this question, we turn now to the issue of the place of deities in the workshops of antiquity.

NEGOTIATING "FALSE" GODS

According to Plutarch, the occupational associations at Rome were the creation of Numa, the legendary second king of Rome in the seventh century BCE. In so doing, he assigned to each association a patron deity:

> He distributed them, accordingly, by arts and trades, into musicians, goldsmiths, carpenters, dyers, leather-workers, curriers, braziers, and potters. The remaining trades he grouped together, and made one body out of all who belonged to them. He also appointed social gatherings and public assemblies and rites of worship befitting each body. (*Num.* 17 [Perrin 1914])

Although clearly legendary, this does point to trends in which specific deities are associated with particular occupations (e.g., Dionysos and wine production). Deities such as Fortuna, Hercules, Jupiter, Mercury, Minerva, Silvanus, and Lares appear frequently in the epigraphic record. At times, however, local gods are invoked as the patron deity of an occupational association (Wojciechowski 2021, 82; Waltzing 1885–1900, 1:200–201; Ausbüttel 1982, 51). Yet there seems to have been no requirement for consistency, since there are also cases where associations comprised of members of the same occupation chose different protective deities (Wojciechowski 2021, 82).

In the Roman imperial period, it would be unlikely for an artisan to work in a shop that did not have at least some acknowledgment of a patron deity or evidence of the cult of the corporate Genius. A carpenter's shop in Pompeii has a façade that provides an idea of how the gods might be construed in the workplace (Regio VI, 7, 8–11).[13] In one of the building's doorways, Mercury and Fortuna face one another, invoking respectively the deity that brought prosperity to tradespersons and shopkeepers and the goddess of wealth and prosperity. The one remaining fragment of the painting depicts the carpenters carrying a statue of Minerva, their patron deity, in a procession. The painting also depicts Daedalus, dressed in a worker's garment and holding a compass in his right hand, a nod to his role as the patron deity and thus protector of carpenters. A separate depiction of Daedalus portrays him making a wooden cow commissioned by Pasiphae out of her love for Zeus. For the customer entering the store, it would signify the great expertise and quality in the products produced therein. Daedalus is depicted both leading the procession and standing over the body of his rival Perdix, whom he has killed, an indication of "his supreme power over the carpenter's skill" (Clarke 2003, 87).

The clothmakers' shop at Pompeii (Regio IX, 7, 5–7), owned by a husband and wife, similarly depicts what went on inside the shop among the workers as they plied their trade. Above the long panel to the right of the doorway, Venus Pompeiana is depicted in regal clothes pointing to her status as protector of the city. On the opposite side of the doorway is Mercury, protector of merchants and travelers, who here also carries in his right hand a sack of money as a "symbol of the financial prosperity that comes from his guardianship over Verecundus's shop" (Clarke 2003, 107). Such paintings depicting scenes of work are essential in establishing how, where, and with what tools artisans plied their trade. But the thick overlay of pious iconography, which would be visible to worker and customer alike, would infuse the workplace with a sense of the presence and protection of the gods throughout the workday. No mere advertisements, such paintings have as their principal message "the celebration and propitiation of the proper gods" (Clarke 2003, 109). It is unlikely that all shops had such lavish paintings as those described here, but given the propensity for dedicatory inscriptions set up for deities by occupational associations, it is difficult to imagine a workplace free of religious iconography and the hopes that placating the gods in this way would bring security and prosperity to owner and worker alike.

---

[13] Clarke provides a detailed description, summarized here, of the notes and watercolor of the now-lost original (2003, 85–87).

Within association life, the documentation around the collection of funds detailed by Last and Harland points to much of it going towards "sacrifices, temple renovations, and other dedications to gods and goddesses," indicative of "the highly important place of deities within the lives of many associations and their members" (2020, 134). We find one such example at Philippi, where association members are recognized for their contributions to the temple of Silvanus in the second century CE:

> Publius Hostilius Philadelphus, on account of the honor of the office of the magistrate of public works (aedile), at his own expense, had inscribed the names of the association members who gave funds for the construction of the temple. Domitus Primigenius gave a bronze statue of Silvanus with a house. Gaius Horatius Sabinus gave 400 roof-tiles towards roofing the temple. Nutrius Valens gave two marble statues of Herakles and Mercury. Paccius Mercuriales gave 250 denarii for concrete in front of the temple and 15 denarii for a painted board of Olympus. Publicius Laetus donated 50 denarii for building the temple. Likewise, Paccius Mercuriales with his sons and freedman donated 50 denarii for building the temple as well as 25 denarii for a marble statue of Liber. Alfenus Aspasius, priest, gave a bronze image of Silvanus with a base and, while he was still living, deposited 50 denarii for his funeral. Hostilius Philadelphus had the rock ascending into the temple quarried at his own expense. (Ascough, Harland, and Kloppenborg 2012, no. 41)

Such activities not only serve to honor the gods but remind the association members that they are seen by the gods even in their daily labor.

In thinking about what this might mean for the earliest Christ adherents, many of whom must surely have worked in such establishments,[14] what is most striking is the silence in the early Christian texts around navigating such commitments in light of their newfound adherence to Christ. As I have noted elsewhere, in writing to the handworkers group at Thessalonike, Paul expresses his joy that news of their revoking "idols" for the "living god" has spread elsewhere (1 Thess 1:8-9), indicative of the replacing of the patron deities of that particular group (see Ascough 2000, 323–24).[15]

---

[14] Given the small size of the Christ groups (see Kloppenborg 2019, 98–123), it is unlikely that there were any exclusively "Christian" workplaces in the early centuries.

[15] Crook (2004, 76–89) rightly notes that "conversion" language in antiquity is framed around terms of divine benefaction and the appropriate human response. Finding a deity that promises greater protection or more fortune would entice a person or group to switch primary allegiance. Outside of situations such as that touted by Paul, we are unlikely to find epigraphic evidence in which a group advertises the switch of primary allegiance—to do so

But to other groups such as those at Corinth, Philippi, and Rome, or in the region of Galatia, Paul gives no direct counsel on how to navigate a workplace, or even a shop, that heavily drips with devotion to gods other than Christ. In large part, I suspect this might either stem from Christ adherents in those places not raising it as a concern with him, since so much of his letters deals with questions or problems that have arisen in the community. And if it is not a problem, then either Paul already addressed this with the Christ adherents when he was among them (except for Rome) or they simply do not need guidance as it is not a concern. In his first letter to the Corinthians, he does address the issue of whether a Christ adherent can eat meat sacrificed to "idols," but in so doing he does not suggest that they abstain from attending meetings and events where this might take place, only that they take care not to offend other Christ believers in what they consume (1 Cor 8:1–11:1).

CONCLUSION

In this essay we have presented evidence to demonstrate how mobile artisans such as Paul and his companions might navigate the process of finding paid work when arriving at a new city. The network connections provided by common ethnicity and common trade were natural conduits to finding opportunities to ply one's skills. Whether on the road or in town, such networks were important, as were the many occupational associations, and for Paul and his companions, those linked to the leather trade in particular. As arbiters of social capital, the associations provided a closed system of trust and reliability that benefited both the migrant worker and the employer alike. Although labor was not necessarily the only means Paul and his companions used to support themselves, given the social dynamics of occupational life and, with it, collegial life, the associations would be a natural draw for Paul. In engaging with workers in such groups, he would have encountered a wide range of people in all social strata save the very bottom and the very top, people who subsequently became Christ adherents, either individually or collectively. They promoted the worship of the one true God of Judaism, but seem not, as far as we can tell, to have challenged the ubiquity of deities that most certainly populated the working environment of anyone who was employed outside of their own home.

---

would be to further risk the wrath of the rejected deity. What we do see are groups that list more than one allegiance, perhaps hedging their bets that at least one of the deities will be looking out for them at any given time.

WORKS CITED

Arnaoutoglou, Ilias. 2016. "Hierapolis and Its Professional Associations: A Comparative Analysis." Pages 278–98 in *Urban Craftsmen and Traders in the Roman World*. Edited by Andrew Wilson and Miko Flohr. Oxford: Oxford University Press.

Ascough, Richard S. 2000. "The Thessalonian Christian Community as a Professional Voluntary Association." *JBL* 119:311–28.

Ascough, Richard S., Philip A. Harland, and John S. Kloppenborg. 2012. *Associations in the Greco-Roman World: A Sourcebook*. Waco, Tex.: Baylor University Press.

Ausbüttel, Frank M. 1982. *Untersuchungen zu den Vereinen im Westen des römischen Reiches*. Frankfurter Althistorische Studien 11. Kallmünz: Michael Lassleben.

Bond, Sarah E. 2016. *Trade and Taboo: Disreputable Professions in the Roman Mediterranean*. Ann Arbor: University of Michigan Press.

Broekaert, William. 2011. "Partners in Business: Roman Merchants and the Advantages of Being a *Collegiatus*." *Ancient Society* 41:215–54.

———. 2012. "Joining Forces: Commercial Partnerships or Societates in the Early Roman Empire." *Historia* 61:221–53.

Casson, Lionel. 1994. *Travel in the Ancient World*. Baltimore: Johns Hopkins University Press.

Clarke, John R. 2003. *Art in the Lives of Ordinary Romans: Visual Representation and Non-elite Viewers in Italy, 100 B.C.–A.C. 315*. Berkeley: University of California Press.

Crook, Zeba A. 2004. *Reconceptualising Conversion: Patronage, Loyalty, and Conversion in the Religions of the Ancient Mediterranean*. BZNW 130. Berlin: De Gruyter.

Foubert, Lien. 2016. "Mobile Women in *P.Oxy.* and the Port Cities of Roman Egypt: Tracing Women's Travel Behaviour in Papyrological Sources." Pages 285–304 in de Ligt and Tacoma, *Migration and Mobility in the Early Roman Empire*.

Goodman, Penelope. 2016. "Working Together: Clusters of Artisans in the Roman City." Pages 301–33 in Wilson and Flohr, *Urban Craftsmen and Traders in the Roman World*.

Hawkins, Cameron. 2016. *Roman Artisans and the Urban Economy*. Cambridge: Cambridge University Press.

Hock, Ronald F. 1980. *The Social Context of Paul's Ministry: Tentmaking and Apostleship*. Philadelphia: Fortress.

Holleran, Claire. 2017. "Getting a Job: Finding Work in the City of Rome." Pages 87–103 in *Work, Labour, and Professions in the Roman World*. Edited by Koenraad Verboven and Christian Laes. Impact of Empire 23. Leiden: Brill.

Holman, Lindsay M. 2015. "Roman Freedwomen: Their Occupations and Identity." Unpublished MA thesis, University of North Carolina at Chapel Hill.

Humphries, Mark. 1998. "Trading Gods in Northern Italy." Pages 203–24 in *Trade, Traders and the Ancient City*. Edited by Helen Parkins and Christopher Smith. Oxford: Routledge.

Kloppenborg, John S. 2019. *Christ's Associations: Connecting and Belonging in the Ancient City*. New Haven: Yale University Press.

———. 2020. "Recruitment to Elective Cults: Network Structure and Ecology." *NTS* 66:323–50.

Krauss, Franklin B. 1928. "The Human Element in Latin Inscriptions." *Classical Weekly* 21:161–63.

Landskron, Alice. 2020. "The Perception of 'Skills' in Ostia: The Evidence of Monuments and Written Sources." Pages 175–202 in *Skilled Labour and Professionalism in Ancient Greece and Rome*. Edited by Edmund Stewart, Edward Harris, and David Lewis. Cambridge: Cambridge University Press.

Larsson Lovén, Lena. 2016. "Women, Trade, and Production in Urban Centres of Roman Italy." Pages 200–221 in Wilson and Flohr, *Urban Craftsmen and Traders in the Roman World*.

Last, Richard, and Philip A. Harland. 2020. *Group Survival in the Ancient Mediterranean: Rethinking Material Conditions in the Landscape of Jews and Christians*. London: T&T Clark.

de Ligt, Luuk, and Laurens E. Tacoma. 2016. "Approaching Migration in the Early Roman Empire." Pages 1–22 in *Migration and Mobility in the Early Roman Empire*. Edited by Luuk de Ligt and Laurens E. Tacoma. Studies in Global Social History 23/7. Leiden: Brill.

Liu, Jinyu. 2017. "Group Membership, Trust Networks, and Social Capital: A Critical Analysis." Pages 203–26 in Verboven and Laes, *Work, Labour, and Professions*.

McDonald, Katherine, and James Clackson. 2020. "The Language of Mobile Craftsmen in the Western Mediterranean." Pages 75–97 in *Migration, Mobility and Language Contact in and around the Ancient Mediterranean*. Edited by James Clackson, Patrick James, Katherine McDonald, Livia Tagliapietra, and Nicholas Zair. Cambridge Classical Studies. Cambridge: Cambridge University Press.

Plutarch. 1914. *Theseus and Romulus. Lycurgus and Numa. Solon and Publicola*. Vol. 1 of *Lives*. Translated by Bernadotte Perrin. LCL 46. Cambridge, Mass.: Harvard University Press.

Ruffing, Kai. 2016. "Driving Forces for Specialization: Market, Location Factors, Productivity Improvements." Pages 115–31 in Wilson and Flohr, *Urban Craftsmen and Traders in the Roman World*.

Still, Todd D. 2006. "Did Paul Loathe Manual Labor? Revisiting the Work of Ronald F. Hock on the Apostle's Tentmaking and Social Class." *JBL* 125:781–95.

Tran, Nicolas. 2017. "*Ars* and *Doctrina*: The Socioeconomic Identity of Roman Skilled Workers (First Century BC–Third Century AD)." Pages 246–61 in Verboven and Laes, *Work, Labour, and Professions*.

Treggiari, Susan. 1976. "Jobs for Women." *American Journal of Ancient History* 1:76–104.

———. 1979. "Lower Class Women in the Roman Economy." *Florilegium* 1:65–86.

Verboven, Koenraad. 2017. "Guilds and the Organisation of Urban Populations during the Principate." Pages 173–202 in Verboven and Laes, *Work, Labour, and Professions*.

Verboven, Koenraad, and Christian Laes. 2017. "Work, Labour, Professions. What's in a Name?" Pages 1–19 in Verboven and Laes, *Work, Labour, and Professions*.

Waltzing, Jean-Pierre. 1895–1900. *Étude historique sur les corporations professionnelles chez les Romains depuis les origines jusqu'à la chute de l'Empire d'Occident*. 4 vols. Leuven: Peeters.

Wilson, Andrew, and Miko Flohr. 2016. "Introduction." Pages 1–19 in Wilson and Flohr, *Urban Craftsmen and Traders in the Roman World*.

Wojciechowski, Przemysław. 2021. *Roman Religious Associations in Italy (1st–3rd Century)*. Toruń: Nicolaus Copernicus University Press.

Woolf, Greg. 2016. "Movers and Stayers." Pages 438–61 in de Ligt and Tacoma, *Migration and Mobility in the Early Roman Empire*.

Zuiderhoek, Arjan. 2017. "Sorting Out Labour in the Roman Provinces: Some Reflections on Labour and Institutions in Asia Minor." Pages 20–35 in Verboven and Laes, *Work, Labour, and Professions*.

5

Stinking Leatherworkers and Noisy Street Criers

Paul, Occupational Stigma, and the Sensory Politics of Associations

Louise J. Lawrence

In her stimulating and thought-provoking book *Trade and Taboo: Disreputable Professions in the Roman Mediterranean* (2016), Sarah Bond traces the perceptions of those trades and occupations frequently stigmatized, disdained, or despised by (predominantly elite) citizens and sources (e.g., street criers, tanners, mint workers, etc.). She traces the ways in which discriminatory attitudes were created and sustained, and how these occupations were consequently positioned in many social imaginations as "dirt" or "pollutants"—or, in William James' terms, "matter[s] out of place" (James 1903, 133, a term frequently used by Mary Douglas [1966]). Bond submits that while on the one hand such occupations often incurred official civic and social disabilities, on the other hand due to their connective function as negotiators between various social strata, individuals performing such roles could also serve as critical "cultural mediators" in ancient societies (2016, 58). In social-scientific terms, those embodying occupational stigma could, at times, function as networking nodes across space and social hierarchies.

Recent scholarship on occupations and trade associations in the ancient world has demonstrated that these identities were frequently used to categorize and assign "specific stereotypes, privileges, burdens, and stigmata" (Bond 2011, 49; see also Joshel 1993). Occupations and trades could be used for rhetorical purposes and, as such, depictions of them and discourses about them have as much to do with "social construction" as with "reality" itself. Through such discourses, individuals and groups had stigma projected onto them, but in turn they could also resist such definitions by exercising "cultural agency to forge their own personal and occupational identities in public contexts" in certain ways (Ferris 2021, 51). Taints associated with certain occupations could variously be refigured and/or subversively commended, and those aspects of an occupation signaled as negative could be rendered insignificant or recalibrated to deliberately accent more positive qualities (Ashforth et al. 2007). Social scientists have also noted the prevalence cross-culturally of occupational metaphors based on hierarchies ("top jobs"/"low-level work") and landscapes ("boundaries and space") and how these often provide means by which "relations, directions, distances, causality, features, and principles" are reimagined (Liljegren 2012, 88). Archaeologists and ancient historians too have observed the importance of conceptual metaphors for constructing social identities, particularly with regard to social organization—things such as image schemas (kin relations, etc.) and/or sensory prompts (aromas and stench; sound and noise; display and spectacle). Such moves map experiences from one domain to another in order to "reason about social order" (Wiseman 2015, 162).

While much energy has been devoted to "thinking with" Greco-Roman trade and/or voluntary associations alongside early Christian groups, it is often the respectable or well-thought-of practices, images, and dynamics of such which have dominated scholarly attention. For example, a prevailing interest has been in internalized positive social capital that networks were presumed to provide for members—"a sense of belonging, honour and achievement" (Kloppenborg and Ascough 2011, 6). Familial conceptual metaphors used within these groups to provide social cohesion and support are also often explicitly mentioned (Harland 2007), and so too are forms of amelioration of social difference operative therein:

> The sociality of associations . . . [created] a form of connectivity that bridged social barriers of ancient society that were particularly sturdy and enduring, between citizen and foreigner, between elite and commoner, and even between free, freedman/freedwoman, and slave. (Kloppenborg 2019, 287)

The assumed mirroring of elite social structures within non-elite groups is also often implied and/or rehearsed: "Mimicry contributed to the integration of sub-elite populations into the city insofar as it reproduced civic practices and values in people who were not citizens" (Kloppenborg 2019, 289-90). John Kloppenborg attests to this predisposition when he writes:

> Since many associations represented non-elite persons, politically disenfranchised in the cities in which they lived, the mimicry of political rituals probably functioned both to create social imaginaries that connected them to the *polis* and to cement affective bonds. (Kloppenborg 2018, 155)

This tendency to view associations (and Christianity's modeling of their dynamics) largely positively is also due in part, perhaps, to perceptions of the "success" or popularity of Christianity as a movement. As a result of these suppositions, much less focus hitherto has been afforded to the study of conceptual metaphors or identity markers based on "disreputable" trades (although "professional" sex work is perhaps one obvious exception) and/or those shadow sides of occupations subject to various taints and slurs from outside the group on account of sensory politics—such as haptic contact with "dirty" material (disgust-inducing sensory prompts such as putrid odors) and/or stigmatized flesh (dead and alive), or "disordered" bodily performances (Drobnick 2006; Classen 2005). Nor has there been much study of how these stigmas could affect occupational self-identities and associative networks for good or ill (Roca 2010, 139). While Philip Harland's work on banquets of the anti-associations and cultural minority groups (2007) does show how associations frequently satirized other groups as dubious, improper, or offensive, much less energy has been focused on how occupational associations themselves responded to a barrage of specifically anti-occupational sentiment or the deployment of sensory distinctions, from external bodies or broader cultural perceptions.

Bond's work underscores that (dis)repute is not endemic to a group, occupation, or individual; rather it is culturally constructed in processes of exchange and encounter being "a dispersed phenomenon that is found in the beliefs and assertions of an extensive number of individuals" (Craik 2008, xvii). Likewise, the mechanics of stigma which render some occupations in certain contexts as "dirty work" are variable on account of physical associations, social relations, and/or moral suppositions (Ashforth and Kreiner 2014), all of which are contextual, dynamic, and shifting, and often generated externally from beyond the occupational group itself.

Building on these various insights and stimulated by Bond's work, discussion here will take examples of two so-called "disreputable" trade associations in the Roman world—(1) tanners/leatherworkers and (2) street criers/announcers—and experimentally read these as conceptual metaphors in relation to selected performances of Paul. These trades are here proposed to function as a social-identity model responsive to, and reflective of, the negotiation of certain occupational stigmas within the New Testament traditions surveyed. Attention will be given to the ways in which receivers of these texts may well have projected occupational stigma onto textual portrayals of these trade associations, but also how the texts and contexts in which they were engaged may also have served to renegotiate or recalibrate the "dirty work" in which Paul and/or early Christians are (at least in some way) perceived to be discursively involved. Crucial too will be the tracing of how these occupational identities could serve as important symbolic/conceptual metaphorical sites from which networking across social divides could be facilitated.

A caveat at the outset: in reading Paul (and early Christians) alongside these trade associations and occupational stigmas, I am not claiming Paul "really was" a member of ancient tanner/leatherworker associations or street crier trade associations (though evidence is more compelling for the former than the latter). Rather, I am experimentally "thinking with" these occupational identities (and their respective stigmas) to evince elements of the emergent social structures and identities of early Christianity which can be discerned from their texts. In Bengt Holmberg's terms, I am creatively curating

> [a] recognizable social profile that is summarized in people's thoughts (usually in narrative form) about who "we" or "they" are, and how we and they typically behave. The developments and fluctuations of a group are reflected in the identity formation process as well. Both insiders and outsiders think about identity and discuss it, and therefore identity is constantly "negotiated." (Holmberg 2008, 28-29)

A brief note too in relation to evidence: scarcity of evidence on disreputable trades undoubtedly inhibits comparative work in this area. Elite literary evidence (marked by prejudicial sentiments against certain occupations) is often the main source of information on such issues; archaeological, epigraphic, visual, and material evidence is variable and dispersed. The online repository entitled *Associations in the Greco-Roman World*, https://philipharland.com/greco-roman -associations/, comprising inscriptions, papyri, and other sources in translation, for example, has only three entries for tanners, none with great detail:

- "Honors by Leather Tanners for Licinius Rufinus" (220 CE, Thyatira)
- "Grave (frag.) with Mention of Tanners" (undated, Smyrna), a funerary text that makes reference to tanners and fines owed to the treasury, but the whole is "too fragmentary to translate"
- "Reservations in the Stadium for Guilds and Other Groups" (second to fourth century CE, Aphrodisias), which comprises a list of seat reservations for occupational groups but gives no further information

For criers (*praecones*) a single reference is offered to the "Building [B27]: Association of the Public Heralds" (200 CE, Rome). Caution in this area is rightly given against generality in favor of specificity (e.g., Ascough 2015, 236), but for some trade associations an exacting or rich dataset is simply not available. As such, rather than the typical "methodological caution and meticulous historical and social analysis of the association inscriptions and papyri . . . as a useful comparanda for the analysis of the New Testament documents and early Christian communities" (Harrison 2019, 299) which has characterized much work in this area hitherto, here a more methodologically experimental approach is purposely adopted, bringing insights from sensory anthropology to bear on selected New Testament traditions, to underscore not only practice or social comparanda, but also affective, sensory, discursive, and ideological dimensions of such parallels.

PAUL AND THE OCCUPATIONAL STIGMA OF TANNERS/LEATHERWORKERS

In her recent ethnographic study of "the violence of odors" and "sensory politics of leather tannery" in India, Shivani Kapoor (2021) posits the materiality of leather as one of knotted affective appeal, jarringly evoking both desire and disgust. She notes the space of the tannery as one "produced through sensuous discourses of caste violence," which mark bodies as "other" through stench and smell. Through sensory means, "affectual and material possibilities of humiliation and discrimination" are made explicit, for

> this violence of odors has no place in the deodorized discourse of law and yet in the sensuous ordering of caste there is nothing more repulsive than to carry the stench of tannery on oneself. (Kapoor 2021, 164)

Similarly, in his study of the "outcast" Buraku people in Japan (who are also subject to occupational stigma on account of their trade in leather and meat production) Joseph Doyle Hankins notes the "aromatic bivalency" of those sniffing luxuriant "real leather" and "the person who inappropriately smells of leather, or animal flesh." Accordingly he submits that a "discriminating nose" is required to "demarcate sets of smell and sets of people" (Hankins 2013, 49–50).

In the ancient world too, smell was often used to demarcate and censor those bodies, professions, or associations rendered "other": "It is axiomatic [in Greek and Roman traditions] that one's own social group, the 'in-crowd,' is odourless, while those outside are malodorous" (Bradley 2015, 133). Bond's analysis of occupational stigma incurred by the "foul associations" of tanners (who variously used urine, excrement, blood, and carcasses in their processes) extends these "odoriferous" assessments to other crafts and trades that used animal products, skin, and hides, and worked with leather in producing a variety of goods (footwear, tents, military dress, weapons and equipment, sails and ropes, etc.).

Unlike some other "disreputable" professions profiled by Bond, tanners (at least from the evidence available) did not seem to be legally outlawed or officially branded; indeed, Bond questions whether elite stereotypes of professions impacted much on the lived experience of those occupying leather trades (2016, 124). For Bond, tanners were broadly public and well-connected: "Tanners and the tanning industry formed a central economic hub within Mediterranean economies that, heretofore, has not been fully understood" (2016, 98). This viewpoint is perhaps corroborated in part by an honorific dedication from a guild of tanners to a patronal benefactor, Ammius Manius Caesonius: "In glorious memory and in all proper justice, the guild of tanners set up (this statue) to their worthy patron" (inscription cited in Kloppenborg 2019, 34). Likewise the "Reservations in the Stadium for Guilds and Other Groups" (second to fourth century CE, Aphrodisias), a roster of seats set aside in public spaces, is evidence that tanners were "seen" and given some measure of approval in public life. It is still probably true, however, that as a group they occupied a "low" place on the "patronage pyramid" of ancient society (Kloppenborg 2019, 35) and were aware of cultural stigma surrounding their occupations.

Practically it would have been evident to many that tanning was a complex and stinking enterprise:

> The hides of animals were tanned using tannic acid. . . . Tanners often worked near the seashore to facilitate the disposal of chemicals, and because they used salt water in the tanning process. Because of the very unpleasant odors the work generated, its practice was not allowed in cities. (Jeffers 1999, 28)

Within the discourses of the elites, discursively the "stench" of the occupation and spatial proximity of other intersecting occupations (which likely included leatherworking, for "where there is tanning, there is leather" [Jeong 2020, 47]) became a sensory tool to barricade them ideologically from others (Bond 2016, 124). Putrid smells frequently served as convenient conceptual ciphers for physical and moral pollution. Illustrative of such sentiments, Artemidorus (the second-century interpreter of dreams) declares:

> The tannery annoys everybody, for the tanner has to meddle with animal corpses, he has to live far from the town and the stench reveals him even when hiding. The vultures love the potters and the tanners as they live far from the towns and deal with dead bodies. (Artemidorus, *Onir.* 1.51, 2.20, cited in Forbes 1966, 51)

As Paul's labor is explicitly mentioned in New Testament evidence in contexts often demonstrating his self-supporting ministry (Acts 18:3; 1 Cor 4:12; 1 Thess 2:9; 2 Cor 12:14), much work has been done on trying to gauge the nature and status implications of his assumed occupation. In Acts, the Greek term σκηνοποιός (Acts 18:3) is often translated as "tentmaker," though it should probably be understood more broadly as a "leatherworker" of sorts. As Stanley Porter notes, "A tentmaker may be too restrictive. Someone of his trade probably worked . . . making not only tents, but sails for boats, canopies for theatres, and various forms of military equipment" (Porter 2016, 24). On the basis of this proposed occupation, J. Albert Harrill posits Paul as a "travelling artisan" who would network through local associations finding work and connections with those in leather-associated trades in workshops (Harrill 2012, 50). Harrill pictures Paul instituting a small group in the space of a workshop, "which mixed rich and poor, workers and customers, and locals and travellers together" (Harrill 2012, 51). Kloppenborg too speculates whether the addressees of 1 Thessalonians themselves "worked with their hands" (4:11)—"perhaps an association of curtain makers or leather cutters" (Kloppenborg 2019, 89; also Ascough 2000)—and that Paul self-consciously uses the identity label of manual trade to "establish common ground" with them. This rhetorical strategy is seen by Kloppenborg as different to the one Paul adopts in the Corinthian correspondence in which he humbly underscores the difference between his own occupational labor and that of the refined Corinthians (Kloppenborg 2019, 88).

Ronald F. Hock, situating Paul in workshops "busy with his trade" and "busy at preaching the gospel" (1979, 450) and reflecting on Paul's (negative) view of his own occupational identity, contends that Paul can be positioned in a "relatively high social class" and seen as one who shares an elite disgust of his trade. Hock sees 1 Cor 9:19 and 2 Cor 11:7 as indicative of one discerning from a "high place" the status inconsistency of the "lowly" tradesman's humbling debasement that he is compelled to occupy. By implication, in Todd Still's words, Hock's version of Paul occupies an identity of "not so much a servant at work, as a snob toward work" (Still 2006, 793). Paul's social status aside, Hock is right to highlight Paul's response to occupational stigma, which includes self-stigmatization and the echoing of the derogatory opinions of others.

One particular set of striking sensory images seemingly used as conceptual metaphors connecting apostolic identity with occupational stigma and conflict appears in 1 Cor 4:11-13. Paul notes the weariness induced by "work of our own hands," also the persecution and slander he and others endure on account of their apostolic status. Jarringly he conceptualizes his and other gospel proclaimers' identities as "the rubbish of the world (περικαθάρματα τοῦ κόσμου), the dregs (περίψημα) of all things" (1 Cor 4:13). Richard Horsley notes that both περικαθάρματα and περίψημα refer to what was removed in the process of cleansing and are therefore metaphors for what is distasteful, noxious, or shameful: "Put simply the apostles (and Paul) are the 'scum of the earth'" (Horsley 2011, 72; also Asano 2016). Astrid Lindenlauf, too, notes that discursively people or things dealt with as disposable are "regarded as unwanted or even dangerous, i.e. refuse in the original sense of the word" (2004, 428).

The discipline of garbology (Scanlan 2005)—including the study of "debris left behind from industry" and the detritus of trade (Griffith 2013, 4)—perhaps can suggest still other layers of meaning within this metaphorical association. The term περικαθάρματα, often translated "rubbish," could also denote filth, dirt, or even excrement. E. Gowers notes that dung and refuse were often synonymous in the ancient mind: the sewers and streets acting as stinking "waste-disposal units" for excrement, city garbage, and at times human and animal remains (Gowers 1995; Liebeschuetz 2015). The term περίψημα, often translated "dregs," is more commonly used in relation to "that which is wiped off" or more specifically "off-scouring and scrapings" (*TDNT* 6:64). While no one seems to have made this connection before, here we could see Paul deliberately invoking waste products involved in technologies of tanning and leatherworking: flaying, trimming horn and sinew, rinsing skin, off-scouring/scraping fat and hair, and cutting (see van Driel-Murray 2009; El Boushy and van der Poel 2000). So too Paul could be deliberately (and sardonically) mimicking elite (Corinthian) opinions that tanners and leatherworkers are little more than animalized "effluence" castigated to "seedy" parts of town. Such opinions are exhibited through comedy in satirical authors such as Aristophanes (*Eq.* 315–21). In her study of "Hippocratic Medicine in Aristophanic Comedy," Sarah Hobe notes that in the story of the sausage seller and the tanner, both characters are graphically displayed as "low-class tradesmen who deal in the most unsavoury, ill-smelling businesses at the city gates," with Aristophanes accordingly picturing these figures (each ridiculed as unsuited for public office) as animalizing and dehumanizing each other through name-calling and slurs: "Paphlagon [the tanner] becomes a pig for the Sausage Seller to slaughter and stuff, while the Sausage Seller becomes nothing more than animal skin that Paphlagon is eager to turn into leather" (Hobe 2018, 65). Most arresting here is the focus on the market products (and wastes) associated with each trade, through which people are metaphorically postured as dehumanized substances.

Could a similar (albeit strategic) self-debasement and self-dehumanization be seen to lie within 1 Cor 4:13? In his materialist Asian American interpretation of Simon the Tanner in Acts, Dong Hyeon Jeong notes that "the proximity of nonhuman skins (from the tanning industry) to the colonized skins . . . [underscores] the affect of animalization which is experienced by both nonhumans and minoritized bodies" (Jeong 2020, 41). For Jeong, material skins are used as performative surfaces on which oppressed identities can be politicized and displayed. This has some resonance with the lower-caste leatherworkers in India who Shivani Kapoor documents responding to accusations of pollution by throwing "carcasses into the public instead of cleaning them up as ritually required" in order to specifically "inaugurate the carcass as a political subject . . . with all its sights, tastes and odours, into the political public" (Kapoor 2018, 5). Could Paul also be engaged in some sort of material, embodied, and metaphorical refiguring of occupational stigma in his encounter with the Corinthians? It is perhaps not insignificant that earlier in his argument in 1 Corinthians 4, Paul specifically uses the language of public display (θέατρον, 4:9; literally, "theater" or "spectacle"), which could be conceived as some sort of performative activism. Moreover, this is directly linked in his discourse to being sentenced to death (ἐπιθανατίους, 4:9), presumably calling to mind the cruciform identity forged for himself and others through Christ's execution:

> For I think that God has exhibited (ἀπέδειξεν) us apostles as last of all, as though sentenced to death (ἐπιθανατίους), because we have become a spectacle (θέατρον) to the world, to angels and to mortals. We are fools

for the sake of Christ, but you are wise in Christ. We are weak, but you are strong. You are held in honor, but we in disrepute. (1 Cor 4:9-10)

Stephen Moore's construction of the crucifixion (itself a materialist assemblage, a mix of the human and nonhuman) seems apropos in this respect. For Moore the event exhibits

> the denuded impaled man; the wood and metal torture device; the divine being erupting from the bowels of a bloody carcass . . . a Christ who in his consummate moment of self-revelation is encountered only as sensate matter, as scoured flesh. (2017, 11)

Could even more explicit links between the crucifixion and the tanners/leatherworkers trade and occupational stigma also be discerned? In his study of "Suspension and Crucifixion in Classical and Hellenistic Greece," David Chapman considers Herodotus' narration of the orders of an Athenian general and the spectacle of death he imposes on an enemy's body: "They took Artayctes the Persian and nailed him still living to a plank with feet and hands extended" (*Hist.* 7.33). Commentators have denoted the event as a "crucifixion" of sorts, as later in the narrative the plank is raised in the air. In a footnote, Chapman cites Liddell and Scott's translation of διεπασσάλευσαν as "stretch out by nailing the extremities" and crucially notes other uses of the term in depicting "an animal hide pegged out for tanning" (Chapman 2015, 457). Here, then, it might be that the public spectacle of a crucified corpse is being conceptually linked to the stinking and stretched skin and waste in the tanner's workshop. In short, occupational stigma from one domain is transferred to another and the "disreputable" techniques and materials of tanning and leather become sensorial metaphors. Perhaps Paul is doing something similar in creating sensorial metaphors of an apostolic identity which likewise occupies a "dehumanized" form as "dregs of the earth" and disposable "waste."

PAUL AND THE OCCUPATIONAL STIGMA OF STREET CRIERS

Like *stench*, *noise* has also been used cross-culturally to mark social boundaries within societies, and is more often than not assigned to those "other" or "disreputable" spaces, groups, and persons (Bailey 1996, 49). Peter Bailey has evocatively defined "noise" as "sound out of place": "a broad yet imprecise category . . . that register[s] variously as incoherent, confused, inarticulate, or degenerate" (1996, 50). In his work on the soundscapes of ancient Rome, Ray Laurence also attests that judgments on sound were made by "perceivers" rather than "emitters" and that "the loudest noises in Latin literature tend[ed] to be associated with disorder" (2017, 13).

Occupational stigmas could, as a result of sound, be cast on account of a subject's "voice," defined as "a set of sonic, material, and literary practices shaped by culturally and historically specific moments and a category invoked in discourse about personal agency, communication and representation, and political power" (Weidman 2014, 37). One particular disreputable trade association which Bond delineates, and which can be numbered among ancient technologies of sound, is the street crier/announcer. *Praeco* was a term derived from the Latin verb *praedicare* (literally, "recite in people's presence" [Lowe 2019, 150]). These figures, variously characterized as criers/heralds and/or auctioneers, publicized or verbally curated events in the forum, political assemblies, auditoria, athletic stadiums, religious festivals, auction halls, and city streets. In the words of one ancient historian, the *praeco* was "a combination of announcer and microphone, one who can make a single word cut through the noise of a crowd" (Lowe 2019, 150). Crucially the *praeco* was never intended to generate his own unique information but rather to faithfully relay the messages of the one who had sent him (see Furnish 1963)—as, for example, in imperial communication. So Duane Litfin writes:

> According to Suetonius (*Life of Augustus* 84.2) even Augustus himself "sometimes because of weakness of the throat . . . addressed the people through a herald (praeconius)." When speaking in his official civic role, the *praeco* was always operating not from his own authority but on behalf of another. (Litfin 2015, 207)

Praecones also played important roles across associations: announcing events, being involved in the curation of funeral rituals, and so on. Bond and others indicate that the forming of a voluntary association seems also to have been a possibility for *praecones* themselves. There is evidence from Ostia in which a *praeco vinorium* (a wine auctioneer), for example, made a dedication to the "genius of the association." So too a group of *praecones*, *librarii*, and *scribae* had a *schola* "east of the temple of Saturn within the Roman Forum" (cited in Bond 2016, 29). Despite these visible identities, Bond ably demonstrates that more often than not *praecones* were considered marginalized and liminal. In elite sources, the *praeco* was frequently derided as a low-status figure: Martial (*Epi.* 5.56.7–8) castigates *praecones* as "dimwits" who could nonetheless become wealthy through their trade; Juvenal (*Sat.* 3.33, 7.5–6) considers their occupations shameful; Cicero (*Pis.* 68) likens their grating voice to cockcrowing (Lowe 2019, 151-52).

Jeffrey Veitch (2017) wonders if coarse voice and loud volume were perhaps among the reasons why these figures were frequently viewed as distasteful. Nonetheless, the multiple contexts in which *praecones* operated, spanning as they did the entire spectrum of life, space, and status hierarchy ("political assemblies, the comitia, funerals, theatrical performances, auction-halls, the open streets"; Lowe 2019, 150), also probably fueled elite fear and suspicion of their reach and influence on account of their many common and/or associational connections. Evidencing some of this status and appeal, an epitaph of a late Republican crier seems designed to underscore his decorum, moderation, and respect: "Here lie the bones of Aulus Granius the *praeco*: modest, discrete, honourable. That is all: He wanted you to have that information. Have a good day" (cited in Lowe 2019, 151). From a similar era, another inscription notes the myriad networks and influences the *praecones* accrued, implicitly evidencing that, due to the nature of their work, the *praecones* who represented the elite could at times amass some degree of respect and standing:

> Publius Cornelius Surus. [Publius Cor]nelius Surus, freedman of Publius, nomenclator, magister of the Capitoline priestly college five times in nine years, magistrate (?) of the collegium of tailors(?), *praeco* for the treasury of the three *decuriae*, magistrate of the association of scribes and poets, directed games in the stone theater, and was an attendant to the consuls and censors. (Inscription cited in Bond 2016, 31)

Bond cites the *Tabula Heracleensis* on municipalities which she (tentatively) connects to the *lex Julia municipalis* (45 CE)—proscribing "exclusion of *praecones* from public office"—as evidence of an elite strategic attempt to censor *praecones* and their influence (2011, 30). Others too have viewed the *Tabula Heracleensis* as intended to guard against "conflicts of interest between contractor and councillor," or profiteering at another's expense, or to serve as a warning to the broader populace that "prostitution of voice" inevitably incurred "*infamia*" and "*indignitas*" (Bond 2011, 30). In short, the censoring of voice seemed to be used as an elite strategy to resist the crier's transmission, spread, and influence.

Certain aspects of Paul's performances and communications could have found resonance for some audiences with street announcers of the sort that Bond profiles. Most prominently Paul self-designates as an announcer of the deity who sent him: "sent neither by human commission nor from human authorities, but through Jesus Christ and God the Father, who raised him from the dead" (Gal 1:1). In his study of Paul's challenge to the (sophistic) art of persuasion in ancient Corinth, Litfin notes that while *praecones* were frequently disdained and ridiculed by elite literary sources Paul nonetheless seems to associate himself with this role not least in representing himself as a messenger of the power of Christ (Litfin 2015, 207). Paul's own awareness of his own devalued speech and voice ("foolishness") in the context of Corinthian elite rhetoric (1 Cor 1:18-3:4)—what Cavan Concannon understatedly refers to as "Paul's perception problem" (2014, 88)—may also indicate strategic managing of an occupational stigma.

In 2 Cor 2:17 Paul also seems to transfer the "crier/announcer" identity (embodied voice, as opposed to literary word) to the community itself, in his statement that the "congregation itself is the speaking letter of recommendation he is carrying with him" (Loubser 1995, 66). They too are *praecones* of their leader: "In Christ we speak as persons of sincerity, as persons sent from God and standing in his presence" (2 Cor 2:17). In the wider context of 2 Corinthians 2, Paul also images Christ leading a "triumphal procession," which through Paul and the Christian community spreads like an aroma (vertically as well as horizontally) across social divides. As such, Paul *kinesthetically* associates the acoustic (sound) of 2 Cor 2:17 with olfactory (smell) in 2 Cor 2:15-16, which reads:

> We are the aroma of Christ to God among those who are being saved and among those who are perishing; to the one a fragrance from death to death, to the other a fragrance from life to life.

Commentators envisage Paul here either as performing a form of self-praise on account of mission or as part of the chattel of war—as the processions often involved the spectacles of prisoners of war being displayed. Whichever interpretation is preferred, the key role of *praecones* in such spectacles has often been unnoticed or underplayed. Significantly, the iconographic framework here (that is, a Roman *pompa triumphalis*, a spectacle of mass communication designed to impress on a city the achievements and renown of a victorious Roman general) directly involved street announcers and heralds as a critical part of the process. Diane Favro, in her study of the *pompa triumphalis* in Rome (1994), notes how often street criers would take part in announcing the procession—controlling arrangements and viewing by the populace. Joe Sheppard too, in his study of mass spectacle as a communication tool in the Roman world, submits that these events were not designed "to transmit particular words or gestures from wealthy benefactors to a captive audience" but rather to facilitate accord and order, since announcing and celebrating "civic identity and political stability" as part of "crisis communications" could help diminish and quash any political turbulence (Sheppard 2019, abstract). Mark Bradley underscores the importance of the sensory and the divine in religious celebrations. He cites one of Varro's Menippean Satires that linked processions with the gates of the city, "allowing people to keep a careful eye, ear, and nose on what entered the community and what left" (Bradley 2021, 125). Such performances, through sensory stimuli, intensified relationships with the gods and were able to effect social transformations. Kloppenborg too pictures such processions as occasions in which association members would "move" (and one could add hear and sense) "together as a single body" despite their differences:

> Like the creation of rosters and the staging of meals, processions are not simply activities in which a group also happens to engage; they are activities that constitute the group as a group and that articulate structures within the group. Belonging is both performed and displayed. (Kloppenborg 2019, 142)

Other statements of Paul may also have drawn vivid conceptual parallels of activities in which *praecones* were traditionally involved. For example, Paul's claim that "you were bought with a price, therefore glorify God in your body" (1 Cor 6:20) could have called to mind the public notice, competition, and arbitration of the sale, all of which were integral to the process of performing conquest and military propaganda in auctions: displaying "submission of booty and prisoners to the victor" (Morcillo 2008, 157)—who, in this instance, is Christ.

Accenting another social context in which Paul's activity can be compared with the disreputable occupation of *praecones*, Steven Muir (2014) in his stimulating study of Gal 3:1 ("It was before your eyes that Jesus Christ was publicly exhibited as crucified") draws resonances of street announcing in Paul's communicative techniques, purposefully designed to produce for the audience an experiential and sensory "re-presentation" of the event. Muir notes that, as a spectator event, crucifixion itself would have routinely been advertised by *praecones*. Muir centers too on the term προεγράφη (a noun related to public notice, advert, or edict) to underscore the force of Paul's communication being to exhibit and advertise the fact of Christ crucified (Muir 2014). Significantly, some ancient historians have claimed the *Tabula Heracleensis* was itself designed to control the pollution posed by criers associated with funerals and death-announcing; Juvenal drew occupational parallels between those collecting rubbish and dead flesh (*Sat.* 3.31). Accordingly Paul's performance as one "crucified with Christ" (Gal 2:19) and participating in Christ's wounds and sufferings (Gal 6:17) could serve to heighten more explicitly, rather than ameliorate or hide, the occupational stigmas of *praecones*. In other respects, however, Muir notes that Paul seems keen to directly rebut an implicit link between occupational taints often associated with *praecone* ("peddling of God's word") and fend off prejudicial reactions that his own performances might incur from others.

Of course, one rebuttal which could be made to reading Paul alongside a *praeco* identity is that he is a writer, an epistolary wordsmith, not specifically an oral performer. However, this too may belie certain text-centric assumptions which could be questioned. Paul visited places and announced his message orally, with letters in most instances used as a follow-up. Muir rightly contends: "What we see in Paul's writings suggest that his oral message fits with what other speakers of his time were doing" (Muir 2014, 85), and in relation to the verbal curation of crucifixion, he may even be using the crier's role for discursive gain.

From a network theory perspective, the very fact that control and suppression seemed to lay behind social injunctions of *praecones* is seen by Bond as (albeit) implicit evidence of their dexterity as "central connectors within associative networks" and key sites for "the dissemination of information within the Roman world" (Bond 2011, 25). So too Pauline Ripat berates the tendency to focus on

> the spread of information in Roman society from the top of the social hierarchy to the bottom . . . [rather than] the spread of information from the lower echelons upwards, and even less has been said about the possible content of this information, its transmitters, or the potential power transmission bestowed. (2012, 50)

Adopting social network theory, Ripat concludes that relationships (rather than material resources) were often preeminent in the spreading of information; so too "those with the closest and most numerous contacts with subcultures or communities of their own enjoy greater importance, and thus power, than their less connected peers" (2012, 50). In mobilizing participation through his voice "from below," Paul too is involved in what

Brandon LaBelle refers to as "acoustic politics" (2010, 186)—marshalling support (subversively) through vocal indecorum and/or weakness. Sebastian Matzner sees in such "complex inferiorities" in ancient literature a "poetics of the weaker voice"—"authorial self-fashioning, hierarchies of genres, and value judgements tied to positions within literary traditions" (Matzner and Harrison 2019, 7)—all purposively defined to invite audiences to reconsider socially typical allegiances, attitudes, or prejudices: in essence as a street crier, being enabled to speak "all things to all people" (1 Cor 9:22).

PAUL, OCCUPATIONAL STIGMA, AND THE SENSORY POLITICS OF ASSOCIATIONS

John Kloppenborg's recent essay on "Recruitment to Elective Cults: Network Structure and Ecology" (2020) uses epidemiology and contagion as a hermeneutical lens to trace early Christian recruitment patterns in Thessaloniki and Corinth. He traces "viable network structures," "ecology of the cult," and "recipients susceptible to diffusion" to account for the spread and distribution of Christ assemblies in these areas. He does not, however, extend the force of his epidemiological metaphor to include "pollution" (or occupational stigma) and the ways and means by which people evade (socially distance!) or stigmatize "viral carriers" of disease, often on account of their presumed power as (biological or ideological) "super-spreaders" across social divides.

Discussion here has experimentally read aspects of occupational stigma encountered by what Bond terms the "disreputable" trade associations of tanners/leatherworkers and street criers alongside Paul and early Christ groups. Key in this regard have been the sensory politics and careful negotiation of occupational stigma (particularly centered on olfactory dimensions and soundscapes) and how these are refracted in Paul's own communications. While some scholars have noted Paul's various disassociations with financial or material support (for both his and their fear of being perceived as "working dirty" in a moral sense), far fewer have noted sensory elements of his "dirty work." Yet sensory aspects of occupational stigma are important to consider—especially with regard to sensory cues and/or elements in network theory. Movements (physical and social, individual and collective) inevitably involved sensory prompts and change, for histories of (social) movements often involve "nodes in a matrix" (Ingold 2000, 219) and "distinct sensory perceptions, and kinaesthetic engagements" (Veitch 2020, 268). Stench and noise as mediating carriers of signification demonstrate potently and "senseibly" the shifting domains of practices, messages, and identities, across both vertical and horizontal axes. Public spectacles often gave associations and individuals marked by occupational stigma (including those who could be deemed "stinking leatherworkers and noisy street criers") a stage on which to challenge and refigure the prejudicial frames in which their techniques, processes, and identities were so often typecast and displayed. Paul and his fellow workers, if subject to occupational stigma of the sort proposed here, may also have sensed, embodied, and employed such performances in their own communications and self-understanding.

WORKS CITED

Asano, Atsuhiro. 2016. "'Like the Scum of the World, the Refuse of All': A Study of the Background and Usage of περίψημα and περικάθαρμα in 1 Corinthians 4.13b." *JSNT* 39:16–39.

Ascough, Richard S. 2000. "The Thessalonian Christian Community as a Professional Voluntary Association." *JBL* 119:311–28.

———. 2015. "What Are They *Now* Saying about Christ Groups and Associations?" *CurBR* 13:207–44.

Ashforth, Blake E., and Glen E. Kreiner. 2014. "Contextualizing Dirty Work: The Neglected Role of Cultural, Historical, and Demographic Context." *Journal of Management & Organization* 20:423–40.

Ashforth, Blake E., Glen E. Kreiner, Mark A. Clark, and Mel Fugate. 2007. "Normalizing Dirty Work: Managerial Tactics for Countering Occupational Taint." *Academy of Management Journal* 50:149–74.

Bailey, Peter. 1996. "Breaking the Sound Barrier: A Historian Listens to Noise." *Body & Society* 2:49–66.

Bond, Sarah E. 2011. "Criers, Impresarios, and Sextons: Disreputable Occupations in the Roman World." PhD diss., University of North Carolina at Chapel Hill.

———. 2016. *Trade and Taboo: Disreputable Professions in the Roman Mediterranean.* Ann Arbor: University of Michigan Press.

El Boushy, A. R. Y., and A. F. B. van der Poel. 1994. 2nd ed., 2000. *Handbook of Poultry Feed from Waste.* Dordrecht: Kluwer Academic.

Bradley, Mark. 2015. "Foul Bodies in Ancient Rome." Pages 133–45 in *Smell and the Ancient Senses.* Edited by Mark Bradley. London: Routledge.

———. 2021. "The Triumph of the Senses: Sensory Awareness and the Divine in Roman Public Celebrations." Pages 125–40 in *Sensorium: The Senses in Roman Polytheism.* Edited by Antón Alvar Nuño, Jaime Alvar Ezquerra, and Greg Woolf. Religions in the Graeco-Roman World 195. Leiden: Brill.

Chapman, David Wallace. 2015. "Suspension and Crucifixion in Classical and Hellenistic Greece." Pages 451–76 in David Wallace Chapman and Eckhard

Schnabel. *The Trial and Crucifixion of Jesus: Texts and Commentary*. Tübingen: Mohr Siebeck.

Classen, Constance, ed. 2005. *The Book of Touch*. Oxford: Berg.

Concannon, Cavan W. 2014. *"When You Were Gentiles": Specters of Ethnicity in Roman Corinth and Paul's Corinthian Correspondence*. New Haven: Yale University Press.

Craik, Kenneth. 2008. *Reputation: A Network Interpretation*. Oxford: Oxford University Press.

Douglas, Mary. 1966. *Purity and Danger: An Analysis of Concepts of Pollution and Taboo*. London. Routledge & Kegan Paul.

van Driel-Murray, Carol. 2009. "Tanning and Leather." Pages 483–95 in *The Oxford Handbook of Engineering and Technology in the Classical World*. Edited by John Oleson. Oxford: Oxford University Press.

Drobnick, Jim, ed. 2006. *The Smell Culture Reader*. Oxford: Berg.

Favro, Diane. 1994. "The Street Triumphant: The Urban Impact of Roman Triumphal Parades." Pages 151–64 in *Streets: Critical Perspectives on Public Space*. Edited by Zeynep Çelik, Diane Favro, and Richard Ingersoll. Berkeley: University of California Press.

Ferris, Iain. 2021. *The Dignity of Labour: Work and Identity in the Roman World*. Stroud: Amberley.

Forbes, R. J. 1966. *Studies in Ancient Technology*. Vol. 5. Leiden: Brill.

Furnish, Victor. 1963. "Prophets, Apostles, and Preachers: A Study of the Biblical Concept of Preaching." *Int* 17:48–60.

Gowers, Emily. 1995. "The Anatomy of Rome from Capitol to Cloaca." *JRS* 85:23–32.

Griffith, Jeremy. 2013. "Garbology: The Beauty of the Items Left Behind." PhD diss., Rochester Institute of Technology.

Hankins, Joseph. 2013. "An Ecology of Sensibility: The Politics of Scents and Stigma in Japan." *Anthropological Theory* 13:49–66.

Harland, Philip A. 2007. "Familial Dimensions of Group Identity (II): 'Mothers' and 'Fathers' in Associations and Synagogues of the Greek World." *JSJ* 38:57–79.

Harrill, Paul. 2012. *Paul the Apostle: His Life and Legacy in Their Roman Context*. Cambridge: Cambridge University Press.

Harrison, James R. 2019. *Paul and the Ancient Celebrity Circuit: The Cross and Moral Transformation*. WUNT 430. Tübingen: Mohr Siebeck.

Hobe, Sara. 2018. "Hippocratic Medicine in Aristophanic Comedy." PhD diss., University of Freiburg.

Hock, Ronald F. 1979. "The Workshop as a Social Setting for Paul's Missionary Preaching." *CBQ* 41:438–50.

Holmberg, Bengt. 2008. "Understanding the First Hundred Years of Christian Identity." Pages 1–30 in *Exploring Early Christian Identity*. Edited by Bengt Holmberg. WUNT 226. Tübingen: Mohr Siebeck.

Horsley, Richard A. 2011. *1 Corinthians*. ANTC. Nashville: Abingdon.

Ingold, T. 2000. *The Perception of the Environment: Essays on Livelihood, Dwelling and Skill*. Abingdon: Routledge.

James, William. 1903. *The Varieties of Religious Experience: A Study in Human Nature*. New York: Longmans, Green.

Jeffers, James. 1999. *The Greco-Roman World of the New Testament Era: Exploring the Background of Early Christianity*. Downers Grove, Ill.: InterVarsity Press.

Jeong, Dong Hyeon. 2020. "Simon the Tanner, Empires, and Assemblages: A New Materialist Asian American Reading of Acts 9:43." *The Bible & Critical Theory* 16:41–63.

Joshel, Sandra R. 1993. *Work, Identity, and Legal Status at Rome: A Study of the Occupational Inscriptions*. Norman: University of Oklahoma Press.

Kapoor, Shivani. 2018. "Your Mother, You Bury Her: Caste, Carcass and Politics in Contemporary India." *Pakistan Journal of Historical Studies* 3:5–30.

———. 2021. "The Violence of Odors: Sensory Politics of Caste in a Leather Tannery." *Senses and Society* 16:164–76.

Kloppenborg, John S. 2018. "Associations, Guilds and Clubs." Pages 154–70 in *The Oxford Handbook of Early Christian Ritual*. Edited by Risto Uro, Juliette J. Day, Rikard Roitto, and Richard E. DeMaris. Oxford: Oxford University Press.

———. 2019. *Christ's Associations: Connecting and Belonging in the Ancient City*. New Haven: Yale University Press.

———. 2020. "Recruitment to Elective Cults: Network Structure and Ecology." *NTS* 66:323–50.

Kloppenborg, John S., and Richard Ascough, eds. 2011. *Attica, Central Greece, Macedonia, Thrace*. BZNW 181. Vol. 1 of *Greco-Roman Associations: Texts, Translations, and Commentary*. Edited by John S. Kloppenborg and Richard S. Ascough. Berlin: De Gruyter.

LaBelle, Brandon. 2010. *Acoustic Territories: Sound Culture and Everyday Life*. New York: Continuum.

Laurence, Ray. 2017. "The Sounds of the City: From Noise to Silence in Ancient Rome." Pages 13–22 in *Senses of Empire: Multisensory Approaches to Roman Culture*. Edited by Eleanor Betts. London: Routledge.

Liebeschuetz, Wolf. 2015. *East and West in Late Antiquity: Invasion, Settlement, Ethnogenesis and Conflicts of Religion*. Leiden: Brill.

Liljegren, Andreas. 2012. "Key Metaphors in the Sociology of Professions: Occupations as Hierarchies and Landscapes." *Comparative Sociology* 11:88–112.

Lindenlauf, Astrid. 2004. "The Sea as a Place of No Return in Ancient Greece." *World Archaeology* 35:416–33.

Litfin, Duane. 2015. *Paul's Theology of Preaching: The Apostle's Challenge to the Art of Persuasion in Ancient Corinth*. Downers Grove, Ill.: InterVarsity Press.

Loubser, J. A. 1995. "Orality and Literacy in the Pauline Epistles: Some New Hermeneutical Implications." *Neot* 29:61–74.

Lowe, Dunstan. 2019. "Loud and Proud: The Voice of the *praeco* in Roman Love-Elegy." Pages 149–58 in *Complex Inferiorities: The Poetics of the Weaker*

Voice in Latin Literature. Edited by Sebastian Matzner and Stephen Harrison. Oxford: Oxford University Press.

Matzner, Sebastian, and Stephen Harrison, eds. 2019. *Complex Inferiorities: The Poetics of the Weaker Voice in Latin Literature.* Oxford: Oxford University Press.

Moore, Stephen. 2017. *Gospel Jesuses and Other Nonhumans: Biblical Criticism Post-poststructuralism.* Atlanta: SBL.

Morcillo, Marta García. 2008. "Staging Power and Authority at Roman Auctions." *Ancient Society* 38:153–81.

Muir, Steven. 2014. "Vivid Imagery in Galatians 2:1: Roman Rhetoric, Street Announcing, Graffiti, and Crucifixions." *BTB* 44:76–86.

Oliver, Isaac. 2012. "The Ritual Insignificance of Tanning in Ancient Judaism." *NTS* 59:50–60.

Porter, Stanley. 2016. *The Apostle Paul: His Life, Thought and Letters.* Grand Rapids: Eerdmans.

Ripat, Pauline. 2012. "Locating the Grapevine in the Late Republic: Freedmen and Communication." Pages 50–65 in *Free at Last! The Impact of Freed Slaves on the Roman Empire.* Edited by Sinclair Bell and Teresa Ramsby. Bristol: Bristol Classical Press.

Roca, Esther. 2010. "The Exercise of Moral Imagination in Stigmatized Work Groups." *Journal of Business Ethics* 96:135–47.

Scanlan, John. 2005. *On Garbage.* Chicago: University of Chicago Press.

Sheppard, Joe. 2019. "Mass Spectacles in Roman Pompeii as a System of Communication." PhD diss., Columbia University.

Stevens, Jeffrey. 2014. "Staring into the Face of Roman Power: Resistance and Assimilation from behind the Mask of Infamia." PhD diss., University of California.

Stewart, Edmund, Edward Harris, and David Lewis, eds. 2020. *Skilled Labour and Professionalism in Ancient Greece and Rome.* Cambridge: Cambridge University Press.

Still, Todd D. 2006. "Did Paul Loathe Manual Labor? Revisiting the Work of Ronald F. Hock on the Apostle's Tentmaking and Social Class." *JBL* 125:781–95.

Veitch, Jeffrey. 2017. "Acoustics of Roman Ostia: Aural Architecture, Noise and Urban Space in the Second Century CE." MPhil thesis, University of Kent.

———. 2020. "Cities and Urbanism." Pages 266–80 in *The Routledge Handbook of Sensory Archaeology.* Edited by Robin Skeates and Jo Day. New York: Routledge.

Weidman, Amanda. 2014. "Anthropology and Voice." *Annual Review of Anthropology* 43:37–51.

Wiseman, Rob. 2015. "Interpreting Ancient Social Organization: Conceptual Metaphors and Image Schemas." *Time and Mind* 8:159–90.

6

Dressing for Deities

Functions and Meanings of Dress within Ancient Associations

Alicia J. Batten

In his book *Stuff*, anthropologist Daniel Miller invites his readers to reconsider the manner in which they think about material culture and clothing in particular. Rather than perceiving dress as merely a surface element of existence that covers or adorns the "true self" that dwells within the person, he observes how in some cultures, "being" is not hidden and embedded somehow deep inside a person—what he calls "depth ontology"—but on the surface, and what appears on the surface, including dress, bears tremendous importance. Depth ontology, Miller demonstrates, is a construction largely of western cultures, but it has contributed to a denigration of materiality and of those interested in material things in western contexts (2010, 13–23). We cannot assume that all peoples view materiality, including dress, as superficial, but must remember that how groups perceive dress is conditioned by all sorts of historical, political, and cultural factors.[1]

---

[1]   For example, Miller (2010, 13–23) discusses squatters living on the Caribbean island of Trinidad, where impoverished women might have a dozen or twenty pairs of shoes, and in which a common leisure activity is to have fashion shows on makeshift runways in the squatters' encampment. These people, claims Miller, were not at all interested in the interiors of persons, but in their freedom to construct themselves through dress, humor, and conversation. The truth of a person, in this context, lies on the surface. Miller postulates that the history of slavery may play a role in the Trinidadian emphasis upon freedom, but his larger point is that here, "how one looks is who one is" (2010, 20).

Likewise, when we think about those who lived in the ancient Mediterranean, including the many who participated in various associations, it is necessary to think about how their contexts affect their attitudes towards self-presentation and materiality and the roles of materiality in that presentation. Many interpreters observe that the cultures of Mediterranean antiquity were much more collectivist than those of contemporary North America or northern Europe, where individualism has emerged more prominently. This emphasis upon the group had implications for comprehending what it means to be a human being. For instance, the needs of the group held priority over individual needs. This means that group activities, such as "processions, sacrifices, festivals, communal meals, and other rituals of expressing 'groupness'—will lie at the center of personhood" (Kloppenborg 2019, 14). Both how one "presented to" but also "represented" the group mattered a great deal.

One cannot assume that such collectivist societies reflected western notions of "depth ontology." Some argue that the Romans, at least, were accustomed to understanding life as a series of roles played, or masks worn, in varied and differing ways depending upon what was taking place (Braund 2005, 391). Dress would have played a crucial role in creating and upholding these roles within the collective sphere. And we know that dress mattered to ancients given the number of texts that refer to some type of dress and/or attempt to regulate it (see Maier 2004; Batten 2010). We also have plenty of artistic and archaeological evidence for all sorts of dress (see Batten and Olson 2021). However, and not surprisingly, it becomes much more complicated when one tries to understand the various purposes and meanings of the images, artifacts, and texts that survive.

This essay explores dress in a variety of ancient associations in an attempt to understand better the diverse ways in which dress could function for these groups. I use a definition of dress developed by Mary Ellen Roach-Higgins and Joanne B. Eicher: "an assemblage of modifications of the body and/or supplements to the body" (1992, 1), which means that "dress" includes clothing, hair, accessories, cosmetics, tattoos and bodily modifications, jewelry, and any other item a person might "wear." Consistent with the focus of the volume, I include examples from Greco-Roman associations and from Christ groups. Inscriptional evidence, of which there is a tremendous amount spanning several centuries, serves as the primary material for Greco-Roman associations whereas the texts for the nascent Christ assemblies are literary.[2] Therefore, I am comparing different kinds of sources. However, such a

---

[2]   Although many Greco-Roman literary texts discuss dress, indicating just how important it was to ancient Mediterranean people.

comparison can still yield insight. We have no choice, moreover, because letters and other literary materials are the main sorts of documents that we have for the earliest members of the Christ cult. They do not begin producing inscriptions until later in the Common Era.

For some analytical leverage, the categories used by Laura Gawlinski from her essay "Theorizing Religious Dress" are helpful. Although she uses the terms "religion" and "religious," Gawlinski is aware that the term *religion* is difficult to apply to the ancient world, as what we might think of today as "religion" was quite different in antiquity, where ritual life was embedded within larger social and cultural activities (2017, 162). "Religion" was not separate from other aspects of life, nor was it focused primarily on beliefs, as it tends to be in some modern contexts, at least in the northern hemisphere.[3] She analyses ancient dress with attention to four different functions or aspects: (1) dress as means of communicating identity; (2) dress and fashion; (3) dress and hierarchy; (4) dress and embodied experience. In this essay, I employ the categories of identity, status and hierarchy, and embodied experience.[4] What a comparison of a limited sampling of evidence indicates, perhaps not surprisingly, is that when it comes to dress and dress practices, Greco-Roman associations and ancient Christ assemblies exhibit some commonalities, but they also differ in significant ways. Their comparison, however, can be very productive.

DRESS AND IDENTITY

Contemporary dress theorists have analyzed the manner in which dress can convey many dimensions of both individual and group identity (Roach-Higgins and Eicher 1992; Davis 1992; Arthur 1999). Gender, status, ethnicity, and kinship are just a few aspects of identity that dress can communicate. In addition, similar dress practices among group members can contribute to a sense of shared identity, and, by maintaining dress practices from former times, or what some have referred to as "fossilized fashion" (Gordon 1987), they can connect the present community members with peoples, memories, and ideas from the past. Contemporary examples of such practices

---

[3]   Today some scholars (for example, Kloppenborg 2019, 10–18) avoid the terms *religion* and *religious* because they can be misleading when it comes to describing the ancient world.

[4]   Although this essay does not employ Gawlinski's category of "fashion," which would mean that questions of changes and stability in dress would be the focus, I do not suggest that such a category is not productive for analysing dress in antiquity. There is simply not space to explore the topic here.

might include the Amish (see Hume 2013, 35–49), but ancients engaged in such practices as well, just in different ways.[5] Moreover, dressing differently from the group, even in a subtle manner, was and is a means of subverting, or resisting, the status quo. Dress has the power to disrupt (see Roach and Eicher 1965) and thus it often requires regulation.

Within the context of ancient associations, dress can be an obvious means of signaling specific roles within the cultic setting, just as it is in many contemporary "religious" or military contexts where there is ritual activity and a performance of some kind. Gawlinski, an expert on an inscription from the first century BCE (or possibly early first century CE) for cultic activities of an association in Messenia near Andania, Greece (*LSCG* 65; see Gawlinski 2012), illustrates how the stipulations about clothes create situational identities within the group. Lines 15–20 of the inscription contain detailed instructions for the type and cost of dress that different groups of females (free adult women versus girls versus female slaves versus sacred women) must wear during the festival for Demeter. The clothing would therefore not only communicate varying identities that are based on gender, age, slave or free, but also the situational identity of whether or not they are "sacred women" (Gawlinski 2017, 163).

Dress regulations in cultic settings could also contribute to a sense of shared identity. The women in the Andanian inscription are prohibited from wearing gold, rouge, white cosmetics, hair bands or braids, and shoes (with some exceptions for certain materials).[6] It is very interesting that the inscription stipulates what the maximum worth of the clothing of each group of women should be. Women could also not wear transparent clothing, presumably because silk, which was usually transparent, could be very expensive. There were also limits on the decoration or borders on their dress (not more than half a finger's width wide). The regulations thus restrict the degree to which the various women could express their economic and social status, even while the rules make distinctions between the different types of women. These restrictions create a certain uniformity (see Ogden 2002) that in turn can contribute to a sense of shared identity. The men participating in

[5] For an analysis of the dress of female workers in bars and inns during the Roman imperial period, and how their dress conveys social status but also communicates cultural memory, see Berg (2019). Special thanks to Dr. Bruce Longenecker for bringing this article to my attention.

[6] These prohibitions against gold and braided hair appear in other inscriptions, such as *LSAM* 14 (Pergamum, third century CE), while some instruct participants to leave their gold at home before they come to the temple of the goddess, as in *LSAM* 6 (Chios, first century CE).

the festival must wear white, which was not uncommon (see *LSAM* 14). The men also don wreaths of laurel, while the sacred women wear white felt caps. These sorts of consistent dress patterns have led Phyllis Culham to suggest that a certain *communitas* is created, at least at an external and visual level (1986, 244; so too Batten 2016, 575–76). Such dress practices are also strictly enforced within the cult, for if anyone violates or deviates from them it is clear that they will be punished by the "controller of women."

Some Christ groups seek to limit women from wearing gold, braided hair, pearls, or expensive clothing as well (1 Tim 2:9-15; 1 Pet 3:1-6), but at least in the case of 1 Peter 3, such modest dress extends to daily life. It is not only during ritual activities that women are forbidden from wearing jewels and lavish dress and hairstyles. Given that the "modest matron" was the ideal within the Roman world, it is perhaps not surprising to observe authors within the Christ associations desiring to limit women's displays of status and wealth, but it is interesting that these limitations extend, presumably, to everyday activities. The explanation for such restrictions is undoubtedly multifaceted. It is possible that as in the Andanian association, the teachings about dress were intended to foster a stronger group identity in which differences in status, at least among women, were mitigated. Another reason could be concern about what sort of identity the Christ group wished to reflect to the broader society. Given the tensions that some of these Christ groups experienced with their neighbors (as is especially evident in 1 Peter), it is likely that they did not want the women to manifest deviations from ancient male constructs of the ideal female for fear it would attract negative attention. Although varied from place to place, it appears that members of Christ groups in the early centuries of the Common Era did not go out of their way to attract disapproval or to distinguish themselves or express their identity through some sort of distinctive dress,[7] as some contemporary groups do. Finally, it is interesting to observe that in the case of 1 Timothy and 1 Peter, there is no mention of the possibility of punishment for dress deviation as there was in the inscription from Andania. Rather, in each case the author provides a theological rationale and appeals to specific interpretations of female figures in the past for why the women should dress in a modest manner (on 1 Peter, see Morrison-Atkins 2021).

The first-century Christ group in Corinth, however, does not evince issues or problems with women wearing jewelry or expensive garb. Here, the subject of dress emerges in the context of praying and prophesying (1 Cor

---

[7] Nor did Judeans, at least not obviously apart from men wearing *tzitzit* or *tefillin*, which they may not have worn in the diaspora so as not to stand out (see Schwartz 2021).

11:2-16) and Paul's famous instruction that women should cover their long hair with a veil while men should not veil nor should they have long hair. Again, there may be multiple factors why Paul expends energy arguing why women need to veil and men should not,[8] but he connects the issue with questions of honor and shame (11:5-6, 14), key values within the ancient Mediterranean (Rohrbaugh 2020; Roberts 2020). These values were often intertwined with gender characterizations, as is the case here. Paul wants to keep gender identities and sexual differentiation clear (see MacDonald 1999) and obvious in the context of praying and prophesying. Stressing the importance of veils and long hair for women and short hair *sans* veil for men was a means of doing so.

DRESS, STATUS, AND HIERARCHY

Paul's instruction about veils and hair in 1 Corinthians 11 also points to the fact that dress was an important tool that could create, reflect, and maintain a hierarchy. In the case of the Christ association in Corinth, Paul is explicit about how these dress instructions reflect a gender hierarchy (1 Cor 11:7-12), although he does acknowledge the interdependence between men and women. In a sense, dress practices followed what some ancient people such as Paul perceived to be a natural gender hierarchy. Although the Andanian inscription delineates different limits on the cost of dress for the various groups of women, these limits would at least lessen the status differences, as mentioned earlier. Liza Cleland has suggested that the dress practices for the different groups of women in Andania create a kind of alternative hierarchy in that they erase or limit some of the status distinctions from the "profane" world for the duration of the festival (2000). It could be that some of the "sacred women" were from a lower socioeconomic status, yet within the cult, they might be "above" wealthier women. The dress as well as the order in which the women would process during the festival would contribute to creating a new hierarchy, at least for a given period of time and within the circumscribed setting of the ritual.

The Andanian inscription is an example that illustrates how dress was tied to status, as was generally the case throughout Greco-Roman society (Olson 2018). In the context of associations, specific robes, belts, and accessories could be symbols of authority and status, but it was often the crown, wreath (στέφανος), and/or diadem or tiara (διάδημα) that signaled

---

[8]   It could be, for example, that Paul also prohibits men from veiling in order to distinguish the Corinthian activities from Roman practices (see Oster 1988).

a financially generous and influential person. These sorts of headpieces were considered sacred to the gods, and we see them in a great range of literary and archaeological materials, spanning all sorts of different groups (Pena 2021, 378). Crowns could be constructed from gold, from flowers, or from laurel, myrtle, olive, or oak leaves. Within the inscriptional and archaeo-logical evidence we observe that priests and priestesses often wore crowns. However, the priesthood generally required no special training, the role was usually not permanent,[9] and priesthoods could be sold to whoever could pay the most (Gawlinski 2017, 166–67). Within Greek cultic life therefore, the widespread use of wreaths was more of an indicator of status than an identity marker (Lee 2015, 145). In fact, the association of crowns with honor was so commonplace that the verb for crowning, στεφανόω, could be employed as a reference to bestowing honor (Gallia 2021, 232).

Crowns were so widespread in associations that honorary crown inscriptions have been described as "a rather fixed institution" (Steven-son 1995, 266) from the fourth century BCE to the fourth century CE. For example, male and female members of a society in the Myrleia area of Bithynia (119 or 104 BCE) crown a woman named Stratonike. This woman was a priestess of Mother Cybele and Apollo, and she receives a crown with a band on a plaque "that was announced and with another crown with a band that was announced in the synagogue of Zeus since she acted in a benevolent manner (φιλαγαθήσας[αν])" (*IApamBith* 35; Harland 2014, 51). Stratonike's benevolence was very likely financial, and thus the crowns she receives were a means of honoring her and granting her status in appreciation for her support of the association. Providing benefaction was a standard means of gaining a degree of authority within these groups, and crowns were used to designate this act of generosity.

There are many examples of people receiving crowns within associa-tions, usually while they were alive, but sometimes posthumously (see *IG* II² 1368; Kloppenborg and Ascough 2011, 241–57), and in some contexts crowns were dedicated to deities (see Stevenson 1995, 262). A decree and membership list from Athens (236/5 BCE) furnishes a list of names of male and female members in an association dedicated to Artemis Kallistē (*IG* II² 1297; Kloppenborg and Ascough 2011, 132–36). It features a person named Sophron, who, it indicates, provided generously to the association in order to provoke rivalry among other people such that they would also contribute to the *koinon* and receive gratitude in return. Sophron is crowned with a wreath

---

[9] Sometimes the priesthood could be for life, as evident in *IG* II² 2361 (see Kloppen-borg and Ascough 2011, 257–61).

of olive leaves and a woolen fillet, and his crowning must be announced publicly when others participate in the rituals of the association. Failure to make this announcement results in a financial penalty. Despite the frequent use of crowns, however, and among the Romans at least, one could not randomly don a crown, and there is evidence that men were sent to prison if they engaged in the unauthorized sporting of crowns in the public domain (Pliny, *Nat.* 21.8; Gallia 2021, 234).

The link between crowns and high status within ancient associations is perhaps most obvious in a short inscription for a Judean association from either Kyme or Phokaia in the third century CE (*IJO* 2.36; Harland 2014, 95–100). Here, a woman named Tation is honored because she has given a building (οἰκός) and a courtyard to a group of Judeans. They honor her not only with a gold crown, but with the right to occupy the front seats. Special seating was a clear honor, whether it was at a banquet, the theater, or an association such as this one (Rohrbaugh 2020, 70). In her golden crown, Tation would occupy a privileged seat within the assembly.

Crowns appear across a range of literature from early Christ groups. The phrase "crown of life" (στέφανον τῆς ζωῆς) appears, seemingly as a reward for those who have withstood trials (Jas 1:12; Rev 2:10). The crown here is eschatological. Whether the imagery derived from the use of crowns to honor benefactors more generally, or from the practice of rewarding victorious athletes who were crowned with organic wreaths, or maybe from the practice of sometimes awarding crowns posthumously, is hard to say. Crowning was associated with the Maccabean martyrs, which might be the best explanation, especially in the case of Rev 2:10 (see Allison 2013, 232, n. 115).

The book of Revelation is an entirely different sort of "text" from that of an inscription that outlines regulations for an association, or one that honors a particular benefactor. Revelation employs very vivid and powerful dress imagery throughout, and this imagery is indebted to a variety of prior texts and contexts (Neufeld 2005; Maier 2021). Crowns and diadems appear in a variety of places, possibly connoting royalty and power (Rev 6:2; 14:14), including threatening power (for example, Rev 12:3). However, there are parallels in the use of crowns in inscriptional evidence for associations and Revelation, despite the fact that the latter is such a different genre. For example, consider the twenty-four elders dressed in white garments with golden crowns on their heads who are seated on thrones around the main throne, but who proceed to cast their crowns on the ground when they worship the one in the center (Rev 4:10). Gregory Stevenson argues that this imagery should be understood within "the context of benefactor relationships" (1995,

270), given the degree to which the language of honor appears in this section of Revelation. The actions of the elders removing their crowns or symbols of honor underscore "God's status as the ultimate benefactor" (1995, 271). The transcendence of the deity is acknowledged, in part, by the elders who forsake their crowns. The scene is a rich example of how dress communicates a divine hierarchy.

Paul also uses crown imagery. In 1 Thess 2:19 he asks, "What is our hope or joy or crown (στέφανος) of boasting before our Lord Jesus at his coming? Is it not you?" Here the crown is the equivalent of the more abstract ideas of hope and joy and appears to have an eschatological element (Peters 2015, 69). The members of the Thessalonian Christ group are the crown, metaphorically speaking. It could be Paul's way of honoring these people as benefactors, given his expressions of appreciation for their generosity and assurance of resurrection in 1 Thessalonians 4 (Ascough 2003, 153). In this case, the designation of the Thessalonians as a "crown" is not to establish or maintain a hierarchy but possibly to encourage a "unified collective," as Janelle Peters has argued (2015, 83). Thus, although Paul is drawing upon the common association of crowns with benefaction, he is not doing so in order to honor a specific person but to honor and assure the group such that, presumably, they would continue to be generous towards others and to maintain cooperation between themselves and with Paul and his associates.

The reference to a crown in Phil 4:1 also refers to the members of the congregation as Paul's "joy and crown." This church had contributed financially to other churches, as Paul acknowledges in Phil 4:15-18, where he uses financial language (Ascough 2003, 113–15). Again, we may be witnessing here the use of "crown" as a recognition of the Philippians for their benefaction to the broader collection of churches. In addition, the language of Phil 4:18 evokes the context of the sacrificial cult, with its reference to a "fragrant offering, a sacrifice acceptable and pleasing to God" (ὀσμὴν εὐωδίας, θυσίαν δεκτήν, εὐάρεστον τῷ θεῷ). The Philippians' monetary gifts have "sacred" value, as Paul evokes the imagery of ritual activity. As in 1 Thessalonians, the use of crown imagery in Philippians indicates that it is the collective that receives honor, not an individual (Peters 2015, 83). In this letter, Paul strives for the recipients to get along (Phil 4:2). There is no indication that he seeks to create or maintain status distinctions between members with his reference to a crown.

Finally, Paul refers to a wreath or crown that athletes compete to win in 1 Cor 9:25. Here the apostle does not identify the crown with the collective but focuses upon the perishable versus imperishable crown. He indicates that although athletes compete to win a perishable crown, members of the Christ group seek an imperishable one. Perhaps this imagery, in addition to drawing from the realm of athletics, is also alluding to the custom of crowning people posthumously, as was practiced sometimes within Greco-Roman associations. In addition, the funerary portraits often depicted people with wreaths of laurel (Peters 2015, 79; Ascough 2003, 63); such individuals were wearing "imperishable" wreaths in a sense. Yet these people were often "crowned" by associations (as well as by the state) because of their influence and generosity while alive. The depiction of these figures with crowns after their death was a means of maintaining honor for them. However, in 1 Corinthians Paul challenges the honor and wisdom of "the strong," who may be economically stronger people (1 Cor 1:26-31). By stressing the imperishable crown over the perishable one that was, in this case, associated with competing in a race, is he implicitly criticizing the practice of crowning the "winner," but also the stronger and wealthier person who could exert more influence in the community? At any rate, it seems clear that in referring to crowns, Paul does not seek to promote the status of any particular individual, as was the case within associations and broader society generally. Rather, Paul attempts to build solidarity and mitigate against some of the status hierarchies that must have characterized some of these Christ assemblies.

DRESS AND EMBODIED EXPERIENCE

We wear dress on our bodies, which means that studies of dress must attend to questions of phenomenology, performativity, and the role of the senses in the experience of getting dressed and being dressed. Most people have had the experience of feeling uncomfortable in a particular item of dress if it does not fit properly or is made of fabric that itches or chafes against the skin. Umberto Eco points out that dress can affect the manner in which we think; does tight fitting or stiff dress make us focus on the external world? Or, like a monk dressed in a loose habit such that he does not have to pay much attention to his physical body, can we center our minds on an interior realm (Eco 2007, 317)? Whatever our experience might be, dress is an embodied practice that can affect day-to-day life. The same was true for the ancients. As Gawlinski writes, "Imagine walking the 14 miles to Eleusis in August in a wool tunic" (2017, 173). This sort of ordeal must have influenced the wearer's experience once they arrived at the location of the mysteries.

Recent work on the senses in antiquity has pointed to the role of dress because of its intimate connection to the body. Adeline Grand-Clément observes how the removal of shoes was sometimes compulsory prior to entering a sanctuary or to participating in a festival (2021, 152–54). Shoelessness was required at Andania, as mentioned above. When these participants processed, they had to walk shoeless through the countryside from Messene to Andania, a distance that could well have been more than ten kilometers. A third-century BCE inscription from Lykosaura stipulates that upon entering the sanctuary of Despoina and Demeter, people could not wear shoes, nor could they wear purple, brightly colored, or black clothes, or rings, or braided or covered hair (*CGRN* 126). On the Greek island of Chios in the first century CE, women at the festival of the goddess could not wear shoes but were required to wear a clean dress (*LSAM* 9). In Lindos the participant was required to shed any footwear prior to entering the shrine in the third century CE (*ILindos* 2.487), and likewise in Pergamon, those spending the night in the shrine of Asclepios had to remove their shoes (*LSAM* 14, third century CE; see Grand-Clément 2021, 152–54).

These are only a few examples, but they point to a reasonably consistent pattern. It is true that removing shoes meant that one was not bringing dirt into a sacred place (Gawlinski 2012, 115–16), a concern also reflected by the instruction, in some instances, to wear clean clothes (see, for example, *LSCGSup* 91). However, Grand-Clément entertains possibilities for the contribution that shoelessness would make to the sensory experience of the worshipper. Perhaps they would feel like a guest in the home of the gods? In addition, maybe the lack of sounds or clatter that shoes tend to make would sustain the silence and assist in creating a soundscape that enhanced the ritual experience? Walking in bare feet would also cause persons to feel much closer to nature and the textures of the ground, which in turn affects their experience of the ritual (Grand-Clément 2021, 153; see also Phillippo 2019, 158–61). It could be, as well, that the lack of shoes was comparable to the absence of other items of dress that were sometimes prohibited, such as jewelry, headbands, veils, belts, and braided hair. Each of these items requires more specific analysis, but by not allowing people to wear them into the sanctuary, perhaps the framers of these regulations were attempting to provide participants with a far less constricted bodily experience than that to which they were accustomed?

The practice of crowning people on the head with a vegetal wreath or metal crown also invites consideration of the effects on the bodies and minds of participants. What sort of comportment and performance would be expected as one accepted the crown and bore it in the presence of others? Would it have, in some way, triggered a sense of value or recognition?

Because wreaths and crowns were associated with the deities, was an effect of being crowned some sort of affinity or identification with the deity? Given the popularity and endurance of these practices, perhaps there was a powerful experiential element beyond the recognition of status, honor, and generosity that the receipt of the crown represented?

Literature from the nascent Christ movement does not exhibit specific rules about shoes, nor do they appear to have practiced crowning people, despite the fact that the central figure of the movement, Jesus, was remembered as being brutally crowned by the state. These texts do, however, evince knowledge of the inextricable links between the body and dress. Perhaps an obvious example is the story of the woman with the flow of blood who is healed as soon as she touches Jesus' garment. Jesus perceives that power has left him when someone simply contacts his clothes (Mark 5:28-30). Another instance appears in Jude 23, which refers to a tunic stained by the flesh. A third example appears in Acts 19:12, which describes how Paul's handkerchiefs and aprons, when taken away from his body, were used to heal the sick of diseases and cleanse others of evil spirits. These cases reflect what some today call the "law of contagion," which refers to the perception that properties of a person are transferred via the object or especially by a garment (Nemeroff and Rozin 1994). The examples discussed in contemporary literature are most often negative, but just as an item of dress could transmit the "badness" of the former wearer to the new person, so could it transmit "goodness."

Transmission not only of positive features but of identity itself may partially explain why we find a few instances of the metaphorical use of garment imagery among Christ groups, whereby believers must "put on" Christ (Gal 3:27; Rom 13:14) or the "new self" (Col 3:10; Eph 4:24) or the "living man" (Gos. Phil. 75:14-26). Paul uses the verb ἐνδύω ("to clothe") in Gal 3:27 when he refers to those who have been baptized and who have "dressed" themselves in Christ. Likewise in Rom 13:14 he instructs his audience to "put on the Lord Jesus Christ, and make no provision for the flesh (σαρκὸς), to gratify its desires." In the latter instance, clothing oneself in Christ affects what the believer does with his or her body; dress and the body are intimately linked. To be sure, there is agency on the part of the believer here, for "neither Paul nor Jesus garbs the baptized in Christ" (Peters 2021, 280), but it is as if wearing Christ transfers a new identity onto or "into" the human being. In both instances, however, it seems clear that the garment of Christ "is the permanent identity of the baptized" (Peters 2021, 280). Furthermore, Col 3:10 and Eph 4:24 use the same verb (ἐνδύω) to describe the "new self," "new nature," or "new human being," which one puts on after having put off the old nature. This old nature produced all sorts of practices associated with the body such as sexual immorality, impurity, passion, evil desire, and covetousness (Col 3:5) or deceitful desires (Eph 4:22). The new nature is in the image of the Creator (Col 3:10; Eph 4:24) and, again, is "embodied" in that it affects what one does with the body. And in Colossians, this "outfit stands in contrast to ethnic and socio-economic status" (Peters 2021, 281). Finally, in the Gospel of Philip putting on the "living man" is associated with ritual activity. Many aspects of the ritual behavior in this gospel are left unexplained, but as Carly Daniel-Hughes observes, "[D]isrobing and acquiring new clothing was an important feature of the sacramental ritual" (Daniel-Hughes 2014, 228). Therefore, it appears that the group associated with the Gospel of Philip went beyond a metaphorical understanding of "putting on" Christ, as in the Pauline and deutero-Pauline texts. Rather, they seem to have engaged in stripping and dressing as part of their ritual activity, which would in turn generate a "new mode of being" (Daniel-Hughes 2014, 230) for participants. Taking into account some of these early texts that speak of "wearing" Christ or the "living man" in some manner, we can perhaps better understand how centuries later, Coptic Christians who donned tunics depicting scenes of Jesus' life while participating in ritual were effectively identifying themselves with Christ. In effect, they were performing "a divinized body, a body visually transformed from corruptibility to incorruptibility by the incarnation of the Word" (Davis 2005, 360).

CONCLUSION

Dress was an important aspect of life within the collective societies of the ancient Mediterranean. This essay has explored some of the ways in which dress could express identity, how it could create, maintain, and challenge hierarchy and status, and finally, how the reality that dress is an embodied practice was important within both Greco-Roman associations and ancient Christ assemblies. We have seen that although there are some similar practices and images, such images and practices could function in a diverse range of ways. In addition, consideration of different sorts of associations enriches the understanding of some of this imagery and practice. For example, the meaning of Paul's references to a crown is enhanced when one is aware of how pervasive crowns were within Greco-Roman associations. Likewise, taking into account the idea of "putting on" Christ or the "living man" within Christ assemblies causes one to attend more to the dress elements of ritual activities in Greco-Roman associations, and the effects that these activities may have had on human experience generally, precisely because they are embodied practices.

As the Christ cult expanded, interest in dress does not wane. Whole treatises devoted to dress questions and controversies, such as some of the works of Tertullian, indicate that all sorts of issues related to dress continued to surface. Many other dimensions of human attire in antiquity, including fashion and change, the importance of color, the significance of knots and braids, the apotropaic functions of clothes and accessories, liturgical dress, as well as the role of certain textile items as dedicatory offerings, have received attention but deserve further study. Engaging in such exploration within a comparative framework that includes multiple types of human groups, who worshipped a variety of deities, can enrich this process of discovery.

WORKS CITED

Allison, Dale C., Jr. 2013. *A Critical and Exegetical Commentary on the Epistle of James*. ICC. London: Bloomsbury T&T Clark.

Arthur, Linda B., ed. 1999. *Religion, Dress and the Body*. Oxford: Berg.

Ascough, Richard S. 2003. *Paul's Macedonian Associations: The Social Context of Philippians and 1 Thessalonians*. WUNT 2/161. Tübingen: Mohr Siebeck.

Batten, Alicia J. 2010. "Clothing and Adornment." *BTB* 40:148–59.

———. 2016. "(Dis)orderly Dress." Pages 567–84 in *Scribal Practices and Social Structures among Jesus Adherents: Essays in Honour of John S. Kloppenborg*. Edited by William E. Arnal, Richard S. Ascough, Robert A. Derrenbacker Jr., and Philip A. Harland. BETL 285. Leuven: Peeters.

Batten, Alicia J., and Kelly Olson, eds. 2021. *Dress in Mediterranean Antiquity: Greeks, Romans, Jews, Christians*. London: T&T Clark.

Berg, Ria. 2019. "Dress, Identity, Cultural Memory Copa and Ancilla Cauponae in Context." Pages 203–37 in *Gender, Memory, and Identity in the Roman World*. Edited by Jussi Rantala. Amsterdam: Amsterdam University Press.

Braund, Susanna. 2005. "The Masks of Satire." Pages 390–97 in *Latin Verse Satire: An Anthology and Reader*. Edited by Paul Allen Miller. London: Routledge.

Cleland, Liza. 2000. "A Hierarchy of Women: Status, Dress, and Social Construction in Andania." Unpublished paper presented at the Celtic Classics Conference, Maynooth, Ireland.

Culham, Phyllis. 1986. "Again, What Meaning Lies in Colour!" *ZPE* 64:235–45.

Daniel-Hughes, Carly. 2014. "Putting on the Perfect Man: Clothing and Soteriology in the *Gospel of Philip*." Pages 215–31 in *Dressing Judeans and Christians in Antiquity*. Edited by Kristi Upson-Saia, Carly Daniel-Hughes, and Alicia J. Batten. Farnham: Ashgate.

Davis, Fred. 1992. *Fashion, Culture, and Identity*. Chicago: University of Chicago Press.

Davis, Stephen J. 2005. "Fashioning a Divine Body: Coptic Christology and Ritualized Dress." *HTR* 98:335–62.

Eco, Umberto. 2007. "Lumbar Thought." Page 315–17 in *Fashion Theory Reader*. Edited by Malcolm Bernard. Oxford: Routledge.

Gallia, Andrew. 2021. "On the Ambivalent Signification of Roman Crowns." Pages 229–45 in Batten and Olson, *Dress in Mediterranean Antiquity*.

Gawlinski, Laura. 2012. *The Sacred Law of Andania: A New Text with Commentary*. Sozomena 11. Berlin: De Gruyter.

———. 2017. "Theorizing Religious Dress." Pages 163–78 in *What Shall I Say of Clothes? Theoretical and Methodological Approaches to the Study of Dress in Antiquity*. Edited by Megan Cifarelli and Laura Gawlinski. Boston: Archaeological Institute of America.

Gordon, Beverly. 1987. "Fossilized Fashion: 'Old Fashioned' Dress as a Symbol of a Separate, Work-Oriented Identity." *Dress* 13:49–60.

Grand-Clément, Adeline. 2021. "Sensorium, Sensescapes, Synaesthesia, Multisensoriality: A New Way of Approaching Religious Experience in Antiquity?" Pages 141–59 in *Sensorium: The Senses in Roman Polytheism*. Edited by Antón Alvar Nuño, Jaime Alvar Ezquerra, and Greg Woolf. Religions in the Graeco-Roman World 195. Leiden: Brill.

Harland, Philip A., ed. 2014. *North Coast of the Black Sea, Asia Minor*. BZNW 204. Vol. 2 of *Greco-Roman Associations: Texts, Translations, and Commentary*. Edited by John S. Kloppenborg and Richard S. Ascough. Berlin: De Gruyter.

Hume, Lynne. 2013. *The Religious Life of Dress: Global Fashion and Faith*. London: Bloomsbury.

Kloppenborg, John S. 2019. *Christ's Associations: Connecting and Belonging in the Ancient City*. New Haven: Yale University Press.

Kloppenborg, John S., and Richard S. Ascough, eds. 2011. *Attica, Central Greece, Macedonia, Thrace*. BZNW 181. Vol. 1 of Kloppenborg and Ascough, *Greco-Roman Associations*.

Lee, Mireille M. 2015. *Body, Dress, and Identity in Ancient Greece*. New York: Cambridge University Press.

MacDonald, Margaret Y. 1999. "Reading Real Women through the Undisputed Letters of Paul." Pages 199–220 in *Women and Christian Origins*. Edited by Ross Shepard Kraemer and Mary Rose D'Angelo. New York: Oxford University Press.

Maier, Harry O. 2004. "Kleidung II." *RAC* 21:1–59.

———. 2021. "Exposed! Nakedness and Clothing in the Book of Revelation." Pages 299–312 in Batten and Olson, *Dress in Mediterranean Antiquity*.

Miller, Daniel. 2010. *Stuff*. Cambridge: Polity Press.

Morrison-Atkins, Kelsi. 2021. "Worn Stories: (Ad)dressing Wives in 1 Peter." Pages 289–97 in Batten and Olson, *Dress in Mediterranean Antiquity*.

Nemeroff, Carol, and Paul Rozin. 1994. "The Contagion Concept in Adult Thinking in the United States: Transmission of Germs and of Interpersonal Influence." *Ethos* 22:158–86.

Neufeld, Dietmar. 2005. "Under the Cover of Clothing: Scripted Clothing Performances in the Apocalypse of John." *BTB* 35:67–76.

Ogden, Daniel. 2002. "Controlling Women's Dress: Gynaikonomoi." Page 203–25 in *Women's Dress in the Ancient Greek World*. Edited by Lloyd Llewellyn-Jones. London: Duckworth and Classical Press of Wales.

Olson, Kelly. 2018. "Status." Pages 105–18 in *A Cultural History of Dress and Fashion in Antiquity*. Edited by Mary Harlow. A Cultural History of Dress and Fashion 1. London: Bloomsbury.

Oster, Richard. 1988. "When Men Wore Veils to Worship: The Historical Context of 1 Corinthians 11:4." *NTS* 34:481–505.

Pena, Joabson Xavier. 2021. "Wearing the Cosmos: The High Priestly Attire in Josephus' *Jewish Antiquities*." *JSJ* 52:359–87.

Peters, Janelle. 2015. "Crowns in 1 Thessalonians, Philippians, and 1 Corinthians." *Bib* 96:67–84.

———. 2021. "Robes of Transfiguration and Salvation in Early Christian Texts." Pages 279–87 in Batten and Olson, *Dress in Mediterranean Antiquity*.

Phillippo, Susanna. 2019. "Stepping onto the Stage: Aeschylus' *Oresteia* and Tragic Footwear." Pages 143–73 in *Shoes, Slippers and Sandals: Feet and Footwear in Classical Antiquity*. Edited by Sadie Pickup and Sally Waite. London: Routledge.

Roach, Mary Ellen, and Joanne B. Eicher, eds. 1965. *Dress, Adornment and the Social Order*. New York: John Wiley & Sons.

Roach-Higgins, Mary Ellen, and Joanne B. Eicher. 1992. "Dress and Identity." *Clothing and Textiles Research Journal* 10:1–8.

Roberts, Ronald D. 2020. "Shame." Pages 79–92 in *The Ancient Mediterranean Social World: A Sourcebook*. Edited by Zeba A. Crook. Grand Rapids: Eerdmans.

Rohrbaugh, Richard L. 2020. "Honor." Pages 63–78 in Crook, *The Ancient Mediterranean Social World*.

Schwartz, Joshua. 2021. "Clothes Make the Jew: Was There Distinctive Jewish Dress in the Greco-Roman Period?" Pages 247–56 in Batten and Olson, *Dress in Mediterranean Antiquity*.

Stevenson, Gregory M. 1995. "Conceptual Background to the Golden Crown Imagery in the Apocalypse of John (4:4, 10; 14:14)." *JBL* 114:257–72.

7

The Prestige of the Gods, the Urban Elites, and the Local Associations

Assessing Honorific Rituals among the Early Christians

James R. Harrison

The preoccupation of the Greco-Roman world with honor, both in terms of its motivational and social expression, has commanded the attention of ancient historians and New Testament scholars since the 1980s. The quest for honor in antiquity has been approached through (1) comparative studies in the anthropology and sociology of modern Mediterranean societies (Peristiany 1965; Adkins 1970; Patterson 2019); (2) the honorific values of Homeric culture operative in the Greek world (Adkins 1970; Cairns 1993; Finkelberg 1998); or (3) the heated competition for ancestral glory among the noble houses of the republic, which molded the persona of the Roman state as an aggressive status seeker (Lendon 1997; 2011; Barton 2001; Galasso 2012; Harrison 2020). Upon the triumph of the Julian house over the traditional Roman noble houses in 31 BCE and the concentration of the quest for glory in the iconic Augustus as *princeps*, leading to the eventual political eclipse of the *nobiles* ("nobles") in the capital, the pace of competition among the civic elites in the Greek East for honor became more heated during the imperial period. The consequence was that the "baroque exuberance of the language of praise" spiraled out of control in inscriptions (Zuiderhoek 2008, 175), along with the extravagance of the monuments honoring powerful civic benefactors[1] and the interminable length of some of their eulogistic decrees.[2]

However, alternative pathways of honor opened up for groups outside of the patronage networks of the eastern provincial elites. The local associations imitated the "bureaucratic" diction and syntax of the late Hellenistic city-state decrees, not only assigning honor to the elite benefactors of their clubs, but also allocating honor to their non-elite members. Members of the associations were of diverse social status, including among their constituency the urban poor, slaves, and freedmen (Wilson 2003, 10–11). But all members appropriated, by virtue of their membership of the association, the honorific titles and rituals that were the currency of prestige in the association's eulogistic decrees and at its meetings (*SIG*³ 1109, ll. 1–10, 117–27; cf. Verboven 2007, 882–86). Danker (1981, 352) highlights the important role that the local associations played in the temporary democratization of honor and civic status that transpired at their meetings. This was the case despite the fact that the association inscriptions were routinely erected in honor of the imperial authorities, elite civic benefactors, and club patrons. The attention accorded to the lower social echelons was also visually reinforced by the elaborate funerary steles occasionally erected in honor of the more ordinary members and their associations (*infra*). Consequently, Danker (1981, 352; cf. Kloppenborg 2019, 206) writes:

> In a world in which ordinary individuals had little contribution to make in the formation of their political destiny, the small groups offered some semblance of corporate dynamics. . . . These clubs and associations affected the diction and syntax of city-states or of the chanceries of the Ptolemies or of the Seleucids. This diction and syntax brought to verbal expression deeply imbedded cultural values. For a brief moment . . . their members could play the role of esteemed civil service officials, of members of councils and planning committees.

But more is involved than just diction, syntax, and honorific roles in the case of the local associations. Kloppenborg (2019, 280–81) correctly maintains that the transfer of elite virtue to association members, effected by eulogies that drew upon the values of the civic moral lexicon, is also a crucial dimension of the culture of association prestige. Furthermore, to confine prestige to just the

---

[1] E.g., Zoilos of Aphrodisias and Philopappos of Athens. See Harrison 2019, 260–61.
[2] E.g., Opramoas of Rhodiapolis (Danker 1982, no. 19 = *IGRR* 3.739). See discussion in Zuiderhoek 2009, 122–25. See also the example of Salutaris of Ephesus (*IEph* 1a 27), available in Rogers 1991.

quest for honor is a truncated understanding of what constitutes "status" in antiquity. Kloppenborg (2019, 237) observes, "The principal values of antiquity were honour, connectivity, and social standing. Money was a means to achieve these, not an end in itself. Financial support for one's collegium was a way to realize those values and a way to materialize one's membership."

The issue of association honorific rituals and the ticklish question of its relation to social prestige in Christian assemblies has commanded less attention than perhaps would have been expected in recent scholarship, given the explosion of monographs on associations.[3] Two scholars have addressed the issue of association honorifics more substantially in relation to the Christ associations.

Firstly, Last (2016, 149–62, 178–81, esp. 150–55) examines three honorific strategies of the associations, arguing that for the Corinthian church "opportunities for status achievements represented an important factor driving recruitment to associations" (156). Last posits that, in spite of "Paul's silence on the routine practice of reciprocating service providers with honorifics" (157), the apostle had to deal with powerful individuals who vied for honor in the Corinthian Christ groups (1 Cor 6:1-8; 11:17-34; 14:2-33). Paul handled this situation by allowing members the opportunity to generate personal status through the provision of services, irrespective of whether they held office or not (Last 2016, 163–212). These opportunities included participation in the Jerusalem collection (1 Cor 16:2; 2 Cor 8:3; 8:11-12), acting as emissaries (1 Cor 16:17-18), and, more controversially in terms of traditional exegesis, the sponsorship of elected officers in banquet administration (1 Cor 11:18-22, esp. v. 19). The contribution of Last is very insightful, but more attention could still be profitably given to Paul's use of honorifics in the Corinthian epistles and more widely throughout his epistolary corpus. Paul's reference to the brothers accompanying the collection as "the glory of Christ" (δόξα Χριστοῦ, 2 Cor 8:23) and the honorifics extended to his co-workers in Romans 16 (vv. 3, 5, 6, 7, 9, 10, 12, 14) are two cases in point (Harrison 2010; 2020, 117–18).

Secondly, Kloppenborg (2019, 43–46, 136–39) discusses the eulogistic language of association decrees, observing that the early believers could not have ignored the ubiquitous honorific practices (46), and highlighting the social

---

[3] Examples of such monographs include Kloppenborg and Wilson 1996; van Nijf 1997; Ascough 2003; Harland 2013; Kloppenborg and Ascough 2011; Ascough, Harland, and Kloppenborg 2012; Harland 2014; Last 2016; Kloppenborg 2019; and, finally, Last and Harland 2020. Exceptions to the tendency to neglect honorific rituals are van Nijf 1997; Ascough 2003; Last 2016; Kloppenborg 2019. See also Harland 1999; 2000. For a coverage of the recent literature on associations, see Harrison 2020, 297–304.

and economic location of early Christian groups (e.g., Macedonian believers) on the basis of the varying association commemorative decrees (88–91, 196–201). The early Christian attention to honorific rituals is seen in 1 Peter (2019, 298–300), which airs the expectation that believers will earn commendation as benefactors (1 Pet 2:12) and also honor the Roman ruler (2:17). Whether the latter involved participation in the hymns of the synod of *hymnodoi* or the performance of sacrifice to the Roman ruler is unlikely: 1 Peter considers such activities as idolatrous (1:14-19; 4:3-5; Harland 2000, 115–16).

While Last and Kloppenborg have adeptly compared the honorific conventions of the association decrees with the practices of the Christ associations, we are left wondering what might have been the distinctive attitudes and practices of the early believers in this regard. In conducting an investigation of the "prestige" culture of antiquity, this study will confine itself to the association epigraphy associated with the first generation of Christian churches: Rome (including, because of its proximity, the harbor port of Ostia), Corinth (including its eastern harbor port Cenchrea),[4] Galatia, Ephesus, Philippi, the Lycus Valley (Colossae, Hierapolis, Laodicea),[5] Thessalonica, Smyrna, Pergamum, Thyatira, Sardis, and Philadelphia. After considering the prestige of the gods, the civic elites, and association members as revealed in the inscriptions, we will be well placed to investigate how the early believers navigated a route through the many demands of honorific culture. For convenience of citation, my epigraphic selection derives from Ascough, Harland, and Kloppenborg 2012, with all enumerated data (i.e., no. 49) referring to that collection unless otherwise specified.

THE PRESTIGE OF THE GODS

The prestige of the association gods was accentuated by the epithets which accompanied their names. Four examples will suffice. First, a Thessalonian association of maritime traders worships Aphrodite *Epiteuxidia* ("Successful": no. 49 [second century CE]), the epithet declaring the success of the deceased and underscoring the protection that the goddess afforded seafarers and merchants during their voyages (Vangeli 2018, 30). Second, the Philadelphian association of initiates of Zeus Dionysos *Gongylos* ("Round":

---

[4]   The sole Corinthian association inscription is highly fragmentary (Ascough, Harland, and Kloppenborg 2012, no. 26). Two Cenchrae association inscriptions (*IG* IV 207; *SEG* 60.329) mention respectively a female "cowherd" (i.e., a member of the Dionysos association) and "the bread-and-meat society."

[5]   There are no association inscriptions among the thirty-one extant Colossian inscriptions (Cadwallader and Harrison 2019, 6–18, esp. 9–11).

no. 50 [first century CE]) honors an official, described as "consecrated to the god," for his bequest of a vineyard for ongoing income for banquet feasts in the sanctuary of Sarapis. The presence of this Greek deity, with its distinctive name, in an Egyptian sanctuary shows how each association sought to distinguish itself from the other associations, no matter its context (Steimle 2006). Third, Dionysios is called "Leader" (*Kathegemon*) at Hierapolis (no. 148 [second century CE]) and at Pergamum in regard to "the divine mysteries" conducted there (no. 115 [first century CE]). The Attalids of Pergamum were the first dynasty to claim the patronage of Dionysos as their divine ancestor, with the Dionysiac Artists acting as priests and the cult being associated with the theater (Kileci and Can 2020, 302). The cult had commenced by the time of Attalus 1 (*SEG* 39.1334 [230–220 BCE]), was maintained by the ensuing Attalid royalty (Welles 1934, nos. 65–67), and was still present at Pergamum in imperial times (*SEG* 37.1020). Dignas (2012, 134) poses the intriguing question whether political rivalry with the Ptolemies, who also traced their decent to Heracles and Dionysios, caused the Attalids to adopt Dionysos as their "Leader." First for consideration are the epithets of Ephesian Demeter (no. 163 [88/89 CE]), *Karpohoros* ("Fruit Bringer"), and *Thesmophoros* ("Law Bringer"). The epithet *Karpohoros* (cf. *IPessinous* 22 [Galatia]) arises from her Olympian status as the fertility goddess of agriculture, grain, and bread (Stallsmith 2008, 116–17). The epithet *Thesmophoros*, from which the Thesmophoria festival perhaps originated, is best understood as the ancient rules and secret rituals revealed by the goddess to humanity regarding grain cultivation and the mysteries (Stallsmith 2008, *passim*).

Thus the association deity epithets either expressed the heated rivalries for status between local associations and their city-states, pointed to the prestigious genealogical and geographical localities of the deities, or functioned as descriptors of the deity's powers and identity. Furthermore, the prestige conveyed by a deity's epithet was reinforced by the architectural expressions of association prestige and the memorialization of foundation stories, as well as by the iconography accompanying the association decrees (*infra*). A fine example of the latter is the relief of the Egyptian jackal-headed god, Anubis, erected by a Thessalonian association of banqueters (no. 47 [first century BCE to first century CE]; see also fig. 6 on p. 44). Sometimes the ritual cry of the worshippers of the deity is stated, as a Pergamum association dedication lets slip regarding Dionysos (no. 113 [post. 158 BCE]): "god of the ritual cry euoi" (Harland 2014, 122). Here distinctive ritual, differentiating one group of worshippers from another, becomes part of the public image and prestige of an association.

Lastly, an important sidelight is worth spotlighting. An Ephesian association inscription makes reference to "throne" rituals involving indigenous deities and the Roman ruler. The Ephesian initiates of Dionysos "co-enthroned [σύ(ν)θρονον] Hadrian with Dionysos" before the city, rendering appropriate honor to the Roman ruler but without diminishing the honor of their patron deity thereby (no. 168 [117–138 CE]). Nevertheless, the reliefs of association inscriptions reinforce the primacy of the indigenous deities, showing Cybele enthroned above an inscription at Prusa by Olympos (*IPrusaOlymp* no. 50 [second century CE]). Further, at Kyzikos (*IMT* 1539 [first century BCE]) Cybele is depicted as enthroned with Apollo (?), both deities being placed above an altar where a slave makes an offering. The Ephesian association inscription is revealing, affording us insight into why Paul (or the pseudonymous author) depicted the risen and ascended Christ as seated (καθίσας) at God's right hand in the heavenly places, exalted above all rule, authority, power, and dominion (Eph 1:20-21). Remarkably, believers have also been seated (συνεκάθισεν) in this present age with God in the heavenly places in Christ Jesus (Eph 2:6). This exalted status stands in contrast to the worshipping slave depicted below Cybele in the Kyzikos relief. Indeed, at Ephesus only the Roman ruler was accorded the prestigious position of sitting enthroned alongside the indigenous deities in association inscriptions. Ephesian auditors could hardly have missed Paul's point about their extraordinary privilege.

THE PRESTIGE OF THE ASSOCIATIONS AND THE ROMAN RULER

Honoring the Roman Ruler

The eastern Mediterranean associations honored the Roman ruler, the members of his house, and his provincial representatives by the erection of statues, inscriptions, and altars (Harland 1999; 2000; 2003; Wojciechowski 2014). They expressed gratitude for the ruler's beneficence to their city, gained prestige over rival associations by dedicating locally built association structures to the ruler, displayed piety by their cultic honors to the imperial gods, and established connectivity with local imperial elites (the provincial proconsul, imperial cult priests).

In terms of gratitude and piety to the ruler, a Pergamon association honors Augustus during his reign as "saviour and benefactor" (no. 114). The synod of Dionysos Breiseus at Smyrna (no. 191 [129–132 CE]) eulogizes Hadrian as "saviour and founder." Livia is honored by the Ephesian Demetriasts as "Augusta Demeter Karpophoros," and the sons of Drusus, Germanicus, and

Claudius have images erected to them as the "new Dioskouroi" (no. 159 [19–23 CE]). The same Demetriasts (no. 163 [88/89 CE]) perform mysteries and sacrifices to "Demeter Karpophoros and Thesmophoros and to the Augustan (*Sebastoi*) gods." The college of Ephesian physicians (no. 165 [102–114 CE]) also sacrifices to Asklepios and to the Augusti (*Sebastoi*). An Ephesian Dionysiac society (no. 105 [early second century CE]) grants Trajan honorary membership in their association (cf. Commodus as the "new Dionysos" at Ephesus, no. 173 [180–192 CE]). Associations adopt for themselves the names of imperial rulers and influential members of the imperial household: "the friends-of-Agrippa companions" at Smyrna (no. 187 [first century to early second century CE]); "the association of friends of the Augusti" at Pergamon (no. 120 [imperial period]); and "the brotherhood of the friends of Caesar" at Ilion (Robert 1960, 220–26; no. 4 [1–50 CE]).

The superiority of an association's prestige over its rivals is established by various means. The "great purity and lawful customs" of the Ephesian Demetriasts regarding their annual celebration of the mysteries (no. 163 [88/89 CE]) is secured by the protection of their rites over a long period of time, supported by the precedents of official documentation. As the inscription states, "These rites were protected by kings and emperors, as well as by the proconsul of the period, as contained in their enclosed letters." Harland rightly observes (2013, 91), "It does not seem that this group is gaining permission to engage in the celebration, but rather seeking the prestige which further acknowledgement by important officials could offer."

Another example of the acquisition of prestige over association competitors at Ephesus is the expansion of the facilities of the Ephesian fishery toll office by the donations of the fishermen and fish dealers (no. 162 [54–59 CE]). A large slab, prominently displayed in the harbor area and inscribed on both sides, lists the Roman and non-Roman donors who had contributed to building the tollbooth. This included their monetary contributions, ranging from the building materials to donations of twelve to fifty denarii, including the structure's bricks and tiles, columns, paving for the colonnade, and adjacent altars. Apart from the "glory" that accrued to the association from this important civic building, deflected glory is acquired by the tollbooth's prestigious dedication to Nero, Julia Agrippina his mother, and Octavia, Nero's wife.

Finally, in terms of social connectivity, the association of dyers at Thyatira (no. 129 [50 CE]) honor a priestess of the Augusti, Claudia Ammon, with this eulogy: "high priestess of the city for life, having served as director of contests in a magnificent and extravagant manner, and having conducted her life in purity and with self-control." Not only does Claudia possess important imperial connections as a priestess, but also she is a wealthy civic benefactor hosting the city's games. The silversmiths of Ephesus (no. 164 [81–117 CE]; cf. Acts 19:23-41) also honor the elite T. Claudius Aristion, "high priest of Asia for the third time . . . president and temple warden, who arranged many great works in our city from his own resources." Was each dignitary a patron of the association or were the members simply seeking relation with the imperial elites of the city by honoring them?

The Synod of the *Hymnodoi*

Associations of "hymn singers" (Friesen 2001, 104–13; Harland 2013, 93–95), which were dedicated to the praise of the imperial gods, arose in several locations in Asia Minor: namely, Pergamum (nos. 117, 120), Ephesus (no. 168), and Smyrna (no. 198). One example will suffice to illustrate how these associations acquired substantial prestige and status by honoring the Roman ruler. On column 1 of an Ephesian association inscription (no. 160 [41–54 CE]) is reproduced a (now fragmentary) letter from Claudius to the hymn singers, which acknowledges their honorific decree praising him. Here we see how enthusiastically the hymn singers memorialize for perpetuity the very considerable social prestige of receiving in the province of Asia a personal response from the Julio-Claudian ruler at Rome. Column 2 replicates a resolution of the provincial assembly of Asia, setting forth its gratitude for the vital role that all the hymn singers from Asia, including Ephesus, played in celebrating the birthday of divine Augustus and his household. The prestige accrued by the synod of the *hymnodoi* through their participation in the imperial celebrations is highlighted in the resolution:

> . . . the hymn singers from all Asia, coming together in Pergamon for the most sacred birthday of Augustus Tiberius Caesar, god, accomplish a magnificent work for the glory of the synod (εἰς τὴν [τῆς συνόδου δόξ] αν), singing hymns to the Augustan household, accomplishing sacrifices to the household gods, leading festivals and banquets.

THE PROVINCIAL ELITES AND THE SOCIAL CONNECTIVITY OF THE ASSOCIATIONS

We will confine ourselves to several epigraphic case studies of association social connectivity with the elites, concentrating upon Ephesus (Ionia), Pessinous and Ankyra (northern Galatia), and Laodicea (Lycus valley).

Admittedly, the connectivity of the associations of Thyatira with powerful elites is remarkable in its scope (nos. 128–33, 135–43). But this rich vein of evidence has to be left for a future occasion and our more limited epigraphic selection mined for its results.

The Associations and the *Vedii Antonini* of Ephesus

The Vedii Antonini, an influential second-century family from Ephesus, are well-known from the epigraphic record (Kalinowski 2002). They held multiple offices and priesthoods, were benefactors of the city—one of whom, P. Vedius Antoninus III, was the builder of the gymnasium and bouleterion (*IEph* 2.285a; 2:460; 3:725; 3:728; 5:1505)—and they received in return substantial civic honors from their beneficiaries, including the local associations. An inscription from Ephesus (*IEph* 7.1.3072) unfolds the remarkable roll call of ancestral glory belonging to the aristocratic Ephesian family of the Vedii. Vedia, a priestess of Artemis, had made the customary distributions to the guilds and completed the mysteries worthily of her family (ll. 28–32). But the inscription also lists all the civic magistracies that her relatives had achieved: asiarch, high priest, priestess and *kosmetira*, *prytenis*, secretary, and agonothete. Here we see the social prestige that attachment to the Vedii secured for the Ephesian associations.

This is demonstrated in the stratospheric honorific accolade that the association of the wool workers render either to P. Vedius Antoninus II or (more likely) his more prestigious son, P. Vedius Antoninus III (no. 171 [mid-second century CE]). The wool workers refer to him as "the founder of the city of the Ephesians," remarkably relegating to insignificance the traditional mythical founder of Ephesus, Adroclus (*IEph* 2.501.1; 3:664; 4:1064; 6:2044; Rathmayr 2010). Furthermore, even in the latrines of the gymnasium the strong connection between the builder of the gymnasium, P. Vedius Antoninus Vedius III, and the Ephesian associations is made plain, with seats being reserved for the bankers, hemp workers, wool dealers, those from Branchiane street, linen workers, and the guild of basket makers. There is a mutual connectivity here: Antoninus Vedius III, in response to the honorific reciprocation of his benefactions by his Ephesian beneficiaries, grants the local civic associations even more privileges at his gymnasium.

The Associations of Galatia and Laodicea

Two association inscriptions from Galatia, one from Pessinous (*IPessinous* 17 [150–220 CE]; cf. *IPessinous* 22), the other from Ankyra (no. 212 [228 CE]), illustrate most effectively the dynamics of honor allocation to the elites. The Ankyra decree makes it clear that the honorific decree, erected for Ulpius Aelius Pompeianus by the sacred theatrical synod, is vitally important "for the sake of preserving honors for both the emperor and Dionysos and maintaining the contest for the city." The beneficent career of Pompeianus, as enunciated in the initial eulogy, provides the grounds for the maintenance of these honors. Pompeianus had (1) provided from his own resources the mystical contest, granted to Pessinous by the Roman ruler, "in a conspicuous manner . . . leaving no brilliant and generous thing undone"; (2) provided benefactions freely, "sparing no expense"; and (3) assisted with all the synod prizes and mystery contests "because he alone preferred to do good for the city." In sum, Pompeianus has mediated the blessings of both the Roman ruler and the god Dionysos to the citizens of Ankyra: but, in reciprocating his beneficence with effusive honor, the association was also honoring the ruler and the god.

In the case of the Attabokaian initiates at Pessinous (*IPessinous* 17), the priest Tiberius Claudius Heras is honored for his previous military experience: he was a prefect of the Iturean cohort and a tribune of two legions. But the military accolade especially highlighted is his highly prestigious imperial honor of the pure spear and *corona vallaris* ("wall crown"), which was awarded to him "for being first on the defensive wall of the enemy camp." Notwithstanding, the real focus of praise at the outset are Heras' multiple priesthoods, even though he was also a gymnasium benefactor: "fifth priest of the Galatians for life of the great mother of the gods," "six times high priest of the Augusti," and "the revealer of the Augusti" in the Pessinous temple. Here we see the complex intersection of the multiple honorific worlds operating in antiquity: military service and courage in battle; civic beneficence; and indigenous and imperial priesthoods. It is impressive how our religious association is acutely aware of each honorific world and renders appropriate eulogies for each activity therein in this inscription.

In sharp contrast, however, the Laodicean group called "The Romans and Greeks in Asia," whose precise nature as an association is difficult to determine, honors Qunitus Pomponius Flaccus exclusively for his civic munificence (*ILaodLyk* 82). Connectivity, as Thyatiran association epigraphy illustrates, can focus exclusively either on the city's military elites (no. 136) or on civic benefactors (no. 133), while elsewhere it celebrates honourees who performed both priestly and civic duties (nos. 130–32, 137–38).

THE PRESTIGE OF THE LOCAL ASSOCIATIONS AND THEIR MEMBERS

The Foundation Story of a Thessalonian and Philadelphian Household Association

There is an extensive dream revelation regarding the foundation of a Thessalonian association of Sarapis (no. 52 [first to second century CE]; Sokolowski 1974; Rollens 2018; cf. Artemidorus, *Onir.* 5.82). There Xenainetos experiences a marvellous dream (θαυμάξαι τε τὸν [ὄ]γειρον, ll. 7–8) in which Sarapis stood beside him. Xenainetos is ordered upon his arrival in Opus to carry a letter, which will be left under his pillow, to his political rival Eurynomos and to ask him "to receive Sarapis and his sister Isis." Upon the miraculous receipt of the letter, Xenainetos meets with his rival Eurynomos and the latter is unexpectedly persuaded to establish Sarapis and Isis among the household gods in the household of Sosinike. Consequently, sacrifices are regularly offered by Sosinike. Moreover, Eunosta, granddaughter of Sosibas, continues the administration of the mysteries of the gods among those not initiated in the cult upon the death of Sosinike. In sum, the considerable difficulty of persuading a political rival to establish a household of association of Sarapis in Opus—the motivation for which would be initially viewed by the rival with great suspicion and subsequently with envy if the association was successfully established—only serves to underscore the divine legitimation of the Sarapis association in the city and the accompanying miraculous power of the god's dream revelation.

In a Philadelphian household association (no. 121 [late second century to early first century BCE]; cf. Barton and Horsley 1981), which worshipped Zeus Eumenes and Hestia his consort, the cultic instructions "were given to Dionysios in his sleep (καθ᾽ ὕπνον)." Significantly, the foundation stories of the household associations mentioned above are both founded upon dream revelations. This poses the question regarding the extent to which dreams and visions provided legitimation of the mission of early Christianity and, concomitantly, the "prestige" associated with its rapid geographic expansion throughout the eastern Mediterranean. Relatedly, initiates of the deities at Thyatira (no. 139 [second to third century CE]) are summoned to learn the truth by approaching the funerary altar of the deceased priestess in order to attain "whatever one wants through a vision (διὰ ὁραμάτος) by day or night." A similar claim to superior revelatory status and the blessing of its Thyatiran recipients is also being made by this association.

Architectural Expressions of Prestige

As noted above, civic prestige for the Ephesian association of fishermen and fish dealers was acquired by the expansion of the facilities of the fishery toll office in the harbor. The size and prominence of the large commemorative slab, inscribed on both sides, visually reinforces the prominence of the association. Another instance of this phenomenon are the lists of fountains used by the mystery associations at Sardis (no. 127 [200 CE]). The mention of the civic sites of the various fountains is impressive. They are opposite the gymnasium of the elders' council, opposite the two mystery halls, and opposite Zeus' sanctuary, into which the fountain flowed. Their proximity to various locations is emphasized: near the Odeion; near a two-story building which has towers; at the guardhouse on a descending road of the marketplace, the precise site of which is now lost due to the inscription's damaged state; near the Menogeneion; near the god Men's sanctuary; and, last, near the gate. The sites represent a blend of civic and sacred space, visually prominent by virtue of their flowing water (often listed in liquid measures), with the source of the water sometimes mentioned ("from the reservoir"). Moreover, the names of fountains are listed: Domitia, Lenaeitis, Lysimachos, Arsinoe, and "the fountain which Rufus and Lepidus built." Not only are fountains mentioned but also the association mystery halls ("the two mystery halls," "the mystery hall of Attis"). This association was publicly prominent throughout the city by virtue of its amenities, not hidden away in temple precincts for banquets or meeting in a private home. The wide geographic spread of this association, based on its amenities at known locations throughout the city, enhanced its prestige.

Memorialization of Association Members, Living and Deceased: The Visual Evidence

Another way associations enhanced their prestige was by commemorating a deceased member with a funerary inscription, while adding to the stele a relief that embodied the ethos of the association members. At Thessalonica (no. 54; see fig. 8 on p. 50) a relief of a donkey driver on a cart, rendered on a stele above the inscription honoring Gaius Julius Crescens, belongs to an association of transport workers devoted to Heron Aulonites, the divine protector of those who crossed narrow passages professionally and privately. A Thessalonian gravestone of a shipper depicts a man steering a boat from Thessalonica who, as the inscription informs us (no. 49; see fig. 7 on p. 47), "died while abroad." At Ostia a black-and-white mosaic at the hall of the grain measurers (van der Meer 2012; no. 23; see fig. 29 on p. 71) has a fragmentary inscription that says, "Six superintendents of the granary of the Agilii (are) here." The prestige and self-assuredness of the Guild of the Grain Measurers is well captured visually by the mosaic's distinctive iconography. To the left a man and a porter carry full sacks of grain. In the middle of the mosaic, a diminutive boy raises his right-hand index finger while holding a ten-branched lead staff: its nine tesserae strips indicates how many *modii* of grain have been measured. To the right a man holds a grain-leveling rod; another has emptied a sack of grain; a final figure gestures that the job is complete. The pivotal mosaic figures for the promotion of the associations' prestige, somewhat unexpectedly, are not the muscular workers performing the heavy lifting but rather those signaling the accurate measuring of the grain and the efficient completion of the task.

Association Lists: Connectivity and Status

In some associations there is a connectivity which at first blush transcends class and economic divisions, embracing equally freedmen and individuals of high social standing, with fictive kinship terminology perhaps pointing to a quasi-familial relationship. An association inscription from Philippi, carved in Latin on the rock face of the acropolis, sets out the contributions of the members to the Temple of Silvanus (no. 41; cf. Abrahamsen 1995, 35–38). Several lists of names identify 105 individuals, though damage to the stone excludes identification of additional members. Not only is the god Silvanus honored by the construction of the temple and the erection of a bronze statue in the second century CE, but other gods and demigods (Herakles, Mercury, Liber) are also honored with statues. Freedmen belong to the association as much as high-status individuals, including the city's magistrate of public works (aedile) and various priests. Consequently, the funds offered to the association coffers range from 250 denarii to 50, 25, and 15 denarii: some of these funds are deposited as funeral funds for various members. Finally, bonds of fictive kinship might exist to some extent, with leaders being designated *pater* ("father"). But since this is a leadership term, it is unlikely that a notion of brotherhood existed among Philippian association members (cf. *phratria*, "brotherhood," nos. 104, 144, 295, ll. 1, 14). Lastly, "the benevolent association of Aesculapius and Salus Augusta" at an imperial estate in Latium, Rome (*CIL* 6.30983 [100–150 CE]), reflects another mixed constituency, mentioning the estate managers and fifty-five plebeian members, among whom are several women, imperial slaves, and freedmen. In sum, social connectivity between diverse social constituencies existed in the Mediterranean associations, but it should not be assumed that this led to an adjustment of hierarchical attitudes and organization within the life of associations.

THE AFFIRMATION AND INVERSION OF HONORIFIC RITUALS AMONG THE EARLY CHRISTIANS

Returning to our question posed in the prolegomenon: what is distinctive about the first believers' negotiation of honor rituals in comparison to the associations? The early Christian attitude to honor and prestige is complex in its continuities and discontinuities with association practice (deSilva 1999; 2002; Jewett 2003; Hellerman 2005; Finney 2013; Harrison 2019, 257–96). The ancient rituals of honor and prestige are affirmed, reconfigured, and critiqued, depending on the social, ecclesial, and theological context of the New Testament documents.

First, in the case of the ancient honor of preferential seating—whether that is the allocation of latrine seats for the Ephesian associations at the Vedius gymasium or the seating of the privileged and powerful at theater spectacles (Jones 2008; Royalty 2016; cf. Xenephon, *Ways and Means* 3.4)— the Gospels are unequivocal in critiquing the operation of this convention at feasts (Matt 23:6; Mark 12:38-39; Luke 14:7-9; cf. Prov 25:6-7). The same stance is taken elsewhere regarding the preferential treatment of the wealthy in ecclesial seating (Jas 2:1-4; 1 Cor 11:20-22).

Second, from the perspective of Jewish and early Christian christologically modified monotheism, no prestige is accorded to the association gods (1 Cor 8:4-6; 10:14-17) due to the dishonoring of the glory of the Creator and his Christ (Rom 1:23; 1 Cor 8:6), as well from a LXX perspective (1 Chr 16:26; Pss 96:5; 106:28; Isa 44:9-20; Jer 10:1-16; Ezek 43:7, 9), the lifelessness of idols (1 Cor 8:4a).

Third, the Roman ruler, who is to be honored (Rom 13:1-7), is nevertheless reduced to the LXX status of "servant" (Rom 13:4, 6) and is stripped of any imperial cult accolades, including Augustan panegyric, to which even Jews like Philo appealed when rhetorically necessary (*Legat.* 143–62; cf. Harrison 2011, 271–323, esp. 300–308).

Flavian auditors of Eph 1:20-21 and 2:6 would have understood their superior status as believers in Christ, over against the honorific co-enthroning of Hadrian with Dionysos in an Ephesian association (*supra*), including Christ's triumph over the magical principalities and powers (Arnold 1992). Notwithstanding John's mimicry of Roman imperial court ceremonial in Revelation 4–5 (Aune 1983), the glorious theophanic depiction of the "one seated on the throne" (Rev 4:2; 5:7) and his Lamb at the center of the throne (Rev 5:6; 7:17; 22:1, 3: "The throne of God and of the Lamb") leads inexorably to the triumphant throne scene in the new creation (21:5; Gallusz 2014).

Fourth, the operation of the ancient honor system and the quest for honor and glory is affirmed (τῷ τὴν τιμήν τὴν τιμήν: Rom 13:7b; cf. 2:7), though its operation is reconfigured in terms of the indebtedness of *agape* (Rom 13:8-10), as opposed to *philia* ("friendship") in the case of the associations (Harrison 2019, 297–329, here 316–21).

Fifth, rivalry over honor is affirmed: but its rationale is redefined. Believers are summoned to strive to outdo each other in giving honor rather than acquiring it (Rom 12:10b). The Corinthians, negligent in keeping their promise regarding the Jerusalem collection in comparison to the impoverished Macedonians (2 Cor 8:1-4), are encouraged—in rivalry with the Macedonians (8:1-2) and in cognizance of contemporary shame culture (8:4)—to fulfill their promise. But Christ's *exemplum* as the impoverished benefactor is the paradigm for the fulfillment of Corinthian promise of beneficence for the collection (8:9; Harrison 2003b, 250–56).

Sixth, the ultimate focus of honor in the Body of Christ is upon the least honored as opposed to the most influential (1 Cor 12:22-25), reflecting not only God's choice of the "nothings of this world" (1:26-29) but also the depths of Christ's cruciform *cursus pudorum* ("course of shame") culminating in the cross (1 Cor 1:23; 2 Cor 13:4a; Gal 3:13; 5:11; Phil 2:5-11; Heb 12:2). The career of the crucified and risen Christ, dishonored and honored, redefines the experience of shame and honor in the lives of his apostles (1 Cor 4:9-13; 2 Cor 6:8-9).

Finally, the association quest for coronal honor is ubiquitous, seen in the crowning of graves (*IHierapJ* 195 [117–212 CE]), the adorning of statues (*IAnkyraM* 140 [128/129 CE]), and the honoring of elites (*TAM* 5.965: "twice crown-bearer, who pursued glory since childhood" [Thyatira, 160–170 CE]; *SEG* 43.773 [Ephesus, second century CE]). But the New Testament writers consistently postpone the allocation of crowns until the eschaton (1 Cor 9:25; Phil 4:1; 1 Thess 2:19; 2 Tim 2:5; 4:8; Jas 1:12; 1 Pet 5:4; Rev 2:10; 3:11). The coronal honor of the Isthmian games is dismissed in 1 Cor 9:25 as "perishable" as opposed to the "imperishable" eschatological crown. Lastly, John's stinging denunciation of idolatry, his multiple-visioned presentation of the grandeur of the throne room of God and his Lamb (Rev 4–5, 7, 14), and his inversion of crowning rituals (Rev 4:10) critiqued the imperial theology of victory and its widespread iconographic rendering of coronal rituals (Harrison 2003a).

WORKS CITED

Abrahamsen, Valerie A. 1995. *Women and Worship at Philippi: Diana/Artemis and Other Cults in the Early Christian Era*. Portland, Maine: Astarte Shell.

Adkins, A. W. H. 1970. "Morals and Values in Homer." *Journal of Hellenic Studies* 90:121–39.

Arnold, Clinton E. 1992. *Ephesians: Power and Magic; The Concept of Power in Ephesians in Light of Its Historical Setting*. Grand Rapids: Baker.

Ascough, Richard S. 2003. *Paul's Macedonian Associations: The Social Context of Philippians and 1 Thessalonians*. WUNT 2/161. Tübingen: Mohr Siebeck.

Ascough, Richard S., Philip A. Harland, and John S. Kloppenborg. 2012. *Associations in the Greco-Roman World: A Sourcebook*. Waco, Tex.: Baylor University Press.

Aune, David E. 1983. "The Influence of Roman Imperial Court Ceremonial on the Apocalypse of John." *BR* 38:5–26.

Barton, Carlin A. 2001. *Roman Honor: The Fire in the Bones*. Berkeley: University of California Press.

Barton, S. C., and G. H. R. Horsley. 1981. "A Hellenistic Cult Group and the New Testament Churches." *JAC* 24:7–41.

Cadwallader, Alan H., and James R. Harrison. 2019. "Perspectives on the Lycus Valley: An Inscriptional, Archaeological, Numismatic, and Iconographic Approach." Pages 3–70 in *The First Urban Churches 5: Colossae, Hierapolis, and Laodicea*. Edited by James R. Harrison and L. L. Welborn. WGRWSup 16. Atlanta: SBL Press.

Cairns, Douglas L. 1993. *Aidōs: The Psychology and Ethics of Honor and Shame in Ancient Greek Literature*. Oxford: Oxford University Press.

Danker, Frederick W. 1981. "On Stones and Benefactors." *CurTM* 8:351–56.

———. 1982. *Benefactor: Epigraphic Study of Graeco-Roman and New Testament Semantic Field*. St. Louis: Clayton.

deSilva, David A. 1999. *The Hope of Glory: Honor Discourse and New Testament Interpretation*. Collegeville, Minn.: Liturgical Press.

———. 2002. *Honor, Patronage and Purity: Unlocking New Testament Culture*. Downers Grove, Ill.: InterVarsity Press.

Dignas, Beate. 2012. "Rituals and Construction of Identity in Attalid Pergamon." Pages 120–43 in *Historical and Religious Memory in the Ancient World*. Edited by Beate Dignas and R. R. R. Smith. Oxford: Oxford University Press.

Finkelberg, Margalit. 1998. "*Timē* and *Aretē* in Homer." *ClQ* 48:14–28.

Finney, Mark T. 2013. *Honour and Conflict in the Ancient World: 1 Corinthians in Its Greco-Roman Social Setting*. LNTS 460. London: T&T Clark.

Friesen, Steven J. 2001. *Imperial Cults and the Apocalypse of John: Reading Revelation in the Ruins*. Oxford: Oxford University Press.

Galasso, Vittorio Nicholas. 2012. "Honor and the Performance of Roman State Identity." *Foreign Policy Analysis* 8:173–89.

Gallusz, Laszlo. 2014. *The Throne Motif in the Book of Revelation*. LNTS 487. London: T&T Clark.

Harland, Philip A. 1999. "Honours and Worship: Emperors, Imperial Cults and Associations at Ephesus (First to Third Centuries C.E.)." *SR* 25:319–34.

———. 2000. "Honouring the Emperor or Assailing the Beast: Participation in Civic Life among Associations (Jewish, Christian and Other) in Asia Minor and the Apocalypse of John." *JSNT* 22:99–121.

———. 2003. "Imperial Cults within Local Cultural Life: Associations in Roman Asia." *Ancient History Bulletin* 17:47–69.

———. 2013. *Associations, Synagogues, and Congregations: Claiming a Place in Ancient Mediterranean Society*. 2nd ed. Kitchener, Ont.: Philip A. Harland.

———, ed. 2014. *North Coast of the Black Sea, Asia Minor*. BZNW 204. Vol. 2 of *Greco-Roman Associations: Texts, Translations, and Commentary*. Edited by John S. Kloppenborg and Richard S. Ascough. Berlin: De Gruyter.

Harrison, James R. 2003a. "'The Fading Crown': Divine Honour and the Early Christians." *JTS* 54:493–529.

———. 2003b. *Paul's Language of Grace in Its Graeco-Roman Context*. WUNT 2/172. Tübingen: Mohr Siebeck.

———. 2010. "The Brothers as the 'Glory of Christ' (2 Cor 8:23): Paul's *Doxa* Terminology in Its Ancient Benefaction Context." *NovT* 52:156–88.

———. 2011. *Paul and the Imperial Authorities at Thessalonica and Rome: A Study in the Conflict of Ideology*. WUNT 273. Tübingen: Mohr Siebeck.

———. 2019. *Paul and the Ancient Celebrity Circuit: The Cross and Moral Transformation*. WUNT 430. Tübingen: Mohr Siebeck.

———. 2020. *Reading Romans with Roman Eyes: Studies in the Social Perspective of Paul*. Paul in Critical Contexts. London: Lexington Books / Fortress Academic.

Hellerman, J. 2005. *Reconstructing Honor in Roman Philippi: Carmen Christi as Cursus Pudorum*. SNTSMS 132. Cambridge: Cambridge University Press.

Jewett, Robert. 2003. "Paul, Shame and Honor." Pages 551–74 in *Paul in the Greco-Roman World*. Edited by J. Paul Sampley. Harrisburg, Pa.: Trinity Press International.

Jones, Tamara. 2008. "Seating and Spectacle in the Graeco-Roman World." PhD diss., McMaster University.

Kalinowski, Angela. 2002. "The Vedii Antonini: Aspects of Patronage and Benefaction in Second-Century Ephesos." *Phoenix* 56:109–49.

Kileci, Senkal, and Birol Can. 2020. "A New Honorific Inscription from Blaundos: Tiberius Claudius Lucius, the Priest of Dionysos Kathegemon." *Adalya* 23:297–309.

Kloppenborg, John S. 2019. *Christ's Associations: Connecting and Belonging in the Ancient City*. New Haven: Yale University Press.

Kloppenborg, John S., and Richard S. Ascough, eds. 2011. *Attica, Central Greece, Macedonia, Thrace*. BZNW 181. Vol. 1 of *Greco-Roman Associations: Texts, Translations, and Commentary*. Edited by John S. Kloppenborg and Richard S. Ascough. Berlin: De Gruyter.

Kloppenborg, John S., and Stephen G. Wilson, eds. 1996. *Voluntary Associations in the Graeco-Roman World*. London: Routledge.

Last, Richard. 2016. *The Pauline Church and the Corinthian Ekklēsia: Greco-Roman Associations in Comparative Context*. SNTSMS 164. Cambridge: Cambridge University Press.

Last, Richard, and Philip A. Harland. 2020. *Group Survival in the Ancient Mediterranean: Rethinking Material Conditions in the Landscape of Jews and Christians*. London: T&T Clark.

Lendon, Jon E. 1997. *Empire of Honour: The Art of Government in the Roman World*. Oxford: Clarendon.

———. 2011. "Roman Honor." Pages 377–403 in *The Oxford Handbook of Social Relations in the Roman World*. Edited by Michael Peachin. Oxford: Oxford University Press.

van der Meer, L. Bouke. 2012. *Ostia Speaks: Inscriptions, Buildings and Spaces in Rome's Main Port*. Leuven: Peeters.

van Nijf, Onno M. 1997. *The Civic World of Professional Associations in the Roman East*. Dutch Monographs on Ancient History and Archaeology 17. Amsterdam: J. C. Gieben.

Patterson, Colin. 2019. "The World of Honor and Shame in the New Testament: Alien or Familiar?" *BTB* 14:4–14.

Peristiany, J. G., ed. 1965. *Honour and Shame: The Values of the Mediterranean Society*. London: Weidenfeld & Nicolson.

Rathmayr, E. 2010. "Die Präsenz des Ktistes Androklos." *AÖAW* 145:19–60.

Robert, Louis. 1960. "Inscriptions d'Asie Mineure au Musée de Leyde." *Hellenica* 11–12:214–62.

Rogers, G. M. 1991. *The Sacred Identity of Ephesos: Foundation Myths of a Roman City*. London: Routledge.

Rollens, Sarah E. 2018. "The God Came to Me in a Dream: Epiphanies in Voluntary Associations as a Context for Paul's Vision of Christ." *HTR* 111:41–65.

Royalty, Robert M. 2016. "Demonic Symposia in the Apocalypse of John." *JSNT* 38:504–25.

Sokolowski, Franciszek. 1974. "Propagation of the Cult of Sarapis and Isis in Greece." *Greek, Roman and Byzantine Studies* 15:441–48.

Stallsmith, Allaire. 2008. "The Name of Demeter Thesmophoros." *GRBS* 48:115–31.

Steimle, Christopher. 2006. "Das Heiligtum der ägyptischen Götter in Thessaloniki und die Vereine in seinem Umfeld." Pages 27–38 in *Religions orientales—culti misterici. Neue Perspektiven—nouvelles perspectives—prospettive nuove. Im Rahmen des trilateralen Projektes "Les religions orientales dans le monde gréco-romain."* Edited by Corinne Bonnet, Jörg Rüpke, Paolo Scarpi, Nicole Hartmann, and Franca Fabricius. Potsdamer altertumswissenschaftliche Beiträge 16. Stuttgart: F. Steiner.

Vangeli, Christina. 2018. "The Cult of Aphrodite in Macedonia." MA thesis, International Hellenic University.

Verboven, K. 2007. "The Associative Order: Status and Ethos among Roman Businessmen in Late Republic and Early Empire." *Athenaeum* 95:861–93.

Welles, C. Bradford. 1934. *Royal Correspondence in the Imperial Period: A Study in Greek Epigraphy.* New Haven: Yale University Press. Repr., Chicago: Ares, 1974.

Wilson, Stephen G. 2003. "Voluntary Associations: An Overview." Pages 1–15 in Kloppenborg and Wilson, *Voluntary Associations in the Graeco-Roman World.*

Wojciechowski, Przemysław. 2014. "The Imperial Cult in Roman Religious Associations." *Electrum* 21:153–62.

Zuiderhoek, Arjan. 2008. "Feeding the Citizens: Municipal Grain Funds and Civic Benefactors in the Roman East." Pages 159–80 in *Feeding the Ancient Greek City.* Edited by Richard Alston and Onno. M. van Nijf. Groningen-Royal Holloway Studies on the Greek City after the Classical Age. Leuven: Peeters.

———. 2009. *The Politics of Munificence in the Roman Empire: Citizens, Elites and Benefactors in Asia Minor.* Greek Culture in the Roman World. Cambridge: Cambridge University Press.

8

The Meals of Christ Groups in Comparative Perspective

John S. Kloppenborg

For over the course of the last two decades, it has gradually become clear that ritual, etiquette, and other strongly habituated forms of practical discourse and discursive practice do not just encode and transmit messages, but they play an active and important role in the construction, maintenance, and modification of the borders, structures, and hierarchic relations that characterize and constitute society itself. (Lincoln 2014, 76)

The epigram from Bruce Lincoln reflects the contemporary approach of ritual, that it is not simply a message encased in a set of physical actions, such that one can distil the message from the ritual without remainder. On the contrary, rituals are performances that materialize identities and social relationships, distinguishing insiders from outsiders, and articulating relationships of both hierarchy and equality within groups. Nowhere is this clearer than in the case of meals, especially communal meals of the city itself, or the meals of demes and phratries, and the meals of associations of various kinds.

Meals of course figured centrally in Christ groups. What is perhaps remarkable is that so little direct evidence remains about those meals, apart from what can be inferred from 1 Cor 11:17-34; Did. 9–10; Justin, *1 Apol.* 1.65, 67; and Pliny's report in *Ep.* 10.96. This dearth of evidence has left ample room for speculation.

Nothing directly is known about the organization of the meals in Christ groups or their funding. Both the Didache and Justin indicate that it was restricted to the baptized (Did. 9.5) or the "illuminated" (*1 Apol.* 65.1). Very little, however, is known of the etiquette that was expected at the meal, and the little that is said is couched in rather opaque theological language: Did. 10.6 requires persons to be "holy" or otherwise to repent; Paul refers to eating unworthily, which is then specified as μὴ διακρίνων τὸ σῶμα (1 Cor 11:29; "without discerning the body" [NRSV]). Thus, he recommends self-scrutiny (δοκιμαζέτω δὲ ἄνθρωπος ἑαυτόν, 1 Cor 11:28; "examine yourselves" [NRSV]). But the basis of this scrutiny is not explained. He even suggests that one might become ill or die from eating unworthily. Since so much of this language is unclear, it is difficult to be certain about what is going on.

By contrast, a good deal is known of most of these topics, mainly from epigraphical and papyrological data from groups that were engaged in the cult of a deity, which conducted meals, and which made efforts to regulate behavior at those meals. The groups, broadly speaking, are what we call "associations."

A TYPOLOGY OF GREEK AND ROMAN MEALS

I begin with a typology of collective meal practices proposed by Claude Grignon (2001) and John Donahue (2003). Grignon's models were developed for modern French society, and these were later adapted by John Donahue to Mediterranean antiquity. Both Grignon and Donahue focus on meals that aim "to accomplish in a collective way some material tasks and symbolic obligations linked to the satisfaction of a biological individual need" (Grignon 2001, 24). (This excludes other possible forms of commensality, including "encounter commensalities"—chance meals with an acquaintance, regular drinks of co-workers in a bar after work, etc.) In varying degrees, collective meals have two aspects: on the one hand, consuming food and drink together is an expression of solidarity and what I will call "fictive equality"; on the other, collective meals confirm, reassert, and sometimes redraw social hierarchies and in that sense are expressions of social power. Four of Grignon's commensalities are relevant to our discussion of associations and Christ groups: ceremonious, exceptional, segregative, and transgressive commensalities.

First, *ceremonious commensalities* for Grignon are those in which invitations to dine serve as means for the host to define and maintain his (or her) place in a social hierarchy and to spread strategic networks of influence. This form of commensality is mainly among peers and indeed depends on invitees being of the same social sector to be able to return honors.

In the Roman world these are the kinds of dining practices described by Pliny and satirized by Juvenal, where meal invitations mapped onto networks of influence, and where meals were expressions of hierarchy and precedence and often involved competitive displays of the wealth, taste, and the social power of the host. The *Cena Trimalchionis* is a satirical exaggeration of such banquets.

There are only a few instances where associations appear to have been the beneficiaries of such ceremonious commensality. An Athenian demesman, Diodoros son of Sokrates, who was credited with founding an association of *Soteriastai* (*IG* II[2] 1343; *GRA* I 48; Athens, 36/35 BCE), was also recognized for having hosted at banquets all of the members (here called *eranistai*) for the year in which he served as priest. All of the members appear to have been demesmen, and thus his social peers.[1] His generosity had the desired effect: the association approved a decree to commemorate his beneficence yearly, and to erect a stele in the precincts of the sanctuary of Artemis Soteira. As Monika Trümper notes, such honorific plaques were the equivalent of modern business cards, permanent reminders of the power and influence of the dedicatee (2006, 119). Diodoros' meals for the *Soteriastai* materialized in one way his status and influence, and the association's reciprocation guaranteed that his influence would not wane.

Second, *exceptional commensalities* are occasional and usually linked to life-cycle events—birthdays, marriages, and deaths. Like ceremonious commensalities, these too function as means to articulate status and precedence. Although there is little evidence that associations celebrated the marriages of their members (or anyone else for that matter), guilds, mainly in the Latin West, routinely celebrated donors' birthdays, and associations in both East and West participated in funerary commemorations. These meals were typically funded by patrons who created an endowment that provided for the distribution of *sportulae* and sometimes a meal.[2] The birthdays that were

---

[1]   Since he is also named as the *archeranistēs* and *tamias*, it is possible that this banquet might have been expected of him as a leader; yet the inscription seems to depict his generosity as exceptional, underscoring the large expenditure of Diodoros' funds that it required.

[2]   *Sportulae* (literally "little baskets") are small coins or sometimes food packages given to those who attend a meal. *CIL* 9.5568 (early second century CE): on the birthday of the donor, a banquet, paid from the interest on HS10,000; *CIL* 14.246 (Ostia, 140–172 CE): on the birthday of Antinous from an endowment; *CIL* 6.10234 (Rome, 153 CE): on the birthday of Antoninus Pius, a banquet and *sportulae* from the interest on HS60,000; *CIL* 6.1872 (Rome, 206 CE): on the birthday of the donor, the distribution of *sportulae* from the interest

usually celebrated were birthdays of the donor or a spouse but could include the birthday of the emperor (or under Hadrian, the birthday of Antinous). These clearly functioned as acknowledgment of the status of the donor (and the emperor) and performances of loyalty on the part of the guild. The well-known collegium of Diana and Antinous (*CIL* 14.2112, Lanuvium, 136 CE) distributed *sportulae* on the birthdays of Diana and Antinous, paid from the donor's endowment, and reciprocated by offering birthday celebrations for the birthdays of the municipal patron (who had given the endowment), and those of his father, brother, and wife, paid for by magistrates of the collegium.

Patrons frequently mandated funerary commemorations to be held by guilds, providing the necessary funds. These were typically conducted either on the birthdays of the deceased, or on the Rosalia (in late May–July) or during the Parentalia (February 13–21). As in the case of the birthdays, the commemorations of the deceased involved both the distribution of *sportulae*, and sometimes banquets.

For example, *CIL* 11.126 (Ravenna, second to third century CE) records a bequest of L. Publicius Italicus, a member of the builders guild (*collegium fabrum*), who established an endowment of HS30,000 to provide for a yearly distribution of *sportulae* in the amount of 2 denarii to each of the *fabri*—probably more than five hundred members.[3] Italicus also stipulated that 150 denarii be spent by the magistrates of his own decuria to decorate with roses the graves of his two sons and his wife (25 denarii), offer a sacrifice (12 denarii), and from the remainder provide a banquet for his decuria. The sums involved are not generous. After subtracting from 150 denarii the costs of roses and the sacrifice, slightly more than 100 denarii remain for the dinner for the members of his decuria (probably twenty-two to twenty-four men). The simple meal of bread, wine, and sardines for the forty-eight *cultores* of Diana and Antinous a century earlier cost 93 denarii. Given the hyperinflation of the third century, 112 denarii would not go much further. Yet despite the modest expenditure, Publicius could expect that his

---

on HS10,000; *AE* 1987, 198 (Ostia Antica, 256 CE): on the birthday of the donor, a banquet and *sportulae* paid from the interest on HS6000. Although no endowment is mentioned by the guild of citrus wood and ivory merchants of *CIL* 6.33885 (Rome, time of Hadrian), it seems likely that an endowment paid for the *sportulae* that were distributed on seven occasions.

[3] An endowment of 30,000 denarii at the usual interest rates would return 1,500 denarii yearly. Assuming that the 150 denarii for his own decuria is deducted, 1,350 denarii would be left for *sportulae* for the remaining *fabri*. This was a large guild, with at least 28 decuria, each with 22–24 members, implying a membership of about 616–672 members. This seems consistent with a distribution of 1,350 denarii, allowing for some increased *sportulae* for decurions and other notables within the guild.

generosity would be remembered in perpetuity by the *fabri* of Ravenna and by his fellow *fabri* of the 28th decuria.

As Donahue notes, the "primary motive of such benefactions was not public charity . . . but the continual need to confirm publicly one's status. These occasions of the life cycle provided a convenient setting for fulfilling such aims" (2003, 428).

Grignon's third model, *segregative commensality*, is the model that is most broadly applicable to the meals of associations, as Donahue recognized. This form of commensality is segregative because it functions to distinguish or segregate the "we" from the "not-we" (strangers, foreigners, enemies, rivals, inferiors, superiors). The result is to strengthen group cohesion.

> Segregative commensality is a group technique and sometimes a group therapy, a way for the group *to make itself visible and concrete to itself*, and, first of all, to number its members, to register recruitments and defections, comers and goers. (Grignon 2001, 29, emphasis added; similarly, Donahue 2003, 432–33)

Associations underscored the importance of group belonging through a number of techniques—by the public display of membership lists (*alba*) set up outside the group's clubhouse or on a stele in the precincts of a temple, and by its opposite, the erasure from the *album* of the names of those who had failed to comply with the group's bylaws. Associations also mounted public processions and, of course, had communal meals.

Whereas ceremonious and exceptional commensalities functioned to underscore the status of the donor, segregative commensality allowed for persons who were not otherwise related to become visible to themselves as members. Whereas in both ceremonious and exceptional commensalities, the status differences between the host or patron and the diners were always visible, eating together in segregative commensalities stressed the equality of diners (Wecowski 2018, 267).

Of course, the degree of social and status diversity differed within guilds and associations. Occupational guilds tended to be gender exclusive and recruited members from the same social catchments. It was in cultic associations that one was more likely to find both genders, persons of a variety of legal statuses (freeborn, freed, slaves), and multiple ethnic identities (although of course some cultic groups had a narrow membership profile). The meal practices of these associations had the effect of segregating them from their identity groups outside the club and creating a fictive equality within the association. Hence, one sometimes finds fictive family language used to describe members.[4]

Meals of this sort were normally governed either by explicit rules that prescribed how dining occurred, or by constraints that in effect disallowed sumptuous dining. For example, the collegium of Aesculapius and Hygia (Rome, 153 CE) was one of the very few associations for which the endowment appears to have paid for all seven meetings. These included two meals at which only *sportulae* were distributed and five that provided for bread, wine, and *sportulae*. The *lex collegii* stipulates how much wine, bread, and *sportulae* each member was to receive, allocating to the *quinquennalis, pater collegii, mater collegii, immunes, curatores*, and plebs differing amounts. These amounts were carefully calibrated to the income that could be expected from HS60,000 and a membership of not more than sixty.

The *cultores* of Diana and Antinous (*CIL* 14.2112; Lanuvium, 135 CE) also prescribed the menu for each of six banquets, two at which *sportulae* were distributed. *Sportulae* of two denarii per pleb appear to have been paid from the endowment income, while four *curatores*, chosen yearly, paid for the dinners.[5] The dinners themselves were modest: bread, slightly more than a sextarius of wine per pleb, and four sardines. In the case of both *CIL* 6.10234 and *CIL* 14.2112, the endowment size limited what each member could receive. In the case of *CIL* 14.2112, the meal itself was provided by the magistrates, and their liability was expressly limited by the *lex*.

A dining club from Tebtynis in the late second century BCE had similar financial constraints (*PTebt* 1.118 = *GRA* III 195). The club account records income and expenditures for three monthly banquets, each serving beer and bread. The cost of each banquet was 2,200 denarii in the debased copper currency of the second century BCE. The large majority of this cost (2,000 denarii) was a six-chous jar of beer (implying 0.88 litres per member). The rest was for bread and wreaths. This meant that in order to fund the meal, twenty-two members were needed, each paying 100 denarii. If insufficient

---

[4]   E.g., the Familia Silvani (*AE* 1929, 161; Trebula Mutuesca, 60 CE). Harland (2005; 2007) discusses the use of ἀδελφός, μήτηρ, and πατήρ (i.e., "brother," "mother," and "father") in associations. The fiction of being "adopted brothers" seems to have been common in the cult of Theos Hypsistos. See *CIRB* 1281.5; 1283.5–6; 1285.5–6; 1286.1 (Tanais, ca. 212–240 CE).

[5]   This assumes an initial membership of forty-eight, and that the *quinquennalis, viator*, and *scriba* received *sportulae* at each of the two distributions commensurate with the portions of food and wine that the *lex* prescribes (ll. 50–54). Since the double portion for the *quinquennalis* is said to apply to anyone who had served as *quinquennalis* in the past (ll. 55–56), this provision would eventually reduce the number of members who could be paid *sportulae* from the endowment, and provided for by the *curatores*.

members attended, the shortfall was made up by inviting four or five guests, who also paid the standard fee of 100 denarii.

These three examples are not only important for understanding the economic constraints under which associations operated (constraints that Christ groups must also have had), but also suggest that the consumption of each member was either controlled expressly by the *lex* of the association or de facto by the financial situation of the club. This is in contrast to the elite meals, where the allocation of food and wine to each participant was at the whim of the host and was used to underscore status differences among the diners. For associations, however, economic constraints meant that food and drink had to be allocated by a rule. The intent was to underscore equality since everyone was constrained by the club's bylaws.

The modest nature of the meal (i.e., bread and wine, which is the case for the majority of associations) suggests that sumptuous dining was not the point. It is true that a few associations are known to have consumed meat.[6] But when the menu is expressly mentioned, especially in collegia of the Latin West, bread and wine are the items most commonly served.[7] The simple nature of the meal should invite us to conclude that the point of the meal was performative: to materialize the value of belonging, which is the nature of segregative commensalities.

Stanley Stowers made the helpful suggestion that the preference for bread and wine over meat as ritual substances had real if unanticipated social consequences for Christ groups. The act of sacrificing within the

---

[6] E.g., *IG* II² 2343 = *GRA* I 1 (Athens, ca. 400 BCE); *IG* II² 1255 = *GRA* I 2 (Piraeus, 337/336 BCE); *IG* II² 1361 = *GRA* I 4 (Piraeus, 330–324/323 BCE); *IG* II² 1283 = *GRA* I 23 (Piraeus, 240/239 BCE); *SEG* 31:122 = *GRA* I 50 (Liopesi, Attica, early second century CE). The excavations at the site of the Hall of the Benches in Pergamon revealed large quantities of bovine, porcine, and bird bones (Radt 1999, 197), and the recently excavated Mithraeum at Tienem (Belgium) revealed a large number of animal remains, all slaughtered in midsummer for a large banquet (presumably not the monthly meetings of the group; Martens 2004). I am indebted to Roger Beck for this reference.

[7] *CIL* 6.10234.12, 13, 16 (Rome, 153 CE); *CIL* 6.33885.11 (Rome, time of Hadrian); *CIL* 14.2112.49 (Lanuvium, 135 CE); *CIL* 5.7920.5 (Cemenelum, first to third century CE), *et oleum* ("oil"); *CIL* 5.8251.11 (Aquileia, second century CE); *CIL* 9.4215.6 (Amiternum, 338 CE); *CIL* 11.5215.16–17 (Fulginiae, 192–235 CE); *CIL* 11.6033.21–23 (Pitinum Pis-aurense, second century CE), *et oleum*; *CIL* 11.6310.3 (Pisaurum, 98–161 CE). For banquets in the East, see Gutsfeld 2011, 165–66: "In den uns interessierenden Vereinen, gleich ob sie wohlhabend oder arm waren, wurde regelmäßig ein Gedeck von Brot und Wein angeboten. Nur bei den *cultores Dianae et Antinoi* sollte jeder Gast zusätzlich noch jeweils vier Sardinen, billige und zeitklassige Fische, erhalten. Hält man sich an diese Tatschen, so kommet man nicht umhin, die Vereinsbankette als eher frugal einzuschätzen, zumindest was die servierten Speisen anbetrifft."

home was normally a gendered activity—males conducted the sacrifices and meat was differentially allocated. Thus, the consumption of meat was an activity fraught with social consequences. Stowers suggests that the adoption by the Jesus movement of a ritual based on substances less implicated in gender and social ranking may have had the effect of creating a new order in which gender and status ranking was somewhat less pronounced than in other groups (1995; 1996). The only qualification I would add to this is that simple meals of bread and wine were not the invention of Christ groups; these kinds of meals are well attested elsewhere and hence it is misleading to think that Christ groups were at the vanguard of social innovation. They, like other non-elite associations, adopted a practice that facilitated the performance of member equality.

But Stowers is right to point to the issue of hierarchy and status. The very physicality of the triclinium meant that some members inevitably reclined in better or worse seats, and may have had food and drink allocated differentially. Rule-based dining, however, had the effect of mitigating status differences, whether magistrates and other officers received twice or one and one-half the normal allocation, or whether (as in the case of a collegium of citrus wood and ivory merchants; CIL 6.33885, Rome, time of Hadrian) all members received exactly the same *sportulae* and food at each banquet. To adhere to rule-based eating is an expression of *eisonomia*, the Athenian notion that rules created a kind of equality among citizens. For those associations that prescribed different amounts of food and wine for magistrates, the effect of the differences in privilege and probably seating were further mitigated by the fact that these groups also typically had a system of rotating leadership, selecting new magistrates either yearly or every five years. Some associations indeed prescribed a rota for the choice of magistrates.[8] If one member enjoyed the benefits of leadership one year, the next he or she would sit with the other plebs.

As John Donahue has recognized, association meals are excellent examples of segregative commensality: membership gave members visibility to themselves and visibility within the polis. It created the space for conviviality that most members could not hope for outside the association. And because associations tended to mimic the political and social

---

[8]   E.g., CIL 14.2112.42–44: "It was agreed that whoever shall be *magister* in his year in the order of the membership list for the preparation of the dinners and fails to comply and prepare (a banquet), he shall pay 30 sesterces into the fund; the man next on the list after him will be required to give the dinner, and he (the delinquent) shall be required to reciprocate in the latter's place."

hierarchies of the city, their meals allowed members to participate in a polity from which, outside the association, they were excluded. According to Donahue (2003, 434), these meals

> provided a setting not only for social interaction but also for creating hierarchies that could not be found outside of the collegium. Only in this context, for example, could a common cult worshiper become a leader and confirm his status through his access to the largest amount of food and drink.

Grignon's fourth mode of commensality is *transgressive commensality*, in which meals allow for the temporary crossing of social boundaries. This form of meal occurs in hierarchical societies, where one of the elite deigns to eat with non-elite: for example, the "invitation au château," or a political leader having lunch with the workers at the factory. Grignon notes (2001, 31):

> For such a meal to fulfil its honorific power and function, the dominant partner must present himself or herself in an authentic manner, be recognisable without any doubt, in short, make for a time a present of himself or herself, as a person, to the other guests. By the same token, on the other hand, he or she cannot share a meal with the common people without showing and recognising that he or she has the same needs and the same tastes, is subject to the same necessities, does not dislike or despise what is commonly liked and praised.

Hence, transgressive commensalities embody a paradox: the elite must be unmistakably recognized as such, yet she or he must also share the same menu. While this appears to efface the boundaries between elite and non-elite, that is only temporary. Because these are exceptional and onetime occurrences, such meals in fact underscore status differences.

One inscription, *AE* 1998, 282 (Lavinium, 227–228 CE), offers an example of transgressive commensality. An equestrian who had served in multiple civic and military roles endowed the *collegium dendrophorum* with HS20,000 so that they might hold an annual banquet (*epulum publicum*) for themselves and for his freedmen in the Caesareum in Lavinium. It is likely that Diodorus attended these banquets, since the dendrophores elected him as patron and his wife as *mater collegii* the following year (228 CE) and since he formally accepted this honor. It is likely that he was present to distribute the *sportulae*. Diodorus' banquet fictively dissolved status differences between the dendrophores and their patron—at least for the duration of the meal.

ASSOCIATIONS AND CHRIST GROUPS

Might knowledge of the commensalities of Greek and Roman associations assist us in thinking about Christ groups? It is obvious that we know much more about some Greek and Roman associations than we know about the finances and meal practices of Christ groups. This is at least in part because of asymmetries in the evidence. Most of the data from Greek and Roman associations is epigraphical or papryological and belongs to the genres of honorific decrees, funerary bequests, *lex collegii, alba*, and occasionally papyri that turn out to be club accounts. These are precisely the kinds of genres that provide information about financial practices, membership size, and meal practices. None of our data from Christ groups belongs to these genres. Instead, what we have for Christ groups is literary—letters and theological treatises. Moreover, those treatises deal with extraordinary issues, not the day-to-day life of Christ groups, and with theological teachings.

Nevertheless, comparison of Christ groups with guilds and associations are illuminating in four respects: (1) both offer examples of segregative commensalities; (2) comparison assists in thinking about the funding of the meals of Christ groups; (3) comparison assists in thinking about how internal tensions might have been negotiated; and (4) comparison also highlights the distinctive aspect in Christ groups as a bookish culture.

(1) *Christ groups as segregative commensalities.* Despite the differences in evidentiary profiles, it seems a reasonable conclusion that the meals of Christ groups belonged to Grignon's model of segregative commensality. This form of meal, as will be recalled, served to materialize "belonging" for persons who were not otherwise related, to mark them off from society in general as in some sense "special," to make them visible to themselves as members of a group, and to create an ethos of fictive equality. This may seem an obvious and banal observation, but it also helps to makes sense of other data.

Christ groups used discursive means to support both belonging and segregation along with a notion of equality, by making copious use of fictive family language and by using such segregating terms as "the elect," "the holy ones." There is no epigraphical evidence of the use of *alba* (since, a fortiori, there is no early Christian epigraphy), but the widespread idea that God keeps a book of life into which names are entered and from which they are erased (Ps 68:28 LXX; Dan 12:1; Phil 4:3; Revelation, *passim*) belongs to the same social imaginary as the use of *alba* by associations. To be named on a list meant that one really belonged.

There is not much evidence in the earlier period of ceremonious or exceptional commensalities among Christ groups, but that is because the evidence of elite involvement in Christ groups is so thin. It is hardly impossible that wealthier Christ followers might have occasionally funded a birthday or a funerary commemoration; but evidence of such practices is lacking before the fourth century, and as Daniel Ullucci has shown, after the fourth century the structure of benefaction seems to have changed, with the church serving as the main node for euergetic activity.[9]

(2) *The funding of meals.* As I have argued elsewhere, analysis of the endowments of 107 associations shows that only two had attracted an endowment able to underwrite the costs of five to seven banquets yearly.[10] The mean size of endowments for cultic associations was HS7,000, and with typical interest of 5–6 percent, able to fund a *single* banquet with *sportulae* but not more than that. Both the median and the mode was HS4,000, which would typically return HS200–240 (50 to 60 denarii). To recall the case of the *cultores* of Diana and Antinous in 135 CE, each meal cost 93 denarii for an association of forty-eight members, for a very modest banquet, without *sportulae.* Fifty to sixty denarii would be enough to fund a single meal for a smaller association of thirty members, without *sportulae.*

This conclusion aligns with the broader conclusions of Arjan Zuiderhoek, who found that during the Antonine and Severan periods the level of elite benefaction to cities was very modest in spite of the effusive commendations that cities lavished on their donors (Zuiderhoek 2009; cf. Liu 2007). Elite benefaction was mainly directed at public distributions and public buildings, not at the basic operating needs of cities. Moreover, Andreau's (1977) analysis of endowment practices indicated that cultic associations were very unlikely to receive endowments from the wealthiest sectors of society (senators, *equites*). Support was more likely to come from municipal magistrates, Augustales, women, and especially wealthier plebs. The elite, if they were inclined to act as patrons, were more likely to endow highly visible civic projects such as the restoration of a public building or public banquets. Our data confirms this: none of the cultic associations with endowments was connected to a person of senatorial or equestrian rank; two were endowed by decurions, two by Augustales, and the remainder by wealthy plebs or by persons of unknown status. This means that while a cultic association might

---

[9] Ullucci 2012; 2015. For example, the pavement of the remains of a fourth-century church below the floor of the Cattedrale di Santa Maria del Fiore in Florence was donated by fourteen named donors. See also Caillet 1993.

[10] Kloppenborg 2019, 226–27.

be able to fund one meal yearly from endowment, they had to rely on other income sources for other meals. These were typically member dues and the obligations of member magistrates to supply meals on a rotating basis.

Of course, we have no epigraphical or papyrological data concerning endowments for Christ groups. But it plainly stretches credibility to assume that Christ groups were able to recruit even wealthier and more generous donors than the norm.[11] Put bluntly, most patrons simply were not that generous. The idea is occasionally mooted that Christ groups could compete with other cultic groups because they had no membership or dinner fees but could supply fifty or more free dinners yearly (Pilhofer 2002; Ebel 2004). This, however, runs aground on the fact that *someone* had to fund those dinners; in the absence of a credible hypothesis that wealthy benefactors did this, we are left to conclude that either membership dues or inputs from member magistrates funded those meals. Both of these mechanisms are very well attested among Greek and Roman associations.[12]

(3) *Equality and hierarchy.* Christ groups, like associations of various types, had to negotiate the social tensions that were inherent within meal settings. At its most basic level, the shared meal was an expression of equality, as Plutarch's brother Timon argues (Plutarch, *Quaest. conv.* 1.2.3 [616E–F]):

> If in other matters we are to preserve equality (ἰσότης) among men, why not begin with this first and accustom them to take their places with each other without vanity and ostentation, because they understand as soon as they enter the door that the dinner is a democratic affair (δημοκρατικόν) and has no outstanding place like an acropolis where the rich man is to recline and lord it over meaner folk?

Athenaeus makes the same point in his sayings about the Homeric meal (*Deipn.* 1.12C):

> The meat was divided into portions, and he [Homer] therefore refers to meals as equal (ἔίσαι) because of the equality (ἰσότης) (practiced); for they called their dinner parties *daites* from the verb δατεῖσθαι ("to divide"), since it was not just the meat that was portioned out but the wine as well:

---

[11] Theissen (1982, 148–55) argues that the issue at Corinth was that the Corinthians had adopted a model of meals where wealthy patrons provided the food and, coming early, consumed most of it, leaving latecomers to be hungry. There are many problems with this model, as detailed in Kloppenborg 2019, 209–42.

[12] I would not, of course, exclude the possibility that, given the culture of euergetism, the occasional meals of some Christ groups received onetime-only funds.

"Now we have had enough of the equal meal" (*Od.* 8.98); and: "Cheers, Achilleus! We are not lacking an equal meal" (δαιτὸς ἐίσης) (*Il.* 9.225).

While the principle of equality was notoriously ignored in ceremonious commensalities (as Pliny and Martial complained), associations appear to have maintained equality, whether it was conceived as arithmetic or geometric.[13] The principle of member quality no doubt came under some stress in some groups, especially those that were gender inclusive and which had members of several legal statuses (free, freed, servile). Another source of tension could arise from the co-opting of a patron of distinguished rank. For example, the election of Herodes Atticus as the priest of the Iobakchoi in 164/165 CE (which required the demotion of the former priest of twenty-three years, Aurelius Nikomachos, to the role of vice-priest) cannot have been as free from tension as *IG* II² 1368 = *GRA* I 51 tries to make out. This inscription amply attests other tensions that arose at table, tensions that required the office of a manager of etiquette (εὔκοσμος) and several bouncers (ἵπποι) able to expel those who misbehaved. Although the membership of the Iobakchoi was likely Athenian demesmen, rivalries among this group could lead to seat stealing, insulting the pedigree of fellow members, and physical violence. The bylaws of the Iobakchoi thus attempted to ensure an atmosphere of conviviality amid the possibility of members competing for precedence.

The very design of dining rooms, with one or more triclinia, automatically marked some diners as of higher status and others as lower. One of the remedies was to adopt a practice of rotating magistracies, such that individuals would serve as presidents for a year (sometimes more), then be replaced by others on the basis of a rota.

I have already suggested that Christ groups adopted discursive ways to assert the equality of members, with fictive family language and confessional formulae such as Gal 3:28. Seating practices among Christ groups are mostly unknown, although James 2 might suggest that the author of James advocated a Timon-like practice of letting diners sit where they wished, without regard to rank and precedence. Nevertheless, it is hardly conceivable that Christ groups could have evaded the issue of negotiating precedence at table, especially in the second and third centuries when a person of rank was present. (One also wonders, for example, about what seating arrangements were made if Phoebe, the patron of the Christ group at Cenchaeae, were present at a Corinthian meal.)

---

[13] On the concept, see Aristotle, *Eth. nic.* 5.3.6 (1131a).

(4) *The distinctives of Christ groups.* Heuristic comparison of Christ groups with a variety of guilds and associations, though it does not manufacture new data about Christ groups, at least allows us to set in perspective some of the meal practices of Christ groups and to invite us to wonder how they might have reacted to the dynamics typical of association meals.

Comparison also highlights some of the ways in which the meals of Christ groups might have been quite different from those of guilds and associations. The most prominent difference has to do with the way that the meal became a venue for the development of a Christian book culture. Justin Martyr describes the meal of the Roman Christ group in *1 Apol.* 67, which began with a reading from the "memoirs of the apostles" or the prophets, an exhortation by the president, and a meal of bread and wine and water. The incorporation of reading and moral exhortation based on the contents of reading marks Christ groups off from most associations. According to Philo, the meals of the Therapeutae featured exposition of texts from the Bible (*Contempl.* 66–77). Such an orientation to book culture is unknown among occupational guilds, and exceptional in most cultic associations. Dionysiac liturgies may have included a discourse about the god (*theologia*) delivered by a priest (*IG* II² 1368.111–17). The fresco of the young boy holding a book in the Villa dei Misteri at Pompeii might indicate some role for reading or recitation in conjunction with the performance of Dionysiac initiation. Richard Last has noted that several associations took time to record the history of their founding on steles.[14] Whether these histories became part of their regular liturgies is unknown.

The bookish practices of Christ groups may not have been entirely unparalleled, but it seems to be a reasonable conclusion that this was one of the features that differentiated Christ groups from occupational guilds and most cultic associations. The adoption of bookish practices might better be compared to the literate practices of Roman elite, who used the reading and discussion of books as a fundamental part of their sociality (Johnson 2010). Of course, Christ groups likely could not afford the deluxe scrolls or the trained readers that the likes of Pliny had. But at a lower social register, they could still engage in literate practices as a fundamental part of their sociality and become what Brian Stock has called a textual community (1983; 1990).

---

[14] Last 2012, with reference to Sarapiastai of Delos (*IG* XI,4 1299) and Thessaloniki (*IG* X,2.1 255); the Iobakchoi (*IG* II² 1368); and a cult group of Agdistis in Philadelphia (Lydia; *TAM* 5.1539 [= *SIG*³ 985 = *GRA* II 117]).

CONCLUSION

Heuristic comparison of Christ groups with the variety of associations attested in Mediterranean antiquity does not manufacture any new data on Christ groups. Nothing short of new discoveries would do that. What comparison does is to create useful reading contexts for the data that we have. To set Christ groups alongside the other examples of segregative commensalities allows us to see that Christ groups employed comparable strategies to create the sense of segregation and belonging that is characteristic of segregative commensalities. Comparison does not tell us how Christ groups funded their meals; but it does foreclose certain possibilities and make plausible others. And although comparison does not help us see all of the strategies that Christ groups employed to address the tensions between equality and hierarchy, it does alert us to the fact that such tensions were endemic of other associations and allows us to see some of the language of Christ groups as discursive means to resolve those tensions. At the same time, comparison can highlight the interesting ways that Christ groups were distinctive. In fact, it is not until one sees the many ways that Christ groups were quite similar to ancient associations that one can appreciate the ways they were also distinctive.

WORKS CITED

Andreau, Jean. 1977. "Fondations privées et rapports sociaux en Italie romaine." *Ktema* 2:157–209.

Caillet, Jean-Pierre. 1993. *L'évergétisme monumental chrétien en Italie et à ses marges: d'après l'épigraphie des pavements de mosaïque (IVe-VIIe s.).* Collection de l'École française de Rome 175. Rome: École française de Rome.

Donahue, John F. 2003. "Toward a Typology of Roman Public Feasting." *AJP* 124:423–41.

Ebel, Eva. 2004. *Die Attraktivität früher christlicher Gemeinden: Die Gemeinde von Korinth im Spiegel griechisch-römischer Vereine.* WUNT 2/178. Tübingen: Mohr Siebeck.

Grignon, Claude. 2001. "Commensality and Social Morphology: An Essay of Typology." Pages 23–33 in *Food, Drink and Identity: Cooking, Eating and Drinking in Europe since the Middle Ages.* Edited by Peter Scholliers. Oxford: Berg.

Gutsfeld, Andreas. 2011. "Das Kollegium bei Tisch. Überlegungen zum Beitrag der Bankette zur sozialen Kohäsion in paganen Vereinen der frühen Kaiserzeit." Pages 161–83 in *Aposteldekret und antikes Vereinswesen. Gemeinschaft und ihre Ordnung.* Edited by Markus Öhler. WUNT 280. Tübingen: Mohr Siebeck.

Harland, Philip A. 2005. "Familial Dimensions of Group Identity: 'Brothers' (ἀδελφοί) in Associations of the Greek East." *JBL* 124:491–513.

———. 2007. "Familial Dimensions of Group Identity (II): 'Mothers' and 'Fathers' in Associations and Synagogues of the Greek World." *JSJ* 38:57–79.

Johnson, William A. 2010. *Readers and Reading Culture in the High Roman Empire: A Study of Elite Communities*. Classical Culture and Society. New York: Oxford University Press.

Kloppenborg, John S. 2019. *Christ's Associations: Connecting and Belonging in the Ancient City*. New Haven: Yale University Press.

Last, Richard. 2012. "Communities That Write: Christ-Groups, Associations, and Gospel Communities." *NTS* 58:173–98.

Lincoln, Bruce. 2014. *Discourse and the Construction of Society: Comparative Studies of Myth, Ritual, and Classification*. Oxford: Oxford University Press.

Liu, Jinyu. 2007. "The Economy of Endowments: The Case of the Roman Collegia." Pages 231–56 in *Pistoi dia tèn technèn: Bankers, Loans and Archives in the Ancient World: Studies in Honour of Raymond Bogaert*. Edited by Koenraad Verboven, Katelijn Vandorpe, and Véronique Chankowski. Studia Hellenistica 44. Leuven: Peeters.

Martens, Marleen. 2004. "The *Mithraeum* in Tienen (Belgium): Small Finds and What They Can Tell Us." Pages 25–56 in *Roman Mithraism: The Evidence of the Small Finds*. Edited by Marleen Martens and Guy de Boe. Archeologie in Vlaanderen 4. Brussels: Museum Het Toreke.

Pilhofer, Peter. 2002. "Die ökonomische Attraktivität christlicher Gemeinden der Frühzeit." Pages 194–216 in *Die frühen Christen und ihre Welt: Greifswalder Aufsätze 1996–2001*. WUNT 145. Tübingen: Mohr Siebeck.

Radt, Wolfgang. 1999. *Pergamon. Geschichte und Bauten einer antiken Metropole*. Darmstadt: Wissenschaftliche Buchgesellschaft.

Stock, Brian. 1983. *The Implications of Literacy: Written Language and Models of Interpretation in the Eleventh and Twelfth Centuries*. Princeton: Princeton University Press.

———. 1990. *Listening for the Text: On the Uses of the Past*. Parallax. Baltimore: Johns Hopkins University Press.

Stowers, Stanley K. 1995. "Greeks Who Sacrifice and Those Who Do Not: Toward an Anthropology of Greek Religion." Pages 299–320 in *The Social World of the First Christians: Essays in Honor of Wayne A. Meeks*. Edited by L. Michael White and O. Larry Yarbrough. Minneapolis: Fortress.

———. 1996. "Elusive Coherence: Ritual and Rhetoric in 1 Corinthians 10–11." Pages 68–83 in *Reimagining Christian Origins: A Colloquium Honoring Burton L. Mack*. Edited by Elizabeth Castelli and Hal Taussig. Valley Forge, Pa.: Trinity Press International.

Theissen, Gerd. 1982. *The Social Setting of Pauline Christianity: Essays on Corinth*. Translated by John H. Schütz. Philadelphia: Fortress.

Trümper, Monika. 2006. "Negotiating Religious and Ethnic Identity: The Case of Clubhouses in Late Hellenistic Delos." Pages 113–40 in *Zwischen Kult und Gesellschaft*. Edited by Nielsen Inge. Hephaistos 24. Augsburg: Camelion.

Ullucci, Daniel C. 2012. *The Christian Rejection of Animal Sacrifice*. Oxford: Oxford University Press.

———. 2015. "Sacrifice in the Ancient Mediterranean: Recent and Current Research." *CBR* 13:388–439.

Wecowski, Marek. 2018. "When Did the Symposion Die? On the Decline of the Greek Aristocratic Banquet." Pages 257–72 in *Feasting and Polis Institutions*. Edited by Floris van den Eijnde, Josine H. Blok, and Rolf Strootman. Mnemosyne, Supplements 414. Leiden: Brill.

Zuiderhoek, Arjan. 2009. *The Politics of Munificence in the Roman Empire: Citizens, Elites and Benefactors in Asia Minor*. Greek Culture in the Roman World. Cambridge: Cambridge University Press.

9

F(r)ee Membership
of Christ Groups

Timothy J. Murray

The recent flourishing of research on associations has invited a reexamination of how scholars reconstruct the early Christian *ekklēsia*. Although primarily driven by a detailed engagement with epigraphic and papyrological evidence, those who have led this field have also criticized perceived methodological and ideological inadequacies in previous scholarship. One question in which all these concerns can be seen is that raised by John Kloppenborg and Richard Last, as to whether it is likely that members of Christ groups were expected to make regular financial contributions to fund the group's activities, as opposed to "free membership."[1] As we will see, this question has clear consequences for other debates, in particular whether and how Christ groups cared for the poor, and the relevance of the *oikos* ("household") for understanding them. These issues are hardly peripheral to our understanding of Christian origins and are areas where Last has been a trenchant critic of "ideological" presuppositions (2016b, 2016c).

---

[1]   See the articles Kloppenborg 2016 and Last 2016b, the conclusions of which are now incorporated into their books: Kloppenborg 2019; Last and Harland 2020.

THE CASE FOR MEMBERSHIP CONTRIBUTIONS

In essence, the argument is quite simple as set out by Kloppenborg: the activities of Christ groups included, at a minimum, regular meals together and these meals needed to be paid for. There are a limited number of ways that any group in the ancient world could finance their activities:

> entrance or initiation fees; monthly (or periodic) dues; required contributions from leaders, analogous to Roman *summa honoraria*; income from patrons and family trusts; endowments owned by associations themselves; and sundry income from rent, fines, charges to non-members for access to a temple, special bequests, and special donations from members. (Kloppenborg 2016, 136)

When all these options are examined, Kloppenborg finds it difficult to imagine any group being able to remain financially solvent without the most common income stream—membership contributions. The reconstruction in previous scholarship which postulates well-resourced Christian patrons funding the meals of Christ groups (perhaps primarily composed of the poor), most of whom ate for free, on an ongoing basis, is rendered highly implausible (Kloppenborg 2016, 153; Last 2016b, 499).

If Christ groups charged some sort of membership fees, this does not necessarily mean that all members were of similar economic means. Kloppenborg has collected evidence that at least some associations were willing to charge differentiated fees to accommodate those who had less (2019, 236). Nor should we assume that members would have resented contributing, as to do so was not only normal but "contributions and service to the group were ways to materialize belonging and commitment and to receive recognition" (239).

One important feature in many reconstructions of Christ groups has been the claim that they cared for the poor in a way that contrasts with other associations, but Last argues that

> none of these idealizations would stand if Pauline groups behaved like typical Greco-Roman associations in closing their doors to people who could not afford membership dues, and penalizing members who were in arrears with fines, shame and expulsion. (2016b, 498)

For Last, the image of a generous Christ group caring for the poor is "not based on data about the groups behaviour" (498) but is constructed by scholars when they read Gal 2:10 and Acts 2:44-45; 4:34-35; and assume they "shaped the financial practices of actual Christ groups" (498). Last then argues that we *do* have data in 2 Thess 3:6-15 that indicates that this Christ group, at least, probably did charge membership fees. The narrower question (how did Christ groups finance their meals and other activities?) is thus presented as important to the broader one (did Christ groups care for the poor?). Finally, the language of the argument has developed over time, with *contributions* now generally preferred to *fees*, for the latter term often carries negative connotations that do not necessarily carry over into the ancient world (Last and Harland 2020, 20).

RECONSTRUCTING MEMBERSHIP CONTRIBUTIONS IN CHRIST GROUPS

The evidence presented by Kloppenborg and Last makes a convincing case for their basic argument that Christ groups must have relied on membership contributions, rather than depending solely on the ongoing generosity of a small number of rich patrons or well-resourced householders within those groups. Nor is this against the grain of the evidence from early Christian writings: in addition to the collection for "the poor among the saints at Jerusalem" (Rom 15:26), which was funded by contributions from most members of Christ groups founded by Paul, texts like Rom 12:13, Eph 4:28, and Did. 4.5–7 evidence the expectation that financial contributions were made within Christ groups. The central concern of this essay is not whether contributions occurred but how we should imagine such contributions and how closely analogous they are to the financial arrangements of other associations.

There are some arguments that may incline us to imagine Christ groups operating similarly to other associations. In addition to Last's detailed argument about 2 Thessalonians we may list the following: Christ groups convened regular meals that included at least bread and wine, which needed to be paid for; they used similar language for their meetings and officers as other associations; there is plenty of evidence for practices of shaming or excluding members in Paul's letters; and, perhaps most importantly, it seems historically likely that they would have organized their groups in line with conventions and structures with which they were culturally familiar. These observations are a welcome corrective to scholarly reconstructions that assume Christ groups were entirely unique in their financial practices, but are they of sufficient strength to convince us that membership contributions in Christ groups differed little (if at all) from those in other associations? To make this judgment we must consider some other observations; simply put, is there evidence that Christ groups may have *differed* from the norms of other associations in their financial matters? If so, then this too must be allowed to shape our historical reconstructions.[2]

The way any group organizes its finances depends on the purpose of its gatherings, which is expressed to large extent through its activities. We have seen how this presupposition (appropriately) underlies the case *for* membership contributions in Christ groups: it is because we have evidence of activities that cost (primarily meals) that we can argue they needed to collect membership contributions. If this is true, then it can also be said that if Christ groups differ in the purpose of their gatherings (which will be reflected in their activities), we have good grounds for asking whether such differences would impact their financial practices. I suggest that this is exactly what we find when we examine the frequency of Christ group meetings and what this consequently implies about their purpose.

The Frequency of Meetings

How often did most associations gather their members? What was the rhythm and frequency of their meetings? The evidence we have suggests that the most common pattern was that of monthly meetings (Kloppenborg 2019, 239). Many inscriptions explicitly tell us that the group met on a certain day of each month (*IG* II[2] 1368; *IG* II[2] 1365 + 1366) and Polybius can refer to association gatherings as "monthly dinners" (*Hist.* 10.5.6). Moreover, some association officials were called monthly officers even when the group did not meet monthly (Last and Harland 2020, 70), an oddity that surely only arises if monthly meetings were the norm. If associations did not meet monthly, it seems that this is because their gatherings were less frequent and were determined by annual festivals, feast days, or commemorative anniversaries (*IG* XII,3 330). Some associations both met monthly and on other annual dates, combining these two features (*IPergamon* 374). None of these observations are, I think, controversial, but they are important: other than the groups that I will go on to discuss (and to anticipate my argument), we should note that we have *no evidence* of associations meeting weekly, which is one area of clear difference between Christ groups and other associations that will be significant when it comes to reconstructing their financial affairs.

The obvious exception to this rule is Jewish groups. Although Jewish associations may have existed in a variety of guises (Last 2016a, 25–31), some of

---

2   The argument of this essay is necessarily general. Although I discuss Christ groups collectively, I accept that each would have differed in various ways and that no two associations were exactly alike. This does not delegitimize broader arguments but rather helpfully qualifies them.

which may have met for monthly banquets like other associations, it is surely incontrovertible that many Jewish groups across the Mediterranean met every week on the Sabbath. The Synoptic Gospels all describe Jewish gatherings on the Sabbath (e.g., Matt 12:9-14 and parr.; Mark 6:2; Luke 4:16, 31) and they are surely implicit in John (e.g., 9:13-34); so too in Acts, Paul is described as attending weekly meetings of Jewish groups (13:14-15; 17:2; 18:4). Philo describes weekly gatherings (*Hypoth.* 7.12; *Spec.* 2.62), as can Josephus (*Ant.* 16.43). Again, to claim Jewish groups met weekly is hardly controversial.

What then of Christ groups? Is the common assumption that they also met weekly well-founded? As with Jewish groups, the evidence for weekly meetings of Christ groups is substantial: Paul's instructions regarding the collection in 1 Cor 16:2 imply a weekly gathering, as does Acts 20:7; so too the reference in Rev 1:10 to "the Lord's Day" (τῇ κυριακῇ ἡμέρᾳ). In the Didache (14.1) we find instructions to gather on the Lord's Day (κατὰ κυριακήν), and Ignatius contrasts this day with the Sabbath (Ign. *Magn.* 9.1), making the Christian gathering equivalent to the Jewish practice with regards to its frequency. This evidence from Christian sources makes it most likely that a weekly rhythm is also the right understanding of Pliny's letter to Trajan, where he recounts that the Christians met "on a fixed day" (*Ep.* 10.96).[3]

If there is any indication of a different frequency of meeting, it is not that Christ groups met less than weekly but that in some cases they met *more* often. Returning to Pliny's letter, he describes two gatherings on the "fixed day": one before dawn for a hymn and ethical admonition, and one later in the day for simple food. In Ignatius' letter to the Ephesians (13.1), he encourages them to "gather together more often" (πυκνότερον συνέρχεσθαι). We already know that Ignatius considered a weekly "Lord's Day" to be an established rhythm for Christ groups, so "more often" here must mean "more than weekly." The Letter of Barnabas (19.10) goes further, encouraging its readers to "seek out the faces of the saints every day" (ἐκζητήσεις καθ ἑκάστην ἡμέραν τὰ πρόσωπα τῶν ἁγίων). These exhortations to meet more than weekly do not cut against the grain of the impression given by other early Christian sources, although they are less explicit. Both Luke's portrayal of Paul's ministry in Acts 19:9 and Paul's own description of his work in 1 Thess 2:9 seem to imply that he did not restrict his teaching to one day of the week but, rather, that this was intertwined with his daily labor. If so, this presents a more complex picture of what a "meeting" of a Christ group might look like. Clearly, such meetings

---

3   For discussion of the evidence including later sources, see Alikin 2010, 42–44.

are not as formalized as the weekly gathering, but that does not render them insignificant. Less formal encouters are also in evidence in 1 Tim 5:13, where they are of enough substance to concern the author about the influence of younger widows who are portrayed as "gadding about from house to house" (περιερχόμεναι τὰς οἰκίας).[4] Christian gatherings in homes and workplaces throughout the week are also observed by Celsus (Origen, *Cels.* 3.55). We may see a similar phenomenon in Paul's reference to the "whole church" in 1 Cor 14:23, i.e., that there were other, less formal gatherings of the church.[5] Finally, we have Luke's description of the Jerusalem Christ group in Acts 2:46 meeting "day by day" (καθ᾽ ἡμέραν), both in the temple and in houses, which, following Last and Harland (2020, 62–63), we may take as a foundation narrative in which the author emphasizes certain practices and ideals that should be embodied by Christ groups.

Clearly the evidence for more than weekly meetings is not as strong as the evidence for weekly gatherings of Christ groups, and I do not wish to argue that most Christ groups met multiple times a week. It is, however, important to register this inclination towards *more* frequent gatherings among Christ groups. Put bluntly, we may say that aside from Jewish groups, we know of no associations that met this often, whereas Christ groups met *at least* weekly.

This observation requires us to ask questions about the purpose of their meetings. Does their different frequency of meeting (weekly instead of monthly) relate to any difference in the purpose of their meetings or was the focus of Christ group gatherings largely indistinguishable from that of other associations? If the latter, we must explain why they met at least four times as often to accomplish similar ends.

The Purpose of Meetings

Why did Christ groups gather? How we answer this question is important for many reasons, including our reconstructions of the groups' financial practices. Unfortunately, this question is given proper consideration far less often than one might expect. When assessing the purpose of association gatherings in general, the discussion often concerns common activities which are usually summarized

---

[4]   This text also uses the term περίεργοι, the verbal form of which plays an important role in Last's article on 2 Thessalonians (see below).

[5]   Last (2016c) has argued vigorously against this kind of reading of 1 Cor 14:23. One of the critical points he makes is that "there is little reason for mini-'churches' to meet daily if the local ἐκκλησία already assembled weekly" (404); that is, the traditional thesis is weak, in part, because he can detect no plausible purpose in the group meeting more regularly than weekly. Given the evidence discussed in this essay, I submit that this objection dissolves with a better grasp of the purpose of their gatherings.

as follows: honoring benefactors, burying members, making offerings to the gods, and holding banquets. Associations funded these activities in a sustainable way with the kind of financial arrangements described by Last and Harland (2020, 99–118)—including collecting membership contributions. Usually, it is the monthly banquet that is presented as the substantial ongoing cost and the main focus of the association gathering (Alikin 2010, 18–23).

Given that Christ groups met more frequently than most associations, what can we say about the purpose of their gatherings? Did they have similar emphases in their time together as other associations, or are there differences that may be important to recognize when we try to reconstruct their approach to membership contributions? To best answer this question, we will need to examine evidence from the first three centuries CE (just as scholars reconstructing association activities tend to work with sources from the third century BCE to the third century CE, e.g., Last and Harland, 2020, 2), paying particular attention to how significant meals were in the gatherings of Christ groups.

We might begin by returning to the weekly meetings of Jewish groups. Our sources are unanimous that the main point of their gatherings was the reading and study of their Scriptures. In Mark 6:2, Jesus enters the synagogue and teaches the community; so too in Luke 4:16-17 where reading the Scripture and teaching are presented as the usual activity. Philo says that Jews are to gather on the seventh day and "in a respectful and orderly manner hear the laws" (*Hypoth.* 7.12); the emphasis is on receiving instruction.[6] So too Josephus claims the day is set aside for "the study of our customs and laws" (*Ant.* 16.43); thus, it is no surprise that Acts describes Paul as debating about the Scriptures on the Sabbath. In none of our sources are these weekly gatherings of Jews related to common meals. This obviously does not prove that meals did not happen, but it does indicate that this was not a comparable focus of their weekly gatherings as a community (or association)—the important thing was reading and instruction from their Scriptures.[7]

It is commonly acknowledged that Christ groups shared regular meals,[8] but the importance of text-related activities to their gatherings has not always been properly accounted for when discussing the purpose of their meetings. It is necessary, then, to briefly outline the main contours of the evidence.

---

[6] According to Fitzpatrick-McKinley (2002, 59), the reading was "educational and not ritualistic"; cf. Philo, *Spec.* 2.62.

[7] The weekly Jewish meal that we find in our sources is the weekly Sabbath family meal, on which see below.

[8] See, e.g., Robinson 2020, 4–5, and the literature cited there.

Several of the early-Christian letters give instructions for the letters to be read aloud and, at times, to be circulated to other Christ groups (e.g., 1 Thess 5:27; Col 4:16; Rev 1:3); other letters clearly expect this (e.g., 1 Cor 3, which assumes all within the church will hear the letter; also Ephesians and James, which are best understood as circular letters).[9] Acts 15:30-31 and 2 Pet 3:14-16 demonstrate that letters were circulating among Christ groups and regularly being read. In all these examples the letters were considered to contain authoritative instruction for their recipients. Not only were texts read in meetings, but other oral contributions were clearly commonplace. We have repeated references to teaching (e.g., Rom 12:7; Gal 1:9; Eph 4:11; Phil 1:15; Col 3:16; 1 Tim 1:3, 3:2; Titus 2:1, 7; Jas 3:1; Did. 10.1-2), praying or prophesying (e.g., Rom 12:6; 1 Cor 11:4-5, 10; Eph 4:11; Col 4:2; 1 Thess 5:17-21; 1 Tim 2:1; Jas 3:13-18; Jude 20; Did. 10.1-7), and other forms of exhortation or inspired speech (e.g., Rom 12:8; 1 Cor 12:8-9; Eph 5:19; Col 3:16; 1 Thess 5:12-14; 1 Pet 4:11). Moreover, beside references to this kind of activity going on at gatherings, we can also reflect on the content of the letters themselves, which are full of theological exposition and ethical instruction.

The reading of authoritative texts becomes even more explicit in the second century, together with prayer, teaching, and exhortation. Justin in his first apology describes Christian gatherings as follows:

> And on the day called Sunday, all who live in cities or in the country gather together to one place, and the memoirs of the apostles or the writings of the prophets are read, as long as time permits; then, when the reader has ceased, the president verbally instructs, and exhorts to the imitation of these good things. Then we all rise together and pray, and, as we before said, when our prayer is ended, bread and wine and water are brought. (*1 Apol.* 67; R. D. trans.)

Here we see reference to a shared meal but only after the importance of prayer, reading, teaching, and exhortation have been rehearsed (cf. Tertullian, *Apol.* 39). Apologetic writing always has to be read critically, but in this case there is a remarkable consistency across all our sources: it may be an obvious point, but if we want to reconstruct Christ group meetings, we must surely account for the tremendous importance that is so clearly attached to these activities.[10]

---

[9] Regarding James, cf. Bauckham 1999 and McCartney 2009; on Ephesians, see O'Brien 1999.

[10] The centrality of these activities has led several scholars (including Kloppenborg 2014) to apply Brian Stock's concept of "textual communities" to Christ groups. See the survey in Heath 2018, esp. 15.

Valeriy Alikin argues that the development of textual practices among Christ groups is best explained as developing from the symposia of other associations rather than from the synagogue: in symposia, a shared meal was often followed by readings from literary works and other oral contributions, whereas Jewish synagogue practice focused exclusively on studying the law (or better, the *Tanakh*; Alikin 2010, 147–55 and *passim*). Alikin also discusses the weekly Sabbath family meal but dismisses its relevance for understanding the Christian gathering:

> The Christian gathering on Sunday was not a continuation of any Jewish gathering on Sabbath. It did not evolve out of the Jewish meeting on Sabbath in the synagogue, for the latter did not include a meal, whereas the Christian gathering was essentially a supper. Nor was the Christian meeting on Sunday evening a continuation of the Jewish family supper on Sabbath, since the latter was essentially a family meal, whereas the Lord's Supper of the Christians was an association meal. (2010, 48–49)

I am not convinced that either of these contrasts are helpful or that Alikin offers the best interpretation of our sources. Generally speaking, it is true that there is evidence for similar activities in both Christ groups and other association symposia, but the evidence itself begs for more nuance. What kind of meal are we talking about? If households and associations could overlap (e.g., Harland 2009, 32–33), labeling Christ group meals as "association banquets" and dismissing the relevance of *oikos* meals may presuppose too much. Regarding texts and oral contributions, we may ask whether the purpose is primarily to instruct or to entertain? What kind of texts are read and how often? Is there any indication of the relative importance of these activities compared with the shared meal?

When we bring these questions to our sources there is plenty of evidence to suggest that Christ groups considered reading and teaching to be more important than shared meals in their gatherings, which our historical reconstructions should take care to account for if they are to be plausible. We may note, with Alikin (2010, 66–67), that second-century sources that describe Christ group meetings tend to invert the usual order of a symposium. Rather than the meal coming first, followed by literary readings or oral performances, Justin (*1 Apol.* 67.3–6), Clement of Alexandria (*Strom.* 6.113.3), and Tertullian (*Apol.* 39) all describe reading and teaching as coming *before* any meal. Alikin suggests this was a practical decision to enable catechumens to hear the teaching while preventing them from sharing in the Eucharist; however, it could equally reflect a different understanding of the purpose and value of such teaching. As opposed to many other symposia, such activities are never described as being primarily about entertainment but rather are focused on instruction and education. Not only is this true of those authors already cited but it can also be seen in the later Acts and the Pseudo-Clementine literature.[11] Some authors explicitly elevate the importance of text-based activities in contrast to meals,[12] and we also find an emphasis on the simple food of Christ groups, which is sometimes compared with the somewhat more lavish banquets of other associations.[13]

EVIDENCE, METHODOLOGY, PLAUSIBILITY

The arguments of the preceding two sections can now be brought together. The best explanation for the greater frequency of the meetings of Christ groups is in their purpose; text-based activities (reading, instruction, moral exhortation, etc.) were more central to their gatherings when compared with most other associations and were aimed both to impart knowledge or understanding to members and to encourage a particular way of life.[14] One can easily see why gatherings were more frequent, for this educative-formational process requires time. If the contours of the argument are accepted (that Christ groups differed in the frequency and focus of their meetings), what might this mean for how we imagine membership contributions?

---

[11] So Acts Thom. 36–38 (Schneemelcher 1992, 354–55), where costly banquets are condemned and immediately contrasted with "the assembly of Christ" which consists of belief in, and instruction about, Jesus; Acts of Paul and Thecla 5–11, where the gathering of a Christ group is described as consisting of prayer, breaking of bread, and the word of God, before being contrasted with the luxurious banquet of the unbelieving Thamyris (Schneemelcher 1992, 239–41); Acts of John 84 (Schneemelcher 1992, 200) describes what characterizes those who "hope in the Lord," where the *agape* comes towards the end of a long list that includes thoughts, mind, souls, practice, counsel, prayers, and Eucharist. By the time of the *Epistula Clementis*, although some concern for shared meals is discernable, it is thrust into the dim background by the concern for teaching, right doctrine, and moral instruction. At some point in the development of the church, collective meals dropped out of the common practice of Christ groups, but reading, teaching, prayer, etc., remained central to their gatherings. There are many reasons for this, like the growth in the number of Christians, but is this not indicative of the relative importance of these activities even at an earlier point?

[12] For example, in the thirteenth chapter of the *Didascalia apostolorum* the importance of "hearing the word of life" is explicitly contrasted with the desire "to be fed with the meat and drink of the belly"; this does not mean meals did not occur, but that they were not of central importance.

[13] Tertullian, *Apol.* 39; cf. Pliny, *Ep.* 10.96.

[14] If this is correct it becomes hard to dismiss synagogue practice as an important analogy for understanding the Christian gatherings.

Did Christ Group Meals Entail "Extra" Expense?

If we agree that the meals of Christ groups were facilitated by the contributions of their members, how should we imagine these meals? On the one hand, we may conceive of these meals as an "extra" cost for members above the usual resources that their normal lives would require (such is connoted by the term *banquet* to describe their meals); this would seem to require similar financial arrangements we know of in many other associations. If this is the case, however, then the weekly gatherings would represent substantial costs for each member to the point where one wonders how many could afford such regular extra expense. On the other hand, we could conceive of these meals as communal but not necessarily "additional," in that the food consumed at the gatherings of Christ groups was largely the same as would have been eaten by each member anyway, perhaps in their household. John Donahue's survey of different kinds of meals notes that although there has been substantial research into the Roman family in recent decades, "largely missing . . . has been any treatment of 'ordinary' everyday domestic meals due to the fact that such meals are simply not very well understood" (2019, 96).[15] The relative paucity of our sources in this area should not prevent us from considering whether this kind of meal (rather than the banquet) may be a better analogy for at least some Christ group gatherings, for it seems more able to explain how members could afford them on a weekly basis. It also invites us to consider whether, despite Alikin's objections, the Jewish Sabbath meal may be a useful point of departure after all, especially if we want to account for the saturation of *oikos* concepts and terminology in the self-understanding of Christ groups.[16]

---

[15] Donahue's survey at least indicates the range of different "meals" that were eaten (cf. Donahue 2015), which creates substantially more conceptual space than, for example, Matthias Klinghardt, whose typology deals only with banquet symposia (Klinghardt 2012). Peter Garnsey's discussion of food and the family similarly struggles with the lack of evidence, but nonetheless helpfully outlines some of the issues concerning food distribution in the household (Garnsey 1999, 100–112).

[16] Philip Harland has demonstrated that the "fictive-kinship" language of Christ groups was not unique and can be found in other associations (2009, 61–96). However, as Harland makes clear, that does not mean it had the same "importance of depth of meaning" (80) whenever it occurred. Thus, we must still investigate the significance of this self-understanding for Christ groups, which seems considerable, given that it extended to central theological beliefs (including "adoption" in Romans, Galatians, and Ephesians and "being born again" in John, 1 John, and 1 Peter), had social implications (e.g., Eph 2:19; Phlm 16), and explains some of their concrete financial practices. On this, see especially Murray 2018, 139–225.

Should We Allow the Ethics of Christ Groups to Aid Our Reconstructions of Their Financial Practices?

We cannot assume that the ethics of a group accurately reflects its behavior (van der Watt 2006), and it is easy to find unnuanced idealizations of the early church (Last 2016b, 499), but it is equally questionable to refuse to let their ethics have any role in our historical reconstructions. These Christ groups wrote, read, copied, and preserved texts that contained substantial ethical material about the use of money and care for the poor; moreover, this teaching was attributed to their deity (Jesus) and their heroes and founders (the first apostles). These concerns are prominent in the earliest Christian documents (both those that became the New Testament and the "apostolic fathers") and continue to be so throughout the second and third centuries and beyond (Rhee 2012). It must also be said that there are important contrasts between this material and what we know of non-Judeo-Christian ethics (Armitage 2016). If this is the case, then it seems entirely reasonable to consider how these values and beliefs may have influenced the actual practices of Christ groups and to ask how they might have differed from other associations which were not connected to the same ethical tradition. Such historical work *may* be apologetic (an accusation found repeatedly in recent secondary literature), but it is not *necessarily* so.[17] Put bluntly, is it plausible to imagine that the ethical and theological tradition that was so dominant in the activities of Christ groups had no impact on their financial practices? I find that unlikely, especially given that on other issues we know that the ethical tradition of Christ groups influenced their behavior.[18]

Has Richard Last Provided the Best Reading of 2 Thessalonians 3:6-15?

Although space does not allow a comprehensive engagement with Last's interpretation of 2 Thess 3:6-15, we must offer some response since Last claims that this verse provides reliable data indicating that this Christ group closely reflected the membership-fee practices of other associations. For Last, the problem reflected in this verse is not that the disorderly ones (ἀτάκτος) have been refusing to work, presuming on the

---

[17] We might suspect that an equally prominent phenomenon is the myth of an ideologically neutral historiography serving to conceal a methodology based on modern naturalistic presuppositions, which lead scholars to systematically underappreciate the importance of beliefs, values, ethics, and religious experience for the subjects of their historical research. Cf. the reflections in Deines 2013, esp. 1–28; Wreford 2021, 44–48.

[18] So especially martyrdom—a fairly drastic behavioral choice related to early Christian theology and ethics, on which see Middleton 2006, *passim*.

brotherly love (φιλαδελφία) of the community and expecting to eat without contributing;[19] instead, they have negotiated (περιεργάζομαι) a temporary suspension of membership dues. Thus, according to Last, rather than conceiving of the group as operating with a system whereby love is expressed partly in the "charitable" provision of food for others, which was being abused, we should imagine a dispute about membership fees for banquets resolved by recording a list of debtors and barring access to further banquets until they settled up. Despite the many contributions of Last's argument, I remain unconvinced that he has explained the features of the text that have led others to see some form of charitable practice as the context of the Thessalonian problem.

For a start, Last resists letting 1 Thess 4:9-12 inform his reconstruction as "the issue in that text is outsiders' perceptions of the group, not the internal financial organization of the Christ group's banquet. . . . Crucially, the issue of *ekklēsia* members working with their own hands is not mentioned at all in 2 Thess 3,6–15" (Last 2016b, 514–15). This is a reductive reading of both texts, for in 1 Thess 4:12 the issue is also about dependence on others within the group and in 2 Thess 3:8-9 Paul presents his own labor and contribution as a model to imitate, clearly implying this was still an issue in the community. It is this unconvincing separation of the two letters that allows Last to dismiss the relevance of φιλαδελφία in 1 Thess 4:9 (and other fictive kinship language), for in 1 Thess 4:9-12 the logic of the text clearly connects brotherly love with work and reciprocity. I know of no examples of φιλαδελφία being used as an ethical norm in other associations (it is usually only applied to real families), but it carries significant ethical weight here. That it refers to practices that go beyond quid pro quo membership rights is further implied in 2 Thess 3:13 where Paul encourages the community not to become tired of doing the good (καλοποιοῦντες) despite the conduct of the disorderly, a verse that Last does not attempt to explain. Furthermore, if the problem was the relatively normal occurrence of members negotiating temporary deferrals on payments, we may ask why the Thessalonians needed such a lengthy intervention by Paul? In both Thessalonian letters Paul works hard to clarify ethical principles concerning work and reciprocity, which seems to me only necessary if the Christ group did *not* simply operate with a normal "fees and benefits" system but one that was perhaps less familiar and carried within it risks of misunderstanding and

---

[19] For a defense of this interpretation and exegetical points made in this paragraph, with summary and discussion of the literature, see Murray 2018, 160–95.

abuse. I think such a reading could incorporate the results of Last's excellent lexical work without needing to accept his more polemical theses.[20]

CONCLUSION

John Kloppenborg writes that "the benefit of careful comparison that identifies similarities is that it in fact allows the differences to stand out with special prominence" (2019, xi). Identifying similarity and/or difference is not only about the evidence we appeal to but our methodology, which can never be detached from our presuppositions. Recent articles on membership contributions in Christ groups have made a cogent case for the likely similarities between Christ groups and other associations; I have begun to explore why and where we may also plausibly postulate difference. My argument has been indicative rather than exhaustive and will require more substantial exposition in the future. All our reconstructions involve unavoidable speculation, but the most plausible theories are surely likely to be those that are guided both by the data of other associations and by the particularities of the Christ groups.

WORKS CITED

Alikin, Valeriy A. 2010. *The Earliest History of the Christian Gathering: Origin, Development and Content of the Christian Gathering in the First to Third Centuries*. VCSup 102. Leiden: Brill.

The Apostolic Fathers. 2007. 3rd ed. Edited and translated by Michael W. Holmes. Grand Rapids: Baker Academic.

Armitage, David J. 2016. *Theories of Poverty in the World of the New Testament*. WUNT 2/423. Tübingen: Mohr Siebeck.

Bauckham, Richard. 1999. *James: The Wisdom of James, Disciple of Jesus the Sage*. London: Routledge.

Deines, Roland. 2013. *Acts of God in History: Studies Towards Recovering a Theological Historiography*. Edited by Christoph Ochs and Peter Watts. WUNT 317. Tübingen: Mohr Siebeck.

Donahue, John. 2015. "Roman Dining." Pages 253–64 in *A Companion to Food in the Ancient World*. Edited by John Wilkins and Robin Nadeau. Chichester: Wiley.

———. 2019. "Roman Meals in Their Domestic and Wider Settings." Pages 93–100 in *The Routledge Handbook of Diet and Nutrition in the Roman World*. Edited by Paul Erdkamp and Claire Holleran. London: Routledge.

---

[20] I am not convinced that Last's rendering of περιεργάζεσθαι as "haggling," and his reading of what that refers to, is ultimately successful, but his lexical research points out some weaknesses in previous scholarship and stimulates us to think about alternative possibilities.

Fitzpatrick-McKinley, Anne. 2002. "Synagogue Communities in the Graeco-Roman Cities." Pages 55–87 in *Jews in the Hellenistic and Roman Cities*. Edited by John R. Bartlett. London: Routledge.

Garnsey, Peter. 1999. *Food and Society in Classical Antiquity*. Cambridge: Cambridge University Press.

Harland, Philip A. 2009. *Dynamics of Identity in the World of the Early Christians: Associations, Judeans, and Cultural Minorities*. New York: Continuum; London: T&T Clark.

Heath, Jane. 2018. "'Textual Communities': Brian Stock's Concept and Recent Scholarship on Antiquity." Pages 5–35 in *Scriptural Interpretation at the Interface between Education and Religion: In Memory of Hans Conzelmann*. Edited by Florian Wilk. Themes in Biblical Narrative: Jewish and Christian Traditions 22. Boston: Brill.

Josephus. 1963. *Books 16–17*. Vol. 7 of *Jewish Antiquities*. Translated by Ralph Marcus and Allen Wikgren. LCL 410. Cambridge, Mass.: Harvard University Press.

Justin. 1885. *First Apology*. Pages 163–87 in vol. 1 of *The Ante-Nicene Fathers: Translations of the Writings of the Fathers Down to A.D. 325*. Translated and edited by Alexander Roberts and James Donaldson. Peabody: Hendrickson.

Klinghardt, Matthias. 2012. "A Typology of the Communal Meal." Pages 9–22 in *Meals in the Early Christian World: Social Formation, Experimentation, and Conflict at the Table*. Edited by Dennis E. Smith and Hal Taussig. New York: Palgrave Macmillan.

Kloppenborg, John S. 2014. "Literate Media in the Early Christ Groups: The Creation of a Christian Book Culture." *JECS* 22:21–59.

———. 2016. "Epigraphy, Papyrology and the Interpretation of the New Testament: Member Contributions to the Eucharist." Pages 129–53 in *Epigraphik und Neues Testament*. Edited by Thomas Corsten, Markus Öhler, and Joseph Verheyden. WUNT 365. Tübingen: Mohr Siebeck.

———. 2019. *Christ's Associations: Connecting and Belonging in the Ancient City*. New Haven: Yale University Press.

Last, Richard. 2016a. *The Pauline Church and the Corinthian Ekklēsia: Greco-Roman Associations in Comparative Context*. SNTSMS 164. Cambridge: Cambridge University Press.

———. 2016b. "The Myth of Free Membership in Pauline Christ Groups." Pages 495–516 in *Scribal Practices and Social Structures among Jesus Adherents: Essays in Honour of John S. Kloppenborg*. Edited by William E. Arnal, Richard S. Ascough, Robert A. Derrenbacker Jr., and Philip A. Harland. BETL 285. Leuven: Peeters.

———. 2016c. "The Neighborhood (*vicus*) of the Corinthian *ekklēsia*: Beyond Family-Based Descriptions of the First Urban Christ-Believers." *JSNT* 38:399–425.

Last, Richard, and Philip A. Harland. 2020. *Group Survival in the Ancient Mediterranean: Rethinking Material Conditions in the Landscape of Jews and Christians*. London: T&T Clark.

McCartney, Dan G. 2009. *James*. BECNT. Grand Rapids: Baker Academic.

Middleton, Paul. 2006. *Radical Martyrdom and Cosmic Conflict in Early Christianity*. LNTS 307. London: T&T Clark.

Murray, Timothy J. 2018. *Restricted Generosity in the New Testament*. WUNT 2/480. Tübingen: Mohr Siebeck.

O'Brien, Peter T. 1999. *The Letter to the Ephesians*. PNTC. Grand Rapids: Eerdmans.

Origen. 1885. *Contra Celsus*. Pages 395–669 in vol. 4 of Roberts and Donaldson, *The Ante-Nicene Fathers*.

Philo. 1941. *Hypothetica*. Translated by F. H. Colson. LCL 363. Cambridge, Mass.: Harvard University Press.

Pliny. 1969. *Books 8–10*. *Panegyricus*. Vol. 2 of *Letters*. Translated by Betty Radice. LCL 59. Cambridge, Mass.: Harvard University Press.

Polybius. 2011. *Books 9–15*. Vol. 4 of *The Histories*. Translated by W. R. Paton. Revised by F. W. Walbank and Christian Habicht. LCL 159. Cambridge, Mass.: Harvard University Press.

Rhee, Helen. 2012. *Loving the Rich, Saving the Poor: Wealth, Poverty, and Early Christian Formation*. Grand Rapids: Baker Academic.

Robinson, Dana. 2020. *Food, Virtue and the Shaping of Early Christianity*. Cambridge: Cambridge University Press.

Schneemelcher, Wilhelm, ed. 1992. *Writings Relating to the Apostles; Apocalypses and Related Subjects*. Vol. 2 of *New Testament Apocrypha*. Rev. ed. Translated by R. McL. Wilson. Cambridge: James Clarke.

van der Watt, Jan G. 2006. "Preface." Pages v–ix in *Identity, Ethics, and Ethos in the New Testament*. Edited by Jan G. van der Watt. Berlin: De Gruyter.

Wreford, Mark. 2021. *Religious Experience and the Creation of Scripture: Examining Inspiration in Luke-Acts and Galatians*. LNTS 641. London: T&T Clark.

10

Women Benefactors and Early Christ Groups

Susan E. Benton

Scholarship on benefactors in the ancient world has sought in recent decades to capture with better precision how women engaged in the patronage systems of the Roman Empire (see Dixon 2001, 100–112). In this, Emily Hemelrijk has broken new ground on women's benefactory roles in civic and associational contexts, by focusing on Latin epigraphic evidence (see especially Hemelrijk 2004; 2008; 2012; 2013; 2015). As Hemelrijk demonstrates, any analysis of women's roles at home and in society that is informed primarily by literary evidence will inevitably lead to underestimating the range of ancient women's activities—a range that epigraphic evidence brings into clearer focus (see Osiek and MacDonald 2006; Schenk 2017; Hylen 2018). Public and private life were not as sharply divided as once thought. In trade and civic associations, in patronage relationships and municipal offices, in homes and in private associations, women participated in influential and sometimes leading capacities throughout the Hellenized world.[1]

Analyzing inscriptional evidence yields resources for reconsidering the named women in early Christ groups. In a Roman inscription recording bylaws for a collegium honoring Aesculapius and Hygiae, Salvia Marcellina

---

[1] On women in civic offices, see Hemelrijk 2015, 11–12; van Bremen 1996; Witherington 1991, 23.

demonstrates the impressive authority attained by a wealthy woman in an association in Rome in 153 CE. This essay will examine the figure of Salvia Marcellina, connect her with additional evidence for women benefactors and leaders in ancient associations, and extrapolate implications for women in New Testament Christ groups. Ultimately, I propose that Salvia Marcellina demonstrates specific leadership functions that women might have exercised in Christ groups, from material provision and general oversight (in accord with prior scholarship) to defining the terms of membership and conditions for group participation. Furthermore, I propose that Salvia Marcellina's title, *mater collegi(i)*, "mother of the association," introduces a useful category for imagining women's roles in early Christ groups, conceptualizing "mothers" and patrons as figures distinct in social rank, in recruitment process, and in role.

SALVIA MARCELLINA AND WOMEN WITH ASSOCIATIONAL POWER

Salvia Marcellina and Other Women Benefactors

Salvia Marcellina's involvement in her association is a vivid example of a woman's influence and benefaction. The translation of the relevant portion from the Latin inscription from 153 CE (*CIL* 6.10234; *ILS* 7213) reads:

> Salvia Marcellina daughter of Gaius (Salvius), in memory of Flavius Apollonius, procurator of the Augusti, who was in charge of the picture gallery in the palace, and in memory of Capito, imperial freedman, his assistant and her most excellent and pious husband, donated as a gift to the association (collegium) of Aesculapius and Hygiae the land for a chapel with a shop and a marble statue of Aesculapius and an attached covered solarium in which the membership (*populi*) of the above-named association can hold a banquet. This is located on the Via Appia near the temple of Mars, between the first and second milestones.[2]

Marcellina, as the inscription also refers to her, was an imperial freedman's widow. With her husband's past imperial enslavement, she likely remained a client to the imperial household (Hylen 2018, 101). Possibly also a freedperson, she is identified customarily, first by her father's name, then further in dedications to the procurator and her husband. Her husband's and father's careers are place markers for her rank; women in the empire had titles conferred through

---

[2] Ascough, Harland, and Kloppenborg 2012, no. 322. For the Latin, see AGRW 322. The inscription itself is pictured in Kloppenborg 2019, 2, fig. 1.

their male relatives' rank.[3] With both her father and husband listed in the inscription, there are more clues about Salvia Marcellina than for most women in extant Latin honorary inscriptions.[4] She may have maintained connections to powerful people through the emperor's household, though this would not be certain; imperial enslavement resulted in a "morbid" number of imperial slaves and freedpeople, with few attaining positions of influence (Flexsenhar 2019, 14). Still, the other recipient of the joint dedication, Flavius Apollonius, was administrator (*proc[uratis]*) of the imperial galleries, and Marcellina's husband Capito was his assistant (*adiutoris*). The dedication to Flavius Apollonius could have helped preserve imperial alliances.

The bequest recorded on the plaque entails land, buildings, a marble statue, and 50,000 sesterces. Noting the building's proximity to the Appian Way and Mars' temple underscores the value of the total gift. Such generosity was exceptional; most gifts to associations provided a few thousand sesterces for banquets.[5] Salvia Marcellina's name appears in large letters at the inscription's top, emphasizing her honors (Hemelrijk 2012, 208). Devoted to the god of healing and the goddess of health, the group could be considered a cultic association; possibly, it was also a stonemasons' collegium.[6] Apart from Marcellina, its members were men.[7] To her benefaction Salvia Marcellina affixed conditions that became part of the association's bylaws. Jinyu Liu proposes two possibilities, favoring the latter: Marcellina was a founder of the group, or Marcellina's donation initiated a reorganization of the group.[8] The bylaws stipulated: no more than sixty members; deceased members' places could be purchased by free men, or bequeathed within a household for half of the funeral dues; money was for specific meetings and supplies; interest on the monetary gift would be *sportulae* (gifts) for members, distributed on the emperor's birthday. The collegium's leadership may have rotated into service, according to John Kloppenborg, but the president,

[3] Hemelrijk 2015, 13: "The surest indication of a woman's social standing is the rank and career of her husband or father as recorded on her, or an adjacent, inscription."

[4] Hemelrijk 2015, 13–14: a majority have no occupational/rank identifiers, or even husbands. I am comparing the evidence in Greek inscriptions for my current research project on ancient women benefactors.

[5] Kloppenborg 2019, 47. More typical examples: 4,000 sesterces in Ostia (*CIL* 14.246); 1,000 sesterces in Umbria (*CIL* 11.5047).

[6] Kloppenborg 2019, 25, with explanation, 353, n. 1.

[7] Hemelrijk 2012, 209. Bequeathed seats could go to sons, brothers, and freedmen.

[8] Liu 2004, 321; 2007, 241. Liu 2007 identifies two other examples, 241–43, of likely reorganizations after gifts, from Lanuvium in *CIL* 14.2112 and *ILS* 7212 (136 CE); and from Mediolanum in *CIL* 5.5612 (ca. 246–268 CE). Additional inscriptions discuss the Mediolanum group before and after its likely reorganization: *CIL* 5.5578, 5738, 5869.

pater, and *mater* appear to have lifelong titles (Kloppenborg 2019, 1). The inscription's latter half clarifies that Aelius Zenon, first identified as the association's father, is also an imperial freedman and the brother of Marcus Publius Capito; that is, he is Salvia Marcellina's brother-in-law.[9] Aelius Zenon also gave an endowment, but his 10,000 sesterces positioned him below Marcellina in the acknowledgments.

Salvia Marcellina's power over organizational structure appears notable, especially given how little is known about associational benefactors' activities.[10] A Greek inscription found near Athens from the second century BCE gives another, earlier example of associational rules rewritten around a significant woman. A cultic association of Magna Mater enforced its rules for its priestesses' rotation by a fine.[11] Part of the translated inscription states, "Whichever priestess has obtained the priesthood shall appoint an attendant from among those who have already been priestesses. But it is not permitted to appoint the same person twice until all have had their turn. Otherwise, the priestess will be liable to the same fines" (Kloppenborg and Ascough 2011, 170). A few sentences later, however, the inscription amends the rules, eight years later, saying Metrodora served so honorably and piously, attending the last *two* priestesses, that the *orgeōnes* and priestesses wished her appointed an attendant for life (Kloppenborg and Ascough 2011, 171, 174). Seemingly, Metrodora would break the prior rule. Yet in an ancient version of "burying the lede," the inscription saves until its final lines the declaration that Metrodora's perpetual priesthood followed the model set by her mother, Euaxis, appointed perpetually and continuing to serve the Mother of the Gods.[12] Clearly, both Metrodora and Euaxis were privileged, exempt from the rules governing other priestesses. Their examples demonstrate, like

---

[9]   Hemelrijk 2012, 209. The final supervisor in the inscription, G. Salvius Seleucus, may be the same Gaius (Salvius) in the top line of the inscription, Marcellina's father. Bruce Longenecker, in personal communication, notes another alternative: that there were two men called Gaius Salvius, Seleucus being one, and Marcellina's father the other, both being freed slaves (and therefore sharing the *praenomen* and *nomen* of their master). Liu (2007, 241) suggests that "C. [*sic*] Salvius Seleucus" may be a relative or a freedman from Salvia Marcellina's household.

[10]   Hemelrijk (2008, 138) identifies another Latin inscription (*CIL* 2.3229 = *ILS* 7308) with Licinia Macedonica, mother in a Laminium collegium, overseeing the erection of a statue, thus functioning as collegium official.

[11]   Kloppenborg and Ascough 2011, 168–74; inscription no. 34, *IG* II² 1328. Portion A dates to 183/182 BCE; portion B dates to 175/174 BCE.

[12]   Kloppenborg and Ascough 2011, 171. Aixone, the current priestess, proposed Metrodora's exception. It seems reasonable to suppose Euaxis' precedent and power also contributed.

Salvia Marcellina, that a woman could influence the structure of an association commensurate with her investment into its flourishing. In Marcellina's case, donation was material. For Metrodora and Euaxis, devotion and excellent service are hailed as investments. Financial outlay being necessary for regular service as priestess, perpetual service probably also extended financial contributions to the cultic association.[13]

Inscriptions show other women occupying benefactor roles like Salvia Marcellina's. Strikingly, women and men are equally attested as "mothers" and "fathers" of associations (Hemelrijk 2008, 137, 143). Women occasionally serve as titled patrons to cities, though with far less frequency than men.[14] Hemelrijk's working theory is that the two designations—patron and mother—are distinct and technical; they should only be used when a benefactor is explicitly named by either title.[15] Local regulations governed the processes for securing municipal patrons; decurions elected notable citizens and recruited them (González 1986, 191). They finalized terms with a *tabula patronatus* delivered to the patron's home, essentially drafting their city's next sponsor (Hemelrijk 2004, 210). A second-century decurial woman and imperial cultic priestess, Abeiena Balbina, served as municipal patron for Pitinum Pisauraense in Italy (Hemelrijk 2004, 212, 238). In the early third century, Vibia Aurelia Sabina, Marcus Aurelius' daughter, was patron to two cities: Thibilis in Numidia and Calama in Africa Proconsularis (Hemelrijk 2004, 214–15, 238). Mostly an honorific role, a city patron also served as an intermediary between city and imperial government (Hemelrijk 2004, 222–24). Women co-opted as city patrons were of high rank, well positioned for advocating their community's interests.

Women served as associational patrons more frequently than as civic patrons. Ancharia Luperca's inscription from Etruria, Italy (*CIL* 11.2702; *ILS* 7217; 224 CE), describes her co-optation in the city of Volsinii by a male builders' association, who placed a bronze statue of her in their meeting place beside her husband's existing statue.[16] The inscription records

[13]   Kloppenborg and Ascough (2011, 170–71) translate the term for Metrodora's service as "co-administer(ing)" the priesthood. She shared the appointed priestess' responsibilities. She supplied significant funds.

[14]   Hemelrijk 2004, 210, 214: out of a total 1,200 city patrons, 19 civic "patronesses."

[15]   Hemelrijk 2008, 119. Explicit use of patron or mother is one of Hemelrijk's criteria for identifying and comparing women benefactors. Following her methodology, this essay treats benefactor as the broad category, with patron and mother as titles within that category.

[16]   Ascough, Harland, and Kloppenborg 2012, no. 332; cf. Hemelrijk 2008, 115–16; 2012, 216–17.

their resolution to attach a patron's plaque to her home. This bronze plaque was discovered in the ruins of the house, leaving traces of the common co-optation practice. Ancharia Luperca's election continued the patronage her husband had previously provided. The sequence of events, Hemelrijk says, implies that titled patrons' financial generosity was "the result of, rather than the reason for, their cooptation" (Hemelrijk 2004, 234). If her observation is accurate, patrons were recognized prior to having performed their benefactions. Moreover, women could back collegia financially even if otherwise ineligible for membership, as in the cases of Ancharia Luperca and Salvia Marcellina. Their benefactions are not unique. Hemelrijk identifies fourteen women patrons of collegia, twenty-six collegia mothers, and thirty civic mothers in inscriptions.[17] By analyzing these women's ancient benefactions, Hemelrijk has contributed a new insight on the subject of ancient women's munificence: a distinction between women patrons and mothers in associations.[18]

Patrons and Mothers

In addition to being a benefactor, Salvia Marcellina is also named a *mater collegi(i)*. The title appears near the middle of the inscription, after the conditions she attached to her gifts. Mothers and fathers of collegia, like Salvia Marcellina and Publius Aelius Zenon, serve their member organizations in an office Hemelrijk proposes was distinct from an external patron (Hemelrijk 2008). Kloppenborg has already observed a distinction between patrons and mothers/fathers on the question of participation in the collegium (Kloppenborg 1996, 25). Hemelrijk concurs: patrons giving benefactions did not participate, but mothers and fathers participated and supported financially. Salvia Marcellina's *mater* role included her regular participation with the association, receiving her *sportula* alongside the president, father, other leaders, and members.

In a second distinction, women patrons were normally elite women; mothers, by contrast, possessed wealth but were non-elite (Hemelrijk 2008, 141). Elite women's ranks alone may have merited their recruitment as patrons, with their names seemingly the main "donations." Assessing the inscriptional evidence, Hemelrijk argues convincingly:

---

[17] Hemelrijk 2008, 144–45 (patrons of collegia); 2012, 203 (mothers of cities), 207 (mothers of associations).

[18] Hemelrijk 2012, 204–7. "Mother" appears a few times with cities, most often applied to imperial family members.

In respect of their benefactions and the public honor they enjoyed, patronesses and "mothers" of *collegia* were poles apart: patronesses left hardly any record of tangible benefactions, but almost all of them were publicly honored. By contrast, despite her benefactions no "mother" seems to have enjoyed public honor. Public honor, it appears, was closely bound up with high social standing but only indirectly related to tangible benefactions. (2008, 127)

Thus, patrons might not always contribute funds but would bring honor through connection to their family name. In return, they were publicly honored: eighteen (possibly twenty) of the women patrons, both of cities and of associations, were honored with statues in their likeness on public display (Hemelrijk 2004, 236–37; 2008, 148–50). Mothers, on the other hand, benefited groups by means of their gifts and their involvement with those groups, and their honors were privately exhibited.

A final distinction between patrons and mothers of collegia lies in the formalities of their elections. The normal procedure was to be "co-opted," or elected to a position by public request of the association, modeled after municipal procedures.[19] Patrons and mothers were both co-opted, but only patrons received a *tabula patronatus* from a delegation. Mothers usually did not receive the permanent patron's plaque. Commemoration of their honor as mothers came through inscriptions displayed in the association's meeting venue. These drew attention to their gifts more than to their person. Some of the mothers, like Salvia Marcellina, erected statues as donations; Marcellina's donation gifted an Aesculapius statue. Other mothers donated statues or altars, but the statues were of objects of worship or of other honored individuals, not representations of the mothers (Hemelrijk 2008, 126–27).

Based on Hemelrijk's research, three distinctions between patrons and mothers emerge, all of which may prove useful in comparison to women in Christ groups. First, patrons were external donors, but mothers were both benefactors and participants in a collegium. Second, patrons were from the elite classes, but mothers were non-elite women with wealth. Third, patrons and mothers were both co-opted, but patrons received an official tablet marking their patronage, and statues were often modeled after them for public display; associational inscriptions recorded mothers' elections, and any involved statues were gifts by mothers honoring others, whether gods or persons.

---

[19]   Kloppenborg (1996, 26) notes the imitation of the cities.

Before proceeding to consider women in early Christ groups, it would be wise to consider potential objections. First, Salvia Marcellina's inscription dates from the mid-second century. Since the Christ groups depicting women leaders appear in literary sources earlier than that, can a mid-second century inscription provide a relevant comparison? Yes, precisely because there are early sources (as well as later ones) testifying to the same phenomenon across a broad temporal spectrum. Hemelrijk's overall summary of 363 Latin inscriptions about women benefactors indicates the following: fewer than 10 are first century BCE; around 65 are first century CE; about 115 are second century CE; and about 80 are third century CE.[20] Her conclusion is "female munificence did indeed start late" relative to male benefaction, but it was established before the second century CE (Hemelrijk 2013, 70). In the Greek East, according to van Bremen, it may have operated earlier, with a few records of women's civic benefactions from the second century BCE and increasing thereafter (1996, 298–300). The influence of Metrodora and Euaxis in their group would be one such early example. In sum, numerous examples of women benefactors are attested before and contemporaneous to the women of early Christ groups, and attestation of female benefaction increases in the second and third centuries.

The second anticipated objection is whether an admittedly remarkable example enables analogy. Salvia Marcellina's gift was unusually large, and her influence in her collegium probably great enough to have shaped its bylaws to her conditions. Using her example for comparison, however, does not require suggesting that all women benefactors were as influential as she. Instead, her example allows for broadening the range of potential activities. Without unambiguous attestation from Christian literature or other evidence, definitive statements cannot be made about women of Christ groups creating membership limits or bylaws. Yet women doing so in other organizations show what was plausible. Comparisons to Salvia Marcellina, other mothers in collegia, attendants like Metrodora, and women patrons like Ancharia Luperca facilitate envisioning women's benefactions, leadership roles, and influence as they overlapped in early Christ groups.

WOMEN IN EARLY CHRIST GROUPS

Women played significant roles in the early Christian movement, with their roles in Acts and the Pauline Epistles long under discussion. Phoebe

---

[20] Hemelrijk 2013, 69, fig. 2. My totals are estimated from Hemelrijk's bar graph. Thirty to thirty-five inscriptions are undated. Elsewhere, Hemelrijk 2004, 238, gives precise data for a set of city patrons; Hemelrijk 2008, 144–45, 151–52, gives precise data for sets of women patrons and mothers of collegia.

is a sister, διάκονος of the Cenchreae assembly, προστάτις of Paul and others (Rom 16:1-2). Mary of Jerusalem and Lydia of Philippi appear in Acts hosting early assemblies, with Lydia also sponsoring Paul's ministry (Acts 12:12-17; 16:14-15, 40). Priscilla, a teacher, also accommodates a group at home (Rom 16:3-5; 1 Cor 16:19). Nympha seems to host a Christ group in Laodicea (Col 4:15); Apphia may serve a role in her local assembly (Phlm 2). Paul references other women vaguely, including Euodia and Syntyche (Phil 4:2-3); Tryphaena, Tryphosa, and Persis (Rom 16:12), all of whom may be leaders of Christ groups or "workers" (Rom 16:12) for their benefit.

For each of these women, Hemelrijk's analysis (outlined above) enables us to think in fresh terms about their roles in early Christian assemblies. In what follows, I will utilize Hemelrijk's insights regarding the role of the "mothers" of associations, a heuristic that easily lends itself to amplifying how we imagine these women functioning in Christ groups.

Since some Christ assemblies likely met in homes, the household setting may have been a significant factor "conducive to their leadership," because ancient women routinely managed household affairs.[21] While a supposed polarity between public and private life for ancient women used to be the prevailing opinion, recent scholarship highlights the permeable boundaries between public and private spheres in antiquity.[22] Business often transpired within the house, and household roles shaped public life. The affection and relationality of the family was projected into public life: family titles became used for municipal roles and symbolized the imperial family's ties to citizens (Hemelrijk 2012, 212). Thus the groups that met in houses can be considered as occupying a kind of liminal space, dwelling at the "crossroads between public and private" (Osiek and MacDonald 2006, 4). Most women named in connection with Christ groups in the New Testament are either described as women with groups meeting in their homes, or they are praised for their work. Neither situation provides satisfying detail about how they functioned in the assemblies. Still, scholars have probed the available data, attempting to understand the roles of these influential women. After first surveying current scholarship, this section will proceed to ponder how Salvia Marcellina and the mothers of collegia may illuminate further potentialities.

In Jerusalem, believers gathered for prayer at Mary's house (Acts 12:12). Peter expected to find fellow believers there, and the narrative has the

---

[21] Hylen 2018, 33. Cf. also Adams 2013 for the likelihood of other meeting places.
[22] For more on the public/private division, see Osiek and MacDonald 2006, 3–4.

community gathered there during the crisis of his imprisonment.[23] The house's linkage only to Mary—not to a husband—implies she is probably widowed and is connected to her well-known son, John Mark (Gaventa 2003, 185; Parsons 2008, 176). Perhaps she can host a Christ group because of her wealth (Miller 2017, 206).

Lydia of Philippi represents the success of Paul's Macedonian outreach (Acts 16:14-15, 40).[24] Her enthusiastic response to the gospel spurs her to host an assembly and to sponsor Paul's ministry. She may or may not have been a freedperson; her occupation and name have been tied to enslavement.[25] Her household's baptism together with her probably signals her independent leadership of it (Hylen 2018, 130). Lydia's involvement in the dyeing trade may have made her wealthy, or she may have had moderate assets.[26] She possessed enough to host Paul and those with him; Mikeal Parsons concludes that she appears to be of low rank but high income (Parsons 2008, 230). With no connections to relatives, her occupation gives her identifying information.

Prisca (known as Priscilla in the book of Acts) hosts an assembly with her husband Aquila in their home (1 Cor 16:19) and works alongside him and Paul "in Christ Jesus" (Rom 16:3).[27] According to Acts, she and Aquila are tentmakers like Paul (Acts 18:3), and they teach Apollos "more accurately" about the "Way of God" (Acts 18:26; see Haenchen 1971, 534). They travel and support themselves; they may initiate and host new Christ groups regularly (Schüssler Fiorenza 1986, 429; cf. Jewett 2007, 957). They have funds to travel and provide meeting space for an assembly, but their trade is non-elite (Jewett 2007, 956; Lampe 2003, 195). They may have been formerly enslaved, with Latin names that were often used for enslaved people (Lampe 2003, 181; cf. also Jewett 2007, 955). Since Prisca's name usually precedes Aquila's (Acts 18:18, 26; Rom 16:3; 2 Tim 4:19), she is more prominent, whether in leadership or social standing.[28] Paul says they intervened to rescue him from danger (Rom 16:4).[29] Their ability to

---

[23] Osiek and MacDonald 2006, 157. There were surely other places of Christian gatherings in Jerusalem. See Adams 2013, 119–200 for a summary of possible location types.

[24] Gaventa (2003, 236) traces this ironic observation to Calvin. Paul's vision expected a Macedonian man. No male Macedonian converts are named, and Lydia is not Macedonian.

[25] See Parsons 2008, 230. Solin (2003, 1:609) names one Lydia, classified as uncertain, not identifiably servile.

[26] On the possibilities, see Gaventa 2003, 237. Cf. Haenchen 1971, 494.

[27] Hylen 2018, 87. MacDonald (1999, 202) observes that only Acts specifies their married relationship.

[28] Jewett (2007, 955) favors social standing.

[29] For possible scenarios, see Fitzmyer 1998, 735. Cf. Wilckens 1978, 134.

intervene suggests influential relationships in the public sphere (Jewett 2007, 957). Prisca exemplifies Roman marital ideals operating alongside women's leadership (Hylen 2018, 87).

Phoebe, as a διάκονος of the Christ group in Cenchreae, is also a well-resourced woman, serving as the personal patron to many people and to Paul himself (πολλῶν . . . καὶ ἐμοῦ; Rom 16:1-2).[30] Phoebe's acclamation by Paul does not supply further information about a father or spouse. She seems to have the money to travel from Cenchreae to Rome (presumably supporting a small entourage to accompany her), and Paul entrusts her with the delivery of his letter to the Christ groups in Rome. In this role, she may also have been the one to read the letter to them, perhaps even serving an interpretative role in its delivery and dissemination (see Gaventa 2016, 12–14).

Relatively little is known about other women associated with Christ groups in the New Testament, apart from names and a single phrase about each of them. Nympha has a Christ group meeting in her Laodicean house (Col 4:15; see MacDonald 2005). Chloe is connected to those who alert Paul to conflicts among Corinth's Christ followers. The meaning of "Chloe's people" (1 Cor 1:11) is debated, a possible conclusion being that they were members of a Christ group she led, but with alternate suggestions that she was entirely uninvolved (Osiek and MacDonald 2006, 9–10; Conzelmann 2016, 82). Euodia and Syntyche labor together with Paul and other co-workers, possibly alluding to evangelism or service to Philippian believers (Phil 4:2-3; Reumann 2008, 610; cf. Holloway 2017, 181–82). Similarly, Tryphaena, Tryphosa, and Persis are all praised for being hardworking in the faith, maybe connecting them to evangelism (Rom 16:12; see Schüssler Fiorenza 1986, 430). The latter three women have names frequent among the formerly enslaved, so it is possible that they are freedwomen (Jewett 2007, 968; Lampe 2003, 169, 183; Solin 2003, 1:619; 2:783, 787). Apphia may serve a leadership role in her local assembly, whether she is wife of the slavekeeper Paul addresses (Philemon) or a woman otherwise connected to the ministry (Phlm 1-2; see Winter 2004, 126–28).

Connecting these women of Christ groups to Salvia Marcellina and women benefactors corroborates elements of existing scholarship. Additionally, based on Marcellina's example, "mothers" of collegia are promising for comparison to women's roles in Christian associations. Against

---

[30] A case might be made that Phoebe was an associational patron in addition to a personal patron to Paul. I do not entertain that scenario in this essay, since Phoebe's case requires more extensive treatment. My ongoing research involves addressing her situation more fully.

interpreters who would assume, without clear evidence, that the named women of Christ groups served differently than men because of their sex, Osiek and MacDonald proceed from the reasonable assumption that women of Christ groups participated in every aspect of the house churches' functioning (Osiek and MacDonald 2006, 9). This coheres with data about mothers actively participating within their collegia; the comparison to collegia mothers thus supports Osiek and MacDonald's overall argument. If Prisca, Phoebe, Lydia, and Mary were women of wealth but no rank, they are comparable to Salvia Marcellina. Benefactions to assemblies converted their wealth to honor; when Paul bestows high praise, these women are among the recipients. References to family members are elided for Phoebe, Lydia, and Mary, and Prisca's name precedes Aquila's; all four cases match patterns for women unable to claim titles.

Considering leading women in Christ groups analogous to collegia mothers offers new windows into their potential influence. Just as Marcellina influenced the bylaws of an assembly, so also leading women in Christ groups may have done the same. Just as Marcellina shaped distributions by the collegium, so also leading women in Christ groups may have been involved in financial planning for group meals, banquets, and later eucharistic practices.[31] Just as Marcellina may have delimited the membership numbers and participation terms, so also leading women in Christ groups could have helped to determine similar membership expectations. Perhaps, given Marcellina's exceptional benefaction, only the wealthiest women in Christ groups—Prisca, Phoebe, Mary, or Lydia—would have managed such group organization. Nevertheless, with the impression of Salvia Marcellina's latitude in setting her collegium's standards, there are concrete suggestions for additional ways that the women in the earliest Christ assemblies may have helped to shape their operations.

CONCLUSION

In the associative social context where early Christ groups flourished, epigraphic evidence allows ongoing comparisons using emerging data about women benefactors. Salvia Marcellina's inscription shows the extent of a wealthy, non-elite woman's imprint on her collegium, even as the only woman participating in it. Metrodora's cultic association from an earlier period demonstrates another occasion when associational rules were reshaped around important women. Contrasts with patronage co-optation

---

[31] Alikin (2010) compares associational banquets and Christian meetings.

for Ancharia Luperca and Hemelrijk's astute proposal for two distinct offices for women benefactors suggest analogously distinct roles for women benefactors in early Christ groups: the external patron and the participant mother. Recruited patrons are elite women co-opted with a patron's plaque, often with an honorific statue. Collegia mothers are elected from the non-elite wealthy, recorded in associational inscriptions, and sometimes gave statues or altars.

In this essay, I have focused on women mentioned in relation to New Testament Christ groups who seem to be fitting counterparts to *matres collegiorum*, serving in localized participatory leadership, joining from the non-elite wealthy, and possibly recruited by a group anticipating benefactions. Commensurate to their investments, the women's views may have helped to determine the groups' plans, established membership expectations and caps, and executed financial oversight.

WORKS CITED

Adams, Edward. 2013. *The Earliest Christian Meeting Places: Almost Exclusively Houses?* Early Christianity in Context. LNTS 450. London: Bloomsbury T&T Clark.

Alikin, Valeriy A. 2010. *The Earliest History of the Christian Gathering: Origin, Development and Content of the Christian Gathering in the First to Third Centuries.* VCSup 102. Leiden: Brill.

Ascough, Richard S., Philip A. Harland, and John S. Kloppenborg. 2012. *Associations in the Greco-Roman World: A Sourcebook.* Waco, Tex.: Baylor University Press.

van Bremen, Riet. 1996. *The Limits of Participation: Women and Civic Life in the Greek East in the Hellenistic and Roman Periods.* Amsterdam: J. C. Gieben.

Conzelmann, Hans. 2016. *1 Corinthians: A Commentary on the First Epistle to the Corinthians.* Philadelphia: Fortress.

Dixon, Suzanne. 2001. *Reading Roman Women: Sources, Genres, and Real Life.* London: Duckworth.

Fitzmyer, Joseph A. 1998. *The Acts of the Apostles: A New Translation with Introduction and Commentary.* AB 31. New York: Doubleday.

Flexsenhar, Michael. 2019. *Christians in Caesar's Household: The Emperors' Slaves in the Makings of Christianity.* Inventing Christianity. University Park: Pennsylvania State University Press.

Gaventa, Beverly Roberts. 2003. *The Acts of the Apostles.* ANTC. Nashville: Abingdon.

———. 2016. *When in Romans: An Invitation to Linger with the Gospel according to Paul.* Theological Explorations for the Church Catholic. Grand Rapids: Baker Academic.

González, Julián. 1986. "The Lex Irnitana: A New Copy of the Flavian Municipal Law." *JRS* 76:147–243.

Haenchen, Ernst. 1971. *The Acts of the Apostles: A Commentary*. Translated by Basil Blackwell. Philadelphia: Westminster.

Hemelrijk, Emily A. 2004. "City Patronesses in the Roman Empire." *Historia* 53:209–45.

———. 2008. "Patronesses and 'Mothers' of Roman *Collegia*." *ClAnt* 27:115–62.

———. 2012. "Fictive Motherhood and Female Authority in Roman Cities." *Eugesta* 2:201–20.

———. 2013. "Female Munificence in the Cities of the Latin West." Pages 65–84 in *Women and the Roman City in the Latin West*. Edited by Emily A. Hemelrijk and Greg Woolf. Leiden: Brill.

———. 2015. *Hidden Lives, Public Personae: Women and Civic Life in the Roman West*. New York: Oxford University Press.

Holloway, Paul A. 2017. *Philippians: A Commentary*. Hermeneia. Minneapolis: Fortress.

Hylen, Susan E. 2018. *Women in the New Testament World*. Essentials of Biblical Studies. Oxford: Oxford University Press.

Jewett, Robert. 2007. *Romans: A Commentary*. Edited by Eldon Jay Epp. Hermeneia. Minneapolis: Fortress.

Kloppenborg, John S. 1996. "Collegia and *Thiasoi*: Issues in Function, Taxonomy and Membership." Pages 16–30 in *Voluntary Associations in the Graeco-Roman World*. Edited by John S. Kloppenborg and Stephen G. Wilson. London: Routledge.

———. 2019. *Christ's Associations: Connecting and Belonging in the Ancient City*. New Haven: Yale University Press.

Kloppenborg, John S., and Richard S. Ascough, eds. 2011. *Attica, Central Greece, Macedonia, Thrace*. BZNW 181. Vol. 1 of *Greco-Roman Associations: Texts, Translations, and Commentary*. Edited by John S. Kloppenborg and Richard S. Ascough. Berlin: De Gruyter.

Lampe, Peter. 2003. *From Paul to Valentinus: Christians at Rome in the First Two Centuries*. Edited by Marshall D. Johnson. Translated by Michael Steinhauser. Minneapolis: Fortress.

Liu, Jinyu. 2004. "Occupation, Social Organization, and Public Service in the *Collegia Centonariorum* in the Roman Empire (First Century BC–Fourth Century AD)." PhD diss., Columbia University.

———. 2007. "The Economy of Endowments: The Case of the Roman Collegia." Pages 231–56 in *Pistoi dia tèn technèn: Bankers, Loans and Archives in the Ancient World: Studies in Honour of Raymond Bogaert*. Edited by Koenraad Verboven, Katelijn Vandorpe, and Véronique Chankowski. Studia Hellenistica 44. Leuven: Peeters.

MacDonald, Margaret Y. 1999. "Reading Real Women through the Undisputed Letters of Paul." Pages 199–220 in *Women and Christian Origins*. Edited by Ross Shepard Kraemer and Mary Rose D'Angelo. New York: Oxford University Press.

———. 2005. "Can Nympha Rule This House? The Rhetoric of Domesticity in Colossians." Pages 99–120 in *Rhetoric and Reality in Early Christianities*. Edited by Willi Braun. Studies in Christianity and Judaism. Waterloo, Ont.: Wilfrid Laurier University Press.

Miller, Amanda C. 2017. "Cut from the Same Cloth: A Study of Female Patrons in Luke–Acts and the Roman Empire." *RevExp* 114:203–10.

Osiek, Carolyn, and Margaret Y. MacDonald. 2006. *A Woman's Place: House Churches in Earliest Christianity*. Minneapolis: Fortress.

Parsons, Mikeal C. 2008. *Acts*. Paidea. Grand Rapids: Baker Academic.

Reumann, John Henry Paul. 2008. *Philippians: A New Translation with Introduction and Commentary*. AB 33B. New Haven: Yale University Press.

Schenk, Christine. 2017. *Crispina and Her Sisters: Women and Authority in Early Christianity*. Minneapolis: Fortress.

Schüssler Fiorenza, Elisabeth. 1986. "Missionaries, Apostles, Coworkers: Romans 16 and the Reconstruction of Women's Early Christian History." *WW* 6:420–33.

Solin, Heikki. 2003. *Die griechischen Personennamen in Rom. Ein Namenbuch*. Rev. ed. 3 vols. Berlin: De Gruyter.

Wilckens, Ulrich. 1978. *Der Brief an die Römer*. EKK 6. Zürich: Benziger.

Winter, Sara B. C. 2004. "Philemon and the Patriarchal Paul." Pages 122–36 in *A Feminist Companion to Paul*. Edited by Amy-Jill Levine and Marianne Blickenstaff. London: T&T Clark.

Witherington, Ben. 1991. *Women in the Earliest Churches*. SNTSMS 59. Cambridge: Cambridge University Press.

11

Aid among Greco-Roman Associations and Christ Groups

Robert E. Moses

In his influential 1895 essay "The Roman Guilds and Charity," Jean-Pierre Waltzing argued that Roman guilds served two main functions for their members: providing a space for the private worship of a god and assisting with the funeral rites of members (1895, 346–47). On the question of charity, Waltzing argued that charity is the legacy of the Christian religion and, since the Roman guilds were not "animated by the Christian spirit," they did not become charitable associations (1895, 361). Modern scholarship, while more nuanced in its approach than Waltzing, has not detected significant charitable initiatives among Greco-Roman associations compared to their Christians counterparts (e.g., Meggitt 1998; Lieu 2004; van der Horst 2016). In their recent work, however, Richard Last and Philip Harland (2020) seek to challenge what they see as an oversimplified contrast between Christ groups and Greco-Roman associations on the subject of care for the poor and mutual assistance. Last and Harland insist that terms such as "charity" and "almsgiving" are unhelpful categories that unfairly stack the deck in favor of the distinctiveness of Jewish groups and Christ groups (2020, 153). They argue that when we employ "neutral terms," such as "mutual aid," "mutual assistance," and "socioeconomic assistance," we will discover that "mutual socioeconomic assistance" was an important principle that was practiced by Jewish and Christ groups and substantial numbers of associations in the eastern Mediterranean (2020, 153). The goal in this essay is to sift through some of the evidence. Our aim is to identify places where aid practices by Christ groups converged with that of Greco-Roman associations, but also where these groups diverged in their practices. We acknowledge with Last and Harland that there were more convergences between Christ groups and Greco-Roman associations than modern scholarship has been willing to allow. However, we also argue that there were significant differences that should allow for the acknowledgment of unique aspects of the aid provided by the Christ groups. In short, we hope to demonstrate that the Christ groups and Greco-Roman associations converged in their practices of in-group support, such as providing burial assistance and bail for prisoners. Nonetheless, the Christ groups' care for what this essay terms "the Old Testament cluster of the vulnerable" (i.e., the poor, widows, orphans, strangers) was not a concern among Greco-Roman associations. We hope to show that, despite the convergences, the Christ groups were engaged in practices that went beyond "mutual aid."

IN-GROUP AID

No group would survive without trust and cohesion. One of the ways to build trust and cohesion is to offer support and assistance to group members who have fallen on hard times. Indeed, it is difficult to see why anyone would define their identity with a group if they do not feel supported by the group, especially during times of difficulty. In-group assistance in times of difficulty creates a sense of responsibility among members and sustains a shared sense of community spirit. In this regard, Greco-Roman associations and early Christ groups were no different. Both groups provided assistance and support to members during times of difficulty. On a papyrus from Tebtynus, Egypt (ca. 145 BCE), is written a rule for members of an association in the region: "The man among us who finds a man among us at the landing post or such a place saying, 'Give to me because of my misfortune,' and he does not give to him, his fine is 25 deben [= 500 drachmas] unless he swears before Sobek saying, 'I could not have given to him'" (*PCair* 2.30605, ll. 22–24; translation in Monson 2006, 229; Spiegelberg 1908, 23; Cenival 1972, 73–78; Last and Harland 2020, 158). Members of this association are mandated to aid fellow members who find themselves in difficulty. The mandate is not dissimilar from the apostle Paul's call to believers in Galatia, "So then, whenever we have an opportunity, let us work for the good of all, and especially for those of the family of faith"

(Gal 6:10).[1] Paul admonishes the Galatians to do good to all people, but especially to members of the Christ group ("family of faith"). Unlike the group in Tebtunis, Paul's admonishment does not come with the threat of a fine. But the underlying message is similar; members of the same group should support and assist one another. In-group assistance among Greco-Roman associations came in several forms, ranging from burial assistance and bail for prisoners to loans. In the rest of this section, we briefly compare these forms of aid to the practices of the Christ groups.

Burial Assistance

Decades before Waltzing wrote his essay, Theodor Mommsen had observed that associations offered aid to their members by covering their funeral expenses (1843, 91). As already noted above, Waltzing argued that one of the main functions of Roman guilds was to provide burial assistance to members. Waltzing, however, was not willing to grant to Mommsen that this sort of assistance constituted "charitable" works (1895, 348). Adopting the language of Last and Harland, burial assistance for members of a group may be considered mutual assistance, for it benefits the group as a whole by building trust and cohesion among group members. Regulations for associations often list funeral assistance at the time of a member's death and support for the family. A demotic Egyptian text from the Ptolemaic period lists the rules of support for a deceased member: "The man among us who dies during the aforesaid period, we will mourn for him and give five deben [= 100 drachmas] per person for his burial and will raise ten rations of grief [for his household] and will invite his son, father, or father-in-law to drink with us in order to sooth his heart" (*PPrague*; translation in Monson 2006, 229; Last and Harland 2020, 161; cf. *PCair* 2.30605; *IG* II[2] 1368, l. 159; Kloppenborg and Ascough 2011, 248). Members of associations could expect assistance for their burial from the group. Such assistance was at times drawn from the common funds, to which the deceased member had contributed with their membership dues.

Evidence for burial assistance among Christ groups in the form that we see practiced by the associations is not attested in Christian documents from the first century, but it is attested in the patristic period by writers like Aristides and Tertullian. Writing in the second century CE, the Christian apologist Aristides sought to enlighten the authorities about the true character of Christianity. Among Christianity's many virtues Aristides lists burial assistance:

---

[1]   Unless otherwise indicated, translations of biblical texts are taken from the NRSV.

"They love one another; and from the widows they do not turn away their countenance; and they rescue the orphan from him who does violence; . . . but when one of their poor passes away from the world, and any of them sees him, then he provides for his burial according to his ability" (Aristides, *Apology* 15; translation in Harris 1891, 49). Aristides writes that the Christ groups offered burial assistance to those without the means to bury their dead. This information is confirmed by Tertullian (third century CE). In his *Apology*, Tertullian discusses the monthly voluntary donations to the "treasure-chest," money that, in his words, is used "to support and bury poor people, to supply the wants of boys and girls destitute of means and parents, and of old persons confined now to the house" (Tertullian, *Apol.* 39, ANF³ 46).

It is important to note here that, in addition to burial assistance, Aristides and Tertullian offer another way in which Christ groups supported the deceased: by helping the families of the deceased through their support of widows and orphans (so also the *Did. apost.* 17–18). Widows and orphans are part of the Old Testament cluster of the vulnerable, which also includes the poor and strangers.[2] While there is no evidence for burial assistance in the New Testament, assistance to families of the deceased is documented. According to Acts, some widows launched a complaint because they were being neglected in the daily allocation of food for widows (Acts 6:1-7). The church sought to rectify this by selecting seven men of honorable reputation to take charge of the daily food allocation. In addition, widows "had been the principal beneficiaries" of Dorcas' ministry (Bruce 1988, 199, referencing Acts 9:36-42). The writer of 1 Timothy distinguishes between older widows and younger widows, the latter of which the author suspects would be drawn to remarriage (1 Tim 5:3-16). The author admonishes members who can assist their widow relatives to do so, in order to free up the church's resources for those who are "real widows" (1 Tim 5:16), presumably those who have no relatives who can assist them. The Christ groups provided assistance when a member died by making orphans and widows a central piece of their aid. As the author of the epistle of James puts it, "Religion that is pure and undefiled before God, the Father, is this: to care for orphans and widows in their distress, and to keep oneself unstained by the world" (Jas 1:27).

Prison Bail

Members of associations who had been imprisoned could at times count on the group to come to their aid. Sometimes the aid took the form of a fellow member using their own personal funds to post bail on their behalf

---

[2] We will discuss the Old Testament cluster in detail later.

(Bauschatz 2007, 9–24; Last and Harland 2020, 159). At times, communal funds were drawn upon to help the imprisoned member. For example, a group in Ptolemaic Egypt included in its bylaws a rule to assist a member unjustly imprisoned: "The man among us who is involved in an unjust legal dispute, we will stand by him and will give him the funds that the members of the associations have agreed on in order to acquit him" (*PCair* 2.30605; translation in Monson 2006, 236; Last and Harland 2020, 159). "Stand[ing] by" the accused meant more than posting bail; the group at times raised funds for legal fees until the case was settled, brought food to the accused in prison, and volunteered to testify on behalf of the accused during the trial (*PPrague*, ll. 25–26; *PCair* 2.30619, l. 7; *GRA* III 188 = *PLilleDem* 29, ll. 14–17; Cenival 1972, 3–10; Monson 2006, 236; Last and Harland 2020, 159–60). It is important to note that some of the associations had an expectation or regulation that the expenses spent on aiding a member in legal trouble (such as posting bail) would be repaid (*PMich* 5.243, l. 9; Ascough, Harland, and Kloppenborg 2012, no. 301 = *GRA* III 212 = *PMich* 5.244, ll. 9–11; Last and Harland 2020, 163–65). In addition to the fact that prison aid was a form of assistance rendered by associations to a member in times of need, standing by an accused member may have been essential to protecting the reputation of the association. The repeated mention of the "unjust" imprisonments of fellow association members in the papyrological record (Bauschatz 2007, 9–24) may suggest that the reputation of the associations was at stake. One member of an association accused of a heinous crime could sully the reputation of the entire association. It was, therefore, incumbent upon all members to do their part to clear the accused of the charges.

It is evident from the records that the Christ groups were also concerned about their reputation. The apostle Paul decries lawsuits among Corinthian believers (1 Cor 6:1-8), citing the need for disputes to be settled within the community, rather than among unbelievers. According to Paul, the presence of lawsuits among believers is itself a "defeat" (1 Cor 6:7). He admonishes the Thessalonian believers to live a quiet life, to mind their own business, to work with their own hands so as not to be dependent on others, and to behave appropriately towards outsiders (1 Thess 4:11-12; cf. 2 Thess 3:6-14). Protecting a group's reputation against outsiders requires group cohesiveness, which in turn requires mutual assistance. Mutual assistance in the form of prison bail is not attested in the first-century Christian documents. However, Justin Martyr, Aristides, and Tertullian mention this is a practice among Christians in the patristic period (see also the *Did. apost.* 19). According to Aristides, if members of Christ groups "hear that any of their number is imprisoned or oppressed for the name of their Messiah, all of them provide for his needs, and if it is possible that he may be delivered, they deliver him" (Aristides, *Apology* 15; translation in Harris 1891, 49; so also Justin Martyr, *1 Apol.* 67). Aristides seems to suggest that aid is provided for the person imprisoned, perhaps in the form of food; and, if there is a possibility that the person may be able to be set free with their aid, they do what they can to free the prisoner. The latter may suggest that Christ groups were willing to post bail or testify in order to free one of their own from prison. Similarly, Tertullian writes that the voluntary donations in the treasure chest were drawn upon to aid prisoners: "If there happen to be any in the mines, or banished to the islands, or shut up in the prisons, for nothing but their fidelity to the cause of God's Church, they become nurslings of their confession" (Tertullian, *Apol.* 39, *ANF*[3] 46). It is possible that the funds were used for only those members who, in the view of the church, had been imprisoned unjustly for their faith. Aristides implies that the Christians come to the aid of the one "imprisoned or oppressed for the name of their Messiah," and Tertullian includes the stipulation that the cause of the imprisonment is "for nothing but their fidelity to the cause of God's Church." These caveats may be their way of defending the Christian faith against the charge that the Christians stood by convicted criminals. In their defense of Christianity both Aristides and Tertullian argue that the Christians stood by only those who had been unjustly imprisoned and oppressed. To the best of my knowledge, there is not much in the records to imply that the Christ groups required repayment of the expenses for aiding an imprisoned member—as practiced among some of the Greco-Roman associations.

Loans

In addition to burial and prison assistance, associations at times provided loans to their members. Many of these loans had to be paid back with interest, though it is possible that some of the loans were interest-free (*GRA* III 286 = *PTexas inv.* 8; Martinez and Williams 1997, 260–61; Last and Harland 2020, 160). The loans were often drawn from the common funds and had to be repaid by a certain date or else the debtor would face serious consequences. The receipts preserved on a Greek papyrus (ca. 182 or 158 BCE) from an unknown location document the terms of three loans. One lists the following agreement: "Asklepiades son of Kasas (?) to Herakles demosiarch, greetings. I agree that I have received from the common funds three thousand . . . ninety-three copper drachmae and three obols, which I will repay in the month of Mesore of the twenty-third year, and if I do not repay, you may seize me without accountability in any way you see fit. Farewell. Phamenoth" (*GRA* III 286 = *PTexas inv.* 8; translation in Martinez and Williams 1997, 260–61). The receipt does not mention interest, but other contracts list interests as high as the customary annual rate in Egypt of 24 percent (e.g., Ascough, Harland, and Kloppenborg 2012, no. 304 = *GRA* III 248 = *PRyl* 4.586, ll. 7–12; Last and Harland 2020, 161). The lack of mention of interest in the papyrus receipts leaves open the possibility that these were interest-free loans. We need to be careful, however, about arguing from silence in cases where no interests are listed; if some groups applied the interest rate of their region, then it is possible that the interest rate was standard and did not have to be mentioned. David Martinez and Mary Williams observe that the practice of giving out loans served two important functions for the associations. First, the practice was in keeping with the aims of the associations to assist its members in times of need. Second, the loans raised revenue for the associations when they were paid back with interest (Martinez and Williams 1997, 260; so also Raubitschek 1981, 98). Loans that were repaid with interest further increased the endowment of the group (Raubitschek 1981, 98).

While Christ groups also engaged in practices of mutual assistance that strengthened group cohesion, to the best of my knowledge, our extant records do not provide evidence of Christ groups issuing loans from the common funds that required repayment (at times with interest). For example, drawing on Jesus' teachings in Luke 6:32-36, the author of the Didache admonishes believers to give without expecting anything in return (Did. 1.5-6). The latter may point to an important difference between the Christ groups and the associations. The associations required dues for membership;[3] and the dues were essential to the practice of mutual assistance among the associations. It was out of the dues that funds for aid were drawn, and those who were not in good standing with respect to their dues did not qualify for much of the assistance provided by the association, including loans. An association at Liopesi in central Attica that designated itself as a "Synodos" demonstrates how essential dues were to the practice of issuing loans. According to the inscription from this group, "The dues are to be brought to the treasurer without fail for the (expenditure or for the) making of loans. He who does not bring his dues is to pay a fine double the amount. He who does not pay at all is to be expelled" (*GRA* I 50 = *SEG* 31.122; ca. 100 CE; translation in Raubitschek 1981, 96; see also *IG* II² 1298; Kloppenborg 2019, 139; Kloppenborg and Ascough 2011, 237). The transfer of dues to the group came with

---

[3]   The subject of membership dues is taken up in detail elsewhere in this volume. We address the topic only briefly in this section.

the expectation of reciprocal benefits from the group, especially in times of hardship. One could even say that, on the basis of their paid dues, association members were entitled to certain benefits. We have already noted that mutual assistance builds trust and cohesion among groups. Part of the foundation of trust for these associations would have been the assurance that one's monthly dues provided some form of safety net, which one could draw upon in times of difficulty. Without this assurance, there could be no trust, which would in turn endanger the survival of the group. The numerous rules concerning dues, which all associations had, were all part of this system of trust (cf. Monson 2006, 237). Those who had contributed could expect the group to come to their aid; but those who did not contribute their fair share should expect no such aid from the group. And this ensured fairness. Members could trust the leadership of the group to apply its rules and use its resources in a way that safeguarded against freeloading. The latter, I suggest, may reveal a fundamental difference with the Christ groups; for, as will be evident shortly, the practices of the Christ groups made it possible for freeloaders to benefit from the community's resources.

The Christ groups solicited voluntary contributions from their members. But it is perhaps best not to characterize these contributions as dues, as they were not required for membership and believers were not refused participation or support because of a lack of payment.[4] Tertullian is firm in his

---

[4]   Kloppenborg has proposed that the Christ groups had required dues based on evidence for contribution to meals among Greco-Roman associations (2019, 209–44). He demonstrates that there is a lack of clear evidence for meals provided exclusively by elite patrons or wealthy members, or for *eranos* meals, i.e., potluck-style dinners. This leaves the Christ groups with two credible models for funding meals: peer benefaction and membership dues (2019, 231). Kloppenborg is correct to reject the argument that Christ groups did not require dues, because they were drawn mostly from lower socioeconomic scales. (The apostle Paul assumes those who were extremely poor could voluntarily contribute—however small their contribution—to his collection effort [2 Cor 8:1-3].) Nonetheless, Kloppenborg has not proven that the Christ groups required the kind of dues one sees among associations—the kind of common-level material contribution from all members that was enforced with contracts detailing legitimate fines and penalties, threats of expulsion, and at times court settlements. Centuries of evidence from Christ groups has not produced any such legal obligations, because it stood against the message, principles, and ideals of the Christ groups. All groups require some type of contribution from their members. Groups are strengthened when all members are expected to contribute. Here, Kloppenborg fails to make an important distinction between material and nonmaterial contributions. The Christ groups expected all members to contribute to the community. Those who could contribute materially were expected to do so. Nonetheless, those who could not contribute materially were expected to contribute in other ways, such as intercessory prayers or thanksgiving that results in blessings for the materially generous (see, e.g., 2 Cor 9:11-15; Herm. Sim. 2.1.5–7). In short, the Christ groups required material and nonmaterial contributions from all

denial that Christ groups accepted dues. He contrasts the Christ groups with other associations in these terms: "There is no buying and selling of any sort in the things of God. Though we have our treasure-chest, it is not made up of purchase-money, as of a religion that has its price. On the monthly day, if he likes, each puts in a small donation; but only if it be his pleasure, and only if he be able: for there is no compulsion; all is voluntary. These gifts are, as it were, piety's deposit fund. For they are not taken thence and spent on feasts, and drinking-bouts, and eating-houses, but to support and bury poor people" (Tertullian, *Apol.* 39, ANF³ 46; so also Justin Martyr, *1 Apol.* 67). The passage is important for its depiction not only of the Christ groups but also of Greco-Roman associations. We have to tread carefully, as apologists tend to denigrate other groups while lifting up their own group. Tertullian's claims, however, can be checked against surviving records; and it is fair to say that his claims are borne out by surviving evidence from the associations. Associations did have a "price" for membership. Each member in an association was required to make regular material contributions to the group in terms of dues. In his study of Egyptian associations from the Ptolemaic period, Andrew Monson finds that the rules contained in the demotic texts from Tebtunis share several similarities with texts from associations in the Ptolemaic Fayyum. The accounts "list the names of the members and the amount of their total annual contribution, which they would pay in monthly installments" (Monson 2006, 223). The ledger of dues suggests that payment of dues was foundational to these associations. Almost all the associations, if not all, set rules for the payment of dues and punishments for lack of payments. Whether Tertullian is correct to characterize these as "purchase-money" is a moot point. (We have already observed that the enforcement of dues was essential to building trust in these communities.) However, the rules around payment of dues suggest that Tertullian's distinction between compulsory and voluntary payments is not farfetched.

What does one make of Tertullian's claim that other groups spend their treasury deposits on eating and drinking? This also contains an element of truth, if one does not read Tertullian as implying that associations spent all of their funds on eating and drinking. We have shown that associations drew on their funds to assist members. But one cannot deny that the funds were also drawn upon for feasting and drinking. For example, the Iobakchoi

---

members; but they did not require legally binding membership dues and initiation fees that one sees among associations. The position articulated here is not an argument from silence; it is based on centuries of extant evidence outlining the message, principles, and ideals of Christ groups.

in Attica (ca. 164–165 CE) set the "entrance fee" to join the group at "fifty denarii" and designated each member's regular contribution as "the monthly dues for wine" (*IG* II^2 1368, ll. 45–46; Kloppenborg and Ascough 2011, 246). Members who were not current on their dues were not permitted to enter the meetings or the group's "feast of the god" (*IG* II^2 1368, l. 44; Kloppenborg and Ascough 2011, 246). In the demotic rules of associations in the Ptolemaic period, Monson finds that "all the associations have rules that make members attend meetings and drink beer or wine together" (Monson 2006, 230). Monson includes a chart of fines for violating the rules of a Tebtunis association (second century BCE). The second-highest fine was for cheating on wine or beer contributions (Monson 2006, 232). The latter offense was only second in degree to cheating on your wife with another member's spouse. Tertullian is, therefore, not caricaturing associations in his characterization of their requirement for dues and their use of their dues for feasting and drinking. Thus, if Tertullian is largely correct in his depiction of the groups to which he does not belong, why should we doubt him in his assertion that the group to which he belongs does not require dues?

We noted briefly that the Christian model allowed room for freeloaders to take advantage of the group.[5] The lack of a payment requirement increased the likelihood of this possibility. The apostle Paul's repeated concern about the "idlers" (1 Thess 5:14) in the Thessalonian community should be read in this light. Paul repeatedly urged each member of the community to work hard and to take care of those among them who were "weak," that is, the economically impoverished (1 Thess 4:10-12; 5:12-14; cf. 1 Cor 1:26-29; see Beale 2003, 166; Longenecker 2010, 143; Moses 2018, 474–79). By the time of the writing of 2 Thessalonians, several "idlers" had joined the community. The apostle had strong words for these idlers:

> Now we command you, beloved, in the name of our Lord Jesus Christ, to keep away from believers who are living in idleness and not according to the tradition that they received from us. For you yourselves know how you ought to imitate us; we were not idle when we were with you, and we did not eat anyone's bread without paying for it; but with toil and labor we worked night and day, so that we might not burden any of you. This was not because we do not have that right, but in order to give you an example to imitate. For even when we were with you, we gave you this command:

---

[5] Cf. Lucian, *The Passing of Peregrinus* 13. The satirist Lucian mocks the Christians, because, in his view, they were susceptible to charlatans and tricksters infiltrating their ranks "as brothers and sisters" and absconding with the group's money.

Anyone unwilling to work should not eat. For we hear that some of you are living in idleness, mere busybodies, not doing any work. Now such persons we command and exhort in the Lord Jesus Christ to do their work quietly and to earn their own living. Brothers and sisters, do not be weary in doing good (καλοποιέω). (2 Thess 3:6-13; NRSV adapted)

The rise in idleness in the community is not easily accounted for by appealing solely to an increased obsession with eschatology. It is also likely the result of the generosity of the Christian model. Thus, Abraham Malherbe, while acknowledging that it is impossible to know with certainty how those who chose to be idle justified their decision, notes: "It is quite possible, perhaps even likely, that they presumed on the extraordinary love of the Christian community for their support" (2000, 456). Malherbe demonstrates that Paul's teachings on sacrificial and brotherly love found practical expression in the community's extension of hospitality to all, including those with no means to secure their livelihood (2000, 255–56).

Such extensive hospitality would have strained the resources of this young community. And yet Paul encourages the community not to grow weary in "doing good" (καλοποιέω; 2 Thess 3:13) and urges the idle members to seek work as their own reciprocal expression of love for the hospitality they had received from the community. The lack of dues among the Christ groups allowed for the participation of many who were destitute or near destitution; and some who came into the community would undoubtedly have tried to take advantage of the generosity of the community (cf. Did. 12.1–5; Ambrose, *Off.* 2.76). The model of the Christ groups, while inevitably focused on community members, did not exclude assistance to nonmembers. As Bruce Longenecker observes in his study of the Pauline communities, "Paul seems to have imagined that, while alleviating the needs of the poor within communities of Jesus-followers was never to be compromised, neither was that practice to be set in opposition to caring for those beyond Jesus-communities" (2010, 292). And the latter constitutes a fundamental distinction from Greco-Roman associations, whose dues requirements ensured that direct benefits went to paying members.

OTHER AID

The Jesus movement saw itself as a continuation of the story of Israel and the family of God which began with the people of Israel (see, e.g., Matt 1:1-17). The God of Israel often commanded his people to care for groups that were often vulnerable to destitution and exploitation. This Old Testament cluster of the vulnerable included the poor, the orphans, the widows, and the stranger or foreigner (e.g., Lev 19:10; 23:22; Deut 14:29; 24:19-21; 26:12-13; Jer 7:6).[6] God is so concerned about these vulnerable groups that he often ties Israel's prosperity or judgment to its treatment of these groups. The prophet Jeremiah connects preservation of the divine presence in the land and the temple to the people's treatment of the vulnerable: "For if you truly amend your ways and your doings, if you truly act justly one with another, if you do not oppress the alien, the orphan, and the widow, or shed innocent blood in this place, and if you do not go after other gods to your own hurt, then I will dwell with you in this place, in the land that I gave of old to your ancestors forever and ever" (Jer 7:5-7). The prophets of Israel often connected the prosperity of the land to how they treated the poor and vulnerable (e.g., Amos 6:4-8; 8:4-14; Isa 6:1-17; 58:6-14). Walter Brueggemann observes that "a predominant theme of the prophetic corpus is the conviction that a predatory economy that permits powerful moneyed interests to prey upon the vulnerable peasant population is unsustainable" (2016, 142). Exploitation of the vulnerable destroys the social order; and the God of Israel will not put up with it. God will bring judgment on those who are engaged in such economic practices.

The Gospel authors present the story of Jesus as a continuation of the story of Israel. Jesus stands in the tradition of the prophets by preaching good news to the vulnerable and oppressed. Like the prophet Isaiah, Jesus proclaims that "the Spirit of the Lord is upon me, because he has anointed me to bring good news to the poor. He has sent me to proclaim release to the captives and recovery of sight to the blind, to let the oppressed go free, to proclaim the year of the Lord's favor" (Luke 4:18-19; cf. Isa 61:1-2; 58:6). Jesus' ministry brings God's love and care to the vulnerable, and he commands his followers to do the same (cf. Matt 25:31-46; 6:1-4). He pronounces blessings on the poor, the hungry, and those who mourn (Luke 6:20-25). He shows concern for widows by sharply criticizing the religious elites for exploiting widows (Mark 12:38-40; cf. Luke 18:1-8; Mark 12:41-44) and raising the only son of a widow (Luke 7:11-17). Jesus warns his disciples against greed (Luke 12:13-21) and commands a rich man to sell all he has, give the money to the poor, and to "follow" Jesus, that is, become a part of a new community where his resources are put in service of the community and where his own needs are met by the community (Mark 10:17-31; cf. Hellerman 2000, 159). In this new community the rich man will gain a hundredfold in this age, including a new father (God himself), "houses, brothers and sisters, mothers and

---

6 The word *cluster* is employed here, because, as shown in the passages, these groups are often listed together in the biblical text.

children, and fields, with persecutions—and in the age to come eternal life" (Mark 10:30; cf. Reploh 1969, 206–7). Jesus sought to establish an alternative community in which each person's resources are made available for the good of the community, especially the most vulnerable in the community.[7]

The Christ groups that followed also showed concern for vulnerable groups. Luke presents the Christian community as sharing their possessions with one another in order to provide for the needs of the poor among them (Acts 4:32-37; 6:1-6). Critical to Paul's ministry was a passionate concern for the poor, embodied in his collection ministry to poor believers in Jerusalem (Gal 2:10). He appealed to different congregations, from Macedonia to Achaia to Rome (Rom 15:25-27; 1 Cor 16:1-4), to contribute to this mission to the poor believers in Jerusalem. It is the case that some of Paul's congregations were in a better position financially than others. Paul, however, appeals to even churches like the Macedonian congregations, which he characterizes as having "extreme poverty" (2 Cor 8:2), to contribute to this collection ministry to poor saints in Jerusalem. The collection ministry was part of a larger theological vision, rooted in Judaism and the ministry of Jesus, that made caring for the vulnerable central to the worship of the God of Israel. Paul promoted care for the poor as integral to the theology and practices of those communities that claimed to follow the Son of God (cf. Longenecker 2010, 135–56). Some of the communities at times fell short of the ideal (e.g., 1 Cor 11:17-34); however, it cannot be denied that care for the vulnerable was important to the identity of the Christ groups as worshippers of the God of Israel. They cared for widows (Acts 6:1-7; 9:36-42; 1 Tim 5:3-16) and orphans (Jas 1:27), welcomed strangers without regard for their status or formal processes that required payment (Jas 2:1-7; Gal 4:13-14; 1 Cor 14:23-25; Did. 4.8; 12.2), and they "remember[ed] the poor" (Gal 2:10; Acts 20:35; 2 Cor 8–9; Jas 2:5-7, 14-17). And as Justin Martyr, Aristides, and Tertullian have revealed, such concern for the vulnerable continued into the postapostolic period.

CONCLUSION

If the Christ groups and Greco-Roman associations both engaged in mutual assistance, then it matters significantly where they diverged. If the Christ groups showed concern for any of the Old Testament cluster of the vulnerable, it would mean they were engaged in practices that went beyond "mutual

---

[7]   The ideas mentioned in this paragraph have been developed in detail in my book *Jesus and Materialism in the Gospel of Mark: Traveling Light on the Way* (Lanham, Md.: Lexington Books / Fortress Academic, 2022).

assistance." We struggle in our attempts to characterize the practices of the Christ groups. Calling it "charity" may be an oversimplification, if by charity we mean top-down assistance, whereby the wealthy or economically secure donated to the needy. Indeed, if we are to take Paul at his word that the Macedonian churches were extremely poor (2 Cor 8:2)—and we have no strong reason to doubt him, as a trip to Macedonia by a member of the Corinthian church would have undermined Paul's collection effort—then it shows that even poor members of the Christ groups found ways to contribute (materially and spiritually) to the needy (see Buell 2008; Downs 2011; Schellenberg 2018). In the words of Aristides, "If there is among them [the Christ groups] a man that is poor or needy, and they have not an abundance of necessaries, they fast two or three days that they may supply the needy with their necessary food" (Aristides, *Apology* 15; translation in Harris 1891, 49; cf. Herm. Sim. 5.3.6). The testimony of Aristides is significant here, for it shows that the poor were determined to contribute materially to the community and found creative ways to do so. Lastly, to all the evidence (OT, NT, patristic) should be added the testimony of outsiders, those who cannot be accused of having Christian bias. The emperor Julian (fourth century CE), even amidst his crusade against Christianity, had to admit that the Christians did good by offering aid to the poor. The emperor writes, "For it is disgraceful that, when no Jew ever has to beg, and the impious Galileans [i.e., Christians] support not only their own poor but ours as well, all men see that our people lack aid from us" (Julian, *Letter* 22, in Wright 1923, 71).

WORKS CITED

Ascough, Richard S., Philip A. Harland, and John S. Kloppenborg. 2012. *Associations in the Greco-Roman World: A Sourcebook*. Waco, Tex.: Baylor University Press.

Bauschatz, John. 2007. "Ptolemaic Prisons Reconsidered." *Classical Bulletin* 83:3–48.

Beale, G. K. 2003. *1–2 Thessalonians*. IVP New Testament Commentary Series 13. Downers Grove, Ill.: InterVarsity Press.

Bruce, F. F. 1988. *The Book of the Acts*. Rev. ed. NICNT. Grand Rapids: Eerdmans.

Brueggemann, Walter. 2016. *Money and Possessions*. Interpretation. Louisville: Westminster John Knox.

Buell, Denise Kimber. 2008. "'Be Not One Who Stretches Out Hands to Receive but Shuts Them When It Comes to Giving': Envisioning Christian Charity When Both Donors and Recipients Are Poor." Pages 37–47 in *Wealth and Poverty in Early Church and Society*. Edited by Susan R. Holman. Holy

Cross Studies in Patristic Theology and History. Grand Rapids: Baker Academic.

Cenival, Françoise de. 1972. *Les associations religieuses en Égypte d'après les documents démotiques*. Bibliothèque d'étude 46. Cairo: Institut français d'archéologie orientale.

Downs, David J. 2011. "Redemptive Almsgiving and Economic Stratification in *2 Clement*." *JECS* 19:493–517.

Harris, J. Rendel, ed. 1891. *The Apology of Aristides on Behalf of the Christians, from a Syriac MS. Preserved on Mount Sinai*. TS 1. Cambridge: Cambridge University Press.

Hellerman, Joseph H. 2000. "Wealth and Sacrifice in Early Christianity: Revisiting Mark's Presentation of Jesus' Encounter with the Rich Young Ruler." *TJ* 21:143–64.

van der Horst, Pieter W. 2016. "Organized Charity in the Ancient World: Pagan, Jewish, Christian." Pages 116–33 in *Jewish and Christian Communal Identities in the Roman World*. Ancient Judaism and Early Christianity 94. Leiden: Brill.

Kloppenborg, John S. 2019. *Christ's Associations: Connecting and Belonging in the Ancient City*. New Haven: Yale University Press.

Kloppenborg, John S., and Richard S. Ascough, eds. 2011. *Attica, Central Greece, Macedonia, Thrace*. BZNW 181. Vol. 1 of *Greco-Roman Associations: Texts, Translations, and Commentary*. Edited by John S. Kloppenborg and Richard S. Ascough. Berlin: De Gruyter.

Last, Richard, and Philip A. Harland. 2020. *Group Survival in the Ancient Mediterranean: Rethinking Material Conditions in the Landscape of Jews and Christians*. London: T&T Clark.

Lieu, Judith M. 2004. *Christian Identity in the Jewish and Graeco-Roman World*. Oxford: Oxford University Press.

Longenecker, Bruce W. 2010. *Remember the Poor: Paul, Poverty, and the Greco-Roman World*. Grand Rapids: Eerdmans.

Malherbe, Abraham J. 2000. *The Letters to the Thessalonians: A New Translation with Introduction and Commentary*. AB 32B. New York: Doubleday.

Martinez, David, and Mary Williams. 1997. "Records of Loan Receipts from a Guild Association." *ZPE* 118:259–63.

Meggitt, Justin J. 1998. *Paul, Poverty, and Survival*. SNTW. Edinburgh: T&T Clark.

Mommsen, Theodor. 1843. *De collegiis et sodaliciis Romanorum. Accedit inscriptio Lanuvina*. Kiel: Libraria Schwersiana.

Monson, Andrew. 2006. "The Ethics and Economics of Ptolemaic Religious Associations." *Ancient Society* 36:221–38.

Moses, Robert. 2018. "Discerning the Body of Christ: Paul, Poverty and the Powers." *JSNT* 40:473–93.

Raubitschek, A. E. 1981. "A New Attic Club (ERANOS)." *J. Paul Getty Museum Journal* 9:93–98.

Reploh, K. G. 1969. *Markus, Lehrer der Gemeinde. Eine redaktionsgeschichtliche Studie zu den Jüngerperikopen des Markus-Evangeliums.* SBM 9. Stuttgart: Katholisches Bibelwerk.

Schellenberg, Ryan S. 2018. "Subsistence, Swapping, and Paul's Rhetoric of Generosity." *JBL* 137:215–34.

Spiegelberg, Wilhelm. 1908. *Die Demotischen Papyrus.* Vol. 2 of *Die Demotischen Denkmäler.* Catalogue Général des Antiquités égyptiennes du Musée du Caire 2. Strasbourg: Dumont-Shauberg.

Waltzing, Jean-Pierre. 1895. "The Roman Guilds and Charity." *Charities Review* 4:345–62.

Wright, C. W. 1923. *The Works of the Emperor Julian.* Vol. 3. New York: G. P. Putnam's Sons.

12

Burial Communities

Associations and Christ Groups

Markus Öhler

Χρυσόπαις Μενεκράτη τῷ τέκνῳ, μουλίωνι μετὰ τῶν κολληγῶν
μνείας χάριν.[1]

Cuique su(um) cip(p)o(m) ("To each his tomb") reads a graffito in the tomb
complex of the Scipiones in Rome (*CIL* 1.2.2660, possibly a modern graffito;
Volpe 2019). In Greco-Roman antiquity, the tomb was a place of remembrance designed according to specific needs, where the connection with the
world of the dead was established and ritual and representation had their
proper space.[2]

A very large proportion of preserved Greek (about 50 percent) and Latin
inscriptions (about 75 percent) come from this sepulchral context. They
range from (1) small tombstones with a few roughly engraved letters, to (2)
monumental tombs on which the merits and achievements of the deceased
person are eloquently highlighted. These epitaphs are all guided more or less
by the same principles: to save the deceased person from oblivion by stating

[1]   "Chrysopais for Menecrates, the child, the mule-driver with his colleagues, for the
sake of memory" (*IG* X,2.1s 1219; Thessalonica, 150–200 CE).
[2]   However, the vast majority of inhabitants of the Roman Empire in imperial times
were denied an individual burial place marked by a gravestone; they were buried anony-
mously in pits (*puticuli*).

his or her name, origin, profession, and relatives, and to communicate to the outside world his or her honor status and thus also that of the bereaved.

The burial, the commemoration of the dead, and the care or protection of the tomb were in most cases carried out by the family.[3] However, it is clear from both grave inscriptions and regulations that this was also part of the activities of many Greco-Roman associations.[4] It goes without saying that this was limited neither to professional associations nor to cultic or ethnically oriented communities.[5]

BURIAL AS AN ASSOCIATION SERVICE

> Clause from the decree of the Senate of the Roman People: "These shall be permitted to [. . .], convene and have a collegium: those who wish to collect a monthly fee [. . .] may gather in this collegium; but [. . .] not [. . .] in the name of this collegium except once a month for the purpose of [. . .], from which they shall be buried after their demise."[6]

In this inscription from a collegium for the worship of Diana and Antinous, a passage from a *senatus consultum* is quoted. According to this legal provision, associations were approved which, in addition to their usual gatherings, also provided funding for the burials of their members.[7] Other regulations of Greco-Roman associations also contain references to this custom.

---

[3]   It is unlikely that families and associations were in competition with each other. Burial was primarily a family affair; cf. van Nijf 1997, 33.

[4]   Instead of numerous individual references to secondary literature, here are the most important contributions on this topic: Poland 1909, 505–13; van Nijf 1997, 31–69; Dittmann-Schöne 2001, 82–93; Perry 2006, 23–60; Schrumpf 2006, 185–98; Bodel 2008, 179–235; Rebillard 2009, 37–56; Ascough 2011, 159–72; Harland 2014, 411–17; Kloppenborg 2019, 265–77; Last and Harland 2020, 93–94.

[5]   The search for specifically "religious" burial sites, including those of Jewish communities, is also superfluous for that reason; see Rebillard 2009, 13–27. Jews, too, were generally not afraid to bury their dead in the midst of pagans and Christians.

[6]   *Kaput ex s(enatus) c(onsulto) p(opuli) R(omani): | quib[us ex s(enatus) c(onsulto) coire co]nvenire collegiumq(ue) habere liceat qui stipem menstruam conferre volen[t unde fiant fune]ra in it collegium coeant neq(ue) sub specie eius collegi nisi semel in mense c[onveniant con]ferendi causa unde defuncti sepeliantur* (*ILS* 7212 = *CIL* 14.2112; Lanuvium 136 CE); trans. Bendlin 2011, 213. Corresponding statements are also found in other inscriptions, mainly from Italy (Bendlin 2011, 238, n. 69; 246).

[7]   Approvals such as the one cited here are the exception; the vast majority of associations had no official authorisation. This collegium from Lanuvium, however, had the most important man of the city, Lucius Caesennius Rufus, as its patron, so that an authorisation by the senate strengthened the reputation of the collegium and its patron. The thesis that so-called *collegia funeraticia* had a special legal status goes back to Theodor Mommsen (1843).

However, the assumption that in many cases this was the only activity of the association is incorrect, as other motives always played a role (sociability, cult, profession, etc.). Moreover, by no means all Greco-Roman associations were dedicated to the task of organizing burials.

Financing Funerals

As for other association activities, contributions were regularly collected for the burial of members. In the abovementioned association from Lanuvium, it was five asses per person, which resulted in about three hundred sesterces for a membership over a period of twenty years.[8] Of this, fifty were set aside for distribution to members attending the funeral service, with the remainder reserved for actual expenses. Similar provisions are also found in other rules and honorary inscriptions. For example, the praise for Theon, the treasurer of a thiasos in Athens, reads:

> Whereas Theon, having been appointed as the treasurer . . . has paid immediately the burial expenses for those who have died . . . [9]

However, a benefactor could also bear the costs, as attested by an honorary inscription for the treasurer Hermaios:

> . . . and also for some who had died, when the treasury had no money, he paid for the tomb so that they might be treated decently even in death.[10]

It is also documented that due to a lack of members, contributions were no longer sufficient to finance a funeral and the association was dissolved.[11] Finally, letters have been preserved from Egypt in which claims were filed by relatives for unpaid amounts for funerals of former association members.[12]

---

[8] The costs for embalming a corpse and the funeral ceremonies are enumerated in an association rule from Egypt; see *PLilleDem* 1.29 = *GRA* III 188; Pisais, 223 BCE; see also *SB* 24.16224 = *GRA* III 291; first to second century CE.

[9] ἐπειδὴ Θέων κατασταθεὶς τ[α]|μία[ς . . . δέδωκεν δὲ καὶ τοῖς μετα[λ]|[λ]άξασιν τὸ ταφικὸν παραχρῆμα (*IG* II² 1323 = *GRA* I 31; Athens, 194/193 BCE).

[10] καί τισιν τῶν ἀπογεγονότων οὐχ ὑπάρχοντος | ἀργυρίου τῶι κοινῶι προιέμενος εἰς τὴν ταφὴν τοῦ | εὐσχημονεῖν αὐτοὺς καὶ τετελευτηκότας (*IG* II² 1327 = *GRA* I 35; Piraeus, 178/177 BCE); see also *IG* II² 1277 = *GRA* I 15; Athens, 278/277 BCE.

[11] "... that now there were not sufficient funds for funerals nor did he have a single coffin" (*modoque autem neque funeraticis sufficerent neque loculum [h]aberet*) (*IDR* 1, no. 31; Alburnus Maior/Dacia, 167 CE).

[12] *PEnteuxeis* 20 = *GRA* III 189 (Fayum/Magdola, 221 BCE) and *PEnteuxeis* 21 = *GRA* III 190 (Magdola, 218 BCE). The accumulated sum for the burial (ταφικόν) could also be paid out to the owner of a corresponding receipt: *PRyl* 4.580 = *GRA* III 287; Egypt, first century BCE (here it is one hundred drachmas).

This system of accumulating a deposit—a kind of insurance—presupposed, of course, that the members of the association could in principle afford it. It is therefore likely that this practice did not primarily serve to provide burial for people who would otherwise have been left without one. This was perhaps relevant for immigrants without families or for slaves.[13] The majority of association members were interested in a larger setting for their burial, in honor and prestige, in better decoration and protection of the grave site, and in a continuing commemoration by the community.

Participation and *Memoria*

Honor and reputation were the social capital of Greco-Roman society, even after death, and the surviving relatives were particularly interested in preserving it. An honorable burial was one that took place on a large scale, to which associations, among others, contributed. It was therefore of particular importance that the members were actually present. Regulations preserved in association laws that obliged members to attend funeral ceremonies show that presence was not a self-evident fact. Accordingly, punitive provisions can be found, such as in a demotic association: it stipulated that those who were absent from the funeral should receive a fine.[14] But incentives were also given for participation: the Iobacchae promised each member a jug of wine (*IG* II² 1368 = *GRA* I 51; Athens, 164/165 CE), while the collegium for Diana and Antinous distributed fifty sesterces among the attendees (*ILS* 7212; Lanuvium, 136 CE).

Beyond these regulations, the social system of reciprocity can also be assumed as a possible background. Whoever attended the funeral of his colleague could assume that the other members would also be present, or vice versa: whoever was noted for his or her absence had to expect to be left "alone" when his or her time came to go to the underworld.

Several documents show that the deceased or their relatives arranged celebrations and rituals to commemorate them. Thus, Valeria Montana, by means of an endowment of 150 denarii, instructed the "Symposium of the God Suregethes" in Philippi to light a fire at her husband's grave on the Feast of Rosalia. Should they fail to do so, they would have to pay

---

[13] Kloppenborg and Ascough 2011, 157. It was also not necessary, of course, for members of the wealthy elite.

[14] *PCair* 30606 = *GRA* III 191 (Tebtynis, 158/157 BCE). This is also maintained in later versions of this rule: *PHambDem* 1 (151 BCE); *PCair* 31179 (147 BCE); *PCair* 30605 (145 BCE), sometimes with the extension that burials of family members must also be visited; likewise *PLilleDem* 1.29 = *GRA* III 188 (Pisais, 223 BCE); see Kloppenborg 2020, 148.

double the amount to another association.[15] In the area around Ephesus, a grain-measurer donated an amount so that an association of workers could procure wine, candles, and wreaths and hold a feast in his honor (*IEph* 3216; second to third century CE). In Hierapolis, P. Aelius Glykon Zeuxianus Aelianus engaged two artisan associations to distribute money on certain occasions. These were two Jewish holidays—the festival of Unleavened Bread and Pentecost—but also the Roman festival of the Kalends. The embeddedness of the Judean Glykon within these associations as well as within the city of Hierapolis, which received a copy of these regulations, is remarkable.[16] The leader of the Association of Hymnods from Pergamon was obliged to donate incense, and the descendants should also receive some.[17] Members of a Dionysiac club had inscribed who among them had donated money so that appropriate celebrations εἰς μνήμην ("in memory of") were held in their clubhouse.[18]

All of these festivities very likely included meals taking place at the grave, the clubhouse, or other locations. A meal at the tomb is indicated for a collegium for the veneration of Aesculapius and Hygia, to which their patroness Silvia Marcellina donates, among other things, a terrace *in quo populus collegi s.s. sepultur* ("so that the collegium can dine there"; *ILS* 7213; Rome, 153 CE).

It was one of the special honors when it was already decided during the lifetime of a member to continue to honor him or her after passing away. This is promised to Dionysodoros on Rhodes, for example:

> Let the honors begin now and continue after his death! . . . It (the association) gives to him the honors both while he is living and when he has spent life on account of the virtue and goodwill.[19]

---

[15]   *IPhilippiP* II 133/G441 = *GRA* I 69 (second to third century CE); see also *IPhilippiP* II 029/G215 (second century CE); *CIL* 3.703 (Philippi, undated); *IG* X,2.1 260 = *GRA* I 81 (Thessalonica, third century CE); *IHierapJ* 133 (after 212 CE); *IHierapJ* 195 (117–212 CE); *IKlaudiupolis* 115 (undated). The festival of Rosalia, which has been documented since the end of the first century CE, served to commemorate the dead (as did the *dies parentales*).

[16]   *IJO* 2.196 = *GRA* II 116 (Hierapolis, after 212 BCE). For a thorough discussion of this inscription, see Harland 2006.

[17]   *IPergamon* 374 = *GRA* II 111; 129–138 CE. The leader was to receive it back from a new member who succeeded the deceased. Cf. also the endowment of money for the somewhat enigmatic custom of ἀποκαυσμὸς τῶν παπων (*IHierapJ* 227; second to third century CE).

[18]   Jaccottet 2003, 2:147 (Magnesia ad Meander, second century CE).

[19]   ἀναγορεύσει τὰν τιμὰν | ἐπὶ τῶν τόπων εἰς τὸν ἀεὶ χρόνον . . . δίδωτι δὲ αὐτῶι τὰς τι‖μὰς καὶ ζῶντι καὶ μεταλλάξαντι τὸν βίον | ἀρετᾶς ἕνεκα καὶ εὐνοίας (*IG* XII,1 155; Rhodes, second century BCE). These two homages were awarded by different associations and were probably celebrated at two grave monuments in their respective gravesites; cf. Gabrielsen 1994, 152–53; Thomsen 2020, 102: "The memory of the benefactor and his areta,

The *memoria* of the deceased was, however, already maintained by the erection of funerary inscriptions alone. From Greek Boeotia, for example, inscriptions from the third to second century BCE have been preserved that quite simply state the name of the deceased and the burying association.[20] Others described more broadly the merits of the deceased, his fate, or other circumstances. In Thessalonica, the Association (δοῦμος) of the Worshippers of Aphrodite Epiteuxidia commemorated one of its members who had died far away.[21] And from Bithynia comes an inscription of a Dionysiac association with a relief that might represent the deceased as charioteer and performer of Pan in the mystery play.[22]

For the relatives, the honors (whether modest or elaborate) bestowed by the association were important for their own status, and this was equally true for the respective associations themselves. By means of inscriptions and associated monuments, they claimed space in the public sphere, even if they had no other facilities like buildings.[23] The burial ceremony itself offered a status-securing effect if the association appeared as a unit and in great strength. In the long run, this status could be preserved if an association entrusted with it properly carried out care and protection of the gravesites.[24] Annual tributes at the grave further supported this.

---

eunoia and philodoxia, was kept alive constantly through announcement at every meeting of the association, his social importance and the gratitude owed to him by the membership being thus continuously reaffirmed."

[20] "Galatas, the Dioniousiastai buried him" (Γαλάτας· | οὗτον ἔθαψαν τὸ | Διωνιουσιαστή; *IG* VII 686 = *GRA* I 57; second century BCE); see also *SEG* 32.488 = *GRA* I 58 (Tanagra, around 100 BCE); *SEG* 26.614 = *GRA* I 59 (Aulis, early second century BCE); *TAM* 5.85 = *GRA* II 118 (145/146 CE); *IEph* 3466a (third to second century BCE); *IG* X,2,1s 1219 (Thessalonica, 150–200 CE; cited in the beginning of this paper); *IBeroeia* 372 = *GRA* I 64 (second century CE); and many more.

[21] *SEG* 42.625 = *GRA* I 75 (90–91 CE). The first half of the inscription is however dedicated to the officials (archisynagogos, secretary, treasurer). The problem of an out-of-town death is also considered in association rules to clarify the question of financing such burials; e.g., in *PCair* 30606 = *GRA* III 191 (Tebtynis, 158/157 BCE) or *ILS* 7212 (Lanuvium, 136 CE).

[22] *IPrusaOlymp* 159; around 200 CE; for a picture, see AGRW 102, https://philipharland.com/greco-roman-associations/grave-prepared-by-fellow-initiates-with-relief/.

[23] Van Nijf 1997, 54: "Private associations used these ceremonies to present an image of themselves as well-ordered organisations." Only a fraction of the associations in a city had their own association buildings at their disposal. The majority had to rent rooms in pubs, temples, or other association buildings, or met in warehouses, outdoors, or at members' homes; see Öhler 2016.

[24] As a rule, the protection was aimed at denying burial to persons outside the association, but sometimes also to other members; see Ascough 2011, 169.

Burial Places

In the Greco-Roman world of the imperial period, burial sites were mostly located along the roads outside the city limits. They served equally as places of remembrance and as opportunities for the representation of families and associations. In the Greek area, some inscriptions have survived that show that associations had their own burial places. For Rhodes, among other things, there is evidence of the ownership of a plot that served for the burial of members of the Aphrodisiastai Hermogeneioi.[25] Certain areas could also be marked by so-called horos inscriptions, like on the island of Kos.[26]

In the west of the empire, this practice was even more widespread. Iulia Monime and others sold a precisely described plot of land on the Via Appia in Rome for the symbolic price of one sestertius to an association of Silvanus worshippers so that they could bury their members there.[27] According to Roman law, however, it was not the collegium as a corporate body that owned the land; instead, the individual members had shares in it, even though this arrangement probably had little significance in reality.[28]

In this regard, the columbaria should also be mentioned, of which numerous examples can be attributed to associations. The majority and the largest of these complexes are located in the city of Rome, which is related to the rather limited space for burials in this city of over a million inhabitants.[29] Three types of columbaria can be distinguished here: Some belonged to large households, in which all relatives were buried. They were practically family tombs. In others, only the urns of slaves and freedmen of a household were buried, but not those of the family members themselves.[30] In the third

---

[25] SEG 65.651 (late second century BCE); see also GRA I 57–59 (Boeotia, third to first century BCE).

[26] Paton and Hicks 1891, nos. 156–59; Bosnakis 2008, no. 276 (Kos, first century CE).

[27] CIL 6.10231 = ILS 7313 (Rome, 71–130 CE); cf. CIL 6.10234 = ILS 7213 (Rome, 153 CE), according to which a plot of land on the Via Appia was likewise donated to the collegium. The regulations of this association also stipulate that relatives or freed persons of members can be buried there if the corresponding contribution is paid; see, e.g., Rebillard 2009, 41.

[28] Cf. Bodel 2008, 230, referring to Dig. 47.22.1.2 and 47.22.3. pr (Marcianus); Osiek 2008, 265.

[29] On the terminology and classification, see Bodel 2008, 195–97, 207–8. On the whole topic, see Borbonus 2014; Hasegawa 2005. Columbaria emerged in the late period of the republic from about 25 BCE and were popular until the time of Hadrian. On smaller columbaria in the Greek East, see Doulfis 2020.

[30] A well-known example of this is the household of Sergia Paullina; cf. Öhler 2016, 525–26. A comparable tomb for freedmen and slaves, donated by the leader of the synagogue Rufina, is found in Smyrna (IJO 2.43; second century CE).

type, the remains of people were buried who were connected in other ways, including through associations.

Columbaria were erected as representative buildings, and their space, even if very large, was limited.[31] The placement and design of the niches for the urns of collegium members had no hierarchical structure, but the information about the functions within the association that the deceased had held was important.[32] The administration of such columbaria was carried out by officers who were often dependent on their patron.[33]

Burial sites in general needed protection against robbery, unauthorized occupation, or damage. An association of which the deceased was a member was often held responsible for this. In addition to cursing formulae that handed over wrongdoers to the vengeance of the gods or the one god, earthly institutions such as the city or associations were also used for this purpose. One of the few Jewish inscriptions from Ephesus for example refers to οἱ Ἰουδαῖοι ("the Jews") as the group responsible for the grave of the physician Julius and his family.[34] In an inscription from Akmoneia (*IJO* 2.171, 212–295 CE), Aurelius Aristeas, son of Apollonios, states that he had paid the neighborhood to place roses on his wife's grave every year, probably on the occasion of the traditional Rosalia festival. Should this not happen, those responsible would be consigned to the justice of God (δικαιοσύνη τοῦ Θεοῦ). This phrase could refer to a Christian or to a Jew.[35] A burial place only for Judeans, which goes back to the donation of a benefactor, is attested for the first century CE in Tlos.[36] From Egypt, moreover, at least one record of a Jewish association dedicated to burial has been preserved: the συνταφιασταῖ ("fellow members of the burial society") met in the local synagogue.[37]

In communal complexes, however, it was also necessary to protect or preserve the burial ground from unauthorized reburial. An association in Cilicia, made up of immigrant craftsmen from Selge, meticulously laid

[31] The monumentum familiae Liviae, which belonged to the imperial family and was used for about seventy years, contained about 1,100 urns.

[32] Cf. Borbonus 2014, 133.

[33] Cf., e.g., *CIL* 6.10237 = *ILS* 7870 (Rome, 16 CE): the renovation and decoration of a columbarium was done by the two quastors of the collegium, two freedmen, "thanks to the kindness and generosity of their patron" (*beneficio et liberalitate T[iti] patroni*).

[34] *IJO* 2.32 (Ephesus, 150–250 CE); see also *IJO* 2.33 on the tomb of a Jewish priest (Ephesus, after 200 CE); *IJO* 1 Mac 15 = *GRA* I 82 (Thessalonica, late third century CE).

[35] See also the discussion in Harland 2014, 154–55 (with literature).

[36] *IJO* 2.223 = *GRA* II 150 (Tlos, first century CE): πάντων τῶν Ἰουδαίων. The penalty payment for infringement should go to the city of Tlos.

[37] *PRyl* 4.590 = *CPJ* 138 = *GRA* III 288 (Egypt, 51–30 BCE); cf. Williams 1994, 174; Kloppenborg 2020, 536–37.

down such rules.[38] Among other things, it stipulated that no place in the complex should be occupied without authorization. Members of the association received sixty drachmas if they did not need the spot because they had moved away. In addition, this regulation stipulated penalties to be paid to temples as well as to the *demos*.

BURIAL IN EARLY CHRISTIANITY: SEARCHING FOR CLUES

Little is known about the burial of Christ believers in the first two centuries. The main reason for this is that they—like Judeans—naturally continued the Greco-Roman burial culture. Theologically, there also was no particular reason to make drastic changes. Concepts about the existence of the dead until the resurrection—sleep (see below), heavenly existence (Rev 6:9-11; 2 Cor 5:1; John 14:2-3), Hades (Rev 20:13; cf. Luke 16:23), paradise (Luke 23:43), being in the presence of Christ (Phil 1:23; cf. Rom 14:8)—did not necessitate renouncing an honorable burial. Moreover, it can be taken for granted that burial was primarily a family matter, even for believers in Christ. Additionally, one may assume that similar to associations, some Christ assemblies also took care of the burial of their members or were at least involved in it. However, sources for this have not been preserved.

Pauline References: Two Notes

Two passages from Paul's letters are interesting in this regard. One is 1 Thess 4:13-17, where Paul gives his addressees in Thessalonica the assurance that those who have died will not miss the parousia: they are only asleep and will rise again. Together with those still alive "in Christ," the risen will go to meet and welcome the Kyrios. While nothing is said about burials, two elements are important for our question: on the one hand, Paul uses κοιμᾶσθαι ("to sleep"), as he does elsewhere when talking about the death of Christ believers (1 Cor 7:39; 11:30; 15:6, 18, 20, 51), to euphemistically describe the condition of the deceased. In this way he adopts a pre-Christian use of language,[39] but the metaphor of sleep is taken up particularly intensively in Christian tradition. This can be seen, among other things, in the designation of the burial place as κοιμητήριον/*coemeterium* ("bedroom"). This is already found in texts of the early third century, although it is disputed whether the "cemetery" is meant in these early testimonies.[40]

---

[38] *ICiliciaBM* 2.201 (Lamos, before 69 CE). On this association, see Öhler 2011, 228–29; Harland 2014, 415–16.

[39] Cf. Hoffmann 1966, 186–206; Peres 2003, 71–72.

[40] Cf. Rebillard 1993; Volp 2002, 152, n. 237.

From the question of the Thessalonians, which Paul answers in 1 Thessalonians 4, we can further conclude that the members of the *ecclesia* were concerned about their deceased brothers and sisters and thus probably also about their own access to salvation if they too died before the parousia. Would they continue to be among the multitude who would be saved and live with Christ (5:9-10)? Paul includes those who are asleep in his answer ("whether we are awake or asleep," 5:10), so that it is ensured that the dead continue to be part of the *ecclesia*. This connection of members beyond death is also evident in the inscriptions of associations, especially where further honors express that affiliation quite ostentatiously.[41]

This idea of community can also be understood as a background to the substitutionary baptism for the dead in 1 Cor 15:29. This is obviously about including those who had not yet been baptized and thus did not yet belong to the *ecclesia* and therefore to the assembly of the saved. Here the belonging of the deceased is achieved through a special ritual. It seems plausible to me that we can recognize here a development of a Christian burial or death ritual. However, it would have its place of performance in the gathering, not at the grave.[42] If it was analogous to the baptism of the living, then it was performed publicly in the *ecclesia*, and hardly as a private rite. It should be added that Paul does not criticize such a ritual, but that it played no further role in the history of late antique Christianity.

Christian Graves in Pagan Company

The claim to exclusivity, which according to the textual testimonies was connected with the conversion to faith in Christ, was generally also to be accompanied by the end of membership in Greco-Roman associations. Although this was not always observed, as can be seen in 1 Corinthians 10 or Revelation 2–3 for example, the majority of believers in Christ would have drawn this conclusion. The exclusions and sufferings of the members of the *ecclesia* could not be explained in any other way than by a detachment from cultic social structures such as associations, mysteries, or *polis*/neighborhood cults.

However, the jurist Callistratus at the beginning of the third century CE held that every co-owner of a tomb (and as such the members of the association were considered) had the right to be buried there as well (*Dig.* 11.7.41). If Christ believers withdrew from the association, they would receive the amount contributed or the sum designated for the burial. Conversely, if they

---

[41] Compare the more detailed discussion in Ascough 2011, 177–84.

[42] The formulation ὑπὲρ τῶν νεκρῶν ("for the dead") is, in my opinion, not to be understood locally, but, as elsewhere in Paul, as an expression of representation in favor of others.

nt. 1994. "The Rhodian Associations Honouring Dionysod-
exandria." *Classica et Mediaevalia* 45:137–60.

, 2006. "Acculturation and Identity in the Diaspora: A Jewish
'agan' Guilds at Hierapolis." *JJS* 57:22–244.

North Coast of the Black Sea, Asia Minor. BZNW 204. Vol. 2 of
Associations: Texts, Translations, and Commentary. Edited
oppenborg and Richard J. Ascough. Berlin: De Gruyter.

o. 2005. *The* Familia Urbana *during the Early Empire: A Study
a Inscriptions*. Oxford: Archaeopress.

1966. *Die Toten in Christus. Eine religionsgeschichtliche und
ntersuchung zur paulinischen Theologie*. NTAbh NF 2. Mün-
lorff.

 françoise. 2003. *Choisir Dionysos: les associations diony-
La face cachée du dionysisme*. 2 vols. Akanthus crescens 6.
thus.

n S. 2019. *Christ's Associations: Connecting and Belonging in
ity*. New Haven: Yale University Press.

Ptolemaic and Early Roman Egypt. BZNW 246. Vol. 3 of
, and Ascough, *Greco-Roman Associations*.

hn S., and Richard S. Ascough, eds. 2011. *Attica, Cen-
Macedonia, Thrace*. BZNW 181. Vol. 1 of Kloppenborg and
co-Roman Associations.

d Philip A. Harland. 2020. *Group Survival in the Ancient Med-
ethinking Material Conditions in the Landscape of Jews and
ondon: T&T Clark.

dor. 1843. *De collegiis et sodaliciis Romanorum. Accedit
nuvina*. Kiel: Libraria Schwersiana.

M. 1997. *The Civic World of Professional Associations in the
Dutch Monographs on Ancient History and Archaeology 17.
J. C. Gieben.

2011. "Ethnos und Identität. Landsmannschaftliche Verein-
nagogen und christliche Gemeinden." Pages 221–48 in *Kult
Religion und Herrschaft im syro-palästinischen Raum—Studien
hselbeziehung in hellenistisch-römischer Zeit*. Edited by Anne
ritz Schipper. WUNT 2/319. Tübingen: Mohr Siebeck.

Meeting at Home: Greco-Roman Associations and Pauline
s." Pages 517–45 in *Scribal Practices and Social Structures
Adherents: Essays in Honour of John S. Kloppenborg*. Edited
. Arnal, Richard S. Ascough, Robert A. Derrenbacker Jr., and
rland. BETL 285. Leuven: Peeters.

2008. "Roman and Christian Burial Practices and the Patron-
en." Pages 243–70 in Brink and Green, *Commemorating the

remained members, they could not be denied burial in the association's tomb or at the association's expense. However, the specific regulations on this were of course left to the association within the framework of its autonomy.

The burial of Christians in the tomb of a pagan *collegium* was first criticized by Cyprian of Carthage (*Ep.* 67.6; 250/251 CE). He objected to the actions of a Spanish bishop who had turned away from faith in Christ during the Decian persecution and became a member of a pagan *collegium*. Moreover, he had also had his deceased sons buried in the *collegium*'s tomb, "burying them with foreigners in a profane sepulchre" (*apud profana sepulcra depositos et alienigenis consepultos*). Cyprian's criticism, however, seems to have been the exception.[43] Although the restriction of burial places to members of the same religious community is also found in inscriptions in pre-Constantinian Christianity, it always concerns a private context. For example, a funerary inscription of a certain M. Antonius Restutus states that he erected the hypogaeum *sibi et suis fidentibus in domino* ("for himself and for those of his [household] who trust in the Lord"; *ILCV* 1597; Rome, 276–300 CE). In general practice, however, Christian, pagan, and Jewish tombs were laid side by side in the catacombs of Rome as late as the third and fourth centuries CE. There was apparently no prohibition of such mixed-religious burials.

Burials by the Community

In his letter to the Romans (Ign. *Rom.* 4.4), Ignatius writes of his martyrdom in the rather morbid hope that the wild beasts would become his grave and leave nothing of his body, "so that after my death I may be a burden to no one" (ἵνα μὴ κοιμηθεὶς βαρύς τινι γένωμαι). Possibly this is an indication that the martyr could expect to be buried by the members of the Roman *ecclesia* or an individual. As a prisoner brought to Rome, he had no family there either.[44] However, this isolated remark cannot serve as evidence for generally organized burials by the community, especially since it represents an exceptional case. Such a situation is also present in the martyrdom of Polycarp (*Mart. Pol.* 18.2–3), the oldest evidence for the burial of a martyr and the celebration taking place at the grave εἴς τε τὴν . . . μνήμην ("for remembrance").

---

[43] Commodianus (mid-third century CE) also polemicized against participation in colleges in order to be buried there: *Incusatus eris qui ob ista collegia quaeris. Sub nigrore cupis vivere: te decipis ipsum* (*Instructiones* 2.33.13–14; ed. Dombart 1887, 105).

[44] Cf. also the burial of John's body in Mark 6:29. The same happens in the burial of Jesus, which is provided by a benefactor (Mark 15:42-46 par.). Origen (*Hom. Jer.* 4.3) speaks of the burial of martyrs, at which the congregation was apparently present.

However, several things are comparable with the *memoria* of benefactors and special members in Greco-Roman associations—not least, the special grave erected by the community, the celebration on the day of his death.

From the end of the second century CE, the burial of ordinary members of the Christian assembly is encountered, mainly in apologetic texts.[45] Quite similar to some of the abovementioned association inscriptions, the Apology of Aristides states that benefactors financed the burial of poor community members.[46] But in general the funding of burials is only rarely alluded to, and the evidence is all disputed. The closest thing to a regular communal burial practice seems to have been established in Carthage. In his *Apology* (written around 197 CE), Tertullian refers to the fact that the burial of the needy was financed from the communal treasury, into which monthly contributions were voluntarily paid (*Apol.* 39.6: *egenis alendis humandisque*).[47] However, the practice is not analogous to that of associations, which financed the burial of all members, not only of those with little resources. Of course, it can be assumed that a funeral for the poor also had to be organized by the community and that certain persons from the community must have been responsible for it.

Besides, Tertullian states that pagans devastated the graves of Christians during the Bacchanalia (*Apol.* 37.2). If this accusation has historical substance, it would prove that Christian graves were obviously recognizable. However, it could also point to specific burial areas that—analogous to associations—were owned by Christian communities (legally by their members) or, more likely, by individual benefactors. And finally, attention should be paid to a passage from the open letter addressed by Tertullian to the enemy of Christians, Scapula, in 212 CE: in it, *areae sepulturarum nostrarum* ("threshing floors of burials") are mentioned, which surely must indicate Christian burial areas. Whether these consisted of private foundations or were administered by communities themselves remains, of course, unclear.[48]

Epigraphic evidence from a somewhat later period points to another thing: the parallelism of communal graves of real and fictitious families.[49] For instance, an inscription from the fourth century CE names "the brothers"

---

[45] The evidence up to the fourth century CE is discussed in Volp 2002, 96–239.

[46] *Apol.* 15.6, but only in the Syrian version; see Volp 2002, 110.

[47] The closeness to the practice of the Lanuvium Association (*ILS* 7212) is also expressed linguistically: *stips menstrua* ("monthly contribution") is also found here; see Kloppenborg 2019, 276.

[48] See Volp 2002, 103–4; Bodel 2008, 204–6; Osiek 2008, 243.

[49] Bodel 2008, 233.

as the donors of a tomb.[50] This ...
acombs of Rome as well. It is ...
joined together to form associ...
the churches themselves were ...
fessional associations in particu...
religious conditions. The devel...
occurred only after Constantine ...

W...

Ascough, Richard S. 2011. "Paul'...
  at Thessalonica and Corinth...
  Corinthians. Edited by Ron ...
  anity and Its Literature 5. Atl...

Bendlin, Andreas. 2011. "Associa...
  The Collegium of Diana and ...
  sidered." Pages 207–96 in *Apo*...
  schaft und ihre Ordnung. Edit...
  Mohr Siebeck.

Bodel, John. 2008. "From *Colum*...
  Pagan and Christian Rome." F...
  Texts and Artifacts in Context. ...
  Berlin: De Gruyter.

Borbonus, Dorian. 2014. *Columbar*...
  tan Rome. New York: Cambrid...

Bosnakis, Dimitris. 2008. Ἀνέκδοτε...
  όροι. Athens: Υπουργείο Πολιτι...
  Σπουδών.

Dittmann-Schöne, Imogen. 2001. ...
  zeitlichen Kleinasiens. Regensb...

Dombart, Bernhard. 1887. *Commo*...

Doulfis, Georgios. 2020. "Building ...
  The Columbaria Monuments."...
  and Social Diversity in Ancien...
  and Burial. Edited by Nikolas ...
  Archaeopress.

---

[50] *IG* X,2.1 607 (Thessalonica, fourth c...
γλυκύ]τατον ₤ οἱ ἀδελφοί; see also *IPer*...
(Korykos, after 350 CE).

[51] Bodel 2008, 230: "There is a significa...
congregations as adapting the administra...
tions to ensure the burial of their member...
a formally constituted legal *collegium* whic...
cemeteries reserved for the burial of Christ...

Gabrielsen, Vir...
  oros from ...
Harland, Philip ...
  Family and ...
  ——, ed. 2014 ...
  Greco-Rom...
  by John S. ...
Hasegawa, Kin...
  of Columb...
Hoffmann, Pa...
  exegetische...
  ster: Asch...
Jaccottet, Anr...
  siaques, o...
  Zürich: A...
Kloppenborg, ...
  the Ancier...
  ——, ed. 20...
  Kloppenb...
Kloppenborg, ...
  tral Greed...
  Ascough, ...
Last, Richard, ...
  iterranea...
  Christian...
Mommsen, ...
  inscriptic...
van Nijf, On...
  Roman E...
  Amsterd...
Öhler, Mark...
  igungen, ...
  und Mac...
  zu ihrer...
  Lykke ar...
  ——. 2016 ...
  Commu...
  among J...
  by Willi...
  Philip A...
Osiek, Carol...
  age of V...
  Dead.

Paton, William R., and Edward L. Hicks. 1891. *The Inscripitions of Cos*. Oxford: Clarendon.

Peres, Imre. 2003. *Griechische Grabinschriften und neutestamentliche Eschatologie*. WUNT 157. Tübingen: Mohr Siebeck.

Perry, Jonathan S. 2006. *The Roman* Collegia: *The Modern Evolution of an Ancient Concept*. Mnemosyne, Supplements 277. Leiden: Brill.

Poland, Franz. 1909. *Geschichte des griechischen Vereinswesens*. Preisschriften 38. Leipzig: Teubner.

Rebillard, Éric. 1993. "*Koimetérion* et *Coemeterium*: tombe, tombe sainte, nécropole." *Mélanges de l'Ecole française de Rome. Antiquité* 105:975–1001.

———. 2009. *The Care of the Dead in Late Antiquity*. Ithaca: Cornell University Press.

Schrumpf, Stefan. 2006. *Bestattung und Bestattungswesen im Römischen Reich. Ablauf, soziale Dimension und ökonomische Bedeutung der Totenfürsorge im lateinischen Westen*. Bonn: Bonn University Press.

Thomsen, Christian A. 2020. *The Politics of Association in Hellenistic Rhodes*. Edinburgh: Edinburgh University Press.

Volp, Ulrich. 2002. *Tod und Ritual in den christlichen Gemeinden der Antike*. Leiden: Brill.

Volpe, Rita. 2019. "Cuique suum? Un insolito graffito nel sepolcro degli Scipioni." Pages 373–76 in *Una lezione di archeologia globale*. Edited by Mirco Modolo, Silvia Pallecchi, Giuliano Volpe, and Enrico Zanini. Bari: Edipuglia.

Williams, Margaret H. 1994. "The Organisation of Jewish Burials in Ancient Rome in the Light of Evidence from Palestine and the Diaspora." *ZPE* 101:165–82.

13

Retiring Religious Associations

Éric Rebillard

Despite a recent urge to abandon the notion of religion altogether when studying the ancient world, religious associations continue to play an important role in the comparison of Christ assemblies with ancient associations. I call to retire the category of "religious associations,"[1] not so much because it carries the inappropriate assumptions of the modern, Western notion of religion but because it cannot be established that the worship of a god or the attendance of a temple is the principal activity or the principal set of connections in any ancient association for which we know more than the name.[2] Though *association* is often used as an etic term,[3] it partially overlaps with the Roman legal notion of collegium. However, there is no category of religious collegium in Roman law, as I will show in the first section. Then, I will argue that certain scholarly traditions created a category of religious associations and that, by so doing, they also created their object of study. Finally, I devote most of this essay to a review not only of

[1]   I borrow the notion of retirement of concepts or categories from Fredriksen 2006.
[2]   Scheid's similar call (2003 = 2011) is too often summarily dismissed: Rohde 2012, 14; Gordon 2017, 279, n. 6; Wojciechowski 2021, 26, n. 16.
[3]   By this, scholars essentially mean that there is no ancient umbrella word comparable to the modern word *association*; see Harland 2009, 36; Ascough 2017, 119–21; Kloppenborg 2019, 18–19.

the criteria that are used for defining a category of "religious association" but of the evidence on the associations defined as such. The conclusion is inescapable, and I briefly sketch how the removal of the category "religious association" can enrich the project of comparison of Christ assemblies with ancient associations.

ASSOCIATIONS IN ROMAN LAW

A *Lex Iulia*, now attributed to Augustus rather than Caesar, introduced a formal authorization by the Senate for the creation of an association.[4] There likely were unauthorized associations, the *collegia illicita* of the jurists, though they probably escape our notice as they would not have displayed their existence on inscriptions. Over time, the emperors took a more positive approach to the forming of associations by the *tenuiores*. Indeed, it is a fundamental contribution of Mommsen (1843) to have brought forward the parallel between an extract of the jurist Marcian (from the Justinian *Digest* 47.22.1), in which *tenuiores* are said to be "allowed to pay a small monthly fee, provided that they meet only once a month, lest an unlawful association be created under this guise," and an extract of a *senatus consultum* quoted on the inscription of the *cultores Dianae et Antinoi* from Lanuvium (*CIL* 14.2112), which in Mommsen's reconstitution authorized a monthly meeting for collecting fees for funerals—hence Mommsen's category of *collegia funeraticia* (a phrase that is not attested in legal texts or inscriptions) that encompasses associations of *tenuiores* formed with the purpose of providing burial to their members.[5] Mommsen's reconstitution of the text of the Lanuvian inscription has been critiqued, and a restitution of *sacra* instead of *funera* changed the purpose of the associations of *tenuiores* from funerary to religious (Ausbüttel 1982, 27–28; cf. Gordon 1958–1965, 2:61–68). A new examination of the inscription and new documents from Ostia, however, now seem to vindicate the restitution *funera* (Bendlin 2011, 248–57; Laubry and Zevi 2012, 320–23).[6] Whatever restitution is adopted, there is no support in the legal evidence for a discrete

---

[4] What follows can be considered a standard account, even if it leaves aside many elements that continue to be discussed; see de Ligt 2000, 243–49; Laubry and Zevi 2012, 314–17.

[5] Mommsen understood *tenuiores* as the poor; we now know that *tenuiores* is an equivalent of *humiliores* and refers to a legal, not economical, status: see Bendlin 2011, 233–35; cf. Ausbüttel 1982, 25.

[6] Furthermore, as all associations have some religious purpose, an authorization for *tenuiores* to create an association for such a purpose would amount to an abrogation of the *Lex Iulia* (Laubry and Zevi 2012, 323; cf. Waltzing 1895–1900, 1:152).

category of either funerary or religious associations. The limitation applies only to one monthly meeting for collecting fees for one purpose or the other; it does not extend to other meetings—when bylaws are preserved, they always list more than one meeting of varied purposes—nor does it apply to the association's activities.

To complicate the matter further, the same extract from Marcian includes the following sentence: "There is, however, no ban on assembly for religious purpose (*religionis causa coire non prohibentur*), so long as there is no contravention of the *senatus consultum* which prohibits unlawful *collegia*" (*Dig.* 47.22.1.1). This extract has been interpreted as providing an explanation for the organization of Christian "communities," which would use the umbrella-status of association *religionis causa* (Reseghetti 1988), and more generally for the development of all foreign cults (Sirks 2006, 25–26). Andreas Bendlin, however, well shows that the notion of a general state recognition of privately organized religious groups results from a modern understanding of the relationship between state and religion that fails to adequately describe the Roman context (Bendlin 2005, 77–82; cf. Eckhardt 2018, 123–24). The exact interpretation of the passage raises many difficulties and will continue to be discussed among specialists.[7] However, it cannot be used as evidence that jurists are familiar with groups founded for religious purpose (contra Gordon 2017, 279). Marcian mentions that people can assemble for religious activities, like members of all associations do, not that they can found groups for this purpose nor that religious activities are their only type of activities (cf. Laubry and Zevi 2012, 323).

To conclude, there is no legal evidence for the existence of a category of associations whose primary, if not exclusive, purpose would be religious.[8]

RELIGIOUS ASSOCIATIONS AND SCHOLARLY TRADITIONS

Different scholarly traditions created a category of religious associations. As Jonathan S. Perry (2006; cf. Tran 2001) well shows for the topic of associative life in general, it is important to understand the historical context in which categories are formed, as they often take a life of their own that opacify their origin. Categories, once in use, also tend to create their own object of study (see Touna 2017, 80–81).

---

[7] Eckhardt (2018, 115–31) discusses many of the issues. Important recent contributions are de Ligt 2001; Bendlin 2005; 2011.

[8] Some scholars understand the phrase *collegia sodalicia* used by Marcian in the same extract mentioned above as religious associations; see Bendlin 2016 for a definitive rebuttal.

A good example of this phenomenon are the so-called Egyptian religious associations from the Ptolemaic period.[9] The technical word for association in demotic has been identified as *swn.t*, the same word that means "the sixth day [of the lunar month]," a festival day. The word is recognized in a number of bylaws or charters of Egyptian associations between the sixth century BCE and the first century CE.[10] Because priests belong to some of the associations and because these associations often meet in temples, they have been categorized as religious associations (Muszynski 1977). It is now established that these associations are independent from the Egyptian temple administration and that their members are not exclusively priests (Monson 2002; 2005; 2007). The activities described in the bylaws are very similar to other associations in the Mediterranean world and are not particularly focused on cult (Paganini 2017, 142–50; Monson 2019, 38–39). When Michel Muszynski (1977) brought together hieroglyphic, demotic, and Greek material on these so-called "religious associations," he wanted to highlight the continuity between these pagan "brotherhoods" and the later Christian "brotherhoods" described by Ewa Wipszycka (1970 = 1996, 257–78). As John Scheid (2003 = 2011) forcefully notes, such an approach is very Christocentric and cannot be sustained anymore. Thus, it is safe to conclude that Egyptian associations should not be studied as constituting a discrete category of religious associations.[11]

Greek associations, especially in the Hellenistic period, are also often described as religious associations. The fact is that, if one leaves aside the *hetaireiai*, most associations known in the Greek world before Roman rule emphasize cult and gods in their self-designation (Gabrielsen 2007, 187, 194–95; cf. Eckhardt 2019, 16). The tradition of calling them religious associations goes back at least to the 1873 monograph of Paul Foucart (1836–1926). In 1909, in what is still today a major monograph on Greek associations, Franz Poland (1857–1945) expressed strong reservations about any taxonomy of associations' activities or purposes based on their names

---

[9] Recently presented in Monson 2019 (who, despite offering a critique of the category, keeps it in his title). A long tradition has maintained (see, for instance, Roberts, Skeat, and Nock 1936, 72–87) that the Greeks imported professional associations in Egypt, while religious associations were typical of the Egyptian tradition, and that Greeks settlers in Egypt would later adopt them; see Paganini (2017, 133–36) for a critique of this tradition.

[10] See Muszynski 1977, 146; on the term, see Hughes 1958. The identification is disputed by Cenival 2006; cf. Cenival 1972, 12–13. The *Chicago Demotic Dictionary* (CDD S [13:1], 81–82) notes Cenival's reading but keeps "cult association" as an extended meaning of *swn.t*, "sixth day festival."

[11] Though he still finds the distinction useful (8–9), Venticinque includes "outwardly religious groups" (2016, 13) at nearly every step of his study of craftsmen and merchants in Roman Egypt.

(1909, 5–6). The label of religious associations, however, is still part of the tradition (see Fröhlich and Hamon 2013, 17–18). Thus, Ilias Arnaoutoglou dedicates his 2003 monograph to "private religious associations," but leaves aside "the reason for the primacy of religion" and "any questions of rituals and celebrations" as they belong to "books about religion" (2003, 22, 30). Paulin Ismard also keeps calling Athenian associations "associations cultu-elles," though he well notes that they are polyvalent (2010, 36–37). In his case, however, the label seems to be extended to all associations. The distinc-tion between professional and religious associations seems to stem from a well-known passage of the *Nicomachean Ethics*.[12] In this passage, Aristotle offers a distinction between associations that form for the sake of a partic-ular advantage—as opposed to the city (*polis*) that is formed for the com-mon advantage—and those that form for the sake of pleasure (Aristotle, *Eth. nic.* 8.9 [1160a]). Among others, he lists maritime merchants as an example of the first category—hence the category of professional association.[13] The second category is illustrated with the *thiasotai* and *eranistai*, "since these are for the sake of sacrifices and fellowship," hence the category of religious associations. Both the integrity and the logic of the passage have been dis-puted (see Pakaluk 1994). Whatever the case, the passage is not meant to be a description, even less a classification, of Greek associations. The passage is in a chapter about friendship (*philia*) that drives people into *koinonia*. The translation of *koinonia* as "associations" is already a modern interpretation (see Touna 2017, 79–80). Thus, one ought to stop taking Greek religious associations as an object of study and instead seek to understand why asso-ciations chose a name that referred to cult and gods.[14]

Roman associations have a more complex tradition of scholarship. Accord-ing to a recent study, Mommsen "'buried' studies on cultic colleges for decades" (Wojciechowski 2021, 6; cf. Perry 2006, 40). The reference is to Mommsen's 1843 monograph *De collegiis et sodaliciis Romanorum*, in which he defended the thesis that Roman associations whose members called themselves *cul-tores* of a god were only perfunctorily religious and were essentially funer-ary associations (1843, 92–95). Mommsen based his demonstration on three *leges collegiorum*, two of which had been published recently: the collegium of Aesculapius and Hygia from Rome, the *cultores* of Diana and Antinous from Lanuvium (Italy), and the collegium of Jupiter Cernenus from Alburnus Maior

---

[12] This is noted, for instance, by Arnaoutoglou (2011, 272–73) and Gabrielsen (2016b, 89).

[13] He also lists soldiers and members of the tribes and demes; see Ismard 2010, 13–15, on the heterogeneity (at least to modern eyes) of the list.

[14] Gabrielsen (2000; 2007; 2016a; 2016b) opens a clear path in this direction; cf. Thom-sen (2020) on Rhodian associations.

(Dacia).[15] All three associations are named after deities but the provisions of their bylaws deal mostly with the funerals and burial of their members. The novelty of Mommsen's thesis is noted by Gaston Boissier (1823–1908), who in an 1872 paper endeavors to verify it through a close study of the associations that present themselves as *cultores deorum*. Boissier emphasizes that the link to a specific deity is not arbitrary but he agrees with Mommsen that religion is at best a secondary purpose in these associations (1872, 85–86, 92). A proof of it for him is that *cultor* came to mean member of an association instead of devotee (1872, 86–87). Boissier, however, suggests that we should not distinguish between religious and funerary associations, because all associations are religious to some extent; consequently, he adopts a bipartition between professional and nonprofessional associations (1872, 87–89). Jean-Pierre Waltzing (1857–1929) tried to test Mommsen's hypothesis on a larger basis, listing all known associations with a theophoric name in order to determine whether their activities were religious and/or funerary (1898; 1899). That study, however, has not been completed (the second installment ends with "À continuer."), and in the index of the fourth volume of his *Étude historique sur les corporations professionnelles chez les Romains*, he considers these associations as *collegia funeraticia*, even, he adds, when funerary activity cannot be established (1895–1900, 4:180). Boissier's nuanced (dis)agreement with Mommsen has barely been noticed, and Waltzing's second "burial" of the religious associations prevailed until Frank M. Ausbüttel's 1982 monograph.[16] The recent monograph of Przemysław Wojciechowski fails to bring any new element to the discussion: he claims that religious associations are "a different type of corporation," but that difference seems to be limited to their self-designation.[17] Indeed, his study of their social composition, their organization, and their activities does not point to any significant difference with other types of corporations. This is a very clear case of a category creating its own object of study.

I now turn to current approaches to categorization. As we will see, once categories are in use, it is difficult to escape their trappings.

---

[15] Mommsen 1843, 92: "Factum enim est ut his annis duae leges collegiorum sacrorum invenirentur, cum adime unam solam collegii Aesculapii et Hygiae cognitam haberemus, quas omnes tres collegiorum funerariorum esse apparuit." The inscriptions are respectively *CIL* 6.10234 (known since 1685), *CIL* 14.2112 (discovered in 1816), and *CIL* 3 pp. 924–27 (discovered in 1788). On the *leges collegiorum*, see Flambard 1987, 213–16.

[16] Ausbüttel 1982; see above. Wojciechowski (2021) does not include Boissier 1872 (nor Waltzing 1898 and 1899 for that matter) in his discussion or in the bibliography. Perry mentions it only in passing (2006, 37), noting the secularized context in which Boissier wrote.

[17] See Wojciechowski 2021, 23–33, on the "terminology."

MEMBERSHIP PROFILES AND RELIGIOUS ASSOCIATIONS

That the name adopted by an association does not necessarily reflect its principal activity, and that associations "inextricably combined" occupational, geographic, religious, burial, and convivial activities is widely accepted and needs not be argued here.[18] A new approach to taxonomy was taken by John S. Kloppenborg when he suggested categorizing associations based on the profile of their membership and distinguishing between household connections, shared occupation, and common cult (1996, 23–26). Philip A. Harland extended the framework to five social networks of membership: household or family connections, ethnic or geographic connections, neighborhood connections, occupational connections, and temple or ritual connections (2013, 19, 23–24; cf. Harland 2009, 31–32). Recognizing that "these sets of social linkages are often inter-related," he nevertheless posits that in many cases "the *principal* set of linkages" can be detected (2013, 19, emphasis in original). In his monograph on Christ's associations, Kloppenborg adopts the five subspecies of Harland without further discussion (2019, 24 and n. 6). Both Kloppenborg and Harland note that the name of an association can be an indication of the principal network of membership but that one ought to be cautious.[19] It is necessary, therefore, to look closer at the associations that they designate as religious or cultic.

Harland gives a few examples of associations in which connections arise from "attendance at places of worship" (2013, 33–42). I discuss only associations that can be dated to the first three centuries CE. A first case is a dedication made by a group of eighteen males to the gods Men and Zeus. It comes from Maionia (Lydia) and is dated to 171–172 CE (*TAM* 5.537 = *CMRDM* 1.54 [AGRW 1209; *CAPInv* 306]). They call their group *hiera symbiosis kai neotera*, thus not referring to a deity but emphasizing the sacred and new character of the group. The epithet *hieros* is not uncommon for associations with an occupational name (Tod 1932, 76–77; cf. Poland 1909, 169). A second inscription that may belong to the same group refers to a *hieros doumos*, a sacred council (*TAM* 5.535 = *CMRDM* 1.53), thus opening the possibility that it is a public institution rather than a private or unofficial association (*CAPInv* 306).

[18] See Flambard 1987, 210, for the phrase. For this wide consensus, see Kloppenborg 1996; van Nijf 1997; Tran 2006; Liu 2009; Verboven 2011; Venticinque 2016.

[19] See Harland 2013, 33: "Nonetheless, there are associations whose membership appears to draw primarily from social networks associated with honoring a specific deity in a given cult or sanctuary, and sometimes such groups highlighted their continuing devotion by including the name of the deity or deities in the self-designation of the association." Cf. same cautious position in Kloppenborg 2019, 25.

Another inscription listed by Harland in relation to the god Men is a list of forty-three men and women responsible for the dedication of a statue of Dionysus (*TAM* 5.351 = *CMRDM* 1.34 [AGRW 830; *CAPInv* 355]). The dedicants call themselves *hoi kataloustikoi*, the ritual-purifiers, and they name several deities. In another inscription, an honorific stele, the dedicants do not link their name to any deity (*TAM* 5.490 = *CMRDM* 1.A3; see Lane 1971–1978, 3:35–36). Both inscriptions come from the Saittai area in Lydia and date to 159–160 and 160–161 CE respectively. Nothing beyond the name they give themselves indicates that the principal set of social linkage between them is religious. It seems that classifying this group as a religious association relies upon the very traditional criterion of its name.

The same is true with an inscription from Teos (Ionia), a grave stele dedicated by *hoi Sabaziastai*, "the Sabazios-devotees" (*SEG* 2.608 = *CCIS* 2.28 [AGRW 12817; *CAPInv* 1681]). Nothing further is known about these Sabaziasts. When we know more about the groups behind the inscriptions, it becomes difficult to establish that the connections arise primarily from attendance at places of worship. The *mystai tou Dios Saouazou* ("the initiates of Zeus Sabazios"), whom Harland mentions next, are a good example. They are known through six inscriptions related to a senatorial estate located in the territory of Kibyra (Pisidia).[20] The inhabitants of the estate formed the *dēmos Ormēleōn* ("the people of the Ormeleis"). One of these inscriptions (*CCIS* 2 43 [AGRW 12468; *CAPInv* 387]) is a dedication for the salvation of the *mystai* themselves, the whole *dēmos* of the Ormeleis, and the senatorial family that owns the estate. The religious linkage is clearly not unique, probably not principal either, given that members are listed according to the hierarchical organization of the administration of the estate.

We see, then, that none of Harland's examples are convincing.[21] His goal seems to strengthen the case he wants to make about the importance and the "genuineness" of the religious purpose of private associations (2013, 47–50). Harland rightly insists, however, that associations of all types were involved in activities honoring gods and goddesses (2013, 50). Indeed, in recent publications, Harland explicitly rejects the category of religious association and does not include places of worship among the potential web of connections (2019,

---

[20] Harland refers to only one of the six inscriptions: Milner 1998, 48–50, no. 114 = *CCIS* 2.43 (AGRW 12468; *CAPInv* 387). The six inscriptions can be found in Corsten 2005, which describes the organization of the estate.

[21] Harland (2013, 37) also mentions groups of *mystai* associated with the cult of Demeter and Kore in Ephesus and Smyrna; it is not certain that they formed a private, or unofficial, association: see Eckhardt and Lepke 2018, 55–58. The same ambiguity applies to the *boukoloi* from Pergamon (Harland 2013, 38; see Eckhardt and Lepke 2018, 59).

210; cf. Last and Harland 2020, 10–11). He explains the shift as a preference to avoid modern, problematic, and inappropriate categories. I applaud the move, but the rationale for it should go beyond mere compliance with a trend in "the disciplines of Cultural Studies and Religious Studies" (Last and Harland 2020, 11; cf. Harland 2019, 210, 213–14). The avoidance of the modern assumptions that come with the use of *religion* and *religious* leaves intact the practice of associations that name themselves after a god or gods.[22]

Kloppenborg does not avoid the use of *religion* and *religious*. He carefully justifies an etic use of the terms and emphasizes that his comparison of Christ's assemblies with associations does not depend on these associations being "religious" (2019, 10–18). He also clearly states that the categories of associations overlap, that all associations have a religious component, and that names can be deceitful. Nevertheless, he maintains that there are analytic purposes to the typology (2019, 24–25). I will show, however, that he fails to produce a convincing example of a cultic association.

The famous Iobakchoi of Athens are mentioned briefly several times as an obvious example (Kloppenborg 2019, 29, 194, and *passim*). Their rule, published when Herod Atticus became their new high priest, lists several religious ceremonies related to the cult of Dionysus but also describes at length the behavioral code for other meetings and banquets (*IG* II² 1368 = *GRA* I 51 [AGRW 496; *CAPInv* 339]). Without denying that religion played a role in the life of the association, it is reasonable to question the assumption that it was formed primarily for religious purpose. The choice of a theophoric name by these exclusive, wealthy, Athenian citizens is noteworthy and not typical for associations in the Greek world under Roman rule (Baslez 2004; Eckhardt 2017). Instead of indicating the purpose of the association, the theophoric name might result from "a strategy of remembering," a conscious continuation of an Athenian local tradition in reaction to Roman rule (Eckhardt 2017, 77–79).

Another well-known inscription related to the cult of Dionysus, the Agrippinilla association from Torre Nova, offers a different example (*IGUR* 160 [AGRW 4194]). Kloppenborg casually refers to it as a cultic or Dionysiac association, though he acknowledges that it fits into the category of domestic associations.[23] Indeed, a careful prosopographical study of the

---

[22] On the assumptions carried by the term *religion*, see Schilbrack 2014, 96–105. Schilbrack also offers a way forward for responsibly using a concept of religion.

[23] Kloppenborg 2019, 89, 116, 194–95, and *passim*. Kloppenborg notes (2019, 38; his emphasis): "We might also consider as a *domestic* [sic] collegium the extremely large Dionysiac association of Pompeia Agrippinilla." Kloppenborg refers to McLean (1993), who unfortunately ignores Scheid 1986 and, though he notes its dependence on the *familia* of Agrippinilla, considers that the scope of the association is wider; see McLean 1993, 255.

more than four hundred *mystai* listed establishes that they all belong to the double *familia* of the Gavii-Pompeii (Scheid 1986, 276–86; cf. Jaccottet 2003, 1:35–38). Membership in this association results from social obligation not from religious choice (Scheid 1986, 286–87; contra Cumont 1933, 237). The choice of Dionysus as a patron deity for the association is the result of a careful calculation by its founder, a calculation that reflects his concern for the glory of his name as much as his religiosity (Scheid 1986, 287–89; cf. Jaccottet 2003, 1:45–51).

The no less famous association of the *cultores* of Diana and Antinous from Lanuvium cannot be presented as a straightforward example of cultic association either, no more than it can serve as paradigm of the funerary associations (*CIL* 14.2112; *AE* 2011, 203). Andreas Bendlin has shown that when the association reorganized itself under the reign of Hadrian, its funerary, religious, and convivial functions are all secondary to its ideological purpose: staking a claim to their place in the local maneuvering of imperial politics (Bendlin 2011, esp. 283–86).

The first-century inscription from Laurion (Attica) that describes how Xanthos founded a temple and a cult of Men Tyrannos does not pertain to an association (*IG* II² 1366 = *CMRDM* 1.13 = *GRA* I 53 [AGRW 3179; *CAP-Inv* 307]). Xanthos stipulates that "those who wish may convene an *eranos* for Men Tyrannos for good fortune" and adds a few rules for the *eranistai* (ll. 21–26). Most scholars understand *eranos* as "association," a meaning that the word receives from the third century BCE in Greek inscriptions. It is not clear, however, that this is what Xanthos had in mind. The word could designate a banquet, with the *eranistai* being its organizers. No permanent structure is required here.[24]

A last inscription highlighted by Kloppenborg pertains to "devotees of Theos Hypsistos."[25] It comes from Beroia (Macedonia) and is dated to the

---

[24] Lane 1971–1978, 3:14; cf. Kloppenborg and Ascough 2011, 277. Horsley (1983, 20–31, no. 6) does not comment on the clause about the *eranos*. On the meaning of *eranos*, see Arnaoutoglou 2003, 70–87, with the reservations of Baslez (2015, 168) on the technical sense of association.

[25] I leave aside *AE* 1929, 161 (= *AE* 2002, 397), about a group calling itself the *"familia of Silvanus."* Kloppenborg (2019, 25) notes, "It was evidently a cultic association devoted to Silvanus; but because Silvanus was associated with agriculture and forests and because their shrine was located outdoors in a grove, they might also have been an occupational guild of some type." Cf. Kloppenborg 2019, 69: "It is possible that the guild was involved in some kind of agricultural pursuit, forestry, or the sale of wood." The four-part inscription includes in its upper part the bylaws of the association and a list of members. It comes from the ancient city of Trebula Mutuesca (Monteleone Sabino, Lazio) and dates to 60 CE. The bylaws do not mention an occupation; nor does the roster include the profession of

second century CE (*SEG* 46.737 = *AE* 1995, 1382 = *IBeroia* 27 [AGRW 20675; *CAPInv* 477]). The inscription is a simple list of names, with no indication of an association, or of a deity, except the iconography of the stele that suggests that it is a dedication to Zeus Hypsistos.[26] Making a series of likely assumptions based on the arrangements of the names on the stele, Kloppenborg suggests that "it is an unlikely scenario that all members are related *solely* by virtue of their devotion" (2019, 78 and n. 56, emphasis in original). He contends nevertheless that this devotion is what unites them all (2019, 77), despite the absence of any strong evidence.

Accordingly, when we consider the associations about which we know more than their name, no compelling case can be made for the identification of cultic associations.[27] Despite all his denials (and all the benefits that come from the comparison of Christ's assemblies with associations), in the end, Kloppenborg's assumption is that Christ's assemblies are more like cultic associations than occupational ones. This becomes clear early on, when he looks into what we can learn about the size of Christ's assemblies. Kloppenborg gathers membership statistics for 141 associations and divides them into occupational guilds and cultic associations (2019, 124–30, table 1). He establishes that occupational associations have a mean size of 164.89 with a mode of 5, while cultic associations have a mean of 29.29 with a mode of 15 (2019, 130). Though he notes that the divide between cultic and occupational associations is artificial, he concludes that "it seems much more likely that Pauline Christ assemblies initially numbered in the 15–30 range—that is, between the mode of 15 and the mean of 29.29" (2019, 110). These are the statistics established for the cultic associations. Thus, it implies that for Kloppenborg Christ assemblies are more like cultic than occupational associations. For Kloppenborg, this also means that the criteria of identification for cultic associations per se are relevant. As I show in the appendix, however, the cultic associations of Kloppenborg's list should be reclassified—or better the category retired altogether—and a recalculation of his figures for the size of associations seems necessary (see below).

---

any member. Neither Vetter (1953) nor Buonocore and Diliberto (2003; cf. Buonocore and Diliberto 2006) offer comments on a possible common occupation.

[26] Mitchell (2010, 170–71) suggests that Zeus Hypsistos is not to be confounded with Theos Hypsistos for Macedonia.

[27] Kloppenborg establishes lists of "cultic associations" in table 1 (membership statistics) and table 6 (endowments); as I show in the appendix to this essay, in most cases for the associations listed in Kloppenborg's table 1, the identification as "cultic" is based solely on the name of the association.

CONCLUSION

When I call for retiring the category of religious associations, I do not claim that honoring the gods is not an important part of the activities of ancient associations. All associations honor the gods. Only scholars with modern assumptions about religion consider the mixing of "religious" activities and other types of activities to be signs of a lesser degree of religiosity on the part of their members.

Note, importantly, that the removal of the category "religious association" from the comparison of Christ assemblies with ancient associations helps eliminate any Christocentric remnant from the comparative project.[28] First, it should be emphasized that Kloppenborg does not need to assume that Paul's groups are more like cultic than occupational associations. The statistics on the size of all 141 associations of Kloppenborg's calculations are a mean of 77.15, a median of 29, and a mode of 15 (2019, 129). The range of 15–30 for Paul's Christ assemblies would therefore still be plausible if the comparison were with all associations.[29] Second, the removal of the category allows historians to consider that Christ followers can belong to associations that are not Christ assemblies. I suggested a while ago that "the Christians who appear to be buried together in Roman catacombs possibly did what other members of the plebs media in the empire did when they formed associations"—that is, they were buried together not necessarily because of their religion but because they belonged to an association owning a burial area and that they likely were buried together with non-Christians.[30] Richard Last finds further evidence that "many of the groups in which Christ followers participated were fully open to individuals with diverse cult practices" (2018, 980). Christ followers may well meet for purposes other than Christ cult and, when they join an association of Christ followers, they may well join neighbors or fellow immigrants as much as they join fellow worshippers.[31]

The lack of evidence about groups of Christ followers, beyond the letters of Paul, however, makes it difficult to draw a line between similarities

[28] See Gruen 2016 on the Christocentric focus of comparisons between Christ groups and Greco-Roman associations, and Ascough's response (2017).

[29] The same is true for the size of association endowments that Kloppenborg compiles to determine if patrons are likely to fund all the meals shared by association members (2019, table 6). The data are divided into occupational and cultic associations, but Kloppenborg (2019, 219), albeit with no explanation for his choice, uses statistics based on all endowments.

[30] Rebillard 2009, 56 (translated from the original [2003, 70]); cf. Rebillard 1999, 280–82 (= 2013, 336–38). For similar conclusions, see Bodel 2008, 226–33; Poe 2007, 124–36; Borg 2013.

[31] I note that these possibilities are not explored in Kloppenborg 2019.

and differences. Indeed, the aspects of Christ assemblies that can be compared with aspects of Greco-Roman associations are limited to what is to the advantage of Paul's rhetorical perspective, which was more often than not dictated by certain circumstances.[32] It is not surprising then that in many cases scholars simply fall back on some preconceived ideas about the differences between Christians and others.[33]

Retiring "religious associations" will make the comparison with Greco-Roman associations an even more powerful tool than it has been so far, as it will promote a comparison of Christians with non-Christians that does not assume their separate grouping in Christ assemblies.

APPENDIX

There is a total of forty-three associations categorized as cultic and dated to the first three centuries CE in Kloppenborg's table 1 (2019, 124–30).

Two have been discussed above: the *familia* of Silvanus from Trebula Mutuesca, Italy (*AE* 1929, 161), and the devotees of Zeus Hypsistos from Beroia, Macedonia (*IBeroia* 27). The synodos of Belela (Piraeus) shares many characteristics of the Iobakchoi mentioned above (*IG* II² 2361).

For eight of them, no deity is named, and no indication of a cultic purpose is contained in the inscription.[34] I will only give the example of the two lists of names from Tebtynis that Kloppenborg identifies as related to cultic associations (*PMich* 5.247, 248). There is no indication of the group's name and therefore no reason to separate them from other lists from Tebtynis.[35]

For another thirteen of them, nothing else is known about the association other than its (theophoric) name.[36]

Then comes a group of eight associations that qualify as religious only because they are known through a dedication to a deity. An association with unknown name from Thessalonike, whose members call themselves *mystai*, offers a dedication to Zeus Dionysos Gongylos (*IG* X,2.1 259 = *SEG* 30.622 [*CAPInv* 716]). Two inscriptions, also from Thessalonike, list members who call themselves "fellow-banqueters" (*synklitai*). One is a stele with a representation of Anubis, the other a dedication to Theos Hypsistos (*IG* X,2.1 58 [*CAPInv*

---

[32] See Kloppenborg 2011, 192–93, on how this constrains the comparison within the household model.

[33] This is well illustrated in some of the studies reviewed in Ascough 2015.

[34] *CIL* 6.7459; *SEG* 46.864; *CIL* 6.1052; *IG* II² 4817; *PMich* 5.247; *PMich* 5.248; *CIRB* 1259; *CIRB* 1262.

[35] *PMich* 5.243–46. Among these, only *PMich* 5.246 belongs to a group associated with a god (Harpocrates). See Venticinque 2016, 77–85, on the multiple links that can be established between members of all these associations.

[36] *CIL* 6.647; *CIL* 3.633; *IDR* 1.31; *CIL* 11.6310; *CIL* 11.5737; *CIL* 6.631; *AE* 1994; 1334; *IGBulg* 1517; *IGBulg* 1626; *PMich* 5.246; *SEG* 49.814; *SEG* 46.800; *SEG* 41.1329.

707] and *IG* X,2.1 68 [cf. *IG* X,2.1 69–70; *CAPInv* 721]). Despite the obvious relation to deities, these two associations emphasize their social activities in their self-designation. In Edessa (Macedonia), members of an association calling themselves *hoi synetheis*, "the companions," offer a stele dedicated to Zeus Hypsistos for the memory of one of their members (*SEG* 46.744 [*CAPInv* 473]). In the case of the graffiti from room 9 in the temple of Gadde at Dura-Europos that list two groups of four men with the offerings they had brought (bread and barley), there is no indication that they form an association (Rostovtzeff, Brown, and Welles 1939, 254, 276, nos. 904, 905). The same is true of the dedication of chapel 38 in the temple of Adonis by a group of eight men (Rostovtzeff, Brown, and Welles 1939, 140, 168, no. 871).

The eight membership lists from Tanais in the Bosporan kingdom may belong to one or more associations of *thiasotai* or *synoditai* of Theos Hypsistos.[37] Given the number of members in relation to the population of Tanais, it does not seem that they ought to be considered as "private associations" (*CAPInv* 1324; Ustinova 1991; 1999, 183–88).

The *collegium salutare* of Aesculapius and Salus Augusta is established on an imperial estate in Rome (*CIL* 6.30983). Its purpose, given its name, the dedication to the imperial household, and the role of the administrator of the estate, is likely to mark the allegiance of the tenants of the estate, whether freedmen, slaves, or freeborn, to the emperor (Kolb 1995; cf. Bendlin 2011, 220).

From Pergamon, Kloppenborg includes rosters of *hymnodoi* and *boukoloi*, associations that do not seem to have been private.[38]

Members of an Athenian association call themselves with a double name (*IG* II² 4817 [*CAPInv* 343])—"those around Aristoboulos the eponymous" and "worshipers of [Artemis] Kolainis"—so their connection clearly is not solely religious.

The case of the inscriptions found in the sanctuary to Jupiter Dolichenus on the Aventine in Rome that look like association *alba* is complex.[39] They are a singularity in the corpus of inscriptions related to the cult of Jupiter Dolichenus. As Jörg Rüpke shows, the lists superpose a collegiate structure to that of the more traditional personnel structure of the cult (2003, 118 [= 2014, 49]). Whether it means that they attest to the existence of an association is a question that I cannot answer in this appendix.

---

[37] More than twenty inscriptions can be related to this or these associations: *CIRB* 1260–91; see *CAPInv* 1324. *CIRB* 1259 and 1262 do not name a deity; see above.

[38] Respectively, *IPergamon* 374 (dedication of an altar to Hadrian by the *hymnodoi theou Sebastou kai theas Rhomes*; *CAPInv* 1653) and *IPergamon* 485 (*IDionysos]* 94; *CAPInv* 927). See Eckhardt and Lepke 2018, 59.

[39] *CCID* 373 (= *AE* 1938, 61; 1940, 75; Zappata 1996, no. 13); *CCID* 375 (= Zappata 1996, no. 14); *CCID* 381 (= Zappata 1996, no. 20).

WORKS CITED

Arnaoutoglou, Ilias. 2003. *Thusias heneka kai sunousias: Private Religious Associations in Hellenistic Athens*. Yearbook of the Research Centre for the History of Greek Law 37. Supplement 4. Athens: Academy of Athens.

———. 2011. "Craftsmen Associations in Roman Lydia—A Tale of Two Cities?" *Ancient Society* 41:257–90.

Ascough, Richard S. 2015. "What Are They *Now* Saying about Christ Groups and Associations?" *CurBR* 13:207–44.

———. 2017. "Methodological Reflections on Synagogues and Christ Groups as 'Associations': A Response to Erich Gruen." *Journal of the Jesus Movement in Its Jewish Setting* 4:118–26.

Ausbüttel, Frank M. 1982. *Untersuchungen zu den Vereinen im Westen des römischen Reiches*. Frankfurter Althistorischen Studien 11. Kallmünz: Michael Lassleben.

Baslez, Marie-Françoise. 2004. "Les notables entre eux: recherches sur les associations d'Athènes à l'époque romaine." Pages 105–20 in *L'hellénisme d'époque romaine. Nouveaux documents, nouvelles approches (Ier s. a C.-IIIe s. p. C.). Actes du colloque international à la mémoire de Louis Robert, Paris, 7–8 juillet 2000 organisé par l'Année épigraphique (USR 710 du CNRS), l'Université de Paris IV (UFR de grec et d'histoire)*. De l'archéologie à l'histoire. Paris: Éditions de Boccard.

———. 2015. "Entraide et mutualisme dans les associations des cités grecques à l'époque hellénistique." Pages 157–68 in *Les régulations sociales dans l'Antiquité*. Edited by Michel Molin. Histoire. Rennes: Presses universitaires de Rennes.

Bendlin, Andreas. 2005. "'Eine Zusammenkunft um der *religio* willen ist erlaubt . . .'? Zu den politischen und rechtlichen Konstruktionen von (religiöser) Vergemeinschaftung in der römischen Kaiserzeit." Pages 65–107 in *Die verrechtlichte Religion: der Öffentlichkeitsstatus von Religionsgemeinschaften*. Edited by Hans G. Kippenberg and Gunnar Folke Schuppert. Tübingen: Mohr Siebeck.

———. 2011. "Associations, Funerals, Sociality, and Roman Law: The Collegium of Diana and Antinous in Lanuvium (CIL 14.2112) Reconsidered." Pages 207–96 in *Aposteldekret und antikes Vereinswesen. Gemeinschaft und ihre Ordnung*. Edited by Markus Öhler. WUNT 280. Tübingen: Mohr Siebeck.

———. 2016. "Sodalician Associations? Digests 47.22.1 pr. and Imperial Government." Pages 435–63 in *Scribal Practices and Social Structures among Jesus Adherents: Essays in Honour of John S. Kloppenborg*. Edited by William E. Arnal, Richard S. Ascough, Robert A. Derrenbacker Jr., and Philip A. Harland. BETL 285. Leuven: Peeters.

Bodel, John. 2008. "From *Columbaria* to Catacombs: Collective Burial in Pagan and Christian Rome." Pages 177–242 in *Commemorating the Dead: Texts and Artifacts in Context*. Edited by Laurie Brink and Deborah Green. Berlin: De Gruyter.

Boissier, Gaston. 1872. "Étude sur quelques collèges funéraires romains: les cultores deorum." *RAr* 23:81–94.

Borg, Barbara E. 2013. *Crisis and Ambition: Tombs and Burial Customs in Third-Century CE Rome.* Oxford Studies in Ancient Culture and Representation. Oxford: Oxford University Press.

Buonocore, Marco, and Oliviero Diliberto. 2003. "L'album e la lex della familia Silvani di Trebula Mutuesca: nuove considerazioni." *Atti della Pontificia Accademia Romana di Archeologia. Serie III, Rendiconti* 75:327–93.

———. 2006. "Approfondimenti sull'album e la lex familiae Silvani da Trebula Mutuesca." *Minima epigraphica et papyrologica* 9:210–54.

Cenival, Françoise de. 1972. *Les associations religieuses en Égypte d'après les documents démotiques.* Bibliothèque d'étude 46. Cairo: Institut français d'archéologie orientale.

———. 2006. "À propos du mot désignant en démotique 'l'association.'" *REG* 57:233–34.

Corsten, Thomas. 2005. "Estates in Roman Asia Minor: The Case of Kibyratis." Pages 1–51 in *Patterns in the Economy of Roman Asia Minor.* Edited by Stephen Mitchell and Constantina Katsari. Swansea: Classical Press of Wales.

Cumont, Franz. 1933. "La Grande inscription bachique du Metropolitan Museum. 2, Commentaire religieux de l'inscription." *AJA* 37, no. 2:232–63.

Eckhardt, Benedikt. 2017. "Heritage Societies? Private Associations in Roman Greece." Pages 71–81 in *Strategies of Remembering in Greece under Rome (100 BC–100 AD).* Edited by Tamara M. Dijkstra, Inger N. I. Kuin, Muriel Moser, and David Weidgenannt. Publications of the Netherlands Institute at Athens 6. Leiden: Sidestone.

———. 2018. "*Religionis causa?* Zur rechtlichen Lage der Vereine 'fremder' Götter in der römischen Kaiserzeit." Pages 113–52 in *Transformationen paganer Religion in der Kaiserzeit. Rahmenbedingungen und Konzepte.* Edited by Michael Blömer and Benedikt Eckhardt. RVV 72. Boston: De Gruyter.

———. 2019. "Private Associations in Hellenistic and Roman Cities: Common Ground and Dividing Lines." Pages 13–36 in *Private Associations and Jewish Communities in the Hellenistic and Roman Cities.* Edited by Benedikt Eckhardt. JSJSup 191. Leiden: Brill.

Eckhardt, Benedikt, and Andrew Lepke. 2018. "Mystai und Mysteria im kaiserzeitlichen Westkleinasien." Pages 39–80 in Blömer and Eckhardt, *Transformationen paganer Religion in der Kaiserzeit.*

Flambard, Jean-Marc. 1987. "Éléments pour une approche financière de la mort dans les classes populaires du haut empire: analyse du budget de quelques collèges funéraires de Rome et d'Italie." Pages 209–44 in *La mort, les morts et l'au-delà dans le monde romain: actes du colloque de Caen, 20–22 novembre 1985.* Edited by François Hinard. Caen: Université de Caen.

Foucart, Paul. 1873. *Des associations religieuses chez les Grecs: thiases, éranes, orgéons, avec le texte des inscriptions relatives à ces associations*. Paris: Klincksieck.

Fredriksen, Paula. 2006. "Mandatory Retirement: Ideas in the Study of Christian Origins Whose Time Has Come to Go." *SR* 35:231–46.

Fröhlich, Pierre, and Patrice Hamon. 2013. "Introduction: Histoire sociale et phénomène associatif dans les cités grecques d'époque hellénistique et impériale." Pages 1–27 in *Groupes et associations dans les cités grecques (IIIe siècle av. J.-C.–IIe siècle ap. J.-C.). Actes de la table ronde de Paris, INHA, 19–20 juin 2009*. Edited by Pierre Fröhlich and Patrice Hamon. Hautes études du monde gréco-romain 49. Geneva: Droz.

Gabrielsen, Vincent. 2000. "The Rhodian Associations and Economic Activity." Pages 215–44 in *Hellenistic Economies*. Edited by Zofia H. Archibald, John Davies, Vincent Gabrielson, and G. J. Oliver. London: Routledge.

———. 2007. "Brotherhoods of Faith and Provident Planning: The Nonpublic Associations of the Greek World." *Mediterranean Historical Review* 22:183–210.

———. 2016a. "Associations, Modernization and the Return of the Private Network in Athens." Pages 121–62 in *Die Athenische Demokratie im 4. Jahrhundert. Zwischen Modernisierung und Tradition*. Edited by Claudia Tiersch. Alte Geschichte. Stuttgart: Franz Steiner.

———. 2016b. "Be Faithful and Prosper: Associations, Trust and the Economy of Security." Pages 87–111 in *Antike Wirtschaft und ihre kulturelle Prägung*. Edited by Kerstin Dross-Krüpe, Sabine Föllinger, and Kai Ruffing. Philippika 98. Wiesbaden: Harrassowitz.

Gordon, Arthur E. 1958–1965. *Album of Dated Latin Inscriptions*. 3 vols. Berkeley: University of California Press.

Gordon, Richard L. 2017. "Projects, Performance and Charisma: Managing Small Religious Groups in the Roman Empire." Pages 277–316 in *Beyond Priesthood: Religious Entrepreneurs and Innovators in the Roman Empire*. Edited by Richard L. Gordon, Georgia Petridou, and Jörg Rüpke. RVV 66. Berlin: De Gruyter.

Gruen, Erich S. 2016. "Synagogues and Voluntary Associations as Institutional Models: A Response to Richard Ascough and Ralph Korner." *Journal of the Jesus Movement in Its Jewish Setting* 3:125–31.

Harland, Philip A. 2009. *Dynamics of Identity in the World of the Early Christians: Associations, Judeans, and Cultural Minorities*. New York: Continuum; London: T&T Clark.

———. 2013. *Associations, Synagogues, and Congregations: Claiming a Place in Ancient Mediterranean Society*. 2nd ed. Kitchener, Ont.: Philip A. Harland.

———. 2019. "'The Most Sacred Society (*thiasos*) of the Pythagoreans': Philosophers Forming Associations." *Journal of Ancient History* 7:207–32.

Horsley, G. H. R., ed. 1983. *A Review of the Greek Inscriptions and Papyri Published in 1978*. Vol. 3 of *New Documents Illustrating Early Christianity*. Edited by S. R. Llewellyn. North Ryde: Ancient History Documentary Research Centre, Macquarie University.

Hughes, George R. 1958. "The Sixth Day of the Lunar Month and the Demotic Word for 'Cult Guild.'" *MDAI* 16:147–60.

Ismard, Paulin. 2010. *La cité des réseaux: Athènes et ses associations, VIe–Ier siècle av. J.-C.* Histoire ancienne et médiévale 105. Paris: Publications de la Sorbonne.

Jaccottet, Anne-Françoise. 2003. *Choisir Dionysos: les associations dionysiaques, ou, La face cachée du dionysisme*. 2 vols. Akanthus crescens 6. Zürich: Akanthus.

Kloppenborg, John S. 1996. "Collegia and *Thiasoi*: Issues in Function, Taxonomy and Membership." Pages 16–30 in *Voluntary Associations in the Graeco-Roman World*. Edited by John S. Kloppenborg and Stephen G. Wilson. London: Routledge.

———. 2011. "Greco-Roman *Thiasoi*, the *Ekklēsia* at Corinth, and Conflict Management." Pages 187–218 in *Redescribing Paul and the Corinthians*. Edited by Ron Cameron and Merrill P. Miller. Early Christianity and Its Literature 5. Atlanta: SBL.

———. 2019. *Christ's Associations: Connecting and Belonging in the Ancient City*. New Haven: Yale University Press.

Kloppenborg, John S., and Richard S. Ascough, eds. 2011. *Attica, Central Greece, Macedonia, Thrace*. BZNW 181. Vol. 1 of *Greco-Roman Associations: Texts, Translations, and Commentary*. Edited by John S. Kloppenborg and Richard S. Ascough. Berlin: De Gruyter.

Kolb, Anne. 1995. "Vereine 'kleiner Leute' und die kaiserliche Verwaltung." *ZPE* 107:201–12.

Lane, E. 1971–1978. *Corpus monumentorum religionis dei Menis (CMRDM)*. 4 vols. EPRO 19. Leiden: Brill.

Last, Richard. 2018. "*Ekklēsia* outside the Septuagint and the *Dēmos*: The Titles of Greco-Roman Associations and Christ-Followers' Groups." *JBL* 137:959–80.

Last, Richard, and Philip A. Harland. 2020. *Group Survival in the Ancient Mediterranean: Rethinking Material Conditions in the Landscape of Jews and Christians*. London: T&T Clark.

Laubry, Nicolas, and Fausto Zevi. 2012. "Inscriptions d'Ostie et phénomène associatif dans l'Empire romain: nouveaux documents et nouvelles considérations." *Archeologia classica* 2:297–343.

de Ligt, Luuk. 2000. "Governmental Attitudes towards Markets and Collegia." Pages 237–52 in *Mercati permanenti e mercati periodici nel mondo romano: atti degli Incontri capresi di storia dell'economia antica (Capri 13–15 ottobre 1997)*. Edited by Elio Lo Cascio. Pragmateiai 2. Bari: Edipuglia.

―――. 2001. "D. 47,22, 1, Pr.-1 and the Formation of Semi-Public Collegia." *Latomus* 60:345–58.

Liu, Jinyu. 2009. *Collegia Centonariorum: The Guilds of Textile Dealers in the Roman West.* Columbia Studies in the Classical Tradition 34. Leiden: Brill.

McLean, Bradley H. 1993. "The Agrippinilla Inscription: Religious Associations and Early Church Formation." Pages 239–70 in *Origins and Method: Towards a New Understanding of Judaism and Christianity; Essays in Honour of John C. Hurd.* Edited by Bradley H. McLean. JSNTSup 86. Sheffield: JSOT Press.

Milner, Nicholas P. 1998. *An Epigraphical Survey in the Kibyra-Olbasa Region Conducted by A.S. Hall.* Regional Epigraphic Catalogues of Asia Minor 3. London: British Institute of Archaeology at Ankara.

Mitchell, Stephen. 2010. "Further Thoughts on the Cult of Theos Hypsistos." Pages 167–208 in *One God: Pagan Monotheism in the Roman Empire.* Edited by Stephen Mitchell and Peter Van Nuffelen. Cambridge: Cambridge University Press.

Mommsen, Theodor. 1843. *De collegiis et sodaliciis Romanorum. Accedit inscriptio Lanuvina.* Kiel: Libraria Schwersiana.

Monson, Andrew. 2002. "Egyptian Priests in Ptolemaic Tebtunis: Administration, Associations, and Economy." MPhil thesis, University College London.

―――. 2005. "Private Associations in the Ptolemaic Fayyum: The Evidence of Demotic Accounts." *Papyrologica Lupiensia* 14:179–96.

―――. 2007. "Religious Associations and Temples in Ptolemaic Tebtunis." Pages 769–79 in *Proceedings of the 24th International Congress of Papyrology, Helsinki, 1–7 August, 2004.* Edited by Jaakko Frösén, Tiina Purola, and Erja Salmenkivi. Commentationes Humanarum Litterarum 122. Helsinki: Finnish Society of Sciences and Letters.

―――. 2019. "Political and Sacred Animals: Religious Associations in Greco-Roman Egypt." Pages 37–57 in Eckhardt, *Private Associations and Jewish Communities.*

Muszynski, Michel. 1977. "Les associations religieuses en Égypte d'après les sources hiéroglyphiques, démotiques et grecques." *OLP* 8:145–63.

van Nijf, Onno M. 1997. *The Civic World of Professional Associations in the Roman East.* Dutch Monographs on Ancient History and Archaeology 17. Amsterdam: J. C. Gieben.

Paganini, Mario C. D. 2017. "Greek and Egyptian Associations in Egypt: Fact or Fiction?" Pages 131–54 in *Hellenism and the Local Communities of the Eastern Mediterranean: 400 BCE–250 CE.* Edited by Boris Chrubasik and Daniel King. Oxford: Oxford University Press.

Pakaluk, Michael. 1994. "Aristotle's Nicomachean Ethics VIII.9, 1160a14–30." *ClQ* 44:46–56.

Perry, Jonathan S. 2006. *The Roman Collegia: The Modern Evolution of an Ancient Concept.* Mnemosyne, Supplements 277. Leiden: Brill.

Poe, Alison Crystal. 2007. "The Third-Century Mausoleum ('Hypogaeum') of the Aurelii in Rome: Pagan or Mixed-Religion Collegium Tomb." PhD diss., Rutgers University.

Poland, Franz. 1909. *Geschichte des griechischen Vereinswesens*. Preisschriften 38. Leipzig: Teubner.

Rebillard, Éric. 1999. "Les formes de l'assistance funéraire dans l'empire romain et leur évolution dans l'antiquité tardive." *Antiquité Tardive* 7:269–82.

———. 2003. *Religion et sépulture: l'église, les vivants et les morts dans l'antiquité tardive*. Civilisations et sociétés 115. Paris: Éditions de l'École des Hautes Études en Sciences Sociales.

———. 2009. *The Care of the Dead in Late Antiquity*. Translated by Elizabeth Trapnell Rawlings and Jeanine Routier-Pucci. Ithaca: Cornell University Press.

———. 2013. *Transformations of Religious Practices in Late Antiquity*. Variorum Collected Studies Series 1028. Farnham: Ashgate Variorum.

Reseghetti, S. 1988. "Il provvedimento di Settimio Severo sui collegia religionis causa e i cristiani." *Rivista di Storia della Chiesa in Italia* 42:357–64.

Roberts, Colin H., Theodore C. Skeat, and Arthur Darby Nock. 1936. "The Gild of Zeus Hypsistos." *HTR* 29:39–88.

Rohde, Dorothea. 2012. *Zwischen Individuum und Stadtgemeinde. Die Integration von Collegia in Hafenstädten*. Studien zur alten Geschichte 15. Mainz: Verlag Antike.

Rostovtzeff, Mihail Ivanovič, Frank Edward Brown, and Charles Bradford Welles, eds. 1939. *The Excavations at Dura-Europos: Preliminary Report of the Seventh and Eighth Seasons of Work, 1933–1934 and 1934–1935*. New Haven: Yale University Press.

Rüpke, Jörg. 2003. "Integration und Transformation von Immigrantenreligion. Beobachtungen zu den Inschriften des Iuppiter-Dolichenus-Kultes in Rom." *Studia historica. Historia antigua* 21:105–18.

———. 2014. *From Jupiter to Christ: On the History of Religion in the Roman Imperial Period*. Translated by David M. B. Richardson. Oxford: Oxford University Press.

Scheid, John. 1986. "Le thiase du Metropolitan Museum (IGUR I,160)." Pages 275–90 in *L'association dionysiaque dans les sociétés anciennes: Actes de la table ronde organisée par l'École française de Rome (Rome 24–25 mai 1984)*. Collection de l'École française de Rome 89. Paris: Éditions de Boccard.

———. 2003. "Communauté et communauté: réflexions sur quelques ambiguïtés d'après l'exemple des thiases de l'Égypte romaine." Pages 61–74 in *Les communautés religieuses dans le monde gréco-romain: essais de définition*. Edited by Nicole Belayche and Simon C. Mimouni. BEHER 117. Turnhout: Brepols.

———. 2011. "Community and Community: Reflections on Some Ambiguities Based on the *Thiasoi* of Roman Egypt." Pages 365–82 in *The Religious*

History of the Roman Empire: Pagans, Jews, and Christians. Edited by John North and S. R. F. Price. Oxford Readings in Classical Studies. Oxford: Oxford University Press.

Schilbrack, Kevin. 2014. *Philosophy and the Study of Religions: A Manifesto*. Oxford: Wiley-Blackwell.

Sirks, A. J. Boudewijn. 2006. "Die Vereine in der kaiserlichen Gesetzgebung." Pages 21–40 in *Vereine, Synagogen und Gemeinden im kaiserzeitlichen Kleinasien*. Edited by Andreas Gutsfeld and Dietrich-Alex Koch. Studien und Texte zu Antike und Christentum 25. Tübingen: Mohr Siebeck.

Thomsen, Christian A. 2020. *The Politics of Association in Hellenistic Rhodes*. Edinburgh: Edinburgh University Press.

Tod, Marcus N. 1932. *Sidelights on Greek History: Three Lectures on the Light Thrown by Greek Inscriptions on the Life and Thought of the Ancient World*. Oxford: Oxford University Press.

Touna, Vaia. 2017. *Fabrications of the Greek Past: Religion, Tradition, and the Making of Modern Identities*. Supplements to Method & Theory in the Study of Religion 9. Leiden: Brill.

Tran, Nicolas. 2001. "Le collège, la communauté et le politique sous le Haut-Empire romain: historiographie du droit à la fin du XIXe siècle, tradition sociologique et quelques recherches contemporaines." *Cahiers du Centre Gustave Glotz* 12:181–98.

———. 2006. *Les membres des associations romaines: le rang social des collegiati en Italie et en Gaules sous le haut-empire*. Collection de l'École française de Rome 367. Rome: École française de Rome.

Ustinova, Yulia. 1991. "The *Thiasoi* of Theos Hypsistos in Tanais." *HR* 31:150–80.

———. 1999. *The Supreme Gods of the Bosporan Kingdom: Celestial Aphrodite and the Most High God*. RGRW 135. Leiden: Brill.

Venticinque, Philip F. 2016. *Honor among Thieves: Craftsmen, Merchants, and Associations in Roman and Late Roman Egypt*. New Texts from Ancient Cultures. Ann Arbor: University of Michigan Press.

Verboven, Koenraad. 2011. "Professional Collegia: Guilds or Social Clubs?" *Ancient Society* 41:187–95.

Vetter, Emil. 1953. "Die familia Silvani in Trebula Mutuesca und die sectores materiarum in Aquileia." Pages 93–119 in *Studi aquileiesi offerti il 7 ottobre 1953 a Giovanni Brusin nel suo 70. compleanno*. Aquileia: Associazione nazionale per Aquileia.

Waltzing, Jean-Pierre. 1895–1900. *Étude historique sur les corporations professionnelles chez les Romains depuis les origines jusqu'à la chute de l'Empire d'Occident*. 4 vols. Leuven: Peeters.

———. 1898. "Les collèges funéraires chez les Romains (1)." *Musée Belge* 2:281–94.

———. 1899. "Les collèges funéraires chez les Romains (2)." *Musée Belge* 3:130–57.

Wipszycka, Ewa. 1970. "Les confréries dans la vie religieuse de l'Egypte chrétienne." Pages 511–25 in *Proceedings of the Twelfth International Congress of Papyrology*. Edited by Deborah H. Samuel. ASP 7. Toronto: Hakkert.

———. 1996. *Études sur le christianisme dans l'Égypte de l'Antiquité tardive*. Studia Ephemeridis Augustinianum 52. Rome: Institutum Patristicum Augustinianum.

Wojciechowski, Przemysław. 2021. *Roman Religious Associations in Italy (1st–3rd Century)*. Toruń: Nicholas Copernicus University Press.

Zappata, Emanuela. 1996. "Les divinités dolichéniennes et les sources épigraphiques latines." Pages 87–256 in *Orientalia sacra urbis Romae: dolichena et heliopolitana. Recueil d'études archéologiques et historico-religieuses sur les cultes cosmopolites d'origine commagénienne et syrienne*. Edited by Gloria M. Bellelli and Ugo Bianchi. Studia archaeologica 84. Rome: "L'ERMA" di Bretschneider.

14

συναγωγή and Semi-public Associations

Greco-Roman, Judean, and *Christos* Followers

Ralph J. Korner

My priority in this essay is to reframe conversations in which the English word *synagogue* (Greek: συναγωγή) is usually delimited only to a Judean group and/or building and/or meeting. I will demonstrate the value of adding two more group entities from the ancient Mediterranean into the relevant discussions: (1) Greco-Roman associations that use the term συναγωγή, and (2) *Christos*-follower groups that use the term συναγωγή and the related term ἐκκλησία ("assembly").

TERMS AND DEFINITIONS

"Synagogue" and Association

In their synagogue sourcebook, Runesson, Binder, and Olsson (2008) include within the semantic range of the English word *synagogue* twenty-two different Greek, Hebrew, and Latin words that were used by Judeans in the land and/or in the diaspora to describe five synagogal entities:[1] (1) a public/civic gathering in the land for administrative, judicial, religious, economic, and/or social activities (e.g., συναγωγή);[2] (2) public or semi-public buildings (e.g.,

---

[1] See also Runesson 2001, 171–73.
[2] Levine 2005, 29.

προσευχή,[3] συναγωγή,[4] *bet ha-midrash*,[5] *bet mo'ed*,[6] *bet ha knesset*,[7] οἰκός[8]); (3) a temporary community identity (συναγωγή) when gathered for public or semi-public purposes; (4) the meeting of a semi-public association (e.g., σύλλογος,[9] συναγωγή[10]); and (5) a collective designation for a semi-public association in the diaspora (ἐκκλησία,[11] πολίτευμα[12]).[13] Gillihan (2012) adds one more example of a semi-public association, but this one being in the land:[14] the (pre-)Covenanters of Qumran,[15] who self-designated corporately as a קהל.[16] קהל is the only Hebrew term that the LXX consistently translates as ἐκκλησία. By contrast, the LXX uses συναγωγή to translate both קָהָל and עֵדָה.[17]

Runesson (2001) gives further nuance to synagogue taxonomy by identifying two types of synagogue institutions: public and semi-public. Judean public/civic synagogue gatherings addressed a broad range of issues relevant to all members of a regional community, usually in rural Judea. According to Levine (2005, 29), the communal functions of public synagogue gatherings included "a courtroom, school, hostel, a place for political meetings, social gatherings, housing charity funds, a setting for manumissions, meals (sacred or otherwise), and, of course, a number of religious-liturgical functions." As for semi-public synagogue gatherings,

---

[3]   A προσευχή is a structure for prayer (Philo, *Legat.* 132) and/or public decision-making (Josephus; in Alexandria [*C. Ap.* 2.10]; in Judea [*Vita* 276–81, 294–95]). It is a regional synonym in Egypt for συναγωγή (Runesson, Binder, and Olsson 2008, 188).

[4]   Philo, *Hypoth.* 7.11–14.

[5]   m. Ter. 11:10. See Runesson, Binder, and Olsson 2008, 105; Runesson 2001, 223–34.

[6]   War Scroll (1QM 3.3–4).

[7]   b. Meg. 26a.

[8]   Ascough, Harland, and Kloppenborg 2012, no. 145 (*GRA* 113; *IJO* 2.168; *MAMA* 6.264; *CIJ* 766). Rajak (1999) suggests three interpretations of οἰκός in the Severa inscription: (1) "house of prayer" (i.e., συναγωγή), (2) a domestic premise, or (3) the main hall in a building.

[9]   The Therapeutae held a σύλλογος ("general assembly") every seventh day (Philo, *Contempl.* 30–33; 30–45 CE; Runesson, Binder, and Olsson 2008, 201).

[10]   For example, the Essenes (Philo, *Prob.* 80–83) and the community behind the Theodotus inscription (*CIJ* 2.1404; see Kloppenborg 2000; Runesson 2001, 171–72, 356–57).

[11]   Philo, *Virt.* 108.

[12]   Josephus speaks of Judean πολιτεύματα in Alexandria (*C. Ap.* 2.164–65; cf. *Ant.* 1.13).

[13]   See the appendix for a collated table of terminological categories.

[14]   See my discussion of Gillihan in Korner 2017b, 175–79.

[15]   For a comparison of the *yaḥad* (in Qumran and beyond) with Greco-Roman associations through the lens of disciplinary measures and "rites of affliction" in the *Community Rule* and the *Damascus Document*, see Krause 2019.

[16]   4QMMT, CD 7.17; 11.22; 12.6; 4Q396 1–21, l. 40; and 1QSa 2.4. See further in Korner 2017b, 235–37.

[17]   For details, see Korner 2017b, 93–94.

Runesson (2001) notes that they were "members-only" meetings usually within an urban setting in the diaspora. It is only these semi-public groupings that fall within the heuristic category *association*.

Last (2016) adds helpful nuance to the classification *synagogue* by looking beyond emic terminology used by Judeans. He surveys the inscriptional evidence of thirty Judean craft guilds that heretofore have not been considered as examples of synagogue communities.[18] If one considers these heterogeneous occupational guilds as synagogue communities, then one "breaks the mold," so to speak, of traditional definitions of ancient synagogues as only reflecting socio-religiously homogenous Judean communities (non-Judean proselytes and "Godfearers" notwithstanding).

While acknowledging Last's important contribution to the conversation on synagogue terminology, Eckhardt (2020, 315) problematizes his approach by noting that if "every association with one or more Jewish members [is] a 'synagogue' of the same right as others [then] there is no room for legal categories here."[19] Eckhardt is concerned here (rightfully) with the need to integrate into the "Greco-Roman associations" model the fact that Judean "synagogue" associations were considered *collegia licita* under Roman law.

Mention should also be made here that the full semantic range of the English word *synagogue* (i.e., the twenty-two terms) is broader than the semantic domain of the *taxon association*. *Association* refers only to a *semi-public communal entity* (e.g., συναγωγή, ἐκκλησία, πολιτεύμα). The semantic range of the English word *synagogue*, however, is broader than that of *association* since it includes two additional concepts: (1) a *public entity* (e.g., συναγωγή) and (2) a *structure/building* (e.g., συναγωγή, προσευχή, *bet ha knesset*).

Associations: Private or Semi-public?

The category *association* is purely a heuristic framework for noting similarities and differences among many small group phenomena in the ancient Mediterranean world. Harland (2003, 29) uses five principal social networks as a basis for classifying and identifying the overlapping functions of at least five types of non-civic associations: (1) household connections, (2) ethnic or geographic connections, (3) neighborhood connections, (4) occupational connections, and (5) cult or temple connections.[20] Ascough (2015) reframes

[18] See the appendix "Selected Occupational 'Synagogues'" in Last 2016.
[19] In order to follow the debate, see Eckhardt 2019c (response to Last 2016) and the reaction in Last and Harland 2020, 6, n. 20. See also the conversations in Gruen 2016 with Ascough 2015 and Korner 2015, and the responses in Ascough 2017 and Korner 2017a.
[20] Instone-Brewer and Harland 2008, 202, 203.

Harland's definition of "association" into an etic meta-category that sub-sumes taxonomical subsets based on factors such as kinship, neighborhood, ethnicity, occupation, or cultic expressions. Thus, as subsets of the word *association* we can include group designations used in antiquity for (1) Judean "synagogue" groups (e.g., by the Covenanters of Qumran, the Theraputae of Egypt, the ἐκκλησία in Alexandria [Philo, *Virt.* 108]), (2) Greco-Roman groups (e.g., θίασοι, collegia, συνόδοι, κοινά), and (3) *Christos*-follower groups (e.g., ἐκκλησίαι, συναγωγαί).

Kloppenborg (2013, 187) adds a cautionary note, though, to our usage of the *taxon association*. He argues that the communal complexity of Christ groups stretches beyond the definitional boundaries of *association*. Thus, thinking about Christ groups through the lens of Greco-Roman associations, while somewhat reductionist, is nonetheless helpful in providing us with "rich data from ancient associations that can generate heuristic questions for interrogating the data from Christ groups."

Eckhardt (2018; 2019a; 2019b; 2019c) echoes Kloppenborg's caution, but from a different angle. He is not convinced that the primacy given to the heuristic model of "Greco-Roman associations" is appropriate. His priority, rather, is to interrogate the growing consensus that Judean groups were essentially a type of Greco-Roman private association. In fact, Eckhardt (2018) critically evaluates the generally received wisdom that Pliny, Lucian, Celsus, and Tertullian perceived Christ groups through the lens of associations and finds that wisdom wanting.

Eckhardt (2019b; 2019c) seeks to move the heuristic conversation forward by advocating for nuanced analyses that acknowledge differentiation not least across time, geography, political regimes, and ethnic/cultural frameworks. Examples include (1) assessing the value of a synchronic approach (e.g., fees, communal meals, or membership structures), favored by scholars of religion, versus a diachronic approach, favored by ancient historians, which has largely marginalized Judean groups; and (2) acknowledging differences between the Greek and Roman worlds, and the "ground-level" variances not least in local contexts, legal statuses, and ancient categories.

I would suggest that another way to move the heuristic conversation forward is through a reevaluation of the three categories that scholars use when assessing participant accessibility to group activities in the ancient world. Runesson (2012, 213) helpfully frames them within the context of the three social levels at which "religion" was integrated: "a. Public level (civic/state/ empire concerns); b. Semi-Public level/Association level (voluntary groups/ cults and their concerns); c. Private level (domestic/familial concerns)."

Scholarship commonly uses *private* as a descriptor for what Runesson terms a "semi-public" association. This issue is not a matter simply of terminological preference, but of precision. Both categories are required when assessing the epigraphic record. *IGUR* 160 (Torre Nova, Italy; ca. 160 CE), for example, describes a "private" θίασος (cultic) association that actually did limit its membership to those with familial connections. It is the second-century CE Dionysus association that was overseen by the priestess Pompeia Agrippinilla and which had four hundred *mystai* ("initiates"), almost all of whom were "household" members, whether familial or servile.[21] However, in most cases, θίασοι have a more diverse membership beyond familial connections (e.g., Egyptian Isis and Serapis θίασοι). These, then, are better described as "semi-public" associations. Runesson's category of "semi-public," thus, provides a more precise "middle ground" for association categorization, particularly in respect of the five principal social networks identified by Harland (2003). The non-civic category of *semi-public* is most broadly representative of the diverse demographics of associations in the Greco-Roman world. A "semi-public" association is one in which communal participation is delimited to members and sympathizers only, none of which need have any familial connections.[22]

But there is yet one more twist to unravel in the search for precision in association terminology. Eckhardt (2020, 316) notes that Judean organizations in Egypt named πολιτεύματα were "created and ultimately controlled by the Ptolemaic bureaucracy, [and so] we cannot treat them as private associations like the ubiquitous groups of *Dionysiastai, Sarapiastai vel sim.* in Greek cities."[23] This being the case, perhaps a differentiation *within* the term *semi-public* is helpful. In this essay, I will use the term *formal semi-public* for associations with direct connections to local, regional, or federal governing authorities. Egypt is one region where this associational classification predominates. Not only can we include Judean πολιτεύματα within the term *formal semi-public* but also Ptolemaic-era Egyptian religious associations (e.g., Isis and Serapis cults/θίασοι).[24] One could also potentially include the first-century CE association that Philo describes as being tasked with

---

[21] See McLean 1993; Harland 2003, 30; 2009, 26, 32.

[22] See the appendix for a collated table of ancient group terminology divided into the three social categories of public, semi-public, and private.

[23] Regarding the evolution of Jewish πολιτεύματα in Egypt from state-sponsored ethnic groups during the Ptolemaic period to private associations, see Czajkowski 2019.

[24] See Monson 2019, whose study of Egyptian religious associations during the Ptolemaic era (330–323 BCE) notes that they were formally recognized in Egyptian law, with their primary function being to promote the ruler cult and the state cults of Isis and Serapis.

initiating Egyptian proselytes into the πολιτεία of the Judean community in Alexandria (*Virt.* 108).[25]

There is, though, yet one more distinction that can be assigned to non-civic "semi-public" groups, both "formal" and "informal," during the Roman period. Eckhardt (2020, 318–19) notes a not insignificant difference between Judean associations in the Roman period and other *collegia licita*: trans-local connections and privilege.[26] He states that "Jewish privileges, through information sharing and precedent, developed into a set of rights given to Jews everywhere. . . . Perhaps the translocal [*sic*] development of Jewish privileges was not foreseen when Caesar recognized Jewish associations as legitimate *collegia*."

The Roman legal category *collegia licita* does seem, however, to complicate terminological precision further: the associations included within the legal category *collegia licita* do not fit the heuristic category *formal semi-public association* since, although being legally sanctioned by Rome, they are not integrally connected with the governance structures of their political regions. Nor would *collegia licita* seem to fit seamlessly within the category *informal semi-public associations* given their elevated legal and social status with (not least) civic authorities. Eckhardt (2020, 316–17) notes three factors that were consistent, from a Roman perspective, of a *collegium licitum*: being "either very old or 'useful,'" the group had "the right to 'convene, assemble, and contribute (money)' (*coire convenire conferre*)." This Roman legal framework meant that even the religious identity of Judeans was particularized through their *collegia licita*: "From a Roman perspective, there was no 'Judaism' outside associations" (Eckhardt 2020, 319). Given the foregoing, it seems that precision is further complicated when seeking a heuristic classification for a Judean *collegium licitum*, not least given their distinctive, but not unique, development of trans-local privileges.

ΣΥΝΑΓΩΓΗ AND GRECO-ROMAN ASSOCIATIONS

In its essence, συναγωγή simply denotes a non-civic or civic gathering/ meeting. As such, it is an *ethnically neutral* term. In its use as a group designation, it sits linguistically within a family of *syn*-compounds used for

---

[25] See Korner 2015, 66–69; 2017b, 129–36. See also Korner 2017b for an extended discussion of Philo's use of ἐκκλησία for Judean association gatherings in Egypt within *Spec.* 1.324–25 (2017b, 136–40) and *Deus* 111 (2017b, 141–45).

[26] See also Eckhardt 2019a on similarities between the "trans-local aspects" of Jewish communities and other *collegia licita* (e.g., Dionysiac *technitai*).

association names (e.g., συνόδος).[27] The Attic spelling is used in non-Judean literary artifacts as early as the fifth century BCE by Thucydides (*P.W.* 2.18.3; ξυναγωγή). Extant epigraphic records use συναγωγή (not ξυναγωγή) within non-Judean contexts, but almost exclusively beginning with the second century BCE.[28] As a side note, it should be acknowledged that προσευχή also is used within non-Judean inscriptional contexts.[29]

From Hellas we find examples of συναγωγή being used as a group designation by a "formal semi-public" association and by an "informal semi-public" association. A second-century BCE inscription from Thessaly (*IG* IX,2 259) describes the "formal semi-public" συναγωγή of the νέοι[30] (τῆς τῶν νέων συναγωγῆς) presenting a civic honorary decree "during a regular civic assembly" (ἐκκλησία<ς> [γενομέ]<ν>ης ἐννόμου).[31] An example of an "informal semi-public" συναγωγή is found in *IPerinthos* 49 (Perinthos, later Herakleia, Thrace; first century CE). It honors the restoration of "the altar to the synagogue (τῆ συναγω||[γ]ῆ) of barbers—namely those gathered around the head of the synagogue (ἀρχισυνάγ||[ωγ]ον)."[32] The most natural way to read the juxtaposition of the phrase συναγωγή τῶν κουρέων with [π]ερὶ ἀρχισυνάγ||[ωγ]ον is that συναγωγή is being used as a group designation/name of the group rather than only as a name for the meeting of the group. While Judean usages of συναγωγή as a group identity are not uncommon, that semantic domain is uncommon with respect to a Greco-Roman association.

From Alexandria in Egypt hails an example of a ("formal"?) non-civic association (συνόδος) of "the principal followers of emperor Augustus Caesar," whose assembly in their building (ἐν οἴκωι συνόδου) is designated as a συναγωγή and whose leadership includes a συναγωγός (*SB* 22.15460; late first century BCE).[33] Ascough, Harland, and Kloppenborg

---

[27]   See Kloppenborg 2019, 371, n. 113, for a list of *syn*-compound association names.

[28]   PHI indicates 276 occurrences of the lexeme συναγωγή. Of these, only three are definitively dated prior to 200 BCE, and they each are from Cos/Kos (*IG* XII,4 1:96; *IG* XII,4 1:298; *IG* XII,4 1:348/*ICosED* 149).

[29]   Harland states that the phrase τῆ κυρίᾳ προσ|ευχῆ refers to a "prayer-house" used by an association dedicated to "Asbameus . . . likely Zeus" in Amastris (AGRW 13788).

[30]   The official age-based group called νέοι incorporated young men whose primary communal venue was the *gymnasium*, and whose political status afforded them occasional participation in honorary decrees alongside civic entities such as civic councilors (βουλευταί), the δῆμος, and the γερουσία (the *polis* elders; Korner 2017b, 57, n. 145).

[31]   *IG* IX,2 259 (Kierion: Sofades, ca. 125 BCE).

[32]   Ascough, Harland, and Kloppenborg 2012, no. 63; *IPerinthos* 49 = *IGRR* 1.782 = *GRA* I 86.

[33]   Ascough, Harland, and Kloppenborg 2012, no. 280 (see also no. 63); *SB* 22.15460 = papyrus written by the same association as the inscription *BGU* 4.1137; 5 BCE (August 21).

(2012, 168) translate the Greek phrase ἐπὶ τῆς γενηθείσης συν|[α]γωγῆς as "at the assembly which met [in the house]," which implies that συναγωγή is a group designation. However, a more preferable translation would be "at the meeting that was convened [in the house]," which is more consistent with Harland's translation of ἐπὶ συναγωγῆς | τῆς γενηθείσης . . . τοῦ πολιτεύματος in *OGIS* 737 as "during the gathering of the corporate body."[34] Even though the honoree's mother was a priestess of Horos, given the Idumean demographic of *OGIS* 737, ambiguity exists as to whether the συναγωγή terminology therein derives from a Judean heritage or from the more ethnically neutral use of συναγωγή among Greco-Roman associations.

Two examples from Asia Minor represent second-century BCE inscriptions of "informal semi-public" associations that use συναγωγή in the sense of "assembly" (*I.Thess* I 16; *IApamBith* 35). Both indicate cultic contexts. Öhler (2018) cites a συναγωγή mention that he claims is "one of the oldest for an association" in Bithynia and Pontus. *IApamBith* 35 (119 or 104 BCE) describes a priestess of Cybele being honored by the male and female members (θιασῖται, θιασίτιδες) of a cultic association within the συναγωγή of Zeus (ἐν τῆι τοῦ Διὸς συναγωγῇ).[35] Elsewhere in Asia Minor there is an even older συναγωγή reference. From the mid-second century BCE (146–133 BCE), we find a posthumous honorary decree by an association of *Attalistai* (τοῦ κοινοῦ τῶν Ἀτταλιστῶ) for the priest of the synod (ὁ <ἱρ>εὸς | τῆς συνόδου) in appreciation for his personal benefaction to them (*CIG* 3069).[36] The priest was proclaimed "worthy of our group's (αἵρεσις) and gathering's (συναγωγή) name."

From the Aegean Islands comes a second-century BCE inscription by a κοινόν of Anthister (Dionysian) in Thera that was established by a Pythian oracle. Their gathering is called τὰν [συναγω]|[γὰ]ν, with the overseers known as ἐπισκόποι.[37] This inscription provides evidence that associations engaged in loans.

---

[34] See Harland's translation of *OGIS* 737 = *SB* 5.8929 = *AGRW* 20335. It is not referenced in Ascough, Harland, and Kloppenborg 2012, nor in *GRA III*. *OGIS* 737 is a late second-century BCE honorary decree by Idumean soldiers in Memphis.

[35] Ascough, Harland, and Kloppenborg 2012, no. 95 = *GRA* 99 = *IApamBith* 35 = *CCCA* 1.25. For text, translation, and commentary, see *AGRW* 52.

[36] Teos (Ionia, Asia Minor), 146–133 BCE; *GRA* 141 = *CIG* 3069 = *OGIS* 326. For text, translation, and commentary, see *AGRW* 12904.

[37] For text, translation, and commentary, see *AGRW* 12910. Thera (southwestern islands, Aegean Islands), ca. 200 BCE; *IG* XII,3 329 + *IG* XII,3Suppl. 1295 on p. 284.

As already noted, aside from ethnically neutral references to the word συναγωγή in Greco-Roman epigraphic records, there are also references to the cognate συνάγωγος (and ἀρχισυνάγωγος) as associational leadership titles. An illustrative example of συνάγωγος usage by a non-Judean θίασος association (society of shippers, θέασος ναυκλήρων) comes from the second-century CE Bosporan Kingdom (*CIRB* 1134).[38] The title ἀρχισυνάγωγος is found in an inscription from second-century CE Macedonia that mentions the dedication of an altar (τὸν βωμόν) by a collegium (κο<λ>λήγιον) that was overseen by ὁ ἀρχισυνάγωγος θεοῦ ἥρωος ("of the hero god").[39]

"SYNAGOGUE" AND JUDEAN ASSOCIATIONS

I move now to an assessment of data related to συναγωγή usage among Judean associations in the diaspora and in the land. My focus here is limited to highlighting a few epigraphic examples that help inform our reading of *Christos*-follower writings.

Diasporic Synagogue Entities

With respect to Egypt and surrounding regions, two observations bear upon our review of συναγωγή usage among Judean associations. First, Runesson, Binder, and Olsson (2008, 188) note that Philo's use of προσευχή for the meeting places of Alexandrian Judeans appears to be a regional synonym in Egypt for συναγωγή. Thus, the paucity of συναγωγή references in Egypt does not justify any word-concept conclusion that there was a paucity of Judean "synagogue" communities.[40] Second, as I have already noted, Eckhardt clarifies that Judean πολιτεύματα were not associations in a strictly non-civic sense since they were regulated and sponsored by Ptolemaic functionaries. Within inscriptions, πολιτεύμα is used as a sociological term ("social network") rather than as a political term ("commonwealth").[41] As a

---

[38] See *GRA* I 93 = Ascough, Harland, and Kloppenborg 2012, no. 84 = *CIRB* 1134. For other examples of συνάγωγος occurrences in non-Judean inscriptions, see Ascough, Harland, and Kloppenborg 2012, nos. 84, 85, 87, 90, 91, 213, 280, 286, 291.

[39] *GRA* I 66 (Macedonia, Kassandreia/Hagios Mamas; *CIG* 2:2007f; *IMakedD* 747). For other examples of non-Judean inscriptions using ἀρχισυνάγωγος, see Ascough, Harland, and Kloppenborg 2012, nos. 45, 54, 63.

[40] Levine (2005, 83, n. 8; 87, n. 41) notes that συναγωγή occurs only once in Egyptian inscriptions (*CIJ* 2.1447 = *JIGRE* 20).

[41] Ascough, Harland, and Kloppenborg (2012, 190–91) note that Lüderitz 1994 (see esp. 192) decisively challenged the view first put forward in Smallwood 1976 that πολιτεύμα necessarily indicates a community that is formally recognized by political institutions, such as the citizenry of a *polis*, or a colony of immigrants with semiautonomous political status.

result, πολίτευμα is most accurately translated as "community"[42] or "corporate body,"[43] and is even used in Cyrenaica of an association of women.[44]

One extant example of a Judean πολίτευμα (Berenike, Cyrenaica) holds primary interest here in that it self-identified collectively as a συναγωγή. It is mentioned in three inscriptions. The earlier one (*IBerenike* 18, first century BCE)[45] indicates that the "formal semi-public" πολίτευμα mimics elements of a civic Greek enactment decree (e.g., the enactment formula is ἔδοξεν τῆι, "resolved by").[46] It reads in part, "The leaders of the corporate body of the Judeans in Berenike resolved" (ἔ[δοξε . . . τῶι πολιτεύματι | τ[ῶν] ἐν Βερνικίδι Ἰουδαίων). The ostensibly later inscription (*IBerenike* 17; 41 BCE or 24 CE) recounts honors ascribed to a Roman provincial official.[47] A distinctive feature of this πολίτευμα reference is that, in later decades, the same group refers to itself as a συναγωγή (and to its meeting structure as a συναγωγή; *IBerenike* 16).[48]

The inscriptional contexts for πολίτευμα usage inform our understanding of Paul's politicized use of πολίτευμα in Phil 3:20 ("our πολίτευμα is in heaven").[49] If one translates Paul's πολίτευμα reference consistent with its inscriptional usage ("community/corporate body"), then Paul may be making a veiled reference to the fact that his ἐκκλησία communities should function "politically" as metaphorical cleruchies of their heavenly community

---

[42]   Runesson, Binder, and Olsson (2008, nos. 131, 132) use "community" to translate πολίτευμα in *IBerenike* 18 and *IBerenike* 17.

[43]   Ascough, Harland, and Kloppenborg (2012, nos. 305, 306) use "corporate body" to translate πολίτευμα in *IBerenike* 18 and *IBerenike* 17. See also Harland (2009, 41) on the πολίτευμα of Phrygians at Alexandria (3 BCE; *IAlexandriaK* 74 = *IG* XIV 701 = *IGRR* 1.458) and of devotees of the goddess Sachypsis in the Fayum in Egypt (3 BCE; *SIG*³ 1107).

[44]   The πολίτευμα of women were invited to participate in the biannual Hera festival. The following inscriptions are from Caria and are undated: *IStratonikeia* 149; *IStratonikeia* 174; *IStratonikeia* 352; *IStratonikeia* 666. For text, translation, and commentary see https://philipharland.com/.

[45]   Ascough, Harland, and Kloppenborg 2012, no. 305 = *IBerenike* 18 = *CJZC* 70 = *SEG* 16 (1976), no. 931, and *SEG* 48 (1998), no. 2048.

[46]   For the five standardized elements within enactment decrees, see Rhodes and Lewis 1997, 551–52; McLean, 2002, 215–27.

[47]   Ascough, Harland, and Kloppenborg 2012, no. 306 = *IBerenike* 17 = *CJZC* 71.

[48]   *IBerenike* 16 (56 CE) reads, "It seemed good to the synagogue of the Judeans [τῆ συναγωγῆ τῶν . . . Ἰουδαίων] in Berenike that they should inscribe . . . the names of those who contributed towards the restoration of the synagogue [τῆς συναγωγῆς]" (Ascough, Harland, and Kloppenborg 2012, no. 307 = *SEG* 17 [1960], no. 823 = *IBerenike* 16 = *CJZC* 72).

[49]   See Sergienko 2011 for an extensive analysis of Paul's usage of πολίτευμα.

that elsewhere he calls the "Jerusalem above" (Gal 4:26).[50] This "political" action involves inculcating their loving ἐκκλησία ethos, which derives from their heavenly πολίτευμα, into all of their "*polis*-tical" engagements, not least within the Roman colony (aka "cleruchy") of Philippi.

Synagogue Entities in the Land

Gruen (2016, 131) questions what we can know "about synagogues in Judea, indeed in Jerusalem itself." He notes that if we accord historical veracity to the book of Acts, then we have evidence in Jerusalem of "the synagogues [*sic*; συναγωγή in singular] of the freedmen (*libertini*), of the Cyreneans and the Alexandrians, and of the Cilicians and Asians" (Acts 6:9).[51] This possibility of multiple συναγωγή associations in Jerusalem gains reinforcement through an integration of inscriptional evidence.

Regarding Cyrenaica, we know that sometime early in the first century CE, the πολίτευμα association in Berenike appeared to have changed their group designation to συναγωγή (*IBerenike* 16). Did immigrants from Berenike carry this practice with them to Jerusalem? For Luke to mention that Alexandrians in Jerusalem used συναγωγή as a group designation is not unexpected since the regional "synagogue" term in Egypt is προσευχή, but it refers to a building, not to a group designation. Regarding Cilicia, it is clear that Saul of Tarsus (Paul), who was present at Stephen's stoning, was intimately acquainted with synagogue contexts. Although Runesson, Binder, and Olsson (2008) do not cite any inscriptional evidence of the word συναγωγή from Cilicia,[52] there is one extant instance of συναγωγέα, which is the title ("leader of the gathering") of the recipient of an honorary crowning by the Σαββατισταί θεοῦ ("Sabbatists of God"). Harland (2003, 49–50) indicates that the Sabbatists seem to be "an association [of gentiles] devoted to the Jewish God with practices relating to the Sabbath (time of Augustus)." Regarding Asia, there are archaeological "synagogue" sites (e.g., Priene; cf. *ASSB* 113) and literary συναγωγή references,[53] but a paucity of inscriptional evidence up to 200 CE.[54] If one assumes that a

---

[50] A cleruchy was an ancient Athenian colony in which the cleruchs, or settlers, maintained their political allegiance to Athens and retained their Athenian citizenship. Two Athenian cleruchies (Delos, Samos) are associated with inscriptional evidence of a Greco-Roman association that names its semi-public assembly an ἐκκλησία (*IDelos* 1519; *ISamos* 119).

[51] Acts 6:9 reads in part, τινες τῶν ἐκ τῆς συναγωγῆς τῆς λεγομένης Λιβερτίνων.

[52] See their map in Runesson, Binder, and Olsson 2008, 330–31.

[53] See Runesson, Binder, and Olsson 2008, esp. 134–51.

[54] *IJO* 2.157 (undated; Nikomedia, Bithynia). It reads in part, τῇ συναγωγῇ τῶν || Ἰουδέων. *IJO* 2.157 = *TAM* 4.377 = *CIJ* 799.

reference to an ἀρχισυνάγωγος implies that his community self-designates as a συναγωγή, then Synnada in Phrygia provides us with one roughly contemporaneous "smoking gun," so to speak (first to second century CE).[55] Although far from conclusive, perhaps my rehearsal of συναγωγή references is illustrative of the possibility that the book of Acts may be listing a number of diasporic συναγωγή associations that existed in Jerusalem during Stephen's time in Jerusalem.

While Gruen grants (1) the existence of diasporic Judean associations in Judea, and (2) the evidence of Levine (2005) that in rural Judea (and regions) there existed public "synagogues," he questions the existence of "synagogue" semi-public associations in Judea (especially Jerusalem) that were comprised solely of local Judeans (2016, 131). He states that his skepticism is congruent with the Theodotus inscription (ca. 70 CE),[56] since Theodotus, the builder of the συναγωγή building, is the son of Vettenus, "a Roman name, thus indicating an Italian [not a Judean] origin" (Gruen 2016, 131). Gruen neglects to note, though, that the assembly places of some Judeans in Judea are called συναγωγαι (or their linguistic equivalent; Philo, Hypoth. 7.11–14; 1QM 3.3–4).

In Prob. 80–83, Philo writes of the Essenes, who could be considered an "informal semi-public" Judean association. He uses συναγωγή for the assembly place of the Essenes in Hypoth. 7.11–14. He claims that the Essenes were found in many cities and villages in Judea (Hypoth. 11.1). Binder (1999, 24) classifies the Essenes as "what we might imprecisely label 'sectarian synagogues.'" The War Scroll (1QM 3.3–4) appears to indicate that the sectarian Essenes used the Hebrew "synagogue" term bet mo'ed ("meeting house")[57] for their assembly place.

Runesson (2010, 464) asserts that there are three examples of "indigenous" Judean synagogue communities in the land: "Essene association synagogues, Pharisaic association synagogues—and the association synagogue of the Mattheans. These association synagogues were all different expressions of first-century Jewish identities."[58]

---

[55] IJO 2.214 (CIJ 2.759; MAMA 4.90). See Runesson, Binder, and Olsson 2008, 148 (no. 116).

[56] Kloppenborg (2000) has conclusively demonstrated that the Theodotus inscription can be dated pre-70 CE.

[57] Runesson, Binder, and Olsson 2008, no. 38.

[58] Regarding the Essene association synagogues, Runesson cites two studies upon which he bases his claim: Klinghardt 1994 and Weinfeld 1986. A more thorough proponent of this view is now Gillihan 2012. Regarding Pharisaic association synagogues, the Gospel of Matthew is his primary source of evidence (Runesson 2001, 486; 2008, 121, 124).

"SYNAGOGUE" TERMINOLOGY AMONG *CHRISTOS*-FOLLOWER ASSOCIATIONS: ἘΚΚΛΗΣΙΑ AND ΣΥΝΑΓΩΓΗ

James: συναγωγή (and ἐκκλησία)

The word συναγωγή occurs only a single time in the epistle of James, in the clause ἐὰν γὰρ εἰσέλθῃ εἰς συναγωγὴν ὑμῶν (2:2). If the phrase συναγωγὴν ὑμῶν refers to the building owned by a semi-public Judean association of non-Jesus followers, within which James' halakhic observant *Christos* followers met, then his *Christos* followers differentiated their "members-only" meeting from other gatherings in the συναγωγή building by naming it an ἐκκλησία (5:14). If (1) the provenance of the epistle of James is Rome, as Allison (2013, 94–98) suggests, and as Kloppenborg (2020, 329, n. 96) now concurs, and if (2) Nanos is correct that the (earlier?) *Christos* followers in Rome socially interacted with the Judean synagogue community, even to the point of using their συναγωγή building(s) for their ἐκκλησία meetings,[59] then James' community becomes another witness to the fact that there was no "parting of the ways" in Rome at least up until the principate of Trajan or Hadrian.[60] Internal evidence also may imply social interaction, since, as Dibelius and Greeven (1976, 134–35) note, "neither the rich nor the poor man seem to belong to the community," as evidenced by their need to be directed to appropriate seats. If non-Jesus-following Judeans as well as *Christos* followers were all meeting in the same building, then it is simple to see how some non-Jesus followers (rich and poor) would take part in the semi-public meetings of *Christos* followers.

Two other interpretations of the word συναγωγή are possible. Bauckham (2007, 58) claims that συναγωγὴν ὑμῶν could refer to a ritual assembly of Judean *Christos* followers. McKnight (2011, 183) suggests that συναγωγὴν ὑμῶν speaks of a building owned by James' community, which is dedicated for their ritual worship assemblies. McKnight's suggestion, however, is anomalous with respect to other New Testament writings.

If one views συναγωγὴν ὑμῶν as referring to a building owned by non-Jesus-following Judeans, then one could interpret James' ἐκκλησία (5:14) as being either a semi-public association gathering ("assembly") or a group designation (e.g., the anachronistic term "church"). If one translates James' phrase τοὺς πρεσβυτέρους τῆς ἐκκλησίας through the lens of

---

[59] See Nanos 1996, 69–71; 1999.
[60] Compositional dates for James range from the mid-60s to the late second century; see Allison 2013, 3–32.

inscriptional usages of the phrase πρέσβεις τῆς ἐκκλησίας, then a translation of ἐκκλησία as a ritual assembly is preferable.

The lexically related phrase πρέσβεις τῆς ἐκκλησίας[61] occurs within numerous inscriptions, one of which is dated to 29 CE (Ephesos; *SE* 210*2).[62] *SE* 210*2 uses ἐκκλησία in the sense of a "meeting": Octavian references both the Ephesian δῆμος and ἐκκλησία in differentiated ways.[63] In at least three inscriptions the collocation of πρέσβεις and ἐκκλησία describes a civic ἐκκλησία assembly within which πρέσβεις are elected by the δῆμος on a time-limited basis to serve as their official emissaries or delegates for a specific mission.[64] Given this civic backdrop, one could suggest that within James' non-civic context the phrase τοὺς πρεσβυτέρους τῆς ἐκκλησίας is best translated "the elders of the assembly" rather than as "the elders of the church/congregation/community."

In summary, (1) if James' phrase συναγωγὴν ὑμῶν refers to the building owned by a Judean synagogue community, within which his halakhic obser-vant *Christos* followers meet, and (2) if ἐκκλησία refers to their semi-public meeting, then (3) James' *Christos* followers differentiate their "members-only" ἐκκλησία meeting from the "members-only" συναγωγή meetings of non-Jesus-following Judeans who also gather in the same συναγωγή build-ing. Such a scenario of social interaction challenges presuppositions of a "parting of the ways" between Judean non-Jesus followers and *Christos* fol-lowers, not least in the region of James' diasporic addressees.

Non-Judean *Christos* Followers and συναγωγαί

There are at least seven instances in patristic-era and later writings where συναγωγή is used in reference to early *Christos* followers. The first four examples use συναγωγή when discussing an assembly/meeting/gathering

---

[61] The term πρέσβυς, whose comparative form is πρεσβύτερος (e.g., Jas 5:14), occurs in Greek inscriptions and refers to official delegates commissioned on behalf of the δῆμος through a vote in an ἐκκλησία (see Bornkamm 1968).

[62] *SE* 210*2 recounts the election of πρέσβεις by the βουλή through decree of the γερουσία for a political mission to Emperor Octavian on behalf of the entire *polis* of Ephesos.

[63] *SE* 210*2 reads [Αὐτ. Καῖσαρ θε]οῦ υἱός . . . [Εφεσίων βο]υλῇ, δήμῳ χαίρειν· . . . πρέσβε[ις][τῆς ἐκκλη]σίας.

[64] (1) *IG* XII,Suppl 143 (Lampsakos; 3 BCE; χειροτόνησαι δὲ ἐν τᾶ ἐκκλη[σία ἐφόδι] ον τῷ πρεσβευτᾶ); (2) *IMT* 579 (Troas, 80–70 BCE; χειρίσαι ἐν τῆι ἐκκλησίαι πρεσβευτὴν πρὸς Θασίους); (3) *IG* XII,Suppl 139 (Miletos, 167 BCE?; ὅππω[ς] δεῖξαι πρεσβεύταν ἐν τᾶι ἐκκλησίαι); (4) *IDelos* 1498 (160–150 BCE; χειροτονῆσαι δὲ καὶ πρέσβεις . . . ἐπὶ τὴν Ἀθήνησιν βουλὴν καὶ ἐκκλησίαν παρακαλέσουσι τὸν δῆμον).

of non-Judean *Christos* followers.[65] Ignatius enjoins Polycarp to "let your assemblies (συναγωγαί) be of frequent occurrence" (Ign. *Pol.* 4.2; late first century CE). The author of the Shepherd of Hermas uses συναγωγή in reference to "the assembly of just men who believe in the divine spirit" (Herm. Mand. 11.9; also 11.13, 14; late first or early second century CE).[66] Mandate 11 uses συναγωγή in reference to a "meeting/gathering" rather than as a group designation. Dibelius and Greeven cite two even later examples of συναγωγή being used in reference to an "assembly/meeting": the Marcionites in Lebaba (318–319 CE) and Shenoute's Coptic monks in the fifth century (Sohag, Egypt).[67]

The next two examples juxtapose the terms συναγωγή and ἐκκλησία within the same text unit when speaking of *Christos*-follower *praxeis*. Justin Martyr in his supersessionistic *Dialogue with Trypho* (ironically?) equates the terms συναγωγή and ἐκκλησία as referring to a single entity: the universal body of *Christos* followers (*Dial.* 63.5; ca. 155 CE). In the Acts of Peter 9 (ca. 200 CE), we find reference to Peter going "out of the assembly (συναγωγή)," meaning thereby most likely a συναγωγή gathering rather than a συναγωγή building. Interestingly, though, in the prior chapter, Peter uses the term ἐκκλησία when speaking of the collective entity known as "the Church" (Acts Pet. 8; cf. also Acts Pet. 4). Thus, συναγωγή and ἐκκλησία are attested as relevant terminology not least for the second-century CE addressees of the Acts of Peter. This duality of term usage appears also to be evident in North Africa among Dionysius' third-century *Christos*-following communities that Eusebius describes.

Eusebius' *Historia ecclesiastica* contains the seventh example of συναγωγή usage among patristic-era and later *Christos* followers. Of great interest is the fact that Eusebius cites the only clear patristic example wherein συναγωγή is used to designate a *group* of *Christos* followers (7.9.2).[68] This collective designation occurs within Eusebius' record of comments made by Dionysius of Alexandria (mid-third century CE). In addition to using συναγωγή as a group designation, Dionysius also is said to use the noun συναγωγή when speaking of *assemblies* of *Christos* followers in Libya and regions (ἢ ἐν συναγωγῇ τινι εὑρεθείη, 7.11.11; see also 7.12, 17). Eusebius' account of Dionysius' banishment to Libya implies that συναγωγή reflects actual insider/

---

[65] See further in Dibelius and Greeven 1976, 133.

[66] See Osiek 1999, 103–56.

[67] Dibelius and Greeven 1976, 132–34.

[68] *Hist. eccl.* 7.9.2: "The blessed Heraclas, [who] was *a member of the congregation* [τῆς συναγωγῆς μετασχών], was present with those who were recently baptized."

emic language for *Christos*-follower assemblies and groups. In addition, Eusebius' juxtaposition of the words συναγωγή (7.11.11, 12) and ἐκκλησία (7.11.12) for *Christos*-follower contexts suggests that they demonstrated both continuity with, and differentiation from, their Judean heritage (and contemporary Judean synagogue communities).

In sum, Eusebius' account of the political ostracization of Dionysius and his communities in North Africa uses (1) the noun συναγωγή as a descriptor both of a meeting/assembly (7.11.11, 12, 17) and of a group designation of *Christos* followers (7.9.2) and (2) the noun ἐκκλησία as an ongoing group designation of *Christos* followers (7.11.12) who met together in συναγωγαί ("assemblies").

Judean *Christos* Followers and συναγωγαί

While the previous seven examples detail συναγωγή usage among non-Judean *Christos* followers, the Judean *Christos* followers known as the Ebionites exhibit a range of synagogue terminology. The patristic sources, beginning with Irenaeus (180 CE), describe the Ebionites as being a Torah-observant *Christos*-following community (e.g., Sabbath, circumcision, dietary restrictions). Skarsaune (2007, 421) asserts that their name "no doubt is based on the biblical Hebrew term *ebionim* (probably via Aramaic *ebionaye*)."

When describing their organizational structure, Epiphanius states that the Ebionites "have elders and heads of synagogues (πρεσβυτέρους καὶ ἀρχισυναγώγους), and they call their church [articular ἐκκλησίαν] a synagogue (συναγωγήν) and not a Church [anarthrous ἐκκλησίαν] and honour Christ in name only" (*Pan.* 30.18.2).[69] Epiphanius' mention of "a συναγωγή" does not seem to refer to a "meeting/assembly" given its use within the context of a discussion about the group's authority structure. Rather, the focus on leadership titles would seem to suggest that συναγωγή and ἐκκλησία address the group's corporate identity, or perhaps simply the name of their building.

It bears mentioning that the Ebionites were not the only *haeresis* of Judean *Christos* followers addressed in patristic sources. The Nazoraeans/Nazarenes evinced not dissimilar intersections with Ebionite theology and *praxeis*,[70] but yet without any patristic indication that they used συναγωγή as a name either for their group or for the building(s) within which they met.[71] The fact that two not dissimilar groups of Judean *Christos* followers, each of which are presented

---

[69] Translation in Klijn and Reinink 1973, 187. Epiphanius, the bishop of Salamis, completed the *Panarion* (*Adversus haereses*) around 378 CE.

[70] See Van Elderen 1994, 97–117; Kinzig 2007.

[71] This reflects a correction of my previous statements in Korner 2020, 71, 74–75, 238–39.

as coexisting both historically and geographically at various points in their life cycle, and are differentiated in their group organizational terminology, lends credence to the historicity of Epiphanius' account that only the Ebionites diverged from other *Christos* followers in using synagogue terms for their leadership and for their group designation and/or buildings.

CONCLUSION

It was my priority in this essay to reframe scholarly conversations in which the English word *synagogue* is usually delimited only to a Judean group and/or building and/or meeting. It has become clear that συναγωγή is an ethnically neutral term that is used for group modalities of non-Judean and Judean associations, and of non-Judean and Judean communities of *Christos* followers. *Christos* followers continued to use συναγωγή as meeting terminology into the fifth century, which should give pause to any blanket assertions of a "parting of the ways" between non-Jesus-following Judeans and *Christos* followers. The word συναγωγή, however, is not the only term that indicates a Judean "synagogue" entity. A well-rounded study of Judean "synagogues" in the Greco-Roman world needs to incorporate into the semantic range of our English word *synagogue* twenty-one other terms related to Judean/Jewish communal modalities (group, building, and/or meeting). Since ἐκκλησία is one of those Judean synagogue terms, then one could say that *Christos* followers' very act of adopting ἐκκλησία as their corporate identity culturally rooted them implicitly both into a Judean heritage and into their Greco-Roman civic contexts.

APPENDIX: TERMINOLOGICAL CATEGORIES

BUILDING	GROUP	GROUP	MEETING
PUBLIC: regional community-center structure that is accessible to the public: συναγωγή, προσευχή (Judea [Josephus, *Vita* 277], Egypt [Philo, *Legat.* 132])	SEMI-PUBLIC: associations (members only): θίασοι, collegia (κολλήγια), συνόδοι, κοινά, αἵρεσις, συναγωγαί, ἐκκλησίαι, πολιτεύματα, קהל	PRIVATE: associations (family/household only): θίασος, Dionysus (*IGUR* 160; Torre Nova, Italy; 160 CE)	PUBLIC: an assembly within a regional community center that is accessible to the public: συναγωγή

BUILDING	GROUP	GROUP	MEETING
SEMI-PUBLIC: local structure accessible to members: συναγωγή, bet ha-midrash, bet mo'ed, bet ha knesset, οικός, προσευχή (Acts 16:13)	Formal: direct connections to civic, regional, or federal governing authorities (e.g., Egypt: Judean πολιτεύματα, Judean ἐκκλησία [Philo, Virt. 108], Isis and Serapis θίασοι)		SEMI-PUBLIC: an assembly that is accessible only to association members: συναγωγή, ἐκκλησία, σύλλογος
	Informal: non-civic, no direct connections to governing authorities (e.g., Judean diasporic συναγωγαί)		
	Collegia licita: e.g., trans-local, non-civic, informal associations such as Judean diasporic συναγωγαί and also Christos-follower diasporic ἐκκλησίαι (?)		

WORKS CITED

Allison, Dale C., Jr. 2013. A Critical and Exegetical Commentary on the Epistle of James. ICC. London: Bloomsbury T&T Clark.

Ascough, Richard S. 2015. "What Are They Now Saying about Christ Groups and Associations?" CurBR 13:207–44.

———. 2017. "Methodological Reflections on Synagogues and Christ Groups as 'Associations': A Response to Erich Gruen." Journal of the Jesus Movement in Its Jewish Setting 4:118–26.

Ascough, Richard S., Philip A. Harland, and John S. Kloppenborg, eds. 2012. Associations in the Greco-Roman World: A Sourcebook. Waco, Tex.: Baylor University Press.

Bauckham, Richard. 2007. "James and the Jerusalem Community." Pages 55–95 in *Jewish Believers in Jesus: The Early Centuries*. Edited by Oskar Skarsaune and Reidar Hvalvik. Peabody, Mass.: Hendrickson.

Binder, Donald. 1999. *Into the Temple Courts: The Place of the Synagogue in the Second Temple Period*. Atlanta: SBL.

Bornkamm, Günther. 1968. "πρέσβυς, πρεσβύτερος." *TDNT* 6:651–683.

Czajkowski, Kimberley. 2019. "Jewish Associations in Alexandria?" Pages 76–96 in *Private Associations and Jewish Communities in the Hellenistic and Roman Cities*. JSJSup 191. Edited by Benedikt Eckhardt. Leiden: Brill.

Dibelius, Martin, and Heinrich Greeven. 1976. *James: A Commentary on the Epistle of James*. Hermeneia. Philadelphia: Fortress.

Eckhardt, Benedikt. 2018. "Who Thought That Early Christians Formed Associations?" *Mnemosyne* 71:298–314.

———. 2019a. "Associations beyond the City: Jews, Actors, and Empire in the Roman Period." Pages 115–56 in Eckhardt, *Private Associations and Jewish Communities*.

———. 2019b. "Introduction: 'Greco-Roman Associations' and the Jews." Pages 1–12 in Eckhardt, *Private Associations and Jewish Communities*.

———. 2019c. "Private Associations in Hellenistic and Roman Cities: Common Ground and Dividing Lines." Pages 13–36 in Eckhardt, *Private Associations and Jewish Communities*.

———. 2020. "Synagogues as Associations in the Greco-Roman World." Pages 313–37 in *Archaeological Finds, New Methods, New Theories: Synagogues in the Hellenistic and Roman Periods*. Edited by Lutz Doering and Andrew Krause. Göttingen: Vandenhoek & Ruprecht.

Van Elderen, Bastian. 1994. "Early Christianity in Transjordan." *TynBul* 45:7–117.

Gillihan, Yonder Moynihan. 2012. *Civic Ideology, Organization, and Law in the Rule Scrolls: A Comparative Study of the Covenanters' Sect and Contemporary Voluntary Associations in Political Context*. STDJ 97. Leiden: Brill.

Gruen, Erich S. 2016. "Synagogues and Voluntary Associations as Institutional Models: A Response to Richard Ascough and Ralph Korner." *Journal of the Jesus Movement in Its Jewish Setting* 3:125–31.

Harland, Philip A. 2003. *Associations, Synagogues, and Congregations: Claiming a Place in Ancient Mediterranean Society*. Minneapolis: Fortress.

———. 2009. *Dynamics of Identity in the World of the Early Christians: Associations, Judeans, and Cultural Minorities*. New York: Continuum; London: T&T Clark.

———, ed. 2014. *North Coast of the Black Sea, Asia Minor*. BZNW 204. Vol. 2 of *Greco-Roman Associations: Texts, Translations, and Commentary*. Edited by John S. Kloppenborg and Richard S. Ascough. Berlin: De Gruyter.

Instone-Brewer, David, and Philip A. Harland. 2008. "Jewish Associations in Roman Palestine: Evidence from the Mishnah." *JGRChJ* 5:200–221.

Kinzig, Wolfram. 2007. "The Nazoreans." Pages 463–87 in Skarsaune and Hvalvik, *Jewish Believers in Jesus*.

Klijn, Albertus Frederik Johannes, and Gerrit Jan Reinink. 1973. *Patristic Evidence for Jewish-Christian Sects*. NovTSup 36. Leiden: Brill.

Klinghardt, Matthias. 1994. "The Manual of Discipline in the Light of Statues of Hellenistic Associations." Pages 251–70 in *Methods of Investigation of the Dead Sea Scrolls and the Khirbet Qumran Site: Present Realities and Future Prospects*. Annals of the New York Academy of Sciences 72. Edited by John J. Collins. New York: New York Academy of Sciences.

Kloppenborg, John S. 2000. "Dating Theodotus (CIJ II 1404)." *JJS* 51:243–80.

———. 2013. "Membership Practices in Pauline Christ Groups." *Early Christianity* 4:183–215.

———. 2019. *Christ's Associations: Connecting and Belonging in the Ancient City*. New Haven: Yale University Press.

———, ed. 2020. *Ptolemaic and Early Roman Egypt*. BZNW 246. Vol. 3 of Kloppenborg and Ascough, *Greco-Roman Associations*. Berlin: De Gruyter.

Kloppenborg, John S., and Richard S. Ascough, eds. 2011. *Attica, Central Greece, Macedonia, Thrace*. BZNW 181. Vol. 1 of Kloppenborg and Ascough, *Greco-Roman Associations*.

Korner, Ralph J. 2015. "*Ekklēsia* as a Jewish Synagogue Term: Some Implications for Paul's Socio-religious Location." *Journal of the Jesus Movement in Its Jewish Setting* 2:53–78.

———. 2017a. "*Ekklēsia* as a Jewish Synagogue Term: A Response to Erich Gruen." *Journal of the Jesus Movement in Its Jewish Setting* 4:127–36.

———. 2017b. *The Origin and Meaning of* Ekklēsia *in the Early Jesus Movement*. Ancient Judaism and Early Christianity 98. Brill: Leiden.

———. 2020. *Reading Revelation after Supersessionism: An Apocalyptic Journey of Socially Identifying John's Multi-Ethnic* Ekklēsiai *with the* Ekklēsia *of Israel*. New Testament after Supersessionism 14. Eugene, Ore.: Cascade Books.

Krause, Andrew. 2019. "Qumran Discipline and Rites of Affliction in Their Associational Context." Pages 58–75 in Eckhardt, *Private Associations and Jewish Communities*.

Last, Richard. 2016. "The Other Synagogues." *JSJ* 47:330–63.

Last, Richard, and Philip A. Harland. 2020. *Group Survival in the Ancient Mediterranean: Rethinking Material Conditions in the Landscape of Jews and Christians*. London: T&T Clark.

Levine, Lee I. (2000) 2005. *The Ancient Synagogue: The First Thousand Years*. 2nd ed. New Haven: Yale University Press.

Lüderitz, Gerd. 1994. "What Is Politeuma?" Pages 183–225 in *Studies in Early Jewish Epigraphy*. Edited by Jan Willem van Henten and Pieter W. van der Horst. AGJU 21. Leiden: Brill.

McKnight, Scot. 2011. *The Letter of James*. NICNT. Grand Rapids: Eerdmans.

McLean, Bradley H. 1993. "The Agrippinilla Inscription: Religious Associations and Early Church Formation." Pages 239–70 in *Origins and Method: Towards a New Understanding of Judaism and Christianity; Essays in Honour of John C. Hurd*. Edited by Bradley H. McLean. JSNTSup 86. Sheffield: JSOT Press.

———. 2002. *An Introduction to Greek Epigraphy of the Hellenistic and Roman Periods from Alexander the Great Down to the Reign of Constantine (323 B.C.–A.D. 337)*. Ann Arbor: University of Michigan Press.

Monson, Andrew. 2019. "Political and Sacred Animals: Religious Associations in Greco-Roman Egypt." Pages 37–57 in Eckhardt, *Private Associations and Jewish Communities*.

Nanos, Mark. 1996. *The Mystery of Romans: The Jewish Context of Paul's Letter*. Minneapolis: Fortress.

———. 1999. "The Jewish Context of the Gentile Audience Addressed in Paul's Letter to the Romans." *CBQ* 61:283–304.

Öhler, Markus. 2018. "Graeco-Roman Associations, Judean Synagogues and Early Christianity in Bithynia-Pontus." Pages 62–88 in *Authority and Identity in Emerging Christianities in Asia Minor and Greece*. Edited by Cilliers Breytenbach and Julien M. Ogereau. Ancient Judaism and Early Christianity 103. Leiden: Brill.

Osiek, Carolyn. 1999. *The Shepherd of Hermas: A Commentary*. Hermeneia. Philadelphia: Fortress.

Rajak, Tessa. 1999. "The Synagogue within the Greco-Roman City." Pages 161–73 in *Jews, Christians, and Polytheists in the Ancient Synagogue: Cultural Interaction during the Greco-Roman Period*. Edited by Stephen Fine. London: Routledge.

Rhodes, P. J., and David M. Lewis. 1997. *The Decrees of the Greek States*. Oxford: Clarendon.

Runesson, Anders. 2001. *The Origins of the Synagogue: A Socio-historical Study*. ConBNT 37. Stockholm: Almqvist & Wiksell.

———. 2008. "Rethinking Early Jewish-Christian Relations: Matthean Community History as Pharisaic Intragroup Conflict." *JBL* 127:95–132.

———. 2010. "Behind the Gospel of Matthew: Radical Pharisees in Post-war Galilee?" *CurTM* 37:460–71.

———. 2012. "Was There a Christian Mission before the 4th Century? Problematizing Common Ideas about Early Christianity and the Beginnings of Modern Mission." Pages 205–47 in *The Making of Christianity: Conflicts, Contacts, and Constructions: Essays in Honor of Bengt Holmberg*. Edited by Magnus Zetterholm and Samuel Byrskog. ConBNT 47. Winona Lake, Ind.: Eisenbrauns.

Runesson, Anders, Donald D. Binder, and Birger Olsson. 2008. *The Ancient Synagogue from Its Origins to 200 C.E.: A Source Book*. AGJU 72. Leiden: Brill.

Sergienko, Gennadi Andreyevich. 2011. "'Our Politeuma is in Heaven!': Paul's Polemical Engagement with the 'Enemies of the Cross of Christ' in Philippians 3:18–20." PhD diss., Fuller Theological Seminary.

Skarsaune, Oskar. 2007. "The Ebionites." Pages 419–62 in Skarsaune and Hvalvik, *Jewish Believers in Jesus.*

Smallwood, Mary E. 1976. *The Jews under Roman Rule: From Pompey to Diocletian.* Leiden: Brill.

Weinfeld, Moshe. 1986. *The Organizational Pattern and the Penal Code of the Qumran Sect: A Comparison with Guilds and Religious Associations of the Hellenistic-Roman Period.* NTOA 2. Göttingen: Vandenhoeck & Ruprecht.

15

Christianization and the Decline of Elective Cults Revisited

Competitors or Cohabitants?

Christina Gousopoulos

In previous narratives of Christianization, the fourth century was often characterized by pervasive conflict between Christians and polytheists—a battle in which the cult of Christ ultimately emerged victorious. The rise of Christianity was inevitable, it was argued, since the cult offered superior answers to the vicissitudes of antique life and provided members a far more rewarding experience than the already stagnant pool of polytheism (Dodds 1965; van der Meer 1961; Burckhardt 1949; Momigliano 1965; Moore 1919). Through this logic, as polytheistic traditions failed to revitalize themselves, the conversion of Constantine solidified the coercive power of the state for the Christ cult, empowering the succession of Christian emperors to suppress dangerous idolatry (Handson 1985; Baker 1930; MacMullen 1981; 1997; Beatrice 1993).

Efforts to take stock of extant literary accounts of Christianization would indeed tell us as much. Testimonies from the evangelists, church historians, and hagiographers alike offer frustratingly quixotic accounts of Christianity's swift acceptance throughout the world,[1] in tandem with

---

[1]   For Eusebius, *Hist. eccl.* 1.3.19, the proof that Jesus was the Savior himself rested upon his designation as the Christ. Of all the prophets and holy men, Jesus was the sole recipient of this title, which he alleges is known and accepted by all men "throughout the world" (καθ᾽ ὅλου τοῦ κόσμου) by his time, including Greeks and barbarians.

the rapid destruction of polytheistic temples.[2] The glory of the Savior had now been proclaimed across the empire, thereby enabling the polytheistic population to be converted (or coerced) with ease until all of their cultic rivals were effectively defeated (Eusebius, *Hist. eccl.* 9.9.1, 9.9.8, 10.8.6–9, 10.9.1–9; *Laud. Const.* 17.4; Sozomen, *Hist. eccl.* 1.7–8, 2.34, 8.1). In the utopian imagination of Christian apologists, Constantine's conversion in 312 CE had finished what the resurrected body of Christ had begun.

While polytheistic traditions officially lost their public role in 380 CE, private associations organized around the cult of deities such as Mithras, Jupiter Dolichenus, Isis and Sarapis, Antinous, and Cybele had coexisted alongside Christianity for centuries as several choices for potential recruits in a cultic "marketplace" (Bendlin 2000). Yet to appraise the relationship between the rise of Christianity and the decline of these elective cults, dependency upon these Christocentric narratives presents significant challenges for the modern researcher to separate discourse from the reality on the ground level (Van Dam 1985; Van Haeperen 2014; Brown 1997). In such accounts, not only do the fates of elective cults become intricately (and negatively) yoked to Christianity's success, but in attempting to make the Christ cult appear *sui generis*, the significance of polytheistic cultic associations becomes invested solely in their proximity and relationship with Christians (Alvar 2008).

To decentralize this Christocentric narrative and re-examine the etiology of polytheism's decline, the present contribution offers a brief investigation of competition and conflict between Christianity and the cults of Mithras, Isis, and Jupiter Dolichenus. Our data for the decline of these elective cults in the fourth century is unfortunately sparse, which may make the paradigm of violent and hostile conflict more attractive. This proves to be particularly tempting in view of the era-defining significance of the Serapeum's destruction in Alexandria or the widespread desecration and abandonment of many *mithraea* by the time of Theodosius I. Nevertheless, the narrative of cultic decline in antiquity is not so straightforward. Upon closer inspection, it is not at all apparent that overt competition with Christianity constituted the chief or decisive factor in the decline of these elective cults.

---

[2] For a detailed list, see von Harnack (1908, 1–22); Eusebius, *Vit. Const.* 3.55–60; Sozomen, *Hist. eccl.* 1.8, 2.34; Jerome, *Epist.* 107.1; Rufinus, *Hist.* 11.22–23; Socrates, *Hist. eccl.* 3.2; Sulpicius Severus, *Vit. Mart.* 13–15; Mark the Deacon, *Vit. Porph.* 59–70.

Although a full examination of these cults is beyond the scope of this essay, several other explanations may prove to be efficacious in mapping out their respective declines, including social network collapse, economic crises and insolvency, and unintentional destruction of cults through natural disasters, barbarian invasions, looting, and accidents. An emphasis upon regional differences in cultic decline additionally urges that locale conditions may have influenced the fortunes of a cult, with the result that there was no uniformity in a cult's decline across the empire as no two regions—or two cultic associations—exhibit identical outcomes.

This research joins a much larger conversation in which there is an increasing acceptance of Christianization as a far more gradual process than previously considered (Talloen 2009; Sweetman 2010; Lavan 2011; Dijkstra 2015; Kahlos 2020; Bremmer 2021). Even in spite of increasingly austere bans on polytheistic practice, large communities of pagans persevered long after the time of Constantine, including at Gaza, the countryside of Gaul, Athens, Rome, and Britain, among others (Mulryan 2009; Belayche 2004; Castrén 1999; Brown 1997; Seaman 2014; Stancliffe 1979; Klingshirn 1994; Harl 1990). Recent research has additionally challenged the notion that coercion through these imperial decrees was sufficient to impose adoption of Christianity, contending that there was no solidified anti-pagan agenda that was uniformly enforced throughout the fourth and fifth centuries (Lee 2000; Demarsin 2011; Engels and Van Nuffelen 2014; Humphries 2018; Stenger 2018). The traditional nexus between Christianization, religious intolerance, and violence has also been called into question (Van Nuffelen 2018; 2020; Mayer 2020). Neither the category of *religious violence* nor the view of ubiquitous Christian intolerance holds up to scrutiny, since acts of violence committed by Christians were significantly less common than our sources would suggest and almost always had other motives than the elimination of religious rivals (Salzman 2006; Dijkstra 2015; 2020).

From the resultant discussion, it is evident that Greco-Roman elective cults did not decline swiftly, uniformly, or inevitably upon the ascendance of Christianity, nor were members of elective cults ostensibly "defenders of a hopeless cause" following Constantine's conversion (Harl 1990, 8). To better understand the complicated processes of Christianization and the decline of elective cults, it is thus crucial to avoid characterizing relations between Christians and elective cults in the fourth century *primarily* in terms of antagonism and hostile competition but rather more accurately as "co-protagonists in a complex religious scene" (Cassia 2019, 38).

THE DECLINES OF MITHRAS, ISIS, AND JUPITER DOLICHENUS: A (VERY) BRIEF OVERVIEW

The Mysteries of Mithras constitute an ideal subject for our first case study. This is not least due to the recent scholarly interest in the so-called "mystery cults" (τὰ μυστήρια) or the auspicious survival of hundreds of *mithraea* and pertinent inscriptions, but patently because the cult has secured an enduring reputation as the prime adversary of Christianity (Vermaseren 1963; Renan 1882; Cumont 1903; Gager 1975; Sauer 1996; Winter 2000). Alongside the apologists' condemnation of the cult's perceived barbarism[3] and alleged imitation of Christian sacraments,[4] we inherit from Jerome a reference to Gracchus, the prefect of Rome in 377–378 CE, who allegedly destroyed a *mithraeum* and the "monstrous images" housed within it,[5] as well as an instance of a violent altercation following the purification of an abandoned Alexandrian *mithraeum*.[6]

Considering the tetrarchs' famous dedication to Mithras as the "Protector of the Empire" just four years before Constantine's conversion (*CIL* 3.4413), previous scholarship posited an inherent enmity between the two cults for the control of the empire. For Eberhard Sauer (1996, 79), the violent fates met by many *mithraea* over the course of the late third through to the early fifth century surely suggested that the Mithras cult constituted the "most hated cult and first victim of the Christian persecution of paganism." As the construction of new *mithraea* had significantly declined by the onset of the fourth century, it appeared at first glance that the triumph of Christianity culminated in the prompt extinction of the Mithraic mysteries. In competition with the superior Christ cult, the power of "the unvanquished god" was utterly enfeebled and had simply lost its *raison d'être* (Vermaseren 1963, 192).

In contradistinction to this narrative, David Walsh (2018) has persuasively argued that competition with Christians and iconoclastic violence are not sufficient to explain the demise of the Mithras cult. Of all the excavated *mithraea* to date, on only four occasions (Hawarte, Doliche, Ša'āra, and Ponza) is there archaeological certainty that Christians were to blame for their destruction. Although it is possible that we have yet to discover the *mithraeum* that was the alleged target of the prefect Gracchus, none of

---

[3] Firmicus Maternus, *Err. prof. rel.* 4; Ambrosiaster, *Quaest.* 113.11; Gregory of Nazianzus, *Or. Bas.* 4.70, 4.89; Socrates, *Hist. eccl.* 3.2; Sozomen, *Hist. eccl.* 5.7.

[4] Justin, *1 Apol.* 66; Tertullian, *Bapt.* 5; *Praescr.* 40; *Cor.* 15; Commodian, *Instr.* 1.13; Firmicus Maternus, *Err. prof. rel.* 20; Jerome, *Jov.* 1.7.

[5] Jerome, *Epist.* 107.2.

[6] Sozomen, *Hist. eccl.* 5.7; Socrates, *Hist. eccl.* 3.2; Rufinus, *Hist.* 11.2.

the *mithraea* excavated at Rome satisfy Jerome's description. There is only a singular instance, however, of the *mithraeum* at Hawarte, in which the structure was abandoned contemporary to the Christian ambush in the early fifth century. Even so, it may be presumptuous to view these violent episodes as clear manifestations of a cultic rivalry. The location of Hawarte, Doliche, and Ša'āra by the Persian border may suggest that the desecration of these *mithraea* was perhaps rather (or additionally) instigated by politically motivated distaste for the cult's connections to the enemy Persians instead of a calculated assault against "heathenish superstition" (Walsh 2018, 75–88).

Walsh's impressive overview of the decline of *mithraea* across the empire illustrates that there was no uniformity in the decline of Mithraic associations following Constantine's conversion (that is, assuming that the cult was not continued elsewhere after the structure's abandonment). Along the Rhine, for instance, support for the construction and restoration of *mithraea* dwindled in the second half of the third century—far too early to be ascribed to the influence of Christianity—whereas *mithraea* in Rome and Ostia continue to be restored and constructed at this time, with an emerging population of senatorial rank members who retained membership into the final decades of the fourth century. As the cult experienced a gradual decline throughout the fourth century, Mithraic congregations certainly did not act as if they were being vigorously persecuted out of existence; despite the dramatic decline in funding for all other temples and civic buildings after the Severan period, tight-knit military communities in Pannonia and Britain enthusiastically supported their *mithraea* into the early fourth century. Nor does the desertion of towns like Aquincum or Poetovio appear to have alarmed the resident Mithraic communities, since the *mithraea* situated there continued to be frequented even into the end of the fourth century (Walsh 2020).

Walsh's most cogent conclusion is his assertion that "in reality, there was little scope for Christians to actively persecute the Mithras cult given that the two groups operated in largely different areas in the fourth century" (2018, 92). It is well-known that the cult of Christ achieved early success in the eastern provinces such as in Egypt or Asia Minor, yet evidence for the Mithras cult in the east is quite lacunary as most Mithraic communities were concentrated around the western provinces, at the northern frontiers, and at Rome. Beyond Rome, there is very little evidence of Mithraic and Christian cohabitation. In fact, in the few locales where we can confirm the presence and cohabitation of both cults, any evidence for intergroup conflict is often lacking in comparison to the plentiful evidence of intragroup competition within Christ cults, such as the clash in Rome between Damasus and Ursinus for the papacy in 366 CE (Ammianus Marcellinus, *Res gestae* 27.3.11–13). It may be tempting to take the apologists' resentment toward Mithras as an indication of wider attitudes in Christ groups, but Christians seemed to take no issue in being buried alongside several Mithraic priests (*sacerdos*) in the catacombs of Vibia along the Via Appia well into the late fourth century (Simón 2018; Johnson 1997). Contrary to the stringent enforcement of the pagan–Christian divide in apologetic literature, cultic affiliation did not appear to be a large concern in choosing one's burial location, with families of different affiliations buried together for convenience rather than solidarity of religious belief (Lewis 2016).

If not for blatant competition with Christians, what alternative factors may have contributed to the decline of the Mithras cult? For one, in place of Christian iconoclasts, the desecration and destruction of many *mithraea* may be better explained by the invasions of so-called barbarian groups in the third century, who may have sought to execute a "ritual killing" of "the unvanquished deity" that was so closely linked with the Roman military (Walsh 2018, 56–60). As a further consequence of these invasions, the mass abandonment of settlements along the frontier regions meant that Mithraic communities at Hadrian's Wall or the Danubian Limes now became socially integrated with fleeing civilians. Through these new social relationships, members of Mithras cults may have been introduced to novel religious innovations that offered more opportunities for social capital accumulation, visibility, and honor, eventually diluting their focus and commitment for the Mithras cult.

We may also consider the role of unintentional destruction through natural disasters and accidents. In the wider Roman world, there is a plethora of archaeological evidence for the abandonment of a cult in a given locale due to external causes: for instance, while the temples of Dea Nehalennia at Domburg and Colijnsplaat were effectively deserted in the fourth and fifth centuries due to flooding from the Dunkirk II Transgression (Verhulst 1999, 14), an earthquake from Galilee in 363 CE not only precipitated the abandonment of the Nabratein synagogue for over two centuries (Meyers and Meyers 2009) but also abruptly halted worship at several temples in the Nabatean kingdom (Al-Nasarat 2018; Ward 2016). There is similar evidence of this sort in Mithraic communities. At the Schachadorf *mithraeum* (*CIMRM* 2.1409–12), an accidental fire best explains the hasty abandonment of the site in the late fourth century at the same time that a large seismic event in the Vienna Basin destroyed the *mithraea* and many other buildings in Carnuntum, resulting in the utter desolation of the town and abandonment of these ritual spaces (Decker, Gangl, and Kandler 2006). An emphasis upon regional differences, however, reveals that some Mithraic groups were able to sustain their association despite the serious hurdles and disincentives that were consequential of accidental destruction. An *album* of a group in Virunum (*AE* 1994, 1334) states that when their *mithraeum* had collapsed of natural causes, thirty-four members were keen to collectively fund its restoration. The accidental destruction of the group's ritual space seemed to have had no long-term impact on the cult's ability to continue recruiting new members, considering the addition of members' names to the *album* nearly two decades afterwards (Beck 1998; Kloppenborg 2019, 108–10).

By elucidating these alternative reasons of decline, I do not mean to argue that the socioreligious transformation of the fourth century had no impact on the fate of the Mysteries of Mithras. It is indeed quite possible that certain members of Mithraic groups did disaffiliate due to the looming pressures of Christianization. As we are met, however, with a dearth of evidence that antagonistic competition or violent confrontations with Christians *directly* caused the decline of Mithraic groups, there is good reason to believe that exploring these alternative routes for cultic decline is fruitful and can help shed light on the complexities of antique cultic decline.

In terms of Isis and Sarapis groups, while recent research has convincingly posited Ptolemaic military operations (Glomb et al. 2018; 2020), familial networks of Italian merchants (Martzavou 2010), and transcontinental trade networks (Talloen 2015, 196–99) as potential vectors of the cult's diffusion, it is far more challenging to identify the dissolution of any given Isiac or Sarapiastic association in the late antique period since the historical record largely falls silent throughout the fourth century. From the few traces we have in our sources, it appears that the worship of Osiris/Sarapis persevered at Canopus in the latter half of the fourth century (Bull 2021) and the temple of Philae famously retained its prominence until the middle of the fifth century (see below). Due to the persistence of polytheism in Rome, the shrine of Isis in Campus Martius was frequented until the early fifth century, and we have at least a cursory indication that in Athens, the notoriously idolatrous (κατείδωλον) city (Acts 17:16), sacrifices to Isis, Cybele, Asclepius, and perhaps even rituals associated with the Eleusinian Mysteries were carried out in upper-class homes despite growing temple closures over the fourth and fifth centuries (Saradi and Eliopoulos 2011, 275–80).

We might question if there is any tenable basis for widespread hostility between Isiac and Christ groups. In contrast to the vitriol launched at Cybele and Attis (Fear 1996), the apologists do not seem to be overly concerned with Isis and Sarapis and frequently affix them to the Greco-Roman or Egyptian pantheons as homogenized entities of vile *superstitio* (Takács 1995, 122). At times when ad hominem attacks are levied against Isis, she is ridiculed for her inefficacy as a divine benefactor, for if she was not able to protect her own consort Osiris, how would she be able to support her supplicants (Aristides, *Apol.* 12)? In comparison to the venerable σύμβολον of the cross, the σύμβολα or "passwords" revealed to initiates of her mysteries were merely false hopes of salvation (Firmicus Maternus, *Err. prof. rel.* 18, 19, 21). Alike the polemical treatment of Mithras, Isis and Sarapis groups were accused of counterfeiting the Christian *religio* for the perceived similarity of their fasting practices. As to be expected of the apologists, the Isiac rites were said to be utterly inefficacious since their practices derived from the devil (Tertullian, *Jejun.* 2.4, 16.7; Jerome, *Jov.* 2.17). Tertullian even goes at length to claim that Sarapis himself was a mere bastardization of Joseph, an assertion that is later adopted by Firmicus Maternus, who deduced that the etymological origins of his name must have derived from Σάρρας παῖς ("great-grandson of Sarah"; Tertullian, *Nat.* 2.8; Firmicus Maternus, *Err. prof. rel.* 13).

Even if there is not overwhelming evidence for hostility between the two cults, the destruction of the Alexandrian Serapeum in 391/392 CE is often taken as much more than the mere coup de grâce to the Sarapis cult. The disastrous fate of the sanctuary would soon become the most famous emblem of Christianity's perceived intolerance of religious dissidents. In retrospect, the church historians asserted that it was only imminent that shrines, temples, and idols across the empire would meet a similar fate, seeing that "after the death of Sarapis, who had never been alive, which temples of any other demon could remain standing?" (Rufinus, *Hist.* 11.28). Recent research has nuanced this narrative with a resounding agreement that the Serapeum incident is indicative of a regional tendency for interethnic violence and tensions as opposed to a symptom of a larger pattern (Hahn 2008; Demarsin 2011; Dijkstra 2015; 2020). Nevertheless, this embellishment of Christian sources is not an isolated incident: the tendency of Christian sources to underscore a triumphalist reading of history is remarkably apparent in the case of the Temple of Isis at Philae, where the traditional Egyptian cults continued to flourish far longer than other temples in Egypt (Bagnall 1988). With Procopius' account cited as primary evidence, past scholarship has taken for granted that the decline and demise of these cults at Philae occurred because of the alleged command of Emperor Justinian (527–565 CE) for the temple to be destroyed and the church of St. Stephen built in its place (*History of the Wars*, 1.19.36–37), a story that is seemingly vetted by an inscription in situ that reads, "✝ Ὁ σταυρὸς ἐνίκησεν, καὶ ἀεὶ νικᾷ ✝·✝·✝."[7] Adopting this narrative, Pierre Nautin noted that with the eradication of the Egyptian cults that had long plagued the Christian population, "désormais l'île entire était aux chrétiens" (1967, 16). Yet it appears that the temple had already been abandoned seventy-five years prior, as the final priestly inscription dates to 456–457 CE. Since the Egyptian priests consistently retained records, the cessation of this practice likely indicates that the cults met their demise concomitantly, even within the year (Dijkstra 2015). The Temple of Isis, of course, was not destroyed, as it still stands quite preserved today; even if one argued that Procopius rather meant that the temple was officially closed by the emperor in the mid-sixth century, this closure would have only been symbolic to publicize Christianity's triumph in retrospect.

Indeed, in many cases across the empire, temples which exhibit evidence of Christian violence had already been abandoned sometime prior, although these texts tend to describe the desecrated sites at active temples at the time of the attack, since "to acknowledge that a bishop's victory was over a dying or long deceased cult makes the achievement sound rather hollow, while active and popular temples play for better in such narratives" (Walsh 2018, 42). Christian apologists and hagiographers may have furnished an image of imperially sanctioned temple destruction and renovation into churches, but conversion into churches was relatively rare as many temples were simply abandoned or repurposed into other civic buildings long after cultic activities had ceased, such as military camps, apartment blocks, or prisons (Bayliss 2004; Dijkstra 2011).

Given the difficulty of tracking the decline of Isiac associations, we may perhaps best utilize this space by positing another tentative factor in cultic decline: insolvency and economic crises. For the survival and continued propagation of any given cultic group, one of the necessary "ecological conditions" (Kloppenborg 2020b) is adequate economic resources to cover a variety of operational expenses which could range from foodstuffs, materials for banquets or for bestowing honorifics upon benefactors, costs associated with cultic or funerary ceremonies, loans or financial support to fellow members in need, or shared property for communal gatherings (Last and Harland 2020). While prestigious and well-connected associations were able to attract the patronage of affluent individuals who might contribute large endowments or provide financial assistance in times of conflict, smaller or less affluent groups relied mainly on membership fees. If groups could not achieve solvency, or if

---

[7]   *IPhilae* 2.201: "The cross [has] conquered; it always conquers!"

members could not (or did not) contribute,[8] long-term success and survival was quite plainly untenable as the group's ability to fund future activities and generate social capital for its members would be greatly threatened.

The demise of the collegium of Jupiter Cernenus at Alburnus Maior illustrates such a case. In 167 CE, although there were once fifty-four members of the group, only seventeen remained, with speculative reasons including the Antonine Plague, the effects of the Marcomannic War, the depreciated mining business in the region, or a combination thereof (Liu 2016; Kloppenborg 2020b). Not even the co-president of the group had attended a meeting. With no funds or coffins for members' funerals due to a lack of member contributions, the association warns its remaining members that "no members should suppose that, should he die, he belongs to an association or that he shall be able to make any request of them for a funeral."[9] The group could no longer financially support itself, and its future was bleak.

It remains pure speculation if any Isis or Sarapis groups failed due to bankruptcy, yet the sharp decline of the important Sarapis sanctuaries at Delos coincides with the economic crises and decline of the island altogether. Following the Mithridatic Wars and the sacking of the island in the first century BCE, Italian merchant families who were prominent patrons of the cult abruptly disappear from the epigraphical record and later appear to have migrated to Thessaloniki. Instead of abandoning the Isiac cult, the cult demonstrates a resurgence on the mainland, suggesting that these communities did not themselves experience the same economic deprivation but were able to retain their interest and resources necessary to revitalize the cult. Without their patronage and presence, however, the sanctuaries on Delos largely fell into decline (Martzavou 2010).

Our final case of Jupiter Dolichenus is unique in the sense that the cult—a Roman form of a storm god from Doliche—did not attract the attention or scrutiny of the apologists. Unlike the Mithraic or Isiac cults, the extant evidence of the Dolichenus' decline offers very little credence to any potential influence of Christianization, particularly since dedications and frequentation of *dolichena* seems to have largely dissipated by the onset of the fourth century. Like the Mithras cult, worship of Dolichenus was particularly popular in military communities and diffused rapidly in the western and northern provinces through the close social relationships ("strong-ties")[10] of military

---

[8] See *GRA* III 238 = *PMich* 9.575.

[9] Ascough, Harland, and Kloppenborg 2012, no. 69 = *IDacia* 1.31; see Kloppenborg 2019, 51.

[10] Per Granovetter 1973; 1983.

officials who traveled frequently and maintained highly communicative networks across the empire (Collar 2013, 131). Dolichenus worship appears to have reached its peak by the Severan dynasty, yet only a few dedications to Dolichenus survive past roughly 250 CE,[11] suggesting a dramatic decrease in the cult's popularity in only half a century. If not for Christian iconoclasm or competition with Christians, what happened to the Dolichenus cult after the mid-third century?

Anna Collar's (2013) research of cultic networks offers a viable answer. Insofar as recruitment to cultic groups may have occurred through existing social relationships (Lofland and Stark 1965; Stark 1992; 1996; Eshleman 2007; Kloppenborg 2020b; Centola 2018; 2021), disaffiliation or decline may occur when the networks which inspired recruitment fail to sustain themselves over time and collapse. In this same vein, Collar attributes the rapid decline of the cult to disintegration of Roman military networks following the Severan period, considering the period was wrought with political and military turmoil, including civil war, barbarian incursions, and the resurgence of the plague which altogether destroyed the military networks which were once hotspots for Dolichenus activity. When these networks of military officials were disrupted, surviving members of Dolichenus cults were left with a fragmented and diminishing reservoir of strong ties to corroborate the advantages of membership and to encourage continued involvement and investment of one's resources.

To make matters worse, soldiers and military personnel, who by the nature of their occupation are transient, have "reconfigured social networks" due to frequent travel. While tight-knit military communities who were stationed together in Britain and Pannonia continued to enthusiastically restore and construct *dolichena* even after other temples fell into decline (Walsh 2020), many worshippers would became spatially separated from the military networks that encouraged participation upon their return home. Since devotion to Dolichenus was not exclusive, there were now more barriers to persist in the cult at home, and in many cases, these men shifted primary allegiance back to the traditional gods of their social networks. Collar employs proximal point analysis and network theory to corroborate this hypothesis of network collapse (Concannon 2017), illustrating that the interior regions of Greece, Italy, Thrace, Asia Minor, France, and Spain display a dearth of evidence for the cult. Even when a rare dedication is found in one of these regions, it is often in isolation, leading Collar to speculate that without the support of the military

[11]   *CCID* 33 (Dura-Europos); *CCID* 48 (Stobi); *CCID* 235 (Gerulata); *CCID* 384 (Rome); *CCID* 3 (Colonia Ulpita Ratiaria); *CCID* 621–623 (Lambaesis).

networks that encouraged participation, the cult was evidently not "in fashion" any longer for individual worshippers. To further obstruct the cult's ability to survive, Dolichenus was not transmitted to many civilian settlements because of their lack of embeddedness in these military networks. When these military networks collapsed during the plague and political turbulence in the mid-third century, the Dolichenus cult simply had no means to retain its current adherents or gain new recruits and largely dissipated afterwards.

While it is difficult to differentiate between temples which have been destroyed by Christians, barbarian incursions, or perhaps even from looting for material resources, the *dolichena* along the Rhine and Danube in the early third century additionally appear to have been pillaged for the riches and cultic objects housed within them under the orders of Maximinus Thrax, who was said to have confiscated the property and wealth of affluent citizens, public treasuries, and temples to fund his military agenda (Herodian, *Hist.* 7.3.5–4.1). The Dolichenus worshippers frequenting these temples seem to have received word of this imminent violence since many cultic objects were hidden. These structures were never revisited, and the objects were never retrieved, which is perhaps an indication that the members were also slain during this destruction. From the scarce evidence for the continued existence of the cult after 235 CE, István Toth (1973) concludes that Dolichenus worship met its end altogether in the region from these instances of violent looting.

This violence, however, was not typical of the fate of *dolichena* across the empire: some temples in Rome, elsewhere in Italy, and North Africa continued to be utilized as places of worship in the latter half of the third century as well as into the fourth century at Vindolanda, with the *dolichenum* there fully equipped with new renovations that included a heated room, perhaps for cult banquets (Birley and Birley 2012; Birley, Meyer, and Greene 2016). For the cult of Jupiter Dolichenus, therefore, it was not simply the case that the cult had failed to compete against Christianity in the cultic "marketplace" of late antiquity. The military networks that had encouraged participation in the cult could not sustain themselves, alongside the violent desolation of the cult along the Rhine and the Danube, which manifested itself in a general decline of Dolichenus worship prior to any possible scrimmages with Christ groups.

REFLECTIONS FOR FUTURE RESEARCH IN CULTIC DECLINE

In future attempts to elucidate the complexity of cultic decline and its intersections with Christianization, lacunary data will undoubtedly present itself as the greatest obstacle. In the same manner that the decline of most Isiac and Sarapiastic associations is opaque, the demise of the cult of Antinous, for instance, is difficult to pinpoint, even when we have direct evidence of cultic groups which had formerly enjoyed a vibrant social life, such as the collegium of Diana and Antinous in Lanuvium (*CIL* 14.2112; Bendlin 2011). It would be interesting to further investigate, should our data permit, to what extent the decline of the Asclepius cult was impacted by competition or violent confrontation with Christians since the polemicists seemed particularly keen to challenge Asclepius' healing abilities. In their treatment of Asclepius, they asserted that Christ was the superior healer since he not only healed without discrimination and without need of payment, but in healing his supplicants, he saw no need for lengthy prescriptions or elaborate incubation ceremonies as his divine authority alone was sufficient (Arnobius, *Adv. nat.* 1.44, 1.48–49; Tertullian, *Nat.* 2.14; *Apol.* 22; Acts John 22; Acts Thom. 156).[12]

Nevertheless, it is ultimately unsurprising that our fragmented data sets often prevent us from probing further; indeed, the rarity of apposite evidence coupled with the secrecy of the so-called "mystery cults" can perhaps make the study of antique cultic decline feel as if it were a "paradoxical study of a concealed object" (Belayche and Massa 2021, 5). This is all the more exacerbated by the fact that groups were not likely to announce defectors or expend more resources to publicize the association's disbandment. They were rather more likely to prioritize broadcasting tales of faithful converts, as was frequently the case in Christ groups (Wilson 2004), or codifying the association's foundation legend, membership *alba*, group bylaws, or honorifics for benefactors (Ascough, Harland, and Kloppenborg 2012; Kloppenborg and Ascough 2011; Harland 2014; Kloppenborg 2020a).

The enduring hope of this research, however, is to nuance and challenge Christocentric narratives which appeal to the teleologically laden terminology of victory, inevitability, and irreparable conflict—of triumphant winners and tragic losers. While there is useful historical information to be extracted from apologetic and hagiographical literature, an uncritical adoption of these testimonies as those of "surrogate researchers" (Platt 1981, 41) complicates the investigation of cultic decline and our understanding of relations between Christianity and elective cults, since these texts often give credence to the reductionist notion that socioreligious transformation can happen in a singular moment of conflict or convergence. To thus identify the institutional adoption of Christianity as a turning point for the *imperial support* of

---

[12]   Other ad hominem attacks of Asclepius: Clement, *Protr.* 2; Tertullian, *Nat.* 2.14; Arnobius, *Adv. nat.* 1.41, 4.24; Tertullian, *Apol.* 14; Eusebius, *Vit. Const.* 3.56; Lactantius, *Inst.* 1.19; Tatian, *Or. Graec.* 21.

polytheism seems to be a given; to identify this development as the definitive catalyst for elective cults in all their various manifestations across the empire seems overly simplistic, if not misguided.

Whereas indisputable evidence of violent and antagonistic competition between associations is lacking (Harland 2005; Van Haeperen 2014), there is often much more evidence of intragroup conflict concerning banquet etiquette, honorific designations, and leadership crises (Ascough 2005; Kloppenborg 2019). That is not to say that peaceful coexistence and cohabitation was always the standard between Christians and elective cults. Yet long after the Constantinian era, Christians, Jews, and polytheists continued to coexist in locales in which piety and devotion to the gods was deeply engrained in the cultural fabric. Certain Christians had stronger attitudes toward this, but there was never a solidified Christian front serving to dismantle polytheism. In truth, acts of iconoclastic violence occurred rarely, differed greatly on a regional basis, and frequently involved factors other than sheer intolerance and antagonism toward non-Christian cults.

In an endeavor to conceptualize a more complex picture of cultic decline, it may be fruitful to further appraise the efficacy of theories outside of Christian iconoclasm and intergroup competition, including alterations or collapses in social networks, insolvency and economic crises, and accidental destruction of temples. Competition between cultic associations in antiquity need not have *always* manifested itself in visible, violent, and hostile ways but as implicit or "healthy competition" for social capital and prestige in the ancient *polis* (Donaldson 2000). Moving forward, prioritization of regional differences in decline and contesting claims that the rise of Christianity necessarily constituted the *sentence de mort* of all elective cults will thus challenge the notion that the demise of Greco-Roman cults was monolithic, swift, or even inevitable upon Constantine's conversion. Christianization and the decline of polytheistic associations were rather lengthy and complicated processes that took place over centuries, whereby an intricate interweaving of causes contributed to the overall decline of elective cults.

WORKS CITED

Alvar, Jaime. 2008. *Romanising Oriental Gods: Myth, Salvation and Ethics in the Cults of Cybele, Isis and Mithras.* Translated by Richard Gordon. RGRW 165. Leiden: Brill.

Ascough, Richard S. 2005. "Religious Coexistence, Co-operation, Competition, and Conflict in Sardis and Smyrna." Pages 245–52 in *Religious Rivalries and the Struggle for Success in Sardis and Smyrna.* Edited by Richard S.

Ascough. Studies in Christianity and Judaism 14. Waterloo, Ont.: Wilfrid Laurier University Press.

Ascough, Richard S., Philip A. Harland, and John S. Kloppenborg. 2012. *Associations in the Greco-Roman World: A Sourcebook*. Waco, Tex.: Baylor University Press.

Bagnall, Roger S. 1988. "Combat ou vide: Christianisme et paganisme dans l'Égypte romaine tardive." *Ktema* 13:285–96.

Baker, G. P. 1930. *Constantine the Great and the Christian Revolution*. New York: Dodd, Mead.

Bayliss, Richard. 2004. *Provincial Cilicia and the Archaeology of Temple Conversion*. BARIS 1281. Oxford: Archaeopress.

Beatrice, Pier Franco. 1993. "L'intolleranza cristiana nei confronti dei pagani: un problema storiografico." Pages 7–13 in *L'intolleranza cristiana nei confronti dei pagani*. Edited by Pier Franco Beatrice. Bologna: Edizioni Dehoniane.

Beck, Roger. 1998. "'Qui Mortalitatis Causa Convenerunt': The Meeting of the Virunum Mithraists on June 26, A.D. 184." *Phoenix* 52:335–44.

Belayche, Nicole. 2004. "Pagan Festivals in Fourth-Century Gaza." Pages 5–22 in *Christian Gaza in Late Antiquity*. Edited by Brouria Bitton-Ashkelony and Aryeh Kofsky. Jerusalem Studies in Religion and Culture 3. Leiden: Brill.

Belayche, Nicole, and Francesco Massa. 2021. "Mystery Cults and Visual Language in Graeco-Roman Antiquity: An Introduction." Pages 1–37 in *Mystery Cults in Visual Representation in Graeco-Roman Antiquity*. Edited by Nicole Belayche and Francesco Massa. RGRW 194. Leiden: Brill.

Bendlin, Andreas. 2000. "Looking beyond the Civic Compromise: Religious Pluralism in Late Republican Rome." Pages 115–35, 167–71 in *Religion in Archaic and Republican Rome and Italy: Evidence and Experience*. Edited by Edward Bispham and Christopher Smith. Edinburgh: Edinburgh University Press.

———. 2011. "Associations, Funerals, Sociality, and Roman Law: The Collegium of Diana and Antinous in Lanuvium (CIL 14.2112) Reconsidered." Pages 207–96 in *Aposteldekret und antikes Vereinswesen. Gemeinschaft und ihre Ordnung*. Edited by Markus Öhler. WUNT 280. Tübingen: Mohr Siebeck.

Birley, Andrew, Alexander Meyer, and Elizabeth M. Greene. 2016. "Recent Discoveries in the Fort and Extramural Settlement at Vindolanda: Excavations from 2009–2015." *Britannia* 47:243–85.

Birley, Andrew, and Anthony Birley. 2012. "A New Dolichenum, inside the Third-Century Fort at Vindolanda." Pages 231–57 in *Iuppiter Dolichenus. Vom Lokalkult zur Reichsreligion*. Edited by Michael Blömer and Engelbert Winter. Orientalische Religionen in der Antike 8. Tübingen: Mohr Siebeck.

Bremmer, Jan N. 2021. "How Do We Explain the Quiet Demise of Graeco-Roman Religion? An Essay." *Numen* 68:230–71.

Brown, Peter. 1997. "Christianization and Religious Conflict." Pages 632–64 in *The Late Empire, A.D. 337–425*. Vol. 13 of *The Cambridge Ancient History*. Edited by Averil Cameron and Peter Garnsey. Cambridge: Cambridge University Press.

Bull, Christian H. 2021. "Prophesying the Demise of Egyptian Religion in Late Antiquity: The Perfect Discourse and Antoninus in Canopus." *Numen* 68:180–203.

Burckhardt, Jacob. 1949. *The Age of Constantine the Great*. Translated by Moses Hadas. Berkeley: University of California Press.

Cassia, Margherita. 2019. "Between Paganism and Judaism: Early Christianity in Cappadocia." Pages 13–48 in *Early Christianity in Asia Minor and Cyprus: From the Margins to the Mainstream*. Edited by Stephen Mitchell and Philipp Pilhofer. AGJU 109. Leiden: Brill.

Castrén, P. 1999. "Paganism and Christianity in Athens and Vicinity during the Fourth to Sixth Centuries A.D." Pages 211–24 in *The Idea and Ideal of the Town between Late Antiquity and the Early Middle Ages*. Edited by G. P. Brogiolo and Bryan Ward-Perkins. Transformation of the Roman World 4. Leiden: Brill.

Centola, Damon. 2018. *How Behavior Spreads: The Science of Complex Contagions*. Princeton: Princeton University Press.

———. 2021. *Change: How to Make Big Things Happen*. New York: Little, Brown Spark.

Collar, Anna. 2013. *Religious Networks in the Roman Empire: The Spread of New Ideas*. Cambridge: Cambridge University Press.

Concannon, Cavan W. 2017. *Assembling Early Christianity: Trade, Networks, and the Letters of Dionysios of Corinth*. Cambridge: Cambridge University Press.

Cumont, Franz. 1903. *The Mysteries of Mithra*. Translated by Thomas J. McCormack. London: Kegan Paul, Trench, Trübner.

Van Dam, Raymond. 1985. "From Paganism to Christianity at Late Antique Gaza." *Viator* 16:1–20.

Decker, Kurt, Georg Gangl, and Manfred Kandler. 2006. "The Earthquake of Carnuntum in the Fourth Century A.D.—Archaeological Results, Seismologic Scenario and Seismotectonic Implications for the Vienna Basin Fault, Austria." *Journal of Seismology* 10:479–95.

Demarsin, Koen. 2011. "'Paganism' in Late Antiquity: Thematic Studies." Pages 3–40 in *The Archaeology of Late Antique "Paganism."* Edited by Luke Lavan and Michael Mulryan. Late Antique Archaeology 7. Leiden: Brill.

Dijkstra, Jitse H. F. 2011. "The Fate of the Temples in Late Antique Egypt." Pages 389–436 in Lavan and Mulryan, *The Archaeology of Late Antique "Paganism."*

———. 2015. "Religious Violence in Late Antique Egypt Reconsidered: The Cases of Alexandria, Panopolis and Philae." *JECS* 5:24–48.

———. 2020. "Crowd Behaviour and the Destruction of the Serapeum at Alexandria in 391/392 CE." Pages 286–305 in *Religious Violence in the Ancient World: From Classical Athens to Late Antiquity*. Edited by Jitse H. F. Dijkstra and Christian R. Raschle. Cambridge: Cambridge University Press.

Dodds, E. R. 1965. *Pagan and Christian in an Age of Anxiety: Some Aspects of Religious Experience from Marcus Aurelius to Constantine*. Cambridge: Cambridge University Press.

Donaldson, Terence L. 2000. "Concluding Reflections." Pages 331–39 in *Religious Rivalries and the Struggle for Success in Caesarea Maritima*. Edited by Terence L. Donaldson. Studies in Christianity and Judaism 8. Waterloo, Ont.: Wilfrid Laurier University Press.

Engels, David, and Peter Van Nuffelen. 2014. "An Introduction in Religion and Competition in Antiquity." Pages 9–44 in *Religion and Competition in Antiquity*. Edited by David Engels and Peter Van Nuffelen. Collection Latomus 343. Brussels: Éditions Latomus.

Eshleman, Kendra. 2007. "Affection and Affiliation: Social Networks and Conversion to Philosophy." *CJ* 103:129–40.

Fear, A. T. 1996. "Cybele and Christ." Pages 37–50 in *Cybele, Attis and Related Cults: Essays in Memory of M. J. Vermaseren*. Edited by Eugene N. Lane. RGRW 131. Leiden: Brill.

Gager, John G. 1975. *Kingdom and Community: The Social World of Early Christianity*. Englewood Cliffs, N.J.: Prentice-Hall.

Glomb, Tomáš, Adam Mertel, Zdeněk Pospíšil, and Aleš Chalupa. 2020. "Ptolemaic Political Activities on the West Coast of Hellenistic Asia Minor Had a Significant Impact on the Local Spread of the Isiac Cults: A Spatial Network Analysis." *PLOS One* 15:1–20.

Glomb, Tomáš, Adam Mertel, Zdeněk Pospíšil, Zdeněk Stachoň, and Aleš Chalupa. 2018. "Ptolemaic Military Operations Were a Dominant Factor in the Spread of Egyptian Cults across the Early Hellenistic Aegean Sea." *PLOS One* 13:1–22.

Granovetter, Mark S. 1973. "The Strength of Weak Ties." *American Journal of Sociology* 78:1360–80.

———. 1983. "The Strength of Weak Ties: A Network Theory Revisited." *Sociological Theory* 1:201–33.

Van Haeperen, Françoise. 2014. "Cohabitation or Competition in Ostia during the Empire." Pages 133–48 in Engels and Van Nuffelen, *Religion and Competition in Antiquity*.

Hahn, Johannes. 2008. "The Conversion of the Cult Statues: The Destruction of the Serapeum 392 A.D. and the Transformation of Alexandria into the 'Christ-Loving' City." Pages 335–65 in *From Temple to Church: Destruction and Renewal of Local Cultic Topography in Late Antiquity*. Edited by Johannes Hahn and Ulrich Gotter. RGRW 163. Leiden: Brill.

Handson, Richard P. C. 1985. *Studies in Christian Antiquity*. Edinburgh: T&T Clark.

Harl, K. W. 1990. "Sacrifice and Pagan Belief in Fifth- and Sixth-Century Byzantium." *Past & Present* 128:7–27.

Harland, Philip A. 2005. "Spheres of Contention, Claims of Pre-eminence: Rivalries among Associations in Sardis and Smyrna." Pages 53–63 in Ascough, *Religious Rivalries and the Struggle for Success in Sardis and Smyrna.*

———, ed. 2014. *North Coast of the Black Sea, Asia Minor*. BZNW 204. Vol. 2 of *Greco-Roman Associations: Texts, Translations, and Commentary*. Edited by John S. Kloppenborg and Richard S. Ascough. Berlin: De Gruyter.

von Harnack, Adolf. 1908. *The Mission and Expansion of Christianity in the First Three Centuries*. 2nd ed. Translated by James Moffatt. Vol. 2. New York: G. P. Putnam's Sons.

Humphries, Mark. 2018. "Christianity and Paganism in the Roman Empire, 250–450 CE." Pages 61–80 in *A Companion to Religion in Late Antiquity*. Edited by Josef Lössl and Nicholas J. Baker-Brian. Hoboken, N.J.: Wiley-Blackwell.

Johnson, Mark J. 1997. "Pagan-Christian Burial Practices of the Fourth Century: Shared Tombs." *JECS* 5:37–59.

Kahlos, Maijastina. 2020. *Religious Dissent in Late Antiquity, 350–450*. Oxford Studies in Late Antiquity. Oxford: Oxford University Press.

Klingshirn, William E. 1994. *Caesarius of Arles: The Making of a Christian Community in Late Antique Gaul*. Cambridge Studies in Medieval Life and Thought 22. Cambridge: Cambridge University Press.

Kloppenborg, John S. 2019. *Christ's Associations: Connecting and Belonging in the Ancient City*. New Haven: Yale University Press.

———, ed. 2020a. *Ptolemaic and Early Roman Egypt*. BZNW 246. Vol. 3 of Kloppenborg and Ascough, *Greco-Roman Associations*.

———. 2020b. "Recruitment to Elective Cults: Network Structure and Ecology." *NTS* 66:323–50.

Kloppenborg, John S., and Richard S. Ascough, eds. 2011. *Attica, Central Greece, Macedonia, Thrace*. BZNW 181. Vol. 1 of Kloppenborg and Ascough, *Greco-Roman Associations*.

Last, Richard, and Philip A. Harland. 2020. *Group Survival in the Ancient Mediterranean: Rethinking Material Conditions in the Landscape of Jews and Christians*. London: T&T Clark.

Lavan, Luke. 2011. "The End of the Temples: Towards a New Narrative?" Pages xv–lxv in Lavan and Mulryan, *The Archaeology of Late Antique "Paganism."*

Lee, A. D. 2000. *Pagans and Christians in Late Antiquity: A Sourcebook*. London: Routledge.

Lewis, Nicola Denzey. 2016. "Reinterpreting 'Pagans' and 'Christians' from Rome's Late Antique Mortuary Evidence." Pages 273–90 in *Pagans and Christians in Late Antique Rome: Conflict, Competition, and Coexistence in the Fourth Century.* Edited by Michele Salzman, Marianne Sághy, and Rita Lizzi Testa. Cambridge: Cambridge University Press.

Liu, Jinyu. 2016. "Group Membership, Trust Networks, and Social Capital: A Critical Analysis." Pages 203–26 in *Work, Labour, and Professions in the Roman World.* Edited by Koenraad Verboven and Christian Laes. Impact of Empire 23. Leiden: Brill.

Lofland, John, and Rodney Stark. 1965. "Becoming a World Saver: A Theory of Conversion to a Deviant Perspective." *American Sociological Review* 30:836–74.

MacMullen, Ramsay. 1981. *Paganism in the Roman Empire.* New Haven: Yale University Press.

———. 1997. *Christianity and Paganism in the Fourth to Eighth Centuries.* New Haven: Yale University Press.

Martzavou, Paraskevi. 2010. "Les cultes isiaques et les Italiens entre Délos, Thessalonique et l'Eubée." *Pallas* 84:181–205.

Mayer, Wendy. 2020. "Religious Violence in Late Antiquity: Current Approaches, Trends and Issues." Pages 251–65 in Dijkstra and Raschle, *Religious Violence in the Ancient World.*

van der Meer, Frits. 1961. *Augustine the Bishop: The Life and Works of a Father of the Church.* Translated by J. H. McNeill and G. R. Lamb. London: Sheed & Ward.

Meyers, Eric M., and Carol L. Meyers. 2009. *Excavations at Ancient Nabratein: Synagogue and Environs.* Meiron Excavation Project 6. Winona Lake, Ind.: Eisenbrauns.

Momigliano, Arnaldo. 1965. "Introduzione: Il cristianesimo e la decadenza dell'Impero romano." Pages 5–19 in *Il conflitto tra paganesimo e cristianesimo nel secolo IV.* Edited by Arnaldo Momigliano. London: Oxford University Press.

Moore, Clifford H. 1919. "The Pagan Reaction in the Late Fourth Century." *Transactions and Proceedings of the American Philological Association* 50:122–34.

Mulryan, Michael. 2009. "'Paganism' in Late Antiquity: Regional Studies and Material Culture." Pages 41–86 in Lavan and Mulryan, *The Archaeology of Late Antique "Paganism."*

Al-Nasarat, Mohammed. 2018. "From Paganism to Christianity: General Remarks on the Religious Changes in Petra (1st–6th Cent. AD)." *Studia Ceranea* 8:209–36.

Nautin, Pierre. 1967. "La conversion du temple de Philae en église chrétienne." *Cahiers archéologiques* 17:1–43.

Van Nuffelen, Peter. 2018. *Penser la tolérance durant l'Antiquité tardive.* Les conférences de l'École pratique des hautes études 10. Paris: Éditions du Cerf.

———. 2020. "Coercion in Late Antiquity: A Brief Intellectual History." Pages 266–85 in Dijkstra and Raschle, *Religious Violence in the Ancient World*.

Platt, Jennifer. 1981. "Evidence and Proof in Documentary Research 1: Some Specific Problems of Documentary Research." *Sociological Review* 29:31–52.

Renan, Ernest. 1882. *Marc-Aurèle et la fin du monde antique*. Histoire des Origines du Christianisme 7. Paris: Calmann Lévy.

Salzman, Michele Renee. 2006. "Rethinking Pagan-Christian Violence." Pages 287–308 in *Violence in Late Antiquity: Perceptions and Practice*. Edited by H. A. Drake. Hampshire: Ashgate.

Saradi, Helen G., and Demetrios Eliopoulos. 2011. "Late Paganism and Christianisation in Greece." Pages 261–309 in Lavan and Mulryan, *The Archaeology of Late Antique "Paganism."*

Sauer, Eberhard. 1996. *The End of Paganism in the North-Western Provinces of the Roman Empire: The Example of the Mithras Cult*. BARIS 634. Oxford: Oxford University Press.

Seaman, Andy. 2014. "Tempora Christiana? Conversion and Christianisation in Western Britain AD 300–700." *Church Archaeology* 16:1–22.

Simón, Francisco Marco. 2018. "A Place with Shared Meanings: Mithras, Sabazios, and Christianity in the 'Tomb of Vibia.'" *ActAnt* 58:225–42.

Stancliffe, C. E. 1979. "From Town to Country: The Christianisation of the Touraine 370–600." *SCH* 16:43–59.

Stark, Rodney. 1992. "Epidemics, Networks, and the Rise of Christianity." *Semeia* 56:159–75.

———. 1996. *The Rise of Christianity: A Sociologist Reconsiders History*. Princeton: Princeton University Press.

Stenger, Jan R. 2018. "The 'Pagans' of Late Antiquity." Pages 391–409 in Lössl and Baker-Brian, *A Companion to Religion in Late Antiquity*.

Sweetman, Rebecca. 2010. "The Christianization of the Peloponnese: The Topography and Function of Late Antique Churches." *Journal of Late Antiquity* 3:203–61.

Takács, Sarolta A. 1995. *Isis and Sarapis in the Roman World*. RGRW 124. Leiden: Brill.

Talloen, Peter. 2009. "From Pagan to Christian: Religious Iconography in Material Culture from Sagalassos." Pages 575–607 in Lavan and Mulryan, *The Archaeology of Late Antique "Paganism."*

———. 2015. *Cult in Pisidia: Religious Practice in Southwestern Asia Minor from Alexander the Great to the Rise of Christianity*. Studies in Eastern Mediterranean Archaeology 10. Turnhout: Brepols.

Toth, István. 1973. "Destruction of the Sanctuaries of Iuppiter Dolichenus at the Rhine and in the Danube Region (235–238)." *ActAnt* 25:109–16.

Verhulst, Adriaan. 1999. *The Rise of Cities in North-West Europe*. Cambridge: Cambridge University Press.

Vermaseren, M. J. 1963. *Mithras, the Secret God*. New York: Barnes & Noble.

Walsh, David. 2018. *The Cult of Mithras in Late Antiquity: Development, Decline and Demise ca. A.D. 270–430.* Leiden: Brill.

———. 2020. "Military Communities and Temple Patronage: A Case Study of Britain and Pannonia." *American Journal of Archaeology* 124:275–99.

Ward, Walter. 2016. "The 363 Earthquake and the End of Public Paganism in the Southern Transjordan." *Journal of Late Antiquity* 9:132–70.

Wilson, Stephen G. 2004. *Leaving the Fold: Apostates and Defectors in Antiquity.* Minneapolis: Fortress.

Winter, Engelbert. 2000. "Mithraism and Christianity in Late Antiquity." Pages 173–82 in *Ethnicity and Culture in Late Antiquity.* Edited by Stephen Mitchell and Geoffrey Greatrex. London: Duckworth.

II

Focal Points

16

From Analogy to Identity

Did an Association of Leatherworkers "Turn" into the Thessalonian Church?

Timothy A. Brookins

If Richard Ascough is correct about the Thessalonian church, then one of the key methodological questions surrounding the study of associations and early Christian groups, at least for this church, becomes irrelevant. While scholarship has increasingly emphasized that associations offer a fitting "analogy" to early Christian groups, Ascough has argued that the Thessalonian church was not just *like* an association, but in fact *was* one, and existed as such *prior* to their encounter with Paul.[1]

Ascough's thesis builds upon several facts about the church's profile that are commonly agreed upon. Interpreters unanimously agree that the church consisted primarily of gentiles (1 Thess 1:9-10; 4:5), and that many or most of them belonged to the artisan class (1 Thess 4:11) and lived at subsistence level or in some degree of poverty (1 Thess 2:9; cf. 2 Cor 8:1-5).[2] As

---

[1] The first publication to propose this thesis was Ascough 2000. This essay, however, anticipates Ascough's first monograph (2003), which is based on his doctoral dissertation, submitted at the Toronto School of Theology in 1997. Continuing this line of argument later are Ascough 2014a; 2014b; 2017.

[2] Ascough adds further arguments in support of this socioeconomic profile based on the evidence of 1 Thessalonians: θλῖψις in 1:6 as a reference to poverty (2003, 168); Paul's repeated references to "work" in 2:9; 3:2, 5; 4:11; 5:12 (2003, 169–72); Paul's uncommonly positive attitude about manual labor (2003, 172–74). Hock (1978) plausibly argues that Paul's attitude about manual labor elsewhere (1 Cor 9:19; 2 Cor 11:7) is indirectly negative.

Ascough observes, Paul too was a manual laborer. Acts' description of Paul as a σκηνοποιός ("tentmaker," Acts 18:3) is corroborated in general terms by Paul's self-description as a manual laborer (1 Thess 2:9; 2 Thess 3:8-9) and his references to self-support (1 Cor 9:6, 14; 2 Cor 11:7, 9; 12:13). Ascough accepts Acts' description of him, sharing the predominant view that this meant he was, more broadly, a leatherworker (though not a tanner; Ascough 2003, 175; see also Hock 1980, 21).

Ascough constructs from this data an innovative new thesis. Since Paul supported himself through his trade, upon entering a new city he would need immediately to find work. When Paul entered Thessalonica, then, as a leatherworker he naturally sought out an association of leatherworkers, and after joining them, worked daily in their workshop (Ascough 2014a, 8–9). In the course of their work, Paul introduced the gospel and eventually succeeded in collectively converting the group. Since most professional associations were also religiously oriented, their conversion consisted in exchanging allegiances, as 1 Thess 1:9 indicates, from one God (or "idols") to another (or "a living and true God"; Ascough 2003, 175, 184–86). And since professional associations were usually gender divided and disproportionately male (2003, 54–59), the Thessalonian association of leatherworkers—the new Thessalonian church—consisted entirely of men. The structures of the association, together with its patterns of leadership and its stipulations of order, remained intact (2003, 176–84).

While Ascough's theory has received both positive and negative attention,[3] to my knowledge the particulars of Ascough's thesis have not been subject to any extended evaluation. In my judgment many of his points are well supported by the evidence (that Paul was probably a leatherworker; that the Thessalonians were predominantly of gentile origin and were predominantly subsistence-level members of the artisan class). Others are reasonable assumptions and likely to be correct (that Paul promptly searched for employment upon entering a city; that he introduced the gospel to artisans within a work setting). However, I would like to discuss several areas in which the balance of evidence in my view lowers the probability that the distinctive claims of Ascough's construction of the situation are correct.

[3]   Bridges bases her reconstruction of the letter on Ascough's theory (2008, 8–11). Others are skeptical, as is Stenschke (2005). Park (2015, 196, n. 78) agrees that Paul's first converts in Thessalonica could have come from a professional association and cites Ascough's 2000 article. See the overview and a short assessment of Ascough's thesis by Gupta (2019, 72–75). Longenecker 2022 builds on Ascough's general thesis without committing to it in all its particulars.

THE CHURCH'S PROFILE ACCORDING TO ACTS, 1 THESSALONIANS, AND ASSOCIATIONAL EVIDENCE

Acts begins its account of Paul's activity in Thessalonica by saying that he visited "a synagogue of the Jews" (17:1). There, after "reasoning with them from the Scriptures," "some of them were persuaded and attached them- selves to Paul and Silas" (τινες ἐξ αὐτῶν ἐπείσθησαν καὶ προσεκληρώθησαν τῷ Παύλῳ καὶ τῷ Σιλᾷ), along with "a large quantity of pious Greeks and not a few of the leading women" (τῶν τε σεβομένων Ἑλλήνων πλῆθος πολύ, γυναικῶν τε τῶν πρώτων οὐκ ὀλίγαι) (17:4).[4] Ascough is skeptical of Luke's account (2003, 205–8). With regard to the conversion of Jews and Godfearers, Ascough argues that 1 Thessalonians contains "no clear references to Jews or things Jewish" (2003, 212). Noting 1 Thess 1:9 ("turned to God from idols to the living and true God"),[5] he suggests that Paul "would not describe Jews (or God-fearers) as turning from idols to God" and thus concludes that the Thessalonians "were not Jews or God-fearers" (2003, 202, and n. 65).[6] Like- wise, Ascough (2003, 206) lends no credence to Acts' description of the con- version of "not a few of the prominent women" (17:4), basing his position in large part on the silence of 1 Thessalonians as to female participants and the directedness of 4:4-6 specifically to men (2003, 187–89).[7]

In many respects Ascough's construction of the church's profile differs lit- tle from what interpreters usually propose. Where it is distinctive, however, it also seems more problematic.

(1) Ascough argues that the church constituted an "already formed" group that Paul persuaded "to switch their allegiance from their patron deity or deities 'to serve a living and true God'" (2003, 185), and he offers an extended discussion of the absence of evidence for Jewish communities

---

[4]   While the items coordinated by τε … τε could be appositional to τινες, this interpre- tation is neither necessary nor most natural. As all modern English translations agree, the two coordinate items are additional to the first group designated as τινες. Translations in this chapter are by the author.

[5]   While the LXX uses the language of "turning" (ἐπιστρεφείν) more often of Jews (re) turning to God (e.g., Hos 5:4; 6:1; Joel 2:13) than gentiles turning to God (e.g., Ps 21:28; Isa 19:22; Jer 18:8, 11), the addition here of "from idols" most likely points to non-Jews. Apocryphal and pseudepigraphical works also apply the verb to both groups: Jews turning to God (T. Iss. 6:3; T. Dan 5:9, 11; T. Naph. 4:3; Jos. Asen. 11:10–11; Tob 14:6); both gentiles and Jews (T. Zeb. 9:7, 8). References are from Malherbe 2000, 119.

[6]   Elsewhere, Ascough's language seems to allow for the possibility that the commu- nity included some among its members: "It seems unlikely that the *core* of the Christian communities at Thessalonica and Philippi is to be found among Jews and/or God-fearers" (2003, 192; my italics; "core" also on p. 202).

[7]   Ascough takes σκεῦος in 4:4 in reference to the male genitalia.

in first-century Thessalonica (see below). Subtle qualifications in Ascough's language, however, reveal that he leaves an opening for the possibility that some Jews or Godfearers, although a minority in number, may have existed in the church (he denies that Jews and Godfearers constituted the "core" or "backbone" of the church; 2000, 312; 2003, 192, 202, 212). Yet he does not anywhere reconcile this possibility with his sharply defined thesis that the church constituted, in whole, a flipped or "already formed" association of gentile leatherworkers.[8]

(2) It could be debated whether "turning from idols" excludes the presence of those whom Luke calls "pious Greeks" (τῶν σεβομένων Ἑλλήνων). Jerome Murphy-O'Connor (1992) has made a close examination of the inscription *IAph* 11.55 (= *SEG* 36.970; second/sixth century CE), and makes a compelling case that the group there attached to the "Jews" (Ἰουδαῖοι) and designated "God-worshippers" (θεοσεβεῖς) are a distinct group from other participants in the synagogue, and more loosely attached to it. As Murphy-O'Connor notes, the entrance beside which the inscription was placed was "that of a soup-kitchen for the benefit of the poor and vagrants" (1992, 422). As apparent donors to the building project, the only connection of this group of god-worshippers to the synagogue was "a willingness to contribute to a good cause initiated by Jews but which had wider social implications" (1992, 423–24).

(3) The emphasis of 1 Thessalonians on men is consistent with Paul's typically androcentric form of address throughout his letters (for instance, the inclusive ἀδελφοί), so the silence about women carries little weight on its own.[9] There is, moreover, a degree of circularity at work in Ascough's thesis about the absence of women: the silence about them in the letter is taken in support of the thesis that the church was an all-male association, and the claim that the church was an all-male association is taken as evidence that the church probably did not contain women (2003, 186).[10] While his thesis

---

[8]   One might consider the possibility that there were Jewish members of the association of leatherworkers, though that scenario would be most difficult to reconcile with Ascough's view that the association was dedicated to a pagan God.

[9]   Granting that 4:4-6 addresses strictly men (assuming that σκεῦος refers to the male sexual member), this could be regarded as a more pronounced *moment* of androcentric focus. Moreover, this passage finds parallel in Paul's comments to one of his other churches: he writes to the Corinthian church regarding sexual immorality, and there overtly addresses his comments to men (1 Cor 6:12-20, esp. vv. 15-16).

[10]   A bit of ambiguity remains at this point in the argument. Ascough says based on the pattern of professional associations that "we *would expect* that the group [the Thessalonian Christian community] would be composed *primarily* of males" (my italics), which seems to leave open the possibility that females made up a portion. Yet Ascough then dissents from "most interpreters," who "see the group as including both men and women."

works similarly to sociological "models," in which the model is tested against the facts, in this case the model seems to be used to tell us what the facts must have been.

In short, Ascough's assessment of the conflict between Acts and 1 Thessalonians as to the church's profile appears to be overstated in such a way as to make room for his hypothetical construction of the church's profile as an association. Put differently, Ascough has used his construction of a typical association of leatherworkers to evaluate the evidence of Acts and 1 Thessalonians and consequently to shape his construction of the church. A weaker version of Ascough's thesis might allow for the inclusion of some Jews and women. Yet, to the extent that Ascough concedes to their inclusion, the basis for the distinctives of his thesis diminishes, for as long as the model is used to exclude certain members, the inclusion of such members could also be used to exclude the model.

EPIGRAPHICAL EVIDENCE FOR LEATHERWORKING ASSOCIATIONS AND JEWISH COMMUNITIES

At the time of Ascough's 2003 publication, there were extant "at least seventy-five voluntary association inscriptions which date from the Hellenistic and Roman periods," most of them indigenous to Thessalonica and Philippi, and most of them dating to the second and third centuries CE (2003, 18–19). According to a slightly more recent study by Nigdelis, forty-four inscriptions from Thessalonica are extant from the imperial era (2006, 14–22). Religious inscriptions are the most numerous (twenty-four of forty-four). While professional associations are also attested (purple dyers, muleteers, garland makers, a gladiatorial school), as even the most recent collection shows (Kloppenborg and Ascough 2011), no association of leatherworkers is attested either in Thessalonica or Macedonia at large in any century in antiquity.

Ascough (2003, 176) acknowledges the lack of evidence for leatherworking associations in Macedonia, though he notes three inscriptions that refer to leatherworker associations elsewhere: one from Phrygia dating to 160 CE (*IGRR* 907 = apparently *IGR* 4.790); one from Lydia dating to 147/148 CE (*SEG* 29.1183); and one from Pisidia dating to 223/224 CE (*IPisidiaHM* 93 = apparently *TAM* 3.114).[11] The last of the three refers ambiguously to tanners/leatherworkers (σκυτεῖς). A fresh search offers a few further results:

---

[11] He also references six other locations attesting to the "leather trade," citing Forbes 1966, 57.

four more inscriptions from Lydia, dating respectively to the late first century CE (AGRW 131 = *TAM* 5.1002), 152/153 CE (AGRW 700 = *TAM* 5.79), 173/174 CE (AGRW 713 = *TAM* 5.81), and second/third century CE (AGRW 12851 = *IGLAM* 656); one from Syria dating 257/258 CE (AGRW 10311 = *IPalmyra* 59); an undated inscription from the Aegean Islands (*SEG* 26.891 = Ascough, Harland, and Kloppenborg 2012, no. 259); and a doubtful one from Lydia dating to the second/third century CE (AGRW 12972 = *SEG* 41 [1991], no. 1033).[12] Significantly, all the evidence gathered so far in the *Greco-Roman Associations* series—which aggregates the ancient evidence for associations from Attica, Central Greece, Macedonia, and Thrace (vol. 1), the north coast of the Black Sea and Asia Minor (vol. 2), and Ptolemaic and early Roman Egypt (vol. 3)—includes testimony of only four associations of "leatherworkers." Of these, one refers rather to an association of "tanners" (σκυτοβυρσεῖς, not σκυτότομοι), one refers most likely to shoemakers (ἡ σύνοδος τῆς σκυτικῆς), and another refers ambiguously to tanners/leather-cutters (σκυτεῖς).[13] As noted above, and as Ascough agrees (2003, 175), Paul was not a tanner.

The lack of evidence for associations of leatherworkers is difficult to assess, for countless associations existed that inevitably we have no record of. The situation, however, reveals an inconsistency in Ascough's use of the evidence. He devotes substantial attention to investigating archaeological evidence for a synagogue of the Jews or a Jewish community in first-century Thessalonica and, against the testimony of Acts, shows that no such evidence has survived (2003, 191–212). While Ascough is reticent to deny the presence of Jews altogether, he concludes that there is "very little evidence" for their presence in first-century Macedonia, advises that it is "wise to be more cautious" in assessing their presence "than has often been the case," and draws from the evidence the inference that it is "unlikely" that the core of the church consisted of Jews (and Godfearers; 2003, 191–92, 202).

Ascough's unwillingness to acknowledge a strong Jewish presence in Thessalonica while at the same time conjecturing the presence of a leatherworking association, when evidence for both is lacking, comes across as a bit tendentious. Were one to appeal to the evidence of such associations

---

[12] An additional inscription from Lycia refers to a guild of "tanners" (σκυτοβύρσεις): AGRW 9724.

[13] (1) *IKibyra* 63 (from Lycia/Phrygia, dating to 150 CE) refers to tanners. (2) *IGLAM* 656.11 (from Lydia, dating to the second/third century CE) could refer (σκυτεῖς) to either leather-cutters or tanners. (3) *SEG* 29.1183 (from Lydia, dating to 147 CE) refers to the "synod τῆς σκυτικῆς"; the adjective, meaning "pertaining to leather," is listed in LSJ only as meaning "skilled in shoemaking." (4) *TAM* 5.1002.1 (from late first-century CE Lydia) refers unambiguously to leather-cutters. Indexed in Kloppenborg 2020, 581.

elsewhere, that would need to be weighed against the fact that the evidence for Jewish communities across the Mediterranean, and for synagogues explicitly, is substantially *more* abundant than evidence for leatherworking associations. Several dozen inscriptions attest to Jewish associations or synagogues across Bithynia, Caria, Lycia, Phrygia, Asia, Bosphorus, and even Macedonia (*IJO* 1 Mac 1) and Thessalonica (*IJO* 1 Mac 15),[14] and several of these date to the first century CE.[15]

TRANS-LOCALITY AND PAUL'S MISSIONARY STRATEGY

As Wayne Meeks memorably remarked, "Paul was a city person" (1983, 9). Among other benefits, cities afforded Paul something he could not have carried on without: employment. Logistically, it seems reasonable to suppose that Paul's first order of business when he arrived some place new was to find work. Ascough imagines that upon entering the city Paul headed immediately for the grid, searching for employment among those who shared his trade, along the row of workshops that lined the streets (2014a, 8–9). That Paul looked promptly for work is perhaps suggested by the book of Acts (18:1-3), which begins its account of Paul's visit to Corinth by describing Paul's connecting with Priscilla and Aquila, "tentmakers" (σκηνοποιοί) with whom Paul shared a "common trade" (being ὁμότεχνος) and in whose workshop he set himself up.

While Paul's first contacts upon arrival in a new city may have been "walk-in" encounters initiated by his search for work, in many places he may have been able to hook himself into preexisting networks based on other common interests or identity, even if he did not know any individuals personally. Initially, we may seriously consider the possibility of "trans-local" connections based on Paul's profession. Ascough argues that associations that were separated geographically sometimes maintained trans-local connections for various mutual interests (1997). Evidence of trans-locality is attested for several kinds of associations, including immigrant groups, merchants of a common trade, and foreign cults. The benefits of such ties were many, including the facilitation of travel, the provision of hospitality, integration into a new locale, and the provision of a central place of worship with which to meet up with one's group.

---

[14] See discussion of the inscriptions in *GRA* I 73, 82; II 95, 106, 113, 135, 139, 144, 150.

[15] A synagogue in late first- / early second-century CE Phrygia (*IJO* 168); a grave for "all the Judeans" in late first-century Lycia (*IJO* 1.223); multiple references to associations of the Ἰουδαῖοι in first-century Bosphorus (*CIRB* 70.19; *IJO* 1 BS 18.18); Judeans (λαός) in first-century BCE Caria (*IJO* 2.26).

Trans-local trade networks, however, tended to involve groups of common ethnicity, which extended diasporically from the central location of their homeland, as the evidence cited by Ascough demonstrates (1997, 228–34). There is little evidence for trans-local links shared on the basis of common profession per se. It may be noted, furthermore, that in contrast to trans-local trade networks it was not primarily Paul's work that directed his travels but his missions, for which his work served as a means. In this regard, it seems judicious to consider also the relevance of his *ethnic* connection with people in his new locales. The relevance of this consideration can be demonstrated by returning to the account of Priscilla and Aquila. The details of Paul's coming to Corinth point to the likelihood that his first personal contact with them was not made solely on the basis of his profession: Priscilla and Aquila happened also to be Jewish (18:2). Thus, both his professional *and* ethnic/religious ties to Priscilla and Aquila establish a first link in the development of a network in his new location.

Connections between geographically separated diaspora Jewish communities are attested in various ways not only through literary but also through epigraphical evidence.[16] (1) Abundantly attested are contributions of the temple tax owed to the temple in Judea from Jews living abroad (in one instance we also have evidence of "Israelites" sending contributions to the temple on Gerizim),[17] revealing a sense of ongoing attachment to the temple and Jewish homeland (Barclay 2016, 113). (2) Jews throughout Palestine made pilgrimages to Jerusalem as often as once a year. Many Jews even in the diaspora made multiple pilgrimages to Jerusalem throughout their lives (Sanders 2016, 210, 215; see also Philo, *Spec.* 1.69–70; Josephus, *Ant.* 4.203; *J.W.* 5.199). Philo describes such pilgrimages as occasions for forming new friendships and creating new bonds between far-flung diaspora communities (*Spec.* 1.69–70). (3) The opening part of 2 Maccabees presents as a letter addressed from Jews in Judea to Jews in Egypt, in which the senders seek both to foster ties between the two communities and to encourage them in their commitment to their common heritage.[18]

In the same way, Paul could follow connections into a preexisting local network based on a common religious heritage and the shared ethnicity of the Jewish people. In the absence of evidence for either a synagogue of the Jews *or* an association of leatherworkers in Thessalonica, based on the

---

[16] For these references I am indebted to Hall 2021.

[17] *SEG* 32.809–10.

[18] Regardless of the question of authenticity, the letter expresses an intention that reveals a sense of connectedness between distant communities.

advantages afforded by trans-local relationships and the common patterns that characterized them, it seems highly likely that Paul would have sought out members of his own people immediately for integration and hospitality,[19] and that if a synagogue did exist in Thessalonica, this would be one of the first places he visited.[20]

THE THESSALONIAN CHURCH AND EXTENDED NETWORKING

Ascough extends his thesis in a more recent article titled "Redescribing the Thessalonians' 'Mission' in Light of Graeco-Roman Associations" (2014b). Here Ascough proposes an analogy between the Thessalonians' activity as described in 1 Thess 1:2-10 and the activities of associations. Specifically, just as associations proclaimed their deity of worship through inscriptions and honorary monuments, so the "report" that "sounded out . . . not only in Macedonia and Achaia but in every place" (1:8) was a report *about* the church's honoring of their new deity. And just as messages traveled between individuals tied to each other throughout associational networks, so the report carried itself through natural networks of traders, artisans, and other travelers.

This reconstruction of the community's extension into the wider world seems intuitively correct. However, it also challenges the neatness of Ascough's construction of the group as proposed in his other publications. Unless Ascough's hypothetical association heard Paul's presentation of the gospel, deliberated over it, and voted on their realignment to their new god all at once, without telling anyone about it, it seems unlikely that the core group with which Paul began consisted solely of members of the association. While the point can be supported by nothing more than common sense, the process of forming the community cannot have been so swift and mechanical (even if a "vote" did finally take place). It seems highly improbable that interest would be taken by members of the guild and only members of the guild. Most members would surely have wives and children, with whom they would converse daily, along with parents and possibly other extended family, as well as friends, frequent customers, and neighbors.

The probable dynamics of networking has further implications also for Ascough's proposal that the Thessalonian community consisted entirely of men. The simple existence of personal relations between men and their wives would likely result in transmission of Paul's message from one to another before

[19] For example, *CIJ* 1404.
[20] A non-Jewish example is described in Apuleius, *Metam.* 11.26, with regard to the character Lucius.

the passage of many days. Apart from other women tied to these households, moreover, even associations that consisted exclusively of men often had "honorary" ties with women known as *matres collegiorum*, who served the associations financially, among other ways (*CIL* 6.10234 [= Ascough, Harland, and Kloppenborg 2012, no. 322]; *IG* II² 1328 [= *GRA* 34]). We find these "mothers of associations" frequently tied to professional associations.[21]

We may infer from Ascough's construction of the group's growth through natural networks that he sees the induction of women occurring eventually. Yet Ascough's theory presents the community as being all-male *even up to* the time 1 Thessalonians was written (4:4-6), an interval that cannot have been less than three to six months after Paul's departure.[22] That the report about the church's faith could have "sounded out throughout all Macedonia and Achaia and every place," traveling over the course of several months the many paths that connected intersecting networks, and not yet to have contained women, seems very difficult to believe.

INSTITUTIONAL STRUCTURE AND RELIGIOUS REALIGNMENT

Were one to assume that the assembly did begin as an association, there might be features of its organization that there would be no sense in changing. The leatherworkers would not have discontinued "meeting" in the workshop (though they would now have at hand an interesting new topic of conversation). Conceivably, many of their rules of "order" stipulated for special meetings or commensal occasions would still apply. For instance, Ascough cites the example of *IG* II² 1368 (Athens, 164/165 CE), which forbids fighting, sitting in another person's seat, or insulting or abusing each other (2003, 181).

In other respects, it is doubtful that the hypothetical group's institutional structures remained fundamentally unchanged.

---

[21] Shipbuilders (*CIL* 14.256); builders (*CIL* 11.5748); launderers (*CIL* 9.5450); timberworkers (*CIL* 2.1355; 3.7505; 14.69, 326; *AE* 1998, 282); reed-bearers (*CIL* 14.37); firemen (*CIL* 3.1207). References are from table 4 in Hemelrijk 2008, 151–52. See also women leaders and benefactors in *GRA* II 99, 106, 108, 123, 138, 147, 153.

[22] Paul has moved from Thessalonica, to Berea, and to Athens (Acts 17:9–18:1 appears to harmonize basically with 1 Thessalonians on these points). After several failed attempts to return (1 Thess 2:18), he then sent Timothy from Athens back to Thessalonica (1 Thess 3:2), where Timothy must have stayed for some time, at least until news of the Thessalonians traveled throughout Macedonia, Achaia, and "every place" (probably Asia, if not further east). At last, Timothy travels from Thessalonica back to Paul, who is now in Corinth, giving him a favorable report. This could not have happened more quickly than two or three months, and may have taken as long as six.

(1) Ascough suggests that the leadership structure remained intact and that offices rotated perhaps on a monthly or annual basis, "as was common in the associations" (2003, 177). Yet it is difficult to imagine Paul leaving alone leadership in the new community of faith as a matter of course. While his assemblies were perhaps more egalitarian than the traditional household or the established structures of the body politic, his letters afford evidence that he wished for his communities to operate under the supervision of those whom he deemed most qualified "in Christ" or according to the gifting of the Spirit. It is certainly relevant that he includes among the different gifts distributed to believers according to the dispensation of the Spirit (1 Cor 12:4-31; Rom 12:6-8) "teachers" and their gift of "teaching" (1 Cor 12:28, 29; Rom 12:7). In 1 Corinthians, Paul "urges" (παρακαλῶ) the church to "recognize" (οἴδατε) the household of Stephanas, and to "be subject" (ὑποτάσσησθε) to them (1 Cor 16:15-16). The implication of the grounding remark (ὅτι) that follows, that they were among "the first-fruit of Achaia" (ἀπαρχὴ τῆς Ἀχαΐας), is undoubtedly that they had been in the faith *longer than others*. In 1 Thess 5:12, moreover, the nature of the leadership role as Paul briefly characterizes it suggests that the routine for appointing group officials (if they appointed their own) cannot have been based on the same criteria as they had been in prior procedure. For while it is conceivable that the legitimacy of "presiding over" (προϊσταμένους) others and enforcing group norms (νουθετοῦντας) could derive from the consensus vote of elections, it is doubtful that Paul would have seen associational *election* procedures as giving leaders special qualification to preside over others specifically, as he puts it, "*in the Lord*."

(2) As Macedonian inscriptions demonstrate, most professional associations were also religious (Ascough 2003, 23–24). Many professional associations devoted themselves to one deity in particular, whom they invoked in their rites and honored publicly through various means (Ascough 2003, 23, citing inscriptions including *CIG* 2082; *CIL* 6.641, 642). Ascough makes the intriguing proposal that the artisan association to which Paul presented his message simply "realigned" themselves, "turning" (ἐπεστρέψατε) from some pagan deity of worship (ἀπὸ τῶν εἰδώλων) to worship "the living and true God" (θεῷ ζῶντι καὶ ἀληθινῷ; 2003, 184–86). Based on the second person plural, ἐπεστρέψατε, Ascough argues that this decision was a collective one agreed upon by the association as a whole.

While Paul's ministry in Thessalonica may have been especially successful among a group of artisans who shared his trade, the particulars of Ascough's proposal on this point present significant problems. First, the fact that Paul describes their "turning" in the second person plural cannot be regarded as a significant indicator of associational group consensus, since Paul's comments in his letters are directed to the churches in the plural nearly 100 percent of the time. Second, Ascough puts forward that Paul managed to persuade the group "over time" (2003, 185; 2014a, 13–17), though, as mentioned above, any length of time would only increase the probability that members were conversing with others in their networks about the matter, and these people cannot all have remained disinterested. The most natural result would be at least a partially eclectic core.

Perhaps more importantly, we have no examples of religious realignment of an association from worship of one deity to exclusive worship of another. Ascough acknowledges this, noting that the Thessalonians' example "stands out as unique" (understandably, since in the polytheistic religious environment exclusive allegiance would not be necessary; 2003, 186). Ascough, however, notes that "in a few cases in antiquity" we find associations adopting a new deity of worship without abandoning devotion to one already worshipped (2003, 185). Ascough cites two inscriptions. The first (SIG³ 985) describes a dream in which Zeus appears to a certain Dionysius ordering him to perform due rituals in the former's honor. It is not clear from the inscription whether Dionysius was to establish a new association in his house or to open up a preexisting cult to new members. The second inscription (IG X,2 1 255 = GRA I 77 = Ascough, Harland, and Kloppenborg 2012, no. 52) describes a dream in which Sarapis appears to a man named Xenainetos (apparently in Thessalonica), enjoining him to send instructions for the founding of a cult of Sarapis and Isis at Opus. Although the inscription dates to the first or second century CE, the alleged story took place in the second century BCE (Ascough 2003, 13, 14; Ascough, Harland, and Kloppenborg 2012, no. 52; GRA I 77). Neither of the two inscriptions offers a close parallel to the proposed origins of Paul's church. In the first case, it is debatable whether the inscription in fact describes the introduction of a new deity *alongside* another within a *preexisting* association. In the second, we quite apparently do not have the introduction of a new deity to a preexisting association but rather the transplanting and extension of a cult from one place (Thessalonica) to another (Opus).

(3) A more general point of consideration is that the question whether the Thessalonian church was drawn *from* an association of artisans can theoretically be separated from the question whether the fundamental operations of the association continued to function as they had. The earliest analogical descriptions of Christian assemblies by outsiders likened them to philosophical schools (in the mid-second century, for instance, Galen compares

Christian groups to the philosophical schools [Galen, *Diff. puls.* 2.4; 3.3]). At some point, this label came to apply no longer as an analogy but rather as a Christian self-description.[23] A plethora of studies have demonstrated that Paul's communities were indeed in many ways akin to "scholastic communities" (Judge 1960; 1961; Conzelmann 1966; Schmeller and Cebulj 2001; Smith 2012; White 2017) or, even more specifically, philosophical schools (Stowers 1984; 2001; Alexander 1995; 2001; Glad 1995). Important similarities with the philosophical schools included, among other items, an emphasis on ethics and exclusive and wholehearted commitment to one's creed, and a unique style of community nurture.

Against Ascough's thesis about associational "realignment," a closer analogue to the Thessalonians' conversion is found in the experience of new devotees to "philosophy." This point was argued extensively by Abraham Malherbe in a long series of publications (1970; 1983; 1987; 2000). Ancient philosophy advocated not only fundamentally different ideas about the universe from popular mythology and cultic religion, but also a profound redefinition of life's "goods." Thus, taking on the philosophical life required deconstruction of a symbolic universe deeply embedded through primary socialization, assimilated from the cradle through our nurses and parents, and later continued through teachers and the domestic, political, and religious institutions that surround us.[24] The simultaneous reconstruction of a new worldview would need to be facilitated by constant repetition of precepts and a rigorous program of behavioral reinforcement, applied gradually and adapted uniquely for each individual (a process that has been described as "psychagogy," or nurture of the soul). All of this required commitment of one's whole self (Cicero, *Tusc.* 5.2.5; Seneca, *Ep.* 53.8; Marcus Aurelius, *Med.* 8.1).

Analogously, conversion for the Thessalonians entailed a comprehensive change of theological perspective (from idols to God) and behavioral norms (from those of the gentiles, "who do not know God"), so that the proselytes' induction into the faith required a similar level of commitment and program of resocialization. The appropriateness of this comparison is confirmed by examining the dynamics of Paul's "parenetic" style in the

---

[23] Justin Martyr (*Dial.* 8.1), Tertullian (*Pall.* 6.4), and Tatian (*Or. Graec.* 31; 42) considered the Christian faith a "philosophy."

[24] The philosophers often blamed vice on bad socialization: influence from the crowd (Seneca, *Ep.* 94.55; 123.6–9; Musonius Rufus, *Diatr.* 6); the teaching of our parents (Seneca, *Ep.* 115.11); Cicero lists nurses, parents, masters, the poets, and public opinion (*Tusc.* 3.1.2–3).

Thessalonian letters. As the philosophers did with their students, Paul constantly reminds the Thessalonians what they already "know" (1:5; 2:1, 2, 5, 11; 3:3, 4; 4:2; 5:2) or "remember" (2:9), and reviews what he had previously taught (3:4; 4:1, 2, 6, 11; cf. 5:2), even when they had "no need" to be reminded (4:9; 5:1); he urges them to repeat the truth to themselves (4:18); he reminds them how he had instructed "each" one of them (2:11); he refers often to positive exemplars (1:5-6; 2:1-12; 2:14-16); and he frequently employs the language of exhortation and instruction (2:3, 12; 3:2, 7, 13; 4:1, 2, 10, 11, 18; 5:11, 12, 14).

The comparison extends also to Paul's professional work alongside the Thessalonians. As was not uncommon among the philosophers, Paul taught while working (Hock 1980; Malherbe 2000), even giving individualized instruction, adapted to meet the varying needs of each individual.[25] Because self-support by trade necessitated prolonged hours of labor every day, most of the community's time would have been spent together in this fashion. If a substantial portion of this time included instruction and reinforcement in the faith, we are a long way from the kind of broad "ethical" emphases of the associations, which generally consisted of rules of order, applicable at *meetings* that occurred not more than weekly or monthly.[26] That is, for the Thessalonians, reinforcement of the community's identity as a group now occurred mostly, not at special meetings, but outside of them.

This is not to advocate the view that the Thessalonian church was a philosophical school rather than an association (although it is worth mentioning that there did exist associations of philosophers),[27] but that even if the church began as an association, the professional association as a model poorly fits the *psychagogic* emphasis of community life in Paul's churches, and that the church's character apparently moved quickly in the direction of the philosophical schools.

---

[25] "Working night and day . . . we preached to you the gospel of God . . . we instructed each and every one of you . . . exhorting and encouraging and invoking you" (2:9-11). See also the varied language of exhortation in 5:14.

[26] Ethical stipulations beyond meetings are attested, but are much more exceptional (e.g., Ascough, Harland, and Kloppenborg 2012, no. 13; cf. no. 295).

[27] Philosophical associations are indicated, for instance, in a second-century inscription from Lycia (*GRA* 146 = *TAM* 2.910 = *IGR* 3.733 = PHI 284800 = AGRW 6120); a second-century CE inscription from Bithynia (*IPrusaOlymp* 17–18 = *IHadrianoi* 51–52 = PHI 278508 = AGRW 16298); Harland's index (*GRA* II), under "occupational associations—philosophers" (II 467), points to several associations of philosophers in the region of Pisidia and Lycia, with text and commentary found at II 367–85.

CONCLUSION

Much can be said in praise of Ascough's work. Ascough has worked at the cutting edge of research on associations and the early Christian movement, and few match his expertise in the wealth of data that offers us a window into ancient associations, and the social lives of much of the non-elite population. His thesis about the origins of the Thessalonian church has made an innovative and intriguing contribution to studies of the Thessalonian letters. The evidence strongly supports the view that the church consisted primarily of gentiles and primarily members of the artisan class. That Paul promptly searched for employment among members of his own trade (which, doubtless, was that of leatherworking), and upon finding them introduced them to the gospel while plying their trade in the workshop, seems wholly plausible. I have pointed out, however, several reasons to doubt the finer distinctives of Ascough's thesis. While we may speculate (given the absence of evidence for leatherworking associations) that many of the Thessalonians could have been participants in an association, once the other distinctives of the thesis are lost, we are virtually back to the original consensus that the church's members belonged largely to the artisan class.

WORKS CITED

Alexander, Loveday. 1995. "Paul and the Hellenistic Schools: The Evidence of Galen." Pages 60–83 in *Paul in His Hellenistic Context*. Edited by Troels Engberg-Pedersen. London: T&T Clark.

———. 2001. "IPSE DIXIT: Citation of Authority in Paul and in the Jewish and Hellenistic Schools." Pages 103–27 in *Paul beyond the Judaism/Hellenism Divide*. Edited by Troels Engberg-Pedersen. Louisville: Westminster John Knox.

Ascough, Richard S. 1997. "Translocal Relationships among Voluntary Associations and Early Christianity." *JECS* 5:223–41.

———. 2000. "The Thessalonian Christian Community as a Professional Voluntary Association." *JBL* 119:311–28.

———. 2003. *Paul's Macedonian Associations: The Social Context of Philippians and 1 Thessalonians*. WUNT 2/161. Tübingen: Mohr Siebeck.

———. 2014a. *1 & 2 Thessalonians: Encountering the Christ Group at Thessalonike*. Phoenix Guides to the New Testament 13. Sheffield: Sheffield Phoenix Press.

———. 2014b. "Redescribing the Thessalonians' 'Mission' in Light of Graeco-Roman Associations." *NTS* 60:61–82.

———. 2017. *1 & 2 Thessalonians: Encountering the Christ Group at Thessalonike.* T&T Clark Studies Guides to the New Testament. London: Bloomsbury.

Ascough, Richard S., Philip A. Harland, and John S. Kloppenborg. 2012. *Associations in the Greco-Roman World: A Sourcebook.* Waco, Tex.: Baylor University Press.

Barclay, John M. G. 2016. *Pauline Churches and Diaspora Jews.* Grand Rapids: Eerdmans.

Bridges, Linda McKinnish. 2008. *1 & 2 Thessalonians.* Macon, Ga.: Smyth & Helwys.

Conzelmann, Hans. 1966. "Paulus und die Weisheit." *NTS* 12:231–44.

Forbes, R. J. 1966. *Studies in Ancient Technology.* Vol. 5. Leiden: Brill.

Glad, Clarence E. 1995. *Paul and Philodemus: Adaptability in Epicurean and Early Christian Psychagogy.* NovTSup 81. Leiden: Brill.

Gupta, Nijay K. 2019. *1 and 2 Thessalonians.* Grand Rapids: Zondervan Academic.

Hall, Josiah. "Translocal Relationships among Associations and Christ Groups, Revisited." *ZNW* (forthcoming).

Hemelrijk, Emily A. 2008. "Patronesses and 'Mothers' of Roman *Collegia.*" *ClAnt* 27:115–62.

Hock, Ronald F. 1978. "Paul's Tentmaking and the Problem of His Social Class." *JBL* 97:555–64.

———. 1980. *The Social Context of Paul's Ministry: Tentmaking and Apostleship.* Philadelphia: Fortress.

Judge, Edwin A. 1960. "Early Christians as a Scholastic Community." *JRH* 1:4–15.

———. 1961. "Early Christians as a Scholastic Community." *JRH* 1:125–37.

Kloppenborg, John S., ed. 2020. *Ptolemaic and Early Roman Egypt.* BZNW 246. Vol. 3 of *Greco-Roman Associations: Texts, Translations, and Commentary.* Edited by John S. Kloppenborg and Richard S. Ascough. Berlin: De Gruyter.

Kloppenborg, John S., and Richard S. Ascough, eds. 2011. *Attica, Central Greece, Macedonia, Thrace.* BZNW 181. Vol. 1 of Kloppenborg and Ascough, *Greco-Roman Associations.*

Longenecker, Bruce W. 2022. "Configuring Time in Roman Macedonia: Identity and Differentiation in Paul's Thessalonian Christ Group." Pages 289–308 in *Greco-Roman Associations, Deities, and Early Christianity.* Edited by Bruce W. Longenecker. Waco, Tex.: Baylor University Press.

Malherbe, Abraham J. 1970. "'Gentle as a Nurse': The Cynic Background to 1 Thessalonians 2." *NovT* 12:203–17.

———. 1983. "Exhortation in First Thessalonians." *NovT* 25:238–56.

———. 1987. *Paul and the Thessalonians: The Philosophic Tradition of Pastoral Care.* Philadelphia: Fortress.

————. 2000. *The Letters to the Thessalonians: A New Translation with Introduction and Commentary*. AB 32B. New York: Doubleday.

Meeks, Wayne A. 1983. *The First Urban Christians: The Social World of the Apostle Paul*. New Haven: Yale University Press.

Murphy-O'Connor, Jerome. 1992. "Lots of God-Fearers: Theosebeis in the Aphrodisias Inscription." *RB* 99:418–24.

Nigdelis, Pantelis M. 2006. *Επιγραφικά Θεσσαλονίκεια. Συμβολή στην πολιτική και κοινωνική ιστολρία της απαρχαίς Θεσσαλονίκης* [Epigraphica Thessalonicensia: Contribution to the Political and Social History of Ancient Thessaloniki]. Thessaloniki: University Studio Press.

Park, Young-Ho. 2015. *Paul's Ekklesia as a Civic Assembly: Understanding the People of God in Their Politico-Social World*. Tübingen: Mohr Siebeck.

Sanders, E. P. 2016. *Judaism: Practice and Belief, 63 BCE–66 CE*. Minneapolis: Fortress.

Schmeller, Thomas, and Christian Cebulj. 2001. *Schulen im Neuen Testament? Zur Stellung des Urchristentums in der Bildungswelt seiner Zeit*. Freiberg: Herder.

Smith, Claire S. 2012. *Pauline Communities as "Scholastic Communities": A Study of the Vocabulary of "Teaching" in 1 Corinthians, 1 and 2 Timothy and Titus*. Tübingen: Mohr Siebeck.

Stenschke, Christoph W. 2005. "Paul's Macedonian Associations: The Social Context of Philippians and 1 Thessalonians." *R&T* 12:74–79.

Stowers, Stanley K. 1984. "Social Status, Public Speaking and Private Teaching: The Circumstances of Paul's Preaching Activity." *NovT* 26:59–82.

————. 2001. "Does Pauline Christianity Resemble a Hellenistic Philosophy?" Pages 81–102 in Engberg-Pedersen, *Paul beyond the Judaism/Hellenism Divide*.

White, Devin L. 2017. *Teacher of the Nations: Ancient Educational Traditions and Paul's Argument in 1 Corinthians 1–4*. Berlin: De Gruyter.

17

Configuring Time in Roman Macedonia

Identity and Differentiation in Paul's Thessalonian Christ Group

Bruce W. Longenecker

We are so bound by time, by its order. . . .
There are days that define your story beyond your life.

(Heisserer 2016)

The Thessalonian Christ followers were members of an association who collectively decided to abandon their deities and adopt devotion to Christ—so argue John Kloppenborg (1993; 2019, 325–26), Richard Ascough (2000; 2003, 162–90; 2014), and others (e.g., Rulmu 2010; Rollens 2016, 127–28). There is scope to question certain aspects of this reconstruction.[1] Nonetheless, the proposal makes good sense of 1 Thess 1:7-9, where the report regarding the conversion of the Thessalonians is said to have spread throughout Macedonia and Achaia, becoming "known everywhere" in those regions.

There are two primary reasons why this proposal regarding the arrival of Christ devotion in Thessalonica has some merit. First, it would be unusual if the Thessalonian Christ followers had been sizeable in number. Recent estimates of the size of Christ groups in the early decades of the Christ movement usually place the membership of Christ groups to below fifty, often

---

[1] See, for instance, Brookins' essay (2022) in this volume. So also Johnson-DeBaufre 2010; Trozzo 2012.

two to three dozen.[2] Second, reconstructions of Paul's ministry permit a period of only a few months (roughly three or so) for Paul's work among the Thessalonians, and 1 Thessalonians seems to have been written within a few months of his departure.[3]

These two factors place considerable constraints on scenarios to explain how Paul could make such an extravagant claim regarding the widespread chatter about the surprising adoption of Christ devotion in Thessalonica. They tend to rule out a scenario in which the Thessalonians had undertaken an active "evangelization" initiative throughout the regions of Macedonia and Achaia[4]—a scenario problematized further by the likelihood that the Thessalonian Christ followers did not have access to the economic resources needed to sponsor such an effort.[5] And in the absence of a widespread mission undertaken by Thessalonian Christ followers themselves, Paul's comments are unlikely to be simply a rhetorical trope of commendation, since the employment of this trope would be effective only if it had some historical foothold, which is unlikely in view of the two constraints noted.[6] Other connective social and/or familial networks may have contributed somewhat to the spread of the news, but those networks were no different in Thessalonica than in any other location, and the spread of the news about the Thessalonians seems, as Paul portrays it, to be somewhat exceptional. Accordingly, Paul's claim in 1:7-9 may well reflect a situation in which knowledge of the Thessalonians' Christ devotion had made its way through the grapevine of associational connectivity.[7]

[2] See, for instance, the extensive discussion in Kloppenborg 2019, 97–123.

[3] See Hengel and Schwemer 1997, 301; Riesner 1998, 414; Brookins 2021, 17–19.

[4] As Brookins (2021, 35) notes, what "sounded out" into the surrounding regions was not the good news itself but a report about the Thessalonians' reception of the good news.

[5] Piecing together hints about their economic well-being from several of Paul's comments, this association must be representative of those numerous associations that we have no material evidence for—associations at the relatively low end of the economic spectrum that left behind no monumental inscriptions, statues, tombs, or the like. On the economic profile of this Thessalonian Christ group, see Longenecker 2010, 255–58, where their corporate economic profile is deemed to be ES5. Jung puts them "mostly [at] PS6 and partly [at] PS5 and PS7" (2020, 472, 474). I think Jung does not take Paul's rhetorical goals into sufficient account, which explains how he arrives at a slightly lower economic profile than I do.

[6] For an example of the effective use of this rhetorical trope, see Rom 1:8 and 1 Clem. 1.1. In both instances, Christ devotion has been in place for decades by the time the authors invoke the trope.

[7] On intercity connectivity between associations, see Ascough 1997 and especially Hall 2021. Moreover, see Rollens 2022, which gives extensive consideration to *PPetaus* 28 (= *GRA* III 239; Ascough, Harland, and Kloppenborg 2012, no. 290). Rollens (p. 314 in this volume, emphasis in original) notes how that letter "reveals a network that facilitated the movement of knowledge trans-locally *among* villages, horizontally *within* villages, and even vertically between people of different statuses within the association/village itself"; similarly,

With this said, however, there are other possibilities than a scenario in which the Thessalonian Christ followers were, without remainder, a converted association *in toto*. A good number of members of a single association may have changed their devotional allegiance, but that may not have included all of the members; perhaps the data can just as easily be explained in relation to a split within the original association—for clearly an association "torn asunder" by the introduction of a new form of controversial devotion could just as easily have been the news that spread through associational networks. Nor is it necessarily the case that an associational core of members would have excluded others from joining in a new corporate identity after the rupture from the original association. Even with nuances of that kind, however, the conversion of (a sizeable portion of) an association has good explanatory force with regard to Paul's comments in 1:7-9.

It is quite possible, then, that (a significant percentage of) the Thessalonian Christ followers had been members of an association and decided to shifted their allegiance exclusively to a powerful deity who, having died and been resurrected, was soon to transform the world in favor of those who were committed to him. Ultimately the argument of this essay does not require that scenario to have been the case; the data from Macedonian associational inscriptions and tombstones that appear below could just as easily shed light on the Thessalonian context even if the Thessalonian Christ followers (or a significant percentage of them) had *not* assembled as (or within) an association prior to their adoption of Christ devotion. But the associational theory seems to me the most likely explanation, even in a modified form, as noted above.

This essay focuses on the organization of time in Macedonia—as evidenced by a number of associational and other inscriptions from that region, and in comparison to the conception of time that Paul was expecting Thessalonians to adopt. As we will see, if in fact Paul converted members of a Thessalonian association of some kind, it also seems that Paul sought to reconstruct the corporate identity of the Thessalonian Christ group by inserting a new ideology of time into a context where temporal orientations were already heavily freighted with ideological commitments.

CONTOURING TIME

Studies of the use of space in the ancient world repeatedly illustrate how social values influenced the construction of space in which people carried

---

"trans-local communication within associative networks could be routine in unofficial associations, even when they had a much more local interest" (p. 318 in this volume).

out their social interactions.[8] Simply put, the organization of social relationships was reflected in the organization of social space.

But what is true of space is also true of time—that is, orientations to time were (and arguably are) constructed and structured in ways that reflect socially shared values of a culture or subculture. Social theorists have repeatedly highlighted that social interaction is performed on a temporal playing field "leveled" to correspond to the constructs of value that are operative within cultures. As Barbara Adam notes, time is "irreducibly social since human culture is a prerequisite to the development of concepts" (1990, 89; see also Giddens 1979, 198–233; 1984, 110–61; Gallois 2007). As Sarit Kattan Gribetz has recently demonstrated, since orientations to time are culturally constructed phenomena, they can serve a unifying function for those who share them while also "differentiat[ing] those who mark their time in certain ways from those who mark their time differently" (2020, 1). She notes (2020, 1–2):

> Time—as it is constructed, interpreted, and enacted—thus creates both shared worlds and different worlds, and through measurements and manners of conceptualizing and organizing time, different groups intertwine with each other in multiple ways. . . . [The organization of time] serves as a powerful mechanism through which to enact difference and forge identity.

For reasons of this kind, clashes of culture often involve clashes in orientations to time (what Gallois [2013] calls "the war for time").

This sculpting of time to reinforce aspects of identity (and cultural forms of power) was a key feature of Roman sociopolitical ideology. As Anthony Grafton (2003, 82) has noted, "The Romans of the late Republic and early Empire were . . . obsessed with time"—precisely for the purposes of documenting the rise of Roman power over the world that mattered. So too, Denis Feeney has illustrated ways that Roman structures of power inevitably contoured "the time of the city and the empire" in a manner that "touched on practically every dimension of their experience . . . [in order] to fix themselves within a worldwide web of time" (2007, 2).[9]

---

[8] For instance, see standard discussions of space in Pompeii: Wallace-Hadrill 1994; Hartnett 2017; for similar studies of space in Rome, see Russell 2015; Davies 2020; and Caldelli and Ricci 2020. On the issue of how space could have impacted the character of early Christ groups, see Oakes 2016.

[9] Forsythe (2012, xi–xii) notes that "many aspects of Roman religious thought and behavior" were "preconditioned or even substantially influenced by concepts of time." For a study of cosmic timekeeping in Greek religious experience, see especially Boutsikas 2020 (in many ways a much-needed update of Cumont 1912).

Attempts to embed the Roman imperial order within the "worldwide web of time" is found in Roman literature such as Virgil's *Aeneid* and on monumental civic pronouncements such as the Priene inscription—the latter (*OGIS* 458, from 9 BCE) crediting "Providence" with the ordering of all things, including the appearance of Augustus on the stage of world history, so that "the birthday of the god Augustus" is identified as "the beginning of the good news for the world." But what we see in Roman epic poetry and civic monuments is also evidenced in inscriptional self-presentations of Macedonian associations in the Roman world—precisely the world of the Thessalonian Christ followers, who themselves had perhaps assembled originally as a somewhat typical Macedonian association. But whether the Thessalonian Christ followers (or many of them) had already been an association or not, Paul seems intent on framing their orientation to time in a way that probably was starkly distinctive from the associations and residents of their city.

ROMANIZED TIME IN MACEDONIA

Two dating systems were commonly used in Macedonia during the Roman imperial period:

1. A provincial-era dating system, which provided dates in accordance with the founding of the Roman Macedonian province in the year 148 BCE (starting on October 15).

2. An imperial-era dating system, which provides dates in accordance with Augustus' emergence as the primary figure in Roman governance—in particular, September 2 in year 31 BCE, the date when the young Octavian defeated his rival Anthony in the Battle of Actium.

Each of these dating systems had pro-Roman narratives attached to them and offer important glimpses into the cultural ethos of Macedonia in the first century. Those narratives are as follows.

The provincial-era dating system was pegged to the victory of Rome over Macedonian forces in 148 BCE. The king of Macedonia at that time was Philippos Andriskos, who, in a short-lived reign, had drummed up anti-Roman sentiment among the Macedonians, leading to a military insurrection against Rome's political influence. The Roman forces under the command of Quintus Caecilius Metellus defeated the Macedonian forces in the autumn of 148 BCE. In the aftermath, Rome not only reorganized the "space" of Macedonia but its "time" as well. Reorganizing its space involved grouping the whole of Macedonia (which previously consisted of smaller administrative units) into one province, with Thessalonica as its administrative center. Reorganizing its time involved imposing the provincial-era calendar on the Macedonians, with its start date coinciding with the defeat of indigenous Macedonian forces. This temporal initiative was an obvious way of organizing Macedonian self-identity around what we might call "Roman-controlled time." Forming time in relation to the defeat of Philippos Andriskos asserted the dominance of Roman power and "temporalized" the futility of rebellion against Rome. The year 148 BCE stood as a watershed signaling "the new era" and inspiring "gratitude commemorating the liberation of the country from the usurper and the restoration of the republic" (Papazoglou 1983, 193). As Bradley Hudson McLean rightly notes, the provincial-era dating system was widespread in Macedonia precisely because the narrative of the inevitability and legitimacy of Roman domination "was deeply rooted in the popular consciousness" of the people of Macedonia (2002, 174, n. 121).

Alongside this provincial-era dating system was the imperial-era dating system. This calendar took its temporal bearings from the year 31 BCE—specifically, September 2 of that year, the day that Octavian defeated his friend-cum-rival Mark Antony in the Battle of Actium. Prior to this battle, Macedonia had been under the jurisdiction of Mark Antony, but that changed with Octavian's victory, which of course concentrated incomparable power in Octavian's hands and acted as a catalyst for his unprecedented rise as the "first citizen" of Rome and ultimately the establishment of the Roman "empire"—with Octavian adopting the honorific "Augustus" in 27 BCE. After the Battle of Actium, Octavian/Augustus effectively had unrivaled control of the Mediterranean (*mare nostrum*), and the chaos of the republican civil wars was ended. This is exactly the way Augustus presented his victory years later in his *Res gestae*, highlighting how he "had put an end to civil wars" (*postqua[m b]el[la civil]ia exstinxeram* / μετὰ τὸ τοὺς ἐνφυλίους ζβέσαι με πολέμους, 34.1).

The Battle of Actium was so important to Octavian that he took various initiatives to mark the event—including (1) the erection of a monument dedicated to Neptune and Mars on the spot where his command post had stood in Actium, (2) the establishment of a new city Nicopolis or "City of Victory" (fed by smaller urban centers in the same area), and (3) the renovation and rejuvenation of the Actian games. Beyond this, the civic elite of

Thessalonica (referenced in an inscription as "politarchs," *CIG* 1967) also erected the "Golden Gate" on the western city wall—a triumphal arch commemorating Octavian's victory at Actium.[10]

But the Macedonians themselves eagerly adopted a further initiative—one that went beyond monumentalized ways of memorializing the turning point in Octavian's (later Augustus') career and Rome's history. This initiative involved the organization of time itself, so that the temporal bearings of Macedonia were pegged to Octavian's Actian victory.[11] In many ways, this was a far more significant initiative than any of Octavian's three localized initiatives (mentioned above). The establishment of the imperial-era dating system ensured that time itself was structured in relation to the watershed in the course of history, brought about by Octavian/Augustus. The imperial-era dating system was an exercise in "the politics of the past," structuring time around a political agenda with Roman imperial reign at the center. But it was also "the politics of the future," since it corresponded to the popular belief that the Roman imperial order was an empire eternally blessed by its deities.[12] And the fact that the imperial-era system (which took its starting point from Octavian's Actium victory) survived well beyond Augustus' death differentiates this system from the usual short-lived calendars that, taking their bearing from the beginning of the reign of a specific emperor (e.g., "the twentieth year of Hadrian Caesar the lord" in *GRA* III 264), also ended with the death of that same emperor. The beginning of Augustus' reign was more than the beginning of a single emperor's sovereignty; it was the beginning of the imperial sovereignty of Rome.

We see the use of these epochal dating systems in various inscriptions from Macedonia—predominantly in associational inscriptions and family tombstones. Table 17.1 gives the data for Macedonian associational inscriptions, while table 17.2 gives the data for non-associational inscriptions based solely in Thessalonica (as an example of a more widespread phenomenon).

---

[10] For this interpretation of the arch, see Burnett 2020b, 157.

[11] This temporal orientation was not simply a Macedonian phenomenon. For instance, the term "the year of Caesar" appears in a dozen Egyptian inscriptions, as well as one from Pompeii that originated from Alexandria (*GRA* III 171), all of which are dated within Augustus' lifetime.

[12] See, for instance, Harrison's discussion of "the Roman sense of time in relation to imperial rule" (2011, 97–108).

INSCRIPTION	DATE	LOCATION	DATING SYSTEM/S	ASSOCIATION
SEG 48 (1998), no. 716ter [#33]	90/89 BCE	Amphipolis	Provincial Era	Artisans (Dionysian Artisans?)
SEG 61 (2011), no. 485	85/84 BCE	Amphipolis	Provincial Era	Artisans (or Performers?)
SEG 48 (1998), no. 751 [#35]	7 BCE	Beroea	Provincial Era	Dionysos Devotees
GRA I 65	52	Edessa	Provincial Era	Zeus Hypsistos Devotees
GRA I 74 [#48]	66/67	Thessalonica	Provincial Era	Banqueters
GRA I 75 [#49]	90/91	Thessalonica	Imperial Era	Shippers
IG X.2.1s 1339	117/118	Thessalonica	Provincial & Imperial Eras	Artemis Devotees
SEG 56 (2006), no. 766	125/126	Thessalonica	Provincial & Imperial Eras	Fishermen? (Immigrants?)
IMakedD 596	154	Thessalonica	Provincial & Imperial Eras	Associates of Herakles
BE (1972) 263 [#54]	159/160	Thessalonica	Imperial Era	Transportation Workers
GRA I 80 [#57]	209	Thessalonica	Provincial Era	Dionysos Devotees
SEG 56 (2006), no. 812	237/238	Thessalonica	Provincial Era	Asklepios & Dionysos Devotees
GRA I 72 [#45]	250	Pydna	Provincial & Imperial Eras	Zeus Hypsistos Devotees

Table 17.1 Inventory of Macedonian Association Inscriptions Incorporating Era Dating Systems[13]

---

[13] Bracketed numbers in the first column indicate the entry in Ascough, Harland, and Kloppenborg 2012.

INSCRIPTION	DATE	LOCATION	DATING SYSTEM/S	CONTEXT
IG X.2.1 573	134/135	Thessalonica	Provincial & Imperial Eras	Family Tombstone
IG X.2.1 285	140	Thessalonica	Provincial & Imperial Eras	Family Tombstone
IG X.2.1 448	141/142	Thessalonica	Imperial Era	Family Tombstone
IG X.2.1 826	145	Thessalonica	Provincial & Imperial Eras	Personal Tombstone
IG X.2.1 608	147/148	Thessalonica	Imperial Era	Family Tombstone
IG X.2.1 923	152/153	Thessalonica	Provincial & Imperial Eras	Family Tombstone
IG X.2.1 483	162/163	Thessalonica	Imperial Era	Family Tombstone
IG X.2.1 450	165/166	Thessalonica	Provincial & Imperial Eras	Family Tombstone
IG X.2.1 457	206	Thessalonica	Imperial Era	Family Tombstone
IG X.2.1 495	224/225	Thessalonica	Provincial & Imperial Eras	Family Tombstone
IG X.2.1 s 1321	236/237	Thessalonica	Provincial & Imperial Eras	Family Tombstone
IG X.2.1 s 1075	260	Thessalonica	Provincial & Imperial Eras	Invitation to Gladiatorial Games

Table 17.2 Inventory of Other Thessalonian Inscriptions Incorporating Era Dating Systems

Obviously the data is somewhat spotty and many of the inscriptions post-date 50, the year that Paul probably wrote 1 Thessalonians (following his initial visit in 49). But what these inscriptions suggest is that an orientation to time had taken root in Macedonia, predating Paul's letter and firmly entrenched enough to be sustained not only across a wide geographical expanse (as evidenced in the associational data)[14] but also across an extensive temporal expanse. Dating systems in the ancient world often came and went with relative frequency—or, as Alan Samuel has noted, "The number of eras which

[14] Amphipolis, roughly fifty-five miles east of Thessalonica; Beroea, roughly forty-three miles west of Thessalonica; Edessa, roughly fifty miles west of Thessalonica; Thessalonica itself; Pydna, roughly thirty-five miles west of Thessalonica.

came into use and then expired to be replaced by yet other eras during Hellenistic and Roman times is probably not infinite, but I have not yet been able to find the end of them" (1972, 246). With regard to the two dating systems used in Roman Macedonia, however, it is notable how durable those systems were. In our sample, inscriptions that incorporate the provincial-era dating system appear between 90/89 BCE to 260 CE,[15] while inscriptions that incorporate the imperial-era dating system appear between 90 CE and 260 CE. In view of the pro-Augustan ethos of Macedonia, there is little reason to doubt that the imperial-era dating system was in usage well before its first attestation among extant associational inscriptions in that region (i.e., 90 CE).[16]

These systems that structured time in Macedonia oriented people's daily lives to the overarching narrative of Roman control. The sense that "Augustus had become the 'lord of time'" (Harrison 2011, 108) was linked to the politico-military interface in which societal power was situated (or, as Carole Newlands [1995, 24] notes, "Control over time was closely linked with military control"). The temporal orientations frequently evidenced on Macedonian associational inscriptions serve as a commentary on their world: it was Roman time because it was a Roman world.

THE TEMPORAL ORIENTATION OF 1 THESSALONIANS

In light of the Romanized temporal orientation of Macedonian cities (not least Thessalonica), certain aspects of 1 Thessalonians come into sharper focus. The temporal orientation of Paul's letter takes its cues from the Thessalonians' turn from idols to serve the "living and true" deity (1:9). Paul uses that simple conversion narrative to highlight the key temporal moments of his good news—both an established point in the past and a corresponding point in the future. The temporal anchor of the past is, of course, the death and resurrection of God's Son, captured in the simple phrase "whom he raised from the dead" (1:10). In the same verse, Paul identifies the temporal anchor of the future, which, of course, is the eschatological coming of

---

[15] The use of this system in Macedonia "persisted at least until the fourth century" (Theodossiou and Mantarakis 2006, 348), as evidenced by data beyond the inscriptional database.

[16] The pro-Roman posture of Macedonia had fostered the establishment of localized imperial cults in several Macedonian cities. With regard to the Thessalonica of Paul's day, the issue is debated. Papazoglou 1983, 206–7, offers a maximalist view of the importance of the imperial cult within Thessalonica; for more skeptical views, see Hoppe 2016, 47; and Miller 2010. Burnett 2020a offers a nuanced view (updating and correcting the influential views of Hendrix 1984; 1991), illustrating the ensconced nature of cultic devotion to the imperial family within Thessalonian expressions of devotion to traditional Greco-Roman deities as the overseers of the Roman imperial order.

the risen Son "who rescues us from the wrath that is coming" (1:10), with the Thessalonian Christ followers identified as those who "wait for [God's] Son from heaven." This future temporal point is highlighted at the close of the letter as well, when Paul speaks of the need for the Thessalonians to be "blameless at the coming of our Lord Jesus Christ" (5:23; cf. 5:9).

These two temporal points in the *mythos* of Paul's deity also appear together (as they do in 1:10) in 4:14 and 5:10. The first of these passages stands in a textual unit (4:13-18) where Paul addresses the Thessalonian confusion regarding the unexpected death of some of their members: "Jesus died and rose again, and so we believe that God will bring with Jesus those who have fallen asleep in him." Paul has prepared the Thessalonians for this claim already in 3:13 by emphasizing the future temporal point in the eschatological narrative of God's Son: "so that you will be blameless and holy in the presence of our God and Father at the coming of our Lord Jesus with all his holy ones" (cf. 2:19; 4:15).

With regard to the Roman imperial order of Paul's day, we might think that there is nothing too radical about all this. A deity is being proclaimed and nothing is said against Roman authority in particular. But, in fact, Paul is articulating a narrative in which the culmination of world history does not have Rome and its deities at the center. That was the whole point of the provincial-era and imperial-era dating systems—that a new era has begun, an era in which Rome's authority is entrenched in an eternal and unrivaled reign. Whatever was backward-looking about those Rome-oriented calendrical systems was simultaneously forward-looking as well, with the confident assurance that Rome's perpetual rule embodied the culmination of the history ordained by the eternal deities of Rome.

For Paul, to look back to the era-defining moments was not to look back to 148 BCE or 31 BCE, with the presumption that the eschatological era had already taken hold with the establishment of Roman rule. Instead, Paul looked back to the death and resurrection of Christ, with the confident assurance of the coming salvation promised to his followers in the time of wrath and the conviction that the high deity of all the world had left his Spirit to guide his followers in the meantime (5:19). Paul assured the Thessalonians that God had called them "into his own kingdom and glory" (2:12). Here he is not simply describing one deity's relationship with a cultic association; in Paul's view this "kingdom" outstrips all other kingdoms, as will be evident at the coming (παρουσία) of the Lord whom Paul proclaimed. With that temporal reorientation around the "Lord Jesus Christ" lay the "hope" of the Thessalonians, according to Paul (1:10; 4:13; 5:8).

In all this, we cannot underestimate Paul's use of the motif of divine wrath (ὀργή), which appears three times in the letter (1:10; 2:16; 5:9).[17] This aspect alone cuts like a knife through the temporal rope that helped to hold Roman imperial ideology together. Any attempt to orient time ultimately around Roman ideology is shattered by Paul's notion of the divine wrath poised against a disobedient world. Paul's confidence that the wrath of his deity is coming punches a hole in the purported eternal reign of Rome. And Paul thinks he already has a case study of the future outworking of God's wrath in a recent occurrence in which the Judean leaders in Jerusalem were not able to assuage the wrath of God (2:14-16). Whatever he means by that, Paul takes that situation as a miniature version of what will happen in the future, when divine wrath explodes upon the world, the world under Roman control, shattering all pretense that Rome is ultimately at the helm of the world's space and time.

It is not surprising, then, that Paul's attempt to realign the Thessalonians' temporal orientation in 1 Thessalonians 4 flows into discourse that is perhaps the most politically transgressive of the Pauline corpus: 1 Thess 5:1-11. Paul begins this textual unit with strong gestures to the temporal reorientation of the Thessalonian Christ followers: "We do not need to write to you about the times and the seasons" (περὶ . . . τῶν χρόνων καὶ τῶν καιρῶν), adding that the Thessalonians "know very well that the day of the Lord will come like a thief in the night" (5:1-2). This potentially transgressive temporal orientation then overspills into explicit discourse that first-century Macedonians could not help but hear as politically transgressive: "When people are saying, 'Peace and security,' destruction will come on them suddenly, as labor pains on a pregnant woman, and they will not escape." The motifs of peace and security were the lynchpins in the ideology behind the provincial-era and imperial-era calendrical systems evidenced in the monumentalized inscriptions of some Macedonian associations and elsewhere. Those calendrical systems perpetuated a sense that peace and security pervaded the empire of the Roman order, firmly in place in the events of 148 BCE (in relation to Macedonia itself) and 31 BCE (in relation to the whole of the world that mattered). The ideology evidenced in those systems must be one aspect of what Paul goes on to talk about in 5:4-10. There he highlights the "darkness" and the "fake news" systems that perpetuate

---

[17] I do not take 2:14-16 to be a scribal insertion, for reasons outlined in Smith 2004. See also Rydelnik 2008. Note in particular that the phrase τῶν Ἰουδαίων τῶν . . . ἀποκτεινάντων in 2:14-15 needs to be translated "the Judeans who killed" (= the Judean leaders) rather than "the Judeans, who killed . . . ," therefore avoiding the "anti-Semitic comma" of some interpretations.

the disinformation of ideological drunkenness and the convictional slumber that stand in opposition to the true narrative that lies at the heart of reality—a narrative about the triumph of the true "deity who brings about peace" (ὁ θεὸς τῆς εἰρήνης, 5:23).[18]

IDENTITY AND DIFFERENCE IN A THESSALONIAN CHRIST GROUP

In this essay, we have analyzed popular Macedonian calendars to see what they reveal about the temporal orientation of Macedonia in Paul's day. We have seen that people's orientation to time had political significance; time itself had been weaponized for political purposes. And we have seen that, in his interactions with Thessalonian Christ followers, Paul articulated a view of time that ran against the grain of popular politicized temporal orientations. Brief consideration is now given to the experiences of the Thessalonian Christ followers in relation to these contrastive temporal orientations.

Although Paul's narrative of the Thessalonian conversion to Christ devotion (1 Thess 1:7-9) is hyperbolic, his account permits us to think (as noted above) that the Thessalonian Christ followers may (predominately) have been members of an association prior to Paul's arrival in Thessalonica. When Paul arrived (probably in 49), he accessed this association and convinced (many of) its members to adopt Christ devotion, so that they evidently abandoned their commitment to any of the traditional deities who were thought to prop up the association.[19] Word of that surprising conversion seems to have spread through an associational network throughout parts of Macedonia and Achaia.[20]

As a consequence of this radical adjustment in their devotional allegiance, the Thessalonians experienced a notable level of "persecution" from their civic peers almost immediately (1:6; 2:2, 14; 3:3-4). Persecution would not have arisen simply because the Thessalonians were adopting notably Judean

---

[18] For a similar study of time, but in relation to 1 Peter, see Horrell and Wan 2016.

[19] Although we should assume that many forms of early Christ devotion were not exclusive (see, for instance, Longenecker 2016; Rebillard 2020; and many others), the abandonment of devotion to the Greco-Roman deities seems to be the best explanation for the persecution being experienced by the Thessalonian Christ followers.

[20] Kloppenborg 2019, 326: "It was natural—indeed, a necessary expression of piety and loyalty—to advertise the benefits provided by a deity. Thus, it is natural to suppose that neighbors of the Thessalonian Christ assembly knew quickly what deity was being worshiped, the benefits that membership provided, and the kinds of behaviors that could be expected of Christ followers." Speedy news that began in the neighborhood seems then to have spread through intercity associational networks within Macedonia and Achaia.

ethical practices and sensitivities (4:3-5); the adoption of Judean sexual ethics (for instance) might have attracted curious comments, at most, but not persecution. Instead, persecution must have had something to do with what was perceived as an aloof stance toward civic-mindedness—a posture that threatened the city's advancement through the channels of protection by the traditional deities in connection with the imperial benefactors of the Julio-Claudian family.

It is easy to see how a radical alteration in the Thessalonians' orientation to time could have played a part in a posture of disengagement from civic-oriented practices and values, as part of their adoption of exclusive devotion to Jesus Christ. As Gribetz (2020, 2) has reminded us, a group's orientation to time serves as "a powerful mechanism through which to enact difference and forge identity"; Thessalonian Christ followers had begun to model a stance toward time that, were it replicated en masse, could easily have been perceived as a threat to the social fabric of Thessalonian society and the city's place within the network of Macedonian urban centers. This was probably a relatively minor association, but its social ruptures were significant enough to attract attention. If the whole association converted (as Ascough and others propose), perhaps the ire of their peers had fallen on them because of their exclusive devotion to Jesus Christ and the temporal orientation that went with it; a pronounced schism within the association (as proposed above) would have had even greater potential of drawing attention to this transgressive form of devotion, with some members denouncing those who had left the membership. In either scenario, the association may have lost the support of its civic patron/s, compromising its social reputation (Kloppenborg 1993, 276; Rulmu 2010, 409). Spreading through the communication networks of associations in Macedonia and Achaia, a report about the dramatic change in the identity of this Thessalonian association may even have provoked civic officials in other cities to send expressions of concern to civic officials in Thessalonica—since associations (and their patrons) were often deeply embedded in the life of their local *polis*, and since Thessalonica was the administrative capital of Macedonia.[21]

---

[21] This would help to explain the implied targets of Paul's discourse in 2:14-16, where civic authorities (in this instance, Judean civic authorities) are the ones who hinder the spreading of the good news—with Judean civic authorities in Jerusalem standing as placeholder figures deemed to resemble the Thessalonian civic officials who were doing much the same to Christ followers in their city. On this interpretation of 1 Thess 2:14-16, see Smith 2004; also Rydelnik 2008. In general, see also de Vos 1999, 123–77; Tellbe 2001, 80–140; and Rulmu 2010. Rulmu makes the interesting suggestion that Paul's advice to "strive to keep quiet" in 4:11 is a call "to become invisible and independent, to remain unnoticed, and to

The motif of persecution that runs throughout much of 1 Thessalonians illustrates the extent to which the advocacy of exclusive devotion to Jesus Christ (with its politically transgressive reorganization of time and the devotional practices that were aligned with that temporal orientation) was perceived by the Thessalonians' contemporaries to be incompatible with the city's ideological allegiance to the Roman imperial order—an allegiance that was thoroughly intermeshed with local religiopolitical structures of the city.[22] With its telic exclusivity, Paul's construction of an alternative orientation to time was socio-politically transgressive, running against the grain of the orientation to time that had become firmly embedded in Macedonian culture.[23] In his letter, Paul seems unrepentant in this regard, especially in the first half of chapter 5. Building on the construct of what God has already done in Christ and what lies on the future horizon (i.e., divine "wrath"), Paul articulated the "hope of salvation" that was soon to come like a thief in the night upon a world blanketed by darkness and under the influence of the false gospel of Roman "peace and security."

In all likelihood, prior to adopting an exclusive form of Christ devotion, the Thessalonians to whom Paul wrote 1 Thessalonians had oriented their lives in conformity with the ideological sentiments of the pro-Roman calendars that were widespread in Macedonia. There is little reason to think, however, that the Thessalonian Christ followers abandoned their use of those

---

give up any progressive socio-political aspirations, even if that meant disqualifying themselves from actively participating in the redistribution of the benefits and goods of urban society" (395). Relatedly, Paul's claim that Satan has prevented him from returning to the city (2:18) is probably a projection of the civic opposition to Paul within Thessalonica.

[22]   This change in the Thessalonian association's identity could have been interpreted as an instance of an otherwise good association gone bad—in conformity with a fairly widespread suspicion of the potential of associations to undermine civic stability. Perhaps the civic-mindedness of an association was always something that needed to be *proved by* the association itself rather than something that could be assumed to be the case *about* an association *by* others. (On this, see Brewer 2022.) Note also that the argument of this essay (along with other historical data) problematizes Das' view that because Christ groups were "religious" groups that met only in people's homes, they would be of no concern to civic authorities (2016, 189).

[23]   This alternative orientation to time differed from typical Judean articulations of temporal orientation in one key aspect: in Paul's articulation of time, the telic point of history was coming soon, with Jesus Christ judging the world in the near future. That was what made it so powerfully dangerous. When a similar expectation spread through Judea and Galilee in the late 60s in the form of Judean zealotry, Rome crushed the fabric of Judean society in the war of 66–70, resulting in the destruction of the city of Jerusalem. Without the expectation of imminence, Judean telic eschatology was, perhaps, tolerable from a Roman point of view. The same would have been true of Isiac contours of time in book 11 of Apuleius' *Metamorphoses*.

calendars as a result of their Christ devotion. This does not contradict the points made above; the data has not been analyzed to answer whether the Thessalonian Christ followers continued to use culturally entrenched calendars after adopting Christ devotion. Even Paul shows no hesitation in this regard. He instructed the Thessalonians "to live quietly, to mind your own affairs, and to work with your hands, as we directed you" (4:11). Paul did not instruct them to shun culturally informed dating systems when drawing up business contracts, nor to go out on the streets and denounce the use of provincial-era and imperial-era dating systems. So the issue is not whether the Thessalonian Christ followers continued to use culturally entrenched calendars; the issue is how they interpreted those calendars and the extent to which Paul's view of time seeped into their problematized social interactions in relation to those calendars.

If the Thessalonians adopted Paul's contouring of time, they would also have come to see those calendars as merely functional constructs. If Paul's temporal ideology seeped into the worldview of the Thessalonian Christ followers, those calendars would have been denuded of their ideological commitments, serving merely as timekeeping mechanisms, overshadowed by a larger and more significant reality determined by the God who had raised Jesus Christ from the dead. And with that recognition, the Thessalonians would have had a radically altered conception of their world—their place and their time within it. No longer was time to be seen as Roman time in a Roman world; time (and space) belonged to the God who raised Jesus Christ from the dead.[24]

Paul was not opposed to Roman rule, as his comments in Rom 13:1-7 would later illustrate; what he opposed was the ideology that displaced the resurrecting God from the place of ultimate sovereignty.[25] He protested making a subsystem of God's reality (i.e., Roman rule) into the ultimate form of

---

[24] Compare the claim that God sent his Son "in the fullness of time" or (paraphrased) "at the point when God's organization of time [i.e., the time appointed by the father, 4:2] had come to the point of perfect culmination," as Paul would go on to say in Galatians (4:4)—his next extant letter, written in 50/51. It is also in Galatians that Paul chides gentile Christ followers interested in Torah observance that they are slipping back under the influence of *ta stoicheia tou kosmou* (Gal 4:3 [cf. 4:9], which I translate as "the formative structures that shape the systems of the world"), and uses the prioritization of certain temporal contours (days, months, seasons, years; 4:10) as an example of the improper attachment to things that undermine Christ devotion. See also Rom 14:5-6 in the context of 14:1–15:6, where certain temporal markers are deemed to be *adiaphora* for those in Christ.

[25] In Rom 13:1-7, Paul sees the governance of the authorities as legitimate, since it is a necessary way that God keeps order within God's world—a position that promotes paying taxes (including taxes to Roman authorities, the ones who wield "the sword") while simultaneously removing the ideological underpinnings of Roman claims to rule by the deities of

divine reality. To the extent that the Thessalonian Christ followers bought into Paul's vision and practiced an innovative form of exclusive devotion, they were being trained in his skill of theological overlay, in which Paul's ideological orientation to time emptied ideologically freighted calendars of their convictional signification.

In sum, in the mid-first century CE, it seems likely that (many) members of an association in Thessalonica shifted their ideological framework by adopting devotion to a powerful deity who deserved exclusive loyalty. A central component of that ideological shift was the reconfiguring of their temporal orientation. Perhaps nowhere is the transgressive nature of the message of early Christ followers more evident than in the narrative of the successive life stages of these members of what was probably a rather insignificant Thessalonian association.[26]

WORKS CITED

Adam, Barbara. 1990. *Time and Social Theory*. Oxford: University of Oxford Press.

Ascough, Richard S. 1997. "Translocal Relationships among Voluntary Associations and Early Christianity." *JECS* 5:223–41.

———. 2000. "The Thessalonian Christian Community as a Professional Voluntary Association." *JBL* 119:311–28.

———. 2003. *Paul's Macedonian Associations: The Social Context of Philippians and 1 Thessalonians*. WUNT 2/161. Tübingen: Mohr Siebeck.

———. 2014. "Redescribing the Thessalonians' 'Mission' in Light of Graeco-Roman Associations." *NTS* 60:61–82.

Ascough, Richard S., Philip A. Harland, and John S. Kloppenborg, eds. 2012. *Associations in the Greco-Roman World: A Sourcebook*. Waco, Tex.: Baylor University Press.

Boutsikas, Efrosyni. 2020. *The Cosmos in Ancient Greek Religious Experience: Sacred Space, Memory, and Cognition*. Cambridge: Cambridge University Press.

Brewer, Eric J. 2022. "Suspicion, Integration, and Roman Attitudes toward Associations." Pages 33–47 in *Greco-Roman Associations, Deities, and Early Christianity*. Edited by Bruce W. Longenecker. Waco, Tex.: Baylor University Press.

Brookins, Timothy A. 2021. *First and Second Thessalonians*. Waco, Tex.: Baylor University Press.

Rome. In this way, the mythological narrative supporting the payment of taxes is novel, in a manner that ran against the grain of Roman mythological constructs.

[26] My thanks to Richard Ascough, Eric Brewer, and Jeff Hubbard for casting a critical eye on this essay at various stages of its development. Any deficiencies remain my own responsibility.

———. 2022. "From Analogy to Identity: Did an Association of Leatherworkers 'Turn' into the Thessalonian Church?" Pages 271–87 in Longenecker, *Greco-Roman Associations, Deities, and Early Christianity.*

Burnett, D. Clint. 2020a. "Imperial Divine Honors in Julio-Claudian Thessalonica and the Thessalonian Correspondence." *JBL* 139:567–89.

———. 2020b. *Studying the New Testament through Inscriptions: An Introduction.* Peabody, Mass.: Hendrickson.

Caldelli, Maria, and Cecilia Ricci, eds. 2020. *City of Encounters: Public Spaces and Social Interaction in Ancient Rome.* RomeScapes. Rome: Edizioni Quasar.

Cumont, Franz. 1912. *Astrology and Religion among the Greeks and Romans.* New York: G. P. Putman's Sons.

Das, A. Andrew. 2016. *Paul and the Stories of Israel: Grand Thematic Narratives in Galatians.* Minneapolis: Fortress.

Davies, Penelope J. E. 2020. *Architecture and Politics in Republican Rome.* Cambridge: Cambridge University Press.

Feeney, Denis. 2007. *Caesar's Calendar: Ancient Time and the Beginnings of History.* Berkeley: University of California Press.

Forsythe, Gary. 2012. *Time in Roman Religion: One Thousand Years of Religious History.* New York: Routledge.

Gallois, William. 2007. *Time, Religion and History.* Harlow: Longman.

———. 2013. "The War for Time in Early Colonial Algeria." Pages 252–73 in *Breaking up Time: Negotiating the Borders between Present, Past and Future.* Edited by Chris Lorenz and Berber Bevernage. Göttingen: Vandenhoeck & Ruprecht.

Giddens, Anthony. 1979. *Central Problems in Social Theory.* London: Macmillan.

———. 1984. *The Constitution of Society: Outline of the Theory of Structuration.* Cambridge: Polity Press.

Grafton, Anthony. 2003. "Dating History: The Renaissance and the Reformation of Chronology." *Daedalus* 132:74–85.

Gribetz, Sarit Kattan. 2020. *Time and Difference in Rabbinic Judaism: How the Rabbis of Late Antiquity Used Time to Define the Boundaries of Jewish Identity.* Princeton: Princeton University Press.

Hall, Josiah. "Translocal Relationships among Associations and Christ Groups, Revisited." *ZNW* (forthcoming).

Harrison, James R. 2011. *Paul and the Imperial Authorities at Thessalonica and Rome: A Study in the Conflict of Ideology.* WUNT 273. Tübingen: Mohr Siebeck.

Hartnett, Jeremy. 2017. *The Roman Street: Urban Life and Society in Pompeii, Herculaneum, and Rome.* New York: Cambridge University Press.

Heisserer, Eric. 2016. Screenplay to the film *Arrival*. Based on "The Story of Your Life" by Ted Chiang. Directed by Denis Villeneuve. Paramount Pictures / Sony Pictures / Stage 6 Films.

Hendrix, Holland Lee. 1984. "Thessalonians Honor Romans." ThD diss., Harvard University.

———. 1991. "Archaeology and Eschatology at Thessalonica." Pages 107–18 in *The Future of Early Christianity: Essays in Honor of Helmut Koester*. Edited by Birger A. Pearson. Minneapolis: Fortress.

Hengel, Martin, and Anna Maria Schwemer. 1997. *Paul between Damascus and Antioch: The Unknown Years*. London: SCM Press.

Hoppe, Rudolf. 2016. *Der erste Thessalonikerbrief. Kommentar*. Freiburg: Herder.

Horrell, David G., and Wei Hsien Wan. 2016. "Christology, Eschatology and the Politics of Time in 1 Peter." *JSNT* 38:263–76.

Johnson-DeBaufre, Melanie. 2010. "'Gazing upon the Invisible': Archaeology, Historiography, and the Elusive Women of 1 Thessalonians." Pages 73–108 in *From Roman to Early Christian Thessalonikē: Studies in Religion and Archaeology*. Edited by Laura Salah Nasrallah, Charalambos Bakirtzis, and Steven J. Friesen. Cambridge, Mass.: Harvard University Press.

Jung, UnChan. 2020. "Paul's Letter to Free(d) Casual Workers: Profiling the Thessalonians in Light of the Roman Economy." *JSNT* 42:472–95.

Kloppenborg, John S. 1993. "Φιλαδελφία, Θεοδίδακτος and the Dioscuri: Rhetorical Engagement in 1 Thess 4.9–12." *NTS* 39:265–89.

———. 2019. *Christ's Associations: Connecting and Belonging in the Ancient City*. New Haven: Yale University Press.

Longenecker, Bruce W. 2010. *Remember the Poor: Paul, Poverty, and the Greco-Roman World*. Grand Rapids: Eerdmans.

———. 2016. "Mark's Gospel for the Second Church of the Late First Century." Pages 197–214 in *The Fullness of Time: Essays on Christology, Creation and Eschatology in Honor of Richard Bauckham*. Edited by Daniel M. Gurtner, Grant Macaskill, and Jonathan T. Pennington. Grand Rapids: Eerdmans.

McLean, Bradley H. 2002. *An Introduction to Greek Epigraphy of the Hellenistic and Roman Periods from Alexander the Great Down to the Reign of Constantine (323 B.C.–A.D. 337)*. Ann Arbor: University of Michigan Press.

Miller, C. 2010. "The Imperial Cult in the Pauline Cities of Asia Minor and Greece." *CBQ* 72:314–32.

Newlands, Carole E. 1995. *Playing with Time: Ovid and the Fasti*. Ithaca: Cornell University Press.

Oakes, Peter. 2016. "Nine Types of Church in Nine Types of Space in the Insula of the Menander." Pages 23–58 in *Early Christianity in Pompeian Light: People, Texts, Situations*. Edited by Bruce W. Longenecker. Minneapolis: Fortress.

Papazoglou, Fanoula. 1983. "Macedonia under the Romans: Political and Administrative Developments, Economy and Society, Intellectual Life." Pages 192–207 in *Macedonia: 4000 Years of Greek History and Civilization*. Edited by M. B. Sakellariou. Athens: Ekdotike Athenon.

Rebillard, Éric. 2020. "Approaching 'Religious Identity' in Late Antiquity." Pages 15–27 in *Rhetoric and Religious Identity in Late Antiquity*. Edited by Richard Flower and Morwenna Ludlow. Oxford: Oxford University Press.

Riesner, Rainer. 1998. *Paul's Early Period: Chronology, Mission Strategy, Theology*. Grand Rapids: Eerdmans.

Rollens, Sarah E. 2016. "Inventing Tradition in Thessalonica: The Appropriation of the Past in 1 Thessalonians 2:14–16." *BTB* 3:123–32.

———. 2022. "Conflict and Honor in the Ancient Epistle: Or, How an Egyptian Funerary Association Illuminates Rivalry at Corinth." Pages 309–24 in Longenecker, *Greco-Roman Associations, Deities, and Early Christianity*.

Rulmu, Callia. 2010. "Between Ambition and Quietism: The Socio-political Background of 1 Thessalonians 4,9–12." *Bib* 91:393–417.

Russell, Amy. 2015. *The Politics of Public Space in Republican Rome*. Cambridge: Cambridge University Press.

Rydelnik, Michael A. 2008. "Was Paul Anti-Semitic? Revisiting 1 Thessalonians 2:14–16." *BSac* 165:58–67.

Samuel, Alan E. 1972. *Greek and Roman Chronology: Calendars and Years in Classical Antiquity*. Munich: Beck.

Smith, Abraham. 2004. "Unmasking the Powers: Toward a Postcolonial Analysis of 1 Thessalonians." Pages 47–66 in *Paul and the Roman Imperial Order*. Edited by Richard A. Horsley. Harrisburg, Pa.: Trinity Press International.

Tellbe, Mikael. 2001. *Paul between Synagogue and State: Christians, Jews, and Civic Authorities in 1 Thessalonians, Romans, and Philippians*. Stockholm: Almqvist & Wiksell.

Theodossiou, Efstratios, and P. Mantarakis. 2006. "The Lost Roman Calendars of Ancient Macedonia." *Astronomical and Astrophysical Transactions* 25:347–54.

Trozzo, Lindsey M. 2012. "Thessalonian Women: The Key to the 4:4 Conundrum." *PRSt* 39:39–52.

de Vos, Craig Stephen. 1999. *Church and Community Conflicts: The Relationships of the Thessalonian, Corinthian, and Philippian Churches with their Wider Civic Communities*. Atlanta: Scholars Press.

Wallace-Hadrill, Andrew. 1994. *Houses and Society in Pompeii and Herculaneum*. Princeton: Princeton University Press.

18

Conflict and Honor in the Ancient Epistle

Or, How an Egyptian Funerary Association Illuminates Rivalry at Corinth

Sarah E. Rollens

PPetaus 28 is an intriguing letter from second-century (CE) Egypt. It appears to be an exchange between two figures within an occupational network that is responsible for transporting, preparing, and burying corpses. In the letter, we catch a glimpse of a dispute between colleagues: the letter's recipient has failed to send a corpse from his village to that of the letter's writer, a situation that has led to significant problems for the writer. The letter is short—one might even say curt—but its few sentences are tinged with impatience and annoyance. While the resolution of this particular dispute is unknown, we can nevertheless tease out the way that honor, reputation, and authority operated in the conflict behind the letter.

A similar dispute about authority and honor, many have argued, lies behind 1 Corinthians, namely, between Paul and Apollos. The conflict between Paul and Apollos has to do with their both being authoritative religious[1] specialists within the *ekklēsia* at Corinth,[2] which provides some

---

[1] Without delving deeply into this tempestuous debate, I maintain that the category of *religion* is a modern academic construct, albeit an analytically useful one, and so here I use this construct to help classify a family of discourses, practices, and exchanges associated with non-obvious beings (i.e., gods).

[2] To avoid the problematic nomenclature of *community* or *church*, I use *ekklēsia* (Gk.: assembly), *group*, and *Corinthian association* interchangeably. On the problems with *community*, see Rollens 2019; on *church*, see Fredriksen 2006.

concern for Paul, especially since it is leading to rivalries within the group. This essay will argue that studying the conflict and the network of knowledge in *PPetaus* 28 and viewing the letter as a space for the sender to defend his honor and reputation can provide a useful analogue for thinking about how Paul manages some of the problems in Corinth, especially how he negotiates his own precarious authority. Just as *PPetaus* 28 reveals a passive-aggressive correspondence that explicitly shames the recipient, so also 1 Corinthians can be seen as a similar sort of communique that implicitly challenges Apollos' authority and tries to subordinate him to Paul.[3] Despite some obvious differences, these two letters may be part of a wider strategy for how male authorities in ancient associations maintained and defended their authority vis-à-vis their constituents.

Though such a comparison is limited, it participates in a wider trend of scholarship on early Christianity that uses unofficial associations[4] from the Greco-Roman world as *comparanda* to early Christ groups; this volume is a testament to the importance of such scholarship. The once-common anxiety about reducing Christ groups to "only" another ancient association has rightly waned, as numerous scholars are beginning to see the need to situate the social formations in earliest Christianity alongside other ordinary social phenomena, instead of arguing that Christianity's social forms were utterly unique.

OVERVIEW OF *PPETAUS* 28

While the contents of Paul's letters are well-known, *PPetaus* 28 is far more obscure, as it is a short papyrus that has only been published in a handful of places. Therefore, it is useful to give a brief overview of this document, before using it to gain some purchase on Paul's situation with Apollos in 1 Corinthians. I reproduce the entire text of the letter before discussing it:

> Papsaus to Asklas, his brother, many greetings. I greet you and your entire household. I am now writing to you a second letter regarding the body of the soldier from Visemtos, (5) a legionary, whose remains [the trans-

---

[3]   This is, of course, not the sole function of 1 Corinthians. The letter is one of the longest extant letters from Greco-Roman antiquity, and without dismissing the other relevant conflicts preserved in the letter, I am admittedly focusing on only a very small situation (the relationship between Paul and Apollos) behind the letter.

[4]   I follow Richard Last and Philip Harland in designating these social forms as "unofficial associations" (Last and Harland 2020, 9). *Voluntary associations* has also been a rather common designation, but given that many of these associations were based on occupational networks or household affiliations—connections that were not necessarily voluntary—the terminology of *unofficial associations* makes better sense. See also Kloppenborg 2011, 191.

porters] from Tmunache and Phebichis, Quintilius and his companion,[5] brought, which they gave to your son. The evidence: they have attached a staff to his back and throwing him (10) on the donkey that belongs to you and your son, together with your son, they brought him to you. Now I am writing all these things to you about him, so that you will bring him to his village. Since I have experienced a great (15) insult, and they almost brought me before the governor (τὸν ἡγεμόνα); was this not on account of what you have done to me? I am writing to you (with) another piece of evidence about him: your wife, when she came out, bought spices for four obols for the sailor from (20) Tmunache named Quintilius. You have not treated me well (by) not bringing him to his proper place. I greet you and your son and your entire house. I pray that you are in good health. Nineteenth day of the month of Pharmouthi.

‹verso›

(25) Deliver this to Ke[rkesoucha Orous] . . . to Asklas, from Papsaus, his friend.[6]

Both Papsaus and Asklas are responsible for transporting the corpse of a legionary through a network of villages in Egypt (Kloppenborg 2020, 349);[7] they are likely part of or interacting with a funerary/mortuary association or guild.[8] Papsaus writes to Asklas because Asklas has not sent the body to him in a timely manner, and so, Papsaus' obligations to the legionary—and probably also to the legionary's family—have been disrupted. Papsaus outlines his specific reasoning for thinking that Asklas has shirked his duties, before appealing to honor and reputation to encourage him to send the body.

The letter employs fictive kinship between the two men, which was common in occupational associations and which likely signals that it is a

---

[5] "The transporters" has been added for clarity. The rather complex phrasing reads: οἱ ἀπὸ Τμουναχῆ καὶ οἱ ἀπὸ Φεβῖχις Κουιτειλεῖς καὶ ὁ μετ' αὐτοῦ, literally meaning "those from Tmunache and Phebichis, [namely] Quintilius and the [unnamed] person with him."

[6] This translation is my own and is drawn from Kloppenborg 2020, 348, which is a collaborative resource that I worked on. I have made some minor changes here for readability.

[7] In this case, the villages mentioned form a "chain" of locations that roughly follow the path of the Nile.

[8] On funerary associations and necropolis workers in Egypt, see Bond 2016, 79–96. Egyptian necropolis associations often included a vast range of figures, including corpse transporters, embalmers, mummy wrappers, buriers, craftspeople, artisans, and similar tradespeople (Bond 2016, 80). Other mortuary associations are attested in *PRyl* 2.65 and *PKöln* 10.414.

letter between equals (Kloppenborg 2020, 349).[9] The language of friendship (φίλου) functions similarly, at least rhetorically.[10] But in addition to establishing a sense of equality, such forms of address also implicitly reminded the men of their obligations to each other. By invoking language of "friend" or "brother," Papsaus is activating specific cultural expectations for how male friends and siblings should treat one another, a point to which I return below.

Asklas and Papsaus are not the only figures involved in this occupational network. The letter also mentions Quintilius (a fellow transporter, who evidently used a boat at least some of the time),[11] his unnamed companion (and fellow transporter), Asklas' son, and Asklas' wife. Given that mortuary guilds in Roman Egypt were typically hereditary and often involved entire families (Bond 2016, 80), it is likely that many, if not all, of these people were part of the same trans-local association based on their common occupation. The identity of the ἡγεμών mentioned in the letter is of some import for envisioning the networks that this letter presupposes. There are three main interpretive possibilities for this figure: a civic official, a military figure, or a guild president (Daniel 1979, 42). The civic official and the guild president are the most likely candidates. If it is the former, we should likely imagine that Papsaus has been reprimanded or punished for not producing the body, which explains the urgency of his letter to Asklas. Indeed, in volume 3 of *Graeco-Roman Associations*, I translated ἡγεμών with the generic term "governor," that is, in line with the civic official option, but I now think it is equally plausible that it is a guild president, especially given Sarah Bond's recent work showing the highly structured nature of Egyptian funerary/mortuary associations (Bond 2016, 80). If we translate this is as a guild leader, the reference to being "almost brought before the ἡγεμών" could imply that Papsaus was facing some sort of punishment (perhaps a fine or censure) within the association itself. Regardless of the precise translation, this feature of the letter implies that the activities of this network were somehow known to a wider group and that there were consequences for not meeting the obligations of their occupation.

[9] On fictive kinship in associations, see Daniel 1979, 40; Harland 2009, 63–96; on fictive kinship in early Christianity, see Murray 2018, 137–57.

[10] On friendship, see Crook 2011. As Crook points out, sometimes language of "fictive friendship" was used to mask or undermine obviously unequal relationships.

[11] Quintilius could be part of the same occupational association, though separate associations of sailors (or shipowners and the merchants associated with them; as in *IG* II² 1012 and *SEG* 42.625, translations of which are found in Kloppenborg 2011) and donkey drivers (as in *SB* 6.9112 and *PAthen* 41, translations of which are found in Kloppenborg 2020) are also attested throughout the Roman Empire.

Thus, this letter is evidence of a trans-local association[12] that was using a complex occupational network of movement and knowledge to facilitate its activities. Their occupational activity mapped across numerous locations in Egypt, and what's more, those within the network evidently had avenues of communication to ensure that people along the pipeline could surveil the activities of their colleagues elsewhere.

THE NETWORK OF KNOWLEDGE IN *PPETAUS* 28

Funerary associations offered essential services and thus intersected with a wide range of people in a given region, which meant that they, in Bond's words, "formed a node for the interaction of numerous associations" (Bond 2016, 68).[13] So, despite being involved in a disreputable trade (Bond 2016, 80), funerary workers could be quite well-connected socially, which facilitated their physical movement and the transfer of knowledge and communication among them. In this section, we will map out the specific movement of knowledge that is presupposed in *PPetaus* 28. The goal, in part, will be to show later that Paul's surveillance of and communication with the Corinthians makes a great deal of sense when placed alongside other unofficial associations that had trans-local connections. In other words, Paul's knowledge of the social problems and rival teachers in Corinth need not only (or even primarily) be read with a lens of pastoralism (that is, early "church" management), but rather, through the typical knowledge networks of an association with mobile members.

Let us first visualize the social actors in this network of corpse transporters. Papsaus is the author of the letter that is addressed to Asklas and his household, and he stands at the end of this transport network, awaiting the arrival of the corpse. One of the transporters is referred to as Quintilius, who is also called a sailor (τῷ ναυτικῷ), while the other transporter remains unnamed. The two transporters deliver the body to Asklas' son, who in turn takes it to Asklas. Asklas' wife is also part of this network: she buys spices for Quintilius (the spices could either be some sort of payment for his transport

---

[12] *Trans-local* is too often supposed to mean that a group identified *only* by means of its universal identity. However, a more realistic use of trans-locality acknowledges the local orientation of the unofficial associations under question, while recognizing that they had connections with other groups and/or that their members were mobile. The feature of trans-locality, understood in this more nuanced way, as Richard Ascough (1997, 224) has shown, is shared by most ancient associations and early Christ groups.

[13] If Quintilius is part of an association of sailors and if the father and son who own the donkey are connected to an association of donkey drivers (see n. 11), such a statement describes the situation in *PPetaus* 28 well.

work, or they could be related to embalming practices).[14] A final possible node in the network behind this letter is the ἡγεμών. If this figure is a guild leader, then we glimpse even more of the associative network. If it is a local civic official, we see this association intersecting with the wider civic networks of the region. In short, we discover here an association that involves at least six people, seven if we count the ἡγεμών. Given the complexities of Egyptian funerary associations during this time (Bond 2016, 80), it is likely that this is only a fraction of the network.

In addition, we can extract the precise moments of communication that have facilitated the movement of knowledge about the legionary's body through this network. For one, Papsaus specifies that this is his *second* letter, so at least two instances of written communication are in view. Papsaus also seems to be receiving oral reports or messages from others operating in the network. Someone has evidently told him that Quintilius and his companion delivered the corpse to Asklas' son, and then accompanied the son in bringing it to Asklas. He emphasizes the specific details of this encounter, probably so that Asklas knows he has been in contact with someone who has witnessed it visually ("they have attached a staff to his back" and thrown him "on the donkey that belongs to you and your son"). Several lines later, he presents more specific details to further attest to his intimate knowledge of what has taken place ("your wife, when she came out, bought spices for four obols for the sailor from Tmunache named Quintilius"). Thus, Papsaus has communicated with at least one person in Asklas' village (possibly more) to learn these particular details. The letter also implies that the network of knowledge had made the delayed body somewhat of a public spectacle, depending on the translation of ἡγεμών: if it is a local civic leader, then the scandal has come to the attention of civic authorities, and if it is guild leader, the scandal has likely reached the "public" view within the association itself. Thus, in a mere twenty-five lines of short text, the letter reveals a network that facilitated the movement of knowledge trans-locally *among* villages, horizontally *within* villages, and even vertically between people of different statuses within the association/village itself.

PAUL AND APOLLOS IN CORINTH

The dispute between Papsaus and Asklas in *PPetaus* 28 provides an interesting analogue to Paul and Apollos and the network of Christ followers in

---

[14] Unlike in Italy, where funeral workers are all male, women appear to have been a crucial part of Egyptian necropolis associations (Bond 2016, 82).

which they operate. In this section, we will analyze the textual evidence for that relationship, with a view toward noticing (1) the implicit competition between the two and (2) the honor and reputation that are at stake, which are quite similar to the concerns that lie behind Papsaus' communication with Asklas. For our purposes, it is important to consider Paul and Apollos to be two fellow teachers or workers[15] in the Corinthian *ekklēsia*. Paul's apparent conflict with Apollos both in the local Corinthian network and in the wider trans-local network managed by Paul, I will argue, is cut from a similar cultural cloth as the exchange between Papsaus and Asklas, and it makes sense within the expected masculine posturing and competition for authority within ancient associations.

We admittedly know very little about Apollos as an historical figure. The primary evidence about him and his relationship with Paul comes in 1 Corinthians 1–4 and 16.[16] There are a few references to Apollos in Acts of the Apostles but they must be treated as secondary, perhaps entirely fictional, in comparison to Paul's testimony.[17] What is most important for our discussion—the primary information that we can glean from 1 Corinthians—is that Apollos, like Paul, is a mobile religious specialist: minimally a baptizer (1 Cor 1:12-16), but perhaps also a teacher responsible for some sort of custodial activity within the group (1 Cor 3:5-9).

Apollos' relationship to Paul is hotly debated among commentators.[18] The relevant question for the present analysis is, Was Apollos a co-worker of Paul or a rival of Paul? In the interest of space, I will not reproduce the scholarly debate and will simply make my position clear: I maintain that Apollos is *both* a co-worker *and also* a competitor of Paul. This, of course, requires a bit of elaboration. Both appear to be figures with some authority in the group; both

[15] It is common to refer to Paul and Apollos as fellow "missionaries" (as in Duff 2017, 137), but I prefer *religious specialists*, a term that makes it easier to discuss the practices of competition between such social actors. In addition, *missionary* often presumes a fully formed, clearly articulated religion, program, or doctrine, all of which I am skeptical existed in the first century.

[16] Apollos is also mentioned in Titus 3:13, but seeing as how that is nearly universally agreed to be non-Pauline, we cannot use it for any evidence about their relationship (not to mention that it offers virtually no new information about him).

[17] I treat Acts as an early second-century, idealized account of the origins of Christianity. In the interest of showing the predestined, divinely guided success of the movement, Acts homogenizes, smooths over, rewrites, and sometimes fabricates the processes involved in this development. Though Paul's letters are the best evidence for his relationship with Apollos, we should bear in mind that he is not a disinterested source. His testimony provides only his own perspective on Apollos' role in the *ekklēsia*.

[18] Useful summaries of this debate can be found in Ker 2000 and Mihalia 2009, 181–212.

appear to have baptized members and carried out other activities as leaders or religious authorities. It is obvious that Paul maintains some regular communication with Apollos, and so I do not imagine Apollos to be like the sneaky "counter-missionaries" that lie behind Galatians, nor like the uppity "super-apostles" that animate parts of 2 Corinthians. On the contrary, it is completely ordinary according to ancient conventions of *paideia*, as well as ancient honor codes and gender dynamics, for someone like Paul to be in explicit competition with someone like Apollos, especially since they are part of the same social network.[19] Both are religious specialists as far as the Corinthians are concerned, and the authority and status of both is subject to continual evaluation. Paul shows awareness of this constant evaluation in passages like 1 Cor 4:6-9, where he acknowledges that his (and Apollos') behavior is on display before the *ekklēsia* to encourage imitation. For this reason, though they are both on the same "side," Apollos can also be understood as a competitor of Paul in terms of authority and status in the Corinthian group.

Moreover, Apollos seems to be intimately involved in the factionalism that is occurring in the Corinthian *ekklēsia*. According to 1 Cor 1:11, Paul has heard reports of factionalism among the Corinthians, amounting to smaller groups being formed based on who had baptized whom (1 Cor 1:12-17). Paul, Apollos, and Cephas (Peter) all appear to have smaller groups orbiting around them (perhaps only a handful of people), based on the members that they had personally baptized. At issue is a fundamental misunderstanding of what baptism is: Paul believes it associates all of them together as a group "in Christ," while others believe that baptism creates smaller networks of affiliation underneath the person who baptized them. These relationships are probably best understood through frameworks of patronage: those who had been baptized were probably treating their baptizer as a new patron or their personal religious specialist, whereas Paul wants them to place Christ in that role. Paul's impatience with this situation leads him to make the pronouncement that he is glad he only baptized Crispus and Gaius "so that no one can say that you were baptized in my name" (1 Cor 1:15), followed by the absurdly dissembling "I did baptize also the household of Stephanas; beyond that, I do not know whether I baptized anyone else" (1 Cor 1:16).

Though all three of these baptizers seem to contribute to the factionalism, Apollos constitutes a special problem for Paul, and we know this because Paul brings him up in subsequent chapters. In 1 Cor 3, he continues the discussion of factionalism, particularly the "jealously and quarreling" (1 Cor 3:3)

---

[19] Competition in *paideia* is discussed well throughout Eshleman 2012; see also Wendt 2016.

involved, because some are claiming to "belong" to Paul or Apollos (1 Cor 3:4). He uses agricultural metaphors to assure the Corinthians that they are both on the same team, so to speak: Paul plants the crops, while Apollos waters them (1 Cor 3:5-9). This is followed by construction metaphors with the same interest: Paul lays the foundation (i.e., Christ) of a building, while Apollos builds upon it (1 Cor 3:10-11). Again later, after offering his reasoning for why he and Apollos should be considered equals, Paul claims that he has "applied all of this to myself and Apollos for your benefit" (1 Cor 4:6). I agree with scholars who maintain that, despite this rhetoric of equality, Paul is implicitly asking the Corinthians to place him in a superior position (Ker 2000, 86; Knox 1989, 80; Welborn 1987). Regarding the agricultural metaphor, for instance, Donald Ker contends that it implies a "priority . . . that should not be missed by his listeners. . . . The one who plants has a greater claim on the work than the one who waters" (2000, 86). As for the building metaphor, "In a situation that clearly involves co-workers, Paul considers himself to be in charge" (Ker 2000, 88). Despite the surface rhetoric of equality, then, these metaphors subtly create a hierarchy in which Apollos is inferior to Paul.

The tension between Paul and Apollos may be based as much on personality differences or disputes over authority within the group than differences over teaching. Paul Duff speculates that Apollos' teaching was not noticeably different than Paul's, because "the apostle does not offer any corrective to his preaching" in the letter, which would be the ideal spot to challenge any of Apollos' teachings that he disagreed with (2017, 100, n. 39).[20] This makes a great deal of sense and fits with my position that their competition is over status and authority within the Corinthian *ekklēsia*. In other words, they both offer essentially the same teachings, but they are jockeying for influence and authority in the group.

The final reference to Apollos comes in 1 Cor 16:12, a statement that Ker notes "lacks any degree of Pauline personal warmth" (2000, 76). Employing fictive kinship (τοῦ ἀδελφοῦ), Paul notes that he "strongly urged" Apollos to visit Corinth but that "he [i.e., Apollos] was not at all willing to come now" (1 Cor 16:12). Paul follows up with the promise that Apollos "will come when he has the opportunity" (1 Cor 16:12). As I note in the final portion of this essay, such statements are indicative of implicit competition between the two and should determine how we interpret the tone of the

[20] Compare this with Paul's vitriol in, for instance, Galatians, where he rejects specific teachings of his rivals. Or, consider 1 Cor 15:12-19, where he articulates clearly and then rejects a position that he disagrees with.

letter. For now, we may note that this reference tells us that Apollos is not at the beck and call of Paul; that is, despite Paul's "strong" request, Apollos has refused to return to Corinth.

In sum, the sparse evidence from 1 Corinthians gives us a window into Paul's perspective on his relationship with Apollos. Like Paul, Apollos travels throughout a trans-local network of Christ associations and baptizes members. And much to Paul's dismay, it seems that "Apollos has sufficient stature as a leader . . . for some to consider him superior to Peter or Paul" (Ker 2000, 77). Since Paul and Apollos are fellow mobile religious specialists, both making claims to expertise over the Jewish tradition and both positioning themselves as dispensers of salvation, their conflict makes the best sense in terms of religious competition.

Returning to *PPetaus* 28, I want to suggest that Paul and Apollos could be considered "workers" in the Corinthian association in the same way that Asklas and Papsaus were in the Egyptian corpse transport network. Like the occupational clash we see in *PPetaus* 28, 1 Corinthians show us something similar: two men in dispute over the "work" done within the association. In the next portion of this essay, I will map out the associative networks that lie behind 1 Corinthians, establishing that, like *PPetaus* 28, this letter reflects the movement of knowledge about in-house "problems" through a trans-local network.

THE NETWORK OF KNOWLEDGE IN 1 CORINTHIANS

How does Paul come to hear about the factionalism that so intimately involves Apollos? We have seen how *PPetaus* 28 evinces a conflict that relies upon a trans-local network of knowledge about the comings and goings of specific members of an Egyptian association. Something similar lies behind the Corinthian correspondence. Numerous scholars have attempted to map out the moments of communication that Paul has with the group, and so we will only do so briefly here. The goal of doing this is to align the practices in the Corinthian group with *PPetaus* 28 in order to demonstrate that trans-local communication within associative networks could be routine in unofficial associations, even when they had a much more local interest.[21]

---

[21] In a compelling article, Richard Ascough shows that (1) unofficial associations often had stronger trans-local links that have hitherto been recognized; and (2) Christian groups, despite their vocal trans-locality, often had a deeply local presence (1997). By eroding two sides of the argument that Christianity's trans-locality is fundamentally different from other Greek and Roman associations, Ascough makes comparing Christ groups to associations a more natural fit.

The first point of contact that Paul had with the Corinthians probably came with his first arrival. This is often referred to as the moment that he "founded" the Corinthian group. The notion of "founding," I would suggest, is misleading: realistically, there were probably already household networks, perhaps even occupational networks, in place before Paul arrived, and the establishment of the Christ *ekklēsia* likely just took advantage of those networks already in place. In any case, the information that Paul gave the Corinthians about the risen Christ in this initial visit appears to have been sparse (perhaps something akin to the creed-like formulation preserved in 1 Cor 15:3-11), especially since they reached out with numerous queries down the road.

There are even other points of contact before the penning of 1 Corinthians, though. Paul evidently sent a letter prior to what came to be known as 1 Corinthians (1 Cor 5:9). In addition, after he left Corinth following the initial visit, he was contacted by "Chloe's people" (1 Cor 1:11 [likely enslaved people acting as messengers]) with a report about what was happening among the members; many scholars have treated this moment as an instance of oral communication instead of formal writing. Finally, a formal letter containing the Corinthians' numerous queries that occasioned the robust response in 1 Corinthians arrived. In other words, the network of knowledge and communication lying behind 1 Corinthians is rather complex, operating through numerous letters and human messengers. Moreover, if we include the correspondence(s) in 2 Corinthians, which is widely considered to be a composite letter, we see at least two, perhaps even more,[22] additional epistolary moments in this network.

Thus, as in *PPetaus* 28, the Corinthian correspondence gives us a window into a network of knowledge within something like an unofficial association with trans-local linkages; the network relies on the movement of various forms of communication through it. Though 1 Corinthians is far more complex than *PPetaus* 28, both letters attempt to manage a conflict between members of the group: in *PPetaus* 28, the conflict is between Asklas and Papsaus, while in 1 Corinthians, one conflict (of the many conflicts) is between Paul and Apollos. As the final section of this essay argues, we should appreciate the "public" nature of these epistles and remember not only that these letters are correspondences between members of the same social network but also that they are efforts at surveillance and the management of relationships in those networks.

[22] The number of letters that comprise 2 Corinthians has long been debated: see Hausrath 1870; Kennedy 1897; more recently, Welborn 1995; Betz 1985; Bornkamm 1962; Schmithals 1973.

HONOR, REPUTATION, AND THE "PUBLIC" LETTER

Letters are not mere transcripts of communication. They are highly stylized rhetorical projects whose authors have carefully chosen their wording and expressions. They are also social "performances" of communication, even those that purport to have a single addressee. In this last section, I will briefly consider another similarity between *PPetaus* 28 and 1 Corinthians: each author uses the (semi-)public space of the letter to manage his honor.

In the Greco-Roman world, honor, the increased reputation that a person achieves when one's social group evaluates them positively in a public setting, is regularly tied to performances of idealized masculinity, wherein the ideal man is a competent and suasive public speaker, a worthy and skilled adversary in debate, a person stoically in control of his emotions and body, and a figure who does not allow himself to be manipulated by others (Conway 2008, 15–34). *PPetaus* 28 and 1 Corinthians are both performances of masculinity and navigations of honor in their own contexts. In the former, Asklas' refusal to send the legionary's body to Papsaus has caused Papsaus great shame because he has been unable to carry out his obligations. Papsaus speaks of the "great insult" that Asklas has done to him and later notes the consequences of "what you have done to me [i.e., Asklas]." The letter ends bluntly, stating outright that "you have not treated me well," before providing a conventional closing formulae.[23] Though Papsaus is the one with the damaged honor (recall: he was "almost brought . . . before the governor [τὸν ἡγεμόνα]"), such statements amount to the shaming of Asklas, essentially challenging him to rectify his actions. In this way, Papsaus reasserts his honor after experiencing shame brought on by Asklas.

Paul's negotiation of honor in 1 Corinthians is slightly more cryptic, but nevertheless, still present. Paul is obviously anxious about the authority that Apollos has achieved in the group, because, in part, it threatens his position. As we have seen, he uses various metaphors to position himself (and his authority) above Apollos. This is all an effort to manage the Corinthians' perception of him, for his honor and reputation are a function of how they see his relationship to Apollos. By 1 Corinthians 16, Paul tries to be the singular authority in the group and attempts to speak for Apollos, promising that Apollos will visit Corinth when he is able (all the while, sidestepping the obvious difficulty that Apollos has refused to visit at present).

---

[23] *PPetaus* 28 contains many stock phrases from ancient letters (Huebner 2019, 19), though as I suggest shortly, we might do well to read such phrases with more varied tones, depending on wider context.

Both letters use fictive kinship in the course of this honor negotiation. Many biblical scholars have, I contend, been too generous in their interpretations of fictive kinship in Paul's letters, often opting to view it solely for its functions of identity formation and social cohesion. I would like to suggest that its use can also be ironic or even slightly aggressive. In addition to creating social cohesion, fictive kinship also makes a quiet appeal to certain kinds of behavior (Bossman 1996). That is, by applying a label of fictive kinship to someone, one is imposing a set of obligations on them, based on the cultural conventions involved in the real kinship relations. When Papsaus calls Asklas "brother," for instance, it could be read as a reminder that they are equal in status and that Asklas has no right to refuse to carry out his part of the work. It also could be a gentle (or not so gentle) prod, encouraging Asklas to remember his obligations. Somewhat differently, when Paul calls Apollos "brother," there may be some irony in the usage: at the level of rhetoric, Paul is suggesting they are equal, but given his other assertions in the letter, he clearly thinks he is in some sort of position of superiority. "Brother" is, therefore, not always the warm, sincere greeting that we might imagine. In short, fictive kinship can be wielded strategically to do such things as assert pressure on the honor system, to make sure that people in a certain network live up to their expectations and obligations, or even to implicitly code the dynamics of power in a particular social relationship.

These experimental readings of fictive kinship raise the question of *tone* in our analysis. Under the interpretive lens I am suggesting, we ought to be alert for passive-aggressive, perhaps impatient or even sarcastic, statements in these letters, too. Perhaps we should read Papsaus' claim that he "pray[s] that you are in good health" as a perfunctory, hollow brush-off, especially since it follows the accusation of personal mistreatment by Asklas. Somewhat differently, maybe we ought to read sarcasm in Paul's statement of "I did baptize also the household of Stephanas; beyond that, I do not know whether I baptized anyone else" (1 Cor 1:16). At the very least, when we keep in mind the competition with rival religious specialists that he is negotiating, such a statement is likely tinged with exasperation and annoyance that the authority stemming from baptism has gotten out of control. Finally, perhaps Paul's curt statement many chapters later that Apollos "will come [to Corinth] when he has the opportunity" (1 Cor 16:12) is a passive-aggressive criticism directed at Apollos ("throwing shade," if you will), for it is a statement that could be taken to both assert his authority over Apollos (that is, to speak *for* Apollos in his absence) and point out that Apollos is being insubordinate (that is, to acknowledge that Apollos has refused to go to Corinth even though Paul "strongly urged" [1 Cor 16:12] him). Scholars of early Christianity are often hesitant to read passive-aggressiveness, sarcasm, irony, and other such subtleties in Paul's letters. We too often assume he must be expressing kindness, compassion, and sincerity, especially since those are the qualities that he champions in his own letters. But reading 1 Corinthians alongside *PPetaus* 28, to my mind, encourages us to look for more tongue-in-cheek subtleties in his discourse. In this case, we see that an unspoken tone may be an important tool for asserting Paul's honor when competing for authority with rival teachers.

A final point: we are reminded of the public dimension of 1 Corinthians when we realize that Paul invites the Corinthians to observe how he has applied his advice to both himself and Apollos for purposes of ethical formation (1 Cor 4:6; see Ker 2000, 93). It is widely agreed that the letter was addressed to the entire group and so was likely read to all of them. For that reason, the letter itself is a public venue where status and honor were on display, where Paul had to contest people who challenged him, and where he leveled veiled insults at his rivals and found new ways to keep them under his authority. *PPetaus* 28, despite being a more private correspondence, also has an implicit public nature, too: Papsaus clearly defends his own honor in the letter and pressures Asklas to live up to the obligations of his occupation. And lest we forget, Papsaus' letter suggests that this conflict with Asklas had become public in some way or another: either public within the association itself or at the civic/village level. Thus, unofficial associations, including Christ groups, can and did use the epistolary form to contest honor and defend statuses. This comparison also suggests that surveillance of members in a trans-local association was not extraordinary in the slightest. Paul keeping tabs on his fellow workers, as well as the groups in each urban locale, is normal in the context of associations and need not be situated within discourse of pastoralism of the early church.

CONCLUSION

Comparative analyses can get out of control, since literally any two things can be compared at the whim of the scholar. The trick is to *discipline* the comparison to be productive. The analytical payoff lies not in either item of comparison but rather in the new knowledge produced *through* the comparison. In this essay, I have been carefully tying threads between these letters to show that similar navigations of honor and authority are taking place in both. If we treat both letters as witnesses to a trans-local association, it helps us see how surveillance throughout these associative networks was accomplished and how authority was crafted, displayed, and contested in the epistolary form. In this way, the genre of the letter itself can be seen as a kind of public space in which members of associations managed their social relationships. Above all, reading these two letters together invites us to notice the competitive tone in each, especially the competitive discourse of honor and shame—something that New Testament scholars have sometimes missed when each letter is viewed only in the context of Paul's other letters.

WORKS CITED

Ascough, Richard S. 1997. "Translocal Relationships among Voluntary Associations and Early Christianity." *JECS* 5:223–41.

Betz, Hans Dieter. 1985. *2 Corinthians 8 and 9: A Commentary on Two Administrative Letters of the Apostle Paul*. Edited by George MacRae. Hermeneia. Philadelphia: Fortress.

Bond, Sarah E. 2016. *Trade and Taboo: Disreputable Professions in the Roman Mediterranean*. Ann Arbor: University of Michigan Press.

Bornkamm, Günther. 1962. "The History of the Origin of the So-Called Second Letter to the Corinthians." *NTS* 8:258–64.

Bossman, David M. 1996. "Paul's Fictive Kinship Movement." *BTB* 26:163–71.

Conway, Colleen M. 2008. *Behold the Man: Jesus and Greco-Roman Masculinity*. Oxford: Oxford University Press.

Crook, Zeba. 2011. "Fictive-Friendship and the Fourth Gospel." *HTS Teologiese Studies/Theological Studies* 67: https://hts.org.za/index.php/HTS/article/view/997.

Daniel, Robert W. 1979. "Notes on the Guilds and Army in Roman Egypt." *BASP* 16:37–46.

Duff, Paul B. 2017. *Jesus Followers in the Roman Empire*. Grand Rapids: Eerdmans.

Eshleman, Kendra. 2012. *The Social World of Intellectuals in the Roman Empire: Sophists, Philosophers, and Christians*. Greek Culture in the Roman World. Cambridge: Cambridge University Press.

Fredriksen, Paula. 2006. "Mandatory Retirement: Ideas in the Study of Christian Origins Whose Time Has Come to Go." *SR* 35:231–46.

Harland, Philip A. 2009. *Dynamics of Identity in the World of the Early Christians: Associations, Judeans, and Cultural Minorities*. New York: Continuum; London: T&T Clark.

Hausrath, Adolph. 1870. *Der Vier-Capitel-Brief des Paulus an die Korinther*. Heidelberg: Bassermann.

Huebner, Sabine R. 2019. *Papyri and the Social World of the New Testament*. Cambridge: Cambridge University Press.

Kennedy, James Houghton. 1897. "Are There Two Epistles in 2 Corinthians?" *The Expositor* 6:231–38.

Ker, Donald P. 2000. "Paul and Apollos—Colleagues or Rivals?" *JSNT* 22:75–97.

Kloppenborg, John S. 2011. "Greco-Roman *Thiasoi*, the *Ekklēsia* at Corinth, and Conflict Management." Pages 187–218 in *Redescribing Paul and the Corinthians*. Edited by Ron Cameron and Merrill P. Miller. Early Christianity and Its Literature 5. Atlanta: SBL.

———, ed. 2020. *Ptolemaic and Early Roman Egypt*. BZNW 246. Vol. 3 of *Greco-Roman Associations: Texts, Translations, and Commentary*. Edited by John S. Kloppenborg and Richard S. Ascough. Berlin: De Gruyter.

Kloppenborg, John S., and Richard S. Ascough, eds. 2011. *Attica, Central Greece, Macedonia, Thrace*. BZNW 181. Vol. 1 of Kloppenborg and Ascough, *Greco-Roman Associations*.

Knox, John. 1989. *Chapters in a Life of Paul*. Rev. ed. London: SCM Press.

Last, Richard, and Philip A. Harland. 2020. *Group Survival in the Ancient Mediterranean: Rethinking Material Conditions in the Landscape of Jews and Christians*. London: T&T Clark.

Mihalia, Corin. 2009. *The Paul-Apollos Relationship and Paul's Stance toward Greco-Roman Rhetoric: An Exegetical and Socio-historical Study of 1 Corinthians 1–4*. LNTS 402. London: T&T Clark.

Murray, Timothy J. 2018. *Restricted Generosity in the New Testament*. WUNT 2/480. Tübingen: Mohr Siebeck.

Rollens, Sarah E. 2019. "The Anachronism of 'Early Christian Communities.'" Pages 307–24 in *Theorizing "Religion" in Antiquity*. Edited by Nickolas P. Roubekas. Studies in Ancient Religion and Culture. Sheffield: Equinox.

Schmithals, Walter. 1973. "Die Korintherbrief als Briefsammlung." *ZNW* 64:263–88.

Welborn, Larry. 1987. "On the Discord in Corinth: 1 Corinthians 1–4 and Ancient Politics." *JBL* 106:86–111.

———. 1995. "The Identification of 2 Corinthians 10–13 with the 'Letter of Tears.'" *NovT* 37:138–53.

Wendt, Heidi. 2016. *At the Temple Gates: The Religion of Freelance Experts in the Roman Empire*. Oxford: Oxford University Press.

19

The Significance of Λογεία for the Meaning of Paul's Collection in 1 and 2 Corinthians

Philip F. Esler

Interest in interpreting the early Christ movement in relation to the numerous voluntary associations of the cities of the first century Mediterranean world is a welcome growth point in recent scholarship. A key component of that advance has been the consideration of financial aspects of associational life—both within individual associations and among associations across a geographical expanse.[1] This essay contributes to that discussion by seeking to explain a salient fact of Paul's presentation of the collection in 1 and 2 Corinthians: the radically different treatment he offers in the two letters.

Firstly, in the Greek text of 1 Corinthians Paul expends sixty-four words on the collection (16:1-4). In 2 Corinthians (8–9) he deploys 693. A tenfold increase in the amount of language Paul felt necessary to devote to this project less than a year later (2 Cor 8:10; 9:2) indicates, at the very least, that his initial approach was inapt at the outset, or became so in the course of time, or both. Secondly, it is notable that whereas in 1 Cor 16:1-4 he describes the collection as both a χάρις (*charis*, "gift"; 16:3) and a λογεία (*logeia*, "collection"; 16:1; plus λογεῖαι; 16:2), in 2 Corinthians 8–9, while retaining χάρις (8:4, 6, 7, 19), he drops λογεία and introduces five other concepts: κοινωνία (*koinōnia*, "close relationship"; 8:4; 9:13), διακονία/διακονεῖν

1   For the former, see for instance Last and Harland 2020; for the latter, see *CIG* 5853.

(*diakonia/diakonein*, "ministry/minister to"; 8:4, 19, 20; 9:1, 12, 13), ἁδρότης (*hadrotēs*, "abundance"; 8:20), εὐλογία (*eulogia*, "blessing"; 9:5 [2x]), and λειτουργία (*leitourgia*, "service"; 9:12). Paul's failure to use λογεία at all in the rich vocabulary related to the collection in 2 Corinthians 8–9 calls for an explanation but has hitherto attracted little attention.[2] This neglect probably stems from the long-standing tendency of critics (discussed below) to attach inappropriately benign meanings to λογεία and thus overlook the contrast with 2 Corinthians 8–9.

Particularly relevant to this essay is John Kloppenborg's recent investigation of collections by voluntary associations and their bearing on Paul's collection (2019, 245–64). He observes (2019, 246) that since there is epigraphic evidence for groups of handworkers and resident aliens (who probably comprised the majority of Paul's Christ groups) in Greece having been engaged in collecting funds, including for special purposes, for at least four hundred years before Paul's arrival in Corinth, his project to arrange a collection could not have been an unknown activity to them. This view is incontestable. So too is Kloppenborg's eloquent defense of the merits of comparative analysis (2019, 5–10). Yet, decades ago, Maurice Duverger observed that when we engage in "close comparisons" of social phenomena from much the same time and place, since we expect similarities, it is the differences that may be more interesting.[3] This has relevance to Kloppenborg's attempt, following a suggestion by Verlyn Verbrugge (1992), to explain the common Greek practice of the ἐπίδοσις (*epidosis*), or voluntary collection for a specific purpose (2019, 248–51), and then to compare this with Paul's collection, *in terms of similarities* (2019, 252). That we might need, rather, to follow Duverger's advice in taking difference seriously is suggested by the circumstance that Paul never uses the word ἐπίδοσις in relation to the collection (indeed the word does not appear in the New Testament), but twice in 1 Cor 16:1-2 employs λογεία, a word Kloppenborg does not address. Paul's use of this word means that we must first consider the meaning of λογεία. Although the word was used in settings other than those connected with voluntary associations, we must investigate its wider semantic range to assess what response it would have elicited from the Corinthian Christ followers in relation to Paul's collection.

---

[2]   Verbrugge 1992, 32–41, 75–77, is a notable exception.
[3]   See Duverger 1964, 261–67, and the discussion of the comparative method in Esler 1987, 9–12.

ΛΟΓΕΙΑ IN THE ANCIENT NONLITERARY SOURCES

Since λογεία does not appear in literary works before Paul, researchers turn to ancient nonliterary sources to shed light on its use in 1 Cor 16:1-2. Those sources comprise papyri and ostraca, almost exclusively from Egypt, and inscriptions on stone, mainly from the cities in the Greco-Roman east, including one from Egypt. A prominent feature of existing scholarship, however, is the limited nature of the evidence discussed, with Ruth Kritzer (2006) and Peter Arzt-Grabner (2013) being the main exceptions. Adolf Deissmann, for example, discussed an ostracon from Thebes in detail (= *OWilck* 413, in Wilcken 1899, 120), while referring to the "numerous instances of the use of the word in Egypt," as well as an inscription from Smyrna and another from Magnesia on the Maeander (Deissmann 1927, 106). Gerhard Kittel (1967) mentions a handful of inscriptions, six papyri, and eight ostraca. David Downs refers to some eight inscriptions, a few papyri, and an ostracon (2008, 129–31). On the other hand, Kritzer (2006, 506–7) and Arzt-Grabner (2013, 389–410) consider a wide array of papyri. Missing from the scholarship so far, however, is a reasonably systematic coverage of the major source of evidence on the meaning of λογεία, namely, the papyri and the ostraca. Fortunately, the website Papyri.info, which came into existence in 2010,[4] contains rich resources for a useful sampling exercise.[5]

The Papyri and Ostraca

The noun λογεία is cognate with the verb λογεύειν (*logeuein*) and it is worthwhile to start with it. Searching Papyri.info for instances of λογευ- across its whole range (beginning in 2100 BCE) produced 156 instances. There are about seventy instances of λογεύειν (excluding prepositional forms of that verb). Most refer to what are taxes. In the papyri λογευτής (*logeutēs*) means a tax collector, λογευτήριον (*logeutērion*) means the office of the tax collector, and τὸ λογευτικόν (*to logeutikon*) means the cost of a collection. These last three words occur frequently. Six examples of λογεύειν will give a flavor of its use. In *PHamb* 2.178, from 241 BCE, the word relates to the collection of the dike-maintenance tax (and λογεία is also used). In *PKöln* 10.412 it is used of the collection of taxes on agricultural products (λογεία is also used).

---

[4]   On this site, see https://classicalstudies.org/scs-blog/michael-zellmann-rohrer/review-papyriinfo-searchable-database-papyri-and-translations.

[5]   The Papyri.info site (https://papyri.info) was accessed from July 19–23, 2021, for this exercise. This site was also used as the main source for the texts of the papyri and ostraca.

BGU 8.1815, from around 60 BCE, employs the word in relation to the collection of burdensome taxes. In *CPJ* 1.33, from 299–200 BCE, there are two instances of the word with respect to taxes. The word signifies the collection of taxes from people living on a certain person's estates in *PCairZen* 2.59206 (from 255 BCE). Finally, in *PCount* 33, from 254–231 BCE, λογεύειν appears in connection with a register of tax receipts. Occasionally, however, the word occurs in non-fiscal contexts, for example in requests in letters to family or friends to collect something (e.g., money) and send it on (e.g., *OKrok* 2.246, from 117–130 CE).

Searching Papyri.info for all instances of λογει- produced 1,422 instances. To generate a more manageable sample, the field was narrowed from 300 BCE to 100 CE, which produced 591 hits, but many were prefixed verbal forms (especially beginning ὁμο- or κατα-), and the total for various forms of λογεία alone in the sample, which includes ostraca and papyri, was 60 (although 17 of these appeared in one papyrus).

A significant proportion of these instances related to taxes imposed by the Hellenistic and then Roman administrations. This was to be expected in view of the frequency with which, as just noted, λογεύειν, λογευτής, and λογευτήριον appear in the papyri. Thus, we have an ostracon dated to 104 BCE from Apollonius (*OEdfou* 2.244) recording a receipt "regarding the holy tax on [wheat]" (ὑπὲρ ἱερᾶς λογείας [πυροῦ]). Four ostraca—the first two from Elephantine, the third from Lagis, and the fourth from Heracleopolis—are receipts for payment of the salt tax.[6] Two other ostraca record receipts for payment of something like a poll tax on the inhabitants of Syene.[7] An ostracon from Thebes from 11 CE (*OLeid* 379) registers the receipt of the wine tax (οἰνιχὴ λογεία). The word λογεία in relation to payment of agricultural products appears in a letter of 246 BCE and a letter dated 197 BCE from Tebtynis.[8] A papyrus of 241 BCE from Oxyrhynchus records payment of a levy tax (*PHamb* 2.178). *PHamb* 2.184 and 186 (from mid-third-century BCE Oxyrhynchus) refer to a λογεία τῶν χλωρῶν ("tax of the greens"), probably meaning a forage tax. In a number of papyri and ostraca that note the receipt of λογείαι the target of the taxes has not survived.[9]

---

[6] *OVleem* 25 and 27, from 219 and 237 BCE, respectively; *PCount* 24, from 254–231 BCE; and *PCount* 45 from 243–217 BCE.

[7] *PBagnall* 21 and 22, from 221 and 219 BCE, respectively.

[8] The first letter is *PCairZen* 3.59346, a letter from Horos to Zenon, and the second is *PTebt* 3.1750, from a tax farmer in Alexandria.

[9] These are: *OEdfou* 3.344 from Apollonius in the third century BCE; *PBagnall* 20 (anostracon) from Elephantine in 222 BCE; *OEdfou* 3.362 from Apollonius in 104 BCE;

Worthy of particular note is *UPZ* 2.175, a papyrus from Thebes from 145 BCE, which concerns the sale from one person to another of one-third of the right to conduct λογεῖαι among the choachytes, the functionaries charged with care of mummified bodies. Arzt-Grabner has suggested that the choachytes formed a voluntary association (2013, 392).[10] Although this is possible, no collective noun denoting an association appears in the document. The feature of this document relevant here is that these λογεῖαι cannot have been voluntary. For someone would only pay the considerable price mentioned if the return on that investment was secure, which it would not have been if the contributions were voluntary. The most probable solution is that all choachytes in Thebes were liable to pay a tax to the state, just as were the weavers,[11] and that this tax was farmed out, so that the right to collect it became a valuable and assignable asset.

Yet while the power of the state stood behind the taxes just mentioned, λογεία often denoted the payment required for a service and, in such cases, designated a compulsory exaction on everyone using that service. Thus, six of the sample are ostraca from Thebes during the period 47–69 CE and record the receipt of payments by individuals of four drachmas (and some obols) for the λογεία τοῦ θεοῦ ("collection of the god"), or similar expressions such as λογεία Ἴσιδος περὶ τῶν δημοσίων ("collection of Isis for the public works").[12] David Klotz (2009) has noted that altogether twenty-three ostraca of this type survive from the period 47–69 CE and argues they refer to payments for the construction or renovation of the temple of Isis at Deir Shelwit. He suggests that the named officials who took payment and those who paid were fellow devotees (2009, 254). While this is possible, the fact that receipts were issued and the amount was standardized at four drachmas (plus some obols) makes it certain that this was a compulsory charge, perhaps the price for entrance to the temple precinct. Perhaps some of those paying the fee were casual visitors? In this case, although Deissmann (1927, 106) observed that these ostraca were "interesting evidence of the extent

---

OWilck 360 from Thebes in 8 BCE; and *PHibeh* 2.210 from Oxyrhynchus in the period 250–240 BCE.

[10] On associations in Egypt during the Principate, see Mitchell 2017, 175–87.

[11] See *POxy* 61.2957 (of 91 CE) for the existence of a tax on weavers in Oxyrhynchus, and *POxy* 76.5097 (discussed below) for their status as a guild.

[12] Only the number "four" appears on the ostraca, but drachma seems the likely amount as four obols would represent a minimal return. The six ostraca in the sample are: *OCair GPW* 67; *OWilck* 402, 412, 413, 414; and *PSI* 3.262. Some of the ostraca are in demotic, not Greek, which partially explains the comparatively small proportion of them appearing on the Papyri.info website.

of the financial claims made upon persons of no great means for religious purposes in the period which saw the rise of Christianity," one might doubt whether "religious" is appropriate.

In addition, of the sixty examples of λογεία in our sample, another five are ostraca from Thebes and acknowledge receipt of payment of an annual charge (probably two drachmas) for entry to the baths (the λογεία βαλανευτική; "bath-tax").[13] PPetr 3.107, dated 226 BCE and from either Krokodilopolis or Ptolemais Hormu in the Arsinoite nome, is a list of fares and freights (= λογεία, appearing seventeen times) for persons and goods transported on boats.

Of great importance for this essay is that some of these papyri concern complaints against people who have organized λογείαι in an illegal or oppressive way. Particularly notable is POxy 76.5097.[14] This is an edict of the Roman Prefect Lucius Iulius Vestinus dated February 27, 62 CE, against one Sarapion, the president (προστάτις) of the guild (πλῆθος) of weavers in Oxyrhynchus, in relation to his organization of apparently illegal collections, and his accomplices. He had been summoned to appear before a court "and had perhaps failed to appear," which might explain the prefect's action in confirming a judgment or threatening some further action against him (Bowman 2011, 197). The appearance of the word στασιώδεις (like στασιώθεις: "seditious," "quarrelsome") shortly before Sarapion's accomplices are mentioned suggests that they had been charged with serious misbehavior. We do not know, however, who was being subjected to Sarapion's exactions or the nature of the disturbances. Another papyrus from Oxyrhynchus and only a few years later provides a different perspective. In POxy 2.239, from 66 CE, a man swears on oath that he has not undertaken any collections in the village of Psobthis and in the future will become its headman, which suggests he will not be able to do so in that office. Thirdly, a papyrus from Thebes in 119 BCE (PTorAmen 6) contains the sentence of a court against someone who had, inter alia, organized improper λογείαι. Lastly, it is worth mentioning one other example from slightly beyond our sample's time range. PGiss 1.61, from 119 CE, contains a complaint to the governor from the inhabitants of the village of Naboo against their village scribe for, inter alia, imposing on them a (compulsory) λογεία (l. 8) by which he extorted (διέσεισεν; ll. 10–11) twenty drachmas from some and eighteen drachmas from others.

---

[13] They are: OBodl 2.650 (12 CE); OBodl 2.651 (13 CE); and OCair GPW 41, 42, 43 (2 BCE).

[14] See Bowman 2011 and Arzt-Grabner 2013, 401.

Finally, just as λογεύειν appears in non-fiscal contexts (see above), in a handful of cases λογεία also features in contexts that have some general sense of a collection and not in reference to a tax or a compulsory fee for service.[15] Apart from these anomalous cases, there is not a single case in the sample where λογεία refers to a voluntary collection. Either they were compulsory in the sense of representing various forms of exactions by the state to raise revenue, or they referred to the cost of a service that would not be provided in the absence of payment, or they were imposed by private citizens practicing a form of unauthorized extortion.

This analysis of our sample provides a basis to assess existing suggestions on the meaning of λογεία. Firstly, the view of Kittel (1967, 283) denying that it meant a "levy" or "imposed tax," supported by Dieter Georgi (1992, 53, 188), is untenable. That is where the primary emphasis does fall, as seen in the details mentioned above. This is also the view of Kritzer (2005, 506): "Das Wort λογεία bzw. bezeichnet in den Papyri zunächst allgemein 'Einhebung' oder 'Einziehung' von verschiedenster Abgaben." Secondly, the suggestion by Downs, supporting the view of Deissmann (1927, 105), that this is "language typically associated with cultic and sacral collections for temples and gods" (2008, 130), a position in turn followed by Roy Ciampa and Brian Rosner (2010, 842), is unsustainable. As just noted, many (the dominant group) were secular taxes, such as on salt, forage, or persons, or for dike maintenance. But there was another broad category relating to the price of services. Even the money payable for admission to the temple at Deir Shelwit may have covered entrants for non-cultic purposes.

The Inscriptions

Having considered the papyrological evidence and established a framework for the meaning of λογεία, we now proceed to five inscriptions that have been prominent in the discussion. Firstly, a third- or second-century BCE inscription from the island of Paros lists contributions made by at least sixty-five women for "the restoration of the fountain, the altar and the shrine" (εἰς ἐπισκευὴν τῆς κρήνης καὶ τοῦ βωμοῦ καὶ τοῦ θαλάμου; ll. 5–6) of a god or, more likely, a goddess, whose name has not survived.[16] The verb ἐλόγευσεν,

---

[15] These include *BGU* 10.1911 (a letter from the mid-third century BCE, with two examples of λογεία) and *PMich* 1.84 (a memorandum from Heracleides to Zenon that apparently refers to the resources to be used on constructing a palisade for animals against the advancing Nile).

[16] *IG* XII,5 186 + addenda p. 310. Wilhelm (1898, 428) suggested as possibilities Aphrodite, Demeter, or Eileithyia.

curiously in the singular,[17] is used of the collection (l. 4), although λογεία does not occur. The contributions ranged from one obol (one-sixth of a drachma) to thirty-one drachmas. Richard Last and Philip Harland suggest that the women "were perhaps members of an association" (2020, 125), but there is no evidence for this, and Adolf Wilhelm doubted it.[18] Certainly, their suggestion that the singular verb ἐλόγευσεν in line 4 had as its subject a singular noun referring to an association is unjustified. More specifically, Wilhelm comprehensively demolished the suggestion by the original editor (Ernst Maas) that the women were members of a voluntary association of prostitutes.[19] That the amounts paid were variable and the names of contributors listed strongly suggest that this was a voluntary collection. Here, then, is a meaning not attested in the papyri.

Secondly, a long inscription (of at least 115 lines) from Magnesia on the Maeander speaks of the award of the people of Magnesia (on referral from the Roman Senate) in a dispute between Hierapytna and Itanus (two cities in Crete) in either 138 or 132 BCE. The dispute concerned ownership of certain land and some islands.[20] Line 72, unfortunately mutilated, contains the expression πρὸς δε τούτοις λογείαις τε σιτικαῖς ἅς . . . ("in addition to these collections of grain which"). Deissmann (1927, 106) notes an earlier suggestion of G. Thieme that here λογείαι refers to "the collecting together of supplies for warlike purposes," which is very likely since the word immediately before this expression is φρουρίου, from φρούριον, a hill fort or garrison, and "soldiers" are mentioned in the previous line. As requisitions for an army, these λογείαι would have conveyed compulsion, even if reimbursement was provided. This meaning comes close to the numerous uses of λογεία in the papyri in connection with state taxes.

Thirdly, an inscription from the Fayum mentions an attempt by local priests in 95 BCE to take a collection from each person in the village of Magdola, παρ' ἕκαστον ἐν τῆι κώμηι λογείαις ἐπιχιρ[ε]ῖν (see ll. 23–25), so that the temple of Heron could be maintained and restored.[21] There is no doubt the priests were intent on a compulsory levy of the villagers. This is a very

---

[17] See the discussion by Wilhelm (1898, 416–17), who notes that ἐλόγευσεν demands a subject and discusses what it might be.

[18] It was an assumption that seemed to him "unproven and unprovable" (Wilhelm 1898, 429–30).

[19] Wilhelm 1898, 418–24.

[20] For the text, see Kern (1900) 1967, no. 105, pp. 95, 97–98. Also see the discussion in Deissmann 1927, 106–7, and, for the Roman dimension, Kallet-Max 1995, 172–81.

[21] For the text, see Étienne Bernand 1975–1981, 3:152. It is available at: https://inscriptions.packhum.org/text/219972?&bookid=376&location=1695. For a discussion, see André Bernand 1992, 1:80–83; 2:70–83.

similar situation to the compulsory and unauthorized levies mentioned in four of the papyri.

Fourthly, an inscription from Physkos in the Rhodian Peraea from ca. 66 BCE records an embassy sent to the mother city of Lindos from the κοινόν (*koinon*), a local political and religious organization embracing the city of Physkos and its surroundings, requesting permission to take up the collection (λογεία) for the common cults in the established way.[22] Clearly this concerned a collection made for a sacred purpose and was probably voluntary, except to the extent that one probably gained honor by contributing. Accordingly, we have a second instance in the ancient evidence of λογεία meaning a voluntary collection.

Fifthly, an inscription from Smyrna associated with the cult of Helios Apollo, and probably from the first century CE, contains an elaborate list of cult objects and structures that a priest named Apollonios Sparos, son of Metrodoros, had dedicated to the god and the city.[23] Although Downs (2008, 130) states that the inscription "speaks of a religious association founded by one Apollonios Sparos," there is no sign of such an association in the inscription; Apollonios was the priest of an established cult. Nevertheless, it does speak of a collection. One of the objects is described as a κλεῖν κεχρυσωμένην καὶ ἐμπεφιασμένην πρὸς τὴν λογήαν καὶ πομπὴν τῶν θεῶν, literally, "a key gilded and clothed for the collection and procession of the gods," where λογήαν is a misspelling of λογείαν. Deissmann (1927, 106) had noted that the word κλεῖν was of doubtful meaning, and Georg Petzl plausibly suggests that the reference here is not to a key, but to a particular type of divine image (1987, 253). Presumably, the object was a focus in some way for donations that were solicited during the procession in honor of certain gods through the city. These must have been voluntary contributions and no doubt varied in amount. This is the third example of λογεία referring to a voluntary collection.

ΛΟΓΕΙΑ IN 1 CORINTHIANS 16

Paul begins 1 Corinthians 16 as follows:

> Now concerning the collection (Περὶ δὲ τῆς λογείας) for the saints, just as I commanded (ὥσπερ διέταξα) the assemblies of Galatia, so also you do (οὕτως καὶ ὑμεῖς ποιήσατε).[24]

---

[22] In a conservative version of the text, the word λογεία appears in ll. 6–7 (Blümel 1991, 119–20). Sokolowski (1958, 138–41; 1962, no. 143) proposed a highly plausible emendation that also inserted λογεία into l. 14.

[23] For the Greek text, translation, and notes, see Petzl 1987, no. 753, pp. 252–56.

[24] Translations from 1 and 2 Corinthians are the author's.

Paul provides no introduction and offers no explanation. His abrupt entry into this topic suggests he had previously informed the Corinthian Christ followers that they too would be participating in the project. The Corinthians had probably asked him for details in a letter, since this is the fifth Περὶ δὲ since 7:1 and each of the previous occasions seems to be the start of a response to a Corinthian question (Fee 1987, 811).

His words constitute a direction encapsulated in the word διατάσσειν. Archibald Robertson and Alfred Plummer underestimate the force of the word when they suggest it has "a tone of authority" (1914, 383). Διατάσσειν is a forceful word Paul employs in reference to his (or the Lord's or an angel's) instructions to his converts. In 1 Corinthians (where his leadership of the Corinthians is very secure) it occurs in 1 Cor 7:7 and 11:34 (in the middle voice) and in 9:14 and 16:1 (in the active), and it also appears in Gal 3:19. It means "to give (detailed) instructions as to what must be done, order" (Danker 2000, 237). Its force is confirmed by blunt imperative at the end of v. 1: "so also you do." Collins (1999, 588) rightly notes "the mandatory nature" of the collection in 1 Corinthians.

Paul next supplies details of the collection, leaving the expression παρ᾽ ἑαυτῷ untranslated for the present:

> On the first day of each week (κατὰ μίαν σαββάτου),[25] let each of you παρ᾽ ἑαυτῷ lay aside, storing up (τιθέτω θησαυρίζων) in respect of whatever success he may have (εὐοδῶται), in order that when I come collections do not then occur (μὴ . . . λογεῖαι τότε γίνωνται).

Two broad positions exist as to the arrangement Paul communicated to his Corinthian addressees in these three clauses. On one view, Paul is directing them to take up a collection at their weekly meetings.[26] This scenario is envisaged, its proponents suggest, by the mention of the first day of the week, which was when Christ-movement meetings allegedly took place, and by the argument that παρ᾽ ἑαυτῷ does not mean "at home" but "individually," with both meanings being well attested in antiquity.[27] On the other view, Paul is directing the Corinthians to each set aside a sum of money in their homes by weekly amounts so that those can all be accumulated into one

---

[25] Here κατὰ with the accusative is used in a temporal and distributive sense (Fee 1987, 813; Danker 2000, 512). The phrase as a whole has a Judean background.

[26] So: Llewelyn 2001, 209–10; Downs 2008, 128–29; Ciampa and Rosner 2010, 843.

[27] For the meaning "individually," see the instances cited in Llewelyn 2001, 209. Instances meaning "at home" include 2 Tim 4:13; also Homer, *Il.* 13.627 and *Od.* 11.490; Herodotus, *Hist.* 1.105; Xenophon, *Mem.* 3.13.3 and *Cyr.* 1.2.15; and Philo, *Cher.* 48 and *Legat.* 271; similarly, the expression οἱ παρ᾽ ἐμοί means "of my household."

collection when he comes back to Corinth.[28] Although Paul's Corinthian correspondence is replete with debated issues for which the evidence is finely balanced, this is not one of them, since the former view is ruled out by what Paul says. Firstly, group collections are irreconcilable with Paul's use of the singular, masculine participle θησαυρίζων, meaning "storing up." How could individual members of the Christ group store up money if they were handing it over at its meetings each week? This scenario suggests that παρ᾽ ἑαυτῷ bears the common meaning of "at home." Yet even if the alternative meaning, "individually," were correct, it would not affect the result, since the only likely place for group members, especially from the non-elite, acting as individuals, to keep an expanding sum of money was at home. Secondly, Paul's direction to individuals is aimed at ensuring that λογεῖαι, *in the plural*, will not have to occur when he arrives, a time emphasized by τότε. Yet if he had a collection at a group meeting in mind, he would have used λογεῖα. He is saying that he wants them to get the job done in advance of his arrival, to avoid the necessity of having to do it then. But if they fail in this, the job will entail collections, meaning from individuals, when he does arrive. Finally, there is little evidence in Paul's letters that his groups met on the first day of the week or even weekly, but even if they did (which is certainly possible: Fee 1987, 813–14; Thiselton 2000, 1320), that would not matter much here, since Paul could have intended to use the fact that this was the day of the meeting to remind them to set aside the money (Fee 1987, 814). Paul could easily have told the Christ followers to bring their contributions to the weekly meetings, but he does not. A reason for this will be suggested below. Nothing in v. 2 suggests group meetings as a context for the project prior to his return.

First Corinthians 16:3-4 concern what will happen when Paul returns to Corinth. Unfortunately, he says nothing about how the individual contributions will be gathered or by whom. We do not know if there would be a collection event in a group meeting, or whether representatives would approach the members individually for their contribution. Nor do we know whether the amount each contributed would be disclosed to the members. Paul's statements focus solely on how the collection, now called "your gift" (τὴν χάριν ὑμῶν), will be conveyed to Jerusalem. He identifies two options. In both cases the bearers of the gift will be people whom the Corinthians accredit for the task. In the first option, Paul says, "I will send these with letters (δι᾽ ἐπιστολῶν) to carry your gift to Jerusalem." In the second, he says that if it seems worthwhile, "they will go with me," in which

---

[28] So: Robertson and Plummer 1914, 384–85 (who also cite Chrysostom in support; the Vulgate, similarly, has *apud se*); Fee 1987, 813; Thiselton 2000, 1321–24.

case, by necessary implication, letters (i.e., from Paul) would not be need-ed.[29] These verses give the impression of Paul being in complete command of the issue; it is a matter in which he issues instructions (cf. διατάσσειν in v. 1); he is not inviting their views.

THE MEANING OF ΛΟΓΕΙΑ AND 1 CORINTHIANS 16:1-4

We now reach the critical issue. How would the Corinthian Christ follow-ers have understood the collection described as a λογεία? What semantic resonances would it have had? As explained above, the overwhelmingly common use of the word was for compulsory exactions, either imposed by the state as a tax or demanded by the provider of services. We have iden-tified only three instances of its use in relation to a voluntary collection. Paul's use of διατάσσειν, the series of instructions that follow and the fact that, apart from accrediting those who will carry the money to Jerusalem, the Corinthians have no input in the matter, all confirm that Paul's collec-tion closely cohered with the common meaning of λογεία: this was a com-pulsory imposition by Paul on the Christ followers of Corinth. It differed, admittedly, in three respects from a λογεία as a tax or fee for service. No amount was fixed, since each was to give according to their current situa-tion (meaning variable amounts were inevitable), clearly no receipts were to be issued and the person requiring the payment was not to benefit per-sonally from it (since its beneficiaries were the saints in Jerusalem). These features do not, however, distract from the fundamental nature of the col-lection as a compulsory exaction. That one individual was requiring this payment may also have reminded the Corinthians of other instances (like those mentioned above) where people had unjustly extorted money from those subject to them. Even though Paul's stated purpose excluded himself as a beneficiary, the situation was one in which the malevolent might allege he was siphoning off some of this money for himself. His allowing the Cor-inthians to accredit their own bearers of the gift may have been intended to quash such a rumor, but even this left hanging the question of who had custody of the collection in Corinth before its dispatch. Such issues were unlikely to be problematic while Paul had a good relationship with the Corinthians, but what if it deteriorated? There were, in short, some extremely negative possibilities inherent in Paul's characterization of the

---

[29]   A far less likely interpretation connects δι᾽ἐπιστολῶν with the Corinthians' accredi-tation process.

collection as a λογεία and we will see below, in discussing 2 Corinthians, how those possibilities were realized.

Prior to that, Paul's collection should be contrasted with the voluntary ἐπίδοσις. Kloppenborg rightly observes that the collection was similar to the ἐπίδοσις in being collected over a period of time (2019, 252). His second similarity, of its involving most or all the Corinthians, is less secure, since a majority of citizens did not contribute to public ἐπιδόσεις (Chaniotis 2013; Ellis-Evans 2013) and it is unclear what percentage of members of voluntary associations did. Of Kloppenborg's third similarity, of issues that could arise between initiating a collection and bringing it to completion, there is no sign in 1 Cor 16:1-4, but there is evidence for it in 2 Corinthians, as we will see. There are also very significant differences. Firstly, in the case of an ἐπίδοσις organized by a city's assembly, contributions were voluntary, although there was social pressure to participate (Chaniotis 2013, 91–93). This was also the case with voluntary associations (Migeotte 2013), which often imitated civic institutions. Inscriptions survive from both civic assemblies and voluntary associations recording the names of the donors and the amounts they gave. This was not the case, however, with the arrangements Paul sets out in 1 Cor 16:1-4. Paul simply directed them all to contribute, as in a λογεία. In 2 Corinthians 8–9, however, we will observe Paul moving to a position of voluntary contributions. Secondly, in an ἐπίδοσις, potential donors would publicly pledge at the outset how much they would contribute and then make regular payments to fulfill the pledge. The "whole procedure was public" (Chaniotis 2013, 91). This allowed richer members to parade their liberality and gain honor therefrom. Although Kloppenborg supports their presence among the Corinthians (2019, 252), such upfront pledges are incompatible with Paul's direction to accumulate money on a weekly basis at home to the extent that circumstances permitted. This meant the members would not be gaining honor from fulfilling their pledge; it is not even clear if the amount of individual contributions would be revealed. Thirdly, the problem, often addressed in an ἐπίδοσις, of taking steps to avoid the non-fulfillment of promises, has no counterpart in Paul's collection. Fourthly, as Kloppenborg (2019, 248) acknowledges, an ἐπίδοσις was usually for a local purpose (typically, for work on cultic sites; Migeotte 2013, 126), and only rarely for a trans-local one.

THE COLLECTION IN 2 CORINTHIANS 8–9

In my view, 2 Corinthians is a unified composition that we possess as Paul intended it.[30] Within that letter chapters 8–9 constitute an integrated argument on the collection. The idea of some scholars that these chapters represent two separate letters (e.g., Betz 1985) is the weakest element of the partition theories.[31] When Paul writes 2 Corinthians, his relationship with the Christ followers in Corinth is not what it was when he wrote 1 Corinthians. It has become seriously strained, both because of his failure to fulfill an undertaking he had made about visiting them and because outsiders have arrived speaking against him and his ministry. Paul devotes much of chapters 1–7 to rebuilding that relationship and confidence in his ministry, especially by stressing the extent to which he and the Corinthians are engaged in a cooperative enterprise (Esler 2021). The social-identity theory of leadership (Turner 2005; Esler 2021) rejects the idea that leaders gain influence by their control over resources and suggests instead that they are able to exercise authority in relation to group resources only by proving that they are prototypical of the group's values and put its interest above their own. Paul's argument reflects this wisdom in that his argument is occupied with the former issues in chapters 1–7 and the latter in chapters 8–9.

The collection had suffered from Paul's deteriorating relationship with the Corinthians, and what he says about it reflects his efforts to rebuild that relationship. The impression Paul gives in 1 Cor 16:1-4 is that the Corinthians were to start the collection immediately. Given that the language of the statement in 2 Cor 8:6 that Titus "had made a beginning" (προενήρξατο) of the collection, matches the observation that the Corinthians had "made a beginning" (προενηρξασθε) "in the previous year" (ἀπὸ πέρυσι; 2 Cor 8:10), it is likely that it was Titus who had carried 1 Corinthians to Corinth (Esler 2021, 239). Now Paul wants Titus to complete that work (2 Cor 8:6). This will be before Paul arrives in the city (9:4), which will be for the third time (2 Cor 12:14; 13:1). But that Titus had anything to complete before Paul's arrival indicates that the collection had not proceeded as Paul had intended when he wrote 1 Corinthians. The situation is somewhat similar to the problems that sometimes arose in gathering moneys promised in an ἐπίδοσις.

---

[30] See Esler 2021, 14–20 and *passim*.
[31] See Esler 2021, 227–68, on 2 Cor 8–9, and 235–38, for the principal evidence for their unity.

Not only does Paul not use the word λογεία in 2 Corinthians 8–9 but, to a quite remarkable extent, he adopts an argument that refutes the idea that his collection was a λογεία at every point. He opens by invoking the Macedonians as a model, who gave of their own free will (αὐθαίρετοι: 8:3), begging Paul for the privilege of taking part (8:4). In other words, their action was voluntary; he did not compel them. Now he is sending Titus to the Corinthians, so "they might abound" in this work of grace, with the verb περισσεύητε in a (gentle) subjunctive, not a (coercive) imperative voice. If this were not enough, he now insists that he says this not as a "command" (ἐπιταγή) but just to test their love (8:8). Yet in 1 Cor 16:1 he had indeed commanded them to participate, although there using the verb διατάσσειν. Soon after, in 8:10, Paul reinforces this point—he is offering "advice" (γνώμη), meaning, by necessary implication, not a command. Perhaps most astonishing in this regard, after his blunt imperative in 1 Cor 16:2 ("let each of you lay aside"; ἕκαστος ὑμῶν . . . τιθέτω), is what Paul says in 9:7: "Each (should do) just as he chooses (καθὼς προῄρηται) in his heart, not out of grief or compulsion (ἐξ' ἀνάγκης)." It is worth noting that the word προαιρέομαι, which Paul selects here, appears in an ἐπίδοσις inscription of a voluntary association in relation to those who freely choose to make a contribution.[32] This voluntary nature of Paul's collection as described in 2 Corinthians 8–9 thus brings it closer to an ἐπίδοσις than a λογεία. Yet the complete absence of any indication in 2 Corinthians 8–9 that the Corinthians stood to earn individual honor for themselves by contributing still remains as a feature strongly differentiating his collection from an ἐπίδοσις. It was probably to avoid the amounts individual members had collected each week becoming common knowledge in the group that Paul had instructed them to store up the money at home. The main reason Paul offers for the collections in 2 Corinthians 8–9 is group oriented in nature: it is the reciprocal benefit (largely material: Welborn 2013) that the Corinthians, as a group, will derive from it (8:12-15; 9:8-12).

Another striking sign of Paul's contradicting any notion of his collection being a λογεία is his rejection of its bringing him financial benefit. He takes pains to disassociate himself from the type of accusations of oppressiveness and extortion that we have noted above were a feature of λογεῖαι organized by individuals. The complete control he trumpeted in 1 Cor 16:1-4 has disappeared, since now a brother has been appointed by the assemblies to travel with Paul (2 Cor 8:19). This is precisely so that no one might blame Paul in

---

[32] See Migeotte 2013, 115–16, on an association of Thiasites from Callatis, on the Black Sea.

relation to the collection (8:20). He is even sending people on ahead so that this will not be "extortion" (πλεονεξία) but a "generous gift" (εὐλογία). Later in the letter he will deny that neither Titus nor himself engaged in extortion (ἐπλεονέκτησεν) when Paul sent him to Corinth the year before to begin the collection (2 Cor 12:18).

Finally, throughout 2 Corinthians 8–9 Paul takes great care to speak of the collection using expressions that align with the language of cooperation and ministry that characterize chapters 1–7 (Esler 2021). Thus, we find him using terms like κοινωνία (8:4; 9:13), διακονία/διακονεῖν (8:4, 19, 20; 9:1, 12, 13), ἁδρότης (8:20), εὐλογία (9:5 [2x]), and λειτουργία (9:12). These concepts, once more, sharply distinguish his project from a λογεία.

CONCLUSION

We are fortunate in knowing that Paul's efforts to complete the collection in Corinth were successful. In Romans 15, when he is writing from Corinth, he indicates that his work "in these regions" (v. 23) is complete and that he is going to Jerusalem "ministering (διακονῶν) to the saints" (v. 25) because "Macedonia and Achaia have been pleased to make a contribution (κοινωνίαν; not a λογεία, it should be noted) for the destitute among the saints in Jerusalem" (v. 26). Yet he makes no mention of any contribution from Galatia, which powerfully suggests that there had been none. Is the explanation for this that, whereas the Galatian assemblies had also reacted adversely to his ordering them to take part in a λογεία (as he states he had done in 1 Cor 16:1), unlike the case of the Corinthians, he had lacked an opportunity to set things right with them?

WORKS CITED

Arzt-Grabner, Peter. 2013. *2 Korinther.* With help from Ruth Elisabeth Kritzer. Papyrologische Kommentare zum Neuen Testament 4. Göttingen: Vandenhoeck & Ruprecht.

Bernand, André, ed. 1992. *La prose dur Pierre dans l'Égypte hellénistique et romaine.* 2 vols. Paris: Éditions du centre national de la recherche scientifique.

Bernand, Étienne. 1975–1981. *Recueil des inscriptions grecques du Fayoum.* 3 vols. Leiden: Brill.

Betz, Hans Dieter. 1985. *2 Corinthians 8 and 9: A Commentary on Two Administrative Letters of the Apostle Paul.* Edited by George MacRae. Hermeneia. Philadelphia: Fortress.

Blümel, Wolfgang. 1991. *Die Inschriften der rhodischen Peraia.* Bonn: Rudolf Habelt.

Bowman, A. K. 2011. "5097. Prefectoral Edict." Pages 197–200 in vol. 76 of *The Oxyrhynchus Papyri.* Edited by D. Colomo and J. Chapa. London: Egypt Exploration Society.

Chaniotis, Angelos. 2013. "Public Subscriptions and Loans as Social Capital in the Hellenistic City: Reciprocity, Performance, Commemoration." Pages 89–106 in *Epigraphical Approaches to the Post-classical Polis: Fourth Century BC to Second Century AD.* Edited by Paraskevi Martzavou and Nikolaos Paparzarkadas. Oxford Studies in Ancient Documents. Oxford: Oxford University Press.

Ciampa, Roy E., and Brian S. Rosner. 2010. *The First Letter to the Corinthians.* Pillar New Testament Commentary. Grand Rapids: Eerdmans.

Collins, Raymond F. 1999. *First Corinthians.* SP 7. Collegeville, Minn.: Liturgical Press.

Danker, Frederick William, ed. 2000. *A Greek-English Lexicon of the New Testament and Other Early Christian Literature.* 3rd ed. Chicago: University of Chicago Press.

Deissmann, Adolf. 1927. *Light from the Ancient East: The New Testament Illustrated by Recently Discovered Texts of the Graeco-Roman World.* Edited and translated by Lionel R. M. Strachan. London: Hodder & Stoughton.

Downs, David J. 2008. *The Offering of the Gentiles: Paul's Collection for Jerusalem in Its Chronological, Cultural, and Cultic Contexts.* WUNT 2/248. Tübingen: Mohr Siebeck.

Duverger, Maurice. 1964. *Introduction to the Social Sciences.* London: George Allen & Unwin.

Ellis-Evans, Aneurin. 2013. "The Ideology of Public Subscriptions." Pages 107–25 in Martzavou and Paparzarkadas, *Epigraphical Approaches to the Post-classical Polis.*

Esler, Philip F. 1987. *Community and Gospel in Luke-Acts: The Social and Political Motivations of Lucan Theology.* SNTSMS 57. Cambridge: Cambridge University Press.

———. 2021. *2 Corinthians: A Social Identity Commentary.* London: T&T Clark.

Fee, Gordon D. 1987. *The First Epistle to the Corinthians.* NICNT. Grand Rapids: Eerdmans.

Georgi, Dieter. 1992. *Remembering the Poor: The History of Paul's Collection for Jerusalem.* Nashville: Abingdon.

Kallet-Max, Robert Morstein. 1995. *Hegemony to Empire: The Development of the Roman Imperium in the East from 148 to 62 BC.* Berkeley: University of California Press.

Kern, Otto. (1900) 1967. *Die Inschriften von Magnesia am Maeander.* Berlin: W. Spemann.

Kittel, Gerhard. 1967. "λογεία." *TDNT* 4:282–83.

Kloppenborg, John S. 2019. *Christ's Associations: Connecting and Belonging in the Ancient City*. New Haven: Yale University Press.

Klotz, David. 2009. "Λογεία-Receipts and the Construction of Deir Shelwit." *ZPE* 168:252–56.

Kritzer, Ruth Elisabeth. 2006. "IKor 16,1." Pages 506–7 in *1 Korinther*. Edited by Peter Arzt-Grabner, Ruth Elisabeth Kritzer, Amfilochius Papathomas, and Franz Winter. Papyrologische Kommentare zum Neuen Testament 2. Göttingen: Vandenhoeck & Ruprecht.

Last, Richard, and Philip A. Harland. 2020. *Group Survival in the Ancient Mediterranean: Rethinking Material Conditions in the Landscape of Jews and Christians*. London: T&T Clark.

Llewelyn, Stephen D. 2001. "The Use of Sunday for Meetings of Believers in the New Testament." *NovT* 43:205–23.

Migeotte, Léopold. 2013. "Les soucriptions dans les associations privées." Pages 113–27 in *Groupes et associations dans les cités grecques (IIIe siècle av. J.-C.–IIe siècle ap. J.-C.). Actes de la table ronde de Paris, INHA, 19–20 juin 2009*. Edited by Pierre Fröhlich and Patrice Hamon. Hautes études du monde gréco-romain 49. Geneva: Droz.

Mitchell, Leo J. E. 2017. "Balancing the Books: The Economic Impact of *Collegia* in the Western Roman Empire." PhD diss., University of Manchester.

Petzl, Georg, ed. 1987. *Die Inschriften von Smyrna*. Part II, 1. Inschriften griechischer Städte aus Kleinasien 24.1. Bonn: Rudolf Habelt.

Robertson, Archibald, and Alfred Plummer. 1914. *A Critical and Exegetical Commentary on the First Epistle of St Paul to the Corinthians*. Rev. ed. ICC. Edinburgh: T&T Clark.

Sokolowski, Franciszek. 1958. "On the *Lex Sacra* of Physcus." *TAPA* 89:138–41.

———. 1962. *Lois sacrées des cités grecques*. École française d'Athènes. Travaux et mémoires 2. Paris: Éditions de Bocard.

Thiselton, Anthony C. 2000. *The First Epistle to the Corinthians: A Commentary on the Greek Text*. NIGTC. Grand Rapids: Eerdmans.

Turner, John C. 2005. "Explaining the Nature of Power: A Three-Process Theory." *European Journal of Social Psychology* 35:1–22.

Verbrugge, Verlyn D. 1992. *Paul's Style of Church Leadership Illustrated by His Instructions to the Corinthians on the Collection: To Command or Not to Command*. San Francisco: Edwin Mellen.

Welborn, L. L. 2013. "'That There May Be Equality': The Contexts and Consequences of a Pauline Ideal." *NTS* 59:73–90.

Wilcken, Ulrich. 1899. *Griechische Ostraka aus Aegypten und Nubien. Ein Beitrag zur antiken Wirtschaftsgeschichte*. Leipzig: Giesescke & Devrient.

Wilhelm, Adolf. 1898. "Die sogenannte Hetäreninschrift aus Paros." *Athenische Mitteilungen* 23:409–40.

20

The Benefaction-Reward Convention in Greco-Roman Private Associations and Paul's Jerusalem Collection

Jin Hwan Lee

The so-called Jerusalem collection (1 Cor 16:1-4; 2 Cor 8–9; cf. Rom 15:25-32) was a project that obviously connected the Pauline Christ groups to the Christ group in Jerusalem. Apart from that initiative, interactions between the two parties are rather blurry. The picture becomes even less clear if we leave out the account of Paul in Acts. What we hear from Paul's letters about the Jerusalem group is limited, and the data appear contradictory on the surface. In one place, Paul describes the Jerusalem group as a spiritual creditor (Rom 15:27) somewhat highlighting the indebted status of the Pauline Christ groups to the Jerusalem group; but in other places, his attitude toward its members is far from positive (2 Cor 11:4-5; 12:11; Gal 2:11-15; cf. Gal 1:7; 2:4; 4:21-31; 5:12; 6:12-13). Given the data we have, Paul's intention behind the Jerusalem collection project piques curiosity. Why did Paul commence the collection project even if he had an uneasy relationship with the Jerusalem group, and what brought him to do so eagerly—even putting himself in a life-threatening situation (cf. Rom 15:31)? Caution is always in order when trying to determine the unstated motivations of ancient (or, for that matter, modern) figures, but careful attention to cultural norms can move such inquiries from the realm of speculation to that of informed conjecture.

In the case of this essay, I will examine benefaction practices in associations in order to identify some crucial motivations for benefiting others and make a suggestion for Paul's purpose for sending the Jerusalem collection.

THE BENEFACTION-REWARD CONVENTION IN PRIVATE ASSO-CIATIONS

Greek εὐεργεσία or Roman *patrocinium* was a widespread social system deeply rooted in ancient cultures and societies. Such terms can generally be translated as "benefaction" (which will be used throughout this essay) and connote both material contributions (notably monetary support) as well as nonmaterial contributions, such as valuable services. For the interests of the present essay, however, the primary focus will be on monetary benefactions in associations.

Associations treated benefactions and benefactors quite seriously. Performing benefactions encouraged a group to be more active and united, while proper responses to benefactor(s) allowed a group to be in good standing. Associations managed their group with what I will call the "benefaction-reward convention." Some honorific inscriptions allow us to better understand this convention.

Benefactions, Nonpermanent Funding

An Attic inscription found in Piraeus, *IG* II² 1327 (= *GRA* I 35), honors a treasurer named Hermaios, the son of Hermogenes of Paionidai, because of his benevolent support of an association. Not only did he pay for the tomb of a deceased member when the group was short of common funds (κοινόν), but he also often paid for periodic sacrifices from his own monetary resources. Another inscription, *IG* II² 1343 (= *GRA* I 48), honors Diodoros, son of Socrates of Aphidnai, who served as the priest of Soteria in his group. He spent his own money—and not a little money, as heralded in the inscription—to hold a banquet for the entirety of the group's members. The inscription praises him as ἀφιλαργύρως, a man who does not love money. These two inscriptions well represent instances in which group members voluntarily make benefactions for their peers in associations. Similar benefactions in association data appear to be recurring, but it is difficult to tell if a permanent benefactor existed in a group (Kloppenborg 2016, 172–79).

Some associations mandated benefactions. Each association had its own governing group—priest, secretary, treasurer, and so on—that we call functionaries or offices. The collegium of Diana and Antinous in Lanuvium (*CIL*

14.2112; Bendlin 2011) enacted rules for newly selected functionaries (*magistri*) regarding communal meals. According to the membership list of the group, four *magistri* were likely appointed every year. These four functionaries were in charge of supplying the dinner with good wine, bread for all members, four sardines, table settings, and warm water. The group levied fines of thirty sesterces on whoever failed to do so and appointed the member who was going to serve as a *magister* in the next term to take over those duties. The member who was originally unable to carry out the functionary duties was nonetheless obligated to fulfill the duties once the appointed member's time of service was completed. In the same way, the association of *IPergamon* 374 (= *GRA* II 111) regulated similar duties for the keeper of order (*eukosmos*), the priest, and the secretary. These functionaries were required to supply funds, bread and wine, and table settings at several important festivals of their association.

It is worth noting, however, that these positions in both *CIL* 14.2112 and *IPergamon* 374 (= *GRA* II 111) were not permanently held. As it is clearly stated in *CIL* 14.2112, functionaries were rotated regularly according to the membership list. This allowed each member to serve as a functionary over time. Such an opportunity had nothing to do with one's social status; as long as a person was listed in the membership, each member could serve as a functionary and fulfill the benefaction duties belonging to the position. Many other associations selected functionaries by lot (*IG* II² 1368 = *GRA* I 51; *IG* II² 1369 = *GRA* I 49; *SEG* 31.122 = *GRA* I 50), but its practical premise was the same because service terms were only temporary. The opportunity to become a functionary was open to each member of a group, roles that most were barred from undertaking outside of associations (Kloppenborg 1996, 18).

A patron/a provided benefactions, often taking the form of *sportulae* ("gifts," "almsgiving") given to associations. *IDelos* 1520 begins by describing a dire financial situation faced by a certain group. The group had undertaken a building project for a temple (οἶκος), but the project was under threat as the common funds were running out. This association was in need of a patron to resume the project and expand the common funds. The inscription recognizes Marcus Minatius, son of Sextus, as the benefactor who resolved the financial issues of the association, enabling the group to resume the building project. He expanded the common funds by offering seven thousand drachmas voluntarily. Moreover, he invited the whole group to a sacrificial offering made on behalf of the group, at which every member enjoyed the banquet at his expense. Marcus Minatius even promised to offer more to the group. This should not be understood, however, as a case supporting the presence of ongoing benefactions since there was no way to guarantee future benefits. According to Marc Gygax, "Promises were not equivalent to contributions" because some individuals could not carry out their promises even if those promises were inscribed on steles (2016, 26). Even if the group could expect Marcus Minatius to supply another endowment for meals, they would not blindly believe that he would keep providing *sportulae* for them since, generally speaking, benefaction was a nonpermanent funding practice.

Rewards, Rivalry, and Recruitment Strategy

Performances of benefactions were closely related to honorary practices. The names of benefactors, together with their benefactions, were inscribed on steles and remembered thereafter (even now, centuries later!). Such a practice itself was to extol their services and support in an honorable fashion. It was critical to show proper response upon receiving benefactions. Benefactions, once provided, must be reciprocated with benefits in other forms. Several honorific inscriptions cited above (cf. *IG* II² 1327 = *GRA* I 35; *IG* II² 1343 = *GRA* I 48; *IDelos* 1520) list honors that the benefactors had received in return for their benefactions.

Upon receiving benefactions from Hermaios, his group (*IG* II² 1327 = *GRA* I 35) decided to set up his image with a plaque, put it in the temple, and crown it whenever the group gathered for its communal meetings. The group took care of all the expenses for the honors awarded to Hermaios. The group of *IG* II² 1343 (= *GRA* I 48) honored Diodoros by crowning him with an olive wreath once a year along with the proclamation of what the group had decided to award him for his benefactions. As patron to the group of *IDelos* 1520, Marcus Minatius enjoyed five rewards upon donating a large sum of *sportulae* for the temple and the group: (1) his statue was erected with an inscription of his name; (2) the group reserved a seat of honor for him whenever he attended a banquet; (3) the group commemorated him annually for his honor, for which he could bring two guests with him; (4) the group announced his honor whenever the group convened official periodic and annual banquet meetings; and (5) the group offered a bull on his behalf in the procession for Apollo. The benefactions that Marcus Minatius provided to this group were extraordinary, as the amount of endowment was large enough to hold more than several banquet meetings. In return, the honors he received from the group were also remarkable. The more a benefactor enhanced benefactions, the more the benefactor received honors. Interestingly, associations with limited financial resources nonetheless still spent a portion of their resources on rewarding those who provided financial aid.

Whenever we see benefactions recognized in inscriptions, we find honors awarded to the benefactor. The practice had reciprocal characteristics and, indeed, was widely attested in the Greco-Roman world. Broader social experience supports such a reciprocity quite straightforwardly. For example, *TAM* 2.910 (= *GRA* II 146) honors Herakelitos for his benefactions made to his homeland. As a known philosopher, as well as a priest of Asklepios and Hygeia, he not only dedicated his works but also donated fifteen thousand silver denarii to his homeland. In return, the city of Rhodia honored him by providing the foremost seats at civic events. In *IJO* 2.36 (= *GRA* II 106) and *IMiletos* 940a–h (= *GRA* II 135), we find similar honorific practices upon receiving benefactions. Generally speaking, therefore, benefactors *anticipated* rewards while practicing benefaction. In this regard, Gygax is correct in noting that "euergetism was not a phenomenon but an *institution*: a *polis*-sanctioned practice of exchanging benefactions and rewards" (2016, 3; emphasis added). And it is worth noting that the rewards were always visible, practical, and realistic, as described above.

Two functional aspects of this benefaction-reward convention are worth further attention: rivalry and recruitment. Practically speaking, associations *generated* them by utilizing the convention proactively for the purpose of bolstering group solidarity. Associations incited rivalry among members by exemplifying how associations treated their benefactors. For example, in *IG* II² 1327 (= *GRA* I 35), after announcing the group decision of rewarding honors to Hermaios for his benefactions, the inscription continues by describing why the group made such a decision: "so that there might be a rivalry (ὅπως ἂν οὖν ἐφάμιλλον εἶ) among the rest who wish to be honored, knowing that they will receive counterbalancing favor for benefiting the association of *orgeones*" (ll. 20–21; translation mine). Kloppenborg and Ascough note that the formula, ὅπως ἂν οὖν ἐφάμιλλον εἶ, was often found in Attic inscriptions from the fourth to the second centuries BCE (Kloppenborg and Ascough 2011, 134; cf. *IG* II² 1262 = *GRA* I 10; *IG* II² 1263 = *GRA* I 11; *IG* II² 1301 = *GRA* I 25; *IG* II² 1324 = *GRA* I 32). But this does not mean that later associations did not utilize the benefaction-reward convention for instigating rivalry among peers in associations. Even if the exact formula disappears in later inscriptions, it seemed likely that associations kept making use of the convention in the same way. We continuously find associations praising benefactors as "zealous (ones)" (φιλοτιμία; σπουδή; ζηλωτής) towards their groups (cf. *OGIS* 326 = *GRA* II 141, second century BCE; *IG* II² 1343 = *GRA* I 48, first century BCE; *IProse* 1.49 = *GRA* III 170, 5 BCE; *IKallatis* 44, 12–15 CE; *IAnkyraM* 141, 128/129 CE). The Iobakchoi

(164/165 CE) pushed members to be zealous in bestowing benefactions, and another second-century inscription, *IG* II² 1369 (= *GRA* I 49), called for members' zealousness in wishing for the prosperity of the group based on their benefactions.

It is worth noting that the rivalry generated from the benefaction-reward convention was a *positive* mode of competition directing the group toward unity. It was not meant to produce segregation between winners and losers. Such an adverse effect of competition could have been alleviated in associations through windows of opportunities to show "zealousness" because rewards were guaranteed upon granting benefactions: *every* "benefactor will receive counterbalancing favor" (τῶν εὐεργετημάτων χάριτας ἀξίας κομιοῦνται; *IG* II² 1301 = *GRA* I 25; translation mine). *IG* II² 1262 (= *GRA* I 10) also guaranteed to "return counterbalancing favor to those who are zealous toward benefactions" (τὸ κοινὸν τοῖς φιλοτιμουμένοις εἰς αὐτοὺς ἀξίας χάριτας ἀποδίδωσιν τῶν εὐεργετημάτων; translation mine).

One of the rewards that associations provided to their benefactors was inscribing their names and benefactions on a stele. As revealed in *IG* II² 1327 (= *GRA* I 35), such steles were placed in front of a sanctuary so that anyone in the public could learn about a benefactor, benefactions he or she had made, and how the group treated them in turn. All such practices derived from the benefaction-reward convention eventually functioned as advertisements for the associations; in other words, the convention itself had the *potential merit* to attract people. And associations made the best use of the merit for their recruitment strategy by producing honorific inscriptions and other inscriptions that had to do with community regulations (cf. *IG* II² 1368 = *GRA* I 48; *IG* VII 2808; Kloppenborg and Ascough 2011, 12; Lee 2018, 72–75). In this way, associations could expand their membership size and enhance their social reputation. By praising a patron/a's honor and listing the favors bestowed in return, as in *IDelos* 1520, associations could increase the possibility of finding external patrons for them as well.

In summary, the practice of benefactions in associations was widespread and, indeed, a key social practice. People naturally expected rewards when performing benefactions since the practice itself was a convention deeply rooted in Greco-Roman societies. Associations enhanced group solidarity with the benefaction-reward convention. The convention fostered a positive form of rivalry in that members could proactively compete with each other with zeal in supporting their group. The convention could be further utilized as an effective recruitment strategy for expanding both regular fee-paying members as well as external patrons. With this in mind, let us turn back to Paul's Jerusalem collection project.

THE JERUSALEM COLLECTION AS A BENEFACTION

The Jerusalem collection (1 Cor 16:1-4; 2 Cor 8-9; cf. Rom 15:25-32) was Paul's voluntary project carried out with Macedonian and Achaian Christ groups. In 2 Cor 8:2, Paul praises the final result of the Macedonian groups' collection, which was generous and flowing with joy even despite their severe poverty and trials. Paul emphasized their voluntary and self-motivated handling of the collection (v. 3). Such voluntary gift giving towards city institutions, festivals, groups, or even individuals was generally regarded as an act of benefaction. Certain scholars identify ἐπίδοσεις ("subscriptions") as similar in form to the Jerusalem collection project (Verbrugge 1992, 95; Kloppenborg 2019, 248–64). According to Gygax, "voluntarism was the core" of ἐπίδοσεις (2016, 204). It is no doubt that, through the lens of Greco-Roman societies, the Jerusalem collection was seen as a benefaction.

Downs rightly observes that the Jerusalem collection was a onetime project (2008, 25), lending credence to it having been a benefaction. Even if we count the Lukan narrative of Paul's earlier collection carried out with Barnabas and the Antioch group (Acts 11:27-30; 12:25),[1] each collection project would still be considered nonrecurring because each initiative was based on Paul's voluntary decision. Paul's claim in Gal 2:10, ἐσπούδασα αὐτὸ τοῦτο ποιῆσαι ("I was zealous to do the same thing"; translations in this chapter are by the author unless otherwise noted), rhetorically supports the case straightforwardly. In fact, many scholars now dispute that the pronouncement in Gal 2:10 is directly related to the Jerusalem collection (e.g., Martyn 1997, 227; Wedderburn 2002, 103; cf. Becker 1989, 24; Downs 2006, 61). Moreover, Longenecker elaborates that "the poor" in Gal 2:10 refers to the indigenous poor without any geographical restriction, arguing the Jerusalem collection has no direct correlation with Gal 2:10 (2010, 157–206). At any rate, the Jerusalem collection was a separate collection project from any earlier financial relief ministry Paul may have undertaken. If Paul undertook two collections, they were not two initiatives of a larger single benefaction project, such as in the way Nickle considers the collection as a Christian version of the Jewish annual temple tax for Jerusalem (Nickle 2009, 74–99). A time gap of about a decade

---

[1] Cf. Knox 1950. Longenecker sees the Lukan accounts as rhetorical narratives rather than historical (2005, 241–52; 2010, 193).

between the collection from Antioch (mid-40s)—if it ever happened—and the Jerusalem collection (53–57 CE; see Longenecker 2010, 338–44) makes the point clearly. Some associations certainly mandated benefactions as duties of functionaries (*CIL* 14.2112; *IPergamon* 374 = *GRA* II 111); but as we have seen, such duties were never expected to be permanently ongoing. Accordingly, the Jerusalem group would not have viewed Paul's collection as something ongoing; they would never have imagined that one collection effort would necessarily have been followed by another, since that was not how benefaction worked within associations.

Assuming the Pauline collection for the Jerusalem group was an act of benefaction, then, we also need to consider the psychological dimension of performing this benefaction. That is, Paul was expecting counterbalancing rewards while preparing and sending off the collection to the Jerusalem group. In 2 Cor 8–9, Paul discusses rationales for the collection. On the one hand, he talks about Christ as the benefactor who became poor by emptying himself in order to make Christ followers rich (8:9-10; cf. 9:9-10). Hence, the collection is the appropriate response for the benefaction they received. On the other hand, however, Paul notes the collection as a benefaction but says that God will provide rewards for it (9:7-8, 11-14). God/Christ plays an important role in Paul's rationale for the collection anyway (9:15). This leads scholars to view the collection mainly as a Jewish almsgiving practice, which placed the onus on giving rather than receiving from the counterpart (Horrell 1995, 76–79; cf. Longenecker 2010, 135–56). However, Paul's Hellenistic heritage, his vocational calling to travel to the Roman West, as well as his immediate social context of pastoral work, where he had to interact predominantly with non-Jews, are worth further consideration. It has long been suggested that Paul's other rationale for the collection, ἰσότης ("equality"; 2 Cor 8:13-15), was from the Greek world, not from the Jewish (cf. Welborn 2013, 73–74). We should not overlook how the collection would be seen by such Christ-group members. For them, the collection would have little to do with a Jewish practice of almsgiving but more likely would seem like a benefaction, as Welborn rightly notes (2013, 78; cf. Joubert 1999, 85–89). And by their social and cultural governance of the so-called benefaction-reward convention, they would surely expect counterbalancing favors for the collection they provided. What Paul wrote in 2 Cor 9:6 would serve as a promise for them as well as Paul: "The one who sows sparingly will also reap sparingly, and the one who sows bountifully will also reap bountifully" (NRSV).

THE PURPOSE OF THE JERUSALEM COLLECTION

Scholars have suggested several purposes for the collection, which can roughly be summarized into the following: (1) charity, (2) seeking for unity among all Christ groups, (3) attempting to get approval of Paul's gospel, (4) fulfilling salvation history, and (5) repaying debts. These purposes are not mutually exclusive; nonetheless, scholarly views vary regarding the fundamental purpose of the collection. Among these five suggestions, the last two seem least probable. Problems with reading the collection project as eschatological events fulfilling salvation history have been well documented in several works (Verbrugge 1992, 323–27; Downs 2008, 3–9; Verbrugge and Krell 2015, 135–38). The fifth reading is based on the misleading argument that the Jerusalem collection was a continuation of the agreement between the Jerusalem group and Paul alluded to in Gal 2:10. This reading has often been suggested with the view that the Jerusalem collection was obligatory (Nickle 2009, 90–93; Joubert 2000, 6–8; cf. Rom 15:27; 2 Cor 9:14). But as we have discussed earlier, the collection was Paul's voluntary, onetime project. Most scholars prefer the first three suggestions—charity, unity, and approval of Paul's gospel—and these three are mutually related to some degree.

One obvious and nominal purpose for the Jerusalem collection was to provide financial support for the Jerusalem group. Paul describes the collection as a service (2 Cor 9:1; Rom 15:25) for "the relief of the saints" (2 Cor 8:4; 1 Cor 16:1). In Rom 15:26, he elaborates that the collection was specifically prepared for the poorer members in the group. By looking at the designation of the recipient, several scholars have noted that charity was the fundamental purpose of the collection (Horrell 1995, 76; Downs 2008, 20; Kloppenborg 2019, 248; cf. Longenecker 2010, 157–82). Its underlying expectation was to seek for unity among all Christ groups by promoting a state of fairness (Cullmann 1958; Talbert 1989, 365–69; Wedderburn 2002, 108). Longenecker puts it in this way: "Paul hoped that the collection would unleash unifying forces among different streams of the early Jesus-movements" (2010, 313). Paul explains in 2 Cor 8:14 that the collection aims for economic balancing (ἰσότης) between abundant groups and needy groups. Pauline groups were more economically wealthy than the Jerusalem group, so through the generosity of sharing their resources they could supply the needs of the group as well as generate much thanksgiving to God (2 Cor 9:12). Paul seemed to believe such equal balancing was God's way of unifying his people since he made use of the collection (κοινωνίας) as a test case for whether the Corinthian group indeed obeyed the gospel of Christ (2 Cor 9:13: "through your approval of this service, *you* glorify God upon obedience of *your* confession for the gospel of God and upon generosity of sharing for them and for all others"; translation and emphasis mine).

However, these goals for the collection do not sufficiently explain certain situations that biblical texts illuminate. According to the book of Acts, Paul himself was driven to travel to Jerusalem—setting aside the motivation of the Holy Spirit for now—even despite possibly being aware of the perilous situation to come in Jerusalem (Acts 21:4-14). And his visiting Jerusalem seems to be more or less related to traveling to Rome, as the author of Acts previews it in 19:21 and 23:11 and finally reviews it at the end of the book. While one should take precautions when assessing Pauline accounts in Acts, Rom 15:30-32 verifies the situation quite well. The only difference is about the collection, which the author of Acts completely omitted in his account of Paul (cf. Downs 2006, 62–68). When writing his travel plan to Jerusalem in Romans, Paul seemed to predict a dangerous situation ahead as he asked for prayer for his safety in Judea (15:31). A question arises, at this point, regarding why he had to travel to Jerusalem, even risking his life—he used ῥύομαι, a strong word that can connote "rescuing" from a life-threatening situation (cf. Matt 27:43). Moreover, Paul further asked for prayer for the joyful reception of the collection by the Jerusalem group (Rom 15:30-31). Scholars tend to read v. 31 as Paul's concern for the rejection of the collection, and indeed, suggest that the Jerusalem group refused to take it (Wedderburn 2002, 110; Achtemeier 1987, 46; Downs 2008, 18). The situation becomes much more complicated as it is revealed that Paul did not hesitate to risk his life for the collection delivery even when recognizing a higher chance of its refusal. Was it simply for the safe delivery of the collection (1 Cor 16:4; 2 Cor 8:19-21)? It appears unlikely that the sole purpose of the collection was just for relieving the distress of the poorer members in the Jerusalem group and to achieve fair balancing among all Christ groups.

What had the collection meant to Paul, then? Or, to put it differently, which *rewards* were being sought by Paul upon the reception of the collection? This is where we find the most controversial yet irrefutable scholarly speculations on Paul's *hidden* intention underlying the collection project. That is, the collection was to get approval of Paul's gospel, which included demonstrating his apostolic efforts and their results. Scholars note that the collection was to make the Jerusalem leaders stop looking down on the Pauline group (Watson 1986, 175). The collection was to showcase that non-Jewish Christ followers, as the people of God, could also perform generosity in sharing (Longenecker 2010, 314). The collection had the vindicating purpose of Paul's law-free gospel for non-Jewish people finding legitimacy within Judaism (Wire 2000). Or, said even more strongly, the collection was to purchase the rights of non-Jewish Christ followers to share the privileges entitled to the people (Jewish) of God, which G. Lüdemann describes as "a polite bribe" (Orlando 2014, 60–61; cf. Hurtado 1979, 51).

Based on the benefaction-reward convention practices in associations, however, I want to draw attention to the driving force Paul had in mind. Rather than desperately desiring the approval of his gospel or his apostolic efforts, the force would have been his *zeal* (σπουδή; ζηλωτὴς; ζῆλος) for fostering unity and solidarity among people of God. He realized that God is one and for both Jews and non-Jews (Rom 3:29-30; 10:12; Gal 3:28). His apostolic missions and efforts were accordingly set forth to encourage a state of oneness among Christ followers. Jews, including some of the Jerusalem Christ-group members, may have considered Paul as an apostate (cf. 2 Cor 11:24; Gal 1:7; 2:4; cf. Acts 21:21), but Paul was not. Even when identifying himself as an apostle called to minister to non-Jewish people (Rom 11:3; Gal 1:15-16), he believed himself to be a Jewish compatriot (2 Cor 11:22; Rom 11:1; Gal 2:15) from Pharisaic heritage (Phil 3:5) striving for his religion, Judaism (Rom 9:1-5; Gal 1:14), yearning for the restoration of *all* Israel in Christ (Rom 11:25-27; cf. Rom 3:29; 1 Cor 12:12-13). Paul himself emphasized zeal (σπουδή) as a leader's virtue (Rom 12:8), exhorting his audience not to lag in zeal for serving the Lord (Rom 12:11). Most of all, in Gal 2:10 he expressed that the collection for the poor was out of zeal (ἐσπούδασα; note that it shares the same lexeme of σπουδή).

His zeal is well expressed in the rivalry with other apostles and leaders. As we have seen in association data, rivalry and zealousness were the same mechanism that fostered acts of benefaction. Paul was in rivalry with Apollos (1 Cor 1:12; 3:1–4:6), Cephas (1 Cor 1:12; 9:5; Gal 2:7-8, 11-14), and other apostles including those he called super-apostles (2 Cor 11:5; 12:11; cf. Gal 2:6, 9). When Paul felt he was losing his ground in the Christ group in Corinth against other leaders, he used a fatherly image to elaborate on his authority over any other leaders (1 Cor 4:15). His technique of employing mimesis rhetoric represents that he was engaged in a power struggle with others (1 Cor 4:16; Castelli 1991, 98–111). Against accusations regarding his apostleship and alleged status compared to other apostles, Paul forcefully claims that he is not inferior to any other apostles (2 Cor 11:5; 12:11), but equal, seeing no difference between himself and them (Gal 2:6). The most prominent passage that presents Paul as being in a rivalry is 1 Cor 9:24-27.

Here, he utilizes an image of athletes who exercise self-control running for the prize. Although he diverges from the athletes regarding the nature of the prize he is striving for—one that is imperishable—his metaphorical language makes it clear that he was zealously engaged in rivalry.

It is worth pointing out that rivalry, when generated from the benefaction-reward convention, functioned positively in associations. It was not meant to filter out winners from losers. Rather, rivalry was a key social practice used to achieve a better state of unity. Some English Bibles translate both ἔρις (Phil 1:15) and ἐριθεία (Gal 5:20) as "rivalry," dismissing its positive connotation. But the two Greek nouns are better to be translated into "strife" or "contentious disposition." In association data, rivalry seems more comparable to how Paul describes his way of preaching the gospel (Phil 1:15-16): "Some proclaim Christ from envy and contentious disposition, but others from *goodwill* (εὐδοκία). The latter do it *out of love*, knowing that *I am put here* for the defence of the gospel." Or similarly, the zealousness (σπουδαῖος) of Titus (2 Cor 8:16-17) and the eagerness (προθυμία) and zeal (ζῆλος) that the Corinthian group had shown (2 Cor 9:2) might be comparable to the sense of φιλοτιμία, σπουδή, and ζηλωτής expressed in associations, which promoted rivalry. Even if Paul at times used harsh language against other competitors, including alleged anti-Semitic language (1 Thess 2:14-16, if not interpolated), the Jerusalem collection itself signals that he was zealously seeking for unity among Christ followers. Paul's use of κοινωνία for denoting the collection (Rom 15:26; 2 Cor 8:4; 9:13) implies, among other things, his zealousness in seeking for unity and solidarity, as correctly observed by Ogereau (2012, 366–73). Κοινός, the lexeme of κοινωνία, connotes partnership; when applied to a person, it denotes "partner," but otherwise it means "common." Certain associations used κοινόν as their self-title (cf. *IDelos* 1520), emphasizing close relationships among members. Hence, by using κοινωνία, Paul draws attention to the partnership among Christ followers as well as oneness of all the Christ groups. It is worth noting that κοινόν was a technical term denoting "common funds" in various associations (cf. *IG* II² 1343 = *GRA* I 48; *PMich* 5.245 = *GRA* III 219; *IG* II² 1368 = *GRA* I 51). Many associations often utilized their common funds for aiding members in difficult situations (*IPergamon* 374 = *GRA* II 111; *IG* II² 1323 = *GRA* I 31). Such practices enhanced a sense of belonging in associations, which could build up trust between members and, eventually, unity and solidarity.

CONCLUSION

Given the considerations above, I think the rewards that Paul would have expected upon the reception of the collection had little to do with approval of his gospel and apostolic effort. His strong conviction on his equal standing with the Jerusalem leaders in terms of apostleship and gospel, as well as his zeal for bolstering unity among Christ groups expressed in rivalry, simply indicate that he had little reason to be under the control of the Jerusalem leaders. Moreover, rewards bestowed in return for benefactions were often visible, practical, and realistic. Rewards were meant to be known in public, validated in present life, and given in a nonabstract form, such as crowning, reclining at a seat of honor, enjoying more and better food, and so forth. Rewards such as the approval of one's gospel or the fulfillment of salvation history are abstract, lacking historical support.

While Paul did not say anything clear about the rewards he was looking for upon successful delivery of the Jerusalem collection, his prayer request in Rom 15:30-32 seems worth further attention. The request (v. 30) is modified by two subordinating clauses using ἵνα in v. 31 and v. 32, where we find the content of his prayer request. The first subordinating clause is about his concern for safety and successful delivery of the collection to the Jerusalem group. The second one is about Paul's wish to travel to Rome with joy. Interpretation issues may apply since the second ἵνα clause (v. 32) can modify either v. 30, Paul's prayer request, or v. 31, Paul's wishing for successful reception of the collection by the Jerusalem group. If we take the latter option, then v. 32 can be read as revealing a specific reward Paul was looking for upon reception of the collection: "Join me in prayer . . . so that (ἵνα) . . . my service to Jerusalem *may be acceptable to the saints* so that (ἵνα) *I may come to you with joy by the will of God.*" Here, the result of a favorable reception of the collection seems to be linked to Paul's fate of traveling to Rome. In other words, upon his benefaction made to the Jerusalem group, Paul seemed to look forward to a reward of honor—that is, missional support, including but not limited to a dispatch to Rome by the Jerusalem group. This interpretation is further supported by the fact that (1) associations spent their common funds for their benefactor(s) even if they were short of the funds, and (2) the author of Acts presents Paul's Jerusalem visit as his necessary travel route to Rome.

This reading has two merits: one is that the alleged reward is not abstract but concrete; the other is that it can provide a response to a question regarding why Paul had to risk his life to deliver the collection to Jerusalem while realizing a higher chance of refusal. We hear from Paul that he was in need of support from the Roman Christ group for his travel plans to Spain (Rom 15:23). When he noticed that conflicts regarding his gospel were underway between Jews and non-Jews within that group, however, he had to do his best to ease the situation. One of the ways to solve the issue was to write an apologetic letter to the Roman group, which is the Letter to the Romans we now have. Another way would have been, as most scholars think, to show-case that he and the Jewish Christ followers in Jerusalem were in good part-nership (Wedderburn 2002, 99; Ogereau 2012, 371). The collection project eventually would have been an efficient way to serve his needs; yet not as for approval of his gospel, but for the ways in which he could recruit Jewish members and promote unity and solidarity among Christ followers in the Roman Christ group. It is worth recalling at this point that the benefaction-reward convention in associations had as one of its functional effects not only rivalry but also a recruitment strategy. Neighbors, passersby, or any nonmember were able to see and learn how a group properly rewarded its benefactors, which could eventually attract those people to become a member of the group. The Jerusalem collection project, in this regard, could have been part of Paul's recruitment strategy for his missional work in Rome, but would be viable only if the Jerusalem group accepted the collection.

WORKS CITED

Achtemeier, Paul J. 1987. *The Quest for Unity in the New Testament Church: A Study in Paul and Acts*. Philadelphia: Fortress.

Becker, Jürgen. 1989. *Paulus. Der Apostel der Völker*. Tübingen: Mohr Siebeck.

Bendlin, Andreas. 2011. "Associations, Funerals, Sociality, and Roman Law: The Collegium of Diana and Antinous in Lanuvium (CIL 14.2112) Recon-sidered." Pages 207–96 in *Aposteldekret und antikes Vereinswesen. Gemein-schaft und ihre Ordnung*. Edited by Markus Öhler. WUNT 280. Tübingen: Mohr Siebeck.

Castelli, Elizabeth A. 1991. *Imitating Paul: A Discourse of Power*. Louisville: Westminster John Knox.

Cullmann, Oscar. 1958. "The Early Church and the Ecumenical Problem." *AThR* 40:181–89, 294–301.

Downs, David J. 2006. "Paul's Collection and the Book of Acts Revisited." *NTS* 52:50–70.

———. 2008. *The Offering of the Gentiles: Paul's Collection for Jerusalem in Its Chronological, Cultural, and Cultic Contexts*. WUNT 2/248. Tübingen: Mohr Siebeck.

Gygax, Marc Domingo. 2016. *Benefaction and Rewards in the Ancient Greek City: The Origins of Euergetism*. Cambridge: Cambridge University Press.

Harland, Philip A., ed. 2014. *North Coast of the Black Sea, Asia Minor*. BZNW 204. Vol. 2 of *Greco-Roman Associations: Texts, Translations, and Commentary*. Edited by John S. Kloppenborg and Richard S. Ascough. Berlin: De Gruyter.

Horrell, David. 1995. "Paul's Collection: Resources for a Materialist Theology." *EpworthRev* 22:74–83.

Hurtado, Larry W. 1979. "Jerusalem Collection and the Book of Galatians." *JSNT* 5:46–62.

Joubert, Stephan. 1999. "Religious Reciprocity in 2 Corinthians 9:6–15: Generosity and Gratitude as Legitimate Responses to the Χάρις Τοῦ Θεοῦ." *Neot* 33:79–90.

———. 2000. *Paul as Benefactor*. WUNT 2/124. Tübingen: Mohr Siebeck.

Kloppenborg, John S. 1996. "Collegia and *Thiasoi*: Issues in Function, Taxonomy and Membership." Pages 16–30 in *Voluntary Associations in the Graeco-Roman World*. Edited by John S. Kloppenborg and Stephen G. Wilson. London: Routledge.

———. 2016. "Precedence at the Communal Meal in Corinth." *NovT* 58:167–203.

———. 2019. *Christ's Associations: Connecting and Belonging in the Ancient City*. New Haven: Yale University Press.

———, ed. 2020. *Ptolemaic and Early Roman Egypt*. BZNW 246. Vol. 3 of Kloppenborg and Ascough, *Greco-Roman Associations*.

Kloppenborg, John S., and Richard S. Ascough, eds. 2011. *Attica, Central Greece, Macedonia, Thrace*. BZNW 181. Vol. 1 of Kloppenborg and Ascough, *Greco-Roman Associations*.

Knox, John. 1950. *Chapters in a Life of Paul*. New York: Abingdon.

Lee, Jin Hwan. 2018. *The Lord's Supper in Corinth in the Context of Greco-Roman Private Associations*. Lanham, Md.: Lexington Books / Fortress Academic.

Longenecker, Bruce W. 2005. *Rhetoric at the Boundaries: The Art and Theology of New Testament Chain-Link Translations*. Waco, Tex.: Baylor University Press.

———. 2010. *Remember the Poor: Paul, Poverty, and the Greco-Roman World*. Grand Rapids: Eerdmans.

Martyn, J. Louis. 1997. *Galatians: A New Translation with Introduction and Commentary*. Illustrated ed. New York: Doubleday.

Nickle, Keith F. 2009. *The Collection: A Study in Paul's Strategy*. Eugene, Ore.: Wipf and Stock.

Ogereau, Julien M. 2012. "The Jerusalem Collection as Κοινωνία: Paul's Global Politics of Socio-economic Equality and Solidarity." *NTS* 58:360–78.

Orlando, Robert. 2014. *Apostle Paul: A Polite Bribe*. Eugene, Ore.: Cascade Books.

Talbert, Charles H. 1989. "Money Management in Early Mediterranean Christianity: 2 Corinthians 8–9." *RevExp* 86:359–70.

Verbrugge, Verlyn D. 1992. *Paul's Style of Church Leadership Illustrated by His Instructions to the Corinthians on the Collection: To Command or Not to Command*. San Francisco: Edwin Mellen.

Verbrugge, Verlyn D., and Keith R. Krell. 2015. *Paul & Money: A Biblical and Theological Analysis of the Apostle's Teachings and Practices*. Grand Rapids: Zondervan.

Watson, Francis. 1986. *Paul, Judaism, and the Gentiles: A Sociological Approach*. Cambridge: Cambridge University Press.

Wedderburn, A. J. M. 2002. "Paul's Collection: Chronology and History." *NTS* 48:95–110.

Welborn, L. L. 2013. "'That There May Be Equality': The Contexts and Consequences of a Pauline Ideal." *NTS* 59:73–90.

Wire, Antoinette C. 2000. "Response: Paul and Those outside Power." Pages 224–26 in *Paul and Politics: Ekklesia, Israel, Imperium, Interpretation; Essays in Honor of Krister Stendahl*. Edited by Richard A. Horsley. Harrisburg, Pa.: Trinity Press International.

21

Reading Hebrews in a Roman *Vicus* with Voluntary Associations

Jason A. Whitlark

The community addressed in the Letter to the Hebrews could have been perceived by its neighbors as a type of cultic association.[1] The group certainly made central the honor bestowed on Jesus Christ as a deified hero who conquered the death-dealing devil and now sits at God's right hand. Jesus is even the group's great high priest of a heavenly cult that bestows God's benefits upon his faithful. The group also worshipped the God of Abraham who created the cosmos and raised Jesus from the dead. There are, of course, numerous examples of cultic groups gathered around a divinized hero or a god. There were cultic groups devoted to Herakles, the Dioscuri, Silvanus, deified Roman emperors, and Dionysius, as well as Zeus, Hestia, and Diana.[2] The

---

[1]   By way of comparison, Lucian describes Peregrinus as a θιασιάρχης of a Christian group (*Peregr.* 11). Origen reports Celsus' indictment that Christians formed secret associations (*Cels.* 1.1; 8.17). Tertullian contrasts Christian dining practices with cult associations of Herakles, Dionysius, Attic mysteries, and Serapis (*Apol.* 38–39).

[2]   For groups devoted to Herakles, see Ascough, Harland, and Kloppenborg 2012, nos. 3, 223, 262, 303, 320, 325; to the Dioscuri, see no. 252; to Silvanus, see no. 308; to deified Roman emperors, see nos. 281, 216, B9, B10, B12, B20; to Dionysus, see nos. 21, 212; to Zeus, Hestia, and Diana, see nos. 121, 331. In this essay, all translations follow Ascough, Harland, and Kloppenborg 2012. Greek and Latin texts of all source material, unless otherwise specified, were consulted in https://philipharland.com/greco-roman-associations/ together with Kloppenborg and Ascough 2011 (*GRA* I) or Harland 2014 (*GRA* II).

author of Hebrews may even entice us in this direction when he draws upon common association language to characterize the community's gatherings: ἐπισυναγωγή (Heb 10:25).[3]

One approach to an examination of Hebrews and voluntary associations would be to adopt a type of heuristic application of parallels. These parallels would then illuminate social dynamics and community practices within the Christ group addressed by Hebrews (e.g., Yuh 2019). This essay, instead, will be a historically imaginative thick description of social dynamics that possibly existed between Christ followers who live under the demands both of the Letter to the Hebrews and of Greco-Roman associations.

To this end, we will first look at Greco-Roman associations and highlight three typical characteristics of associations—namely, cultic elements and honors, Roman imperial expressions of allegiance, and surveillance and discipline of their members. Second, Greco-Roman associations often met in neighborhoods and from there drew their membership. We will specifically consider *vici* (neighborhoods) in Rome after the Augustan reforms in 7 BCE. The reason for this is that this essay works with the assumptions that the community addressed in Hebrews is made up of converted pagans who lived and gathered in one of the Roman neighborhoods in the latter half of the first century, likely post-70 CE (Whitlark 2014, 4–16). Finally, we will consider what may have proved problematic to these Christ followers, who heard the Christ-exalting, deliberative focus of Hebrews and are living in one of these neighborhoods with its resident associations. Moreover, we will consider what recourse these neighborhoods with their associations might take towards a dissident group in their midst that would explain the type of encounters with suffering which are described in Hebrews. For convenience of citation, my epigraphic selection derives from Ascough, Harland, and Kloppenborg 2012, with all enumerated data (i.e., no. 84) referring to that collection unless otherwise specified.

GRECO-ROMAN ASSOCIATIONS

Three common aspects of Greco-Roman associations could prove problematic for Christ followers. (1) Cultic honors given to the gods are not

---

[3]   Kloppenborg 2019, nos. 20, 28. Cf. Ascough, Harland, and Kloppenborg 2012, nos. 39, 45, 49, 54 (ἀρχισυνάγωγος); nos. 84, 85, 87, 90, 91, 280, 281 (συναγωγός); nos. 63, 238, 243, 287, 295 (συναγωγή). None of these examples are Jewish ethnic associations. Some of the most interesting inscriptions are no. 95 (*GRA* II 99)—synagogue of Zeus; no. 229—the goddess gathers (συνήγαγε) an association of Syrians; no. 280—synagogue of a synod of principal followers of Emperor Augustus Caesar.

only characteristic of cultic groups but are ubiquitously present in occupational guilds, ethnic societies, household groups, and neighborhood associations. (2) With the rise of the Augustan Principate and afterwards, expressions of Roman imperial allegiance are frequently found among the various Greco-Roman associations. (3) Associations surveil and discipline delinquent members.

Ubiquitous Cultic Elements and Honors

The first aspect to take up is the cultic elements and honors observed by associations. It goes without saying that cultic groups engaged in cultic honors toward their patron deities. Occupational guilds, as well, participated in cultic honors to deities (Harland 2013, 50–60). Meeting spaces were commonly devoted to worship (Tran 2020, 214, 217). For instance, a society of shippers dedicated images and built a temple to Poseidon (no. 84).[4] An association of Berytian Poseidoniasts that was constituted of shippers, merchants, and warehouse workers sponsored festivities in honor of Poseidon (no. 224). Another group of shipowners supported the shrine of Zeus Xenios (no. 5). A group of Tyrian merchants and shippers, who gathered around Herakles, and oil merchants dedicated a statue and temple to the hero (nos. 223, 234). An association of craftsmen in Amphipolis crowned priests of Athena (no. 33).[5] One society's treasurer in a second-century BCE Greek association gave funds for sacrifices (no. 2). Moreover, communal meals of associations were typically ritualized and connected to cultic honors (Harland 2013, 62).

Additionally, workshops and households were keenly interested in the upkeep of public sacred places—an upkeep that could be coerced, as a matter of religious duty. An inscription from Magnesia is instructive:

> And it is good for owners of houses or for those who built workshops to provide according to [their] means for the decorations of the altars before the [temple] entrance, and for those who make inscription[s] for Artemis Leukophryene Nikephoros. And if someone should fail to accomplish [these things], it will not be good for him. (*Syll*[3] 695 [trans. Ascough 1996, 597])

Those households and workshops thus had a civic obligation to honor Artemis. The nonparticipation of any of these groups in funding of the temple upkeep was not neutral but incurred negative consequences.

---

[4] Cf. Ascough, Harland, and Kloppenborg 2012, B8, B17.
[5] Cf. no. 179.

Imperial Allegiances

The second aspect to consider is how associations related to Roman rule. With the growing power of Rome in the Mediterranean basin and the rise of the Augustan Principate in the latter part of the first century BCE, many associations found ways to signal their allegiance and support for Roman rule. Such signaling provided respectability to the association and a sense of closeness to power for its members (Tran 2020, 214–15, 221–22). Occupational guilds of Roman merchants, of textile workers, of couch workers, of linen workers, of fishermen and fish dealers, and of slave traders left various dedications (including altars, statues, buildings, and meeting places) to the Roman emperors (deified and alive) and to those who honored the emperors with festivals or Augustan days (the day of the emperor's birth or accession; Harland 2013, 134; nos. 32, 70, 143, 162, 210, 276; *TAM* 4.22; *TAM* 5.862). A synod of Alexandrian athletes in the Campanian town of Neapolis describe themselves as "emperor loving (φιλοσέβαστος)," "Roman loving (φιλορώμα[ιος])," and "pious (εὐσεβὴ[ς])" (no. 312). Ethnic groups as well inscribed honors to the Roman emperor (nos. 64, 71). Hymn singers of Asia Minor at Pergamon's imperial cult celebration honored the god Augustus (who is identified with Zeus Patroos) and Roma by singing hymns, accomplishing sacrifices, and leading festivals (no. 160).[6] A group of singers at Rome honored Zeus Helios, the great Sarapis, and the Augusti gods (no. 319). Various groups could also engage in joint projects to honor Rome and its emperor such as the dedication to Augustus and Roma by Milyadians, Roman businessmen, and Thracian settlers (no. 208).

Likewise, cultic groups also gave honors to the emperor and his family, often embedding the emperor with the group's cultic deity or deities. Some Ephesian Demetriasts had a priestess for Augusta Demeter Karpophoros and a priest of the new Dioskoroi (sons of Drusus). They also made images of these members of the imperial family for public display. There is a dedication found in Pompeii from a group of Phrygians that honored Phrygian Zeus on Augustan day (no. 316). In Ephesus, there were both physicians who sacrificed to Asklepios and the Augusti and a synod that was given funds to offer sacrifices to Roma and Artemis on the sacred city hearth (no. 165; *IEph* 859a). Indeed, there could be associations gathered around the emperor or the deified emperors such as the "association of the friends of the Augusti" in Pergamon, the "principal followers of emperor Augustus

---

[6] Cf. nos. 72, 117.

Caesar" in Alexandria, or the Augustales in Herculaneum (nos. 120, 280; *AE* 1979, 169; *CIL* 10.977, 1411–12).

What is important to note is that the observance of the imperial cult or other demonstrations of imperial loyalty in which associations might participate were regularly included in the honors given to deities among the pagan pantheons (Galinsky 2011, 4–8). When Pliny tests Christians in Bithynia, the emperor's image is placed among the images of the gods, both of whom must be honored (*Ep. Tra.* 10.96.4–6). Even the divine powers identified with the cult of Virtues become joined to "Augusta" in nomenclature to indicate that the benefits of these powers are experienced in the world through the rule of the Roman emperor (Fears 1981, 886–89). For example, wool workers in Pompeii dedicated a statue to Concordia Augusta because the divine benefits of Concordia were being realized through the Roman emperors' rule. By making dedications to Rome, its gods, and its emperors, associations signaled that they participated in a cosmic order set up for Rome and maintained by Rome (Harland 2013, 115–16, 137). These dedications were then not just mere signals of allegiance offered by associations but an acknowledgment of the place of the community and individual within the cosmic framework where the blessings of the gods are manifest in the rule of Rome and its emperor. Of course, on a more practical level, signaling loyalty to Rome and the cosmic order that established its rule could give groups access to resources, preferred locations, and legal assistance (Harland 2013, 130–32).

Surveillance and Discipline of Delinquent Members

The last aspect considered here typical of associations was the group's surveillance and discipline of delinquent members. Absenteeism from meetings and funerals and violating an association's rules could be sanctioned either by erasing the group member's name from an *album* or by leveeing fines. Disciplinary fines were one of the most consistent features of associations. Moreover, attendance roles were meticulously kept. As Kloppenborg notes, attendance was important for two primary reasons: (1) financial considerations such as offsetting the expenses of banquets; and (2) honorific considerations, since banquets were semi-public events and special recognitions could be affected by the number of members present (Kloppenborg 2019, 155–58). Absenteeism ultimately threatened the "communal health" of the association (Yuh 2019, 873–74).

There were several additional mechanisms used by associations to enforce initiatives and attendance. (1) One mechanism of enforcement of an association's rules was informants. An inscription by the Berytian Poseidoniasts allows for members of the society to bring accusations against those who violate the group's decree (no. 224). If successful, the informant would be given one-third of the fine, thus incentivizing group surveillance of one another.[7] (2) Another mechanism for members who had been fined or not paid their dues could be property seizure. An inscription of the association of Epikteta's relatives regularly threatens the seizure of property for unpaid fines or dues. In fact, a member who suggests dissolution of the association, maligns it, or creates divisions within it must pay five hundred drachmas—a fine seemingly paid through seizure because the member is also expelled (no. 243). (3) As Epikteta's group demonstrates, a group might choose to expel a delinquent member. A Bacchic association shut out from its gatherings members who did not pay their dues for wine (no. 7). (4) A group might also hand over a member to the authorities to collect fines or dues owed. An association of Apolysimoi left instructions that if a member did not pay his dues or the head tax or some expenses, then Kronion had authority to exact the pledge and hand over (παραδίδωμι) the delinquent members (no. 301).[8] Though the document does not say to whom the person is handed over, the language is suggestive of being handed over to authorities (e.g., Mark 13:11). Again, regulations of a group of salt merchants state that "if someone fails to pay his dues and does not pay any of the public charges or fines (?) laid against him, Apychnis [who is also a collector of public taxes] has the authority to arrest him . . . and hand him over" (no. 302). While some kind of public tax is included in both examples and Apychnis holds both a public and association position, delinquencies in fines, funds, or dues for an association also seem to subject the member to official action if the association was unable to enforce its own fines (Yuh 2019, 871). Officials could also be solicited by group members if the association failed in its responsibility to provide funds or services such as funeral expenses.[9] (5) Finally, a group could threaten divine curses such as a household group that issued curses by the group's

---

[7] Informant culture was a common feature of Roman imperial society; see Whitlark 2014, 37–43.

[8] It is not clear from the instructions if the exacting of dues, expenses, or head tax is related to the group standing in surety for a member arrested for a debt.

[9] Cf. no. 292; also no. 293.

gods for those who disregard the inscribed ordinances (no. 121).[10] Again, the Berytian Poseidoniasts pronounce a curse over those who do not abide by the inscribed decree (no. 224).

The policing of group members was part of an ethos of competitive zeal for the honor of the association, the increase of the size of the group, and the increase of the honor of the associations' deities (nos. 7, 8, 74). Indeed, a Bacchic association exhorts its members to "speak, act, and be zealous for the association." One association requires that the members be "pure, pious, and good." The subsequent exhortation of zeal for the association's increase certainly must entail the ongoing demonstration of these qualities by its members (no. 8). Kloppenborg (2020, 347) notes from sociological studies of communes that costly requirements of belonging to a group increased the group's longevity and reinforced the value of belonging. Zeal for the group and for the adherence to the group's rules or way of life strengthened group bonds, but also could make leaving the group more costly, as we have seen, through public shame, fines, confiscations, and possibly trouble with authorities.

ROMAN NEIGHBORHOODS

With some features of associations writ large, we next need to imagine the life of associations in the neighborhoods of Rome.[11] We will consider how neighborhoods are defined and how they functioned after the Augustan reforms. What follows will draw significantly upon J. Bert Lott's work (2004) on Roman neighborhoods and the Augustan reforms of these neighborhoods.

Definition

A Roman neighborhood, or *vicus*, could be defined by two geographic features. First, the *vicus* was constituted by the dwellings that lined either side of a street. Second, the *vicus* terminated at a crossroad, or *compitum*, where the central shrine of the *vicus* was located. From a Flavian census in 73 CE, Pliny the Elder identifies 256 *vici* in Rome based on the number of *Compita Larum* because each neighborhood had its own *compitum*, or crossroad shrine (*Nat.* 3.66). If the population of Rome in the first century CE was between 750,000 and 1 million inhabitants, then each *vicus* was possibly between 2,800 and

---

[10] Yuh (2019, 877–79) notes that Hebrews uses this type of incentive for group loyalty.

[11] Inscriptional evidence shows that residents of urban neighborhoods formed associations based upon their shared locale in the city (nos. 118, 172; *IPergamon* 434). Various types of associations, such as occupational groups, could also identify themselves based upon their neighborhood of residence (no. 55; *IGR* 4.791). Thus, neighborhood identity could play a significant role in an urban environment.

3,800 residences. The neighborhood association for each neighborhood had two main functions. One was to oversee the maintenance and administration of the neighborhood. The other was to tend to the compital cult, that is, the ritual worship of the protective deities at the neighborhood shrine.

Augustan Reforms

In 7 BCE, Augustus reorganized the Roman *vici* into fourteen administrative regions. During the late republic the *vici* were often organized to gain political support for various factions thus becoming a source of political unrest in Rome. The reorganization by Augustus was an attempt to align the urban population with Augustus' leadership of Rome by integrating the Principate into all levels of society.

The administration of each neighborhood was placed under four *magistri vici*, who were drawn from the lowest caste of citizens (freedmen) and were chosen from among the residents of the neighborhood. They led the *vicus* in observing the compital cult and attending to the neighborhood's municipal administration such as keeping neighborhood lists of those eligible for grain distributions. While performing their official function they were allowed to wear the *toga praetexta* and have two lictors (cf. Livy, *Ab urbe cond.* 34.7.3–10; Dio Cassius, *Hist. rom.* 55.8.6–7).[12] Thus, the *magistri vici* were recognized and honored as public officials who resembled officers of the state. They were assisted in their duties often by slave officers (*ministri vici*), who dressed like freedmen. The *magistri vici* were then organized under the regional officials of aediles, tribunes, and praetors. Augustus then assigned the *praefectus urbi* with oversight of all aspects of the city's administration including the dispensation of justice.

As mentioned, Roman neighborhoods celebrated the *Compitalia*, which was an ancient custom first attributed to Servius Tullius, who ordered chapels to be erected to heroes on every street. The deities of the crossroads were honored as the protective spirits for each neighborhood (cf. Dionysius of Halicarnassus, *Ant. rom.* 4.14.3–4; Pliny, *Nat.* 36.204). The *Compitalia* became a state holiday celebrated between December 17 and January 5. Livy recounts the plague in Rome in 428 BCE that demonstrates the central importance that these compital shrines held. According to Livy, Roman residents gathered in desperation around and made propitiations to the protective deities at the compital altars. City authorities also surveilled these activities. Aediles were commissioned to make sure that only Roman gods were worshiped in ancestral ways at these altars (*Ab urbe cond.* 4.30.7–11).

---

[12] See the compital altar of the Vicus Aesculeti (Lott 2004, 142–43).

Under Augustus' reforms, the compital altars of each *vicus* became the locus of both imperial beneficence and expressions of loyalty. Augustus, at the time of his reorganization, dedicated new, expensive cult statues for the compital altars of each neighborhood (cf. Suetonius, *Aug.* 57; Dio Cassius, *Hist. rom.* 54.35.2). These statues became the Lares Augusti, the protective spirits for each *vicus*. As Lott (2004, 106) notes, "It is impossible to overestimate how much importance the neighborhoods placed on the imperial gift visit and statuettes of the Lares Augusti." As with all Augustus' renovations in the city, emphasis fell upon inspiring loyalty to the new dynasty. Prominence in a neighborhood also likely hinged on participation in the neighborhood cult built around implicit and overt displays of loyalty.

Indeed, new compital altars and statues were dedicated as signs of support for the Augustan regime. Often reliefs of oak wreaths and laurels were engraved on the altars. These were symbols that Augustus had been allowed to display permanently on his doorposts since 27 BCE. With these decorations, along with the donation of the Lares Augusti, Augustus and subsequent emperors effectively became residents of the *vicus*. Augustus also reinstituted the *ludi Compitalicii* as a part of the *Compitalia*. This local entertainment was likely funded by occupational guilds or other associations in the neighborhoods. Augustus also ordered that the compital altars be decorated twice annually during the city's celebration of Lares Praestites and Lares of the Sacra Via (Suetonius, *Aug.* 43).

Identifying with these new imperial realities was a means of enhancing one's social capital in a Roman neighborhood where, for many, there were limited opportunities to increase one's status. Associations in Rome could develop and enhance the neighborhood shrines and participate in civic processions (Tran 2020, 207–8). Leadership in the *vicus* or public enhancement of the local shrine were all competitive acts aimed at prestige in the neighborhood and were expressions of both local pride and imperial loyalty. In a *vicus* near the Forum Boarium, a freedman, Humeros, is illustrative of these social dynamics. Humeros served as a *magistri vici* at least three times. While his upward mobility was limited, the elected role of *magistri vici* for the neighborhood association was a space in which he could pursue political opportunities and build his honor. He made public donations of a statue of Mercurius Augustus, of gold and silver scales, of a shrine to Hercules, and of a statue of Venus Augusta. For his scales and shrine he was also given the honorific cognomen of Aequitas (fairness) by the neighborhood. As a result, Humeros' political life seems to imitate that of Augustus in Rome. Humeros honors the same Augustan gods; he makes donation of statues to his *vicus*;

he takes on an honorific title for his beneficence; and he holds an elected office of leadership multiple times.

Continued and even renewed attention was given to Roman *vici* during the Flavian period where extensive construction projects were undertaken and neighborhood divisions were recertified after a census in 73 CE. New rounds of compital shrine construction and renovation were undertaken during this period and afterwards. It is then in this setting of voluntary associations inhabiting the Augustan-reformed neighborhoods of Rome that we encounter the community addressed in Hebrews.

THE COMMUNITY OF HEBREWS

From Paul's Letter to the Romans, the indications we get of Christ groups in Rome in the 50s CE is that they were independently organized groups with little unified oversight. By the turn of the century, the Christ groups in Rome appear to have had a more cohesive and organized identity, though centralized leadership had yet to emerge. For example, both Clement and Ignatius can speak of one ἐκκλησία in Rome instead of the one ἐκκλησία that meets in the house of Priscilla and Aquila, who are in Rome with other Christ groups (1 Clem. 1.1; Ign. *Rom.*, intro par.; Rom 16:5; see Tobin 2004, 38–40). These groups likely gathered in shared neighborhood locales in Rome. As Richard Last notes, people often joined associations based upon proximity, and recruitment to the Jesus movement likely grew out of neighborhood-based social relationships and occupancy (Last 2016, 413–19). We will then assume that the group addressed by Hebrews, if in Rome in the latter half of the first century, lived in one of these neighborhoods or possibly drew its community members from adjacent neighborhoods. Moreover, the group remains loosely affiliated to the other Christ groups living in this city.

A Neighborhood Group in Conflict

The community we encounter in the Letter to the Hebrews has and continues to suffer physical, economic, and status hardships for its confession of Jesus Christ. The early days of the community are characterized as "a great contest of sufferings," which included being made a spectacle of reproach and affliction, imprisonment, and property seizure (10:32-34; translations in this chapter are by the author). They continue to experience imprisonment, torture, shame, and anxiety (13:3, 5-6). Moreover, the pall of death seems to be an ever-present threat that hangs over the community for its ongoing identification with Jesus (2:14; 12:4; 13:7). Certainly, key exemplars to which the author points the community emphasize fidelity to God in the face of death, including Jesus, the exemplum par excellence (11:23-27, 35b-38; 12:2-3). Under these pressures, some of the former members have quit identifying with the community (10:25) and instead may have recanted and exposed the Son of God to public shame (6:6).

What dynamics in the neighborhoods of Rome might explain these phenomena? Insight may be gained by looking at Hebrews' agonistic perspective toward pagan deities and imperial rule which, as noted above, were elements of neighborhood and association life in Rome. We can also look at the nature of the penalties for absenteeism from association participation and the neighborhood cult. These tensions could then threaten to escalate against members of a perceived, dissident group in Rome.

Resisting Idolatry: Withdrawal from Associations and Neighborhood Cultic Activities

One reason pagan converts to the Jesus movement could be at odds with associations and their neighborhoods stemmed from their rejection of the traditional pantheon of deities to worship the one God through Jesus Christ. Atheism was not an uncommon charge leveled against Christ followers, at least by the second century (e.g., Mart. Pol. 9.2; 12.2). Moreover, rejecting the ancestral deities to worship only the one God of Jesus Christ was integral to Paul's missional message among gentiles and part of early Christian ethics (1 Cor 10:7; Gal 5:20; 1 Thess 1:9; 1 Pet 4:3; 1 John 5:21; Rev 21:8; see Fredriksen 2015, 645–50). This first-commandment loyalty to God certainly would have put pressure on Christ followers to consider withdrawing from neighborhood cultic rites and from membership in associations which were ubiquitously connected to one or more pagan deities or heroes. By the third century CE, Cyprian disparages Christian participation in associations because of the ethos of the banquets and profane burials with strangers which, as Cyprian possibly implies, led to apostasy by obtaining certificates of idolatry (Ep. 67.6.2).

The author of Hebrews exhorts his community to this first-commandment loyalty pointing to the group's rejection of idolatry ("dead works") to serve the living God of Jesus Christ (6:1; 9:14). The author adapts some of his strongest warnings against apostasy from Old Testament texts that warn against committing idolatry (Whitlark 2014, 49–76). Indeed, some of the primary heroes the author holds forth in Hebrews 11 are praised for their resistance to pagan idolatrous societies such as Moses (Egypt), Rahab (Canaanite Jericho), and the Maccabean martyrs (Seleucid kingdom; 11:23-31, 35). Hebrews 13:13 ("going outside the camp ... bearing his reproach") could be understood as an exhortation to separate from idolatrous (and imperial) culture that stands under God's judgment. This could certainly include association life that was inseparable from honoring the gods. Seeing that many associations were located in neighborhoods and took their constituency from there, such withdrawal would not have gone unnoticed and, as we will see, would have been unwelcomed. Additionally, participation in the neighborhood compital cult in Rome would have proved problematic for the original audience of Hebrews. Of course, honoring the lares of the compital cult was a way of securing the health and well-being of the neighborhood. Such withdrawal, understandably, could be perceived as misanthropy (Tacitus, *Ann.* 15.44; 1 Pet 4:4).

Resisting Empire: Diminishing Imperial Honors and Neighborhood Pride

The Christ followers in the Letter to the Hebrews also appear to be at odds with imperial honorifics that would have been typical in the *vici* of Rome from Augustus onward. Associations in the Roman Empire, as we have seen, often signaled that they shared in the benefits of the divinely ordained Roman rule through the honors they gave to Rome and its emperor. Moreover, after the Augustus' reorganization of the Roman neighborhoods, the central cult of the neighborhood was closely tied to imperial honors and expressions of imperial loyalty. The lares of these shrines had become the Lares Augusti.

In Hebrews, Rome and its emperor have completely been decentered. Indeed, they are not even directly named, which has the effect of diminishing Rome's own self-importance (Whitlark 2014, 98, 198). Jesus is God's chosen ruler over the cosmos (1:5-14; 13:20). God's benefits of the new covenant and salvation in the coming world are through Jesus. Rome is not the eternal city, but the community looks for a city to come whose architect and builder is God (13:14). In the cosmos of Hebrews, Rome and its emperor exercise the power of the devil through the fear of death, which Jesus has defeated through his death on a Roman cross and his resurrection to God's right hand (2:14-15; Whitlark 2014, 122–41). Only God, who is a consuming fire, is to be feared. The imperial cosmos where the emperor rules by the consent of the gods and ushers in peace and salvation is ultimately in conflict with a cosmos that is ruled by Jesus who is chosen by the God of Abraham and promises peace and salvation to those who wait for him. Such competing narratives are implicitly seen in an association's identification as "the principal followers of Emperor Augustus Caesar son of god Zeus Eleutherios" (no. 280, 5 BCE) over against a group identifying itself as the followers, even siblings, of the Lord Jesus, Son of the living God.

Nonparticipation in association and neighborhood honorifics for Rome and its emperor is certainly a probable response. The community gives obeisance with angels to God's exalted Son, not the emperor. Hebrews contains no exhortations to honor the emperor or even pray for him (cf. 1 Pet 2:17; 1 Tim 2:1-2). This type of agonistic ethos is evident at the beginning of the third century CE when Tertullian states that Christ followers do not give emperors vain and false honors and, thus, were counted public enemies because of the nonparticipation in imperial celebrations (*Apol.* 35).

Penalties and Persecution

The exhortations to perseverance alongside resistance to idol worship and imperial honorifics in Hebrews point to a community, from its inception, whose members would likely have separated themselves from both voluntary associations and the compital cult of the Roman *vicus*. Could the withdrawal from such activities explain the type of responses, sufferings, and fears to which the Letter to the Hebrews points?

Fines and Honor Deficit. First, as described above, absenteeism could result in a fine by the group. An association leader could demand attendance, and ignoring the summons could result in a fine (no. 301). Departing from the association may even have been prohibited (no. 295). Fines for rule violations could also be aggressively prosecuted by informants in the association against delinquent members who had identified with the Christ group of Hebrews. These financial penalties alone would have made it problematic for any member of Hebrews' community to withdraw from former memberships in other associations. We should also note that withdrawal from an association could have also resulted in loss of free meals or the loss of *sportulae* at association gatherings and thus a diminishment in benefits and resources of the Christ follower (Yuh 2019, 873).

Absenteeism also made problematic the conferring of honors. Nonattendance in the competitive honorifics of a neighborhood's compital cult or association activities could be taken as a slight by the absentee. Zeal for the association or the neighborhood, rewards for informants, and meticulous role keeping could have made the stakes of nonattendance high for the Christ followers of Hebrews.

Association membership could provide a sense of prestige, and association spaces could provide the non-elite a measure of leisure that imitated the privileges of the elite (Tran 2020, 210–11). Withdrawal from association participation or even expulsion could result in the loss of social capital for members of the Christ group in Hebrews (Kloppenborg 2019, 56).

Furthermore, membership in the Christ group described in Hebrews did not do anything to increase the honor status of the members. In fact, the author indicates that membership in the Christ group has negatively affected the honor of its members. It has become a source of shame to their status in society. The community is to bear Christ's reproach by renouncing opportunities for wealth and status and by performing faithful service to others. It is to despise the shame of public persecution, like Jesus did. It is to recall the spectacle of social reproach they experienced at their conversion (Heb 10:33; 11:26; 12:2; 13:13; see Koester 2001, 571). Thus, the group was not likely to attract the resources or protection of a patron—whether a local magistrate, Augustale, or well-to-do commoner (Kloppenborg 2019, 219). Instead, the group was to rely upon help from God (Heb 2:18; 4:16; 13:5-6).

Confiscation, Imprisonment, and Martyrdom. Second, the collection of fines (for absenteeism from the association, for instance) could escalate to the confiscation of personal property, imprisonment, and exile from the civic community. Certainly, such an escalating situation could become more perilous as information was gathered (or trumped up) about the absentee's decision to withdraw from the association.

Nonparticipation in civic festivals and sacrifices was especially precarious since these rites protected the neighborhood and affirmed that Rome and its emperor ruled the cosmos by divine consent. The centrality of imperial rule through the emperor was part of the new-year festivities of the compital cults in Rome after the Augustan reorganization of the neighborhoods. We have already seen in an inscription from Magnesia that households or workshops were expected to contribute to the upkeep and decoration of the sacred precinct of Artemis in the city. A similar expectation is likely for the upkeep and contribution to the yearly compital festivals among households and guilds in the Roman *vicus*. The elected *magistri vici* took a special interest in the promotion of neighborhood recognition and its compital cult, as a matter of personal and communal honor.

Displays of loyalty to Roman rule and the gods could be aggressively enforced. An inscription from Gytheion during the reign of Tiberius promises death and the confiscation of property to any resident who violates the established sacred law that was implemented to honor the emperors and gods through cult rituals (Levick 2000, 131–33). Again, nonparticipation in the annual festivities surrounding the compital cults could raise suspicions and introduce a shadow of fear over those who abstained. These penalties, such as confiscation and imprisonment, exile, or even execution, would then not have arisen from failure to pay fines but from the appearance of disloyalty to Rome and her gods—namely, treason.[13] This potential danger of not participating in public rites for the emperor and Rome is illustrated by Tacitus who recounts the execution of the Thrasea Paetus under Nero. Thrasea had been accused of treason because he avoided taking the customary oath of allegiance to the emperor and avoided participating in the customary sacrifices and vows made on the emperor's behalf (thus implying he had no care for the emperor's safety; *Ann.* 16.22). As mentioned above, this fear of the infliction of the death penalty seems to be present in the community or anticipated by the author. The experience of martyrdom among former leaders of the community may already be indicated in Heb 13:7 ("considering the outcome of their way of life, imitate their faith"). Hebrews 12:4 suggests that the "shedding of blood in the struggle against sin" presents a real possibility for the audience. Hebrews 6:6 ("holding up the Son of God to public contempt") could point to public loyalty tests where the denial of Jesus as God's enthroned ruler was required.

Escalation. In both cases, whether the imposition of fines or withdrawal from the local compital cult, the *magistri vici* and other officials could have been solicited to help with the dissident members who had joined the Christ group. The urban bureaucracy of Rome was responsible for managing the life and peace of the city. We see how an escalation beyond the neighborhood could potentially happen from Livy's account of the Bacchanalia. To remove Bacchanalia from Roman *vici* around 186 BCE, informants were rewarded for identifying offenders or those who harbored them, triumvirs were posted at the gates to catch fugitives, curile aediles searched for cultic priests, and the plebian aediles policed the *vici* for observance of Bacchic rites. As a result, members of the cult fled the city, some were retained in prison, some publicly executed, some committed suicide, and some handed over to relatives (*Ab urbe cond.* 39.14–18).

Of course, it also may be the case that each neighborhood tolerated Christ groups at different levels and punitive measures may have just been carried out at the level of the association or neighborhood. Thus, in the latter part of the first century, we can imagine sporadic, uneven, and variegated responses against the loosely connected Christ groups residing in Rome that did not reach the level of the pogrom ascribed to Nero. Moreover, a few severe responses by some *vici* can still be damaging to another Christ group's psyche elsewhere in Rome (like the localized, brutal lynchings were to the black communities across the Jim Crow South; see Cone 2011).

---

[13] Cf. Herm. Sim. 1.1–6.

CONCLUSION

If the audience of Hebrews is living in Rome in the latter part of the first century CE, we can see how voluntary groups and neighborhood associations in Roman *vici* might have lived in tension with Christ groups that formed among them. These tensions arose from Christ group's potentially strong response against community members' participation in idolatry and against displays of imperial loyalty. The suffering of the community in Hebrews anticipates the kind of responses encountered by delinquent members in associations and by those who had withdrawn from neighborhood cultic rites and festivities. These responses could be localized within one of the neighborhood locales in Rome but always with the potential to escalate beyond the neighborhood to involve urban officials who administered the Roman populace. Finally, within the New Testament canon, Hebrews resembles the anti-assimilation perspective present in Revelation that would make problematic any compromise with participation in associations and neighborhood cultic life (Harland 2013, 212, 214, 221–22, 231).

WORKS CITED

Ascough, Richard S. 1996. "The Completion of a Religious Duty: The Background of 2 Cor 8.1–15." *NTS* 42:584–99.

Ascough, Richard S., Philip A. Harland, and John S. Kloppenborg. 2012. *Associations in the Greco-Roman World: A Sourcebook*. Waco, Tex.: Baylor University Press.

Cone, James H. 2011. *The Cross and the Lynching Tree*. Maryknoll, N.Y.: Orbis.

Fears, J. Rufus. 1981. "The Cult of Virtues and Roman Imperial Ideology." *ANRW* 17:827–948. Part 2, *Principat*, 17.2. Edited by H. Temporini and W. Haase. New York: De Gruyter.

Fredriksen, Paula. 2015. "Why Should a 'Law-Free' Mission Mean a 'Law-Free' Apostle?" *JBL* 134:637–50.

Galinsky, Karl. 2011. "The Cult of the Roman Emperor: Uniter or Divider?" Pages 1–21 in *Rome and Religion: A Cross-Disciplinary Dialogue on the Imperial Cult*. Edited by Jeffrey Brodd and Jonathan L. Reed. WGRWSup 5. Atlanta: SBL.

Harland, Philip A. 2013. *Associations, Synagogues, and Congregations: Claiming a Place in Ancient Mediterranean Society*. 2nd ed. Kitchener, Ont.: Philip A. Harland.

———, ed. 2014. *North Coast of the Black Sea, Asia Minor*. BZNW 204. Vol. 2 of *Greco-Roman Associations: Texts, Translations, and Commentary*. Edited by John S. Kloppenborg and Richard S. Ascough. Berlin: De Gruyter.

Kloppenborg, John S. 2019. *Christ's Associations: Connecting and Belonging in the Ancient City*. New Haven: Yale University Press.

———. 2020. "Recruitment to Elective Cults: Network Structure and Ecology." *NTS* 66:323–50.

Kloppenborg, John S., and Richard S. Ascough. 2011. *Attica, Central Greece, Macedonia, Thrace*. BZNW 181. Vol. 1 of Kloppenborg and Ascough, *Greco-Roman Associations*.

Koester, Craig R. 2001. *Hebrews: A New Translation with Introduction and Commentary*. AB 36. New York: Doubleday.

Last, Richard. 2016. "The Neighborhood (*vicus*) of the Corinthian *ekklēsia*: Beyond Family-Based Descriptions of the First Urban Christ-Believers." *JSNT* 38:399–425.

Levick, Barbara. 2000. *The Government of the Roman Empire: A Sourcebook*. 2nd ed. New York: Routledge.

Lott, J. Bert. 2004. *The Neighborhoods of Augustan Rome*. Cambridge: Cambridge University Press.

Tobin, Thomas H. 2004. *Paul's Rhetoric in Its Contexts: The Argument of Romans*. Peabody, Mass.: Hendrickson.

Tran, Nicolas. 2020. "The Meeting Places of Associations in the City of Rome." Pages 197–227 in *City of Encounters: Public Spaces and Social Interaction in Ancient Rome*. Edited by Maria Caldelli and Cecilia Ricci. RomeScapes. Rome: Edizioni Quasar.

Whitlark, Jason A. 2014. *Resisting Empire: Rethinking the Purpose of the "Letter to the Hebrews."* LNTS 484. London: T&T Clark.

Yuh, Jason N. 2019. "Abandonments and Absenteeism in the Letter to the Hebrews and Greco-Roman Associations." *JBL* 138:863–82.

22

Julian Christ Worshippers and Their Connection to a Collegium in First-Century Lyon

Reintroducing the Epitaph of Julia Adepta

Richard Last

REINTRODUCING JULIA ADEPTA'S EPITAPH

Prior to vanishing, Julia Adepta's mid-first-century funerary altar was seen by the renowned seventeenth-century archaeographer, Jacob Spon, in a garden on the property of the Mascrany house on Bellecour Square in Lyon. In 1673, Spon published a majuscule of the epitaph in his important study of ancient Lyonnais artifacts, *Recherche des antiquités et curiosités de la ville de Lyon*.[1] All later publications relied on his transcription.[2] The epitaph is, like so many others, terse though revealing of the deceased's most dear social connections. On the basis of Spon's majuscule, the text can be transcribed as follows:

> *Iulia Adepta | hic adquiescit | L(ucius) Iulius Cupitus | matri et sodales || de suo et Perpetua | fil(ia)* (CIL 13:2177)

> Julia Adepta rests here. Lucius Julius Cupitus for his mother, the *sodales* from their own resources, and Perpetua her daughter (made this).[3]

[1] For the discovery location, see Spon 1685, 171. For Spon's commentary, see Spon 1685, 172; (1673) 1858, 228. On Spon himself, see the comments in Le Mer and Chomer 2007, 111–12.

[2] See, for example, Menestrier 1696, 98; de Boissieu 1846–1854, 281; Allmer and Dissard 1890, 48.

[3] All translations are my own.

Spon's brief description of the stone highlighted resemblances with the funerary monument of her spouse, the imperial freedman Nobilis (*CIL* 13.1820): both stones were of a similar shape and quality, and both shared the same style of lettering. He suggested, moreover, that the *sodales* who purchased the stone were members of an association organized for workers and officials in the Lugdunese mint, where Nobilis was appointed a quality control official (Spon [1673] 1858, 228).

The view that these *sodales* were organized as a collegium is reasonable on philological grounds[4] and in light of the financial role they shared in funding Julia's funerary monument (see Kloppenborg 2019, 265–77). Indeed, Jean-Pierre Waltzing includes the *sodales* of *CIL* 13.2177 in his list of "collèges Chrétiens" (Waltzing 1895-1900, 4.235). Since Spon makes no mention of Julia's membership in this collegium, his suggestion seems to be that the *sodales* funded a funerary stone for a nonmember (Julia) who was the spouse of a mint official. But, given the context of the inscription, it is more likely that Julia was fully affiliated with the group.[5] In fact, the phrasing of Julia's epitaph leaves open the possibility that she functioned as *mater* of the collegium.[6] As for Julia's husband, Nobilis, there is no evidence he held membership in the association or even that the collegium existed during his lifetime. Julia's children, Cupitus and Perpetua, though, may well have been affiliated

---

[4]   On modern definitions and Latin terminology, see Tran 2006, 3–9. Note especially Gaius' remark (*Dig.* 47.22.4) that *sodales sunt qui eiusdem collegii sunt, quam graeci ἑταιρίαν vocant. His autem potestatem facit lex, pactionem quam velint sibi ferre, dum ne quid ex publica lege corrumpant*: "*Sodales* are (those) who are of the same *collegium*, which Greeks call ἑταιρίαι. Moreover, a law provides power to them to produce a Rule which they wish among themselves so long as they do not corrupt anything from the public law." For a collegium of wagonmakers known as *sodales carpentarii*, see *AE* 1927, no. 129 (Patavium, Venetia, first to second century CE); for a collegium of wool carders known as *lanari(i) pectonar(ii) sodales*, see *CIL* 5.4501. For similar funerary gifts by *sodales* (as indicated by the phrase *sodales de suo* in funerary inscriptions), see *CILA* 3.62 (Baesucci, Hispania Citerior); and *CIL* 15.8007 (Rome, Latium).

[5]   There is, however, some evidence for collegium members commemorating members' families in the middle of the first century (the date of the inscriptions under examination in this chapter) in Tebtynis, even if not the precise scenario Spon proposes. For examples, see *PMich* 5.243, l. 12 (Tebtynis, Arsinoite, 14–37 CE); *PMich* 5.244, ll. 16–18 (= *GRA* III 212; Tebtynis, Arsinoites, 43 CE). I am grateful to John Kloppenborg and Philip Harland for pointing out these analogies.

[6]   See, for comparison, *AE* 2009, no. 1190 (Tetovo, Moesia Superior): *Cassandr|a h(ic) s(ita) e(st) | vixit an(nos) | [. . .] Iul(ius) Sym||machus Augusta[l(is)] | col(oniae) Scup(inorum) | matri et | collegiu[m] | Herculi[s] | [i]dem matri || b(ene) m(erenti)*: "Cassandra is buried here. She lived [. . .] years. Julius Symmachus, Augustalis, from the colony of Scupi (made this) for his mother, and the *collegium* of Hercules (made) the same for their *mater*. Well deserving."

with the *sodales*. Perhaps the *sodales* even planned to appoint Cupitus or Perpetua as a patron following Julia's death.

Fascinatingly, Spon was sure that Julia and Nobilis practiced Christ worship ([1673] 1858, 228–29). While it is true that some worshippers of Christ opted to join collegia, as Nobilis apparently did according to Spon's reading, this broader reconstruction requires closer scrutiny.[7] The most vigorous defender of Spon's thesis, Alphonse de Boissieu, published his arguments in the middle of the nineteenth century, assisted by evidence not available to Spon (de Boissieu 1846–1854, 281–84, 534). More recently, I updated the discussion on Nobilis' funerary altar specifically, bringing to the fore data not available to previous interpreters. In light of this new evidence, I found Spon's (and de Boissieu's) assessment more plausible than alternatives (Last 2022). Understandably, a majority of nineteenth- and twentieth-century interpreters judged the stones too early for Julia and Nobilis to have practiced Christ worship, a sentiment that can be traced back to Edmond Le Blant in the third volume of his series on Christian inscriptions from Gallia. Le Blant outright refused to accept that an inscription attesting to Christ worship would ever be discovered from the first century (1856, 175). A priori judgments against de Boissieu's position were made by all those who rejected it, but de Boissieu's actual arguments had not been engaged until recently (Last 2022).

Although both aforementioned stones disappeared from discussions on Christian origins and collegia after 1890 (Allmer and Dissard 1890, 47–48), they remain highly significant: with them, we have potentially the first known inscriptional attestations to Christ followers (Julia and Nobilis in *CIL* 13.1820), as well as the earliest epigraphic notice of a collegium member (or even *mater*), namely Julia Adepta (*CIL* 13.2177), with strong ties to a worshipper of Christ (i.e., her spouse, Nobilis). The task of this chapter is to provide a case study of Julia's familial social network, with whom the *sodales* were connected through Julia. It aims to chart the process of this network's gradual transformation, including the possible expansion of Christ worship through it, as well as the eventual formation of a collegium that included Julian freedpersons and their acquaintances.

---

[7] For collegia with members who worshipped Christ, see Cyprian, *Ep.* 67.6; *CIL* 14.251 (Ostia, Latium, 192 CE) with *CIL* 14.1900 (Ostia, Latium, 192–200 CE); *POxy* 1.103, 45.3261-62 (Oxyrhynchus, Upper Egypt, fourth century); *PSI* 12.1265 (Oxyrhynchus, Upper Egypt, 426 or 441 CE); *IOSPE* 5.331 (Hermonassa, North Black Sea, 470–480 CE); *PStrass* 6.287 (Hermopolis Magna, Upper Egypt, sixth century) with Last 2016, 515–16. For others, see Kloppenborg 2019, 274–76; and Harland 2014, 434–41.

NOBILIS AND THE FUNERARY PHRASE, *HIC ADQUIESCIT*, IN FIRST-CENTURY LUGDUNUM

One of Julia's strongest ties was her spouse, Nobilis. His now-lost tomb-stone was first recorded in unpublished manuscripts by Claude Bellièvre ([1525–1556] 1846, 118) and Gabriele Simeoni (1560, 40).[8] Guillaume Paradin saw the funerary altar in Saint-Vincent, while Simeoni and several others recorded its location in the vicinity of Hotel de la Ville.[9] Spon proposed that its original location was likely beside Julia's monument in a now unknown spot. Simeoni's 1560 work, *Le Origine e le Antichità di Lione*, provides our only illustration of the stone (40).[10] Aside from de Boissieu (and possibly Otto Hirschfeld [*CIL* 13.1820, 279]), no other commentators saw his drawing because Simeoni's manuscript remained unpublished until Jean-Baptiste Monfalcon reproduced the text (but not illustrations) nearly three hundred years later (1846, 1–55). As can be seen from figure 22.1, de Boissieu's reproduction of Simeoni's majuscule depicts a curious ligature-shaped character in line 3.[11]

I have discussed Simeoni's illustration and scrutinized various explanations for the ligature-shaped character at the end of line 3 elsewhere (Last 2022). In summary of the findings from that study, de Boissieu's contention that Simeoni's symbol represents a cross is viable, and the alternatives, that it is a ligature or standard tall *t*, are not defensible.[12]

On the basis of de Boissieu's expansions (1846–1854, 281–84), which I also found to be more plausible than alternatives (Last 2022), the text can be transcribed as follows:

---

[8] Bellièvre's manuscript remained unpublished until Jean-Baptiste Monfalcon published it in 1846.

[9] Paradin 1573, 441; Spon (1673) 1857, 22; Bellièvre (1525–1556) 1846, 118; Monfalcon 1846, 29 (for Simeoni); Menestrier 1696, 97; de Colonia 1728, 36.

[10] For a description of Simeoni's career and publications, see Cooper 2016, 297–332. More briefly: Le Mer and Chomer 2007, 110 (Chomer). The past decade has seen renewed interest in Simeoni thanks to the 2011 discovery of an illustrated poem he authored. On the whole, Simeoni's *Le Origine e le Antichità di Lione*, which made a lasting contribution to the study of the origins of the city (including locating the city's amphitheater), continues to be seen as one of Simeoni's most methodologically erudite. Moreover, as the essays in D'Amico and Magnien-Simonin 2016 illustrate, Simeoni's transcriptions were often precise.

[11] A photograph of Simeoni's original illustration was first published in Last 2022.

[12] Early reception of de Boissieu was mixed; some found his interpretation persuasive (e.g., Ravenez 1861, 12–13).

NOBILIS TIB
CAESARIS AVG
SER · AEQ · MONET
HIC ADQVIESCIT
IVLIA ADEPTA CONIVX
ET PERPETVA FILIA D · S · D

Fig. 22.1 De Boissieu's Reproduction of Simeoni's Majuscule
(from de Boissieu 1846–1854, 281)

Nobilis Tib(eri) | *Caesaris Aug(usti)* | *ser(vator) aeq(uatatis) monet(ae)* |
hic adquiescit | *Iulia Adepta coniunx* | *et Perpetua filia d(e) s(uo) d(ant).*[13]

Nobilis, freedman of Tiberius Caesar Augustus, supervisor of equality for
the mint. Here he rests. Julia Adepta his wife, and Perpetua his daughter,
made this from their own resources.

Among witnesses to these monuments, only Spon troubled a date. Based
on the two stones' supposedly poor quality, he argued that the emperor in
lines 1–2 of the Nobilis inscription was Tiberius II Constantine (578–582),
which would place both Nobilis and Julia in the sixth century (Spon [1673]
1858, 23). De Boissieu was the earliest to see that the inscriptions fit better in
the first century. His argument was based on orthography and letter styling,
on the authority of Simeoni's illustration (de Boissieu 1846–1854, 283). Le
Blant agreed, and strengthened the case by adding that the names in the texts
(Nobilis, Julia, Lucius Julius Cupitus) suggest a first-century date (Le Blant
1856, 174). We can now confirm de Boissieu's dating: the funerary phrase,

---

[13] The miniscule had previously been printed conventionally as: *Nobilis Tib(eri)* | *Cae-
saris Aug(usti)* | *ser(vus) aeq(uator) monet(ae)* | *hic adquiescit* | *Iulia Adepta coniunx* | *et
Perpetua filia d(e) s(uo) d(ant)*.

hic adquiescit, found in both Julia's and Nobilis' epitaphs, falls into disuse after the first century in Lugdunum (see below).

Dating the two epitaphs relative to each other is more difficult—though Julia's is obviously later. The legal status of Julia is unstated in both her and also Nobilis' epitaph, but presumably she was free(d) when her son Lucius Julius Cupitus was born; the single name of her daughter, Perpetua, tells us little about Julia's status.[14] Le Blant proposed that Cupitus—who takes Julia's *nomen gentilicium*—may have been born from a union that preceded her marriage with Nobilis.[15] This differs from the standard reconstruction, according to which Julia remarried after Nobilis' death, gained her freedom in that time, subsequently had her son Cupitus, and died several decades after Nobilis.[16] There are, however, three circumstantial reasons that give the edge to Le Blant over the traditional reconstruction: (1) both Nobilis and Julia instructed their *lapidarii* to engrave the rare phrase *hic adquiescit* on their tombstones, indicating a connection between the two stones; (2) Spon, the only observer of *both* stones, highlighted material similarities between Nobilis' and Julia's tombstones with respect to size, shape, and even paleographical similarities (Spon [1673] 1858, 228); and (3) Julia is not commemorated by a second husband after Nobilis. On point 3, it is possible that a second husband died sometime after Nobilis, but this cannot be the preferred explanation in light of the other two points; Julia is associated with no husband other than Nobilis at the time of her death.

It was not only the ligature-shaped symbol in Simeoni's illustration of Nobilis' funerary altar that led de Boissieu to conclude that both Nobilis and Julia were practitioners of Christ worship. The presence of the phrase *hic adquiescit* on both epitaphs was also crucial—both Spon ([1673] 1858, 229) and also de Boissieu (1846–1854, 282) intuited that the formula was used mainly by Christians. This phrase must be analyzed in some detail here, for in addition to

[14] It is not obvious that Perpetua, the daughter of Nobilis and Julia, is a slave. Her mother has a nomen (Julia) and there are no status indications for Julia or Perpetua. For examples of freeborn children with single personal names or with their *nomina* otherwise missing, see *CIL* 6.9077 (Rome, Latium, second century CE) and *CIL* 3.4065 (Poetovio, Pannonia Superior, 161–300 CE), and the discussion of other possible examples in Weaver 1972, 143. For Perpetua in *CIL* 13.1820, 2177, it would appear that we have a case where "the simplest account of children with a single name without [status] indication is that they are not of slave status at all but freeborn with nomen omitted" (Weaver 1972, 143). The praenomen (Lucius) of Julia's son may indicate that she is not from the imperial family (see Weaver 1972, 40, 140–43).

[15] Allmer and Dissard 1890, 48; de Boissieu is less descriptive but still heads in this direction (1846–1854, 282).

[16] See Weaver 1972, 143; and Laubry 2005, 301.

confirming Spon's and de Boissieu's instincts, it also helps reveal Julia's familial and other connections. The phrase is a relatively uncommon funerary formula that metaphorizes death as sleep or rest, and incidentally (considering the cross Simeoni found on Nobilis' funerary altar) such an idea coheres with Christian eschatological convictions and notions of survival after death (not exclusively Christian ideas, granted).[17] But who was using this phrase in Lugdunum? Neither Spon nor de Boissieu documented the cases.

There are eighty-four uses of *quiescere* and cognates (*requiescere* and *adquiescere*) in Lugdunese prose funerary inscriptions from all eras.[18] Most are Christian (sixty-four) or probably Christian (six). The fifteen additional inscriptions, including Julia's and Nobilis' epitaph, may well be Christian but are early enough (first to second centuries CE) for most interpreters to classify them as pagan a priori.[19] Eleven of these early inscriptions use the cognate *adquiescere*, and so this variation of the phrase is the only of the three (*hic adquiescit, hic requiescit, hic quiescit*) in Lugdunum to be deemed categorically pagan now. The problem with this traditional manner of classification is that these phrases were interchangeable in first-century Lugdunum. For example, on the Modesta stone (discussed at length below), one first-century epitaph uses *hic adquiescit* (the variation used by Julia and Nobilis) and another from the same century

[17] While related to the common formula *hic situs/sita est*, the phrase *hic adquiescit* generally differs in that it portrays death as a temporary state—though the metaphor may have occasionally connoted death as a static (Brelich 1937, 62–65; cf. Laubry 2005, 301). The phrase can be compared with Hippolytus' (*Haer.* 9.12.14) use of τὸ κοιμητήριον ("sleeping place") for a hypogeum located at the third milestone on the Via Appia. It was possessed by Zephrynius when he was bishop (199–217) and put into the management of Callistus, his advisor at the time, who later became bishop (217–222). This is now associated with Area 1 of S. Callisto. The term κοιμητήριον is here used for the first time in Greek literature to designate a *metaphorical* "sleeping" place (e.g., an individual tomb or collective burial ground). See also Hippolytus, *Comm. Dan.* 4.51. This sense of the word is found even earlier in Latin literature—Tertullian with *coemeterium* (*An.* 5.17). De Boissieu was the first to highlight the significance of the phrase for understanding the inscriptions (1846–1854, 282). Le Blant (1856, 176–77) rejected de Boissieu's interpretation and pointed out that four other monuments were known to him that used the phrase *hic adquiescit* (or cognates). These, Le Blant argued, would need to be assessed as Christian if de Boissieu's interpretation of *CIL* 13.1820 were followed: one each in Lugdunum (*CIL* 13.2178) and Vienna (*CIL* 12.2016 = *ILCV* 3095 [*hic quiescit*]); and two from Arles (*CIL* 12.845; *CIL* 12.8555a). None of them appear to predate the formation of Pauline *ekklēsiai*.

[18] In this section, there are too many sources to cite due to space limitations, but they are all documented in Last 2022.

[19] For the assessment that they are pagan, see, for instance, Laubry 2005, 304–5. All use *hic adquiescit* unless otherwise indicated. *CIL* 13:1820, 1914, 2047, 2059, 2177, 2178, 2333, 2236 (*hic requiescit*); *AE* 1961, no. 70 (*hic quiescit* and *hic adquiescit*); *AE* 2005, no. 1040; Le Mer and Chomer 2007, 283; *AE* 1973, no. 333 = Audin 1974, 99; *ILTG* no. 278 = Le Mer and Chomer 2007, 677 (*hic requiescit*).

has *hic quiescit*, the latter using a verb (*quiescere*) rarely found in Lugdunum but only ever in Christian inscriptions (*AE* 1961, no. 70).[20] The Epigraphik-Datenbank Clauss/Slaby online database (http://www.manfredclauss.de/gb/index.html) classifies this first-century epitaph as Christian (correctly, I think), presumably because of the appearance of *quiescere*.

Quiescere and cognates were used *often* by Christians of Lugdunum. Almost 65 percent of all Christian verse epitaphs have it.[21] So, not only was *quiescere* and its cognates exclusively used by Christians in Lugdunum (with the concession that interpreters typically judge first- and second-century epitaphs with it as pagan without argumentation), these verbs were also predominant in Christian epitaphs. Based on this throughline we can surmise that when someone in Lugdunum had the idea to put the phrase on their funerary monument, it arose in the social contexts of family members, neighbors, collegium co-members, and other acquaintances who were using the phrase. Regardless of what is made of the entire catalogue of fifteen uses of the phrase in first- and second-century Lugdunum (see n. 19 for the list), users of the formula after the second century are all Christian, and we have seen that there is evidence pointing to Christ worship among at least two of the epitaphs with it from the first century, too (i.e., *CIL* 13.1820; *AE* 1961, no. 70).

So far, an analysis of the small grouping of mid-first-century funerary inscriptions from Lugdunum that use the rare funerary formula *hic adquiescit* has led to two identifiable marks of Christ worship: (1) the cross in Simeoni's illustration of the Nobilis inscription, and (2) the phrase *hic quiescit* in one of the two inscriptions on the Modesta funerary stone. Of all the Lugdunese stones that Simeoni may have found with a cross-shaped symbol, it was one (*CIL* 13.1820) that has an infrequent funerary formula closely associated with Christians in late antiquity, and now earlier (e.g., *AE* 1961, no. 70). On Spon's and de Boissieu's identification of Julia and Nobilis as early practitioners of Christ worship, the burden of proof is on proponents of the traditional interpretation, which neglects the epigraphic evidence of users of *quiescere* and variants on Lugdunese funerary monuments, and dismisses without data-driven argumentation de Boissieu's interpretation of Simeoni illustration.

---

[20] See *NewDocs* III 99 = Le Mer and Chomer 2007, 512; *CIL* 13.2391, 2407, 2428; and for *hic quiescit* specifically, *ILTG* 279 = Le Mer and Chomer 2007, 677. In other locations, there are a few uses that may predate Christ worship. See *AE* 1971, no. 181 (Corduba, Baetica, 30 BCE–30 CE); and possibly *CIL* 8.7159 (Cirta, Numidia, 30 BCE–117 CE).

[21] See Last 2022 for the bibliography.

A NETWORK OF JULIAN FREEDPERSONS

Although the phrase *hic adquiescit* is generally very rare, it is strikingly more common in first-century Lugdunum (eleven occurrences) than anywhere else in Gallia, even from the first three centuries.[22] The Gallic town with the most finds after Lugdunum is Arelate (Gallia Narbonensis) with three.[23] Population size does not account for the discrepancy; in Strabo's time Narbo was larger than Lugdunum, for instance, and yet the phrase is known only from one inscription there (*Geogr.* 4.3.2). Rather, the high frequency of this uncommon formula in Lugdunum compared to anywhere else in Gallia reveals some sort of social network of people with strong enough ties to be gradually encouraging the adoption of ideas behind the phrase *hic adquiescit*, and perhaps also attendant practices in communicating with (new?) gods. The eleven epitaphs from first-century Lugdunum (and one additional epitaph with *hic quiescit*) are as follows:[24]

1. epitaph of unknown individual (Julio-Claudian era; *CIL* 13.2333)[25]

2. epitaph of Ancharia Bassa, freedwoman of Quintus (Julio-Claudian era; *CIL* 13.2059)

3. epitaph of Caius Julius Seleucus, freedman of Cotta (Julio-Claudian era; *AE* 1973, no. 333; Audin 1974, 99)

4. epitaph of Julia Clara, daughter of P(h)ilargurus (Julio-Claudian era; *CIL* 13.2178)

5–6. epitaphs of unknown person and [Jul]ia (?) Modesta (Julio-Claudia era; *AE* 1961, no. 70)

7. epitaph of Claudia Suavis, imperial freedwoman (Claudian or Neronian era; *CIL* 13.1914)

8. epitaph of Nobilis, imperial freedman (Neronian era?; *CIL* 13.1820)

---

[22] Laubry (2005, 303–4) briefly discusses most of them. Dating these epitaphs to specific decades of the first century is difficult. Some are occasionally put in Augustus' reign on the basis of orthography: namely, use of *EI* for long *I*'s (e.g., *CIL* 12.870). However, for the date of Greek and Latin texts that use *EI* for long *I*'s—which can be as late as the second century CE—see Anderson, Parsons, and Nisbet 1979, 132–43.

[23] *CIL* 12.870 (Augustan era); *CIL* 12.845 (first century CE); *CIL* 12.855a (Claudian era); once in Nîmes, Gallia Narbonensis (*CIL* 12.3325). Laubry first compiled all occurrences from Gallia in 2005.

[24] For discussion of each except Le Mer and Chomer 2007, 283, and *CIL* 13.2333, see Laubry 2005, 301–3.

[25] On the problem of dating the epitaph by its spelling of *hic* with *heic*, see n. 24 above.

9.   epitaph of Julia Adepta (Neronian-Vespasian era; *CIL* 13.2177)

10. epitaph of Lepida, freedman of Priscus (second half of first century CE; currently unenumerated; see Laubry 2005)

11. epitaph of unknown individual (first century CE?; *CIL* 13.2047)

12. epitaph of Nicephorus (first century CE?; see Le Mer and Chomer 2007, 283)

The odds that users of this rare phrase were socially connected are strengthened by three considerations: (1) all twelve epitaphs can be dated to the middle quarters of the first century and so the commemorated were contemporaries; (2) about half the commemorated individuals were either themselves Julian freedpersons or associated with Julian freedpersons; and (3) four epitaphs (*CIL* 13.1820, 2177; *AE* 1961, no. 70) demonstrate without question that users of this funerary phrase shared strong ties. The latter four epitaphs are those of spouses Julia (*CIL* 13.2177) and Nobilis (*CIL* 13.1820), which have been explored already, and also the two epitaphs on the Modesta stone (*AE* 1961, no. 70).

The Modesta stone is too fragmentary for reconstructing the two commemorated individuals' relationship. It is a single broken funerary stele discovered in 1958 in situ on Montée Saint-Barthélemy (*AE* 1961, no. 70). Only the right side survives.

> [---? *hic*] *adquiescit.* | [---] *Quartio fratri* | *pio* || [---]*ia Modesta hic quiescit.* (*AE* 1961, no. 70 = Le Mer and Chomer 2007, 501)

> [---] rests here. [---] Quartio for his pious brother. [Jul?]ia Modesta rests here.

The fragmented titulus in the top panel probably originally included a missing first line that may have featured the *tria nomina* of the deceased.[26] It is supported by two columns topped with flowers. A second inscription, very similar to the one in the titulus, was centrally placed below the molded frame. Both have been dated to the Julio-Claudian period on paleographical grounds.[27] All things considered, the commemorated individuals were likely buried in the same tomb.[28]

---

[26] This is the suggestion of Laubry 2005, 302.
[27] Audin and Guey 1961, 111–27 (esp. 119–27); cf. Laubry 2005, 302.
[28] Audin and Guey 1961, 120. Followed by Le Mer in Le Mer and Chomer 2007, 501.

If the name Quartio is in the dative, he would be the deceased in the first epitaph. However, Quartio is a nominative cognomen (see e.g., *CIL* 12.870), and so Nicolas Laubry rightly identifies him as the dedicator—the rest of his *tria nomina* would have preceded the cognomen. The name of the deceased, he argues, may have been placed on a missing line above *adquiescit* (Laubry 2005, 302). The name of the commemorated person in the second epitaph survives partially. Laubry suggests the *gentilicium*, Julia, which would fit and would represent a fourth Julian on these *hic adquiescit* epitaphs. The Julian nomen also appears, of course, in the epitaphs of Julia Adepta (*CIL* 13.2177); Nobilis (*CIL* 13.1820); Julia Clara, daughter of P(h)ilargurus (*CIL* 13.2178); and C(aius) Julius Seleucus, freedman of Cotta (*AE* 1973, no. 333).

In all, we seemingly have four Julians, as well as the spouse of Julia Adepta, to whom the rare term *hic adquiescit* appealed, and in addition to them also an individual with a very strong tie to Julia (?) Modesta. These Julians likely formed the core of the network as their epitaphs are on balance earlier than the others. The network expanded beyond its original core, as can be seen even in our very small list, after the time of Julia Adepta, when there are signs of a shift to acquaintances (neighbors, co-workers, friends) who gradually came to share the small Julian network's perspective on death as a temporary state.

CHRIST WORSHIP AND THE *SODALES*

Now that a Julian familial network has been connected through Julia Adepta to the *sodales* that funded her funerary stone, we can turn to the question of how open the collegium may have been to incorporating Christ worship into their routines. If Julia functioned as their *mater*, perhaps pressure from her would carry a lot of weight. Her spouse, Nobilis, is of course, a user of the funerary formula in question and has been suspected of worshipping Christ on other grounds, too.

The susceptibility of a *sodalis* to Christ worship depends on the threshold of social pressure or persuasion essential for activating the individual's adoption of the practice. The threshold depends on whether Christ worship in mid-first-century Lugdunum was a "simple" or "complex contagion," to use an epidemiological metaphor John Kloppenborg recently applied to the expansion of Christ worship and other worship practices in antiquity (2020). A simple contagion, Kloppenborg highlights, is one with a low threshold for reception and which can be transmitted to a passive recipient. An example of a simple contagion might be an attractive practice that really has very few social consequences and requires little effort on the part of the recipient, such as the idea to use the *hic situs est* formula in one's epitaph. The recipient of a complex contagion, by contrast, must actively reorient their behavior on a grander scale and could suffer serious social consequences for doing so (Kloppenborg 2020, 330–34).

The plainness of Nobilis' and Modesta's self-representations on their funerary stones might provide a clue to the costs of adopting Christ worship in mid-first-century Lugdunum. Their frankness would generally indicate the presumption of societal openness and an inclusive disposition among peers. These stones can be contrasted with a second-century votive altar from Rome dedicated to Jupiter by a (doubly) anonymous worshipper of Christ.[29] The double anonymity in the dedication from Rome suggests hesitancy to publicize one's practice of Christ worship, and the possible danger in doing so.

Since the Nobilis stone has been studied elsewhere (Last 2022), I will focus here on plain self-representation of Christ worship in the Modesta stone. It was already shown that one of the epitaphs on this stone is especially fascinating for its use of the phrase *hic quiescit* in the first century—a funerary formula largely characteristic of Christian epigraphs, and a verb found only on Christian epitaphs from Lugdunum. But the stone's decoration also merits attention, in particular the depiction of a peculiarly placed large tool between the two pilasters.

The surviving portion of the image (fig. 22.2) shows a large tool: most of the handle as well as most of the iron except for a portion of the cutting edge. Since the stone is from Lugdunum, a natural interpretation is that this tool is the *ascia*, an instrument for stonecutting and shaping (see fig. 22.3). *Asciae* are pictured or referenced in funerary formulae[30] in Lugdunensis far more than in any other Roman province.[31] One of many examples is the funerary stele of Puice or Pulchra, from late second-century Lugdunum (see fig. 22.3). This stele features an engraved *ascia* in the pediment as well as the *ascia* formula at the end of its inscription. The inscription reads:

> D(iis) M(anibus) | et requieti (a)etern(a)e / Puice (= Pulchrae?) | civeis Trax [sic]|| qu(a)e vixit annos | LXXX, Aristonia | Maxsimina et | Aristonia | Valen(t)ina fil||li(a)e matri pon|endum qurav|erunt et sub | ascia dedica|vit [sic]. (AE 1991, no. 1227; Lugdunum, 171–200 CE)

---

[29] See *CIL* 6.390 = 30752 with Last 2020.
[30] The formulae vary between *sub ascia* ("under the *ascia*") and *sub ascia dedicare* ("to dedicate under the *ascia*").
[31] For a catalogue of all occurrences by geography, see Mattsson 1990.

Fig. 22.2 Surviving Fragment of Modesta's Funerary Stele—*AE* 1961, no. 70 (from Audin and Guey 1961, 118, fig. 3)
https://creativecommons.org/licenses/by-nc-nd/4.0/.

For the departed spirits and eternal rest of Puice (or Pulchra), a Thracian citizen who lived 80 years. Aristonia Maxsimina and Aristonia Valentina, her daughters, saw to the setting up (of this tombstone) for their mother and they dedicated (it) under the *ascia*.

Unfortunately, there is no consensus on what the *ascia* symbolized. The favored theory is that this tool (in the form of both the image and also the formulae) might have indicated the grave was consecrated by a rite that made the tomb inviolable and warned tomb violators they would suffer divine punishment.[32] However, these *asciae* may not represent a consecration ritual or a warning to tomb violators, but rather could depict the idea of eternal life.[33]

In any case, Amable Audin has observed that Modesta's funerary stele is too early for the *ascia*; this tool does not appear in Lugdunum until the fourth

---

[32] Hatt 1951, 85–107. A similar reading is offered by de Visscher 1963, 277–94. See Panciera 1960; Mattsson 1990.

[33] See the review of literature in Mattsson 1990.

Fig. 22.3 Funerary Stele of Puice
(or Pulchra)—*AE* 1991, no. 1227
Courtesy of Manfred Clauss.

Fig. 22.4 Funerary Stone of Titus
Valerius Puden—*CIL* 7.185
(photo: Anne Kolb)
Courtesy of Manfred Clauss.

quarter of the first century (Audin and Guey 1961, 123).[34] More importantly, the tool in the Modesta stone is not in the shape of an *ascia*, as can be seen by comparing what remains of the picture with an actual *ascia* in figure 22.3. Specifically, the metal blade of the tool pictured on the Modesta stone does not break sharply downward after the handle as an *ascia* would, nor does the left side (the cutting edge) widen (Audin and Guey 1961, 123).

Instead, Audin argues, the tool on the Modesta stone appears to be a *dolabra*—an ax used in mining, trench-digging, and gardening (Audin and

---

[34] Audin is the sole author of the comments on the Modesta stone. It should be noted that the *ascia* can be found earlier in Dalmatia.

HIC·ADQVIESCIT
QVARTIO·FRATRI
PIO
QVARTIA·MODESTA·HIC·QVIESCIT

Fig. 22.5 Amable Audin's Reconstruction of
Modesta's Funerary Stone
(from Audin and Guey 1961, 126, fig. 4)
https://creativecommons.org/licenses/by-nc-nd/4.0/.

Guey 1961, 124). For comparative purposes, the *dolabra* can be seen decorating the base of the limestone funerary monument of Titus Valerius Puden, a soldier from Savaria (fig. 22.4).[35]

Having identified the tool pictured on the Modesta stone, Audin provides a helpful artistic reconstruction (fig. 22.5). Audin proceeds by inquiring why the owners of this stele decorated it so prominently with the *dolabra*. The possibility that the *dolabra* represents the occupational identity of the two deceased individuals commemorated in the inscriptions (names lost) seems unlikely—the image is too conspicuously placed for that; a peripheral location is standard for the tools of one's profession. For comparison, several stones from Lugdunum can be viewed, including the funerary monument of a blacksmith, whose professional tools (pliers and a hammer) are placed on the pediment (*CIL* 13.2036), and the monument of a potter, which features his pots above the inscription panel (*CIL* 13.2033; see fig. 22.6).[36]

---

[35] For the inscription, see *CIL* 7.185 (Lindum, Britannia, 76 CE).
[36] Cf. Audin and Guey 1961, 124.

Fig. 22.6 Funerary Stone of Murranius Verus—*CIL* 13.2033 Courtesy of Manfred Clauss.

So, if not the occupational identity of the deceased, what could the *dolabra* have signified? The location of the tool in the central part of the stone—its significance further underscored by the pilasters that frame it—is key to narrowing the interpretive options. Working from Émile Espérandieu's twelve-volume collection of artifacts from Roman Gaul, Audin observes that among the peoples of Gallic tribes (i.e., Bituriges, Aedui, Lingones, Mediomatrici) there are several other stelai with double registers, whose lower (central) inscription panels are framed by columns and feature engraved objects instead of text (see fig. 22.7). A majority of these are found around Avaricum.[37] The image depicted in most is an altar, and so whatever the connotation, this style of stele foregrounds communication with the gods. The same is likely of the *dolabra* on the Modesta stone.

---

[37] See, for instance, *CIL* 13.5758, 5740, 5801, 5834, 5736.

Fig. 22.7 Funerary stele of Publicius Satto—*CIL* 13.5834 (photo: Kresimir Matijevic) Courtesy of *CIL* 13: Project Flensburg-Trier.[38]

None of the stones collected by Espérandieu feature a *dolabra*[39] (though some depict tools including axes, hammers, and anvils) and most if not all date later than the Modesta stone (Audin and Guey 1961, 125). Audin reasons that the specific images foregrounded in these steles symbolize rebirth (e.g., pine cones, leaves, fruit). The *dolabra* likewise symbolizes rebirth as

---

[38]   *CIL* 13.5834 (Andematunum, Germania Superior, second century CE).

[39]   Audin suggests that *CIL* 13.3367 is of this stele type and features an *ascia*. However, the central image of the *ascia* is not framed by pilasters in that stone. There are, in fact, several funerary stones with prominently placed engravings of the *ascia*, somewhat analogous to the Modesta stone, but missing the columns. See *CIL* 13.5626 (Tilena, Germania Superior, 151–300 CE); *CIL* 13.5634 (Tilena, Germania Superior); *CIL* 13.3367 (Durocortorum, Belgica, 171–250 CE); and *CIL* 13.3407 (Durocortorum, Belgica, 171–230 CE).

a gardening tool, but the peculiarity of the image still must be explained (Audin and Guey 1961, 126).

Since none of the stelai in Espérandieu's collection depict the *dolabra*, the Modesta stone stands out from Audin's *comparanda*. In light of what has been discovered about users of the phrase *hic adquiescit* (or at least some of them) in mid-first-century Lugdunum, it could be posited that Julia (?) Modesta—who chose the variant, *hic quiescit*, in her epitaph—made the unusual choice of a *dolabra* because it put her and the individual commemorated by the other epitaph on the stone in communication with their god, Christ, analogously to the function of the altars in the stelai of a similar style. At this very early date, there was, as should be expected, only the slightest evidence of a vocabulary or artistic tradition associated with Christ worship. The prominence of the symbol on the Modesta stone might reveal that the cost of worshipping Christ by a *sodalis* in the association that funded Julia Adepta's funerary monument was low—but any assessment depends on whether cross-shaped symbols were relatively well-known markers of Christ worship at the time (see Gal 5:11; 1 Cor 1:23; cf. Origen, *Cels.* 6.34).[40]

CONCLUSION

If Nobilis and Julia (?) Modesta conceptualized death as rest or sleep prior to practicing Christ worship, they may be understood as "recipients susceptible to diffusion" of Christ worship, for their practices were presumably more closely aligned with the veneration of Christ than were most of their peers.[41] Their closest connections may have been the ones who found Christ worship most appealing—for Nobilis it would be Julia Adepta and Perpetua among others, and for Julia (?) Modesta it would be the individual with whom she shared a funerary stone, among others. Many scenarios for how and whether members of the Julian network transferred Christ worship to the collegium are imaginable. One possibility is that the formation of this collegium marked a transformation of the Julian network into a more formal and durable organization, for the earliest eight *hic adquiescit* funerary stones include all four Julians, the spouse of a Julian, an unknown individual close enough to Julia (?) Modesta to share a funerary stone, and one other unknown individual. In any case, Julia Adepta's connection to this collegium represented one point in what must have been a constantly evolving urban social life.

[40] On this, see now Longenecker 2015; 2016; and my discussion (Last 2022) of Tarquinius Pollio's funerary stone and epitaph, which also uses the phrase *hic adquiescit* (*CIL* 9.5331; Cupra Maritima, Picenum, first century CE).

[41] Quote from Kloppenborg 2020, 334.

WORKS CITED

Allmer, Auguste, and Paul Dissard. 1890. *Musée de Lyon, Inscriptions antiques.* Vol. 3. Lyon: Delaroche.

Anderson, Robert D., Peter J. Parsons, and Robin George Murdoch Nisbet. 1979. "Elegiacs by Gallus from Qasr Ibrîm." *Journal of Roman Studies* 69:125–55.

Audin, Amable. 1974. "Note d'épigraphie lyonnaise." *Latomus* 33:98–104.

Audin, Amable, and Julien Guey. 1961. "Deux inscriptons lyonnaises de l'époque Julio-Claudienne." *Cahiers d'histoire* 6:109–27.

Bellièvre, Claude. (1525–1556) 1846. *Lugdunum priscum, recueil de notes rédigées entre 1525 et 1556.* Edited by Jean-Baptiste Monfalcon. Collection des Bibliophiles Lyonnais. Lyon: Imprimerie de Dumoulin et Ronet.

Le Blant, Edmond. 1856. *Inscriptions chrétiennes de la Gaule antérieures au VIIIe siècle.* Vol. 1. Paris: Imprimerie impériale.

de Boissieu, Alphonse. 1846–1854. *Les inscriptions antiques de Lyon: reproduites d'après les monuments ou recueillies dans les auteurs.* Lyon: Perrin.

Brelich, Angelo. 1937. *Aspetti della morte nelle iscrizioni sepolcrali dell'Impero romano.* Dissertationes Pannonicae 1.7. Budapest: Institute of Numismatics and Archaeology of Pázmány University.

de Colonia, Dominique. 1728. *Histoire littéraire de la ville de Lyon avec une bibliothèque des auteurs lyonnois, sacrés et profanes, distribuée par siècles.* Vol. 1. Lyon: François Rigollet.

Cooper, Richard. 2016. "Gabriele Simeoni et les antiquités de Lyon." Pages 297–332 in *Gabriele Simeoni (1509–1570?): un Florentine en France entre princes et libraires.* Edited by Silvia D'Amico and Catherine Magnien-Simonin. Geneva: Droz.

D'Amico, Silvia, and Catherine Magnien-Simonin, eds. 2016. *Gabriele Simeoni (1509–1570?): un Florentine en France entre princes et libraires.* Geneva: Droz.

Harland, Philip A., ed. 2014. *North Coast of the Black Sea, Asia Minor.* BZNW 204. Vol. 2 of *Greco-Roman Associations: Texts, Translations, and Commentary.* Edited by John S. Kloppenborg and Richard S. Ascough. Berlin: De Gruyter.

Hatt, Jean-Jacques. 1951. *La tombe gallo-romaine.* Paris: Presses universitaires de France.

Kloppenborg, John S. 2019. *Christ's Associations: Connecting and Belonging in the Ancient City.* New Haven: Yale University Press.

———. 2020. "Recruitment to Elective Cults: Network Structure and Ecology." *NTS* 66:323–50.

Last, Richard. 2016. "The Myth of Free Membership in Pauline Christ Groups." Pages 495–516 in *Scribal Practices and Social Structures among Jesus Adherents: Essays in Honour of John S. Kloppenborg.* Edited by William

E. Arnal, Richard S. Ascough, Robert S. Derrenbacker Jr., and Philip A. Harland. BETL 285. Leuven: Peeters.

———. 2020. "The Silence of a God-Fearer: Anonymous Dedication in *CIL* 6.390a = 30752." *Religion in the Roman Empire* 6:75–103.

———. 2022. "A First-Century Inscription? The Nobilis Funerary Altar (*CIL* 13.1820) and a Return to Alphonse de Boissieu." *Journal of Epigraphic Studies* 5: forthcoming.

Laubry, Nicolas. 2005. "Une nouvelle inscription funéraire de Lyon: remarques sur le formulaire *hic adquiescit* dans l'Occident romain." *Revue archéologique de l'Est* 54:299–309.

Longenecker, Bruce. 2015. *The Cross before Constantine: The Early Life of a Christian Symbol*. Minneapolis: Fortress.

———. 2016. *The Crosses of Pompeii: Jesus-Devotion in a Vesuvian Town*. Minneapolis: Fortress.

Mattsson, Bengt. 1990. *The Ascia Symbol on Latin Epitaphs*. Studies in Mediterranean Archaeology and Literature / Pocket-book 70. Gothenburg: Åströms.

Menestrier, Claude-Françoise. 1696. *Histoire civile ou consulaire de la ville de Lyon*. Lyon: Jean-Baptiste & Nicolas de Ville.

Le Mer, Anne-Catherine, and Claire Chomer. 2007. *Lyon*. Carte archéologique de la Gaule 69/2. Paris: Académie des Inscriptions et Belles-Lettres.

Monfalcon, Jean-Baptiste. 1846. *Mélanges sur l'histoire ancienne de Lyon*. Lyon: Imprimerie de Bajat.

Panciera, Silvio. 1960. "*Deasciare, exacisclare, exasciare*." *Latomus* 19:701–7.

Paradin, Guillaume. 1573. *Mémoires de l'histoire de Lyon*. Lyon: Gryphius.

Ravenez, Louis W. 1861. *Essai sur les origines religieuses de Bordeaux et de Saint Seurin d'Aquitaine*. Paris: Dumoulin et Ducot.

Simeoni, Gabriele. 1560. *Le Origine e le Antichità di Lione*. J.A.X. 16. Turin: State Archives.

Spon, Jacob. (1673) 1858. *Recherche des antiquités et curiosités de la ville de Lyon*. 2nd ed. Lyon: Perrin.

———. 1685. *Miscellanea eruditae antiquitatis*. Lyon: Thomas Amauldry.

Tran, Nicolas. 2006. *Les membres des associations romaines: le rang social des collegiati en Italie et en Gaules sous le haut-empire*. Collection de l'École française de Rome 367. Rome: École française de Rome.

de Visscher, Fernand. 1963. *Le droit des tombeaux romains*. Milan: Giuffrè.

Waltzing, Jean-Pierre. 1895–1900. *Étude historique sur les corporations professionnelles chez les Romains depuis les origines jusqu'à la chute de l'Empire d'Occident*. 4 vols. Leuven: Peeters.

Weaver, P. R. C. 1972. *Familia Caesaris: A Social Study of the Emperor's Freedmen and Slaves*. Cambridge: Cambridge University Press.

23

"Many Have Sold Themselves into Slavery"

Voluntary Imprisonment and Slavery, Survival Strategies among Associations, and the Reception of 1 Corinthians in 1 Clement 55

David J. Downs

In the autumn of 1732, two Moravians—Leonhard Dober, a potter, and David Nitschmann, a carpenter—left their community in Saxony and journeyed to St. Thomas, a Danish colony in the Caribbean.[1] Their intent was to sell themselves as slaves in order to live among slaves as missionaries to them. Ultimately, however, these two Moravian missionaries were prevented from selling themselves into slavery. The reasons for the censure of their voluntary enslavement are multifaceted, but prominent among them was the conviction among many early eighteenth-century European Protestants that neither whites nor Christians could be slaves. The senior chamberlin of the Danish West India Company is said to have responded to the Moravians' plan for voluntary enslavement by saying, "[We] don't let white people do that!"

Among European planters on the island of St. Thomas in the early 1730s, the very notion of a Christian mission to slaves was controversial, even unimaginable, because of the conviction that a Christian identity and a slave identity were incompatible. Christians could not be slaves and slaves could not be Christians. Katharine Gerbner calls this the ideology of "Protestant Supremacy" (2018, 2). Thus, while Dober and Nitschmann's plan to live as

---

[1] The summary here draws on the account and interpretation in Gerbner 2018, 172–202; see also Sensbach 1998, 19–47.

slaves among slaves was rejected in part because they were white, it was also disallowed because they were Christians. Indeed, Gerbner demonstrates that the Moravian missionaries were early proponents of what she terms "Christian Slavery," namely, "an attempt to Christianize and reform slavery" while maintaining its basic structures (2018, 3).

The tale of Dober and Nitschmann (only briefly recounted here) is known as one of the few instances of voluntary slavery for missional purposes in the Christian tradition, even though the "Moravian slaves" were never actually slaves. Yet there is an ancient, and perhaps more historically compelling, reference to Christian self-enslavement from the letter known as 1 Clement. Christ followers in the first and second centuries did not have the luxury or the power to debate whether slaves could be Χριστιανοί ("Christians," to use a term that might be anachronistic in some contexts), nor would such a question have made sense to them. The earliest literary evidence indicates that slaves were indeed participants in Christian associations (Philemon; 1 Cor 7:21-24; Eph 6:5-9; Col 3:22–4:1; 1 Tim 6:1-2; 1 Pet 2:18-21; Ign. *Pol.* 4.3; Did. 4.10-11; Barn. 19.7). How exactly slaves participated in nascent Christ groups and to what extent their freedom was either supported or discouraged are questions that have generated much debate (Glancy 2002; Harrill 2006). In the present essay, I shall consider a somewhat overlooked text that offers a window into the practice of voluntary enslavement for the purpose of providing material assistance to other members of a religious association with the proceeds from the sale of one's body.

First Clement, the second-century letter from Christ followers in Rome to the ἐκκλησία, or "assembly," in Corinth, provides this reference to voluntary enslavement among early Christians. In the context of an appeal for schismatics among the Corinthians to be willing to depart in order to cease an ecclesiastical conflict in Corinth (54.1–4), the Roman authors of 1 Clement allude to practices of self-imprisonment and self-enslavement among Christ followers: "We know that many among us have handed themselves over into bonds, so that they might ransom others. Many have sold themselves into slavery, and with the price received for themselves have fed others" (55.2).[2]

In this essay, I shall attempt to locate this reference to voluntary imprisonment and enslavement in light of 1 Clement's deliberative rhetorical strategies and in the context of practices of group survival among associations in the ancient Mediterranean. Second, I shall explore the commendation of

---

[2] Although it is customary to write of "the author" of 1 Clement, in order to emphasize the letter's own claims to collective authorship by "the assembly of God that resides in Rome" (inscr.; cf. 62.1–63.4), in this essay I shall refer to "the authors" of 1 Clement.

self-enslavement in 1 Clem. 55.2 in connection with the letter's reception of the Pauline Epistles, especially 1 Corinthians. The practice of selling oneself into slavery would, at first glance, seem to violate Paul's directive in 1 Cor 7:23: "Do not become slaves of human masters." Yet the writers of 1 Clement, who clearly esteem 1 Corinthians, appear to have viewed the willing sacrifice of one's freedom for the material benefit of others as a justifiable concession to the principle of remaining in the state in which one is called (1 Cor 7:20, 24), perhaps similar to the exception advocating that slaves seek freedom, if possible, in 1 Cor 7:21. Finally, the essay will conclude with a consideration of the particular survival strategy of voluntary slavery in light of Orlando Patterson's influential thesis that slavery be understood as social death, a status characterized by violence, natal alienation, and dishonor (Patterson 1982). I shall suggest that 1 Clem. 55.2 offers a brief glimpse into an experience of slavery among some Christ followers that challenges the model of slavery as social death.

1 CLEM. 55.2 IN THE RHETORICAL CONTEXT OF 1 CLEMENT

Should we view 1 Clem. 55.2 to be reliable in its assertion that many Christ followers have allowed themselves to be imprisoned and sold into slavery in order to benefit others? Or is this an exaggeration, perhaps even an invention, for rhetorical effect? In their excellent monograph *Group Survival in the Ancient Mediterranean*, Richard Last and Philip Harland are critical of a scholarly tendency to contrast practices of collective socioeconomic support among Jewish and Christian assemblies, on one hand, with an alleged absence of mutual assistance among "pagan" associations, on the other. One of the points that Last and Harland raise is the need for caution in evaluating literary evidence from Christ followers when considering practices of mutual assistance. They write:

> Unfortunately for the social historian interested in cultural practices and social interactions, this literary evidence is prescriptive or reactionary, coming from the perspective of a particular literate individual, rather than the group as whole (unlike collectively established association regulations). This literature is prescriptive in advocating certain behaviours among adherents. . . . Or the literature is reactionary in defending adherents of Jesus against the negative perceptions or accusations of "crimes" by some outsiders. . . . Neither type of source is particularly helpful for the historian who aims to reconstruct a likely scenario regarding social practices among participants in the groups in question. (2020, 178)

With regard to a carefully rhetorically constructed text like 1 Clement, caution is indeed in order. Yet I would suggest that 1 Clem. 55.2 does offer reliable, if brief, evidence for practices of voluntary imprisonment and slavery among early Christ followers. Not only is the letter framed as representing the perspective of a group rather than an individual, and not only is 1 Clement 55 neither prescriptive nor reactionary in its references to voluntary imprisonment and slavery for the sake of others, but there are also other reasons to believe that the authors of 1 Clement assume that their readers will be familiar with real examples of these sacrificial acts.

As a whole, the letter of 1 Clement offers a fine illustration of deliberative rhetoric that makes an extended appeal for "peace and harmony" (63.2; Bakke 2001). A distinguishing feature of the tradition of deliberative rhetoric was the use of examples, both historical and contemporary, to encourage a desired course of action. It is not surprising, therefore, that the argument of 1 Clement is replete with positive examples to imitate and negative examples to avoid (e.g., 1 Clem. 4.1–6.4 is a roll call of negative and positive examples from the ancient and recent past; Bakke 2001, 54–61; Breytenbach 2014, 22–33).

The reference to voluntary imprisonment and enslavement in 1 Clem. 55.2 appears in the context of the author's appeal for those responsible for the schism in Corinth to remove themselves from the situation through voluntary exile (54.1–4; Welborn 2014). Having proposed that the leaders of the faction responsible for the division in Corinth should—with nobility, compassion, and love—depart willingly, the authors provide examples (ὑποδείγματα; cf. 5.1; 6.1; 46.1) of sacrificial love, beginning with "some examples of the nations," which includes the claim that "many kings and rulers, being prompted by some oracle, have given themselves over to death, so that they might rescue their subjects through their own blood" (55.1). Since no specific examples are provided, the authors may assume that readers will fill in the gap with awareness of well-known cases of leaders sacrificing themselves for the sake of their subjects.[3] For instance, before citing numerous instances of rulers who sacrificed for their people, Cicero writes, "Noble deaths, sought voluntarily, for the sake of country, are not only commonly reckoned glorious by rhetoricians but also happy" (*Tusc.* 1.116). The same may be said of the reference to "many" kings and rulers who "have departed their own cities, so they might not rebel any more" in 1 Clem. 55.1b: the

---

[3]   It has sometimes been suggested that the wording of 1 Clem. 55.1, including the phrase χρησμοδοτηθέντες, evokes the story of the Theban Menoeceus, who, in Euripides' *Phoenissae*, throws himself from a parapet to save his city in response to an oracle from the seer Teiresias (834–1092; Bremmer 2015; Lona 1998, 561–62).

authors rely on shared cultural knowledge of the practice of voluntary exile for the sake of civic harmony.

In this context, the authors of 1 Clement write of those who "have handed themselves over into bonds" and those who "have sold themselves into slavery" in 55.2. In the next section, we will consider practices of voluntary imprisonment and slavery in historical context. For now, assuming that these were things that one could theoretically do in the second century CE, it is sufficient to make a few points regarding the plausibility of the authors' claim that "many among us" have done these things. First, the Romans explicitly draw upon shared knowledge of these sacrificial acts, employing the first-person plural form of a verb, ἐπίσταμαι, that has recently and emphatically been used in the letter to underscore the readers' shared knowledge of the sacred Scriptures (53.1: Ἐπίστασθε γὰρ καὶ καλῶς ἐπίστασθε τὰς ἱερὰς γραφάς; Kujanpää 2020, 132). As Keener observes, "Ancient rhetoricians often appealed to common knowledge to make a point; although this information may have sometimes been gossip, it seems unlikely that it was normally simply a rhetorical deception" (2012, 187). Second, the agents of these vicarious practices are specifically said to be "many among us" (πολλοὺς ἐν ἡμῖν). The phrase ἐν ἡμῖν both binds together Christ followers in Rome and Corinth by highlighting their participation in a united community (cf. 6.1; 21.9; 27.3; 63.3), which may extend beyond these two cities, and indicates that those who have willingly had themselves imprisoned to ransom others and sold themselves into slavery are members of Christ assemblies, in contrast to the examples of pagan rulers cited in 55.1 and the scriptural figures in 55.3–6.

It is difficult to know how inclusive the πολλοί is intended to be in this context. The adjective is repeated seven times in 1 Clem. 55.1–3, including anaphoric repetition at the beginning of five separate clauses, an indication that this is a carefully crafted piece of deliberative rhetoric. It is true that the authors go on to proclaim the examples of "many women, being strengthened by the grace of God, performing many courageous deeds" (55.3), and yet then describe the actions of only two women, Judith and Esther (Peters 2021). This should not be taken to indicate that Judith and Esther are the only women who have provided brave examples, however (*pace* Glancy 2002, 82; cf. the examples of valorous women in 6.2 and 12.1–8). Thus, it seems unlikely that the authors of 1 Clement have offered these examples of Christian sacrifice as a rhetorical fiction. Had these self-sacrificial acts been unknown to readers in Corinth, or even if readers would have suspected the examples of being untrue, the point of highlighting these acts of vicarious sacrifice, if not the appeal of the entire letter, would be undermined (Osiek 1981, 370).

Moreover, this characterization of self-giving love fits with the portrayal of the Corinthians elsewhere in the letter, even if this reflects an idealized depiction of the past aimed at promoting ὁμόνοια in Corinth. In the opening *exordium* of the missive, for example, the Corinthians are praised for, among other things, "the impressive habit of [their] hospitality" (1.2) in the past, and they are said to have been "more glad to give than to receive" (2.1). Additionally, the authors of 1 Clement appear to allude to the practice of sacrificial mutual aid among the Corinthians in 2.6–7, where they write, "All rebellion and all schism were detestable to you. You used to mourn because of the offences (done) to your neighbors; you considered their needs (τὰ ὑστερήματα αὐτῶν) to be your own. You were without regret in every act of doing good, ready for every good work."[4] That 1 Clem. 2.6 refers to practices of socioeconomic assistance among the Corinthians—instead of a more spiritualized sense of "(moral) shortcomings"—is confirmed by the use of the noun ὑστέρημα, which is found only one other time in 1 Clement. In 1 Clem. 38.2, ὑστέρημα clearly means "material needs." There, the authors advocate a relationship of mutual exchange between the "strong" (ὁ ἰσχυρὸς) and "the weak" (ὁ ἀσθενὴς): "Let the rich person provide for the poor person; and let the poor person give thanks to God because God gave him one through whom he might supply his need (αὐτοῦ τὸ ὑστέρημα)." Thus, according to 1 Clem. 2.6, before the schism the Corinthians were known for taking on as their own the material needs of their abused neighbors. While this praise for the Corinthians' past behavior is clearly part of the authors' rhetorical strategy in the letter's *exordium* in 1.1–2.8 (Bakke 2001), it would not be effective if it were a fabrication.

1 CLEM. 55.2 AND GROUP SURVIVAL STRATEGIES AMONG GRECO-ROMAN ASSOCIATIONS

If the references to voluntary imprisonment and slavery for the sake of others in 1 Clem. 55.2 allude to things actually done by, or at least known to, Christ followers in Corinth and Rome, it is worth considering these practices in light of survival strategies among associations in the ancient world. Among group survival strategies highlighted by Last and Harland, two

---

[4]   I have followed Codex Alexandrinus (A), which offers τοῖς πλησίον in 2.6, in contrast to τῶν πλησίον of Codex Hierosolymitanus (C) (*pace* Lightfoot, who states that τῶν πλησίον is "a brachylogy for τοῖς τῶν πλησίον" [1890, 19]).

are especially noteworthy for the present study, namely, (1) the provision of funds or assistance to group members who had come into legal trouble, including imprisonment; and (2) the use of community funds to pay for the manumission of slaves (2020, 151–86).[5] While there are parallels between the survival strategies that Last and Harland identify among Greco-Roman associations and the deeds mentioned in 1 Clem. 55.2, it does appear that voluntary enslavement for the sake of other members is distinctive among known practices from associations in the ancient Mediterranean.

In the first instance, the authors of 1 Clement report an awareness that "many among us have handed themselves over into bonds, so that they might ransom others." In this statement δεσμά ("bonds") is a metonym for imprisonment (Curbera 2018, 10). Care for prisoners features as a valued practice in a number of early Christian texts (e.g., Matt 25:31-46; Phil 2:25-30; 4:10-20; Col 4:7; Heb 10:34; 13:3; Ign. *Eph.* 2.2; Ign. *Smyrn.* 6.2; Ign. *Trall.* 12.1; 1 Clem. 59.4; Justin, *1 Apol.* 67.6–7; Lucian, *Peregr.* 11–13; Tertullian, *Apol.* 39; *Did. apost.* 19; Osiek 1981; Wansink 1996; Nicklas 2016). How exactly the voluntary imprisonment of some might result in the ransom of others is not explicitly detailed. Perhaps the most plausible situation would involve some Christ followers standing surety for others imprisoned due to outstanding debts. Although Livy recounts that Roman legislation to eliminate debt bondage was passed in 326 BCE (*Roman History* 8.28; cf. Cicero, *Rep.* 2.59), and later laws attempt to offer protection to debtors from physical coercion (Cod. justin. 4.10.9; 7.71.8; Cod. theod. 11.7.5), the practice of imprisoning debtors is nevertheless well attested (Krause 1996; Bauschatz 2007; Hillner 2015; Eubank 2018). One legal note from Oxyrhynchus from 23 CE, for example, records the willingness of a certain Theon to stand surety for a prisoner named Sarapion, with Theon agreeing either to produce Sarapion within a month or else pay the debt or be imprisoned himself (*POxy* 2.259; cf. Sir 29.15; Lucian, *Tim.* 49; Eubank 2018, 166).

The authors of 1 Clement then refer to voluntary slavery: "Many have sold themselves into slavery, and with the price received for themselves have fed others" (55.2). The practice of selling oneself into slavery was known in antiquity, although the extent to which the slave population

---

5   Space constraints prohibit a consideration of slavery in the wider context of 1 Clement; see, e.g., the reference to Claudius Ephebus, likely a freedman, who is among those said "to have lived blameless lives among us from youth to old age" (63.3; 65.1; cf. 60.2). It is somewhat curious that slaves are not mentioned in the household code in 21.6–8, an omission that might challenge claims that 1 Clement represents elite attitudes toward poverty and slavery (a point I owe to Dr. Jeremiah Bailey).

was supplied by self-sale is debated (Glancy 2002, 80–85). Voluntary enslavement is not mentioned frequently in extant literary sources, perhaps because the subject was taboo or because it represented a challenge to ideals of freedom (Ramin and Veyne 1981; Harris 1999). Later Roman legal tradition suggests that individuals may have sold themselves into slavery in order to attain employment that could offer a path of economic improvement, such as management of an estate, or destitute free persons may have viewed slavery as a means of providing for themselves and/or family members.[6]

The few instances in which voluntary slavery is mentioned in extant literary sources have been well discussed (Lampe 2003, 85–87; Glancy 2002, 80–85; Herrmann-Otto 2001).[7] The acerbic freedman Hermeros, for example, while arguing with a fellow diner at Trimalchio's banquet in Petroninus' *Satyricon*, indicates that he had been a slave because, as he asserts, "I sold myself into slavery, preferring to be a Roman citizen rather than a taxpayer" (57.4–5; cf. Livy, *Ab urbe cond.* 41.9.11). Hermeros goes on to describe the economic advantages he enjoys as a Roman freedman, having purchased his own freedom for one thousand denarii (57.5–11). In this instance, Hermeros appears to have become a slave from a position of relative privilege in order to enhance his economic prospects (Winter 1994, 156–58). Yet it is difficult to know how representative this fictional and satirical portrayal is of the experience of those real persons who did sell themselves into slavery.

I am not aware of evidence of voluntary slavery for the benefit of other members of a religious association in the Mediterranean world. Perhaps the closest possible parallel comes from the Qumran community, for it has been suggested that 4QInstruction prohibits "voluntary self-enslavement," an interdiction that might be interpreted as an indication that voluntary

---

[6] This is the interpretation of *Dig.* 28.3.6.5 offered by Ramin and Veyne (1981, 488–89). It is striking that Winter, in his discussion of voluntary slavery, never considers the possibility that self-enslavement might have been a terrible choice faced by those in dire economic straits; according to Winter, the reason for "the voluntary selling of oneself into slavery" was "to secure enhanced social status, with its attendant financial advantages" (1994, 147). Conversely, Engerman's insightful discussion of voluntary slavery in conversation with Amartya Sen's concepts of freedom and capability tends to assume that those who "have been willing to sacrifice their liberties and those of their family members in exchange for the ability to survive" have done so out of self-interest or for the benefit of immediate family members (2011, 187); voluntary enslavement for the sake of other members of a religious association is not discussed.

[7] Cf. Philostratus, *Vit. Apoll.* 8.7.12; Dio Chrysostom, *Or.* 15.22–23; Seneca, *Ben.* 4.13.3; *Dig.* 1.5.21; 1.5.5.1; 40.12.7.

slavery was practiced among some members of this Jewish association (Strugnell, Harrington, and Elgvin 1999, 105). The text of 4Q416 2 ii 17–18 reads, "[Do not se]ll yourself for wealth. It is good that you are a slave in spirit and without wages you serve your oppressors. For a price do not sell your glory and do not pledge wealth for your inheritance lest he (God?) dispossess your body" (trans. Goff 2013, 60). Yet, as the literary context indicates, the specific concern in 4Q416 2 ii 3–18 is the situation of debt bondage that may occur when someone has stood surety for a neighbor who has defaulted on a loan (Goff 2013, 85–86). Thus, 4QInstruction does not address a situation in which a member of the elect sells himself directly into slavery; instead, the document offers advice for those who find themselves in debt bondage because they have stood surety for a defaulted loan (cf. Prov 6:1-5; 17:18).

While historians ought to be wary of asserting the "uniqueness" of early Christian practices of mutual aid in contrast to an alleged lack of charity within "pagan" associations, the reference to beneficent voluntary slavery in 1 Clem. 55.2 is unusual when considered in light of practices of group survival among associations in the ancient Mediterranean, even though 1 Clem. 55.1 praises pagan kings and rulers for similar acts of sacrificial love. The authors of 1 Clement reveal very little about the circumstances that led some Christ followers to sell themselves into slavery, aside from the fact that the price they received (τὰς τιμὰς αὐτῶν) was used to feed others. Glancy assumes that 1 Clem. 55.2 refers to "free persons who were so desperate that they would sell themselves into slavery because self-sale was the only way they could provide food for others" (2002, 82–83). Yet while poverty could certainly be a reason for voluntary enslavement, the text of 1 Clem. 55.2 does not actually indicate that those who gave themselves into slavery were destitute. Nor are readers told of those to whom these Christ followers sold themselves. Did they sell themselves to other members of an ἐκκλησία in hopes of avoiding the sexual violations or idolatry that would befall those whose bodies belonged to pagan masters? Much is left unsaid.[8] Yet this positive example of voluntary slavery in 1 Clem. 55.2 is perhaps even more surprising given what the founder of the Christ group in Corinth instructed the ἐκκλησία there in the letter called 1 Corinthians.

---

[8]   It is interesting that the authors of 1 Clement indicate that Christ followers gave *themselves* into slavery (ἑαυτοὺς παρέδωκαν εἰς δουλείαν); there is no hint here of selling children as slaves, although the practice was more common than self-sale (Laes 2008; Sigismund-Nielsen 2013).

VOLUNTARY SLAVERY IN 1 CLEM. 55.2 AND THE RECEPTION OF 1 CORINTHIANS

There is little doubt that the authors of 1 Clement possessed the letter known as 1 Corinthians (Gregory 2005, 144–48; Rothschild 2017, 35–60). The Roman authors' exhortation to "take up the epistle of the blessed Paul, the apostle" (47.1), almost certainly a reference to 1 Corinthians, assumes that readers in Corinth had access to the epistle as well. As an earlier text, penned by an esteemed apostolic figure, that corrects σχίσματα ("being divided into rival groups," 1 Cor 1:10; author's translation) driven by competing allegiances to ecclesiastical leaders in Corinth, 1 Corinthians offers the writers of 1 Clement an ideal literary template and a rich source of argumentation for their own deliberative appeal for peace and harmony among the Christ group in Corinth (Welborn 2002, 350; cf. 1 Clem. 13.1; 24.1–5; 34.8; 37.3, 5; 38.1; 48.5; 49.5). It is all the more interesting, then, that the endorsement given to those Christ followers who sold themselves into slavery in 1 Clem. 55.2 seems to contradict the apostle Paul's own instructions regarding the avoidance of slavery in 1 Cor 7:23. For in a discussion of God's calling in 1 Corinthians 7, Paul provides this teaching to the Christ group in Corinth:

> Let each of you remain in the condition in which you were called. Were you a slave when called? Do not be concerned about it. But if you can gain your freedom, avail yourself of the opportunity. For whoever was called in the Lord as a slave is a freed person belonging to the Lord, just as whoever was free when called is a slave of Christ. *You were bought with a price; do not become slaves of human masters.* In whatever condition you were called, brothers and sisters, there remain with God. (7:20-24, NRSV rev.)[9]

How do we reconcile the commendation of those who had sold themselves into slavery in 1 Clement with Paul's directive not to become slaves of human masters in 1 Corinthians, especially in light of the ostensible reverence given to 1 Corinthians by the authors of 1 Clement?

One proposal is that behind Paul's comments in 1 Cor 7:20-24 and 1 Clem. 55.2 stands the custom of "ecclesial manumission," or "the practice of obtaining the freedom of enslaved members by marshalling their collective funds to pay the price of said member's manumission" (Callahan 1989–1990, 113). Some early Christ groups appear corporately to have manumitted slaves with collections of assembly funds. Ignatius of Antioch, for example, expresses his

---

9   Paul does, of course, speak metaphorically of making himself a "slave to all" in 1 Cor 9:19.

disapproval of this practice in a letter to Polycarp: "[Slaves] should not desire to be set free from the (assembly's) common fund (ἀπὸ τοῦ κοινοῦ), lest they be found to be slaves of (their) desire" (Ign. *Pol.* 4.3; Harrill 1993). There is earlier evidence for Greek associations providing loans for the manumission of slaves (e.g., *IG* II² 1553–78; Harrill 1993, 117–21) and later evidence for collective funds from a Jewish association being used to fund the manumission of enslaved Jews (*POxy* 9:1205; *CII* 683; Harrill 1993, 122–28; Last and Harland 2020, 176–77). A major difficulty for this proposal, however, is that there is no indication that funds from a community chest were used for the corporate manumission of slaves in the earliest Pauline assemblies, and it is problematic to read evidence from Ignatius' letters back into the middle decades of the first century. Moreover, the situation described in 1 Clem. 55.2 differs significantly from the practice of corporately funded manumission that Ignatius seems to oppose, for in the letter from the Romans to the Corinthians it is not collective funds from the ἐκκλησία that are used to ransom prisoners and to feed others. Instead, it is the willing imprisonment and voluntarily enslaved bodies of Christ followers that fund these beneficent acts. Finally, this proposal still leaves us with a puzzle: Paul declares "do not become slaves of human masters," yet the authors of 1 Clement praise and highlight the noble example of those who have given their bodies over to human masters.

A solution may be found in connections between 1 Corinthians 13 and 1 Clement 55. Linguistic and conceptual parallels between 1 Cor 13:3 and 1 Clem. 55.2 have often been interpreted as an indication that the latter is alluding to the former (Lampe 2003, 85–87; Rothschild 2017, 56–57).

> 1 Cor 13:3: If I give away all my possessions (ψωμίσω πάντα τὰ ὑπάρχοντά μου), and if I hand over my body (παραδῶ τὸ σῶμά μου) so that I may boast, but do not have love, I gain nothing.

> 1 Clem. 55.2: We know that many among us have handed themselves (παραδεδωκότας ἑαυτοὺς) over into bonds, so that they might ransom others. Many have sold themselves (ἑαυτοὺς παρέδωκαν) into slavery, and with the price received for themselves have fed others (ἑτέρους ἐψώμισαν).

If either the variant καυθήσομαι (C, D, F, G, L, Tert, Ambst) or καυθήσωμαι (K, Ψ) in 1 Cor 13:3 were known to the authors of 1 Clement, they might have interpreted Paul's statement "if I hand over my body so that I may be burned" as an allusion to voluntary slavery, with the burning of the body signifying the practice of branding slaves (Hays 1997, 225). The connection is intriguing. Yet the text-critical issue in 1 Cor 13:3 makes it difficult to know whether the Romans were aware of a statement from Paul about delivering his body for burning. Even if the Roman authors were aware of a version of 1 Cor 13:3 that referred to burning the body, it is not entirely clear that this would have been interpreted as a reference to self-enslavement and, if so, how such a reference might have been reconciled with Paul's ostensible prohibition of becoming slaves of human masters in 1 Cor 7:23.

Whatever may have been the relationship between 1 Clem. 55.2 and 1 Cor 13:3, it is also evident that the authors of 1 Clement drew upon the wider context of 1 Corinthians 13 to frame their appeal to love (ἀγάπη), especially in the "encomium to love" in 1 Clem. 49.1–6 (Bakke 2001, 191):

> Let the one who has love in Christ practice the precepts of Christ. Who can describe the bond of God's love? Who can sufficiently express the greatness of its beauty? The height to which love leads is indescribable. Love binds us to God; love covers a multitude of sins; love endures all things, is patient in all things. There is nothing vulgar in love, nothing proud. Love has no schism; love does not cause division; love does all things in harmony. In love everyone chosen by God has been made perfect; without love nothing is pleasing to God. In love the Master has received us; on account of the love he had for us Jesus Christ our Lord gave his blood for us by God's will—his flesh for our flesh and his life for our life.

With clear reference to 1 Cor 13:4-7 (and also 1 Pet 4:8; Downs 2014, 495–98), the authors of 1 Clement recall and reshape Paul's own memorable reflections on ἀγάπη in order to address the context of schism and division in Corinth.

This evocation of 1 Corinthians 13 will be remembered when, a few chapters later, the authors turn to the issue of voluntary exile for those responsible for the division in Corinth, opening with the questions, "Therefore, who among you is noble? Who is compassionate? Who is filled with love?" (54.1). The authors aim to promote these virtues among the schismatics in Corinth, for the appropriate answer to these rhetorical questions is then given: "Let that one say, 'If there is rebellion and strife and schism on account of me, I will depart; I will go away wherever you wish, and will do whatever is ordered by the people; only let the flock of Christ be at peace with its appointed elders'" (54.2). The examples of self-sacrifice for the sake of others provided in 1 Clem. 55.1–6 are, therefore, specifically framed as noble (γενναῖος), compassionate (εὔσπλαγχνος), and loving (ἀγάπη) acts done for the benefit of others, deeds that serve as paradigmatic examples for the Corinthians to imitate.

In this sense, those who have willingly sold themselves into slavery in order to feed others might be said to have demonstrated the greatest of the virtues of 1 Corinthians 13, namely, love (13:13). In giving themselves over to human masters, these Christ followers may have done something that runs counter to Paul's instruction in 1 Cor 7:23, but they have done so, from the perspective of the authors of 1 Clement, in an implicit imitation of Christ Jesus, who is said to have given "his flesh for our flesh and his life for our life" (49.6).

VOLUNTARY SLAVERY AND SOCIAL DEATH IN 1 CLEMENT

Nowhere in 1 Clement do we clearly hear the perspective of enslaved persons themselves. The references to voluntary imprisonment and slavery in 1 Clem. 55.2 are tantalizingly fleeting. Yet this passing allusion to what is framed as two practices known well to Christ followers in Corinth and Rome offers an opportunity to reconsider some fundamental frameworks through which slavery in early Christianity has often been viewed. Among the most influential perspectives on slavery in antiquity (and in other eras as well) is Orlando Patterson's thesis that slavery be understood as social death, a status characterized by violence, natal alienation, and dishonor (Patterson 1982). Drawing on common experiences among slaves of violence, personal violation, and namelessness and invisibility, Patterson describes slavery as "the permanent, violent domination of natally alienated and generally dishonored persons" (1982, 13). In concentrating his study of slavery on the "relation of domination" by which slaveholders maintained power over the enslaved, Patterson shifted the focus from slavery as defined exclusively by questions of property rights to slavery as a "social death" by which the "desocialized new slave" became incorporated into a personal relation and an institutional process in which a "slave no longer belonged to a community [. . . and] had no social existence outside of his master" (38). According to Patterson, social death is imposed and supported by two primary "symbolic instruments": natal alienation, which means the slave is cut off from all previous social ties, and pervasive dishonoring, which means that the slave "could have no honor because he held no power and no independent social existence, hence no public worth" (10).

Patterson's model for viewing slavery as social death has been challenged on the grounds that it does not satisfactorily highlight the agency of the enslaved and that Patterson's comparative approach does not sufficiently attend to the diverse experiences of slaves, including the lives of honor and communal support that slaves managed to build despite brutal conditions imposed upon them (Brown 2009; Culbertson 2011; Sweet 2013; Bodel and Scheidel 2016; Freeburg 2021). Although the evidence is allusive and fragmentary, 1 Clem. 55.2 would appear to offer one small glimpse into an experience of the enslaved that is not marked by "social death," at least not entirely. Voluntary slavery (along with self-imprisonment) in 1 Clement 55 is imaged as a practice that solidifies social bonds among Christ followers. Not only are those who have sold themselves into slavery still counted among the community of Christ believers ("many among *us*"), but those who have made this sacrifice are honored by having their vicarious deed highlighted as an example of a noble, compassionate, and loving action. In this way, "social death" cannot adequately capture the experience of those Christ followers who sold themselves into slavery in order to feed others.

Like many members of "pagan" associations, a majority, perhaps the overwhelming majority, of Christ followers in the first and second centuries CE eked out a subsistence-level existence (Friesen 2004; Longenecker 2010; Last and Harland 2020, 15–32). First Clement 55 momentarily bears witness to the hardships of imprisonment and hunger, as well as to two practices—voluntary imprisonment and slavery—aimed at providing material assistance for those suffering these privations. One of the strengths of Last and Harland's study of group survival in antiquity is its reminder of the tenuous nature of continued existence, not only for individual members of associations in the ancient Mediterranean but also for the groups themselves. Since collective action was often imperative, close bonds between members of associations were crucial to group survival. Last and Harland write:

> The degree to which members were tied to one another, and to the group as a whole, could closely correspond to a group's level of success and potential longevity. Associations relied on the ongoing commitment and material contributions of their members. In return, such members received a number of benefits beyond the most obvious social attachments the group offered. Communal collections aimed at honouring deities and other purposes illustrate well the collective action and material procedures that were the lifeblood of many associations of various types, immigrant associations included. The fact that associations could themselves be a magnification of commonly accepted principles of reciprocity and mutual aid within society is, therefore, closely linked to material circumstances and survival. As a local, more or less tightly knit social network, an ongoing association provided participants access to social capital in the form of resources of various kinds, both material and non-material. (2020, 187)

Christ followers in Rome and Corinth were aware of examples of sacrificial love that may have gone beyond "commonly accepted principles of reciprocity and mutual aid within society." To allow oneself to be imprisoned in order to ransom a brother or sister in Christ, or to sell oneself into slavery in order to feed others with the price of the sale—these acts would seem to have exceeded normal practices of reciprocity, although the authors of 1 Clement are certainly aware that there is nothing distinctively "Christian" about this kind of sacrifice, as the "examples of the nations" in 55.1 demonstrate.

To what extent, if any, the practices of voluntary imprisonment and slavery, and the rhetorical invocation of them in 1 Clement, forged and solidified bonds among association members in Rome and Corinth, and elsewhere, is difficult to say. In the immediate context of 1 Clement, these sacrificial acts are cited in 1 Clem. 55.2 to encourage the Corinthian schismatics to abandon their divisive ways and voluntarily remove themselves from Corinth. It is interesting, however, that one of the earliest extant conjurings of 1 Clement alludes to communal bonds between Rome and Corinth fashioned through mutual assistance, including care for slaves. Sometime in the second half of the second century (ca. 166–175 CE), the Roman assembly appears to have sent a gift to Christ followers in Corinth. In response, Dionysius, bishop of Corinth, wrote a letter to the Roman church, fragments of which are preserved by Eusebius (*Hist. eccl.* 4.23.9–12). In his letter, Dionysius acknowledges the regular and universal beneficence of the Romans:

> For from the beginning this has been a custom for you, always acting as a benefactor to siblings in various ways and sending financial support to many assemblies in every city, thus relieving the poverty of those in want and supplying additional help to the siblings who are in the mines. (4.23.10; trans. from Concannon 2017, 197)

While metals were not exclusively extracted by slave labor in the Roman imperial period, Dionysius' phrase "the brothers in the mines" (ἐν μετάλλοις δὲ ἀδελφοῖς ὑπάρχουσιν ἐπιχορηγοῦντας) should be taken as a reference to Roman support for Christian slaves, although it is not clear if this care included the manumission of slaves condemned to this difficult work (Concannon 2017, 198).

Dionysius goes on to observe that 1 Clement was still being read in Corinth during his time as bishop: "Today we passed through the Lord's holy day, in which we read your letter. When we read it, we will always have an admonishment (ἕξομεν ἀεί ποτε ἀναγινώσκοντες νουθετεῖσθαι), as also with the former [letter] written to us through Clement" (4.23.11).[10] The preservation and continued reading of 1 Clement in Corinth, perhaps a generation or so after the epistle was first received, will have strengthened ties between the Christ-following associations in Rome and in Corinth. And the memory of the noble, compassionate, and loving acts of voluntary imprisonment and slavery served as examples for the Corinthians to follow, both at the time 1 Clement was written and in the period of its earliest reception.

WORKS CITED

Bakke, Odd Magne. 2001. *"Concord and Peace": A Rhetorical Analysis of the First Letter of Clement with an Emphasis on the Language of Unity and Sedition.* WUNT 143. Tübingen: Mohr Siebeck.

Bauschatz, John. 2007. "Ptolemaic Prisons Reconsidered." *Classical Bulletin* 83:3–48.

Bodel, John P., and Walter Scheidel, eds. 2016. *On Human Bondage: After Slavery and Social Death.* Malden, Mass.: Wiley-Blackwell.

Bremmer, Jan. 2015. "The Self-Sacrifice of Menoeceus in Euripides' *Phoeissae, II Maccabees*, and Statius' *Thebaid.*" *ARG* 16:193–207.

Breytenbach, Cilliers. 2014. "The Historical Example in 1 Clement." *ZAC* 18:22–33.

Brown, Vincent. 2009. "Social Death and Political Life in the Study of Slavery." *AHR* 114:1231–49.

Callahan, Allen. 1989–1990. "A Note on I Corinthians 7:21." *Journal of the Interdenominational Theological Center* 17:110–14.

Concannon, Cavan W. 2017. *Assembling Early Christianity: Trade, Networks, and the Letters of Dionysios of Corinth.* Cambridge: Cambridge University Press.

Culbertson, Laura. 2011. "A Life-Course Approach to Household Slaves in the Late Third Millennium B.C." Pages 33–48 in *Slaves and Households in the Near East.* Edited by Laura Culbertson. Chicago: Oriental Institute of the University of Chicago.

Curbera, Jaime. 2018. "Lexical Notes on Greek Prisons and Imprisonment." *Revue de philologie de littérature et d'histoire anciennes* 92:7–37.

Downs, David J. 2014. "'Love Covers a Multitude of Sins': Redemptive Almsgiving in 1 Peter 4:8 and Its Early Christian Reception." *JTS* 65:489–514.

Engerman, Stanley. 2011. "Slavery, Freedom, and Sen." *Feminist Economics* 9:185–211.

---

[10] To be sure, Eusebius' own decisions about which letters of Dionysius to summarize and which portions to cite reflect his own rhetorical aims and therefore do not provide neutral access to the writings of Corinth's bishop in the late second century.

Eubank, Nathan. 2018. "Prison, Penance or Purgatory: The Interpretation of Matthew 5.25–6 and Parallels." *NTS* 64:162–77.

Freeburg, Christopher. 2021. *Counterlife: Slavery after Resistance and Social Death*. Durham, N.C.: Duke University Press.

Friesen, Steven J. 2004. "Poverty in Pauline Studies: Beyond the So-Called New Consensus." *JSNT* 26:323–61.

Gerbner, Katharine. 2018. *Christian Slavery: Conversion and Race in the Protestant Atlantic World*. Early American Studies. Philadelphia: University of Pennsylvania Press.

Glancy, Jennifer. 2002. *Slavery in Early Christianity*. Oxford: Oxford University Press.

Goff, Matthew J. 2013. *4QInstruction*. WLAW 2. Atlanta: SBL Press.

Gregory, Andrew F. 2005. "*1 Clement* and the Writings That Later Formed the New Testament." Pages 129–57 in *The Reception of the New Testament in the Apostolic Fathers*. Vol. 1 of *The New Testament and the Apostolic Fathers*. Edited by Andrew F. Gregory and Christopher M. Tuckett. Oxford: Oxford University Press.

Harrill, J. Albert. 1993. "Ignatius, *Ad Polycarp* 4.3 and the Corporate Manumission of Christian Slaves." *JECS* 1:107–42.

———. 2006. *Slaves in the New Testament: Literary, Social, and Moral Dimensions*. Minneapolis: Fortress.

Harris, William V. 1999. "Demography, Geography and the Sources of Roman Slaves." *JRS* 89:62–75.

Hays, Richard B. 1997. *First Corinthians*. Interpretation. Louisville: Westminster John Knox.

Herrmann-Otto, Elisabeth. 2001. "Soziale Mobilität in der römischen Gesellschaft. Persönliche Freiheit im Spiegel von Statusprozessen." Pages 171–83 in *Fünfzig Jahre Forschungen zur antiken Sklaverei an der Mainzer Akademie, 1950–2000. Miscellanea zum Jubiläum*. Edited by Heinz Bellen and Heinz Heinen. Forschungen zur antiken Sklaverei 35. Stuttgart: Steiner.

Hillner, Julia. 2015. *Prison, Punishment and Penance in Late Antiquity*. Cambridge: Cambridge University Press.

Keener, Craig S. 2012. *Introduction and 1:1–2:47*. Vol. 1 of *Acts: An Exegetical Commentary*. Grand Rapids: Baker Academic.

Krause, Jens-Uwe. 1996. *Gefängnisse im Römischen Reich*. Heidelberger Althistorische Beiträge und Epigraphische Studien 23. Stuttgart: Steiner.

Kujanpää, Katja. 2020. "Scriptural Authority and Scriptural Argumentation in 1 Clement." *NTS* 66:125–43.

Laes, Christian. 2008. "Child Slaves at Work in Roman Antiquity." *Ancient Society* 38:235–83.

Lampe, Peter. 2003. *From Paul to Valentinus: Christians at Rome in the First Two Centuries*. Edited by Marshall D. Johnson. Translated by Michael Steinhauser. Minneapolis: Fortress.

Last, Richard, and Philip A. Harland. 2020. *Group Survival in the Ancient Mediterranean: Rethinking Material Conditions in the Landscape of Jews and Christians*. London: T&T Clark.

Lightfoot, J. B. 1890. *The Apostolic Fathers. Part 1: S. Clement of Rome. A Revised Text with Introductions, Notes, Dissertations, and Translations*. London: Macmillan.

Lona, Horacio E. 1998. *Der erste Clemensbrief. Übersetzt und erklärt*. Kommentar zu den Apostolischen Vätern 2. Göttingen: Vandenhoeck & Ruprecht.

Longenecker, Bruce W. 2010. *Remember the Poor: Paul, Poverty, and the Greco-Roman World*. Grand Rapids: Eerdmans.

Nicklas, Tobias. 2016. "Ancient Christian Care for Prisoners: First and Second Centuries." *Acta Theologica* Supplementum 23:49–65.

Osiek, Carolyn. 1981. "The Ransom of Captives: Evolution of a Tradition." *HTR* 74:365–86.

Patterson, Orlando. 1982. *Slavery and Social Death: A Comparative Study*. Cambridge, Mass.: Harvard University Press.

Peters, Janelle. 2021. "Judith and the Elders of *1 Clement*." *Open Theology* 7:60–68.

Ramin, Jacques, and Paul Veyne. 1981. "Droit romain et societe: les hommes libres qui passent pour esclaves et l'esclavage volontaire." *Historia* 30:472–97.

Rothschild, Clare K. 2017. *New Essays on the Apostolic Fathers*. WUNT 375. Tübingen: Mohr Siebeck.

Sensbach, Jon F. 1998. *A Separate Canaan: The Making of the Afro-Moravian World in North Carolina, 1763–1840*. Chapel Hill: University of North Carolina Press.

Sigismund-Nielsen, Hanne. 2013. "Slave and Lower-Class Roman Children." Pages 286–301 in *The Oxford Handbook of Childhood and Education in the Classical World*. Edited by Judith Evans Grubb and Tim Parkin. Oxford: Oxford University Press.

Strugnell, John, Daniel J. Harrington, and Torleif Elgvin. 1999. *Qumran Cave 4. XXIV: Sapiential Texts, Part 2*. DJD 34. Oxford: Clarendon.

Sweet, James H. 2013. "Defying Social Death: The Multiple Configurations of African Slave Family in the Atlantic World." *William and Mary Quarterly* 70:251–72.

Wansink, Craig S. 1996. *Chained in Christ: The Experience and Rhetoric of Paul's Imprisonments*. JSNTSup 130. Sheffield: Sheffield Academic.

Welborn, Larry L. 2002. "'Take Up the Epistle of the Blessed Paul the Apostle': The Contrasting Fates of Paul's Letters to Corinth in the Patristic Period." Pages 345–57 in *Reading Communities, Reading Scripture: Essays in Honor of Daniel Patte*. Edited by Gary A. Phillips and Nicole Wilkinson Duran. Harrisburg, Pa.: Trinity Press International.

———. 2014. "Voluntary Exile as the Solution to Discord in 1 Clement." *ZAC* 18:6–21.

Winter, Bruce W. 1994. *Seek the Welfare of the City: Christians as Benefactors and Citizens.* First-Century Christians in the Graeco-Roman World. Grand Rapids: Eerdmans.

24
Mystery Cults and Christian Associations in Early Alexandrian Theology

The Case of Clement of Alexandria

T. J. Lang

Mystery cults permeated the religious landscape of Roman Egypt, but their influence extended beyond the domain modern scholars designate "religion."[1] Vocabulary and motifs from "the mysteries" were readily incorporated within that region's "philosophical" imagination. This includes the "theological" interventions of Christian intellectuals.[2] The task for these intellectuals was sociologically complex but can be formulated simply: to forge a distinctly Christian associational identity amid the panoply of rival religious associations. One of the earliest and most creative architects of such

[1] Helpful introductions to this subject include Haas 1997 and Frankfurter 1998. The most important mysteries in Egypt were those of Isis and Osiris. For a collection of primary texts related to these cults, see Meyer 1987, 157–96. Though not from Egypt, Plutarch nonetheless provides one of the most interesting reflections on Egyptian religious life by way of an intriguing allegorical interpretation of the Egyptian mysteries in his *De Iside et Osiride*. Also helpful is Sly 1996, esp. 100–119, 133–34. The standard introduction to mystery cults is Burkert 1987. See also now Bremmer 2014. On mystery terminology in relation to Philo and Clement, see Riedweg 1987.

[2] The scare quotes around "religion," "philosophy," and "theology" are meant to signal the inadequacies in neatly distinguishing these categories and the questions concerning their conceptual utility. "Religion" is widely contested as a category for describing ancient ways of life and forms of devotion (see Nongbri 2013). The bifurcation of "philosophy" and "theology" is also problematic. It obscures the fact that multiple facets of Christian thinking are in fact serious interventions in long-standing philosophical debates (see Edwards 2021).

a social project was also one of ancient Alexandria's most impressive thinkers: Titus Flavius Clemens, or Clement of Alexandria (ca. 150–215 CE). In his own way, Clement typifies a posture toward mystery cults that endured among ensuing Christian theologians of Alexandria. First, there is unqualified condemnation of all cultic associations. Never are the rites and gods of mystery associations admired. In his Προτρεπτικὸς πρὸς Ἕλληνας (*Exhortation to the Greeks*) this posture of condemnation is the "dissuasion" in his protreptic discourse—"to turn from" (ἀποτροπή) so as "to turn to" (προτροπή) Christian truth.[3] But, at the same time, Clement still readily reproduces technical vocabulary and motifs from these cults to express his own ideas about Christian assembly structures. For Clement, the Christian society is still very much a matter of celebrating sacred mysteries involving gradual induction through secreted rites. He unhesitatingly depicts Christian practices such as baptism, catechesis, and the exegesis of sacred texts as forms of initiation into hidden mysteries, and so very much akin to the cultic associations he derides. Clement thus exploits fundamental structures from his ambient religious culture to depict Christianity's own communal formations. As a sociological strategy, his is one of synchronized social *rupture* and cultural *recapture*. This complements the rhetorical strategy of the protreptic genre on display across Clement's corpus, but especially in his *Exhortation to the Greeks*, also known as the *Protrepticus*. Clement's undertaking in the *Protrepticus* is to balance "dissuasion" (ἀποτροπή) for the purposes of "persuasion" (προτροπή). This protreptic rhetoric assumes a common religious space with numerous homologous characteristics. Within this competitive space of associational rivals, however, Clement insists on the exclusivity of the Christian "sacred guild" (θίασος) (*Protr.* 12.119.2). Every other society is a depraved imitation.

It is important at the outset to say a bit more about the rupture/recapture relation. The *rupture* (the ἀποτροπή, or "turn from") is the distancing of the Christian associations and non-Christian forms of communal life. It is the task of distinguishing true and false forms of social organization. The *recapture* is Clement's unyielding insistence on the intellectual and religious priority of the Christian way of life. The Christian society alone preserves eternal truth. Insofar as Christian and non-Christian religious assemblies would seem to coincide, this is simply because the non-Christian religious language and structural forms depend on and distort an original Christian truth. On Clement's terms, a Dionysian θίασος is not simply an alternative

---

[3] The *Logos Protreptikos* was a common rhetorical strategy to persuade others to alternative ways of life, especially in the context of philosophical discourse.

association, as though all things were equal, but a derivative and distorted one. Christian truth always has priority. This rupture/recapture dynamic is critical for Christian social formation in ancient Alexandria, as it is for many minority groups across time who seek to carve space in cultural worlds variously at odds with their own.[4]

MYSTERY ASSOCIATIONS AND THE ALEXANDRIAN CONTEXT

Clement exemplifies many distinctive features of the Alexandrian intellectual tradition. His interaction with Greek literary culture is second to none in early Christianity. His writings also rank among the most important sources for reconstructing details of many mystery associations across the Roman world. But Clement is much more than just a witness to ancient Mediterranean religious cultures. His own Christian social and theological lexicon incorporates much conventional terminology from the religious world around him—and from mystery cults in particular.[5] Despite this correspondence of language and ideas, however, Clement remains ferociously critical of the common mystery religiosity, and indeed every religious association that is not devoted to Christ. This is the subtlety in Clement's construction of the Christian society: even when his linguistic usage appears on the surface to analogize Christian and non-Christian associations, his actual aim is to sharpen the relation in order to sharpen their opposition—which is to sharpen the truthfulness of Christian associations and the disfigurement of everything else.

Clement is not idiosyncratic in this. Philo of Alexandria, Clement's Jewish predecessor in Alexandria, also deftly absorbs and transforms religious language and communal structures from the world around him, and from mystery associations in particular.[6] But again, as with Clement, Philo's denun-

---

[4]   For more on such sociological dynamics, and with respect to Judaism in particular, see Barclay 1996.

[5]   On "mystery" terminology in Clement, see Marsh 1936. For "mystery" discourses and appeals to divine secrecy more generally in Judaism and early Christianity, see Bockmuehl 1990; Lang 2015.

[6]   For Philo's total intellectual profile, see Niehoff 2018. Niehoff discusses Philo's interaction with themes from the mysteries on pp. 183–85. Philo's interaction with the mystery cults is a matter of long-standing interest. Some have argued that Philo envisions Judaism itself as such a cult. At the center of this debate is Goodenough 1935. Goodenough's thesis is that Philo's Judaism has been thoroughly transformed according to the pattern of the Hellenistic mystery religions. This leads him to conclude that "Judaism in the Greek Diaspora did, for at least an important minority, become primarily such a mystery" (5). For a thorough summary of the debate on this topic, see Lease 1987. The response to Goodenough's thesis has remained consistent, and there is now widespread agreement that "the

ciation of all cultic mysteries is resolute, even while his positive transformation of their vocabulary and practices is extensive. Philo never wavers in his censure. He maintains that Israel's sacred code of laws abolishes "initiations and mysteries" (τὰ τελετὰς καὶ μυστήρια). By the fiat of Torah, the matter is settled. The allure of these "mystical forgeries" distracts a person from truth, and so followers of Moses must "neither initiate nor become initiated" (μήτε τελείτω μήτε τελείσθω) into such impiety (*Spec. Laws* 1.319). In *Spec. Laws* 3.40, Philo again excoriates the theses cults, but now by pointing to the impious and effeminate men of the mysteries who lead processions in the marketplaces and oversee rites of initiation.[7] Such men are also deemed responsible for promoting depraved practice such as pederasty (3.37–42). Other instances of denunciation could be added, but Philo's judgment is everywhere the same.[8] Mystery associations are depraved institutions forbidden by Torah. This is the social *rupture* in Philo's insistence on Jewish exclusivity.

Then there is the *recapture*. Philo has no qualms about depicting Jewish associations and practices using technical terminology and imagery annexed directly from mystery associations.[9] While allegorically interpreting the births of Cain and other biblical figures, Philo exhorts his reader: "O initiates (ὦ μύσται) whose ears have been purified, receive these mysteries (μυστήρια) in your own souls as sacred, and you should not divulge them to the uninitiated (μηδενὶ τῶν ἀμυήτων)" (*Cherubim* 48). Philo offers himself as an example of the dogged pursuit of mysteries, explaining how when he had already been initiated into the great mysteries (μυηθεὶς τὰ μεγάλα μυστήρια) by Moses he came across the prophet Jeremiah. Upon learning that Jeremiah was also an "initiate" (μύστης) and "sufficient hierophant" (ἱεροφάντης ἱκανός), Philo resolved to visit him often (*Cherubim* 49).[10] This is all language and imagery drawn explicitly from the religiosity of ancient mystery associations. It is without scriptural precedent.

---

existence of a peculiarly Jewish mystery cult, conceptualized and patterned after the Hellenistic mystery cults, is without evidence and unsupportable" (874). This does not mean, of course, that the "widespread agreement" is necessarily correct in its estimation of what Philo thought Judaism was and the sociological complexities involved in his thinking on this. For mystery terminology in Philo, see Cohen 2004; Mazzanti 2003.

[7] He specifically mentions in this passage the mysteries of Demeter (τὰ Δήμητρος ὀργιάζοντας).

[8] See the denunciation of τελετή (*Names* 107; *Cherubim* 94) and ὄργια (*Embassy* 78).

[9] For a more detailed analysis of Philo's exegetical style, see Dawson 1992, 73–126.

[10] The ἱεροφάντης is the authorized religious expert who gives instructions for the proper execution of sacred rites. The ἱεροφάντης is most identifiable as the name for the initiating priest (or high priest) at the Eleusinian cult, but it is also used in other cults for the priestly office, appearing often in associational inscriptions.

Philo writes positively about "the Jewish mysteries" in multiple places (see *Alleg. Interp.* 1.104; 3.3; 3.27; *Sacrifices* 33; 60; 62). He also frequently characterizes the process of learning those mysteries as a sacred initiation (see esp. *Alleg. Interp.* 3.71; 3.100; *Unchangeable* 61). He appropriates the language of the Eleusinian mysteries to describe his own exegetical offerings as the difference between initiation into "the greater mysteries" (τὰ μεγάλα μυστήρια) and "the lesser mysteries" (τὰ μικρὰ μυστήρια; *Alleg. Interp.* 3.100; *Cherubim* 49; *Sacrifices* 33; 62).[11] Philo even goes so far as to depict an actual Jewish group (the ascetic association known as the Therapeutae) as exemplifying the ideals and practices of the mysteries in their austere life of sacred study (Deutsch 2008). He describes their monasteries as holy shrines and maintains that in their occupation of allegorical exegesis "they sacredly perform the mysteries of a venerable life" (τὰ τοῦ σεμνοῦ βίου μυστήρια τελοῦνται) (*Contempl. Life* 25). Their carefully regimented associational life is regarded as the ideal embodiment of cultic practice and mystical experience.[12]

These passages exhibit the ease with which Philo articulates his own exegetical procedure by utilizing vocabulary and imagery extracted directly from the associations he otherwise denounces. Although Philo views the cults themselves as spurious and perverse, their ritual structures and terminology remain suitable for constructive social and theological use. It would be incorrect to conclude that Philo's usurpation of mystery terminology and motifs amounts to the "complete transformation of Judaism in the Greek world" (Goodenough 1935, 5), as though processes of acculturation necessarily entailed betrayal. Philo rather aims to transform the language and practices of mystery cults by absorption, by purifying them within the differently determinative domain of Jewish thought and practice in the Alexandrian context. To judge his success in this is a separate, second-order matter.

THE MYSTERIES AND CHRISTIAN SOCIETIES

Like Philo, Clement repeatedly censures the gods and initiates of the mysteries for their immorality and general folly. This is most sustained in the

---

[11]   For more on these designations for the two grades of mystery initiation at Eleusis, see Dowden 1980.

[12]   For six days of the week the various members of the group perform their liturgy in solitude. On the seventh day they gather together in a carefully orchestrated "general assembly" (κοινὸν σύλλογον; *Contempl.* 30) in their meticulously arranged "common sanctuary" (τὸ κοινὸν σεμνεῖον; *Contempl.* 32). The rules and customs of the assembly are extensive. The whole of Philo's *De vita contemplativa* offers fascinating insight into this carefully ordered religious association.

Protrepticus.[13] Clement begins his reproof (his ἀποτροπή) of the mysteries in *Protr.* 2.12.1, which also anticipates the design of his ensuing argument:

And what if I were to recount at length the mysteries (τὰ μυστήρια) to you? I will not burlesque them, as they say Alcibiades did,[14] but I will expose—thoroughly according to the principle of truth—the deceitful magic they conceal. And as for your so-called gods to whom the mystic rites (αἱ τελεταὶ μυστικαί) belong, I will display them also, as it were, on the stage of life for the spectators of the truth.[15]

Clement commences his exposé of the mysteries in the remainder of 2.12, first by ridiculing the frenzied orgies of the Bacchants and then by doing the same to the supposedly shameful stories of Demeter's wanderings and her daughter Persephone's rape.[16] In 2.13.1 he turns to etymology, inventively reckoning that both μυστήρια and ὄργια (secret rites)[17] have ignoble derivations. He alleges that the latter originates from the ὀργή (or wrath) of Demeter for Zeus and the former from the μύσος (or pollution) associated with Dionysus.[18] In the remainder of 2.13, Clement briefly speculates on who was responsible for first instituting the mysteries ("who implanted the mysteries in life as a seed of evil and corruption"), and then in 2.14, and through to the end of that chapter, he mounts his extensive case-by-case demonstration of the ignominious origins and practices of the various mystery groups. He castigates all the major cults—Aphrodite, Attis, Cybele, the Corybantes, Demeter, Dionysus, the Cabeiri, Eleusis—and others. As with Philo, the denunciation of non-Christian mystery assemblies is resolute.

---

[13] For an efficient summary of the total terrain of the *Protrepticus*, and with particular concern for Clement's interaction with the mystery cults, see Mitchell 2020, 97–108.

[14] For the details of this infamous event, see Thucydides, *P.W.* 6.27–29, 53, 60–61; Andocides, *On the Mysteries* 11–24; Plutarch, *Alc.* 19–22.

[15] The text of *Protrepticus* follows Marcovich 1995.

[16] The stories of Demeter and Persephone are celebrated in the Eleusinian cult. For an analysis of the ways in which Clement derides Dionysus and then appropriates aspects of this god and his cult, see Jourdan 2006. See also Halton 1983, which goes so far as to suggest that the *Protrepticus* represents "a new, non-Dionysiac poetics . . . in which Clement assumes the role of stage director casting a new play, a Christian *Bacchae*" (197).

[17] This term for secret rites is used across multiple mystery cults, including those devoted to Demeter in Eleusis and those associated with Dionysus. It sometimes appears to be synonymous with μυστήρια, and so a catchall term for mystery associations.

[18] He does not develop this purported etymology or account for it in his later positive appropriation of the terminology. This would appear to be a case of polemical opportunism.

MYSTERY RITES AND CHRISTIAN RITUAL INITIATION

Alongside invective, however, there is again, similar to Philo, a distinctively Christian reapplication of language and ideas drawn from the cults of ridicule. *Protrepticus* is again the place to begin. Clement once more accents the conventional cultic overtones associated with τὰ μυστήρια. But now, instead of invoking cultic mysteries solely for the purpose of derision, he appropriates their customs of secrecy and initiation. He does this to fashion constructive images for conversion to the Christian assembly—the only *true* guardian of *true* and blessed mysteries. At the end of Clement's exhortation, mystery associations discover their own technical language and traditions repossessed and repaired by Clement's own standards of divine truth. True mysteries are exclusively Christian mysteries, and only accessed among Christ-devoted assemblies.

Having exposed the alleged immoralities and absurdities of the mysteries in chapter 2, and then of the rest of Greek culture in chapters 3–7, Clement shifts to his defense of Christianity in chapters 8–12. He insists in these chapters that Christian associations alone possess mysteries of salvation. His apology reaches a peak in 12.118–20, where he promises his reader that through Christ and the Holy Spirit it is possible to be initiated into the truly divine mysteries that have been kept hidden in heaven:

> The Word of God will steer you (κυβερνήσει),[19] and the Holy Spirit will anchor you in the harbors of heaven (τοῖς λιμέσι καθορμίσει τῶν οὐρανῶν).[20] Then comes the vision of my God, and you will be initiated into those holy mysteries (τοῖς ἁγίοις ἐκείνοις τελεσθήσῃ μυστηρίοις), and you will enjoy those things hidden (ἀποκεκρυμμένων) in the heavens, the things that have been guarded for me, "which neither ear heard nor did they enter the heart" (ἃ οὔτε οὖς ἤκουσεν οὔτε ἐπὶ καρδίαν ἀνέβη)[21] of anyone. (*Protr.* 12.118.4)

[19] For the connection of this verb with mystery rites, see, for instance, *IGR* 1.187.

[20] In the immediately preceding context, Clement develops his thought in relation to Odysseus and the Sirens from book 12 of the *Odyssey*, exhorting his reader to "sail past the song; it works death" (12.118.1–3). The nautical image of a pilot steering an initiate to safe shores for anchor may, however, also allude to the cult of Isis. The "Ship of Isis" (the Ploiaphesia, or *Navigium Isidis*) was one of the goddess' most important festivals. It is described by Apuleius in *Metam.* 11.8–11. This festival marks the opening of the sailing season. In Apuleius' account, Lucius observes the festival and during the procession is healed by eating from a wreath of roses carried by one of the priests. This is what precipitates his decision to become an initiate in Isis' mysteries. For more on the festival itself, see Witt 1997, 165–84.

[21] Presumably a free quotation of 1 Cor 2:9.

The images here are straightforward: conversion to the Christian society is an initiation ceremony involving hidden divine mysteries; Christ and the Holy Spirit serve as co-hierophants; Clement's God constitutes the final revelatory vision. The rhetorical consequences of this redescription are likewise clear: although true heavenly revelation cannot be had in Eleusinian assemblies or among the retinue of Dionysus, the non-Christian is not without hope. Holy mysteries are indeed to be had, but in the Christian society alone. It is this strong insistence on exclusivity that distinguishes Clement's mystery religiosity from the other manifold cults. Only among Christian assemblies are any true mysteries revealed and a morally credible way of life discovered.

Immediately following this promise of a heavenly *epopteia* (the "seeing," the final rite in the Eleusinian mysteries; Bremmer 2014, 11–16), Clement next addresses the non-Christian worshipper directly, beckoning revelers of Dionysus to turn from their lascivious Bacchic mania in order to receive the Word's authentic and sober mysteries. This is the culminating προτροπή in his deliberative argument for the exclusive authenticity of the Christian society:

> Come, O frenzied one, not propped up by the thyrsus, nor wreathed with ivy. Cast off your headband; cast off your fawn skin; come to your senses! I will show you the Word and the Word's mysteries (δείξω σοι τὸν λόγον καὶ τοῦ λόγου τὰ μυστήρια), describing them with respect to your own image (κατὰ τὴν σὴν διηγούμενος εἰκόνα). (*Protr.* 12.119.1)

A depiction of Christ "with respect to the image" (cf. Gen 1:11) of the mystery cult is just what Clement proceeds to offer. It is an account of Christ confronting the Dionysian εἰκών. It is not a picture of Christ reshaped in relation to Dionysus but a picture of Dionysus as the distorted negative of Christ—Christ's debauched doppelgänger. In order to intensify the distortion that is the Dionysian cult, Clement juxtaposes the discordant revelries of Bacchus' mysteries with the lucid music of heaven's own "sacred guild" (τὸν θίασον) (*Protr.* 12.119.2). The Christian *thiasos* is an association of maidens, prophets, and angels who guide initiates up to the mountain (not Cithaeron but Zion)[22] where "dramas of truth" are performed. The liturgy is carefully ordered. The maidens, angels, and prophets all have defined roles. And on that holy mountain the Word himself sings the new song

---

[22] For Cithaeron, see Euripides, *Bacch.* 62–63. This is the mountain range associated with Dionysus and his band of Bacchants.

of salvation. The Father's (instead of Dionysus') mysteries are then finally unveiled to initiates:[23]

O truly holy mysteries (ὦ τῶν ἁγίων ὡς ἀληθῶς μυστηρίων)! O incorruptible light! I carry the torches (δᾳδουχοῦμαι)[24] to heaven to have the vision (ἐποπτεῦσαι)[25] of God. I become holy by being initiated (ἅγιος γίνομαι μυούμενος), and the Lord is a hierophant (ἱεροφαντεῖ) as he seals the initiate (τὸν μύστην σφραγίζεται),[26] providing enlightenment (φωταγωγῶν). And he commends to the Father the one who has trusted, this one being protected for eternity. These are the Bacchic revelries of my mysteries (ταῦτα τῶν ἐμῶν μυστηρίων τὰ βακχεύματα). If you want, be also initiated (μυοῦ), and you will dance with angels around the unbegotten and indestructible and only true God, the Word of God singing with us. (*Protr.* 12.120.1–2)

Once again, conversion to the Christian assembly is ritual initiation into the greatest and truest of mysteries. Clement thus simultaneously subverts and converts corresponding cults—here the cult of Dionysus specifically.[27] Neither Isis nor Dionysus nor any other alternative goddess or god represents truth. The cure to the corruptions of those cults is the Christian God who hides *truly* sacred secrets and reveals them to righteous initiates. The Son is the hierophant of those mysteries and the chief minstrel in Christianity's temperate and melodious chorus. To complete the contrast: Christ is the true anti-Dionysus—the Λόγος who sings in harmony instead of discord and leads his initiates as a *thiasos* of sober Bacchants to the mysteries of eternal salvation. Such are Christianity's "Bacchic revelries" (τὰ βακχεύματα).

In picturing Christ and his association of righteous inductees "with respect to the image" of the Dionysian mysteries, Clement does not mean to modify Christianity in relation to a rival religious guild. His intent is seditious. It is to undermine mystery associations on their own terms by

[23] The entirety of *Protr.* 12.119–20 is full of allusions to Euripides' *Bacchae*, each of which is contrasted with a Christian reality.

[24] This verb, and the activity of proceeding with torches, is often used for mystery celebrations.

[25] Again, the verb used for initiation into the highest level of the mysteries (the *epopteia*). It is particularly associated with the Eleusinian cult. See Clinton 2003, esp. 51–65; Bremmer 2014, 11–16.

[26] The language of sealing also has baptismal overtones in early Christianity. For the early Christian deployment of "sealing" terminology, see Lang 2020.

[27] In *Strom.* 1.1.15.4 Clement refers to himself, like Paul before him, as "becoming a Greek for the sake of the Greeks" in order to win them all (cf. 1 Cor 9:20-21). Paul thus supplies a *raison d'être* for Clement's treatise.

rendering their cults as depraved inversions of the Christian society and, accordingly, distorted simulacra of the truth. The revisionary cultural poetics at work in *Protrepticus* is not an accommodationist attempt at comparison in service of equation. Clement's art aims to define the line between the "pagan" mysteries and Christian assemblies by highlighting the division between true and false, sanctity and depravity. But at the same time, Clement recaptures and converts the pagan εἰκών, in effect Christianizing what is retainable from it and purging what is not. This conversion of the cultic εἰκών is, however, not simply a case of cultural usurpation. It is also something of a *praeparatio* for the conversion of the deceived cultic worshipper, whom at times Clement addresses directly. By creating cultural and conceptual links between the cultic mystery associations and the Christian mysteries, Clement presents a bridge for the non-Christian worshipper to traverse, to discover truth and achieve eternal salvation within the Christian society. Clement states this invitation to conversion (and so restoration) plainly. Salvation does not replace the distorted non-Christian εἰκών but restores it to conformity with the eternal form of righteousness—the archetype from which it derives but deviates:

> O all the images (εἰκόνες), but not all resemble (ἐμφερεῖς) [God]![28] I want to restore you to the archetype (τὸ ἀρχέτυπον) in order that you might become like me . . . So I will reveal the unveiled form of righteousness, through which you ascend to God (γυμνὸν δικαιοσύνης ἐπιδείξω τὸ σχῆμα, δι' οὗ πρὸς τὸν θεὸν ἀναβαίνετε). (*Protr.* 12.120.4–5)

CULTIC MYSTERIES AND CHRISTIAN CATECHESIS

As many scholars have rightly emphasized, the subject of divine pedagogy—and παιδεία more generally—is a central theme in Clement's work and occupies a fundamental place within his larger theological understanding (Kovacs 2001).[29] One key feature of Clement's social program—perhaps *the* key feature—is the pedagogical use of concealment and revelation, which Clement frequently develops in the language of hidden and revealed mysteries.[30] The progressive unveiling of mysteries is a characteristic feature of

---

[28] This is Marcovich's (1995) conjecture. He appeals to *Protr.* 12.1–2 (θεοείκελα . . . ἀγάλματα) and *Strom.* 6.126.4 (ἐμφεροῦς δὲ τῷ κυρίῳ) in support.

[29] Indispensable on this general subject of παιδεία is Jaeger 1961. For his discussion of Clement, see esp. 46–62.

[30] Cf. Riedweg 1987, 137–47, which defines this as the "Christlich-philosophischer Lernprozess."

societal induction among ancient mystery assemblies (Bremmer 2014), and similar processes of induction are also fundamental in Clement's way of organizing the internal structures of Christian assemblies.[31]

Clement repeatedly emphasizes in the *Stromateis* that the mysteries of God are consecrated teachings that must be guarded by initiates from the uninitiated. This scheme of concealed and revealed information (including rites and objects) is axiomatic in Clement's presentation of the Christian associational structure, as it is among the non-Christian mysteries. Clement even ensures that his own writings are intentionally obscure and full of enigmas in order "to speak in a hidden way, to reveal without uncovering, to disclose silently" (*Strom.* 1.1.15.1), lest the uninitiated reader glimpse "greater mysteries." In contrast to someone like Tertullian, who is at pains to prove that the mysteries of Christianity are open secrets, public and available to all,[32] Clement insists that the Christian society is replete with mystical secrets that must be strictly guarded by members of the guild. If written, they must be composed in code so as to be accessible only to initiates. Clement does not, however, distinguish between the initiated and the uninitiated only in terms of insiders and outsiders of Christian associations. Even among Christians there are degrees of induction that involve new catechetical instruction and culminate in the rank of "Gnostic."[33] One should, therefore, expect that sacred writings (such as Scripture) or theological treatises (such as Clement's) will have multiple levels of meaning available to multiple gradations of induction.

To illustrate the associational functions of concealment strategies, Clement first appeals to Jesus at the outset of the *Stromateis*:[34]

[The Lord] has granted to impart the divine mysteries (τῶν θείων μυστηρίων) and that holy light to those who are able to advance. Furthermore, he did not reveal (ἀπεκάλυψεν) to the many the things that were not for the many, but to the few, to those he believed worthy, to those able to understand and be conformed to these things. The sacred

---

[31] It is unsurprising that "mystery" language is ultimately applied to sacraments—"the mysteries"—and the structures of progressive induction through sacred rites and catechetical formation. For just one especially developed and influential discussion of the shape and rationale of the Christian sacramental mysteries, see Ambrose of Milan's *The Mysteries* (*De mysteriis*) and *The Sacraments* (*De sacramentis*).

[32] See, for instance, Tertullian, *Praescr.* 26.2–5.

[33] I use the uppercase for Clement's elite class of Christians. This should not be confused with what is usually termed *gnosticism*.

[34] Clement also frequently appeals to the examples of Paul (*Strom.* 5.4.25.2–26.5; 5.10.60.1–62.4) and of Plato (*Strom.* 1.1.14.4; 5.9.58.6).

secrets (τὰ ἀπόρρητα), like God, are entrusted in word, not in writing. If someone should say it has been written, "There is nothing hidden that will not be revealed, nothing veiled that will not be unveiled" (οὐδὲν κρυπτὸν ὃ οὐ φανερωθήσεται, οὐδὲ κεκαλυμμένον ὃ οὐκ ἀποκαλυφθήσεται),[35] let such a person listen to us, because to the one who understands in a secret way (τῷ κρυπτῶς ἐπαίοντι), the hidden thing will be revealed (τὸ κρυπτὸν φανερωθήσεσθαι), which is why he foretold (προεθέσπισεν) this saying. And to the person who is of the concealed sort (τῷ παρακεκαλυμμένως), these things are handed over, and that which has been hidden (τὸ κεκαλυμμένον) will become clear (δηλωθήσεται) as the truth. Thus to the many it is hidden, and to the few this is revealed (τὸ τοῖς πολλοῖς κρυπτόν, τοῦτο τοῖς ὀλίγοις φανερὸν). . . . The mysteries are handed over mystically (τὰ μυστήρια μυστικῶς παραδίδοται) so that they should be spoken on the lips of the one speaking—or rather not in voice, but in comprehension. (Strom. 1.1.13.1–4)

The same claims are made again in Strom. 1.12.55.1, and again in relation to Jesus' supposed manner of teaching, but with an added allusion to Paul:

Since our tradition is not common and open to all people—especially in terms of comprehending the magnificence of the teaching (τοῦ λόγου)— "the wisdom which is being spoken in a mystery" (τὴν ἐν μυστηρίῳ λαλουμένην σοφίαν),[36] which the Son of God was teaching, appears in a concealed way (ἐπικρυπτέον).

The basic point is straightforward and consistent: Christian doctrine is a repository of sacred mysteries that are not publicly obtainable. Since these mysteries should be imparted only to worthy members of the sacred guild, they are transmitted in veiled forms. Again, this social schema is fundamental to the internal structures of ancient mystery associations, and Clement correlates Christianity explicitly with them.

The Gnostic, Clement's most elite Christian initiate, is repeatedly singled out as the one to whom "the greater mysteries"—à la the Eleusinian mystery cult—have been disclosed.[37] As Clement explains in 7.1.4.2–3, the Gnostic is the only Christian "able to hand over venerably the things hidden in the truth" because the Gnostic alone "learns thoroughly the divine

---

[35] Clement must have in mind Matt 10:26//Luke 12:2//Mark 4:22. Cf. also Gos. Thom. 5, 6.

[36] Cf. 1 Cor 2:7.

[37] Cf. Philo, Alleg. Interp. 3.100; Cherubim 49; Sacrifices 33; 62.

mysteries from the only begotten Son himself" (τὰ θεῖα μυστήρια παρὰ τοῦ μονογενοῦς παιδὸς αὐτοῦ ἐκμαθών). As for the ways in which other Christians are instructed, Clement describes three methods by which Christ, the Pedagogue par excellence, trains various grades of initiates (*Strom.* 7.2.6.1). The Gnostic, having ascended to the highest level of initiation, is trained "in mysteries" (μυστηρίοις), whereas the Pedagogue teaches "the believer by good hopes" and "the hard of heart by corrective discipline." A very similar alignment of the knowledge of divine mysteries with hierarchical divisions among the elect appears in *Salvation of the Rich*, but instead of labeling the highest initiate a Gnostic, Clement speaks of those who are "more elect than the elect" (τῶν ἐκλεκτῶν ἐκλεκτότεροι). What differentiates these "elect of the elect" is that they "hide in the depth of their mind the unutterable mysteries" (ἐν βάθει γνώμης ἀποκρύπτοντες τὰ ἀνεκλάλητα μυστήρια; *Quis div.* 36.1).

This conception of Christian initiation as a mystery pedagogy is so fundamental to Clement's social program that he even arranges his writings according to the principles of concealment and progressive induction. It appears that Clement's so-called trilogy (*Protrepticus, Paedagogus, Stromateis/Didaskalos*) was intentionally designed as a curriculum for gradual induction into the Christian guild.[38] This is at least the case for individual documents. In *Strom.* 4.1.3.1, for instance, Clement likens the order of *Stromateis* to Eleusinian initiation into greater and lesser mysteries. The Christian must "be initiated into the lesser mysteries before the greater ones, so that having been purified in advance nothing impedes the truly divine hierophant" (τὰ μικρὰ πρὸ τῶν μεγάλων μυηθέντες μυστηρίων, ὡς μηδὲν ἐμποδὼν τῇ θείᾳ ὄντως ἱεροφαντίᾳ γίνεσθαι προκεκαθαρμένων). Clement invokes a similar hierarchical ordering of teaching in 1.28.176, where he divides Moses' philosophy into four stages through which a disciple gradually progresses. He defines the fourth and highest part as the ἐποπτεία, and so "as among the truly great mysteries" (μεγάλων ὄντως εἶναι μυστηρίων) (*Strom.* 1.28.176.2).[39] This fourth level of philosophy is concerned with "theological form" (τὸ θεολογικὸν εἶδος), and the people who ascend to this fourth grade of initiation are those who can say, with Paul in Eph 3:3-4, that

---

[38] Clement provides a rationale for the arrangement of Προτρέπων, Παιδαγωγῶν, Ἐκδιδάσκων in *Paed.* 1.1.3. There is debate as to whether *Stromateis* corresponds to the *Didaskolos*. For the case against this equation, see Bucur 2009.

[39] Ancient philosophy was regularly ordered in a set curriculum, and epoptics was a common designation for the final portion of the philosophical program. For the claim that Plato and Aristotle designated this part of the philosophical curriculum epoptics, see Plutarch, *Is. Os.* 382D. See also Hadot 1979.

they have come to know "the mystery through revelation, as I wrote briefly earlier, which when reading you are able to know my understanding in the mystery of Christ" (*Strom.* 1.28.179.1).

Clement's highly developed mystery pedagogy further illustrates the degree to which the contours of his associational sensibilities coincide with those of the cultic mysteries and are markedly shaped in conscious relation to those societies. Once again, however, such correspondences do not mean that Clement's social enterprise aims to translate Christianity into these associational models. Clement regards the mystery pedagogy as a universal technique for societal induction and, as Clement explains in other places, insofar as non-Christian associations similarly perform initiating customs, they merely represent deviations from true worship.[40] As opposed to the priests and hierophants of the cultic mysteries, Clement points to Jesus and Paul in order to substantiate his catechetical designs. As Clement reads them, the Gospels and Paul's letters provide ample evidence that the instructional techniques and rites of his mystery pedagogy lie at the very heart of how Christian associations function. Rival expressions of mystery religiosity are simply deviations from Christian truth and the social program on offer in the Christian ἐκκλησία, the only true θίασος.

CONCLUSION: MYSTERY ASSOCIATIONS AND THE ASSOCIATIONAL IDENTITY OF CHRIST GROUPS

Given Clement's extensive and sophisticated engagement with mystery associations, the pointed question becomes: What sort of association would Clement have a Christian ἐκκλησία be? It has long been fashionable to pinpoint Clement, and the ensuing Alexandrian tradition along with him, as paragons of the so-called "Hellenization of Christianity," that stubborn declension narrative wherein the sweet Palestinian message of Jesus gives up its soul on "Greek" soil. The primary supposition of this thesis is that as Christianity expanded into primarily non-Jewish territory, the ideal and original form begotten by Jesus further eroded, confusing itself with the culture around it. The Alexandrian forms of Christianity represented by Clement and others exemplify what Harnack described as the "promiscuous confusion"[41] of Christianity with non-Christian sensibilities and ideas (often dubbed, with a promiscuous lack of nuance, as "Platonic"). The merger of

---

[40] For lengthier reflections on non-Christian plagiarism and Hebrew (and so also Christian) priority, see *Strom.* 5.14; 6.2–5.

[41] The German is more elaborate but less evocative than Moffatt's 1908 translation: "wogen freilich überall durcheinander" (von Harnack 1908, 237).

mystery language and motifs in Christianity thus represents just one of the many unmistakable symptoms of this syncretistic muddling. A reply to this tired but intractable hypothesis is still required.

First, setting aside the theoretical and historical problems that accompany postulating an ideal (or original) type of "Christian association," it is important to recognize that Clement himself does not believe there is anything from which his social theory departs. Christianity is for him—as he believes Jesus and Paul before him modeled it—an association of mystical revelation, vigilantly guarded theological secrets, sacred rites, progressive illumination, worship of the God of Israel, and worship of that God as revealed in Jesus the Christ. As "Hellenized" as this may be judged to be, it is nonetheless Clement's understanding of what Christian associations are and have always been. Even if, in second-order analytic terms, the Hellenization thesis is deemed serviceable as an explanatory framework for organizing societal development in the Alexandrian tradition, it cannot be confused with Clement's own understanding of what Christian assemblies are.

Second, insofar as the Hellenization thesis misapprehends Clement on Clement's terms, it also obscures what is in fact a subtle but complex strategy of cultural subversion. This is most overt in *Protrepticus*. Clement's approach to alternative gods and cults is much more cunning than simple antagonism. He does not simply underscore what he believes is the divergence between non-Christian falsity and Christian truth. Clement insists that the whole of Greek culture is nothing more than a derivative distortion of the truth to be discovered upon induction into Christian mysteries. Far from single-minded hostility, Clement's social undertaking is also one of recovery as he works to reappropriate and restore alternative associational institutions to what he believes is properly Christian, and so true. To read Clement's social enterprise as "Hellenizing" an ideal type of the Palestinian Jesus movement is to misconstrue what for him is the true transforming agent in his thought. It is Christ who refigures the Dionysian cult, and the rest of the mysteries with him. Christ is the archetype, Dionysus the distorted image.

There is no questioning the fact that Clement is an Alexandrian of his own time and place. The motions of his mind, his social predispositions, and his cultural instincts are all very much shaped by the world to which he belongs. He could belong to no other. But these facts in no way controvert what Clement aspires to make the most constitutive fact of Christian identity: a society loyal to true sources of revelation and to the associations that guard the truth of that revelation. It is the Christian assembly that Clement introduces as leaven to the world around him. Rather than the Hellenization of Christianity, Clement ventures to Christianize Hellenism, even when that venture inevitably involves cultural confrontation and amalgamation in turn. It would be an error for the modern scholar to reduce cultural interaction to the *x*-ization of this or the *y*-ization of that. Cultural change and identity formation are far more multifaceted. And change is always inevitable if any culture or tradition is to persist through time with some sense of common identity across that time. This is where the creative and conservative pulsations in the heart of a tradition push and pull—and push and pull they must if the tradition is to remain alive and intelligible to itself across that time.

In innumerable ways—complex and often undetectable to those involved—subtilties of "Hellenization" (whatever that means precisely, given the fact the whole of the New Testament is written in Greek) surely occurred in various ways as the ideas and story of an Aramaic-speaking criminal variously coalesced among sometimes scattered and sometimes interconnected Christian associations across a multicultural Mediterranean landscape (and, of course, in the Greek language). This always occurs when cultural worlds collide. Such is the story of Christianity's global expansion in arenas of opposing ways of organizing social lives in ever-changing and always complex social worlds.

Given all this, the question with which this conclusion began—what sort of association would Clement have a Christian ἐκκλησία be?—should now be sharpened: Does Clement think Christian assemblies are just another variety of ancient mystery cults? As is required with so many social realities, it seems to me the reply must be subtly crafted: "No, of course not (ἀποτροπή)! And yes, the exclusively true one (προτροπή)!"

WORKS CITED

Barclay, John M. G. 1996. *Jews in the Mediterranean Diaspora: From Alexander to Trajan (323 BCE–117 CE)*. Berkeley: University of California Press.

Bockmuehl, Markus N. A. 1990. *Revelation and Mystery in Ancient Judaism and Pauline Christianity*. WUNT 36. Tübingen: Mohr Siebeck.

Bremmer, Jan N. 2014. *Initiation into the Mysteries of the Ancient World*. MVAW 1. Berlin: De Gruyter.

Bucur, Bogdan G. 2009. "The Place of the *Hypotyposeis* in the Clementine Corpus: An Apology for 'The Other Clement of Alexandria.'" *JECS* 17:313–35.

Burkert, Walter. 1987. *Ancient Mystery Cults*. Cambridge, Mass.: Harvard University Press.

Clinton, Kevin. 2003. "Stages of Initiation in the Eleusinian and Samothracian Mysteries." Pages 50–78 in *Greek Mysteries: The Archaeology and Ritual of*

Ancient Greek Secret Cults. Edited by Michael B. Cosmopoulos. London: Routledge.

Cohen, Naomi G. 2004. "The Mystery Terminology in Philo." Pages 173–87 in *Philo und das Neue Testament. Wechselseitige Wahrnehmungen. I. Internationales Symposium zum Corpus Judaeo-Hellenisticum, 1.–4. Mai 2003, Eisenach/Jena.* Edited by Roland Deines and Karl-Wilhelm Niebuhr. WUNT 172. Tübingen: Mohr Siebeck.

Dawson, David. 1992. *Allegorical Readers and Cultural Revision in Ancient Alexandria.* Berkeley: University of California Press.

Deutsch, Celia. 2008. "Visions, Mysteries, and the Interpretive Task: Text Work and Religious Experience in Philo and Clement." Pages 83–103 in *Inquiry into Religious Experience in Early Judaism and Christianity.* Vol. 1 of *Experientia.* Edited by Frances Flannery, Colleen Shantz, and Rodney A. Werline. SymS 40. Atlanta: SBL.

Dowden, Ken. 1980. "Grades in the Eleusinian Mysteries." *RHR* 197:409–27.

Edwards, Mark, ed. 2021. *The Routledge Handbook of Early Christian Philosophy.* London: Routledge.

Frankfurter, David. 1998. *Religion in Roman Egypt: Assimilation and Resistance.* Princeton: Princeton University Press.

Goodenough, Erwin R. 1935. *By Light, Light: The Mystic Gospel of Hellenistic Judaism.* New Haven: Yale University Press.

Haas, Christopher. 1997. *Alexandria in Late Antiquity: Topography and Social Conflict.* Baltimore: Johns Hopkins University Press.

Hadot, Pierre. 1979. "Les divisions des parties de la philosophie dans l'antiquité." *MH* 36:201–23.

Halton, Thomas. 1983. "Clement's Lyre: A Broken String, a New Song." *SecCent* 3:177–99.

von Harnack, Adolf. 1908. *The Mission and Expansion of Christianity in the First Three Centuries.* 2nd ed. Translated by James Moffatt. Vol. 1. London: Williams and Norgate.

Jaeger, Werner. 1961. *Early Christianity and Greek Paideia.* Cambridge, Mass.: Harvard University Press.

Jourdan, Fabienne. 2006. "Dionysos dans le *Protreptique* de Clément d'Alexandrie: initiations dionysiaques et mystères chrétiens." *RHR* 223:265–82.

Kovacs, Judith L. 2001. "Divine Pedagogy and the Gnostic Teacher according to Clement of Alexandria." *JECS* 9:3–25.

Lang, T. J. 2015. *Mystery and the Making of a Christian Historical Consciousness: From Paul to the Second Century.* BZNW 219. Berlin: De Gruyter.

———. 2020. "Sealed for Redemption: The Economics of Atonement in Ephesians." Pages 155–70 in *Atonement: Jewish and Christian Origins.* Edited by Max Botner, Justin Harrison Duff, and Simon Dürr. Grand Rapids: Eerdmans.

Lease, Gary. 1987. "Jewish Mystery Cults since Goodenough." *ANRW* 20:858–80.

Marcovich, M., ed. 1995. *Clementis Alexandrini: Protrepticus.* VCSup 34. Leiden: Brill.

Marsh, H. G. 1936. "The Use of ΜΥΣΤΗΡΙΟΝ in the Writings of Clement of Alexandria with Special Reference to His Sacramental Doctrine." *JTS* 37:64–80.

Mazzanti, Angela Maria. 2003. "The 'Mysteries' in Philo of Alexandria." Pages 117–29 in *Italian Studies on Philo of Alexandria.* Edited by Francesca Calabi. Boston: Brill.

Meyer, Marvin W. 1987. *The Ancient Mysteries: A Sourcebook.* San Francisco: Harper & Row.

Mitchell, Margaret M. 2020. "On Comparing, and Calling the Question." Pages 95–124 in *The New Testament in Comparison: Validity, Method, and Purpose in Comparing Traditions.* Edited by John M. G. Barclay and B. G. White. LNTS 600. London: T&T Clark.

Niehoff, Maren R. 2018. *Philo of Alexandria: An Intellectual Biography.* New Haven: Yale University Press.

Nongbri, Brent. 2013. *Before Religion: A History of a Modern Concept.* New Haven: Yale University Press.

Riedweg, Christoph. 1987. *Mysterienterminologie bei Platon, Philon und Klemens von Alexandrien.* Untersuchungen zur antiken Literatur und Geschichte 26. Berlin: De Gruyter.

Sly, Dorothy. 1996. *Philo's Alexandria.* London: Routledge.

Witt, R. E. 1997. *Isis in the Ancient World.* Baltimore: Johns Hopkins University Press.

Contributors

Richard S. Ascough is a Professor of Religious Studies at Queen's University, Kingston, Canada.

Alicia J. Batten is Professor of Religious Studies and Theological Studies, Conrad Grebel University College, University of Waterloo, Canada.

Susan E. Benton is a doctoral candidate in the Department of Religion at Baylor University, Texas, USA.

Eric J. Brewer is a doctoral student in the Department of Religion at Baylor University, Texas, USA.

Timothy A. Brookins is Associate Professor of Classics at Houston Baptist University, Texas, USA.

David J. Downs is Clarendon-Laing Associate Professor in New Testament Studies at the University of Oxford and Laing Fellow in Theology and Religion at Keble College.

Philip F. Esler is the Portland Chair in New Testament Studies at the University of Gloucestershire, Cheltenham, UK.

Christina Gousopoulos is a doctoral student at the Department for the Study of Religion, University of Toronto, Canada.

James R. Harrison is Professor of Biblical Studies and the Research Director at the Sydney College of Divinity, Australia.

John S. Kloppenborg is a University Professor and Professor of Religion in the Department for the Study of Religion, University of Toronto, Canada.

Ralph J. Korner is Professor of Biblical Studies at Kairos University's Taylor Seminary, Edmonton, Canada.

T. J. Lang is Senior Lecturer in New Testament at the University of St Andrews, Scotland, UK.

Richard Last is Assistant Professor in the Ancient Greek and Roman Studies program at Trent University, Peterborough, Canada.

Louise J. Lawrence is Professor of New Testament Interpretation at the University of Exeter, UK.

Jin Hwan Lee is the Academic Supervisor at Canada School of Theology, Canada.

Bruce W. Longenecker is the W. W. Melton Chair of Christian Origins at Baylor University and Professor of New Testament in Baylor's Department of Religion, Texas, USA.

Robert E. Moses is Associate Professor of Religion at High Point University, North Carolina, USA.

Timothy J. Murray is a visiting lecturer at Newman University and a pastor at Amblecote Christian Centre, West Midlands, UK.

Peter Oakes is Rylands Professor of Biblical Criticism and Exegesis at the University of Manchester, UK.

Markus Öhler is Professor for New Testament Studies at the Faculty for Protestant Theology, University of Vienna, Austria.

Éric Rebillard is the Avalon Foundation Professor in the Humanities, Professor of Classics and History, at Cornell University, New York, USA.

Sarah E. Rollens is R. A. Webb Associate Professor of Religious Studies at Rhodes College, Tennessee, USA.

Jason A. Whitlark is Professor of New Testament in the Honors College of Baylor University, Texas, USA.

Index of Modern Authors

Index of Ancient Sources

GREEK AND ROMAN LITERATURE

CPSIA information can be obtained
at www.ICGtesting.com
Printed in the USA
LVHW032113041022
729978LV00001B/1